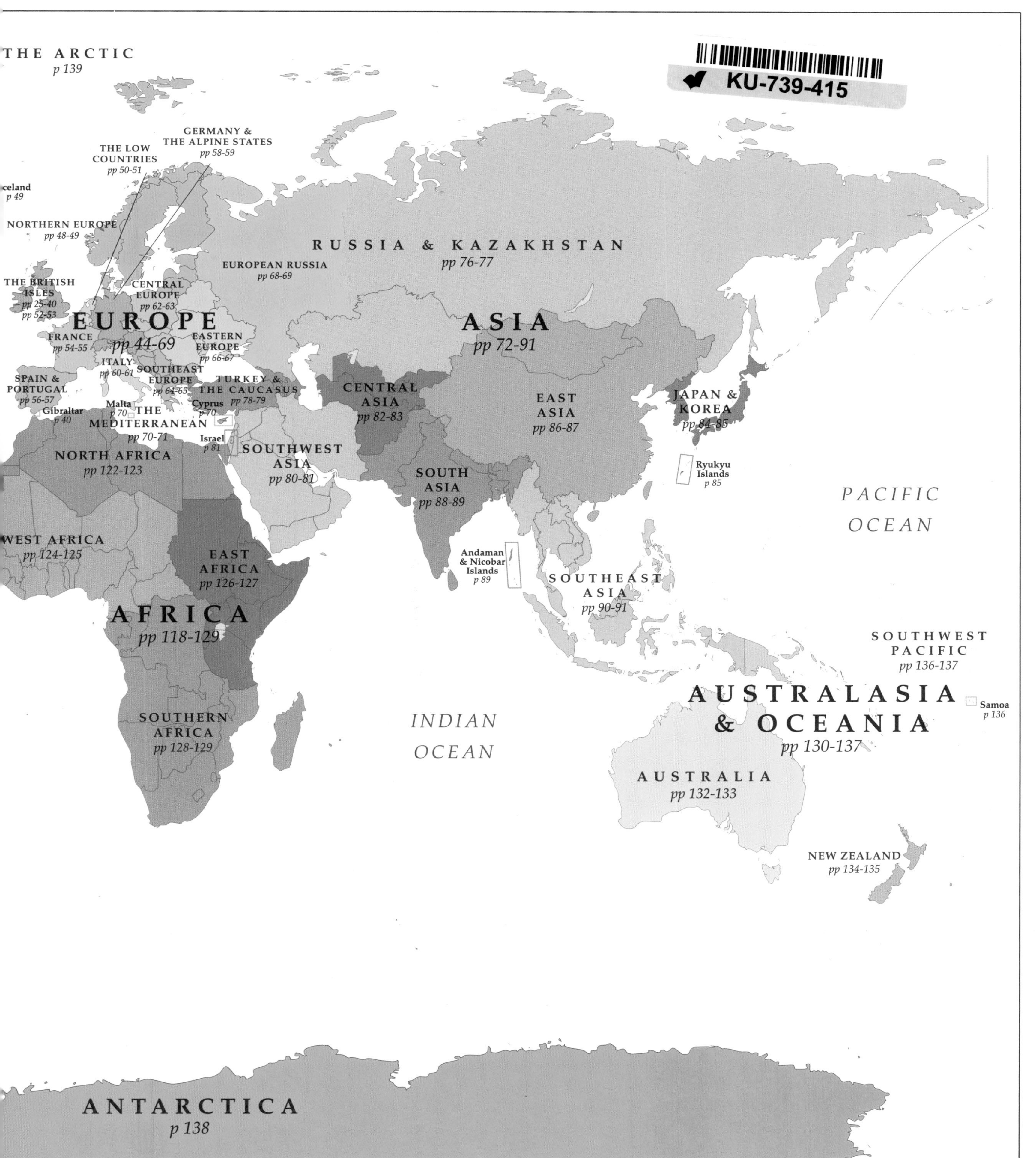
THE ARCTIC
p 139
KU-739-415
GERMANY & THE ALPINE STATES
pp 58-59
THE LOW COUNTRIES
pp 50-51
celand
p 49
NORTHERN EUROPE
pp 48-49
RUSSIA & KAZAKHSTAN
pp 76-77
EUROPEAN RUSSIA
pp 68-69
THE BRITISH ISLES
pp 25-40
pp 52-53
CENTRAL EUROPE
pp 62-63
EUROPE
pp 44-69
ASIA
pp 72-91
FRANCE
pp 54-55
EASTERN EUROPE
pp 66-67
ITALY
pp 60-61
SOUTHEAST EUROPE
pp 64-65
SPAIN & PORTUGAL
pp 56-57
TURKEY & THE CAUCASUS
pp 78-79
CENTRAL ASIA
pp 82-83
EAST ASIA
pp 86-87
JAPAN & KOREA
pp 84-85
Malta
p 70
Gibraltar
p 40
THE MEDITERRANEAN
pp 70-71
Cyprus
p 70
Israel
p 81
NORTH AFRICA
pp 122-123
SOUTHWEST ASIA
pp 80-81
SOUTH ASIA
pp 88-89
Ryukyu Islands
p 85
PACIFIC OCEAN
WEST AFRICA
pp 124-125
EAST AFRICA
pp 126-127
Andaman & Nicobar Islands
p 89
SOUTHEAST ASIA
pp 90-91
AFRICA
pp 118-129
SOUTHWEST PACIFIC
pp 136-137
AUSTRALASIA & OCEANIA
pp 130-137
Samoa
p 136
SOUTHERN AFRICA
pp 128-129
INDIAN OCEAN
AUSTRALIA
pp 132-133
NEW ZEALAND
pp 134-135
ANTARCTICA
p 138

student ATLAS

DORLING KINDERSLEY
LONDON • NEW YORK • MUNICH • MELBOURNE • DELHI
www.dk.com

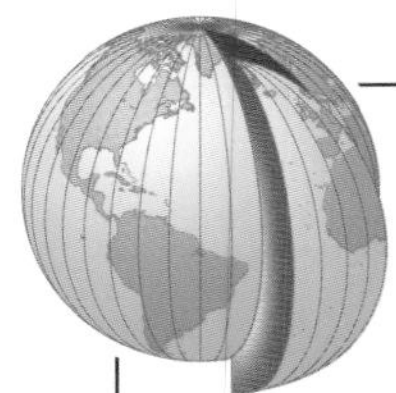

A DORLING KINDERSLEY BOOK
www.dk.com

EDUCATIONAL CONSULTANT
Dr. David Lambert, Institute of Education, University of London

MAP SKILLS CONSULTANT
David R Wright, BA MA

TEACHER REVIEWERS
Kevin Ball, Langdon School, London, Pat Barber, Poynton County High School, Cheshire
Stewart Marson, Guilsborough School, Northampton

ACKNOWLEDGEMENTS
Geography students at Poynton County High School, Cheshire

MANAGING EDITOR
Lisa Thomas

MANAGING ART EDITOR
Philip Lord

PROJECT EDITORS
Debra Clapson, Wim Jenkins

PROJECT DESIGNERS
Rhonda Fisher, Karen Gregory

EDITORIAL CONTRIBUTORS
Thomas Heath, Kevin McRae, Constance Novis, Siobhan Ryan

DESIGNERS
Carol Ann Davis, David Douglas
Nicola Liddiard

MANAGING CARTOGRAPHER
David Roberts

SENIOR CARTOGRAPHIC EDITOR
Roger Bullen

DORLING KINDERSLEY CARTOGRAPHY
CARTOGRAPHERS
Pamela Alford, James Anderson, Chris Atkinson, Sarah Baker-Ede, Dale Buckton, Tony Chambers, Jan Clark, Martin Darlison, Damien Demaj, Sally Gable, Jeremy Hepworth, Michael Martin, Ed Merritt, Simon Mumford, John Plumer, Gail Townsley, Julie Turner, Jane Voss, Peter Winfield

DATABASE MANAGER
Simon Lewis

DIGITAL MAPS CREATED IN DK CARTOPIA BY
Phil Rowles, Rob Stokes

PLACENAMES DATABASE TEAM
Julia Lynch, Natalie Clarkson, Margaret Stevenson

PICTURE RESEARCH
Louise Thomas

EDITORIAL DIRECTION
Andrew Heritage

PRODUCTION
Jo Bull

First published in Great Britain in 1998 by Dorling Kindersley Limited,
80 Strand, London WC2R ORL

A Penguin Company

Second Edition (revised) 2002, Third Edition (revised) 2004

A CIP catalogue record for this book is available from the British Library

ISBN 1405310103

Reproduction by Colourscan, Singapore, and The Printed Word, London.
Printed and bound in China by Toppan Printing Co. (Shenzen) Ltd.

ACKNOWLEDGEMENTS

The publishers are grateful for permission to reproduce the following photographs:
t=top, b=bottom, a=above, l=left, r=right, c=centre

Axiom: J Spaull 74br. **Bridgeman Art Library**: Hereford Cathedral, Trustees of the Hereford Mappa Mundi 8tr. **J Allan Cash**: 120cr. **Bruce Coleman Ltd:** C Ott 92cr (below); Dr E Pott 4bc; H Reinhard 19cr; J Murray 194bl; Peter Terry 19crr. **Colourific**: Black Star/R Rogers 113br; Frank Herrmann 119bc. **Comstock**: 17tc. **James Davis Travel Photography**: 26cr (above), 27bl, 44tr, 119tr. **Robert Harding Picture Library**: 6tr (below), 21c, 21cr, 22br, 74cr (above), 92bl, 94cr, 94br, 95bl, 118bl; A Tovy 120br; Adam Woolfitt 44br; C Bowman 112tr; Charcrit Boonson 72cr (below); David Lomax 20tr; Franz Joseph Land 19tr; G Boutin 120cl (below); G Renner 17c, 118cr(above); Gavin Hellier 95tr; H P Merten 23tl; Jane Sweeney 23bl; Louise Murray 75tr; Philip Craven 28cl; Peter Scholey 73tr; Robert Francis 23cr; Schuster/Keine 44cr (above); Simon Westcott 72br. **Hutchison Library:** A Zvoznikov 19cl; J Nowell 75bl; R Ian Lloyd 10cl. **Image Bank:** Carlos Navajas 17bl; M Isy-Schwart 17bc; P Grumann 46cr (below); Steve Proehl 94cr (below); Terje Rakke 17br. **Images Colour Library**: 19c, 26br, 44cr (below), 118br. **Impact:** Bruce Stephens 26cr (below); Jeremy Nicholl 121cl (below); Mark Henley 20bl; Paul O'Driscoll 45cr; Robin Lubbock 118br. **Frank Lane Picture Agency:** D Smith 19bc; W Wisniewsli 17cr. **Magnum:** Chris Steele Perking 120tr (below); Ian Berry 46br; Jean Gaumy 47cl. **N.A.S.A**: 9tc. **N.H.P.A**: M Wendler 4cl, 110bl. **Oxford Scientific Films:** Konrad Wothe 19tc; L Gould 4tr; Nobert Rosing 92cl. **Panos Pictures**: Alain le Garsheur 74cr; Alain le Garsmeur 95cl (below); Alberto Arzoz 45tr; Bruce Paton 121bl; Jeremy Hartley 120bl; Maria Luiza M Cavalho 112cl (below); Paul Smith 111cr; Rhodri Jones 113bl; Ron Gilling 119cr; Trygve Bolstad 22bl. **Edward Parker:** 17cr (above). **Pictor International**: 4tc, 10bc, 18tr, 20br, 26tr, 26bl, 29bc. **Planet Earth Pictures**: J Waters 113bc. **South American Pictures**: Robert Francis 93br; Tony Morrison 110cr, 111cl. **Spectrum Colour Library:** 93br. **Frank Spooner Pictures**: Gamma/E Baitel 73cl. **Still Pictures**: J Frebet 113cr; R Seitre 72cr (above). **Tony Stone Images:** 17tr, 112cl; A Sacks 92cr; Alan Levenson 74cr; D Austen 195cr; D Hanson 17cl; Donald Johnson 44bc; Earth Imaging 6tr (above); G Johnson 72bl; H Strand 113tr; J Jangoux 19bcr; J Warden 110bc; John Garrett 121br; L Resnick 121tr; P Chesley 194tr; Randy Wells 19br; Robert Frerck 47tr; Tony Craddock 47cr. **Telegraph Colour Library**: 93tr. **Travel Ink**: Colin Marshall 22bc; Ian Booth 27cl. **Trip**: A Kuznetsov 74bc; H Rogers 72cr; M Barlow 112bl; N Ray 10tr; Robert Belbin 74bl; V Kolpakov 75cr (below); V Sidoropolev 46cr; W Jacobs 194c. **World Pictures:** 195tr. **ZEFA Picture Library**: 19bcl, 19cll, 45bc; Bramaz 94bl; Damm 119cl; Heilman 110cr (below); K Siewert 110cl; Kitchen 19bll; Sunak 73cr; Surpress 111tr. **Jacket:** Front cover image: Science Photo Library/NOAA

CONTENTS

LEARNING MAP SKILLS

AMAZING EARTH 4

MAPPING THE WORLD 6

HOW MAPS ARE MADE 8

READING MAPS 10

USING THE ATLAS 12

THE WORLD

THE PHYSICAL WORLD 14

THE EARTH'S STRUCTURE 16
Dynamic Earth, Plate Boundaries, Shaping the Landscape, The World's Oceans

CLIMATE AND LIFE ZONES 18
Winds, Ocean Currents, Life Zones

WORLD POPULATION 20
Population Structure, Population Density, Urban Growth, Population Growth

THE WORLD ECONOMY 22
Measuring Wealth, Types of Industry, Patterns of Trade, Developing Economies, Tourism

BORDERS AND BOUNDARIES 24

THE BRITISH ISLES

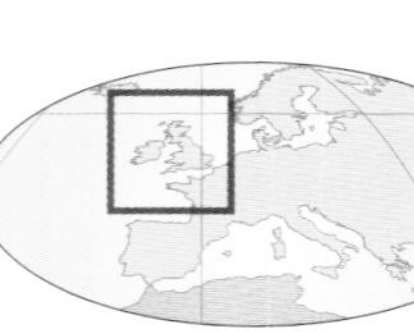

PHYSICAL BRITISH ISLES 26

POLITICAL BRITISH ISLES 28

IRELAND 30

SCOTLAND 32

NORTHERN ENGLAND 34

SOUTHERN ENGLAND 36

WALES 38

UK OVERSEAS TERRITORIES 40

THE WORLD ATLAS

THE NATIONS OF THE WORLD 42

EUROPE

CONTINENTAL EUROPE 44

EUROPEAN GEOGRAPHY 46

NORTHERN EUROPE 48
Denmark, Estonia, Finland, Iceland, Latvia, Lithuania, Norway, Sweden

THE LOW COUNTRIES 50
Belgium, Luxembourg, Netherlands

THE BRITISH ISLES 52
United Kingdom, Ireland

FRANCE 54
Andorra, France, Monaco

SPAIN AND PORTUGAL 56
Portugal, Spain

GERMANY AND THE ALPINE STATES 58
Austria, Germany, Liechtenstein, Slovenia, Switzerland

ITALY 60
Italy, San Marino, Vatican City

CENTRAL EUROPE 62
Czech Republic, Hungary, Poland, Slovakia

SOUTHEAST EUROPE 64
Albania, Bosnia and Herzegovina, Bulgaria, Croatia, Greece, Macedonia, Serbia & Montenegro (Yugoslavia)

EASTERN EUROPE 66
Belarus, Moldova, Romania, Ukraine

EUROPEAN RUSSIA 68

THE MEDITERRANEAN 70

ASIA

CONTINENTAL ASIA 72

ASIAN GEOGRAPHY 74

RUSSIA AND KAZAKHSTAN 76

TURKEY AND THE CAUCASUS 78
Armenia, Azerbaijan, Georgia, Turkey

SOUTHWEST ASIA 80
Bahrain, Iran, Iraq, Israel, Jordan, Kuwait, Lebanon, Oman, Qatar, Saudi Arabia, Syria, United Arab Emirates, Yemen

CENTRAL ASIA 82
Afghanistan, Kyrgyzstan, Tajikistan, Turkmenistan, Uzbekistan

JAPAN AND KOREA 84
Japan, North Korea, South Korea

EAST ASIA 86
China, Mongolia, Taiwan

SOUTH ASIA 88
Bangladesh, Bhutan, India, Maldives, Nepal, Pakistan, Sri Lanka

SOUTHEAST ASIA 90
Brunei, Burma, Cambodia, East Timor, Indonesia, Laos, Malaysia, Philippines, Singapore, Thailand, Vietnam

NORTH AMERICA

CONTINENTAL NORTH AMERICA 92

NORTH AMERICAN GEOGRAPHY 94

WESTERN CANADA AND ALASKA 96
Alberta, British Columbia, Manitoba, Northwest Territories, Nunavut, Saskatchewan, Yukon Territory, Alaska

EASTERN CANADA 98
New Brunswick, Newfoundland and Labrador, Nova Scotia, Ontario, Prince Edward Island, Québec

EASTERN USA 100
Alabama, Connecticut, Delaware, District of Columbia, Florida, Georgia, Illinois, Indiana, Kentucky, Maine, Maryland, Massachussetts, Michigan, Mississippi, New Hampshire, New Jersey, New York, North Carolina, Ohio, Pennsylvania, Rhode Island, South Carolina, Tennessee, Vermont, Virginia, West Virginia, Wisconsin

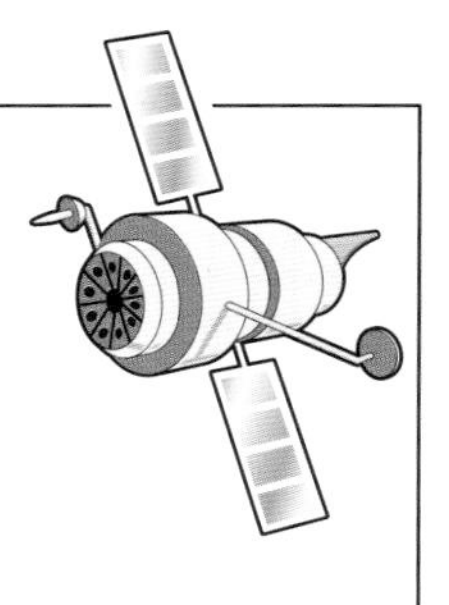

WESTERN USA 102
Arizona, Arkansas, California, Colorado, Hawaii, Idaho, Iowa, Kansas, Louisiana, Minnesota, Missouri, Montana, Nebraska, Nevada, New Mexico, North Dakota, Oklahoma, Oregon, South Dakota, Texas, Utah, Washington, Wyoming

MEXICO 104

CENTRAL AMERICA 106
Belize, Costa Rica, El Salvador, Guatemala, Honduras, Nicaragua, Panama

THE CARIBBEAN 108

SOUTH AMERICA

CONTINENTAL SOUTH AMERICA 110

SOUTH AMERICAN GEOGRAPHY 112

NORTHERN SOUTH AMERICA 114
Brazil, Colombia, Ecuador, Guyana, Peru, Surinam, Venezuela

SOUTHERN SOUTH AMERICA 116
Argentina, Bolivia, Chile, Paraguay, Uruguay

AFRICA

CONTINENTAL AFRICA 118

AFRICAN GEOGRAPHY 120

NORTH AFRICA 122
Algeria, Egypt, Libya, Morocco, Tunisia

WEST AFRICA 124
Benin, Burkina, Cameroon, Central African Republic, Chad, Equatorial Guinea, Gambia, Ghana, Guinea, Guinea-Bissau, Ivory Coast, Liberia, Mali, Mauritania, Niger, Nigeria, Sao Tome & Principe, Senegal, Sierra Leone, Togo

EAST AFRICA 126
Burundi, Djibouti, Eritrea, Ethiopia, Kenya, Rwanda, Somalia, Sudan, Tanzania, Uganda

SOUTHERN AFRICA 128
Angola, Botswana, Comoros, Congo, Dem. Rep. Congo, Gabon, Lesotho, Madagascar, Malawi, Mozambique, Namibia, South Africa, Swaziland, Zambia, Zimbabwe

AUSTRALASIA & OCEANIA

AUSTRALASIA & OCEANIA 130

AUSTRALIA 132

NEW ZEALAND 134

SOUTHWEST PACIFIC 136

POLAR REGIONS

ANTARCTICA, THE ARCTIC 138

GLOSSARY AND INDEX-GAZETTEER 140

KEY TO MAP SYMBOLS ON FRONT ENDPAPER

FLAGS ON BACK ENDPAPER

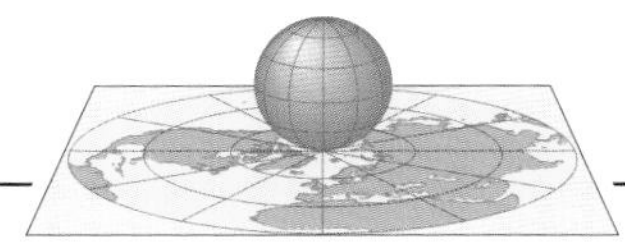

AMAZING EARTH

Earth is unique among the nine planets that circle the Sun. It is the only one that can support life, because it has enough oxygen in its atmosphere and plentiful water. In fact, seen from space, the Earth looks almost entirely blue. This is because about 70% of its surface is under water, submerged beneath four huge oceans: the Pacific, Atlantic, Indian and Arctic oceans. Land makes up about 30% of the Earth's surface. It is divided into seven landmasses of varying shapes and sizes called continents. These are, from largest to smallest: Asia, Africa, North America, South America, Antarctica, Europe and Australia.

WATERY WORLD

The Earth's oceans and seas cover more than 367 million sq km – that is twice the surface of Mars and nine times the surface of the moon.

Beneath the ocean waves lies the biggest and most unexplored landscape on Earth. Here are coral reefs, enormous, open plains, deep canyons, and the longest mountain range on Earth – the Mid-Atlantic Ridge – which stretches almost from pole to pole.

THE SHAPE OF THE EARTH

Photographs taken from space by astronauts in the 1960s, and more recently from orbiting satellites, have proven beyond doubt what humans had already worked out long ago – that the Earth is shaped like a ball. But it is not perfectly round. The force of the Earth's rotation makes the world bulge very slightly at the Equator and go a little flat at the North and South poles. So the Earth is actually a flattened sphere, or a 'geoid'.

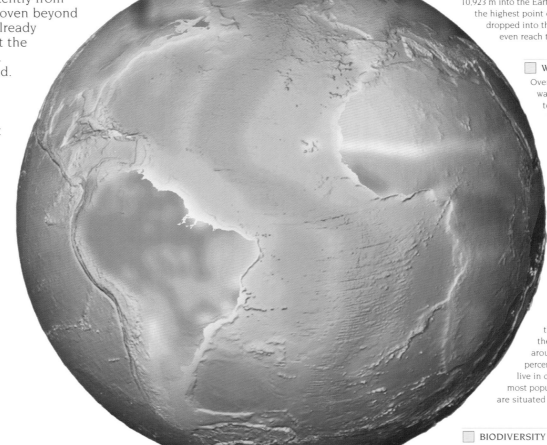

HEIGHTS AND DEPTHS

The Pacific Ocean contains the deepest places on the Earth's surface – the ocean trenches. The very deepest is Challenger Deep in the Mariana Trench which plunges 10,923 m into the Earth's crust. If Mount Everest, the highest point on land at 8,850 m, was dropped into the trench, its peak wouldn't even reach the surface of the Pacific.

WATER

Over 97% of the Earth's water is salt water. The total amount of salt in the world's oceans and seas would cover the whole of Europe to a depth of five km. Less than 3% of the Earth's water is fresh. Of this, 2.24% is frozen in ice sheets and about 0.6% is stored underground as groundwater. The remainder is in lakes and rivers.

COASTS

The total length of the Earth's coastlines is more than 500,000 km – that is the equivalent of 12 times around the globe. A high percentage of the world's people live in coastal zones: of the ten most populated cities on Earth, eight are situated on estuaries or the coast.

BIODIVERSITY

Today, almost six hundred million humans, approximately one million animal species and 355,000 known plant species depend on the air, water and land of planet Earth.

VANISHING FORESTS

10,000 years ago, thick forests covered about half of the Earth's land surface. Today, 33% of those forests no longer exist, and more than half of what remains has been dramatically altered. During the 20th century, more than 50% of the Earth's rainforests have been felled.

WET EARTH

Tropical rainforests grow in areas close to the Equator, where it is wet and warm all year round. Although they cover just 7% of the Earth's land, these thick, damp forests form the richest ecosystems on the planet. More plant and animal species are found here than anywhere else on Earth.

DRY EARTH

Deserts are among the most inhospitable places on the planet. Some deserts are scorching hot, others are freezing cold, but they have one thing in common – they are all dry. Very few plant and animal species can survive in these harsh conditions. The world's coldest and driest continent, Antarctica (*left*), is a cold desert.

DIFFERENT WORLD VIEWS

Because the Earth is round, we can only see half of it at any one time. This half is called a hemisphere, which means 'half a sphere'. There are always two hemispheres – the half that you see and the other half that you don't see. Two hemispheres placed together will always make a complete sphere.

Equator 0°

North Pole

NORTH AMERICA

EUROPE

AFRICA

SOUTH AMERICA

NORTH AND SOUTH

The Equator is an imaginary line drawn around the middle of the Earth, where its circumference is greatest. If we cut along the Equator, the Earth separates into two hemispheres: the northern and southern hemispheres. Most of the Earth's land is the northern hemisphere. Europe and North America are the only continents which lie entirely in the northern hemisphere. Australia and Antarctica are the only continents that lie wholly in the southern hemisphere.

The southern hemisphere contains three of the Earth's four great oceans: the Pacific, Indian and Southern oceans.

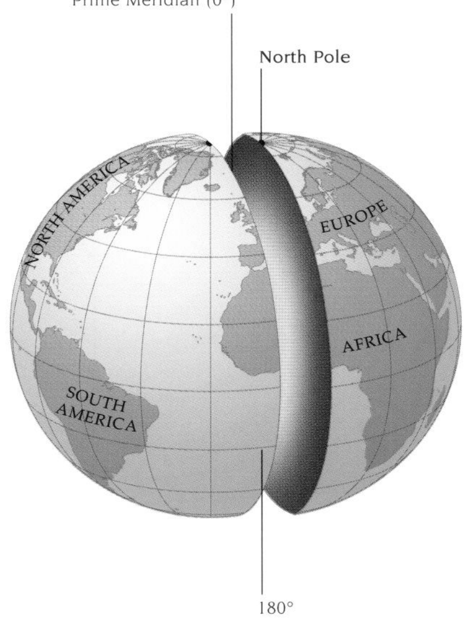

EAST AND WEST

The Earth can also be divided along two other imaginary lines – the Prime Meridian (0°) and 180° – which run opposite each other between the North and South poles. This creates eastern and western hemispheres. The continents in the eastern hemisphere are traditionally called the Old World while those in the western hemisphere – the Americas – were named the New World by the Europeans who explored them in the 15th century.

PLANET WATER, PLANET LAND

The Earth can also be divided into land and water hemispheres. The land hemisphere shows most of the land on the Earth's surface. The water hemisphere is dominated by the vast Pacific Ocean – from this view, the Earth appears to be almost entirely covered by water.

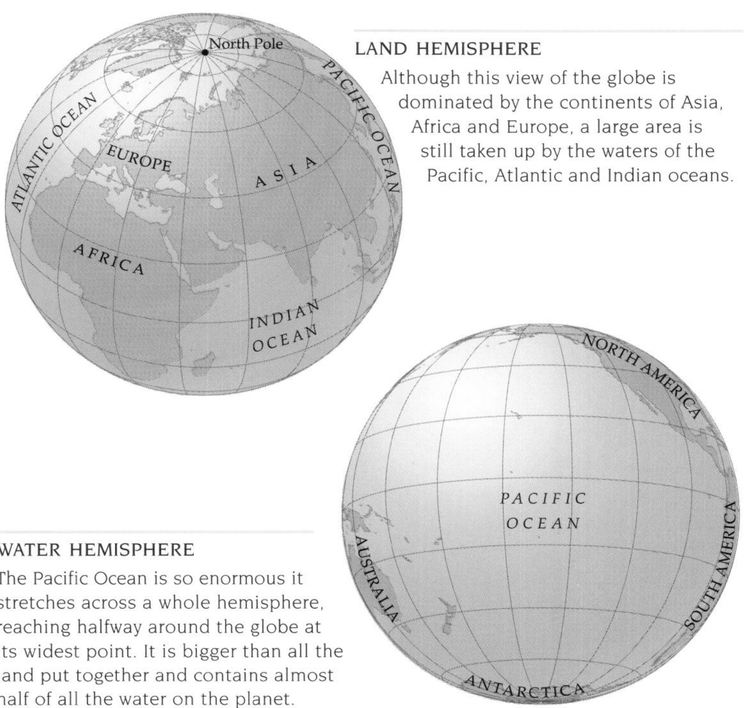

LAND HEMISPHERE

Although this view of the globe is dominated by the continents of Asia, Africa and Europe, a large area is still taken up by the waters of the Pacific, Atlantic and Indian oceans.

WATER HEMISPHERE

The Pacific Ocean is so enormous it stretches across a whole hemisphere, reaching halfway around the globe at its widest point. It is bigger than all the land put together and contains almost half of all the water on the planet.

THE SEASONS

As the Earth orbits the Sun, it is also spinning around an imaginary line called its axis, which joins the north and south poles. The Earth's axis is not quite at right angles to the Sun, but tilts over at an angle of 23.5°. As a result, each place gradually moves closer to the Sun and then further away from it again. Summer in the northern hemisphere is when the north is closest to the Sun. In winter, the northern hemisphere tilts away from the Sun, receiving far less heat and light. In the southern hemisphere the seasons are reversed, with summer in December and winter in June.

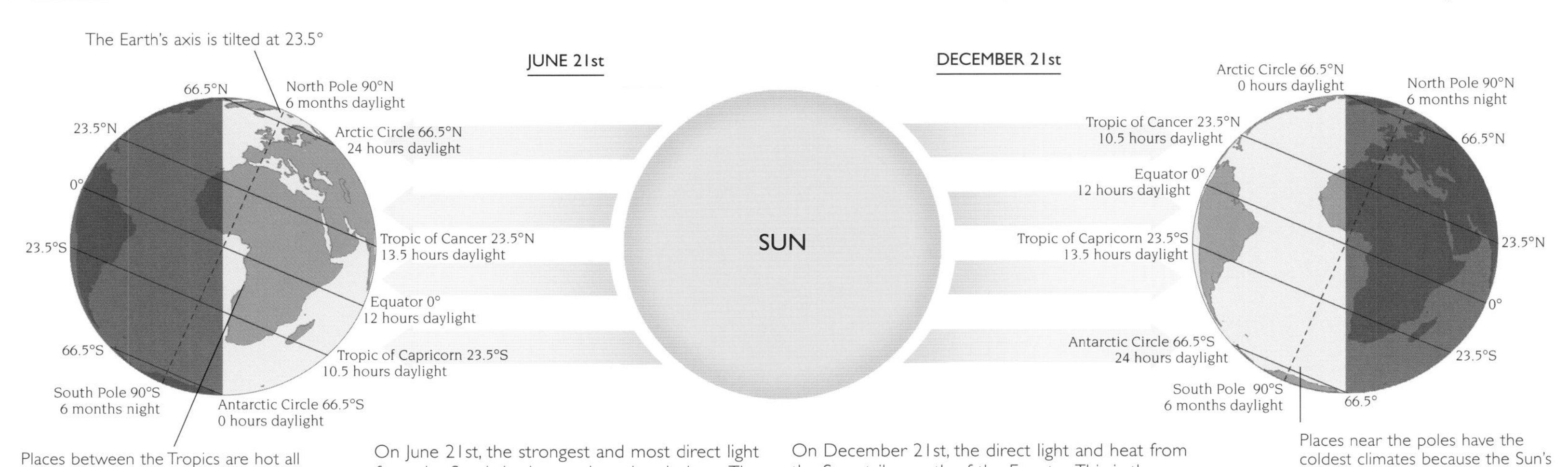

Places between the Tropics are hot all year round. This is because the Sun's rays strike the Equator almost vertically, heating the land more intensely.

On June 21st, the strongest and most direct light from the Sun is in the northern hemisphere. The Arctic Circle has 24 hours of daylight, and the northern hemisphere has its longest day.

On December 21st, the direct light and heat from the Sun strike south of the Equator. This is the longest day in the southern hemisphere. The northern hemisphere has its shortest day and longest night.

Places near the poles have the coldest climates because the Sun's rays hit them at an angle. The Sun's warmth is therefore spread out over a much wider area.

Mapping the World

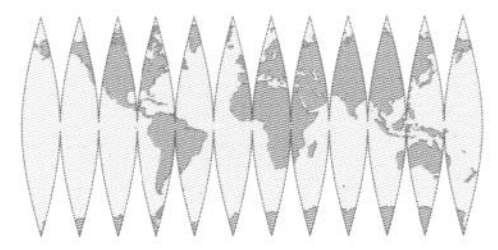

The main purpose of a map is to show, or locate, where things are. The only truly accurate map of the whole world is a globe – a round model of the Earth. But a globe is impractical to carry around, so map-makers (cartographers) produce flat paper maps instead. Changing the globe into a flat map is not simple. Imagine cutting a globe in half and trying to flatten the two hemispheres. They would be stretched in some places, and squashed in others. In fact, it is impossible to make a map of the round Earth on flat paper without some distortion of area, distance or direction.

Models of the World

Satellite images can show the whole world as it appears from space. However, this image shows only one half of the world, and is distorted at the edges.

A globe (*right*) is the only way to illustrate the shape of the Earth accurately. A globe also shows the correct positions of the continents and oceans and how large they are in relation to one another.

LATITUDE

We can find out exactly how far north or south, east or west any place is on Earth by drawing two sets of imaginary lines around the world to make a grid. The horizontal lines on the globe below are called lines of latitude. They run from east to west. The most important is the Equator, which is given the value 0°. All other lines of latitude run parallel to the Equator. and are numbered in degrees either north or south of the Equator.

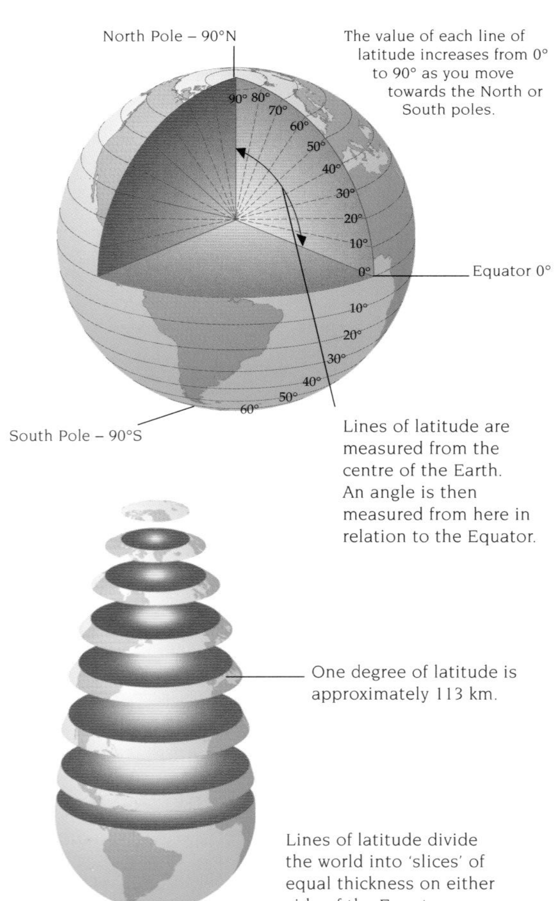

The value of each line of latitude increases from 0° to 90° as you move towards the North or South poles.

Lines of latitude are measured from the centre of the Earth. An angle is then measured from here in relation to the Equator.

One degree of latitude is approximately 113 km.

Lines of latitude divide the world into 'slices' of equal thickness on either side of the Equator.

LONGITUDE

The vertical lines on the globe below run from north to south between the poles. They are called lines of longitude. The most important passes through Greenwich, London and is numbered 0°. It is called the Prime Meridian. All other lines of longitude are numbered in degrees either east or west of the Prime Meridian. The line directly opposite the Prime Meridian is numbered 180°.

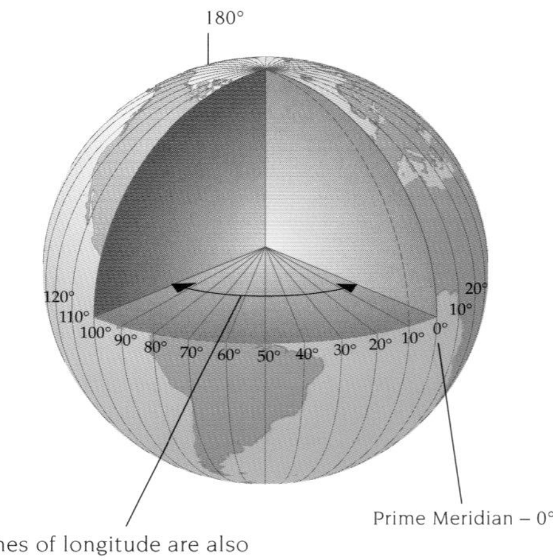

Lines of longitude are also measured from the centre of the Earth. This time, the angle is taken in relation to the Prime Meridian.

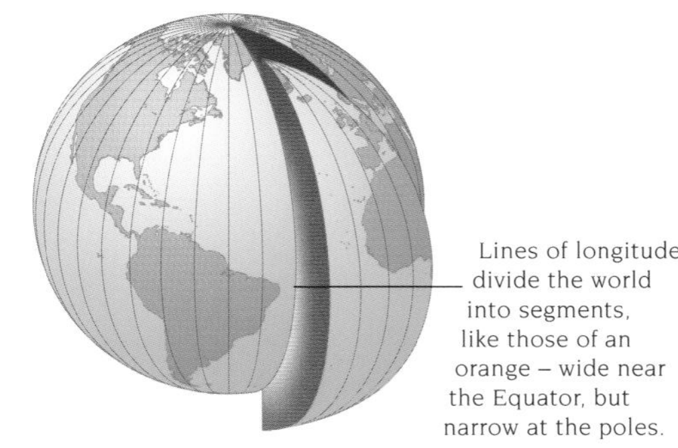

Lines of longitude divide the world into segments, like those of an orange – wide near the Equator, but narrow at the poles.

WHERE ON EARTH?

When lines of latitude and longitude are combined on a globe, or as here, on a flat map, they form a grid. Using this grid, we can locate any place on land, or at sea, by referring to the point where its line of latitude intersects with its line of longitude. Even when a place is not located exactly where the lines cross, you can still find its approximate position.

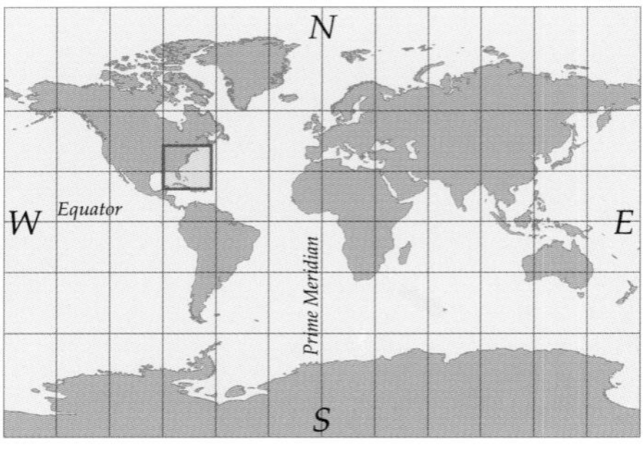

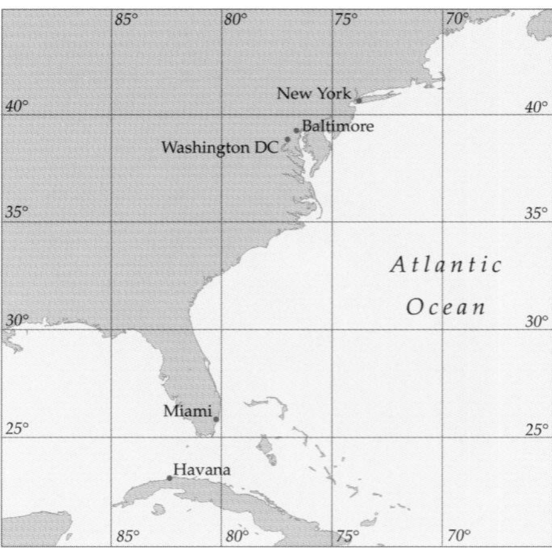

The map above is of the eastern USA. It is too small to show all the lines of latitude and longitude, so they are given at intervals of 5°. Miami is located at about 26° north of the Equator and 80° west of the Prime Meridian. We write its location like this: 26°N 80°W.

MAKING A FLAT MAP FROM A GLOBE

Cartographers use a technique called projection to show the Earth's curved surface on a flat map. Many different map projections have been designed. The distortion of one feature – either area, distance, or direction – can be minimized, while other features become more distorted. Cartographers must choose which of these things it is most important to show correctly for each map that they make. Three major families of projections can be used to solve these questions.

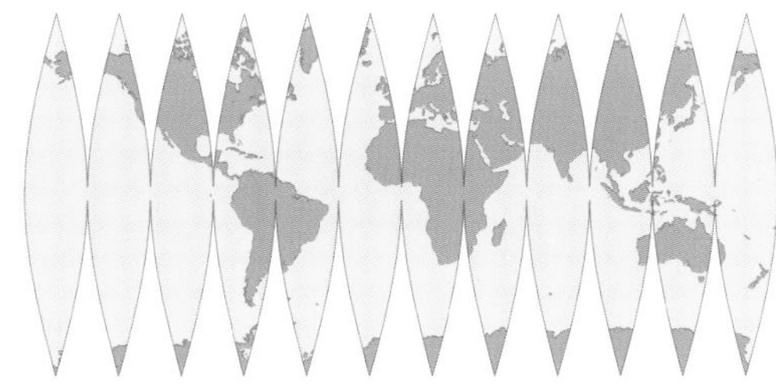

To make a globe, the Earth is divided into segments or 'gores' along lines of longitude.

1 CYLINDRICAL PROJECTIONS

These projections are 'cylindrical' because the surface of the globe is transferred onto a surrounding cylinder. This cylinder is then cut from top to bottom and 'rolled out' to give a flat map. These maps are very useful for showing the whole world.

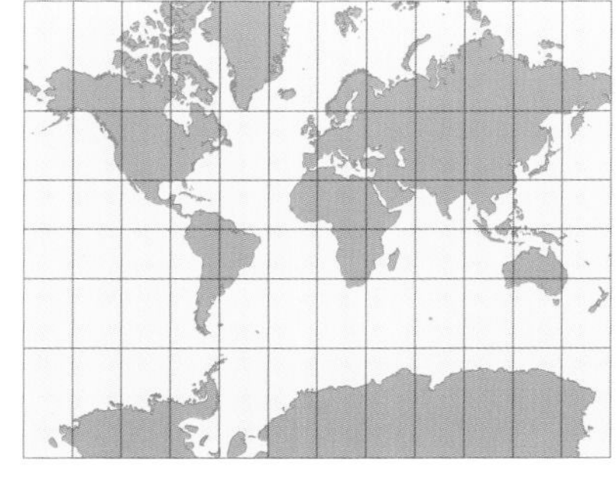

The cylinder touches the globe at the Equator. Here, the scale on the map will be exactly the same as it is on the globe. At the northern and southern edges of the cylinder, which are furthest away from the surface of the globe, the map is most distorted. The Mercator projection (*above*), created in the 16th century, is a good example of a cylindrical projection.

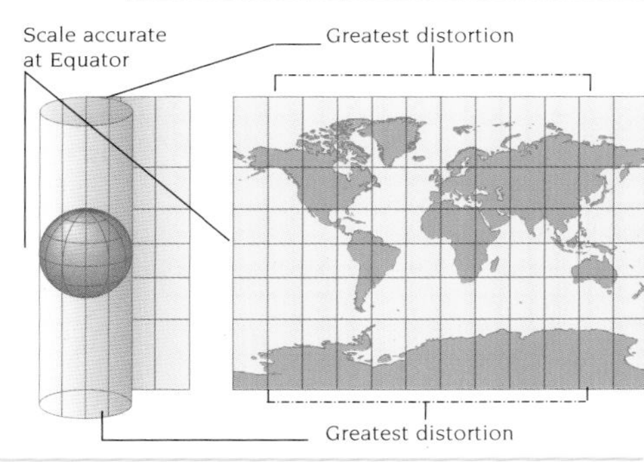

2 AZIMUTHAL PROJECTIONS

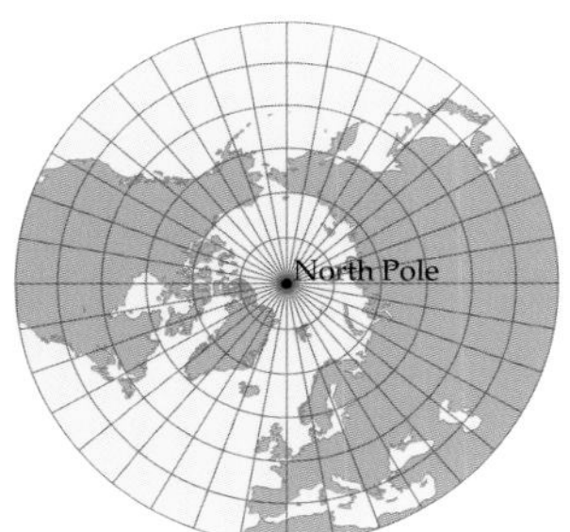

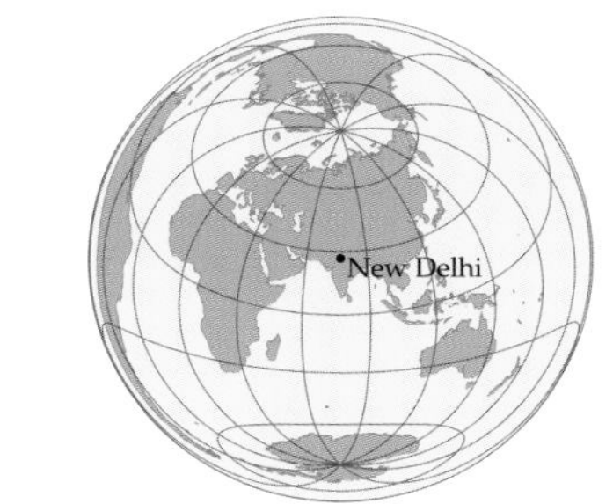

Azimuthal projections put the surface of the globe onto a flat circle. 'Azimuthal' means that the direction or 'azimuth' of any line coming from the centre point of that circle is correct. Azimuthal maps are useful for viewing hemispheres, continents and the polar regions. Mapping any area larger than a hemisphere gives great distortion at the outer edges of the map.

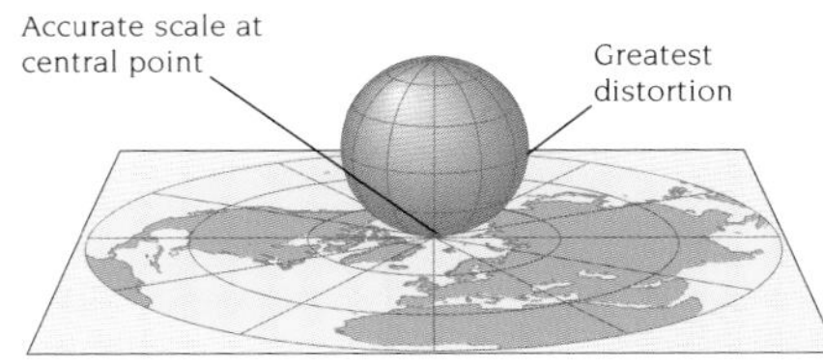

The circle only touches the globe's surface at one central point. The scale is only accurate at this point and becomes less and less accurate the further away the circle is from the globe. This kind of projection is good for maps centering on a major city or on one of the poles.

3 CONIC PROJECTIONS

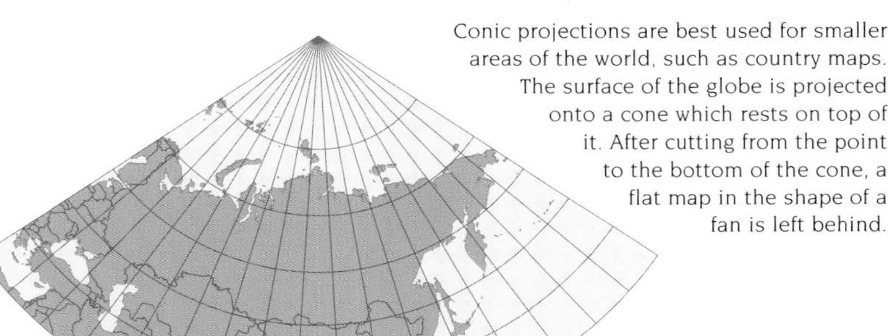

Conic projections are best used for smaller areas of the world, such as country maps. The surface of the globe is projected onto a cone which rests on top of it. After cutting from the point to the bottom of the cone, a flat map in the shape of a fan is left behind.

The conic projection touches the globe's surface at one latitude. This is where the scale of the map will be most accurate. The parts of the cone furthest from the globe will be the most distorted and are usually omitted from the map itself.

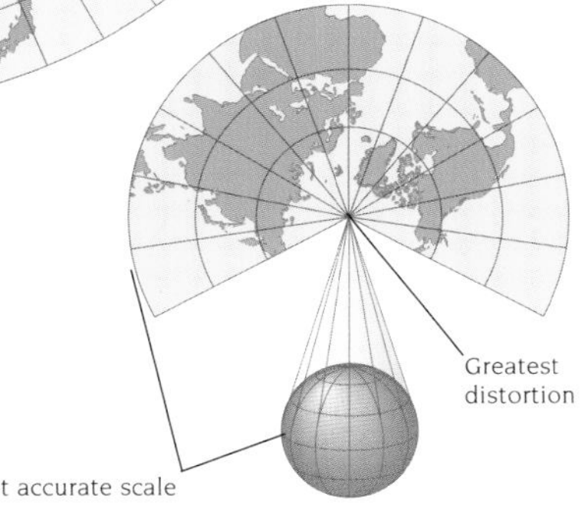

PROJECTIONS USED IN THIS ATLAS

The projections which are appropriate for showing maps at a world, continental or country scale are quite different. The projections for this atlas have been carefully chosen. They are ones that show areas as familiar shapes and ensure that they are distorted as little as possible.

1 World Maps

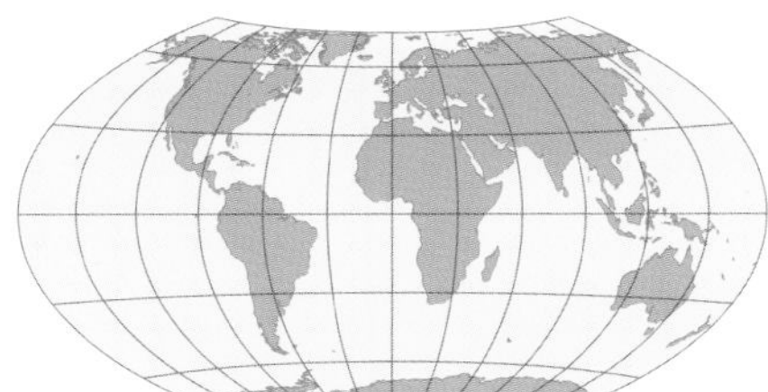

The Wagner VII projection is used for our world maps as it shows all the countries at their correct sizes relative to one another.

2 Continents

The Lambert Azimuthal Equal Area is used for continental maps. The shape distortion is relatively small and countries retain their correct sizes relative to one another.

3 Countries

The Lambert Conformal Conic shows countries with as little distortion as possible. The angles from any point on the map are the same as they would be on the surface of the globe.

How maps are made

New technologies have revolutionized map making. Computers and information from satellites have replaced drawing boards and drafting pens, and the process of creating new maps is now far easier. But map making is still a skilled and often time-consuming process. Information about the World must be gathered, sorted and checked. The cartographer must make decisions about the function of the map and what information to select in order to make it as clear as possible.

The Mappa Mundi

Maps have been made for thousands of years. The 13th century Mappa Mundi, meaning 'known world' shows the Mediterranean Sea and the Don and Nile rivers. Asia is at the top, with Europe on the left, and Africa to the right. The oceans are shown as a ring surrounding the land. The map reflects a number of biblical stories.

HISTORICAL MAP MAKING

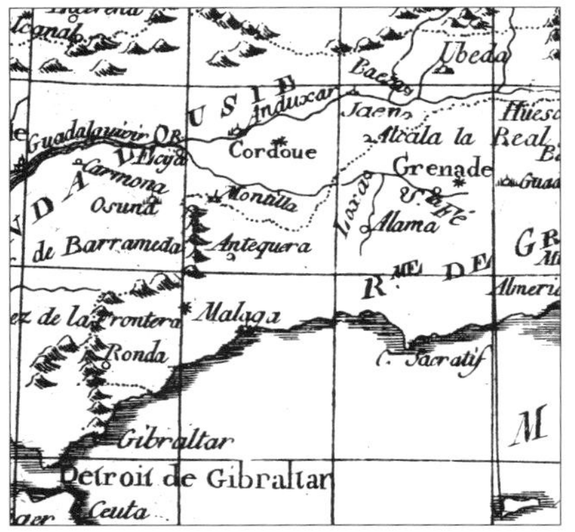

This detailed hand-drawn map of the southern coast of Spain was made in about 1750. The mountains are illustrated as small hills and the labels have been hand lettered.

For centuries, maps were drawn by hand. Very early maps were no more than a pictorial representation of what the surface of the ground looked like. Where there were hills, pictures were drawn to represent them. Later maps were drawn using information gathered by survey teams. They would carefully mark out and calculate the height of the land, the positions of towns and other geographical features. As knowledge and techniques improved, maps became more accurate.

NEW TECHNIQUES

Computers make it easier to change map information and styles quickly. This map of the southern coast of Spain, made in 1997 has been made using digital terrain modelling (see below) and traditional cartography.

Today, cartographers have access to far more data about the Earth than in the past. Satellites collect and process information about its surface. This is called remote-sensed data. Further information may be drafted in the traditional way. Locations can be verified by GPS (Global Positioning Systems) linked to satellites. Computers are now widely used to combine different sorts of map information. Any computerized map is produced using a GIS (Geographical Information System).

MODERN MAP MAKING

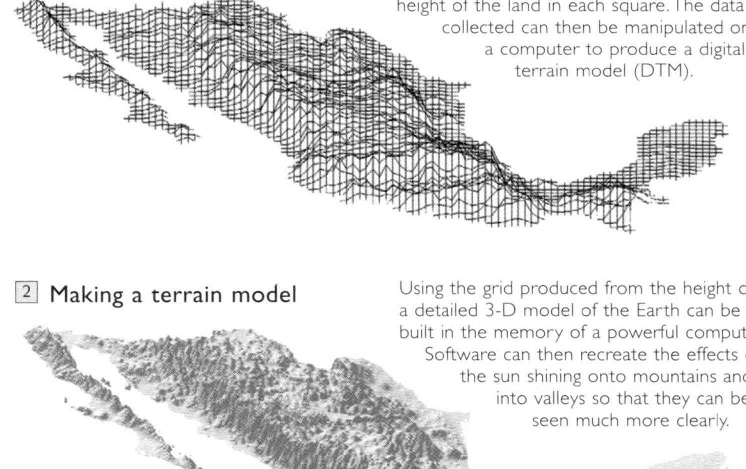

1 Measuring the Earth's surface

The surface of the Earth is divided up into squares. Satellites take measurements of the height of the land in each square. The data collected can then be manipulated on a computer to produce a digital terrain model (DTM).

2 Making a terrain model

Using the grid produced from the height data, a detailed 3-D model of the Earth can be built in the memory of a powerful computer. Software can then recreate the effects of the sun shining onto mountains and into valleys so that they can be seen much more clearly.

3 Adding detail to the land surface

The height of the land can be shown using bands of colour, or by contour lines, which are applied to the digitally-created surface of the Earth. Colour can also be used to show different kinds of vegetation, such as deserts, forests and grasslands.

4 Adding map detail

Features such as roads, rivers, towns and cities can now be added to the map. They are selected, and compiled and scanned digitally into the computer. The information can then be 'draped' on top of the terrain model to create a map.

SHOWING INFORMATION ON A MAP

A map is a selective diagram of a place. It is the cartographer's job to decide what kind of information to show on a map. They can choose to highlight certain kinds of features – such as roads, rivers and land height. They can also show other features such as sea depth, place names, and borders which would be impossible to see either on the ground or from a photograph. The information that can be shown in a map is influenced by a number of factors, most notably by its scale.

This is a satellite photograph of the harbour area of Rio de Janeiro in Brazil. Although you can see the bay and where most of the housing is, it is impossible to see roads or get any sense of the position of places relative to one another.

This is a map of the same area as you can see in the photograph. Much of the detail has been greatly simplified. Towns are named and marked; contours indicate the height of the land; and roads, railways and borders between districts have been added.

SCALE

To make a map of an area it needs to be greatly reduced in size. This is known as drawing to scale. The scale of the map shows us by how much the area has been reduced. The smaller the scale, the greater the area of land that can be shown on the map. There will be far less detail and the map will not be as accurate. The maps below show the different kinds of information that can be shown on maps of varying scales.

WAYS TO SHOW SCALE

When using a map to work out what areas or distances are in reality, we need to refer to the scale of that particular map. Map scales can be shown in several ways.

1 Representative fraction

One unit on the map would be equal to 1,000,0000 units on the ground.

1:1,000,000

2 Linear scale

The line is marked off in units which represent the real distances of the map, given in both miles and kilometres.

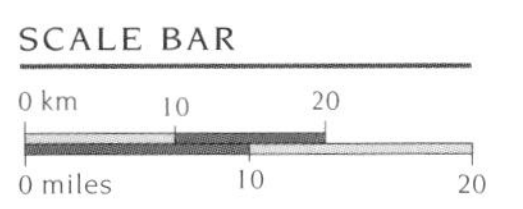

3 Statement of scale

It means that 1 mm on the map represents 1 km on the ground.

1 mm represents 1 km

LONDON 1:21,000,000

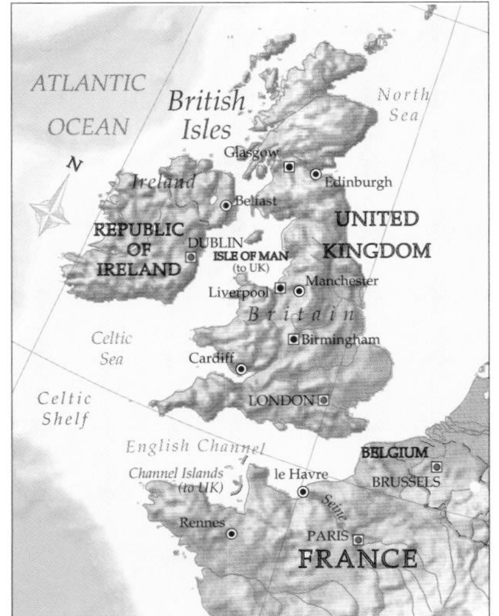

This small-scale map shows the position of London in relation to Europe. Very little detail can be seen at this scale – only the names of countries and the largest towns.

LONDON 1:5,500,000

At a scale of 1 to 5,500,000 you can see the major road network in the southeast of the UK. Many towns are named and you can see the difference in size and status.

LONDON 1:900,000

This map is at a much larger scale. You can see the major roads that lead out from London and the names of many suburbs, places of interest and airports.

LONDON 1:12,500

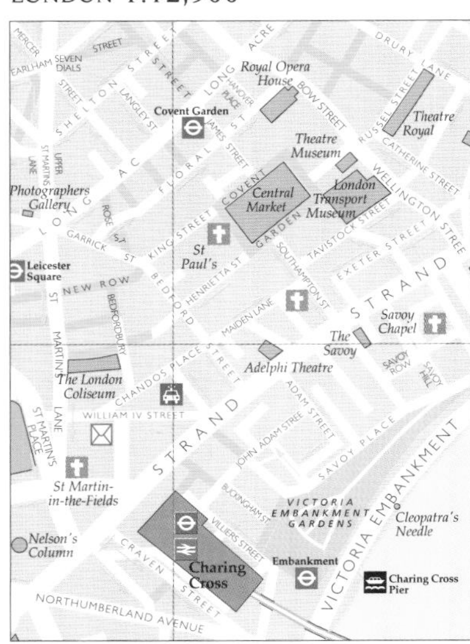

This is a street map of central London. The streets are named, as are places of interest, train and underground stations. The scale is large enough to show plenty of detail.

READING MAPS

Maps use a unique visual language to convey a great deal of detailed information in a relatively simple form. Different features are marked out using special symbols and styles of print. These symbols are explained in the key to the map and you should always read a map alongside its key or legend. This page explains how to look for different features on the map and how to unravel the different layers of information that you can find on it.

PHYSICAL FEATURES

All the regional and country maps in this atlas are based on a model of the Earth's surface. The computer-generated relief gives an accurate picture of the surface of the land. Colours are used to show the relative heights of the land; green is for low-lying land, and yellows, browns and greys are for higher land. Water features like streams, rivers and lakes are also shown.

On this map extract, the blue lines show a number of rivers, including the Salween and the Irrawaddy. The Irrawaddy forms a huge delta, splitting into many streams as it reaches the sea.

These mountains are in the north of Southeast Asia. The underlying relief on the map and the coloured bands help you to see the height of the land.

HUMAN FEATURES

Maps also reveal a great deal about the human geography of an area. As well as showing where towns and roads are, different symbols can tell you more about the size of towns and the importance of a road. Borders between countries or regions can only be seen on a map.

SCALE BAR
0 km 200 400
0 miles 200 400

3 BORDERS

Borders on the map are marked by a thick purple line. The boundary between Laos and Vietnam is in sparsely populated mountainous terrain, with the border generally running along a mountain range.

KEY TO MAP SYMBOLS

Boundaries

- Full international border
- Disputed border

Communication features

- Major road
- Minor road
- Railway
- International airport

Drainage features

- Major river
- Minor river
- Lake
- Wetland

Landscape features

- Mountain

Populated places

- Less than 50,000
- 50,000–100,000
- 100,000–500,000
- Greater than 500,000
- Capital city

Names

BURMA	Country
PARACEL ISLANDS (disputed by China, Taiwan & Vietnam)	Dependent territory
JAKARTA	Capital city
Sarawak	Cultural region
Chin Hills	Landscape feature
Puncak Jaya 5040m	Mountain/pass
Red River	River/lake
Java Sea	Sea feature

LAND HEIGHT	SEA DEPTH
Above 4000 m	0–250 m
2000–4000 m	250–500 m
1000–2000 m	500–1000 m
500–1000 m	1000–2000 m
250–500 m	2000–3000 m
100–250 m	3000–4000 m
0–100 m	Below 4000 m

CITIES AND TOWNS

- Over 500,000 people
- 100,000–500,000
- 50,000–100,000
- Less than 50,000

4 SETTLEMENTS

The symbol for a settlement can tell you its position, population and political status. Most towns are shown by a circle or a square. These represent the size of their population. Where a town is coloured red, this shows that it is a capital city such as Kuala Lumpur in Malaysia.

FINDING PLACES

Alphanumeric grid references

All the maps in this book are indexed using their alphanumeric grid reference – for example, G4. To find a place you must first look up its page number and then its grid reference. Read the letters and numbers off the bottom and side of the grid. Using rulers held at right angles to one another you will find the point where the lines meet. The place will be located within this square.

Latitude and longitude references

The lines of latitude and longitude are known as graticules. They are shown on the map as thin blue lines with the value of their latitude or longitude given as a blue number at the edge of the map.

5 ROADS AND RAILWAYS

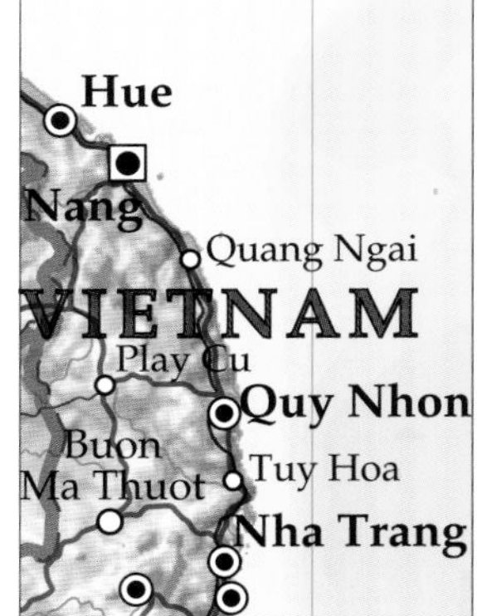

a The major road and railway links between Hue and Nha Trang hug the Vietnamese coast. A string of coastal towns is often connected by road and rail in this manner.

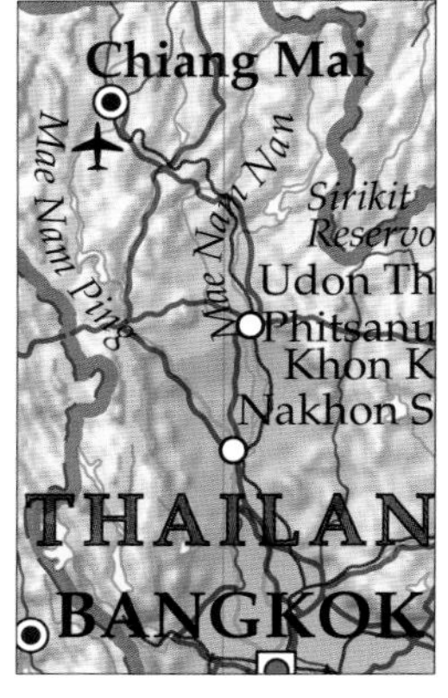

b Chiang Mai, in northern Thailand, is linked to the capital Bangkok to the south by railway and road. At Chiang Mai, the mountains are too high for the railway to continue, and only roads go north into Burma.

USING THE ATLAS

This Atlas has been designed to develop map-reading skills and to introduce readers to a wide range of different maps. It also provides a wealth of detailed geographic information about the world today. The Atlas is divided into four sections: **Learning Map Skills**; **The World About Us**, covering global geographic patterns; the **World Atlas**, dealing with the world's regions, and an **Index-Gazetteer**.

THE WORLD ABOUT US

These pages contain a series of world maps which show important themes, such as physical features, climate, life zones, population and the world economy, at a global scale. They give a worldwide picture of concepts which are explored in more detail later in the book.

Text introduces themes and concepts in each spread.

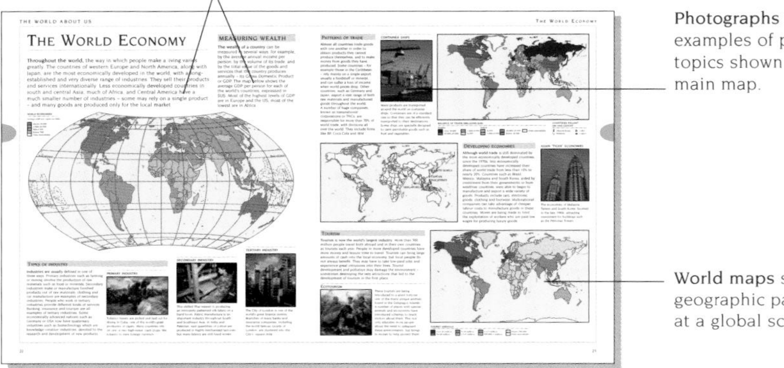

Photographs illustrate examples of places or topics shown on the main map.

World maps show geographic patterns at a global scale.

LEARNING MAP SKILLS

Maps show the Earth – which is three-dimensional – in just two dimensions. This section shows how maps are made; how different kinds of information are shown on maps; how to choose what to put on a map and the best way to show it. It also explains how to read the maps in this Atlas.

Introduction to projections: different projections and how they work.

Choosing the best projections: the map projections used in this book.

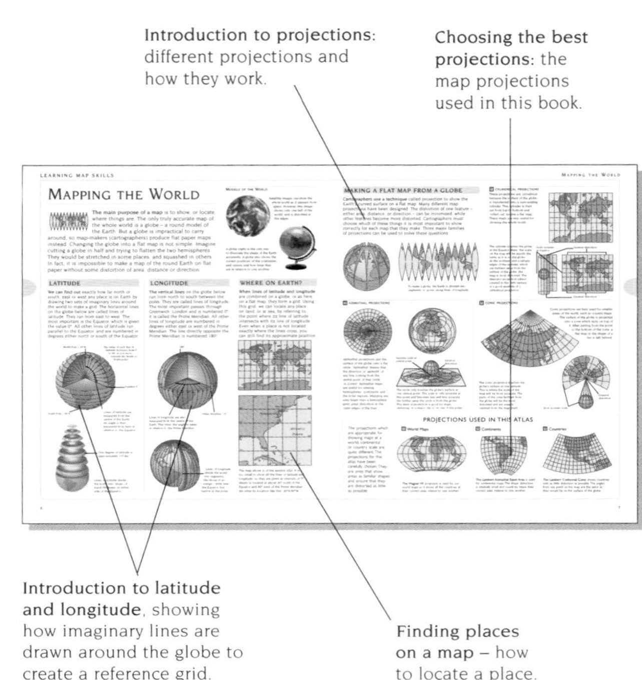

Introduction to latitude and longitude, showing how imaginary lines are drawn around the globe to create a reference grid.

Finding places on a map – how to locate a place.

CONTINENTAL MAPS

A cross-section through the continent shows the relative height of certain features.

A detailed physical map of the continent shows major natural geographic features, including mountains, lakes and rivers.

Photographs and locator maps illustrate the main geographic regions and show you where they are.

The political map of the continent shows country boundaries and country names.

The industry map shows the main industrial towns and cities and the main industries in each continent. It also shows the wealth of each country relative to the rest of the world.

CONTINENTAL PAGES

These pages show the physical shape of each continent and the impact that humans have made on the natural landscape – building towns and roads and creating borders between countries. They show where natural features such as mountain ranges and rivers have created physical boundaries, and where humans have created their own political boundaries between states.

CONTINENTAL GEOGRAPHY PAGES

Humans have colonized and changed all the continents except Antarctica. These pages show the factors which have affected this process: climate, the availability of resources such as coal, oil, and minerals, and varying patterns of land use. Mineral resources are directly linked to many industries, and most agriculture is governed both by the quality of the land and the climate.

The climate map shows the main types of climates across the continent and where the hottest and coldest, wettest and driest places are.

The mineral resources map shows where the most important reserves of minerals, including coal and precious metals, are found.

The land use map shows different types of land and the main kinds of farming that take place in each area.

REGIONAL MAPS

The main part of the Atlas contains detailed maps of countries and regions. Each of these is accompanied by a series of small thematic maps, models and charts, which give information about the climate, where people live, how they use the land, the different kinds of industry, and important environmental issues.

TERRAIN MODEL

A computer-generated landscape model shows what the land really looks like. There are no roads or towns to mask the physical geography of the country or region. Mountain ranges, plains and river basins can be easily seen.

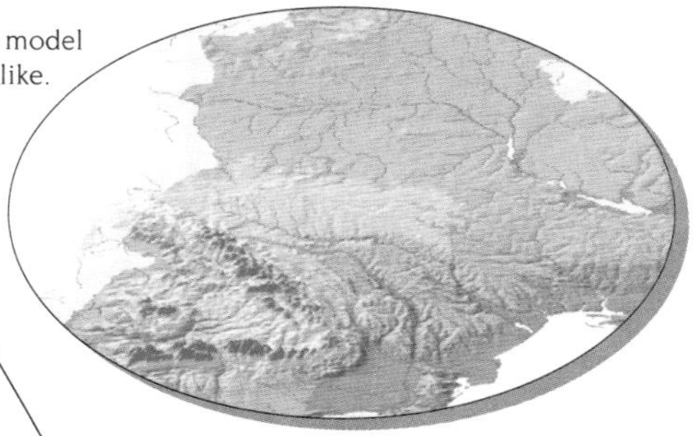

CLIMATE MAPS

These maps show the temperature and rainfall patterns in January and July. Coloured bands indicate temperatures: blue for low temperatures, orange for high ones. Rainfall is represented by black lines with a number giving the average amount of rain. These are called isohyets.

Isohyets show the rainfall patterns in millimetres per year. The areas between the lines are either over or under the figures shown on the ishohyets.

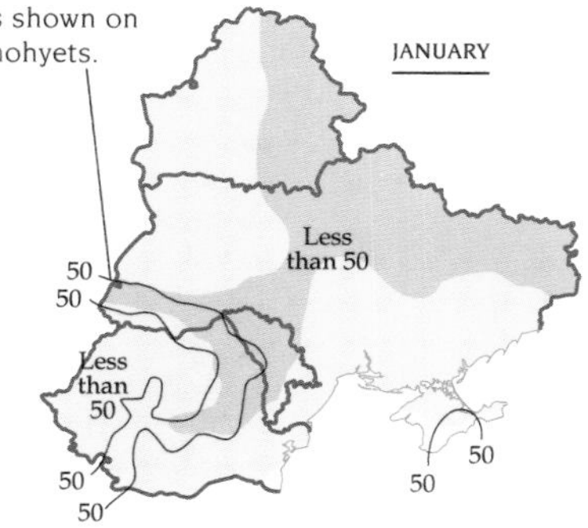

JANUARY
Less than 50
50
50
Less than 50
50
50
50
50

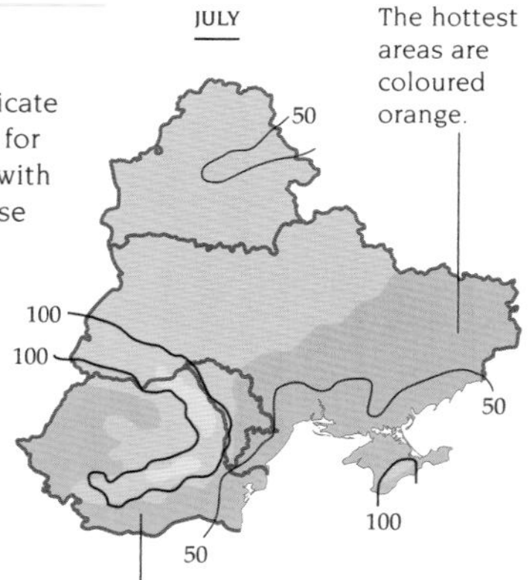

JULY
The hottest areas are coloured orange.
50
100
100
50
100
50
Here the rainfall is between 50 and 100 mm per year.

COLOURED THUMB TAGS

Each section has its own colour code.

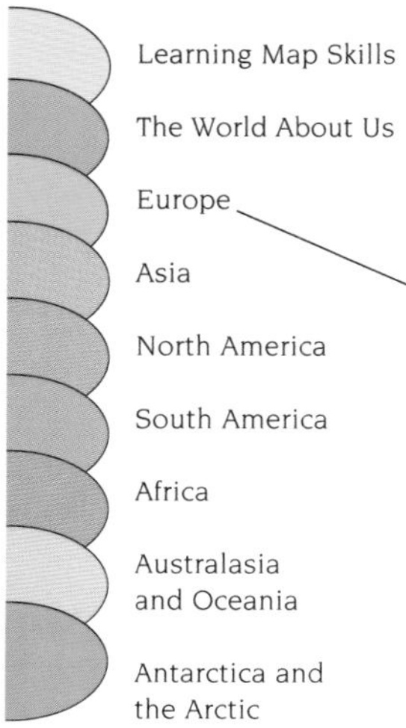

Learning Map Skills
The World About Us
Europe
Asia
North America
South America
Africa
Australasia and Oceania
Antarctica and the Arctic

LOCATOR GLOBE

This shows the location of the country or region both within its continent, and in relation to the rest of the world.

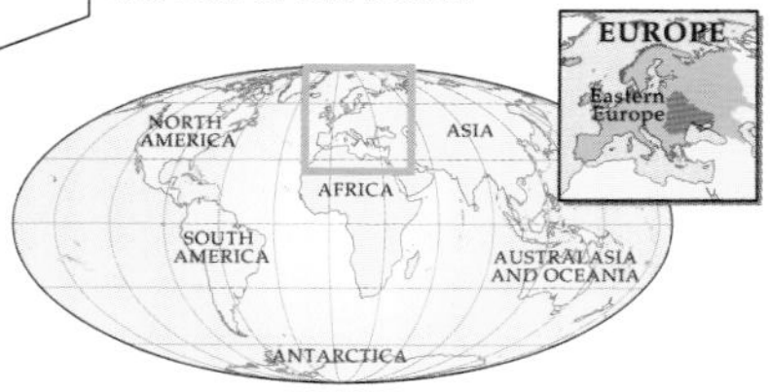

EUROPE
Eastern Europe
NORTH AMERICA
ASIA
AFRICA
SOUTH AMERICA
AUSTRALASIA AND OCEANIA
ANTARCTICA

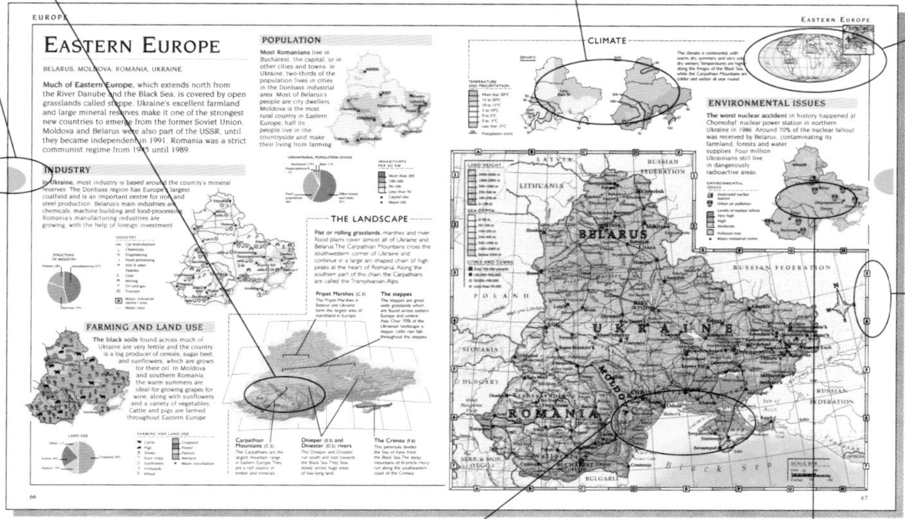

EASTERN EUROPE
BELARUS, MOLDOVA, ROMANIA, UKRAINE
POPULATION
INDUSTRY
CLIMATE
ENVIRONMENTAL ISSUES
THE LANDSCAPE
FARMING AND LAND USE
BELARUS
UKRAINE
ROMANIA

MAP GRID

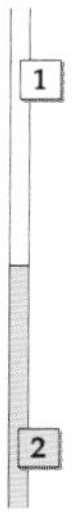

1
2

Each main map has a grid. Using the grid will help you to find a place on the map. Grid references are expressed as letters (running from left to right across the frame), and numbers (running from the top to the bottom of the frame), for example, A 4, G 6. Everything on the map is referenced in the **Index-Gazetteer** at the back of the book.

REGIONAL MAPS

The main map on each regional page shows the main topographical features of the area: the height of the land, the major roads, the rivers and lakes. It also shows the main cities and towns in the region – represented by different symbols.

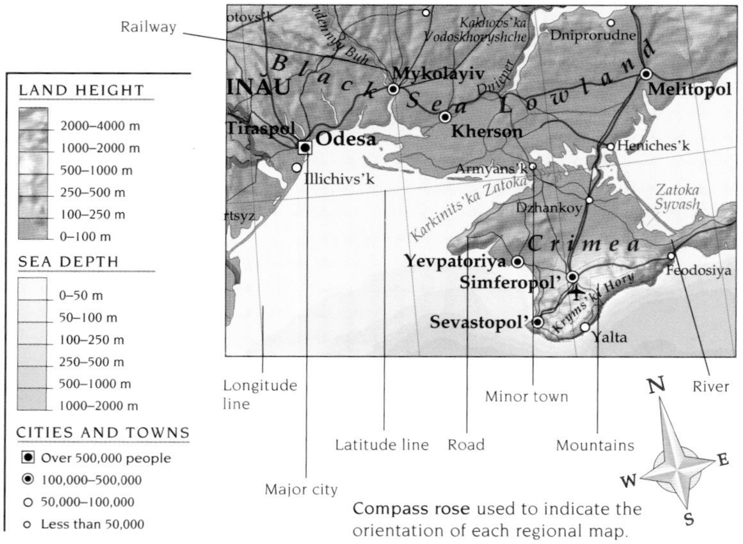

Railway
LAND HEIGHT
2000–4000 m
1000–2000 m
500–1000 m
250–500 m
100–250 m
0–100 m
SEA DEPTH
0–50 m
50–100 m
100–250 m
250–500 m
500–1000 m
1000–2000 m
CITIES AND TOWNS
Over 500,000 people
100,000–500,000
50,000–100,000
Less than 50,000
Mykolayiv
Melitopol
Odesa
Kherson
Black Sea Lowland
Dniprorudne
Heniches'k
Illichivs'k
Armyans'k
Dzhankoy
Zatoka Syvash
Crimea
Yevpatoriya
Simferopol'
Feodosiya
Sevastopol'
Yalta
Longitude line
Latitude line
Road
Minor town
Mountains
River
Major city
N
E
W
S
Compass rose used to indicate the orientation of each regional map.

THEMATIC MAPS

These small maps show various aspects of the geography of the country or region. The environment maps cover topics such as the effects of pollution. Industry, land use and population maps locate the major industries, types of agriculture and the distribution of population.

Diagrams are used to show the geographic information on the map statistically.

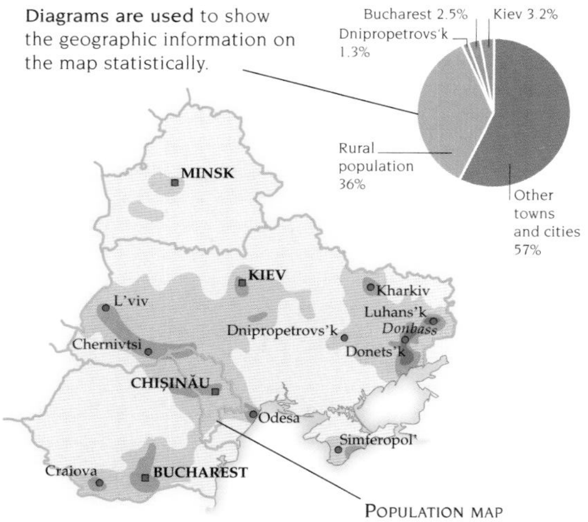

Bucharest 2.5%
Kiev 3.2%
Dnipropetrovs'k 1.3%
Rural population 36%
Other towns and cities 57%
MINSK
KIEV
L'viv
Kharkiv
Luhans'k
Donbass
Dnipropetrovs'k
Donets'k
Chernivtsi
CHIŞINĂU
Odesa
Simferopol'
Craiova
BUCHAREST
POPULATION MAP

INDUSTRY MAP

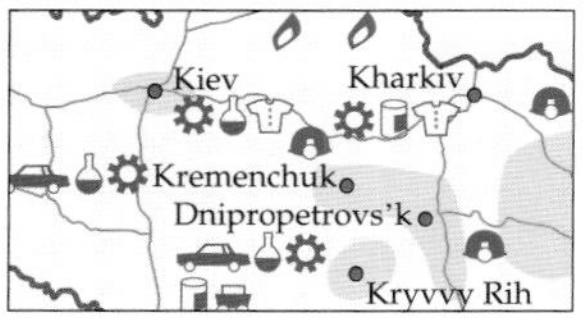

Kiev
Kharkiv
Kremenchuk
Dnipropetrovs'k
Kryvyy Rih

LAND USE MAP

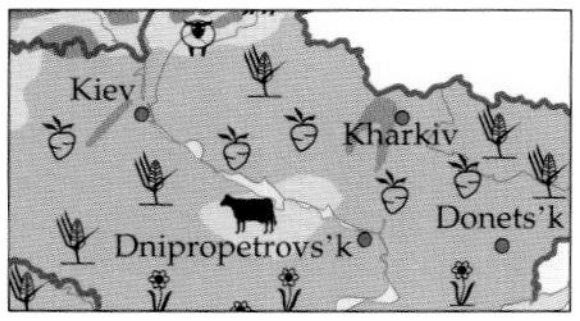

Kiev
Kharkiv
Donets'k
Dnipropetrovs'k

ENVIRONMENT MAP

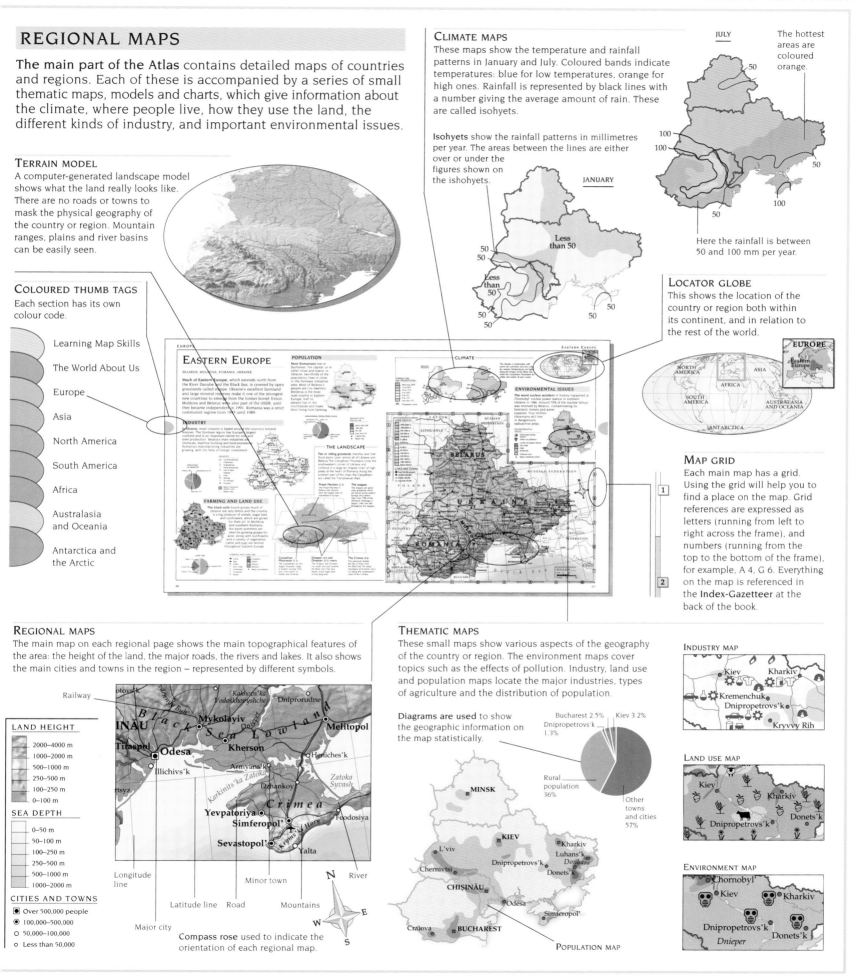

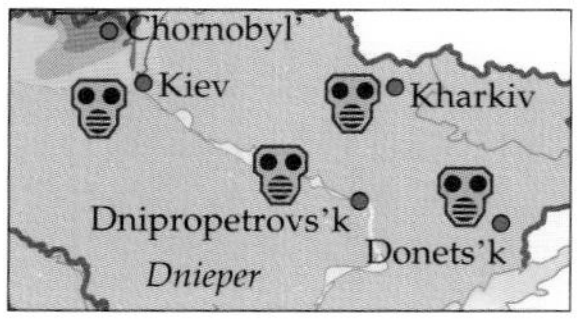

Chornobyl'
Kiev
Kharkiv
Dnipropetrovs'k
Donets'k
Dnieper

THE PHYSICAL WORLD

This map shows the main physical features of the world: the mountain ranges, the great rivers and lakes, deserts, grassland plains, seas and oceans. No human settlements are named on this map – only the physical or landscape features.

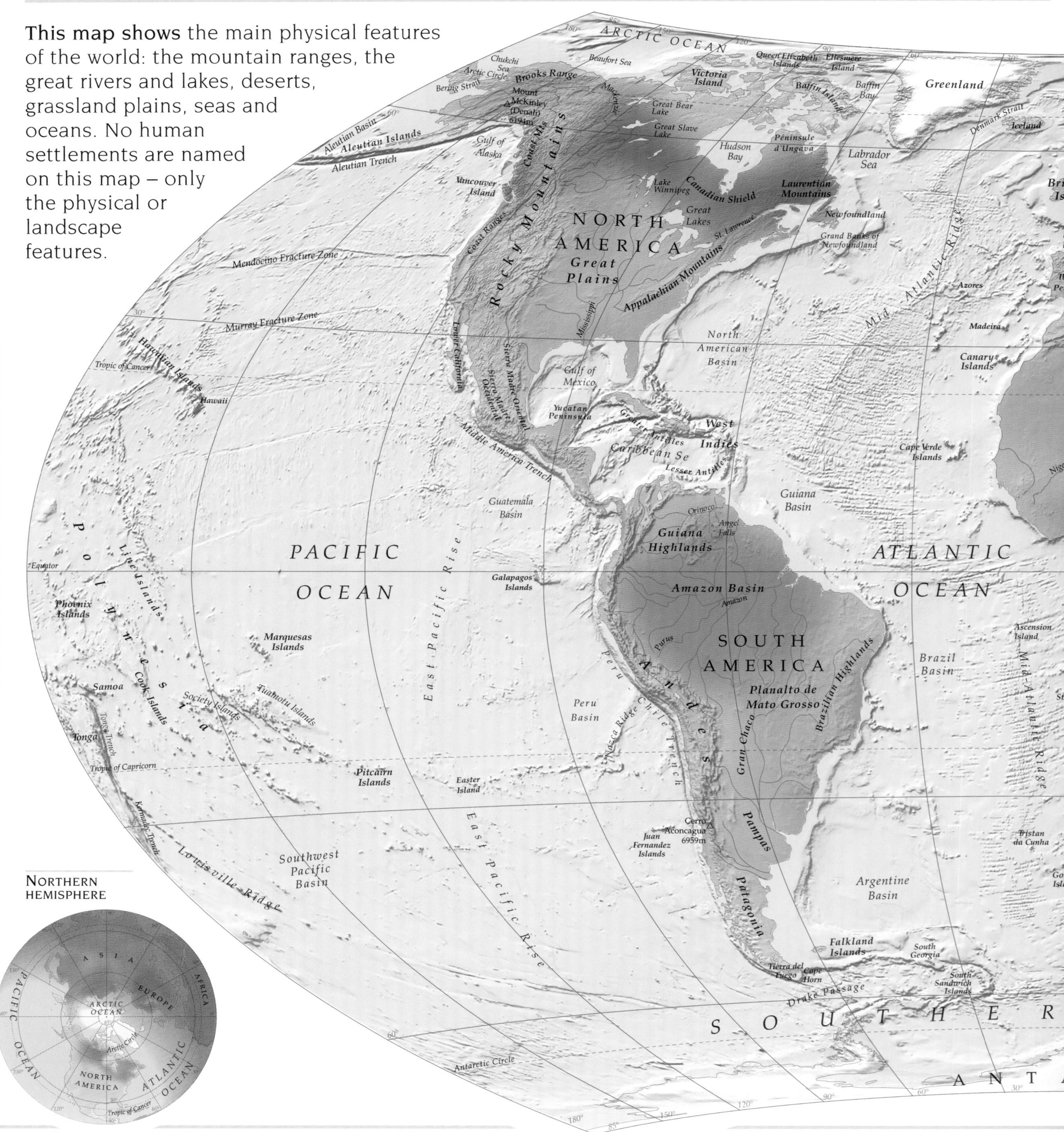

THE WORLD: FACTS AND FIGURES

- **LOWEST POINT ON LAND:** Dead Sea, West Asia 392 m below sea level
- **HIGHEST POINT:** Mount Everest, China/Nepal 8,850 m
- **LOWEST POINT (OCEAN):** Mariana Trench, Pacific Ocean 10,923 m below sea level
- **LONGEST RIVER:** Nile, Africa 6,650 km
- **LARGEST OCEAN:** Pacific Ocean 165,384,000 sq km
- **LARGEST LAKE:** Caspian Sea, Asia 371,000 sq km

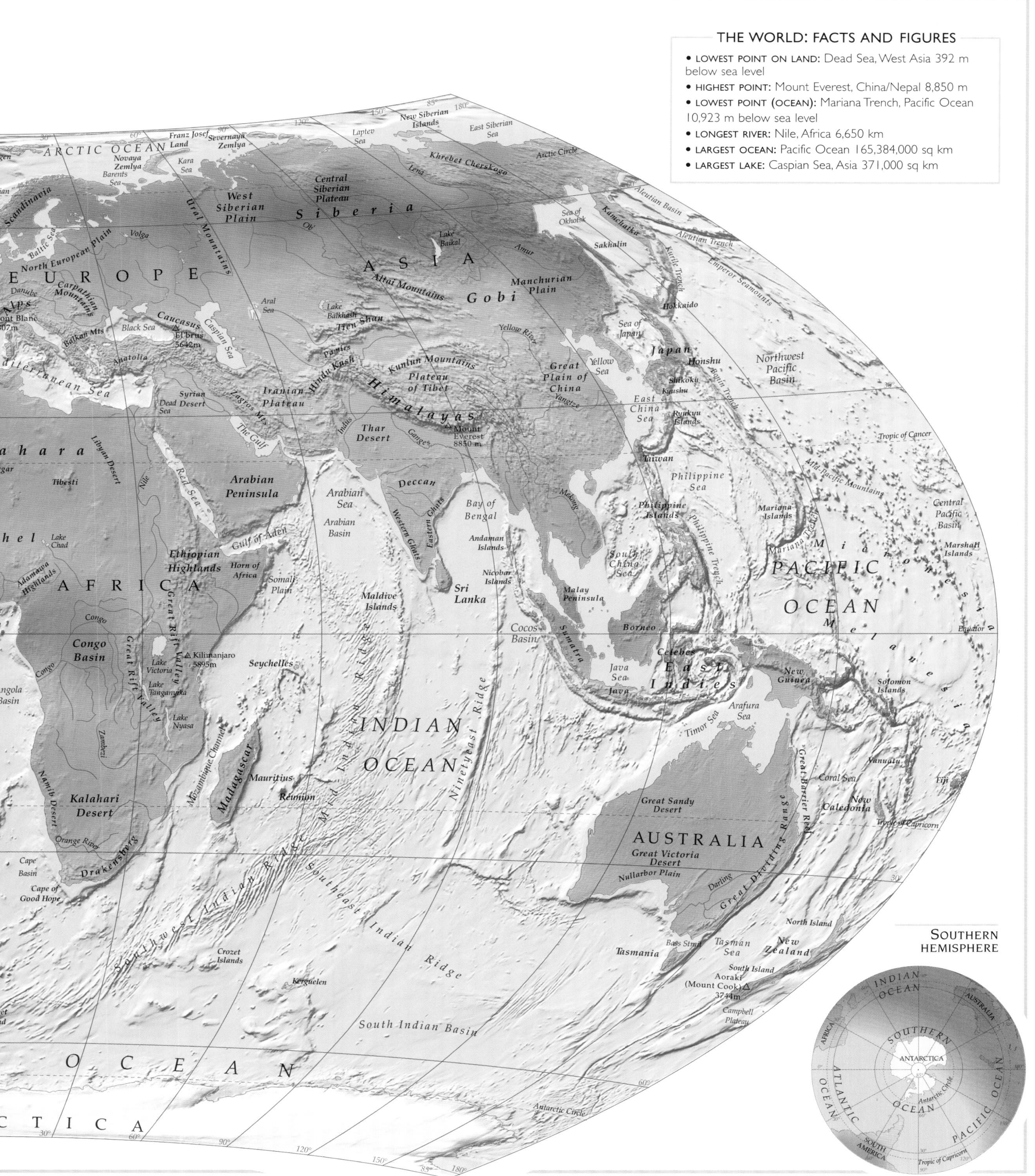

THE EARTH'S STRUCTURE

The shape and position of the Earth's oceans and continents make a familiar pattern. This is just the latest in a series of forms which the Earth has taken in the hundreds of millions of years since its creation. Massive forces inside the Earth cause the continents and oceans to move apart and together again, forming larger landmasses and then breaking them apart – a process known as plate tectonics. The movement is very slow – but over millions of years, the changes can be enormous.

DYNAMIC EARTH

The heart of the Earth is a solid core of iron surrounded by several layers of very hot – sometimes liquid – rock. The crust is relatively thin and is made up of a series of 'plates' which fit closely together. Movement of the molten rock deep within the mantle of the Earth causes the plates to move, creating changes in the surface features of the Earth.

THE EARTH'S PLATES

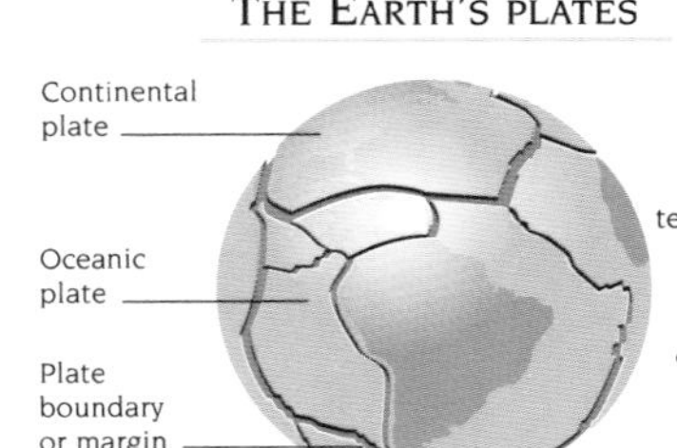

INSIDE THE EARTH

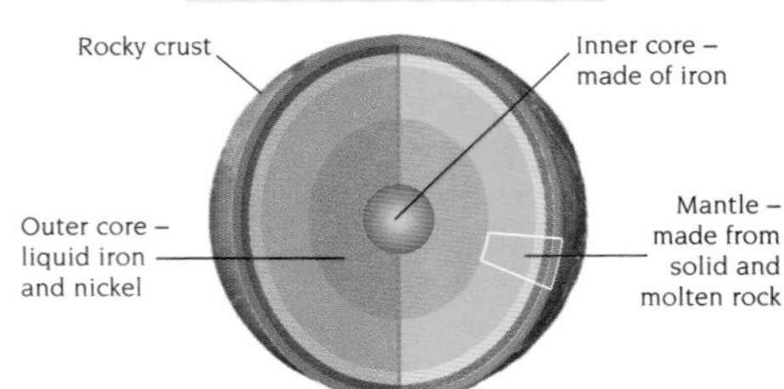

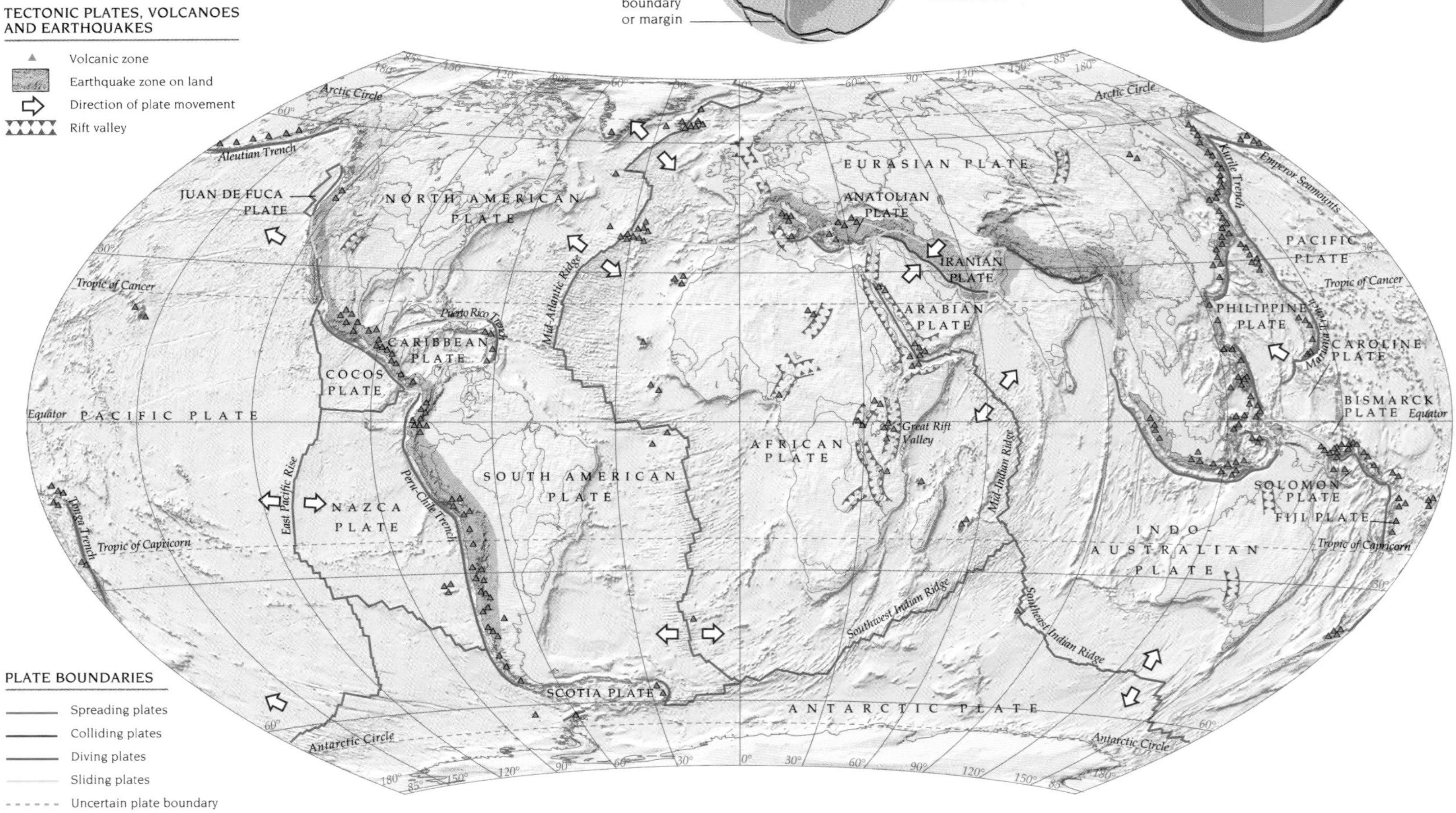

TECTONIC PLATES, VOLCANOES AND EARTHQUAKES

- Volcanic zone
- Earthquake zone on land
- Direction of plate movement
- Rift valley

EURASIAN PLATE
NORTH AMERICAN PLATE
JUAN DE FUCA PLATE
ANATOLIAN PLATE
IRANIAN PLATE
ARABIAN PLATE
PACIFIC PLATE
PHILIPPINE PLATE
CAROLINE PLATE
CARIBBEAN PLATE
COCOS PLATE
PACIFIC PLATE
AFRICAN PLATE
SOUTH AMERICAN PLATE
NAZCA PLATE
BISMARCK PLATE
SOLOMON PLATE
FIJI PLATE
INDO-AUSTRALIAN PLATE
SCOTIA PLATE
ANTARCTIC PLATE

PLATE BOUNDARIES

- Spreading plates
- Colliding plates
- Diving plates
- Sliding plates
- Uncertain plate boundary

PLATE BOUNDARIES

The point where two plates meet is known as a plate boundary. As the Earth's plates move together or apart or slide alongside one another, the great forces which result cause great changes in the landscape. Mountains can be created, earthquakes occur and there may be frequent volcanic eruptions.

SPREADING PLATES

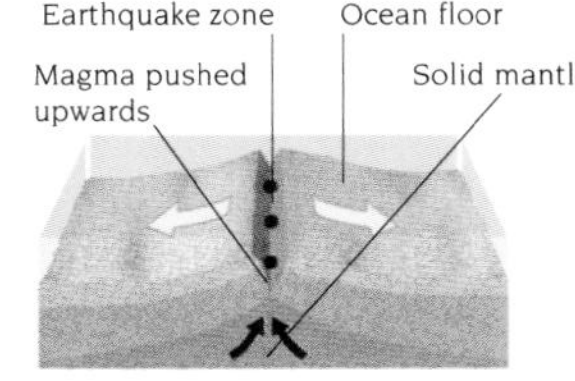

As plates move apart, magma rises through the outer mantle. When it cools, it forms new crust. The Mid-Atlantic Ridge is caused by spreading plates.

COLLIDING PLATES

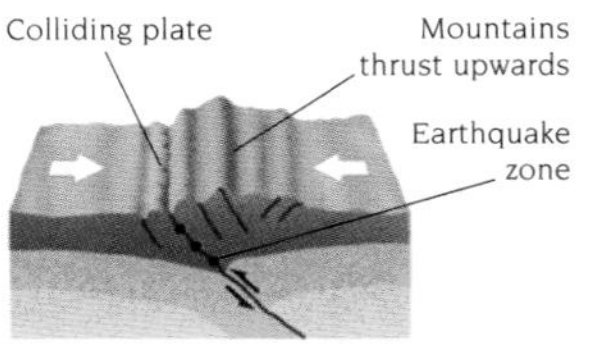

When two plates bearing landmasses collide with one another, the land is crumpled upwards into high mountain peaks such as the Alps, and the Himalayas.

DIVING PLATES

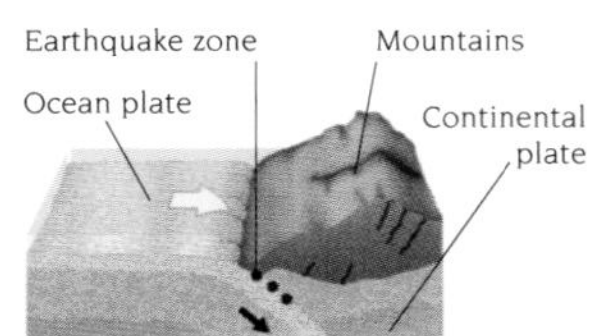

When an ocean-bearing plate collides with a continental plate it is forced downwards under the other plate and into the mantle. Volcanoes occur along these boundaries.

SLIDING PLATES

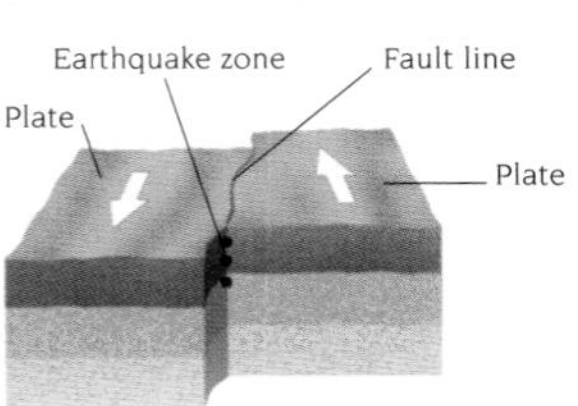

As two plates slide past each other, great friction is set up along the fault line which lies between them. This can lead to powerful earthquakes.

SHAPING THE LANDSCAPE

The Earth's surface is made from solid rock or water. The land is constantly re-shaped by external forces. Water flowing as rivers or in the oceans erodes and deposits material to create valleys and lakes and to shape coastlines. When water is built up and compressed into solid sheets of ice, it can erode more deeply, creating deeper, wider valleys. Wind also has a powerful effect; stripping away vegetation and transporting rock particles vast distances.

RIVERS

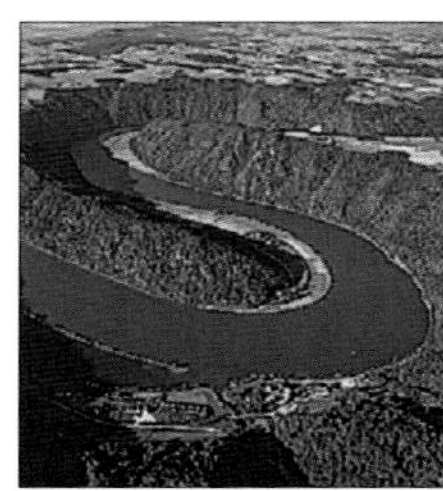

Most rivers have their sources in mountain areas. They flow fast through the mountains, eroding deep V-shaped valleys. As they reach flatter areas they begin to meander in great loops, both eroding and then depositing rock particles as they slow down.

GLACIERS

In cold areas, close to the poles or on mountain tops, snow is built up into rivers of ice called glaciers. They move slowly, eroding deep U-shaped valleys. When the glacier melts, ridges of eroded rock called moraines are left at the sides and end of the glacier.

SEA ACTION

The oceans change the landscape in two major ways. They batter cliffs, causing rock to break away and the land to retreat, and they carry eroded material along the coast, to make beaches and sand bars.

WIND

Wind can erode and break down rock into smaller boulders and stones and eventually into sand. Desert sand dunes are shaped by the force of the wind and vary from ripples to hills 200 m high.

LANDSLIDES

Heavy rain can loosen soil and rock beneath the surface of slopes. As this moves, the top layers slip forward, to form heaps of rubble at the base of the slope.

THE WORLD'S OCEANS

Just over two-thirds of the Earth's surface is covered by water and more than 98% of this water is contained in the oceans. Movements within the Earth shape the ocean floor in the same way as they do the land surface, creating mountain ranges, trenches and plateaus, and changing the shape and size of the oceans. The difference between an ocean and a sea is simply its size; oceans are much bigger.

POLAR OCEANS

The Southern and Arctic Oceans contain large icebergs, that have broken away from the ice shelf.

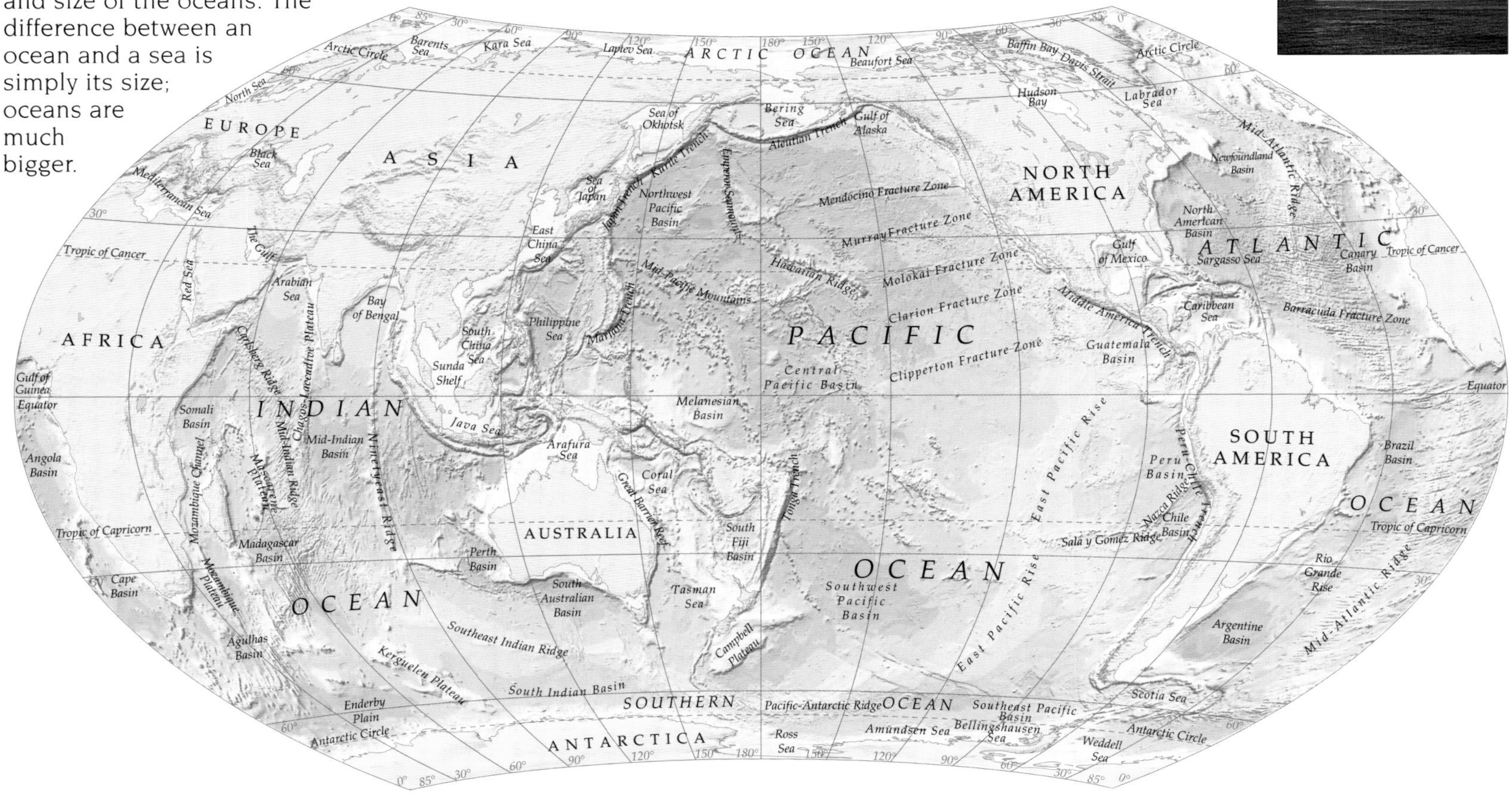

ARCTIC OCEAN, PACIFIC OCEAN, INDIAN OCEAN, ATLANTIC OCEAN, SOUTHERN OCEAN, EUROPE, ASIA, AFRICA, NORTH AMERICA, SOUTH AMERICA, AUSTRALIA, ANTARCTICA

INDIAN OCEAN

The Indian Ocean covers about 20% of the world's surface. Ocean swells, starting deep in the Southern Ocean, often cause flooding in Sri Lanka and the Maldives.

PACIFIC OCEAN

The Pacific is the largest and deepest ocean in the world. It contains an arc of volcanic islands, including Japan, Indonesia and New Guinea, known as the 'Ring of Fire'.

ATLANTIC OCEAN

The Atlantic Ocean was formed about 180 million years ago. The land which now forms Europe and Africa pulled apart from the Americas to create an ocean 3,000 km wide.

CLIMATE AND LIFE ZONES

This map shows the different climates found around the world. Climates are particular combinations of temperature and humidity. Climates are affected by latitude, the height of the land, winds and ocean currents. Climates can change, but not overnight. Weather is local and consists of short-term events such as thunderstorms, hurricanes and blizzards.

HURRICANES

Hurricanes are violent cyclonic windstorms, driven by heat energy gathered from tropical seas. The Caribbean islands and the east coast of the USA are particularly prone to hurricanes.

WORLD CLIMATE

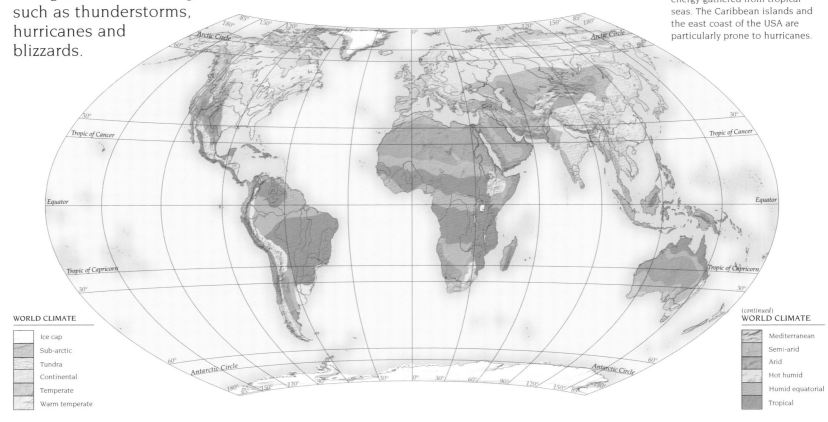

- Ice cap
- Sub-arctic
- Tundra
- Continental
- Temperate
- Warm temperate

(continued)
WORLD CLIMATE

- Mediterranean
- Semi-arid
- Arid
- Hot humid
- Humid equatorial
- Tropical

WINDS

All over the Earth there are a series of large-scale wind patterns called prevailing winds which have a direct effect on weather and climate. The direction of the wind depends on global air pressure. Winds travel from areas of high pressure to areas of low pressure. The westerlies, polar easterlies, and the northeast and southeast trade winds are all prevailing winds. The Equator is known for its light winds – known as the Doldrums. Changes in the direction of the prevailing winds can have a serious impact on the weather all over the planet.

WINDS

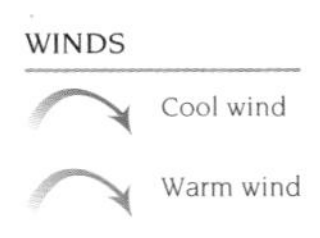

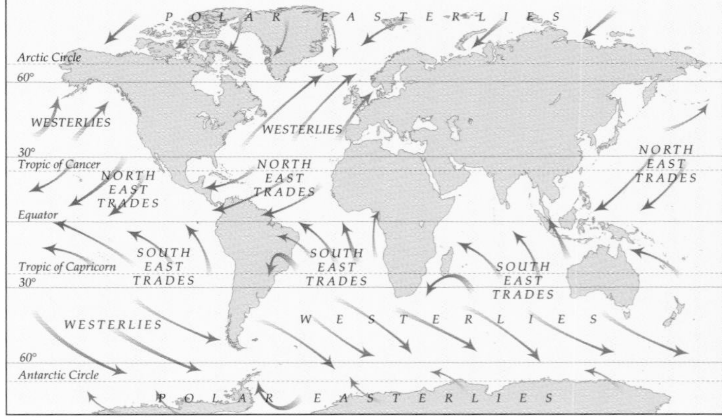

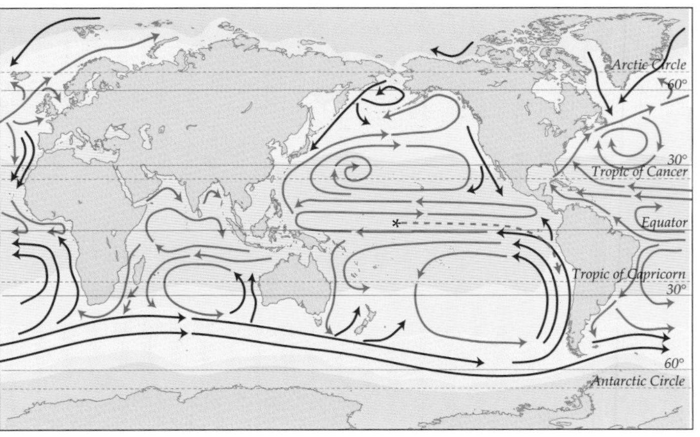

OCEAN CURRENTS

Ocean currents help to distribute heat around the Earth and have a great influence on climate. Convection currents circulate massive amounts of warm and cold water around the oceans. Warm water is moved away from the tropics to higher latitudes and cold water is moved toward the tropics.

OCEAN CURRENTS AND SURFACE TEMPERATURES

- Cold currents
- Warm currents
- El Niño

- 20 – 30°C
- 10 – 20°C
- 0 – 10°C
- Sea-water –2° – 0°C
- Sea-ice (average) below –2°C

LIFE ZONES

The map below shows the Earth divided into different biomes – also called biogeographical regions. The combination of climate, the type of landscape, and the plants and animals that live there, are used to classify a region. Similar biomes are found in very different places around the world.

POLAR REGIONS

The North and South poles are permanently covered by ice. Only a few plants and animals can live here.

TUNDRA

Tundra is flat, cold and dry with few trees. Plants such as mosses and lichens grow close to the ground.

DESERTS

Very little rain falls in desert areas, whether they are hot deserts such as the Sahara or cold deserts like the Gobi.

NEEDLELEAF FORESTS

Tall coniferous trees such as pine and spruce, with spines or needles instead of leaves, grow in the far north of Scandinavia, Canada and the Russian Federation.

BROADLEAF FORESTS

Broadleaf or deciduous forests once covered temperate regions over most of the northern hemisphere. They contain trees of many varieties – all of which shed their leaves every year.

TEMPERATE RAINFORESTS

Evergreen, broadleaved trees need a warmer, wetter climate than deciduous trees. They are known as temperate rainforests.

MEDITERRANEAN

Close to the shores of the Mediterranean Sea, the vegetation consists mainly of herbs, shrubs and drought-resistant trees.

BIOME TYPES

- Mountains
- Polar regions
- Tundra
- Tropical rain forests
- Dry woodlands
- Savanna
- Temperate grasslands

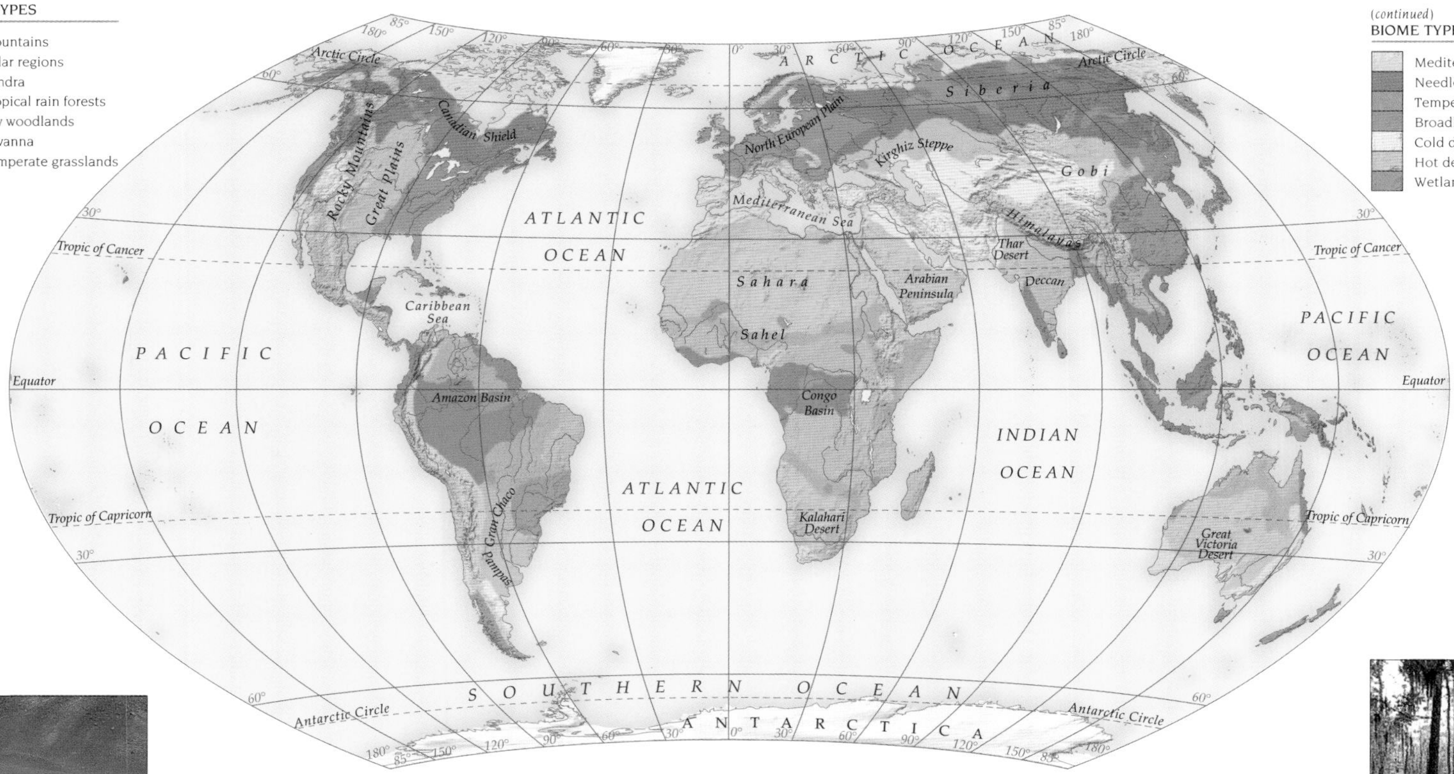

(continued)
BIOME TYPES

- Mediterranean
- Needleleaf forest
- Temperate rainforest
- Broadleaf forest
- Cold desert
- Hot desert
- Wetlands

Arctic Ocean · Arctic Circle · Rocky Mountains · Great Plains · Canadian Shield · North European Plain · Siberia · Kirghiz Steppe · Gobi · Mediterranean Sea · Himalayas · Thar Desert · Deccan · Atlantic Ocean · Sahara · Arabian Peninsula · Sahel · Caribbean Sea · Pacific Ocean · Amazon Basin · Congo Basin · Indian Ocean · Gran Chaco · Pampas · Kalahari Desert · Great Victoria Desert · Tropic of Cancer · Equator · Tropic of Capricorn · Southern Ocean · Antarctic Circle · Antarctica

TEMPERATE GRASSLANDS

Grasslands cover the central areas of the continents. They are known in the middle latitudes as prairies, steppe and pampas.

SAVANNAH

The savannah consists of woodland, interspersed with grassland. These regions lie between the tropical rainforest and hot desert regions.

DRY WOODLANDS

Dry woodlands are found at the edge of grasslands. They contain small trees and shrubs adapted to dry conditions.

TROPICAL RAINFORESTS

Around the Equator, where temperatures are high and there is plenty of rain, tropical rainforests can flourish. Trees grow continuously and are tall with huge, broad leaves.

WETLANDS

Low-lying swamps and marshes are known as wetlands. They are often home to a rich variety of animal, plant and bird species.

WORLD POPULATION

There are now nearly six thousand million people on Earth. The population has increased more than three times since 1900. Before that date, the number of people increased slowly as people were born and died at similar rates. With improved living conditions, better medical care and more efficient food production, more people survived to adulthood and the population began to grow much faster. If growth continues at the present rate, the world's population is likely to reach 8.5 billion by the year 2020.

OVERCROWDING

Favelas – or shanty towns – have grown up many South American cities because of overcrowding.

POPULATION STRUCTURES

Measuring the numbers of old and young people gives the age structure of a country or continent. If there are large numbers of young people and a high birth rate, the population is said to be youthful – as is the case in many African, Asian and South American countries. If the birth rate is low but many people survive into old age, the population distribution is said to be ageing – this is true of much of Europe, Japan, Canada and the USA. Extreme events like wars can distort the population, leading to a loss of population in certain age groups.

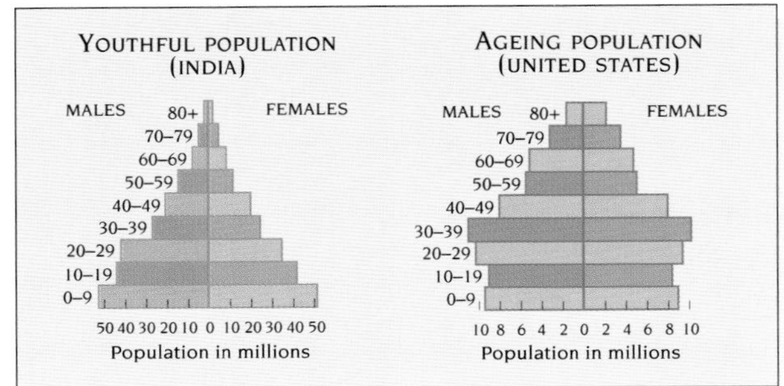

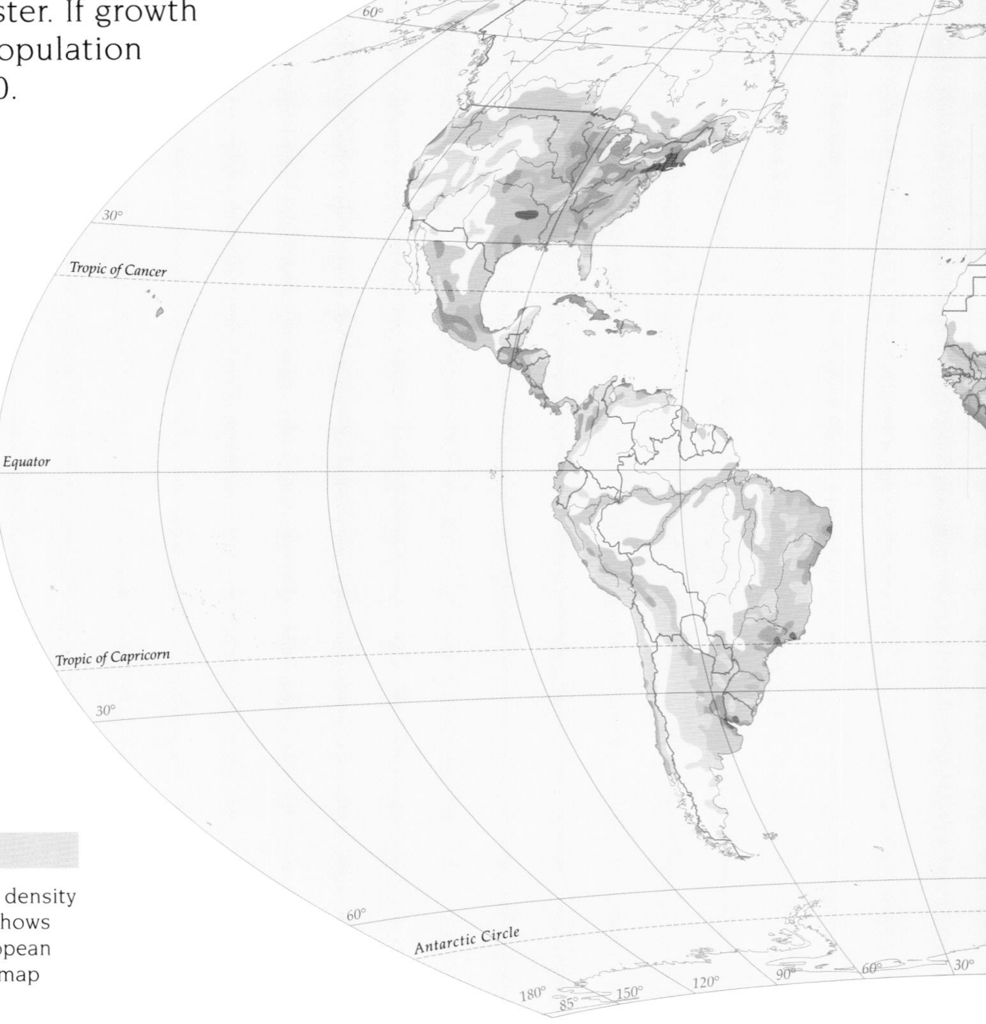

POPULATION DENSITY

The main map (centre) and the map below both show population density – the number of people who live in a given area. The map below shows the average population density per country. You can see that European countries and parts of Asia are very densely populated. The large map shows where people actually live.

While the average population density in Brazil and Egypt is quite low, the coasts of Brazil and the areas close to the River Nile in Egypt are very densely populated.

POPULATION DENSITY

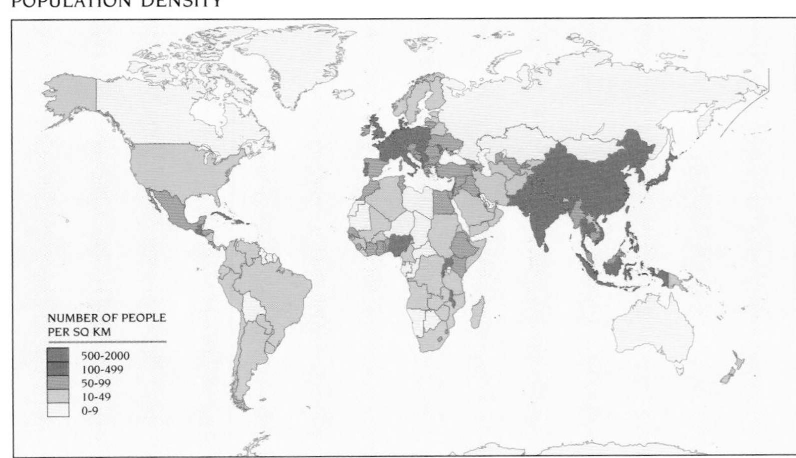

DENSE POPULATION

Huge crowds near the Haora Bridge in Kolkata (Calcutta), India – one of the world's most densely populated cities.

SPARSE POPULATION

The cold north of Canada has one of the lowest population densities in the world. Some people live in extreme isolation, separated from others by lakes and forests.

URBAN GROWTH

The 20th century has seen a huge increase in the number of people living in cities. This has led to more large cities and the development of some 'super cities' such as Mexico City and Tokyo, each with more than 20 million people. In 1900, only about 10% of the population lived in cities. Now it is closer to 50% and soon the figure may be nearer two in three people. Some continents are far more 'urbanized' than others: in South America nearly 80% of people live in cities, whereas in Africa the figure is only about 30%.

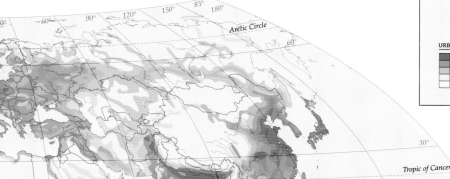

LEVELS OF URBANIZATION

URBANIZATION
- 90-100%
- 60-89%
- 40-59%
- 0-39%
- data unavailable

Arctic Circle
Tropic of Cancer
Equator
Tropic of Capricorn
Antarctic Circle

POPULATION DENSITY (People per sq km)
- Below 1
- 1–5
- 6–10
- 11–20
- 21–50
- 51–100
- 101–200
- Above 200

POPULATION GROWTH

The rate of population growth varies dramatically between the continents. Europe has a large population but it is increasing slowly. Africa is still sparsely populated, but in some countries such as Kenya, the population is growing very rapidly, increasing pressure on the land. China and India have the world's largest populations. Both countries now have laws to try and curb the birth rate.

CONTROLLING GROWTH

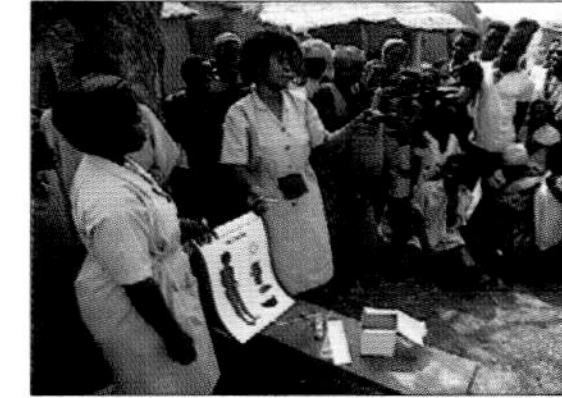

In 1980, fewer than 25% of women in less developed countries used birth control. Education programmes and more widely available contraceptives are thought to have doubled this figure. But many families still have no access to contraception.

AN AGEING POPULATION

In some countries, a low birth rate, and an increasingly long-lived elderly population has greatly increased the ratio of old people to younger people, putting a strain on health and social services. For example, in Japan, most people can now expect to live to at least 80 years of age.

BIRTH RATE

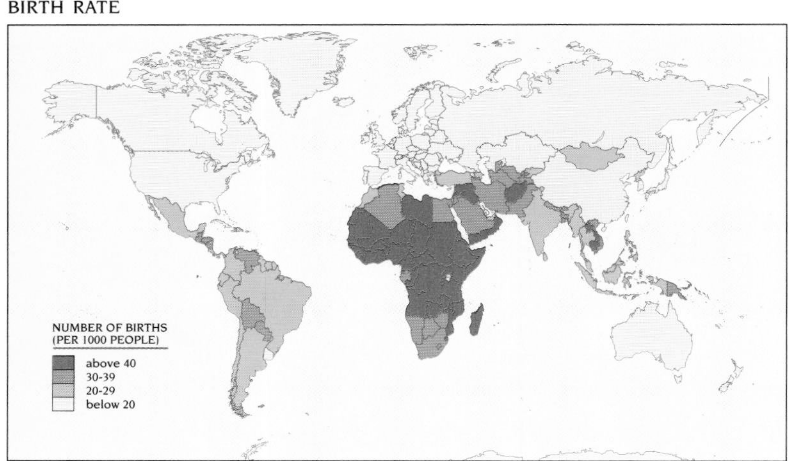

LIFE EXPECTANCY

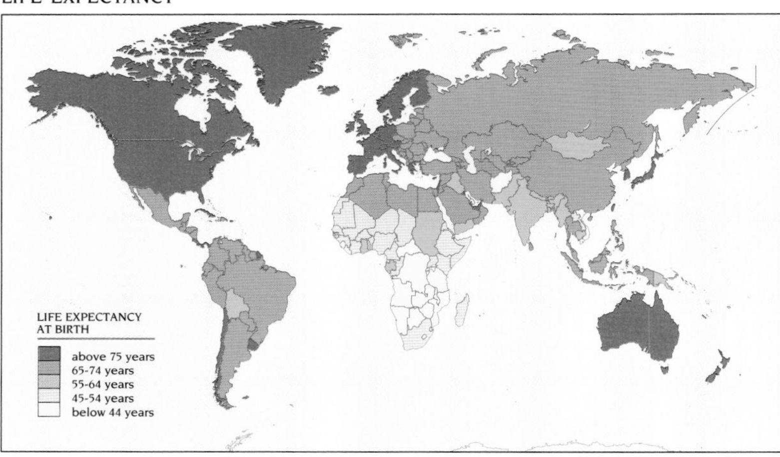

THE WORLD ECONOMY

Throughout the world, the way in which people make a living varies greatly. The countries of western Europe and North America, along with Japan, are the most economically developed in the world, with a long-established and very diverse range of industries. They sell their products and services internationally. Less economically developed countries in south and central Asia, much of Africa, and Central America have a much smaller number of industries – some may rely on a single product – and many goods are produced only for the local market.

MEASURING WEALTH

The wealth of a country can be measured in several ways: for example, by the average annual income per person; by the volume of its trade; and by the total value of the goods and services that the country produces annually – its Gross Domestic Product or GDP. The map below shows the average GDP per person for each of the world's countries, expressed in $US. Most of the highest levels of GDP are in Europe and the US; most of the lowest are in Africa.

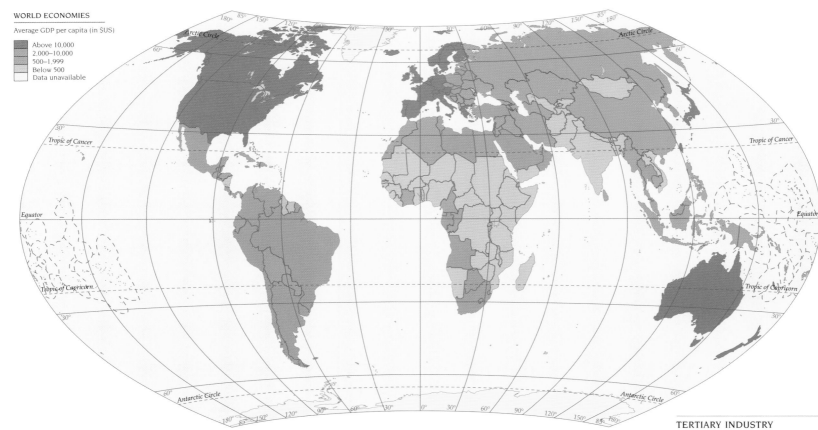

WORLD ECONOMIES

Average GDP per capita (in $US)

- Above 10,000
- 2,000–10,000
- 500–1,999
- Below 500
- Data unavailable

Arctic Circle

Tropic of Cancer

Equator

Tropic of Capricorn

Antarctic Circle

TYPES OF INDUSTRY

Industries are usually defined in one of three ways. Primary industries such as farming or mining involve the production of raw materials such as food or minerals. Secondary industries make or manufacture finished products out of raw materials: clothing and car manufacture are examples of secondary industries. People who work in tertiary industries provide different kinds of services. Banking, insurance and tourism are all examples of tertiary industries. Some economically advanced nations such as Germany or USA now have quaternary industries such as biotechnology which are knowledge-creation industries, devoted to the research and development of new products.

PRIMARY INDUSTRY

Tobacco leaves are picked and laid out for drying in Cuba, one of the world's great producers of cigars. Many countries rely on one or two high-value 'cash crops' like tobacco to earn foreign currency.

SECONDARY INDUSTRY

This skilled Thai weaver is producing an intricately patterned silk fabric on a hand loom. Fabric manufacture is an important industry throughout South and Southeast Asia. In India and Pakistan, vast quantities of cotton are produced in highly mechanized factories, but many fabrics are still hand woven.

TERTIARY INDUSTRY

The City of London is one of the world's great finance centres. Branches of many banks and insurance companies, including the world famous Lloyds of London, are clustered into the City's 'square mile'.

PATTERNS OF TRADE

Almost all countries trade goods with one another in order to obtain products they cannot produce themselves, and to make money from goods they have produced. Some countries – for example those in the Caribbean – rely mainly on a single export, usually a foodstuff or mineral, and can suffer a loss of income when world prices drop. Other countries, such as Germany and Japan, export a vast range of both raw materials and manufactured goods throughout the world. A number of huge companies, known as transnational corporations or TNCs, are responsible for more than 70% of world trade, with divisions all over the world. They include firms like BP, Coca Cola and IBM.

CONTAINER SHIPS

Many products are transported around the world on container ships. Containers are of a standard size so that they can be efficiently transported to their destinations. Some ships are specially designed to carry perishable goods such as fruit and vegetables.

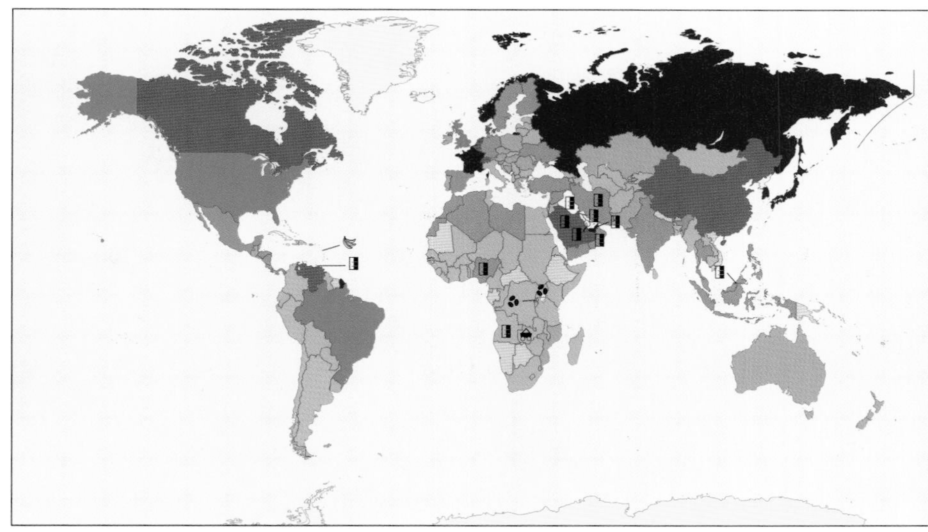

BALANCE OF TRADE (MILLIONS $US)

Surplus
Over 30,000
10,000–29,000
1,000–9,999
0–999

Deficit
0–999
1,000–9,999
10,000–29,999
Below 30,000

Data unavailable

COUNTRIES RELIANT ON ONE EXPORT

oil/petroleum
bananas
coffee
copper

DEVELOPING ECONOMIES

Although world trade is still dominated by the more economically developed countries, since the 1970s, less economically developed countries have increased their share of world trade from less than 10% to nearly 20%. Countries such as Brazil, Mexico, Malaysia and South Korea, aided by investment from their governments or from wealthier countries, were able to begin to manufacture and export a wide variety of goods. Products include cars, electronic goods, clothing and footwear. Multinational companies can take advantage of cheaper labour costs to manufacture goods in these countries. Moves are being made to limit the exploitation of workers who are paid low wages for producing luxury goods.

ASIAN 'TIGER' ECONOMIES

The economies of Malaysia, Taiwan and South Korea, boomed in the late 1980s, attracting investment for buildings such as the Petronas Towers.

TOURISM

Tourism is now the world's largest industry. More than 500 million people travel both abroad and in their own countries as tourists each year. People in more developed countries have more money and leisure time to travel. Tourism can bring large amounts of cash into the local economy, but local people do not always benefit. They may have to take low-paid jobs and experience great intrusions into their lives. Tourist development and pollution may damage the environment – sometimes destroying the very attractions that led to the development of tourism in the first place.

ECOTOURISM

These tourists are being introduced to a giant tortoise, one of the many unique animals found in the Galapagos Islands. A number of places with special animals and ecosystems have introduced schemes to teach visitors about them. This not only educates more people about the need to safeguard these environments, but brings in money to help protect them.

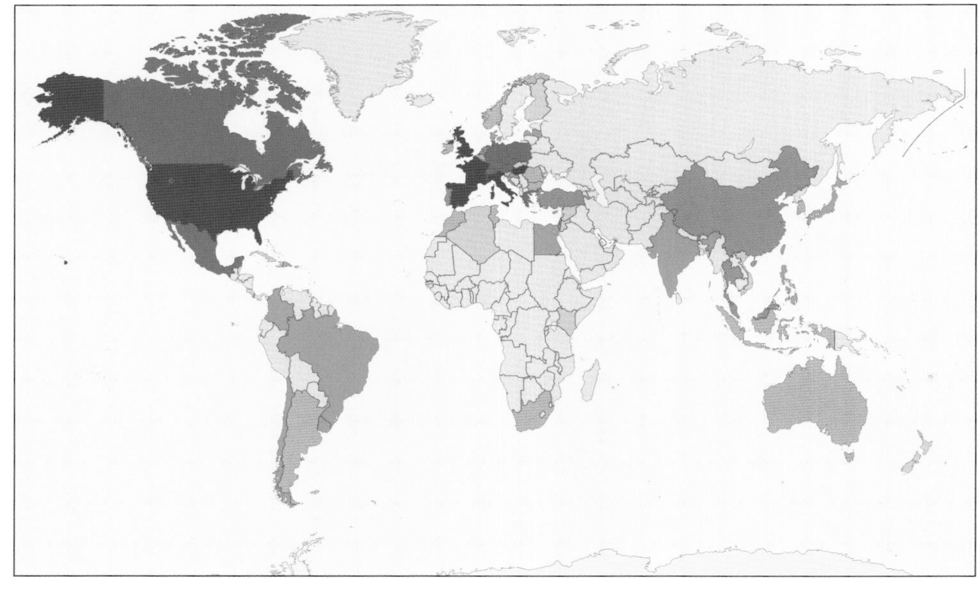

TOURIST ARRIVALS

Over 20 million
10–20 million
5–10 million
2.5–5 million
1–2.5 million
700,000–1 million
Under 700,000
Data unavailable

BORDERS AND BOUNDARIES

There are more countries in the world today than ever before – over 190 – whereas in 1950, there were only 82. Since then, many former European colonies and Soviet states have become independent. The establishment of borders for each of these countries has often been the subject of disagreement.

Military borders

At the end of wars, new borders are often drawn up between the countries – frequently along ceasefire lines. They may remain there for many years. At the end of the Korean War in 1953, North and South Korea were divided close to the 38° line of latitude. This border has remained heavily fortified.

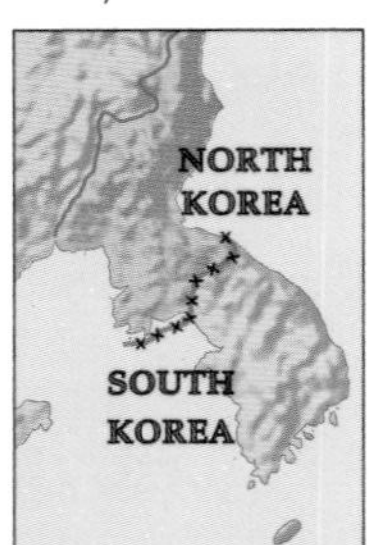

The longest border

The border between the USA and Canada is the longest continuous border in the world. It cuts through the centre of the Great Lakes. To the west of the Great Lakes, the border runs along the 49° line of latitude.

Enclaves

If part of a country's territory has become separated from the rest of the country, and is surrounded by foreign territory, it is called an enclave. Kaliningrad is part of the Russian Federation, but is cut off from it by Lithuania and Belarus.

River borders

Over one-sixth of the world's national borders are formed by rivers. Long stretches of the Danube form natural borders in southeastern Europe.

Mountain borders

Mountain ranges such as the Pyrenees, Alps and Himalayas form natural borders between many countries. In the Andes, border disputes between Chile and Argentina centred on finding the highest point in the mountain range which divided them.

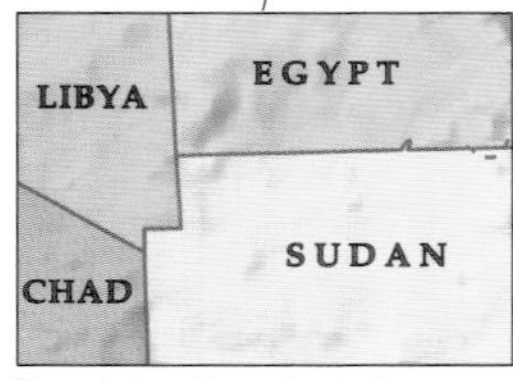

Straight line borders

The borders of many countries in Africa and other former colonial territories are straight lines. This was the simplest solution for colonial administrators, who often knew little of the country's geography or population.

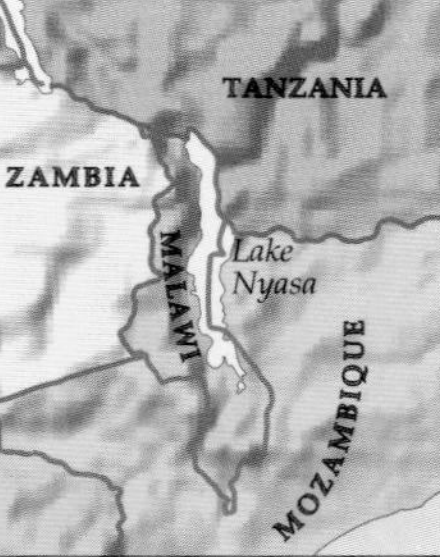

Lake boundaries

Countries which lie next to lakes usually fix their borders in the middle of the lake. Complicated agreements between colonial powers led to the awkward division of Lake Nyasa in Africa.

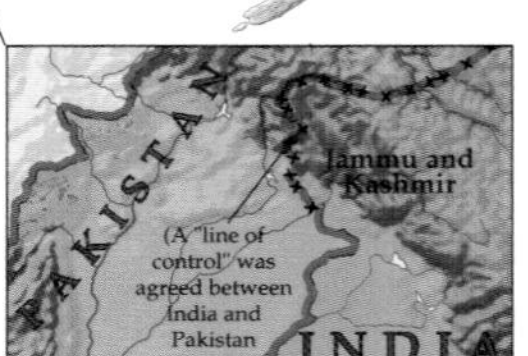

Territorial disputes

There are still many disputed territories and borders. One of the most serious territorial disputes is between India and Pakistan over Jammu and Kashmir, which has led to three wars since 1947.

THE BRITISH ISLES

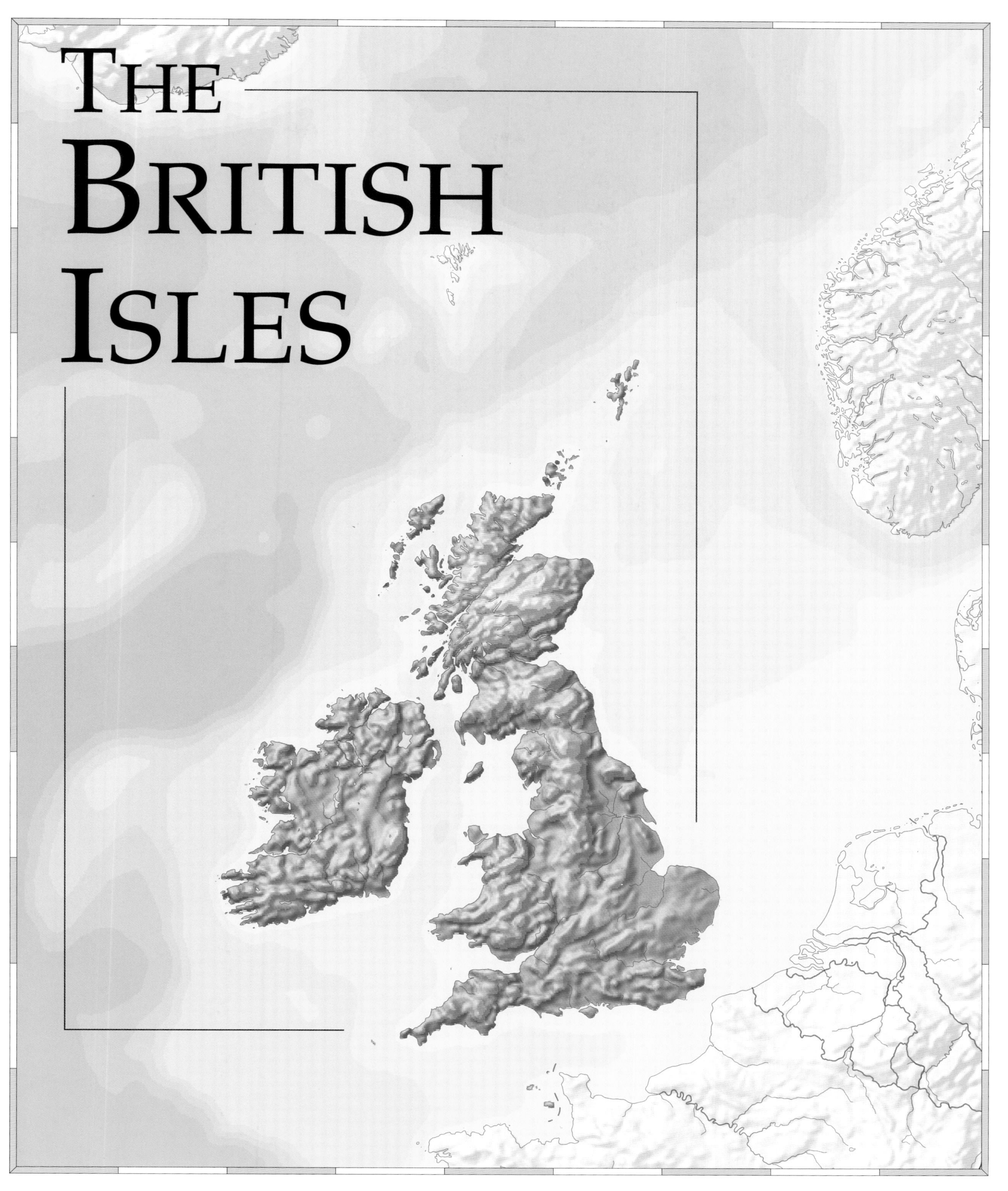

Physical British Isles

The British Isles contain two of the largest islands in Europe and numerous smaller ones. They lie to the northwest of the continent. The rugged north and west of the British Isles is an extension of the mountain range that runs through western Scandinavia. The movement of continents and oceans over millions of years has given the British Isles a very interesting and complicated geological structure, with some of the world's oldest rocks – more than 2,500 million years old, found in both England and southeast Ireland.

LANDSCAPE OF THE BRITISH ISLES

Much of the landscape of the British Isles has been shaped by the ice which covered the Britain and northern Europe for almost 8,000 years during the last ice age, until about 10,000 years ago. The ice scoured and eroded the highlands, smoothing the peaks but deepening valleys and depositing piles of rock and clay in the lowlands. The coastline is indented and constantly changing. Drowned glaciated valleys or fjords are found on the west coast of Scotland. In the southwest of England long inlets called rias are drowned river valleys

5 HIGHLANDS

The British Isles have no true mountains to compare with the Alps of mainland Europe. The highest peaks are found in the highlands of Scotland, in southwest Ireland, Wales and northern England.

ISLANDS 1

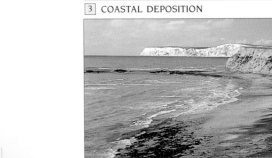

Thousands of small islands lie off the coast of the British Isles – the majority off Scotland. These Scottish islands – the Shetlands, Orkneys and the Hebrides – are part of the same mountain chain that runs through Scandinavia.

2 LOCHS

Up until about 10,000 years ago, most of Britain was covered by ice. Glaciers carved deep, wide valleys in the highlands of Scotland and northern England. Where water has accumulated in glacial valleys, huge long lakes, known in Scotland as lochs, have been formed.

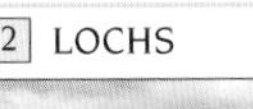

3 COASTAL DEPOSITION

Along the east coast of England there are many large sand dunes, sand bars and spits which have been formed by erosion and deposition along the coast.

4 LOWLANDS

The Fens of eastern England are some of the flattest parts of the British Isles. Some of the land lies below sea level and areas close to the sea are at risk from flooding. Artificial drainage helps to prevent flooding.

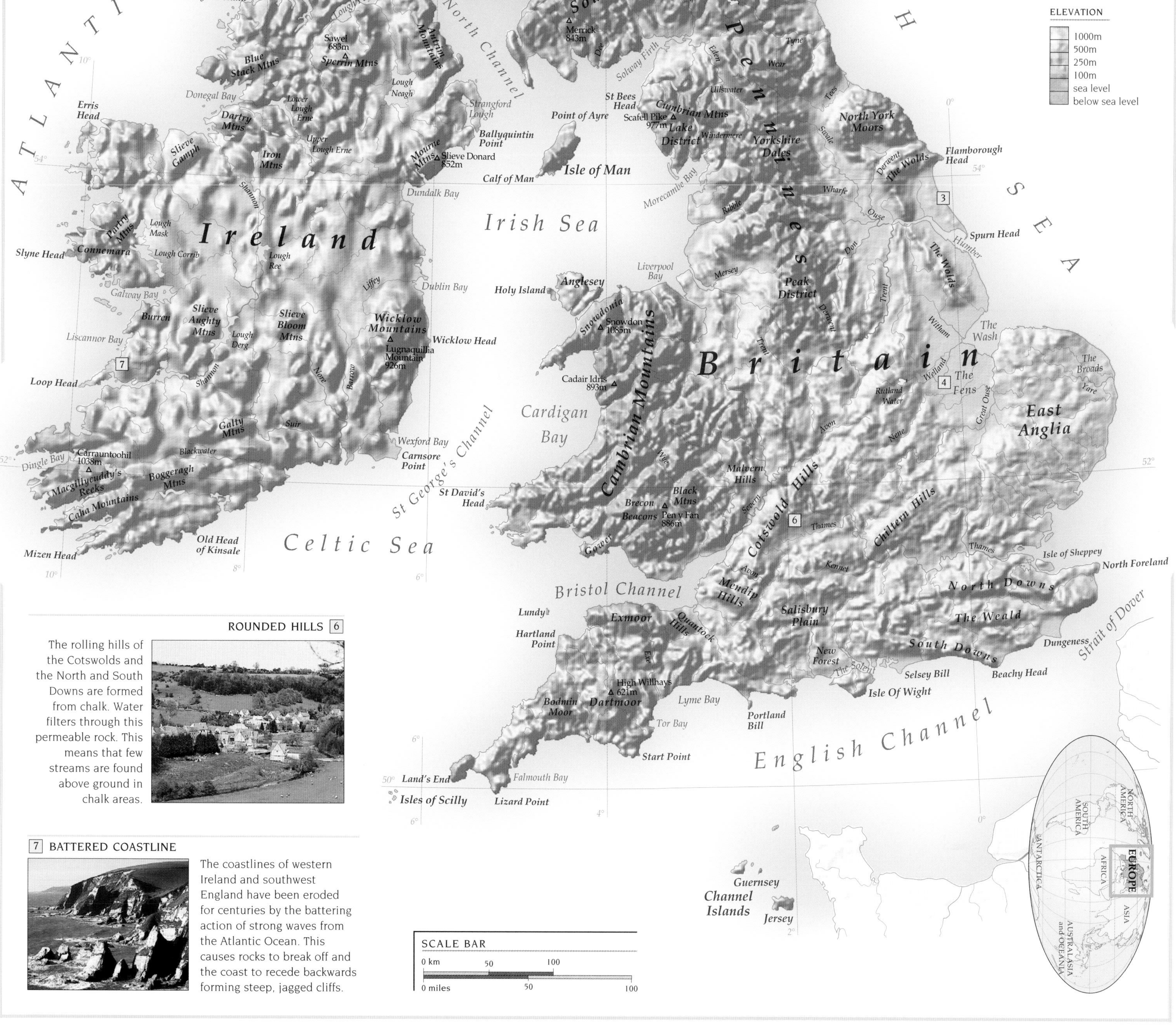

ROUNDED HILLS 6

The rolling hills of the Cotswolds and the North and South Downs are formed from chalk. Water filters through this permeable rock. This means that few streams are found above ground in chalk areas.

7 BATTERED COASTLINE

The coastlines of western Ireland and southwest England have been eroded for centuries by the battering action of strong waves from the Atlantic Ocean. This causes rocks to break off and the coast to recede backwards forming steep, jagged cliffs.

Political British Isles

The British Isles contain two separate countries: the United Kingdom – including the nations of England, Scotland, Wales and the province of Northern Ireland – and the Republic of Ireland. The United Kingdom has one of the longest-lasting systems of government in the world. The Queen is the head of state. There are two Houses of Parliament: the House of Lords, and the more important House of Commons, whose representatives are elected by the people. The issue of the reunification of Northern Ireland with the Republic has led to bloodshed – particularly since 1969.

LOCAL GOVERNMENT

The map below shows the counties and administrative districts of the United Kingdom. The boundaries have changed greatly since the mid-1990s. In densely populated regions – such as the conurbations of London, and Greater Manchester – all aspects of local government are dealt with by single bodies known as unitary authorities. In more rural areas there is a two-tiered system. The county administers services such as schools and the local councils administer services such as refuse collection.

1 CENTRAL SCOTLAND

CLACKMANNANSHIRE
WEST DUNBARTONSHIRE
EAST DUNBARTONSHIRE
NORTH LANARKSHIRE
FALKIRK
WEST LOTHIAN
CITY OF EDINBURGH
INVERCLYDE
GLASGOW CITY
RENFREWSHIRE
EAST RENFREWSHIRE
MIDLOTHIAN

EDINBURGH

Edinburgh is the capital of Scotland. A new 'devolved' Scottish Parliament was elected in May 1999, with strong powers to run Scottish affairs independently of the government in London.

DUBLIN

The Dáil and the Seanad – the two chambers of the Irish parliament – have been based at Leinster House in Dublin since 1922 when the Irish Free State, later the Republic of Ireland, was inaugurated.

2 THE NORTHEAST

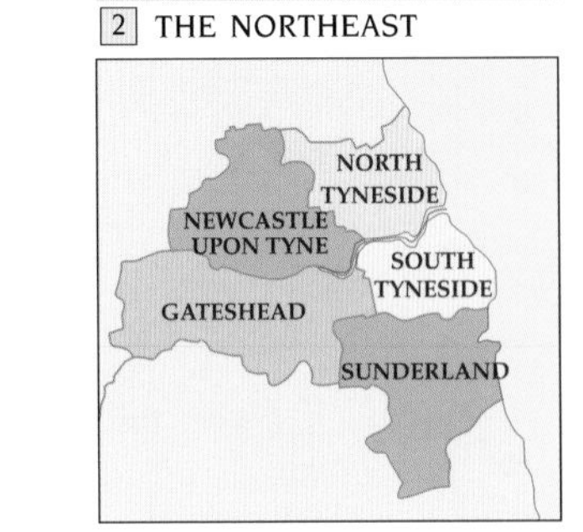

3 TEESSIDE

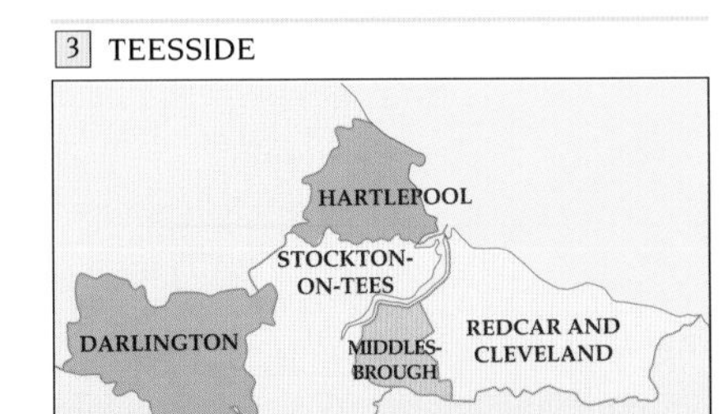

4 THE NORTHWEST

ROCHDALE
BOLTON
BURY
OLDHAM
WIGAN
SEFTON
ST HELENS
SALFORD
TAMESIDE
KNOWSLEY
TRAFFORD
MANCHESTER
WIRRAL
LIVERPOOL
STOCKPORT

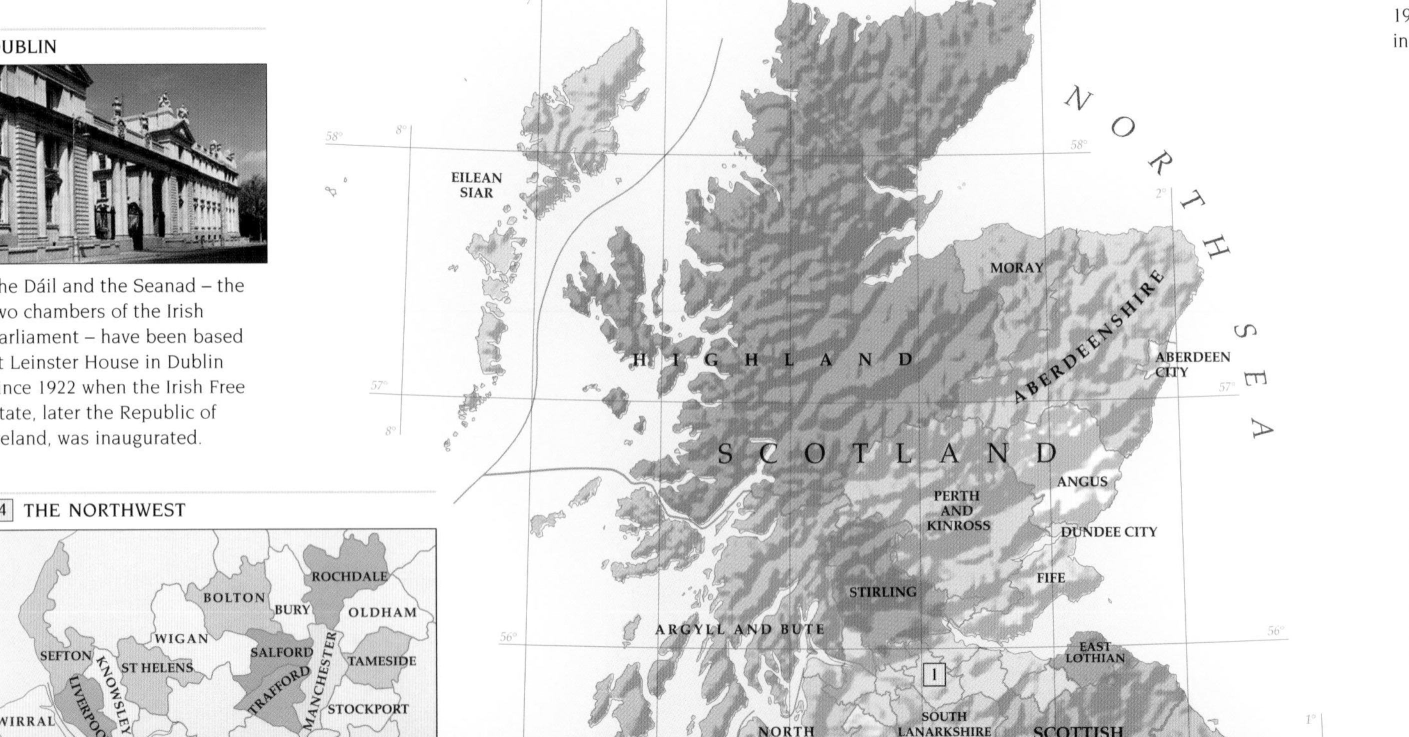

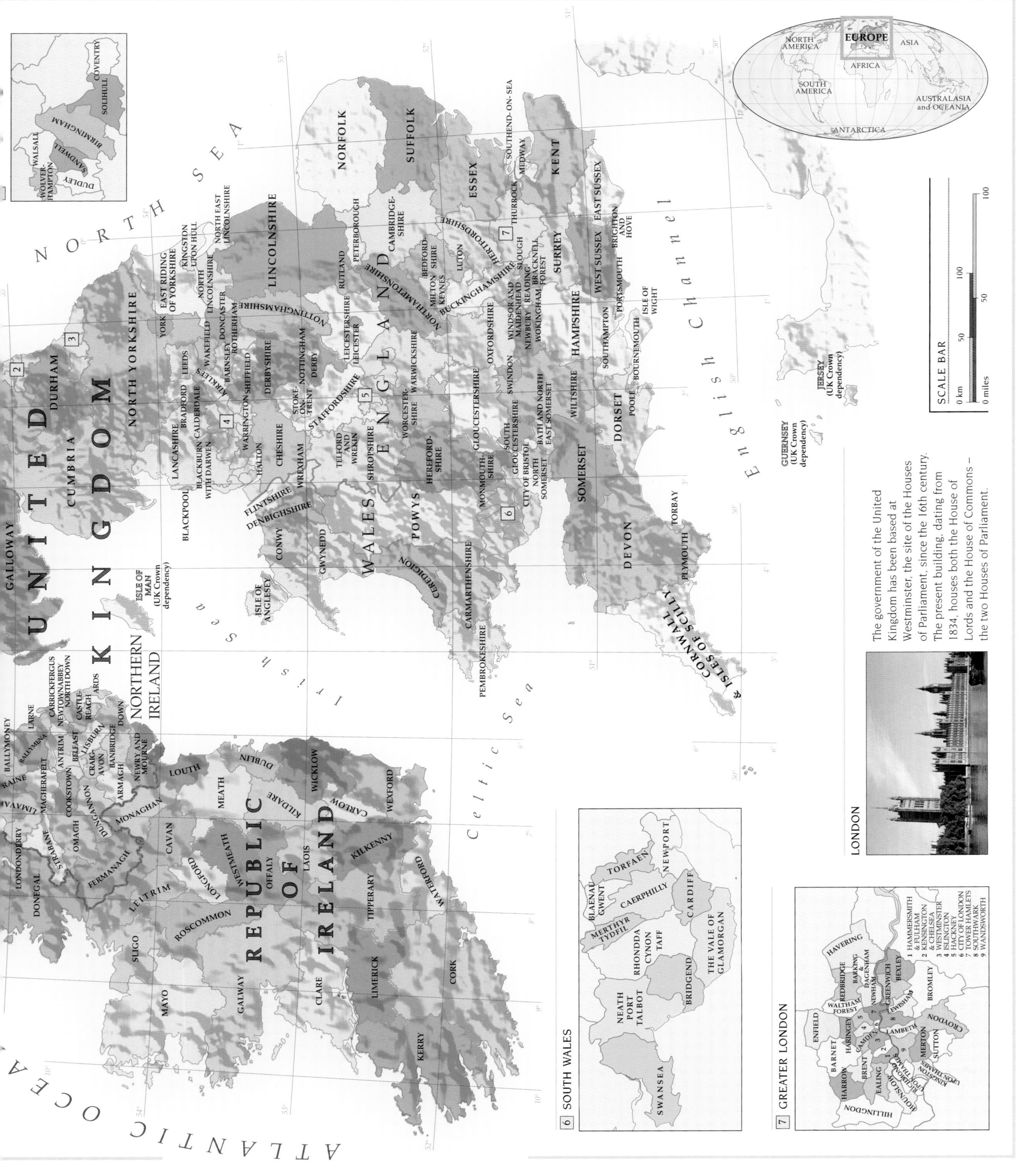

LONDON

The government of the United Kingdom has been based at Westminster, the site of the Houses of Parliament, since the 16th century. The present building, dating from 1834, houses both the House of Lords and the House of Commons – the two Houses of Parliament.

IRELAND

NORTHERN IRELAND, IRELAND

Ireland faces the north Atlantic Ocean and is one of the remotest parts of the European Union. Since 1921 the island has been divided into two separate states: Northern Ireland, which is part of the United Kingdom, and Ireland, which has its own government in Dublin. The eastern side of the island has more people and industry. In the west, traditional ways of life based on farming remain strong and the native Irish language is still spoken by some people.

FARMING AND LAND USE

Potatoes were once the traditional staple food of the Irish; potatoes and cereals flourish in the drier east. The climate is too wet for many types of crop, particularly in the west, where the soils are thin and the land is mostly used for sheep grazing. In bog areas a type of soil called peat is cut from the ground and dried to be burned as fuel.

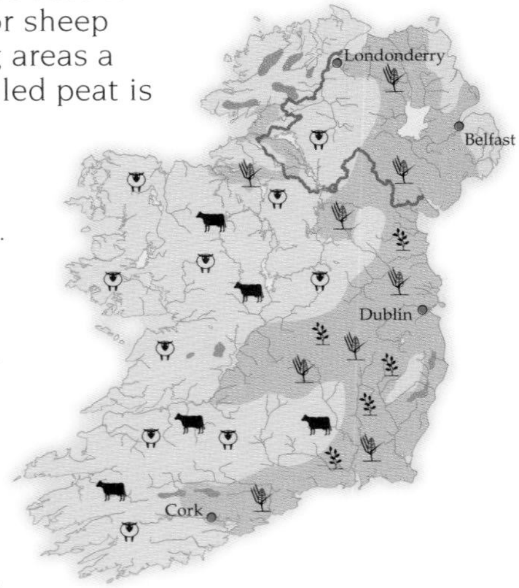
Londonderry
Belfast
Dublin
Cork
FARMING AND LAND USE
Cattle
Sheep
Cereals
Potatoes
Cropland
Forest
Pasture
Major conurbation

INDUSTRY

Ireland has few mineral resources and much of its electricity is produced by burning peat. In the last 20 years the European Union has given money to help the Irish economy and many new factories have been set up, mainly in the area around Dublin. Hi-tech industries expanded rapidly, as a result of low set-up costs and tax benefits.

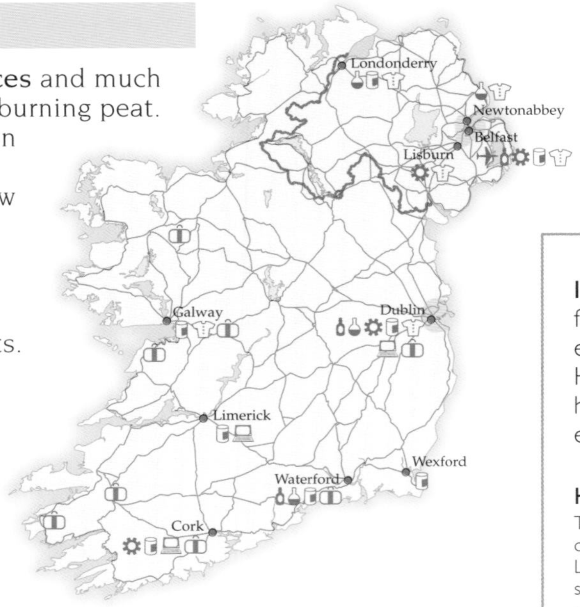
Londonderry
Newtonabbey
Belfast
Lisburn
Galway
Dublin
Limerick
Wexford
Waterford
Cork
INDUSTRY
Aerospace
Brewing
Chemicals
Engineering
Food processing
Textiles
Hi-tech industry
Tourism
Major industrial centre / area
Major road

POPULATION

The population of Ireland has actually fallen over the last century as a result of mass emigration, mainly to North America. The rate of people leaving the country to live abroad is still high, although a very high birth rate and economic immigration is finally causing the population to rise again, with one person in every three being less than 20 years old.

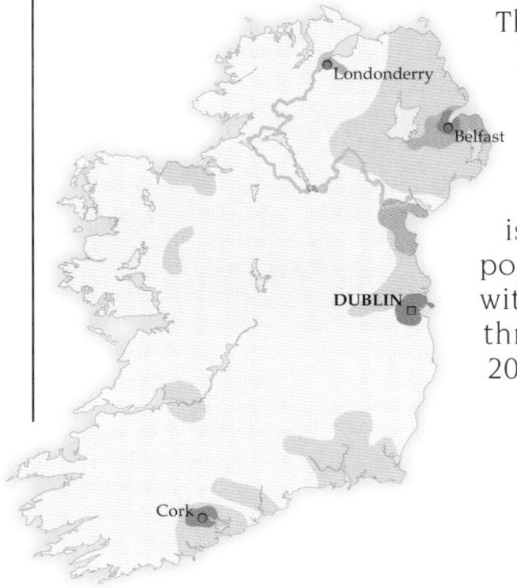
Londonderry
Belfast
DUBLIN
Cork
INHABITANTS PER SQ KM
More than 250
100–250
50–100
Less than 50
Capital city
Major city

THE LANDSCAPE

Ireland's mountains are nearly all close to the sea. They form a ring of high ground – broken in only a few places – encircling a lower lying plain which fills the central areas. Hundreds of lakes, large areas of bogland and low, grassy hills cover this central plain. The west coast follows an extremely irregular line, with many long bays and headlands.

High cliffs (C2)
The cliffs of Donegal are some of the highest in Europe. Slieve League has been half cut away by sea erosion, so that the cliff rises vertically, all the way up from the shore to its 670 m summit.

Lakes made by glaciers
The central plain is covered with lakes of many different sizes. Most of these lakes were formed by huge blocks of ice which remained lying around as the last Ice Age came to an end, slowly melting over hundreds of years to leave sunken pits in the land surface.

Flooded river valleys (A6)
Dingle Bay extends deep inland. Rising seas have flooded the old river valley. Bays formed when the sea floods a river valley are known as rias.

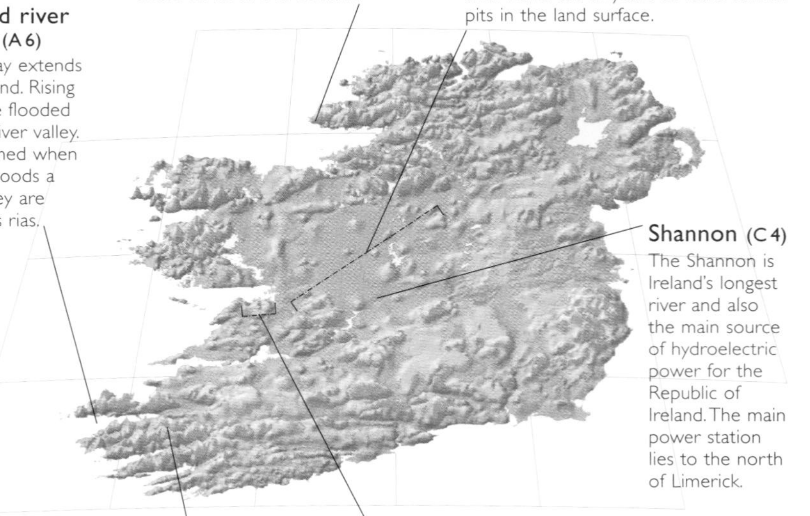

Shannon (C4)
The Shannon is Ireland's longest river and also the main source of hydroelectric power for the Republic of Ireland. The main power station lies to the north of Limerick.

Macgillycuddy's Reeks (B6)
This is the highest mountain range in Ireland. The jagged peaks and steep-sided valleys were cut from the highly resistant rocks by glacial erosion, during the last Ice Age.

Burren (B4)
The Burren is a large plateau of limestone rock. Limestone is permeable, which means that water sinks below the surface and flows underground. The bare rock is visible at the surface in many places, where it is called a limestone pavement.

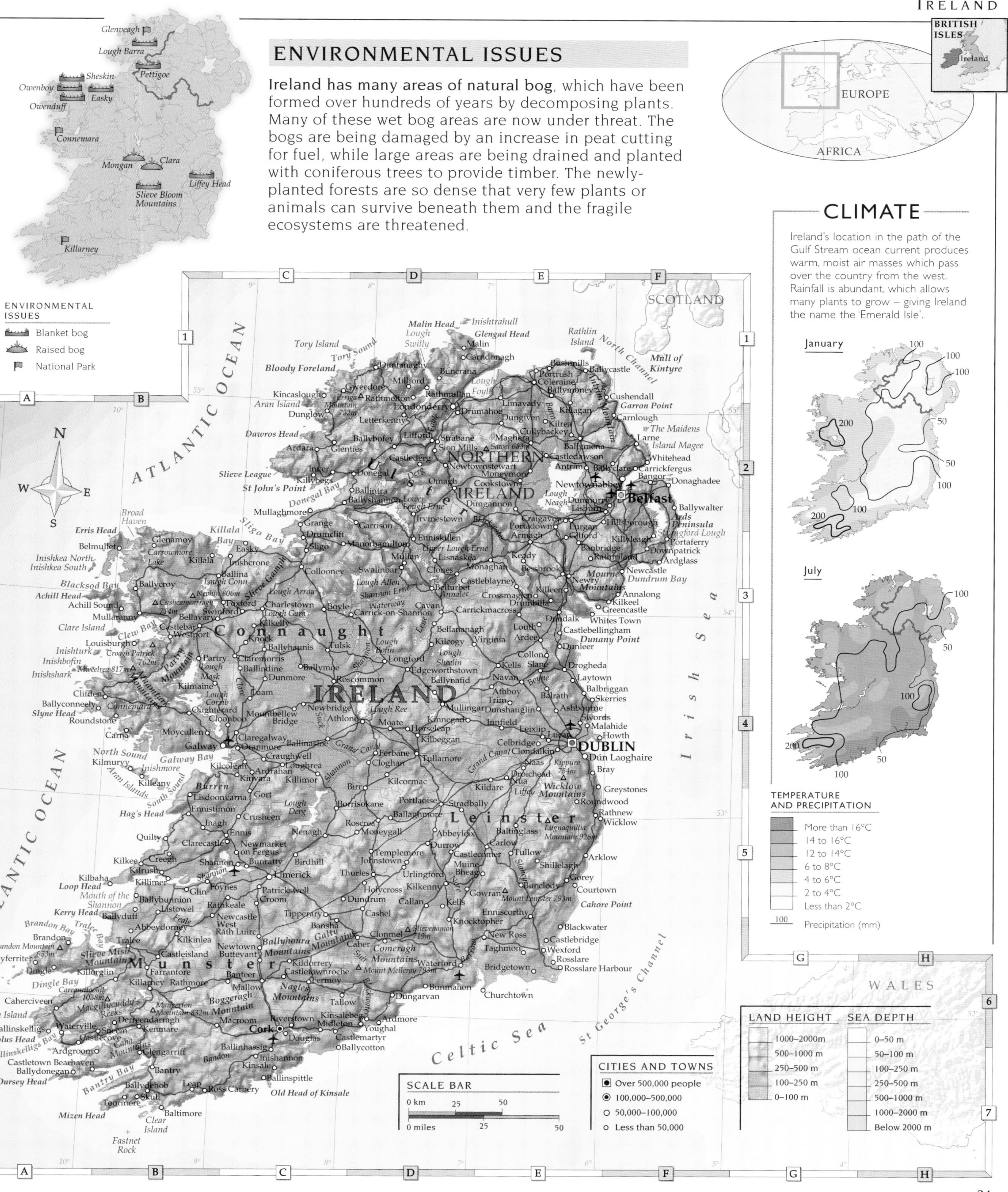

ENVIRONMENTAL ISSUES

Ireland has many areas of natural bog, which have been formed over hundreds of years by decomposing plants. Many of these wet bog areas are now under threat. The bogs are being damaged by an increase in peat cutting for fuel, while large areas are being drained and planted with coniferous trees to provide timber. The newly-planted forests are so dense that very few plants or animals can survive beneath them and the fragile ecosystems are threatened.

CLIMATE

Ireland's location in the path of the Gulf Stream ocean current produces warm, moist air masses which pass over the country from the west. Rainfall is abundant, which allows many plants to grow – giving Ireland the name the 'Emerald Isle'.

Scotland

Scotland occupies the northern third of Britain and has three main regions: the northern highlands and islands, the Southern Uplands and, between these two mountain areas, the central lowlands, where around three quarters of the population live and work. Scotland was once an independent country and, after nearly 300 years of union with England, has regained its own parliament, with certain autonomous powers. Scotland's economy has been boosted over the last 20 years by the North Sea oil industry.

INDUSTRY

A century ago, the area around the River Clyde was one of the great industrial regions of the world. The old heavy industries have since declined and been replaced by hi-tech and electronics industries, earning the area the name of 'Silicon Glen'. North Sea oil has brought many jobs and attracted new, oil-based industries such as chemicals and plastics production to the east coast.

INDUSTRY

- Aerospace
- Brewing
- Chemicals
- Engineering
- Fish processing
- Food processing
- Textiles
- Oil and gas
- Hi-tech industry
- Printing and publishing
- Tourism
- Major industrial centre / area
- Major road

Stornoway, Wick, Banff, Inverness, Peterhead, Aberdeen, Fort William, Perth, Dundee, Glasgow, Dunfermline, Greenock, Edinburgh, Paisley, Kilmarnock, East Kilbride, Ayr, Prestwick, Dumfries, Lerwick

ENVIRONMENTAL ISSUES

During a storm in January 1993, the Braer oil tanker struck the cliffs of southern Shetland. The ship broke up, shedding its entire load of crude oil into the sea. Although the oil was washed away within weeks, the long-term effects are not yet known. Scotland's fledgling skiing industry, in the highlands, has declined sharply, although tourism continues to cause mild environmental damage.

Aviemore, Caringorms, Glen Coe, Braer – 1993

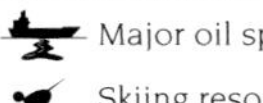

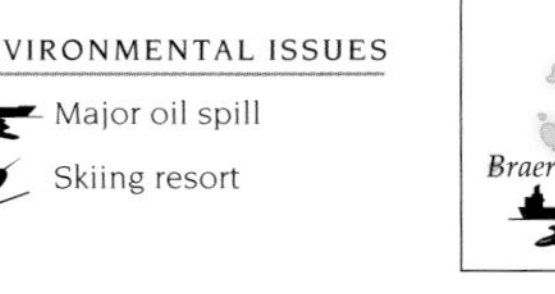

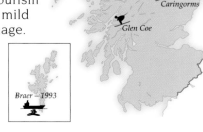

FARMING AND LAND USE

The eastern side of Scotland has a drier climate than the west and is suitable for growing cereal crops and vegetables. Most of the mountain areas are too wet and barren for arable farming and are put to a variety of uses, which include sheep and deer farming, game-keeping, forestry, tourism and recreation. Scottish fishermen currently land about two-thirds of all the fish caught by the UK.

FARMING AND LAND USE

- Cattle
- Deer
- Fishing
- Sheep
- Cereals
- Root crops
- Timber
- Cropland
- Forest
- Mountains
- Pasture
- Major conurbation

Aberdeen, Dundee, Glasgow, Edinburgh

THE LANDSCAPE

Much of Scotland is rugged and mountainous. During the last Ice Age, around 18,000 years ago, glaciers and great sheets of ice attacked Scotland's hard, ancient rocks, leaving behind a landscape of high moorlands and steep-sided mountains separated by deep valleys, often filled by lakes known as lochs.

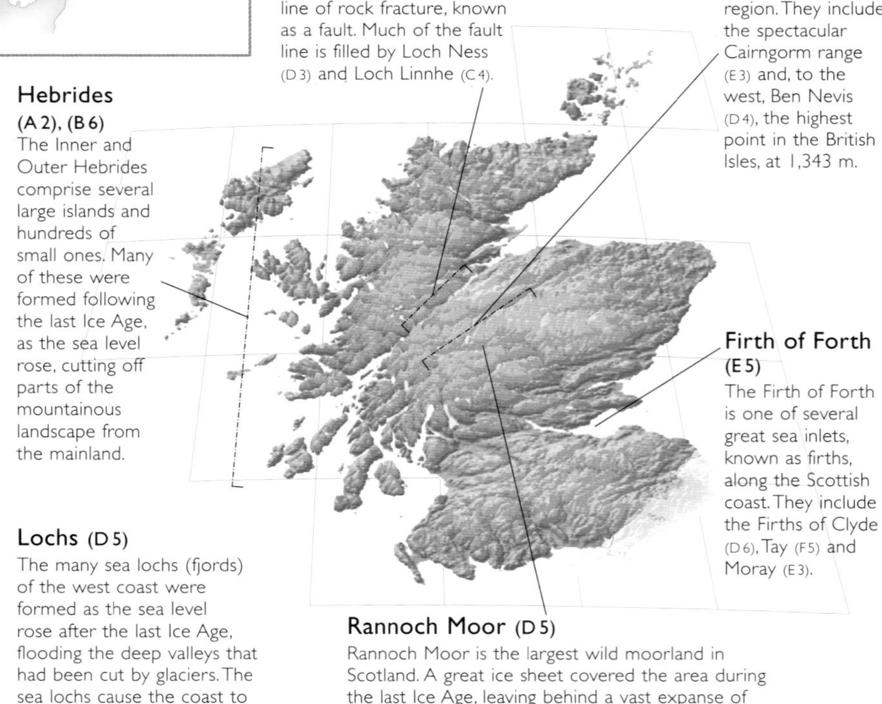

Glen Mor (D 3)
Glen Mor is a deep valley which runs right across Scotland. It marks a major line of rock fracture, known as a fault. Much of the fault line is filled by Loch Ness (D 3) and Loch Linnhe (C 4).

Grampians (D 4)
The Grampians are Britain's largest and highest mountain region. They include the spectacular Cairngorm range (E 3) and, to the west, Ben Nevis (D 4), the highest point in the British Isles, at 1,343 m.

Hebrides (A 2), (B 6)
The Inner and Outer Hebrides comprise several large islands and hundreds of small ones. Many of these were formed following the last Ice Age, as the sea level rose, cutting off parts of the mountainous landscape from the mainland.

Firth of Forth (E 5)
The Firth of Forth is one of several great sea inlets, known as firths, along the Scottish coast. They include the Firths of Clyde (D 6), Tay (F 5) and Moray (E 3).

Lochs (D 5)
The many sea lochs (fjords) of the west coast were formed as the sea level rose after the last Ice Age, flooding the deep valleys that had been cut by glaciers. The sea lochs cause the coast to follow a highly irregular line.

Rannoch Moor (D 5)
Rannoch Moor is the largest wild moorland in Scotland. A great ice sheet covered the area during the last Ice Age, leaving behind a vast expanse of bleak, bare ground, pitted with small depressions.

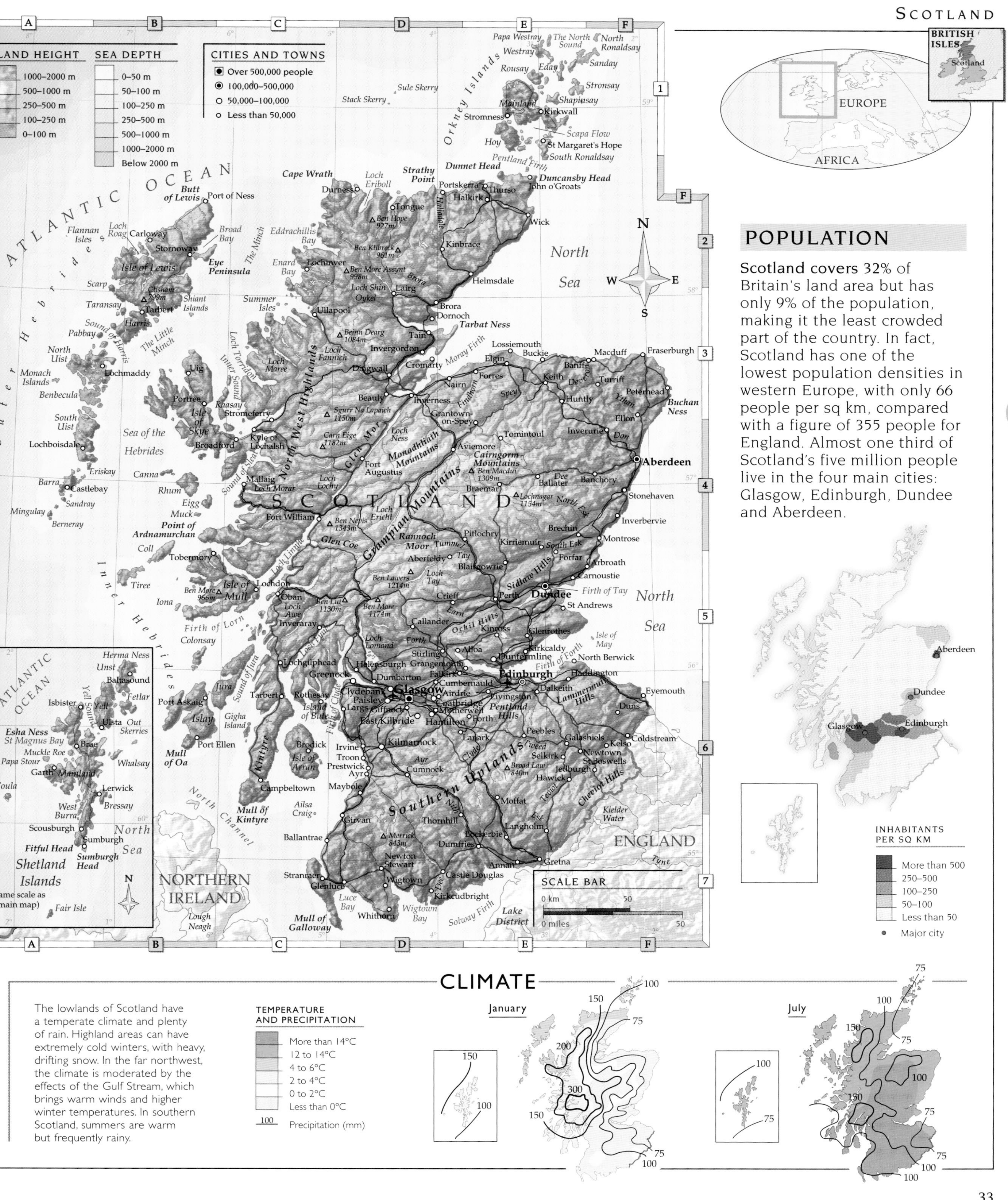

POPULATION

Scotland covers 32% of Britain's land area but has only 9% of the population, making it the least crowded part of the country. In fact, Scotland has one of the lowest population densities in western Europe, with only 66 people per sq km, compared with a figure of 355 people for England. Almost one third of Scotland's five million people live in the four main cities: Glasgow, Edinburgh, Dundee and Aberdeen.

CLIMATE

The lowlands of Scotland have a temperate climate and plenty of rain. Highland areas can have extremely cold winters, with heavy, drifting snow. In the far northwest, the climate is moderated by the effects of the Gulf Stream, which brings warm winds and higher winter temperatures. In southern Scotland, summers are warm but frequently rainy.

NORTHERN ENGLAND

The Industrial Revolution of the 18th and 19th centuries began in northern England. Rich coalfields and new developments in iron and steel and textile production started a new era of mass production – encouraging the growth of cities such as Liverpool and Manchester. Today, these industries have declined, but despite a number of difficult years, northern England is becoming more prosperous again. The magnificent scenery is attracting many tourists and new service industries are thriving.

INDUSTRY

Traditional industries such as iron and steel, coal-mining and textiles have been declining in northern England for over half a century. The region is still the industrial heartland of the UK, although the type of industries have changed. New light engineering and car production plants have developed in and around the region's cities, alongside hi-tech industries producing microchips and computers, and service industries such as insurance and retailing, printing and publishing.

INDUSTRY

- Aerospace
- Brewing
- Car manufacture
- Ceramics
- Chemicals
- Engineering
- Fish processing
- Food processing
- Iron & steel
- Metal refining
- Pharmaceuticals
- Shipbuilding
- Textiles
- Hi-tech industry
- Printing and publishing
- Tourism
- Major industrial centre / area
- Major road

ENVIRONMENTAL ISSUES

Some of England's most dramatic scenery is found in northern England, and National Parks have long been established to protect the environment. The National Parks have proved so popular that in some places tourists are in danger of destroying the environment. Coal-fired power stations in the region power the large cities, but also contribute to acid rain in the UK and Scandinavia.

ENVIRONMENTAL ISSUES

- Coal-fired power station
- National Park
- Major industrial city

FARMING AND LAND USE

The eastern lowlands have an ideal climate for arable crops, while oats and potatoes grow in the north and west. Market gardening is concentrated along the Humber and Mersey estuaries. The southwest is used mainly for grazing cattle and sheep, which also graze rough in upland areas such as the Pennines.

FARMING AND LAND USE

- Cattle
- Sheep
- Cereals
- Market gardening
- Root crops
- Cropland
- Forest
- Pasture
- Major conurbation

THE LANDSCAPE

Northern England has a higher and more rugged landscape than the south, dominated by the bleak hills and moors of the Pennines. The Aire and Ouse rivers have cut a broad flood plain between the Pennines and the North York Moors. In the far northwest, Cumbria's Lake District has many long, deep lakes, which were formed during the last Ice Age.

Limestone pavements
Bare 'pavements' of weathered limestone are also known as karst scenery. They have a block-like appearance, with deep cracks between the blocks which have been dissolved by rainwater.

Spurn Head (F 4)
Spurn Head is a long sand bar at the mouth of the Humber estuary called a spit. It was formed by waves which deposited sand across the mouth of the bay. Recent heavy storms have made Spurn Head almost inaccessible from the mainland.

Kielder Water (C 2)
Kielder Water lies close to the Scottish border. With a perimeter of 44 km, it is the largest man-made lake in Europe.

Isle of Man (A 3)
The Isle of Man is about 50 km long. It has a deeply indented coastline eroded by strong waves in the Irish Sea.

North York Moors (D 3)

Morecambe Bay (B 4)
The bay is renowned for its tides which rise and fall rapidly. A barrage scheme has been proposed to harness this tidal energy.

Lake District (B 3)
The Lake District covers a small area of the Cumbrian Mountains. The 15 lakes here form a radial pattern, spreading out from a central zone of volcanic rock.

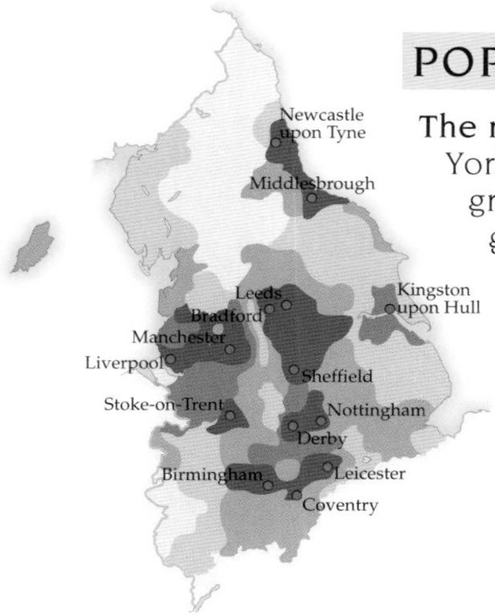

POPULATION

The northwestern cities of Liverpool and Manchester and the Yorkshire cities of Leeds and Bradford have spread out to form great conurbations. In the West Midlands, large populations grew up in and around the industrial cities of Coventry and Birmingham. The northeastern coast from Middlesbrough to Newcastle upon Tyne is also densely populated. The upland regions are more sparsely populated, with small villages in the valleys and lowland areas.

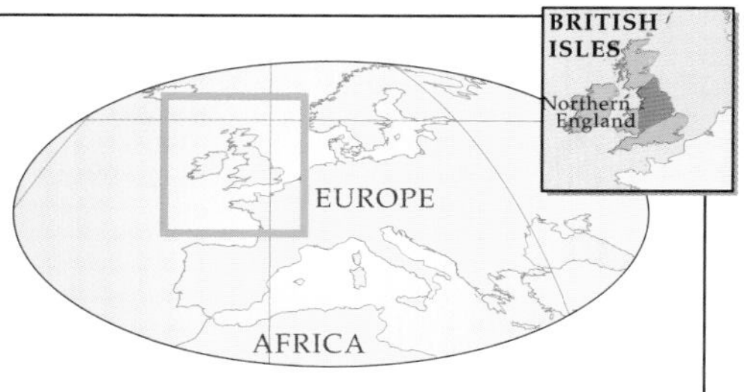

INHABITANTS PER SQ KM

- More than 500
- 250–500
- 100–250
- 50–100
- Less than 50
- Major city

CLIMATE

Northern England tends to be cooler and wetter than the south, especially in the summer months. High rainfall totals are recorded in the upland areas of the west. The east, in the 'rainshadow' of the Pennines, is drier.

January

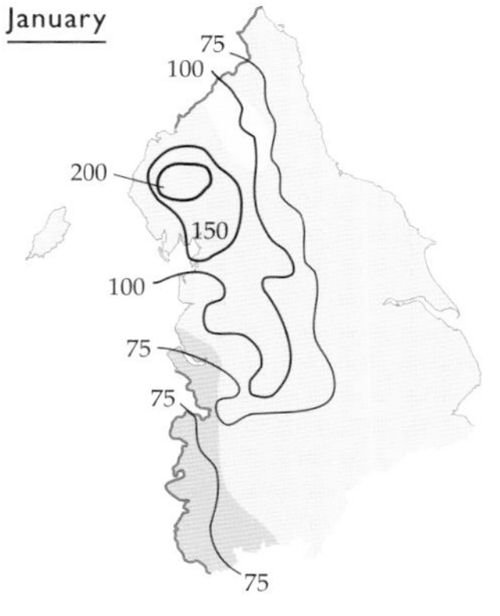

July

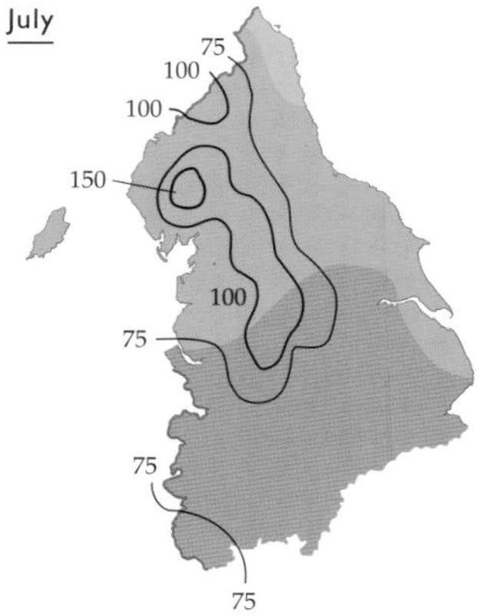

TEMPERATURE AND PRECIPITATION

- More than 16°C
- 14 to 16°C
- 12 to 14°C
- 4 to 6°C
- 2 to 4°C
- Less than 2°C
- 100 Precipitation (mm)

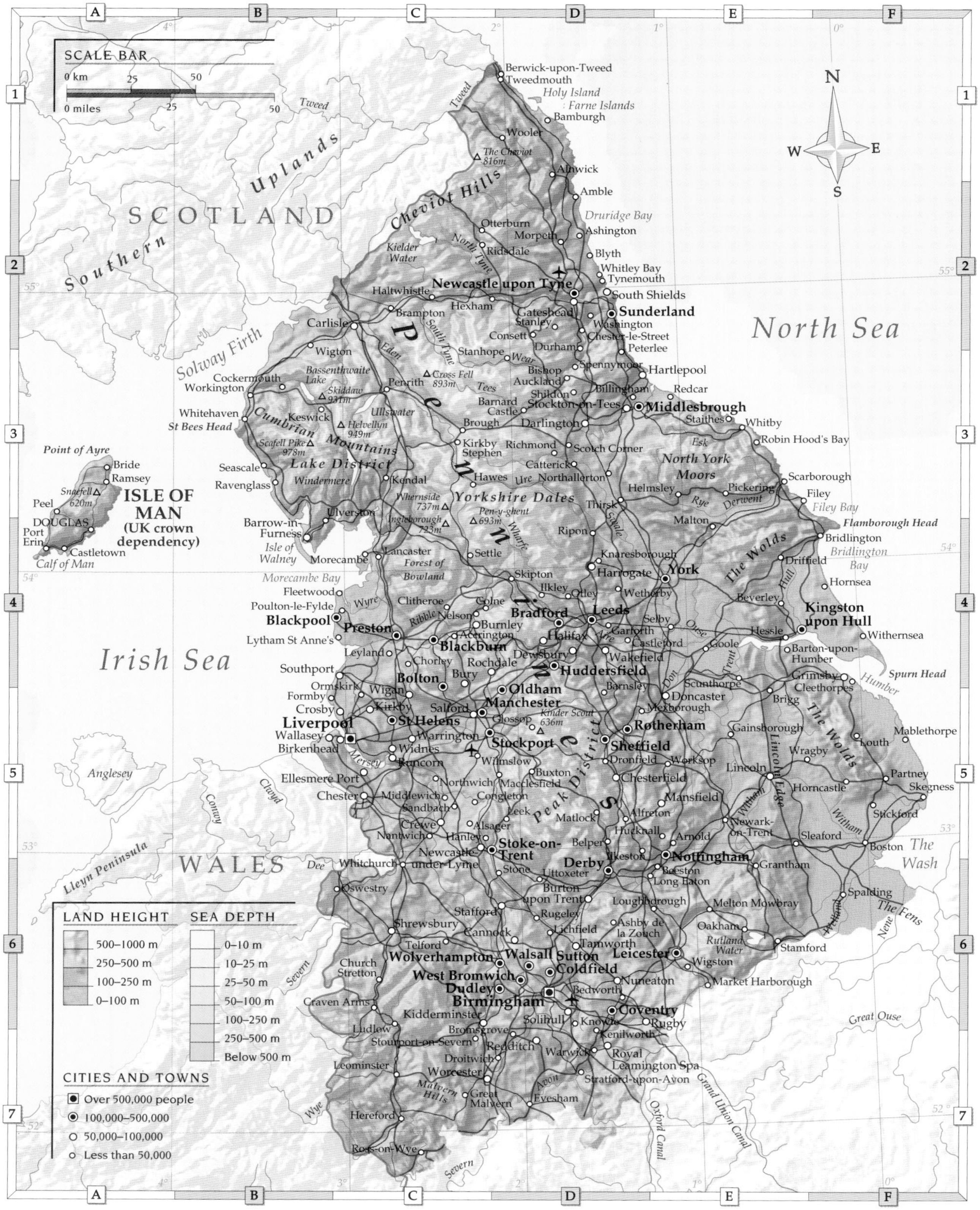

SOUTHERN ENGLAND

The southern counties of England, and particularly Greater London, are the most densely populated part of the British Isles. There are more industries and more jobs here than anywhere else in the UK. In contrast, the counties of the far west and east are much less heavily populated and more rural, although towns in the eastern counties have been growing rapidly since the 1980s. Following the completion of the Channel Tunnel, the UK has had a direct rail link to Europe.

INDUSTRY

London is one of the world's top financial centres and is also a leading centre for other service industries including insurance, the media and publishing. Many car manufacturers are based in southern England, though the numbers of people employed have greatly decreased. Several cities, including Cambridge and Swindon, are centres for hi-tech industry. Thousands of tourists visit the historic and cultural centres in southern England every year.

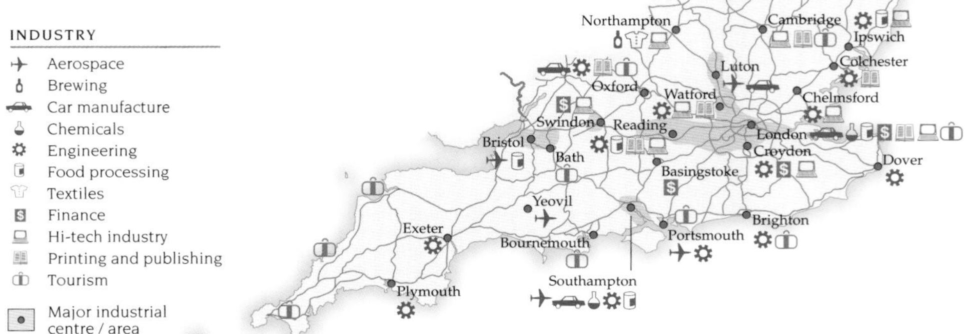

ENVIRONMENTAL ISSUES

The large, and growing population of southern England has put pressure on 'green belt' land; infilling, brownfield redevelopment, building on flood plains, and many new towns required new infrastructure. Road and rail upgrading, and further development of London's five airports, has led to increasing public concern and heated debate.

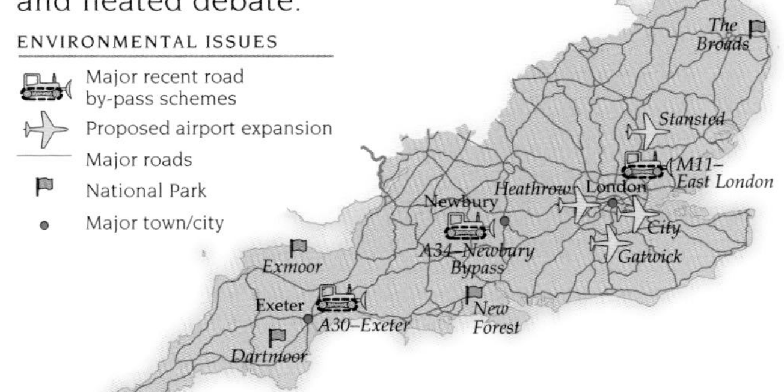

FARMING AND LAND USE

Fertile soils and reliable rainfall mean that a wide range of crops can be grown in southern England. Large arable farms growing wheat and barley are found in the flat eastern counties, and a great variety of soft and orchard fruits and vegetables are grown in market gardens in the far southeast. Beef and dairy cattle and large flocks of sheep are grazed throughout the south.

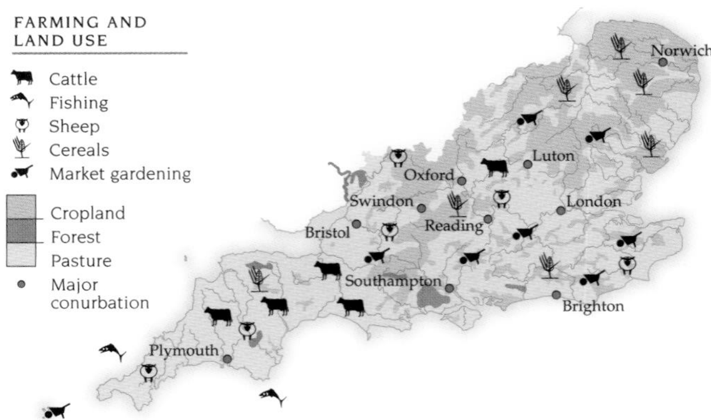

THE LANDSCAPE

The landscape of southern England is very varied. Cornwall in the far west has craggy hills, and a jagged coastline shaped by the Atlantic Ocean. The Cotswolds and the North and South Downs are gentle hills, while towards the east, the land becomes flatter. Near the east coast, low-lying areas are occasionally prone to flooding.

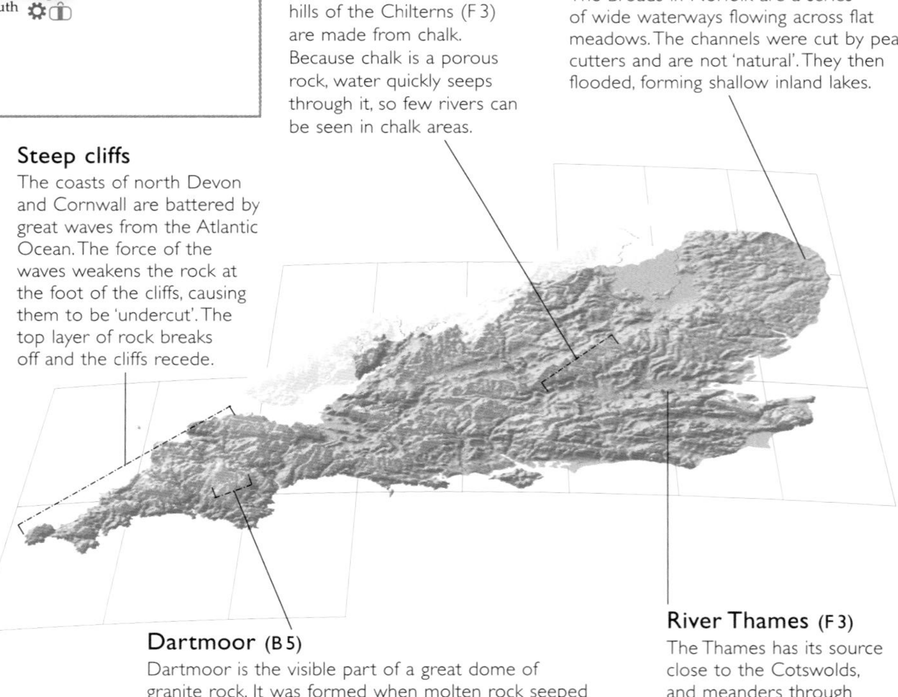

Chalk hills The rounded hills of the Chilterns (F 3) are made from chalk. Because chalk is a porous rock, water quickly seeps through it, so few rivers can be seen in chalk areas.

The Broads (H 2)
The Broads in Norfolk are a series of wide waterways flowing across flat meadows. The channels were cut by peat cutters and are not 'natural'. They then flooded, forming shallow inland lakes.

Steep cliffs
The coasts of north Devon and Cornwall are battered by great waves from the Atlantic Ocean. The force of the waves weakens the rock at the foot of the cliffs, causing them to be 'undercut'. The top layer of rock breaks off and the cliffs recede.

Dartmoor (B 5)
Dartmoor is the visible part of a great dome of granite rock. It was formed when molten rock seeped into and cooled in the Earth's crust. Because granite is so hard it erodes very slowly, so outcrops of rock known as *tors* can be seen all over Dartmoor.

River Thames (F 3)
The Thames has its source close to the Cotswolds, and meanders through Oxford and London before reaching the North Sea in a wide estuary.

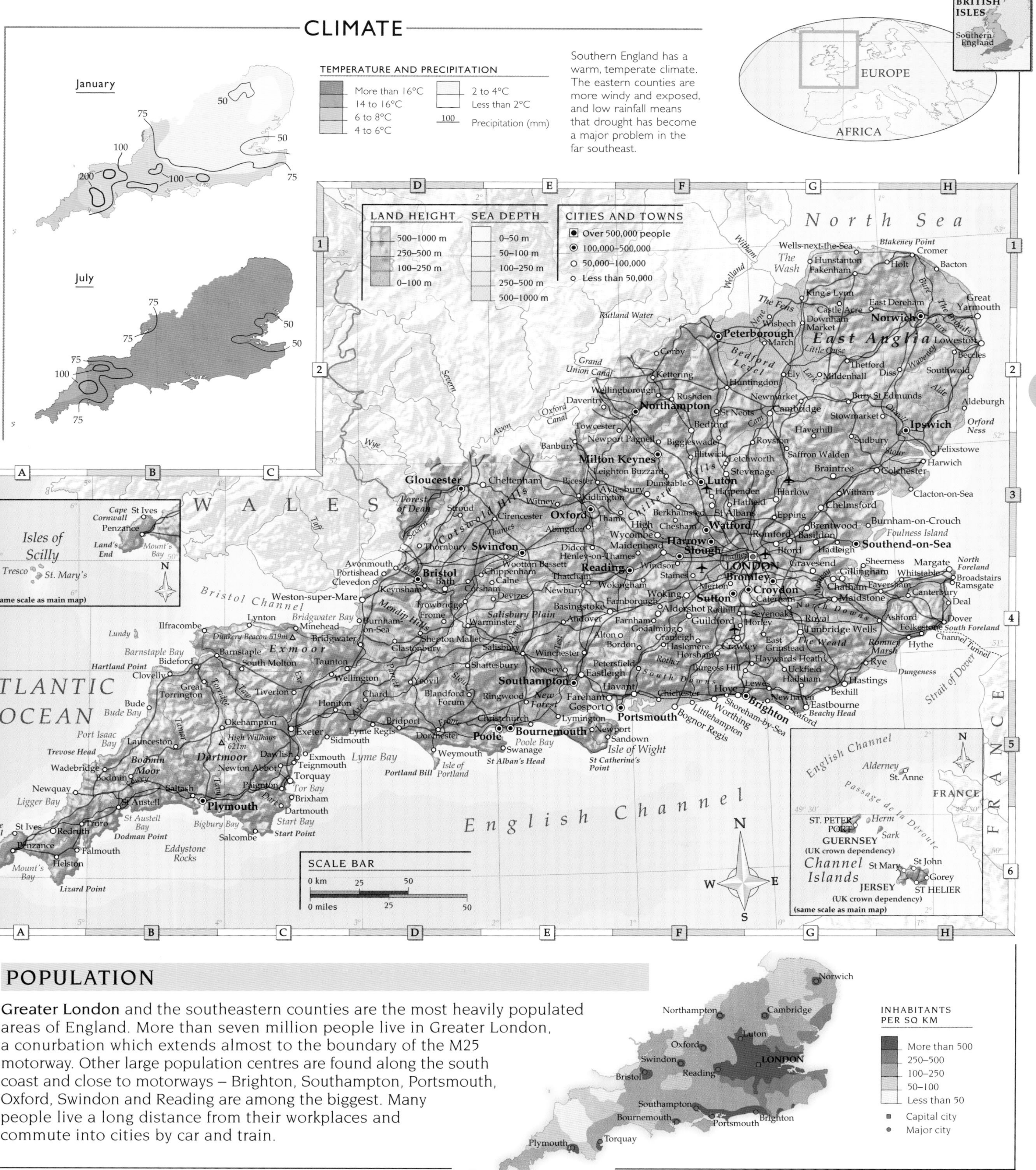

CLIMATE

Southern England has a warm, temperate climate. The eastern counties are more windy and exposed, and low rainfall means that drought has become a major problem in the far southeast.

POPULATION

Greater London and the southeastern counties are the most heavily populated areas of England. More than seven million people live in Greater London, a conurbation which extends almost to the boundary of the M25 motorway. Other large population centres are found along the south coast and close to motorways – Brighton, Southampton, Portsmouth, Oxford, Swindon and Reading are among the biggest. Many people live a long distance from their workplaces and commute into cities by car and train.

WALES

Wales has been governed by England since 1535, yet it remains a distinctly different nation. Over a fifth of the people speak the native Welsh language of their Celtic ancestors. Wales has a strong artistic and musical tradition, celebrated in events such as the Eisteddfod festival. Large areas of the country are sparsely populated, with small and often isolated hill farming communities. South Wales is the main urban area and was once a major coal-mining and heavy industrial region. Wales's wild mountain scenery attracts many tourists and outdoor enthusiasts.

INDUSTRY

Vast quantities of slate, coal and other minerals were mined from the Cambrian Mountains during the Industrial Revolution, supplying the factories of south Wales. Very little mining takes place today but new hi-tech and service industries have grown rapidly in the south. Government assistance has helped these industries to spread into more rural places. Tourism is important in Wales, and large numbers of people visit its National Parks each year.

INDUSTRY

- Car manufacture
- Engineering
- Iron and steel
- Metal refining
- Oil refining
- Hi-tech industry
- Tourism
- Major industrial centre / area
- Major road

Llandudno
Wrexham
Aberystwyth
Milford Haven
Tenby
Llanelli
Merthyr Tydfil
Swansea
Port Talbot
Bridgend
Pontypool
Cwmbran
Newport
Cardiff

POPULATION

The area around Newport, Cardiff and Swansea is home to more than 60% of the 2.9 million people living in Wales. Rising numbers of people have been moving into rural areas in north and central Wales over the last ten years. In old mining and industrial towns such as Merthyr Tydfil and Port Talbot, the population has fallen.

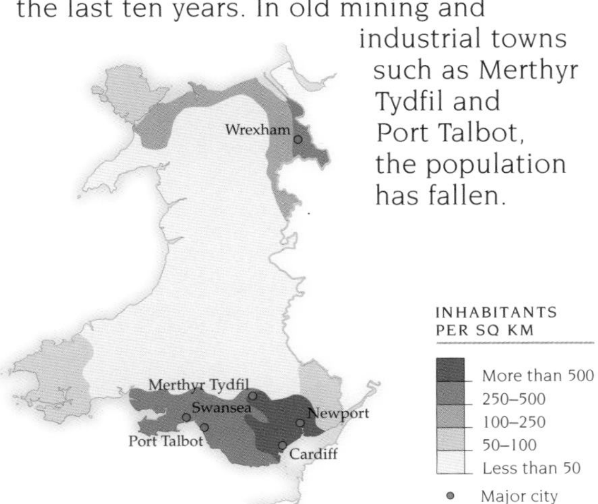

FARMING AND LAND USE

More land is used for farming in Wales than in England, yet only a few parts of Wales, such as the Conwy and Clwyd river valleys, are suitable for growing crops. The main land use is pastoral farming, with dairy cattle in more sheltered areas and sheep farmed on the more exposed uplands. Coniferous forests are now being planted in many mountain areas.

FARMING AND LAND USE

- Cattle
- Sheep
- Root crops
- Cropland
- Forest
- Mountains
- Pasture
- Major conurbation

Swansea
Newport
Cardiff

THE LANDSCAPE

Mountains, plateaus and hills make up most of the Welsh landscape. The only lowland areas are the river valleys and parts of the coast and the English border. The Cambrian mountain range forms the backbone of the country and includes the rugged peaks of Snowdonia in the north, the rounded uplands of mid-Wales and the Brecon Beacons in the south.

The Brecon Beacons (D 6) **and the Black Mountains** (E 5)
These mountains are less steep than the jagged peaks of Snowdonia. This is due to the softer sandstone rock from which they were formed.

Sandy beaches
The coastline of mid and north Wales has large sandy beaches, many with sand dunes. Most of the sand was originally formed from the erosion of cliffs further south along the coast. The beach material is then carried north by longshore drift.

Anglesey (C 1)
The flat, low island of Anglesey is separated from the mainland by the Menai Strait. The flat land surface is believed to be a wave-cut platform, eroded by the sea. It is now exposed because the land has risen since the end of the Ice Age.

Snowdonia (C 2)
These spectacular mountains include Snowdon, the highest point in England and Wales, at 1,085 m. The spectacular sheer sides and jagged ridges were carved by glaciers during the last Ice Age.

The Vale of Glamorgan (D 7)
The Vale of Glamorgan is a fertile coastal plateau, dissected by a number of streams which have cut down into the land surface. The plateau ends abruptly at the coast, with sheer cliffs 33 m high.

Cambrian Mountains (D 5)
The Cambrian range runs the whole length of the country and contains some of the oldest rocks in Britain. The rock is rich in minerals. Slate was also once mined in great quantities in northern and central areas.

Plynlimon (D 4)
This mountain in central Wales is the source for two of the country's most important rivers: the Severn and the Wye.

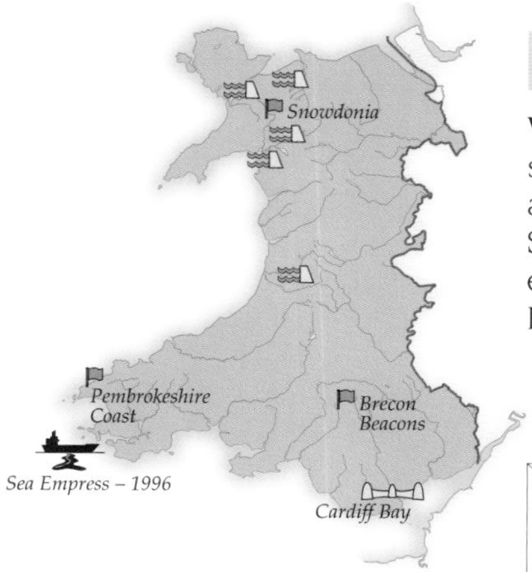

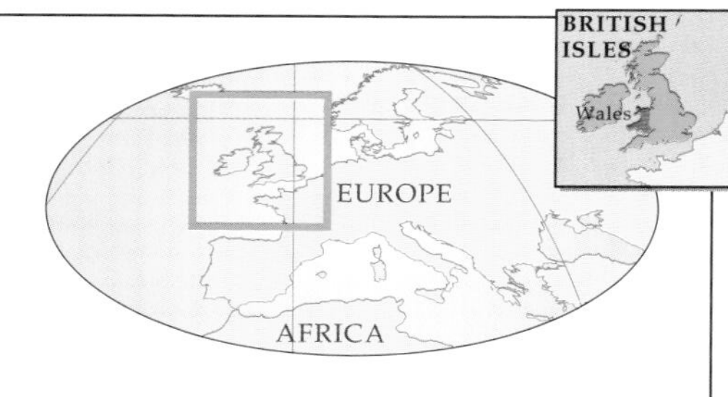

ENVIRONMENTAL ISSUES

Wales's high rainfall is stored in large reservoirs which supply water to major cities in England and Wales, and are also used to generate electricity. The natural splendour of Snowdonia and the Brecon Beacons has been conserved by establishing National Parks. The rugged coastline of Pembrokeshire was hit by a large oil spill in 1996, although much of the oil was cleared away successfully. Recently, tidal Cardiff Bay was dammed to create a huge lake.

Snowdonia
Pembrokeshire Coast
Brecon Beacons
Sea Empress – 1996
Cardiff Bay

ENVIRONMENTAL ISSUES

- Barrage scheme
- Major hydro-electric scheme
- Major oil spill
- National Park

CLIMATE

Wales has a generally temperate climate, with plenty of rain all year round. The mountains are much colder than coastal areas, and some of the higher peaks may be covered by snow for much of the year.

January

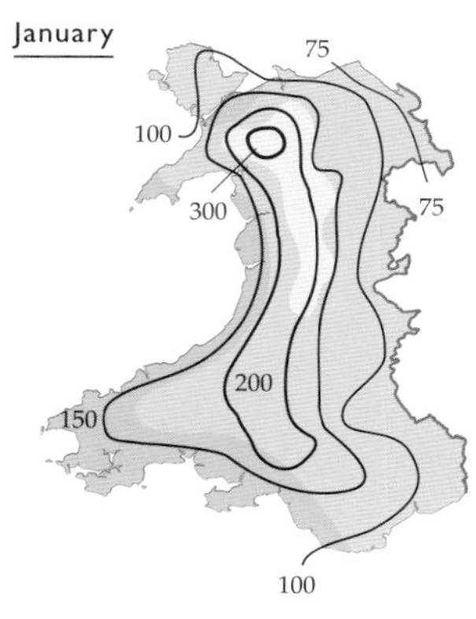

July

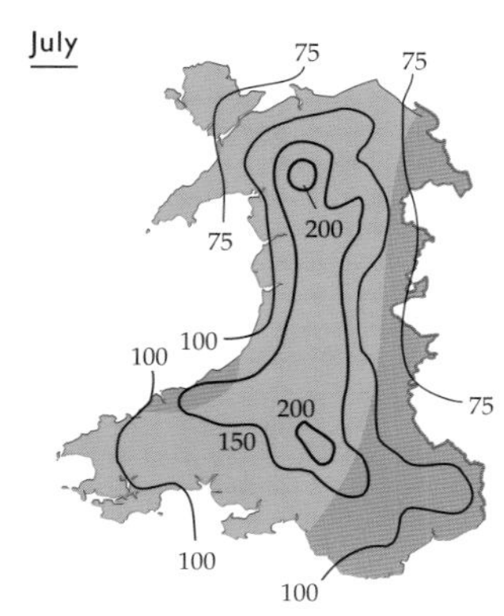

TEMPERATURE AND PRECIPITATION

- More than 16°C
- 14 to 16°C
- 6 to 8°C
- 4 to 6°C
- Less than 4°C
- 100 Precipitation (mm)

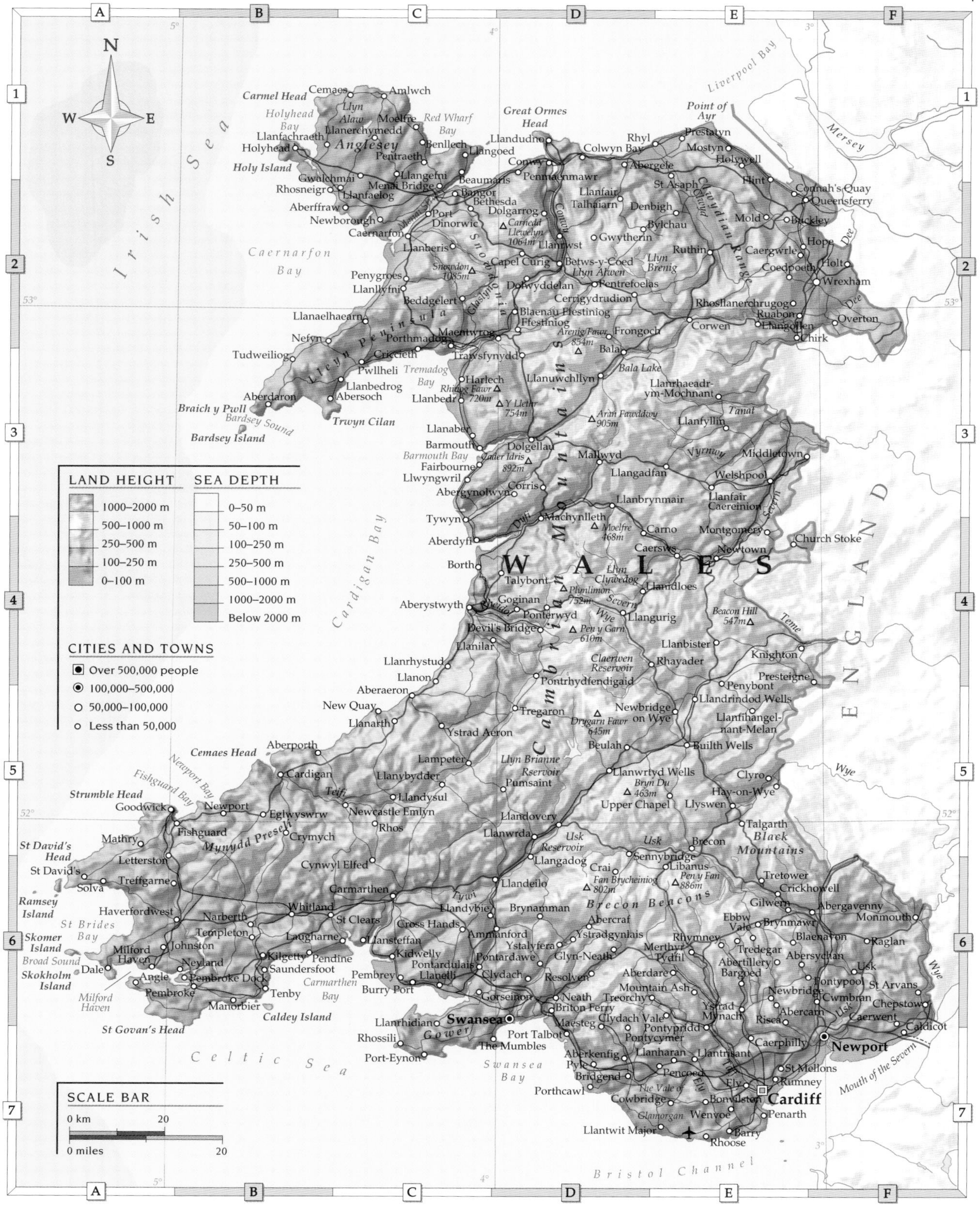

WALES

LAND HEIGHT

- 1000–2000 m
- 500–1000 m
- 250–500 m
- 100–250 m
- 0–100 m

SEA DEPTH

- 0–50 m
- 50–100 m
- 100–250 m
- 250–500 m
- 500–1000 m
- 1000–2000 m
- Below 2000 m

CITIES AND TOWNS

- Over 500,000 people
- 100,000–500,000
- 50,000–100,000
- Less than 50,000

SCALE BAR

0 km 20

0 miles 20

UK Overseas Territories

The UK has the largest number of overseas territories in the world. They still exist for a variety of reasons: some are of strategic or economic importance; others are considered too small or remote to be able to survive as independent countries. UK overseas territories are split between Crown colonies, Crown dependencies and dependent territories but, regardless of their status, most have a high degree of local responsibility for government.

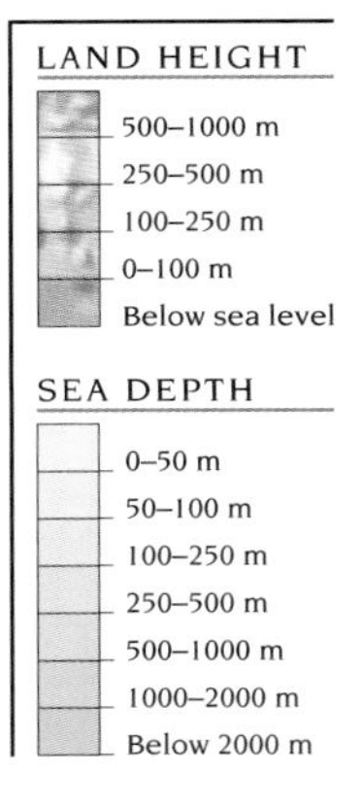

TURKS AND CAICOS ISLANDS

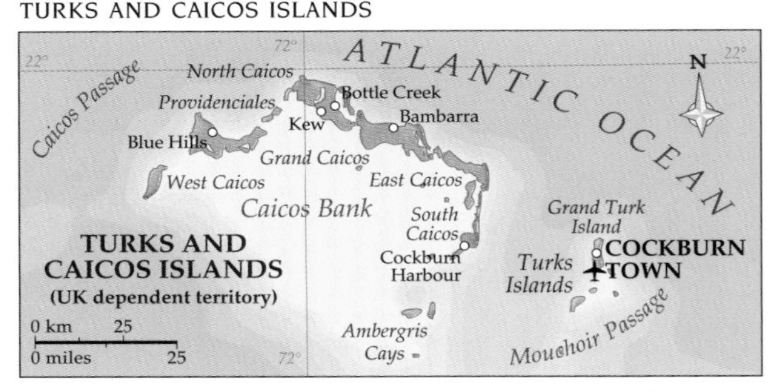

The Turks and Caicos Islands lie to the southeast of the Bahamas. Eight of the 30 islands are inhabited. Tourism and offshore banking are the most important economic activities, but many skilled islanders seek work in the Bahamas.

BERMUDA

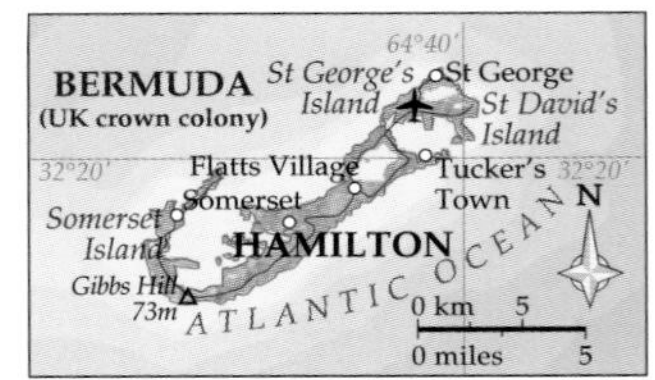

Bermuda consists of more than 150 coral islands in the Atlantic. The most important industry is tourism but Bermuda is also an international insurance market.

BRITISH INDIAN OCEAN TERRITORY

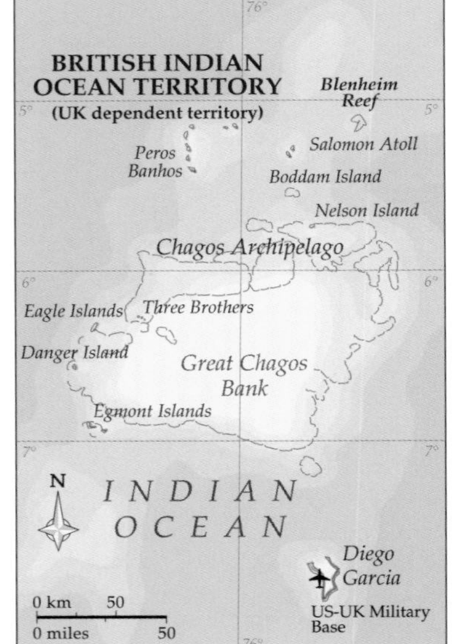

These islands are also known as the Chagos Archipelago. Most are uninhabited except for the US–UK military base on Diego Garcia. The islands will become part of Mauritius when no longer required by the UK.

FALKLAND ISLANDS

Just over 2,000 British citizens live in these windswept islands in the South Atlantic. Since the Argentine invasion of 1982, the British army has maintained a military presence here.

BRITISH VIRGIN ISLANDS

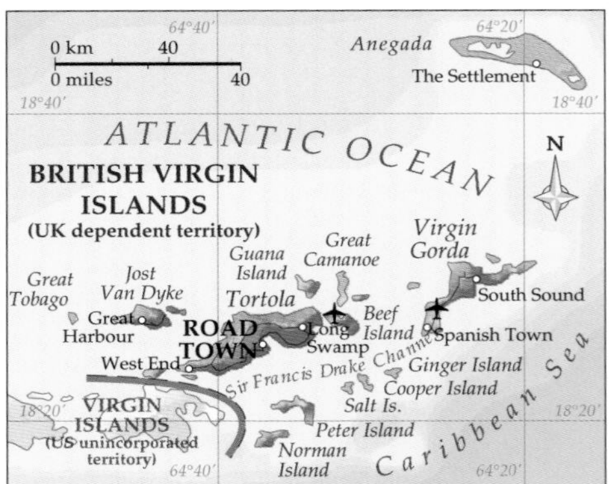

There are 40 islands in the British Virgin Islands; 15 of them are inhabited. Tourism is now the main economic activity, and the government has developed the Virgin Islands as an offshore tax haven.

MONTSERRAT

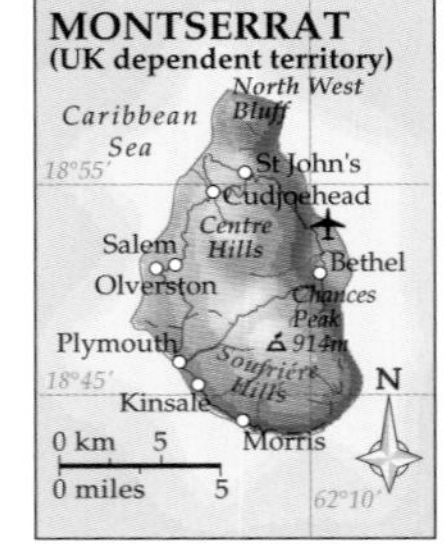

The southern part of Montserrat, including the capital, Plymouth, was devastated by the eruption of the Soufriére Hills volcano in the mid-1990s. The capital is currently at Olverston.

CAYMAN ISLANDS

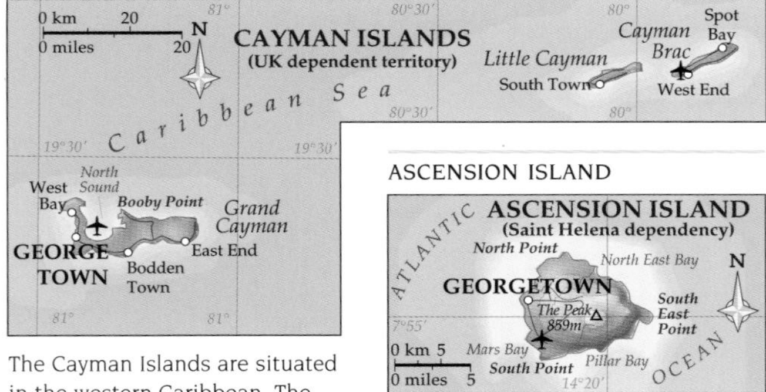

The Cayman Islands are situated in the western Caribbean. The islanders are keen to retain links with the UK and the Caymans are one of the world's largest offshore finance centres.

ASCENSION ISLAND

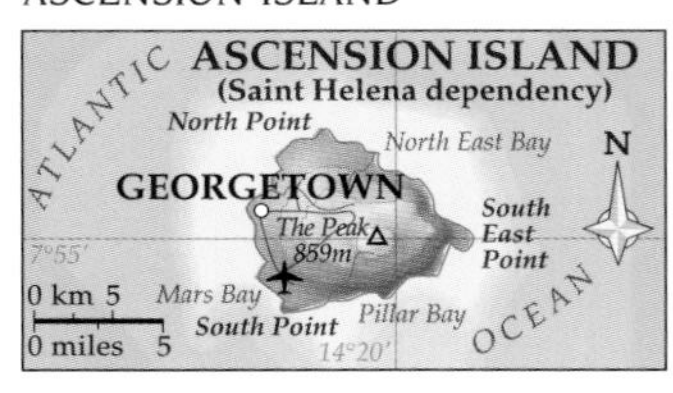

Ascension Island operates mainly as a military base and communications centre. It has a permanent resident population of around 250 people.

SAINT HELENA

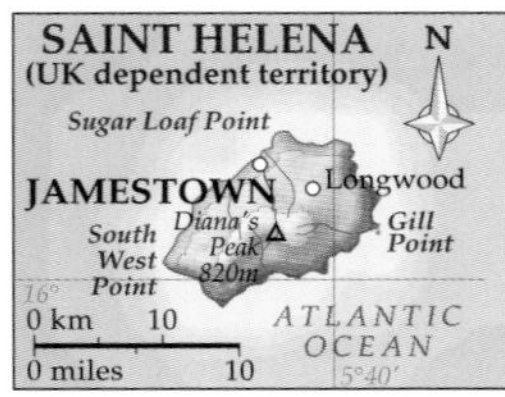

Saint Helena is a small island in the South Atlantic. Its economy is unable to support the population, so many people are forced to seek work elsewhere. Ascension and Tristan da Cunha are part of Saint Helena.

TRISTAN DA CUNHA

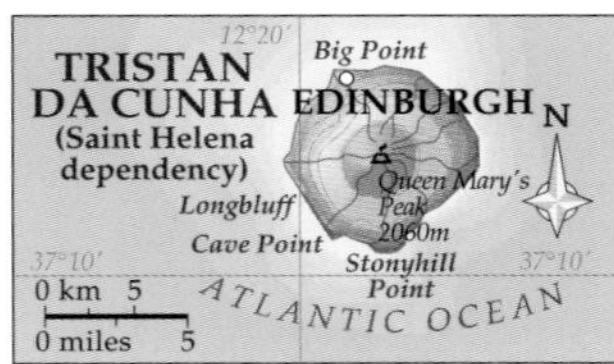

Tristan da Cunha is a volcanic island, 2,000 km to the south of Saint Helena. It has a small, close-knit farming community.

GIBRALTAR

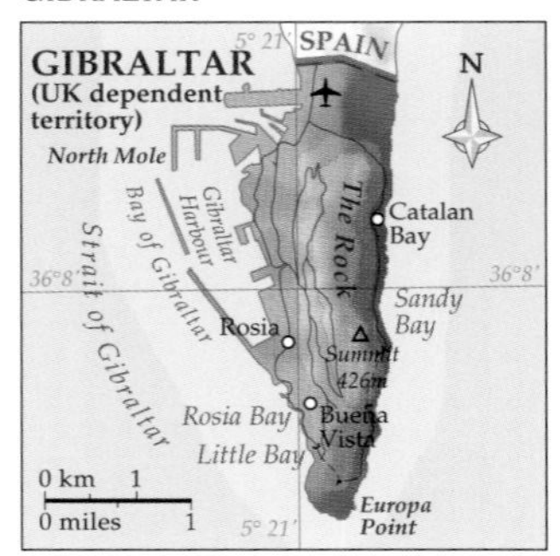

Gibraltar guards the western entrance to the Mediterranean. Some local people want independence, and Spain also claims control of the territory.

THE ATLAS OF THE WORLD

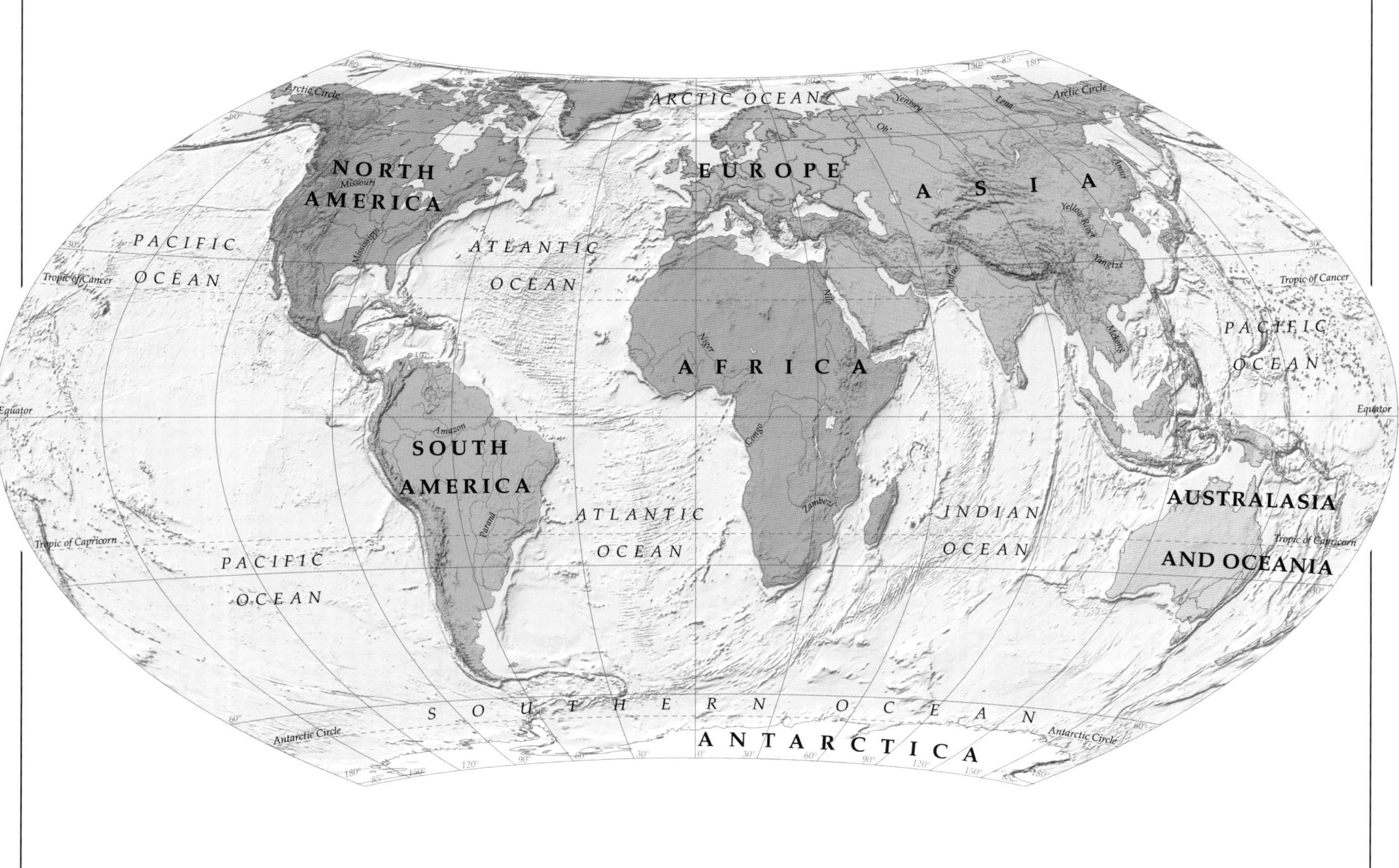

The Nations of the World

The world is divided into 193 independent countries, and about 60 overseas territories or dependencies. The largest country is the Russian Federation covering 17,075,200 sq km; the smallest is Vatican City in Rome, with an area of 0.44 sq km.

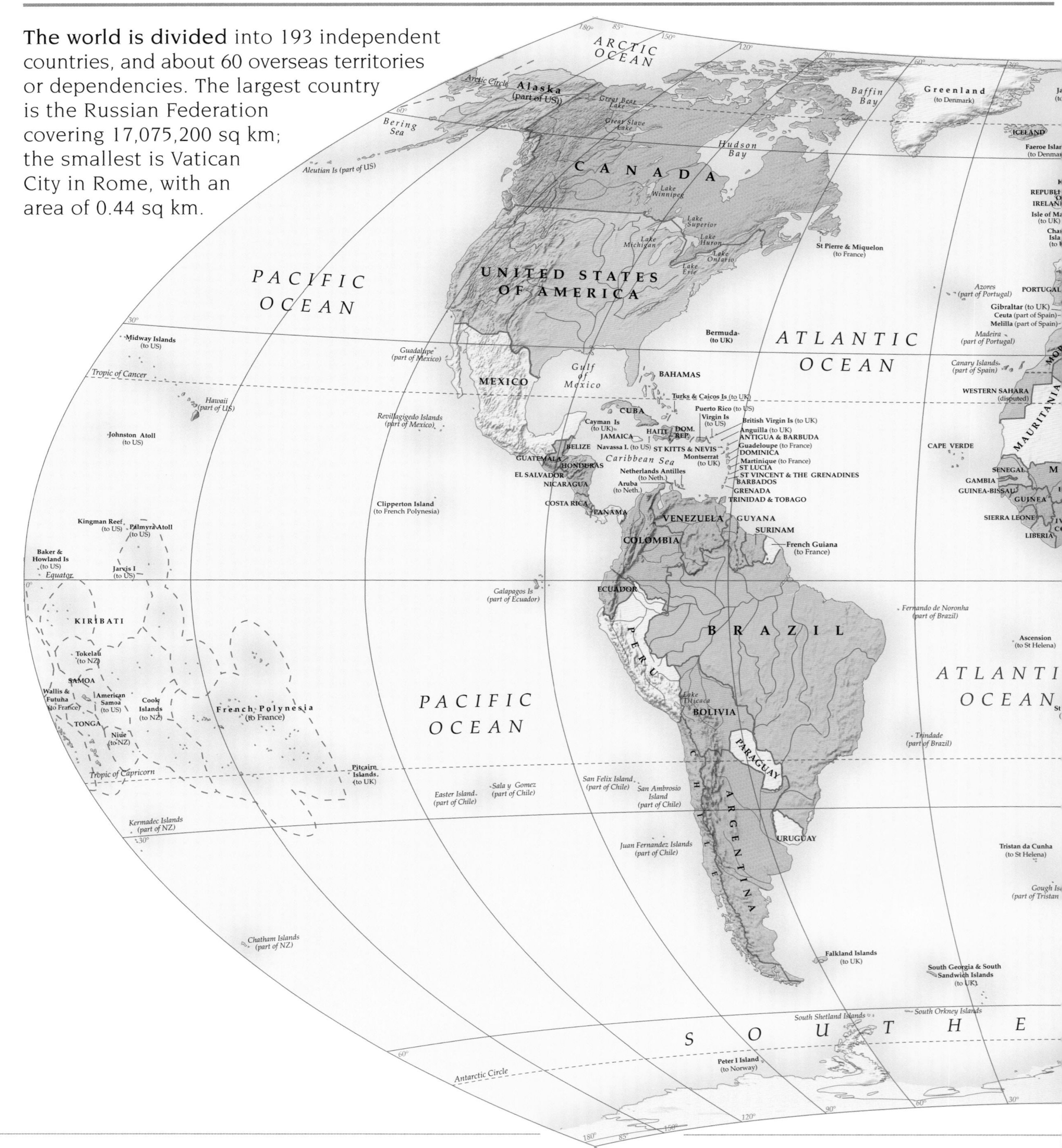

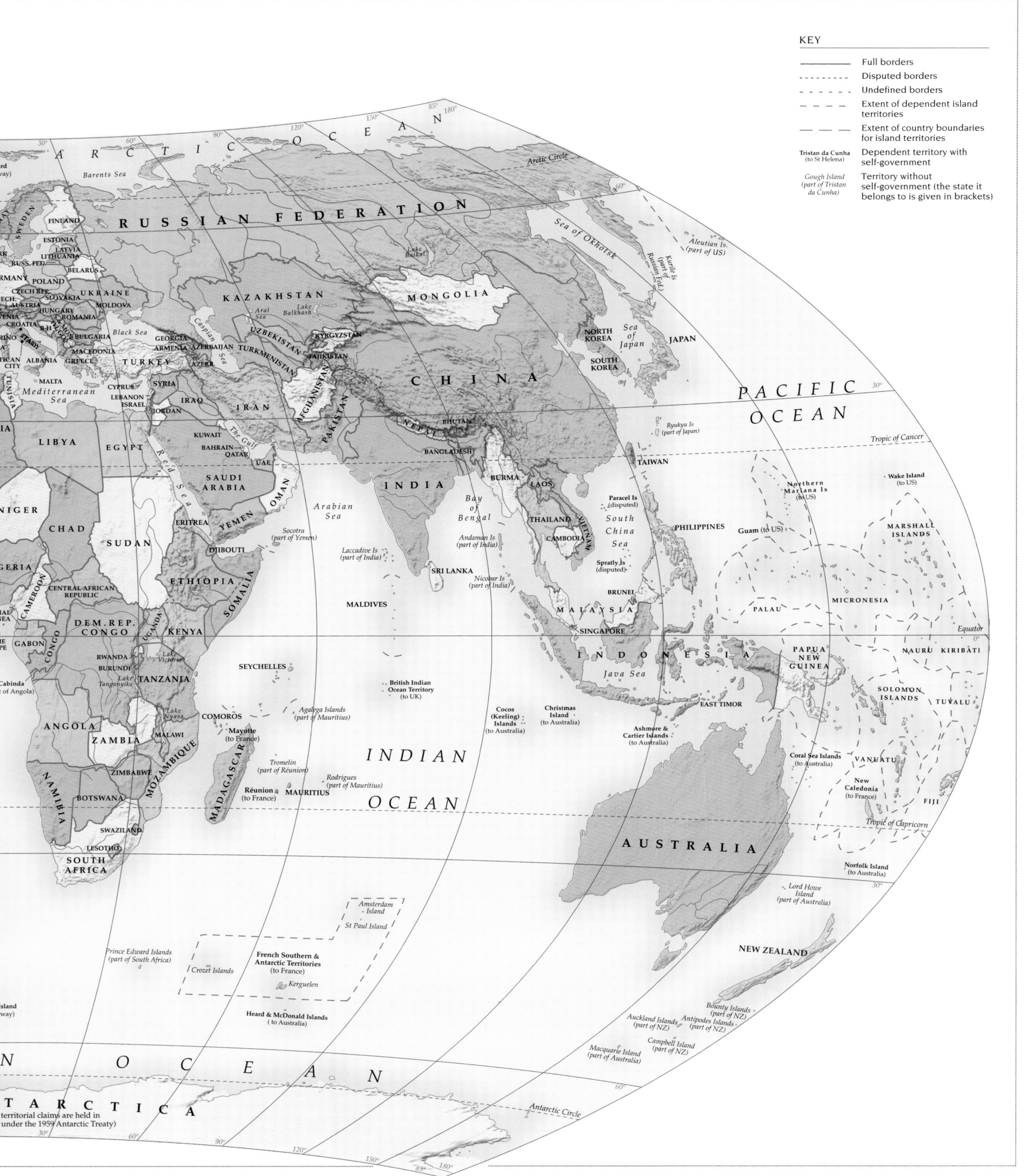
KEY
Full borders
Disputed borders
Undefined borders
Extent of dependent island territories
Extent of country boundaries for island territories
Tristan da Cunha (to St Helena)
Dependent territory with self-government
Gough Island (part of Tristan da Cunha)
Territory without self-government (the state it belongs to is given in brackets)
ARCTIC OCEAN
Barents Sea
Arctic Circle
RUSSIAN FEDERATION
FINLAND
ESTONIA
LATVIA
LITHUANIA
RUSS. FED.
BELARUS
POLAND
UKRAINE
CZECH REP.
SLOVAKIA
AUSTRIA
HUNGARY
MOLDOVA
ROMANIA
CROATIA
BULGARIA
Black Sea
MACEDONIA
ALBANIA
GREECE
TURKEY
GEORGIA
ARMENIA
AZERBAIJAN
KAZAKHSTAN
Aral Sea
Lake Balkhash
Caspian Sea
UZBEKISTAN
TURKMENISTAN
KYRGYZSTAN
TAJIKISTAN
AFGHANISTAN
PAKISTAN
MONGOLIA
Lake Baikal
Sea of Okhotsk
Aleutian Is. (part of US)
Kurile Is (part of Russian Fed.)
NORTH KOREA
SOUTH KOREA
Sea of Japan
JAPAN
CHINA
PACIFIC OCEAN
MALTA
Mediterranean Sea
CYPRUS
SYRIA
LEBANON
ISRAEL
JORDAN
IRAQ
IRAN
KUWAIT
The Gulf
BAHRAIN
QATAR
UAE
NEPAL
BHUTAN
BANGLADESH
Ryukyu Is (part of Japan)
Tropic of Cancer
TAIWAN
LIBYA
EGYPT
Red Sea
SAUDI ARABIA
OMAN
YEMEN
INDIA
BURMA
LAOS
Bay of Bengal
Arabian Sea
NIGER
CHAD
SUDAN
ERITREA
Socotra (part of Yemen)
DJIBOUTI
Andaman Is (part of India)
THAILAND
VIETNAM
CAMBODIA
Paracel Is (disputed)
South China Sea
PHILIPPINES
Northern Mariana Is (to US)
Wake Island (to US)
Guam (to US)
MARSHALL ISLANDS
Laccadive Is (part of India)
ETHIOPIA
SOMALIA
CENTRAL AFRICAN REPUBLIC
CAMEROON
SRI LANKA
Nicobar Is (part of India)
Spratly Is (disputed)
BRUNEI
MALAYSIA
SINGAPORE
MALDIVES
PALAU
MICRONESIA
DEM. REP. CONGO
GABON
CONGO
UGANDA
KENYA
Equator
RWANDA
BURUNDI
Lake Victoria
Lake Tanganyika
TANZANIA
SEYCHELLES
British Indian Ocean Territory (to UK)
INDONESIA
Java Sea
PAPUA NEW GUINEA
NAURU
KIRIBATI
SOLOMON ISLANDS
TUVALU
Cabinda
ANGOLA
ZAMBIA
Lake Nyasa
MALAWI
COMOROS
Mayotte (to France)
Agalega Islands (part of Mauritius)
Cocos (Keeling) Islands (to Australia)
Christmas Island (to Australia)
EAST TIMOR
Ashmore & Cartier Islands (to Australia)
Coral Sea Islands (to Australia)
VANUATU
New Caledonia (to France)
FIJI
ZIMBABWE
MOZAMBIQUE
NAMIBIA
BOTSWANA
MADAGASCAR
Tromelin (part of Réunion)
Réunion (to France)
MAURITIUS
Rodrigues (part of Mauritius)
INDIAN OCEAN
Tropic of Capricorn
SWAZILAND
LESOTHO
SOUTH AFRICA
AUSTRALIA
Norfolk Island (to Australia)
Lord Howe Island (part of Australia)
Amsterdam Island
St Paul Island
Prince Edward Islands (part of South Africa)
Crozet Islands
French Southern & Antarctic Territories (to France)
Kerguelen
NEW ZEALAND
Heard & McDonald Islands (to Australia)
Bounty Islands (part of NZ)
Auckland Islands (part of NZ)
Antipodes Islands (part of NZ)
Campbell Island (part of NZ)
Macquarie Island (part of Australia)
OCEAN
ANTARCTICA
Antarctic Circle
territorial claims are held in
under the 1959 Antarctic Treaty)

Continental Europe

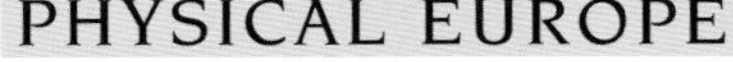

Europe is the world's second smallest continent, occupying the western tip of the vast Eurasian landmass. To the north and west are old highlands, with the high peaks of the Alps in the south. Most people live on the densely populated North European Plain, which runs from southern England, through northern France, across Germany into Russia.

Cross-section through Europe

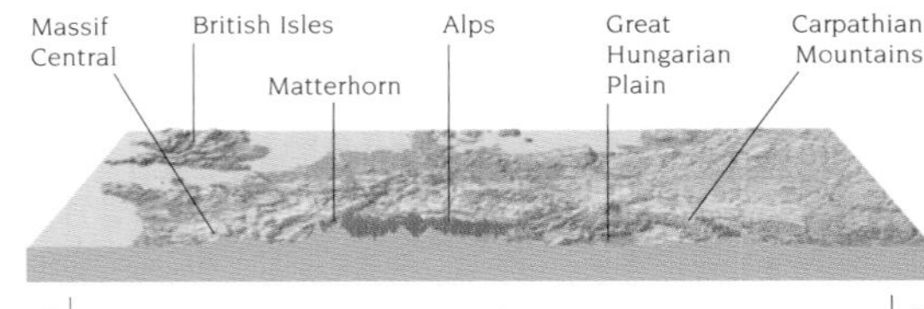

In the west, the land rises up from the Atlantic coast towards the Massif Central in France, and the high peaks of the Alps. Between the Alps and the Carpathian Mountains is the Great Hungarian Plain, where the River Danube flows on its way to the Black Sea.

Physical Europe

The ancient mountains of northwest Europe were scoured and smoothed by glaciers in the last Ice Age. The Alps are newer and more jagged – pushed up when Africa collided with Europe. In between is the North European Plain, where thick layers of fertile soils allow many different crops to be grown.

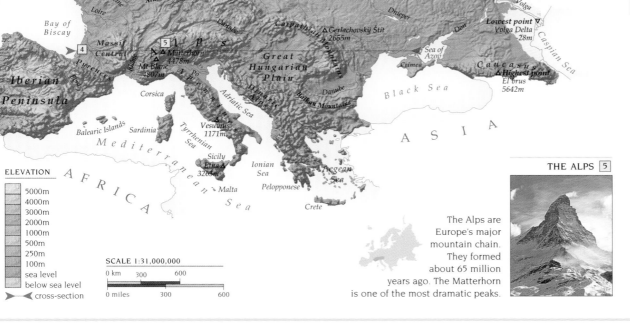

1 The Frozen North

Europe's northern coastline stretches deep into the Arctic Circle. Here in Norway, icebergs drift into the deep, wide-bottomed fjords.

The North European Plain 2

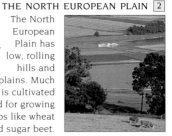

The North European Plain has low, rolling hills and plains. Much of the area is cultivated and used for growing crops like wheat and sugar beet.

3 Ancient Highlands

Some of the world's oldest rocks are found in northwest Europe. Erosion by glaciers in the last Ice Age created smoothed hills such as the mountains of Wales.

The Alps 5

The Alps are Europe's major mountain chain. They formed about 65 million years ago. The Matterhorn is one of the most dramatic peaks.

4 The Atlantic Coast

On Europe's Atlantic coast, the force of waves and winds has created striking landforms like this huge sand dune in southwest France.

POLITICAL EUROPE

Europe's population increased rapidly during the 18th and 19th centuries, following the Industrial Revolution. In the 20th century, Europe suffered a series of wars which redrew the political map. From 1989–1991, communist governments in eastern Europe and the former Soviet Union collapsed, as political reform swept through the countries behind the 'Iron Curtain'. In 2004 the European Union took a further step towards expansion.

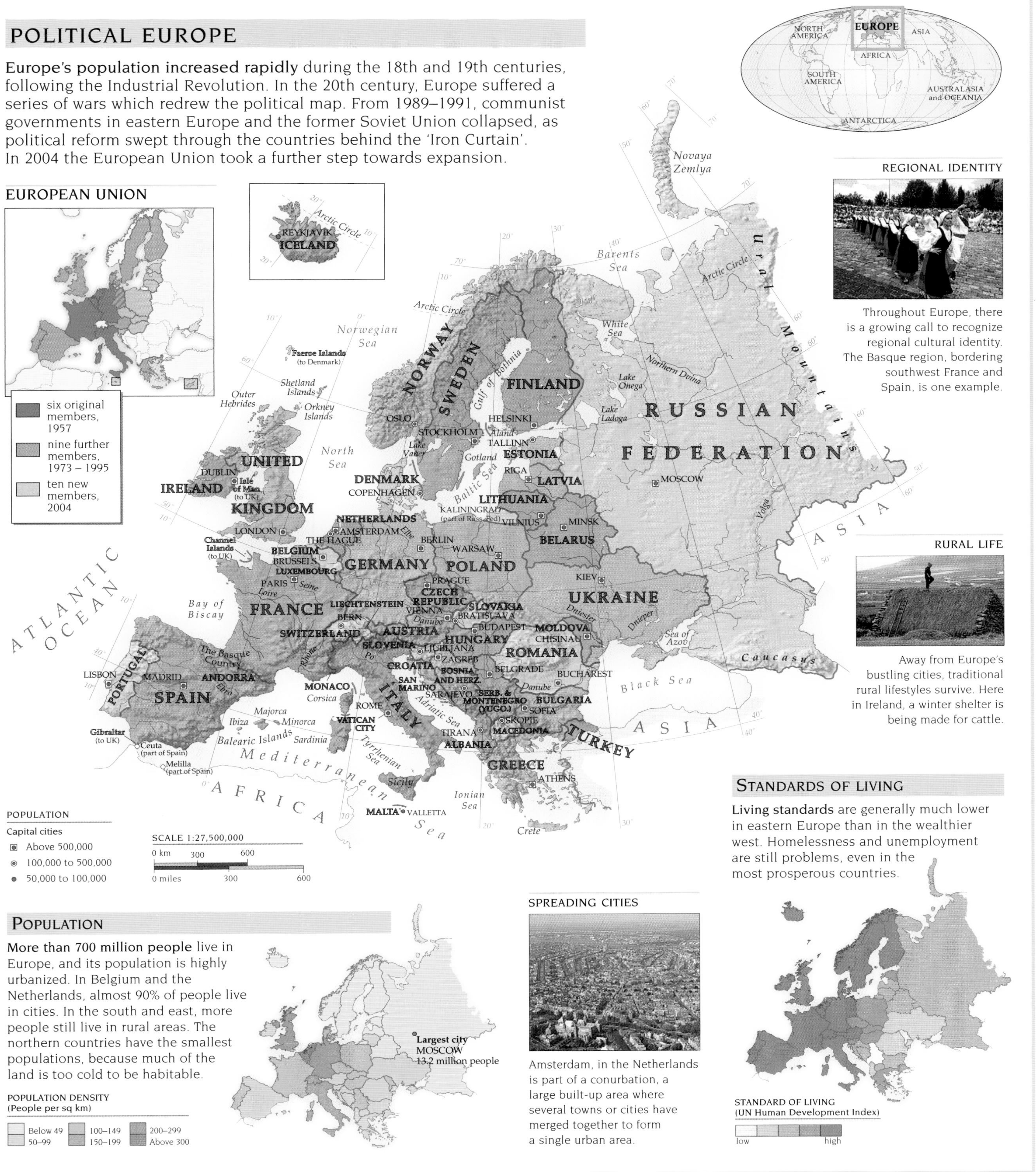

REGIONAL IDENTITY

Throughout Europe, there is a growing call to recognize regional cultural identity. The Basque region, bordering southwest France and Spain, is one example.

RURAL LIFE

Away from Europe's bustling cities, traditional rural lifestyles survive. Here in Ireland, a winter shelter is being made for cattle.

STANDARDS OF LIVING

Living standards are generally much lower in eastern Europe than in the wealthier west. Homelessness and unemployment are still problems, even in the most prosperous countries.

POPULATION

More than 700 million people live in Europe, and its population is highly urbanized. In Belgium and the Netherlands, almost 90% of people live in cities. In the south and east, more people still live in rural areas. The northern countries have the smallest populations, because much of the land is too cold to be habitable.

SPREADING CITIES

Amsterdam, in the Netherlands is part of a conurbation, a large built-up area where several towns or cities have merged together to form a single urban area.

European Geography

Europe is blessed with a temperate climate, ample mineral reserves, and good transport links. During the 18th and 19th centuries the continent was transformed, as new methods of production made industry and farming more efficient and productive. Today, in many countries, 'heavy' industries have been replaced by hi-tech and service industries. Agriculture is still important and many crops thrive on Europe's fertile plains.

Mineral resources

Europe has few sizeable reserves of metallic minerals; most were used up by industry during the 19th century. Oil, gas and coal are found in large quantities – gas in the North Sea and oil in the Volga basin. Coal, though abundant, is being steadily depleted.

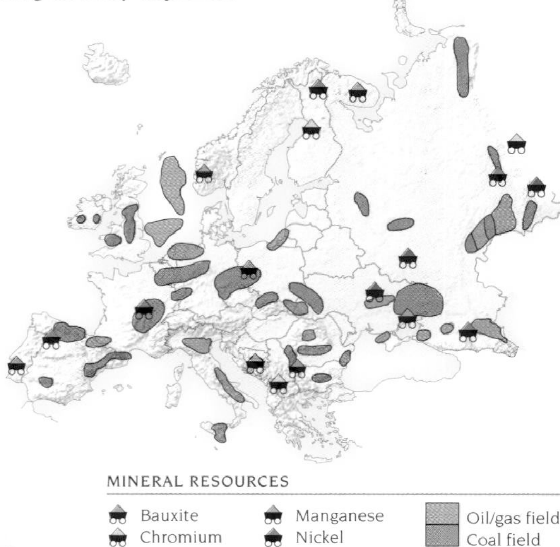

Industry

Western Europe has some of the world's wealthiest countries. In countries such as France, Germany and the UK, traditional industries like iron and steel-making are now being replaced by light industries such as electronics, and services like finance and insurance. In Eastern Europe, industry was subsidized by the communist governments for years. Many factories are old fashioned and need investment to improve their equipment and production methods.

GNP per capita (US$)

- Below 1999
- 2000-4999
- 5000-9999
- 10,000-19,999
- 20,000-24,999
- Above 25,000
- Industrial centre

OIL AND GAS

Oil and gas reserves are plentiful in the Russian Federation. South of Rostov-on-Don, oil is pumped from the ground and piped to nearby refineries.

CAR MANUFACTURE

Germany is one of the world's largest and oldest manufacturer of cars. Companies like BMW, Mercedes-Benz and Volkswagen export cars across the world.

FINANCE

London, Frankfurt and Paris are among the most important financial centres in the world. Many banks and financial institutions have their headquarters here. At the London Stock Exchange, people buy and sell stocks and shares.

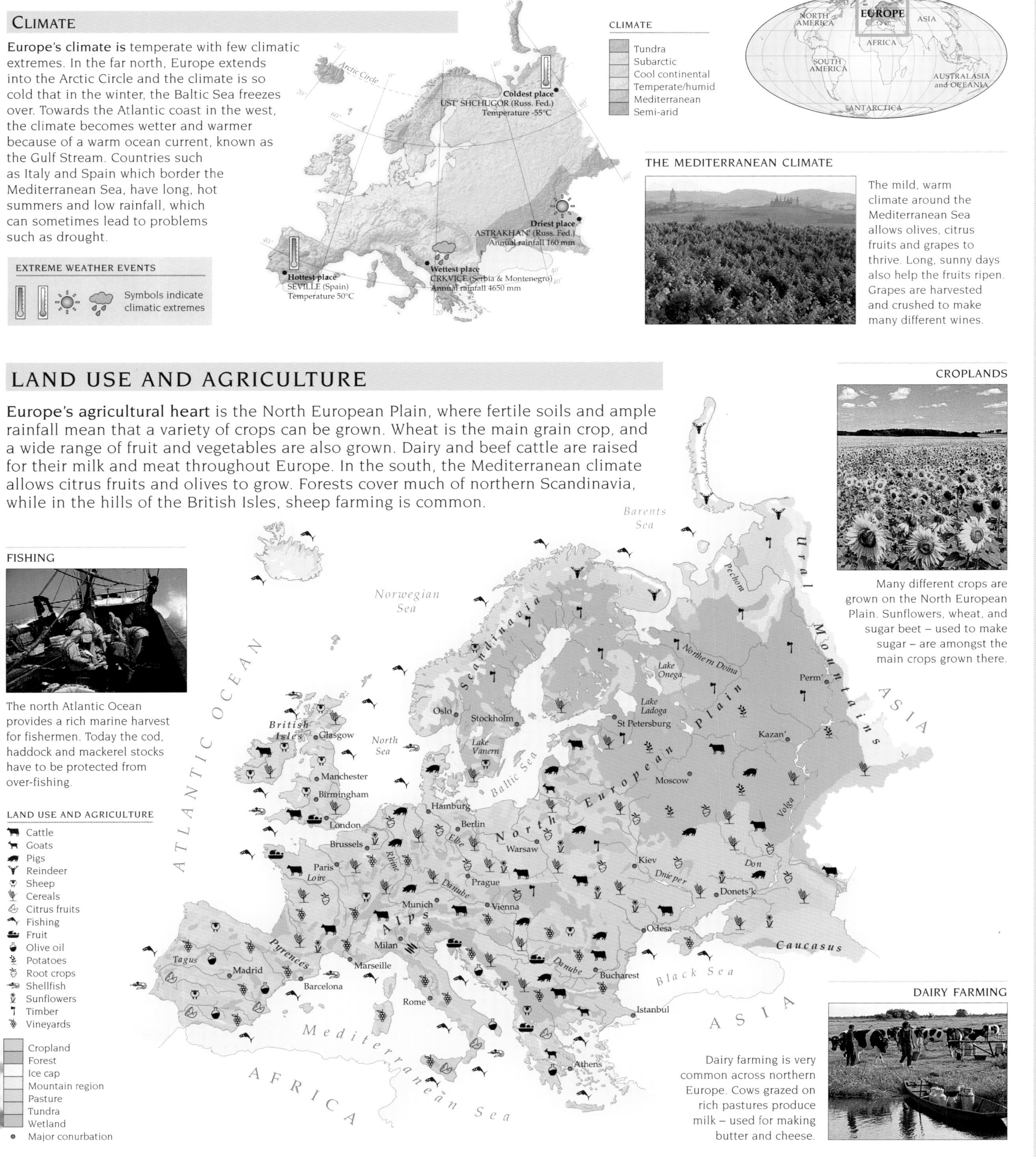

CLIMATE

Europe's climate is temperate with few climatic extremes. In the far north, Europe extends into the Arctic Circle and the climate is so cold that in the winter, the Baltic Sea freezes over. Towards the Atlantic coast in the west, the climate becomes wetter and warmer because of a warm ocean current, known as the Gulf Stream. Countries such as Italy and Spain which border the Mediterranean Sea, have long, hot summers and low rainfall, which can sometimes lead to problems such as drought.

EXTREME WEATHER EVENTS

Symbols indicate climatic extremes

CLIMATE

- Tundra
- Subarctic
- Cool continental
- Temperate/humid
- Mediterranean
- Semi-arid

THE MEDITERRANEAN CLIMATE

The mild, warm climate around the Mediterranean Sea allows olives, citrus fruits and grapes to thrive. Long, sunny days also help the fruits ripen. Grapes are harvested and crushed to make many different wines.

LAND USE AND AGRICULTURE

Europe's agricultural heart is the North European Plain, where fertile soils and ample rainfall mean that a variety of crops can be grown. Wheat is the main grain crop, and a wide range of fruit and vegetables are also grown. Dairy and beef cattle are raised for their milk and meat throughout Europe. In the south, the Mediterranean climate allows citrus fruits and olives to grow. Forests cover much of northern Scandinavia, while in the hills of the British Isles, sheep farming is common.

FISHING

The north Atlantic Ocean provides a rich marine harvest for fishermen. Today the cod, haddock and mackerel stocks have to be protected from over-fishing.

LAND USE AND AGRICULTURE

- Cattle
- Goats
- Pigs
- Reindeer
- Sheep
- Cereals
- Citrus fruits
- Fishing
- Fruit
- Olive oil
- Potatoes
- Root crops
- Shellfish
- Sunflowers
- Timber
- Vineyards

- Cropland
- Forest
- Ice cap
- Mountain region
- Pasture
- Tundra
- Wetland
- Major conurbation

CROPLANDS

Many different crops are grown on the North European Plain. Sunflowers, wheat, and sugar beet – used to make sugar – are amongst the main crops grown there.

DAIRY FARMING

Dairy farming is very common across northern Europe. Cows grazed on rich pastures produce milk – used for making butter and cheese.

NORTHERN EUROPE

DENMARK, ESTONIA, FINLAND, ICELAND, LATVIA, LITHUANIA, NORWAY, SWEDEN

Denmark, Sweden and Norway are together known as Scandinavia. These countries, along with the North Atlantic island of Iceland, have similar languages and cultures. Finland has a very different language and a separate identity from its Scandinavian neighbours. Estonia, Latvia and Lithuania, known as the Baltic states, were part of the Soviet Union until 1989, when each became an independent country.

INDUSTRY

In Scandinavia, many natural resources are used in industry: timber for paper and furniture; iron ore for steel and cars; and fish and natural gas from the seas. Hydro-electric power is generated by water flowing down steep mountain slopes. The Baltic states still rely on Russia to supply their raw materials and energy.

INDUSTRY

- Car manufacture
- Chemicals
- Engineering
- Fish processing
- Hydro-electric power
- Shipbuilding
- Timber processing
- Tourism
- Major industrial centre / area
- Major road

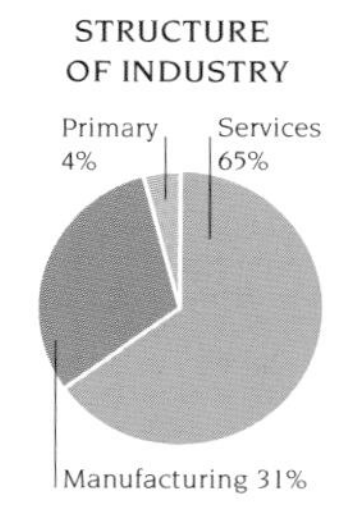

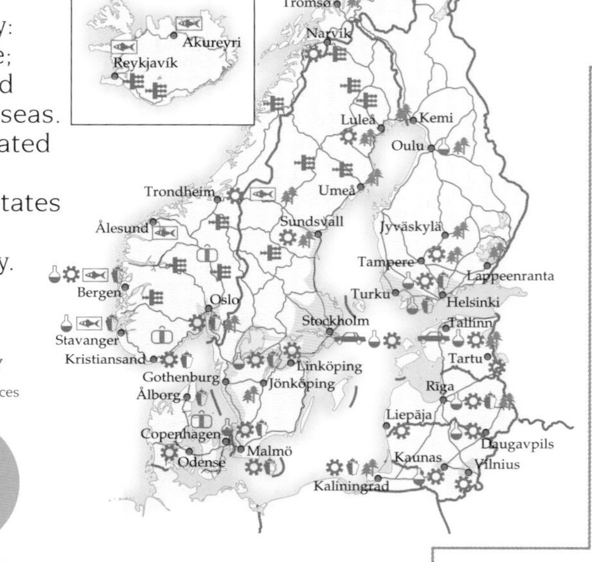

FARMING AND LAND USE

Southern Denmark and Sweden are the most productive areas, with pig farming, dairy-farming and crops such as wheat, barley and potatoes. Sheep farming is important in southern Norway and Iceland. In the Baltic states, cereals, potatoes and sugar beet are the main crops and cattle graze on damp pasture.

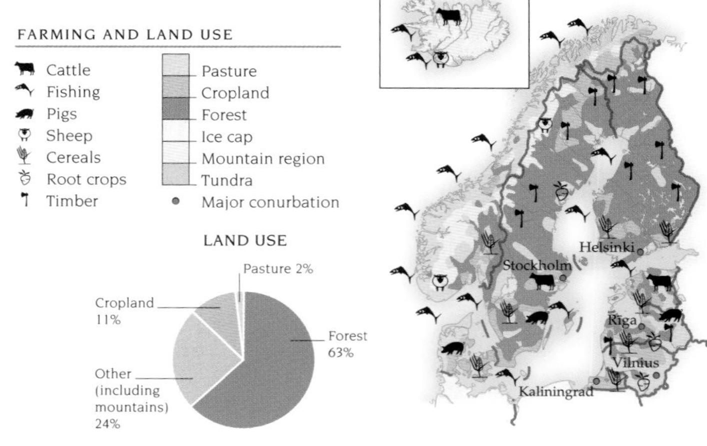

THE LANDSCAPE

The north and west of Scandinavia is extremely rugged and mountainous, with landscapes eroded by ice. In the south of Scandinavia the land is flatter, with fertile soils deposited by glaciers. Much of Finland, Norway and Sweden is covered by dense forests. The Baltic states are much lower, with rounded hills and many lakes and marshes.

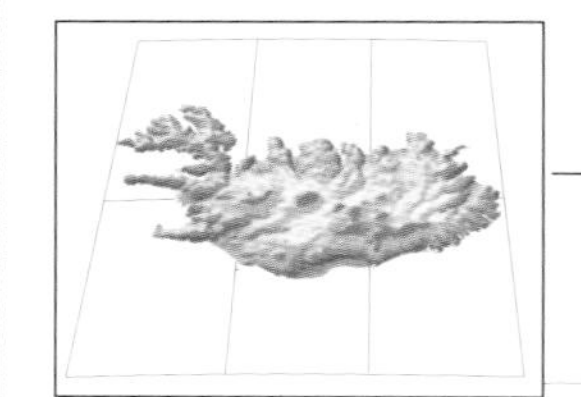

The land of ice and fire. Iceland is one of the world's most active volcanic areas. There are about 200 volcanoes on the island, along with bubbling hot springs, mud-holes, and geysers which spurt boiling water and steam high into the air.

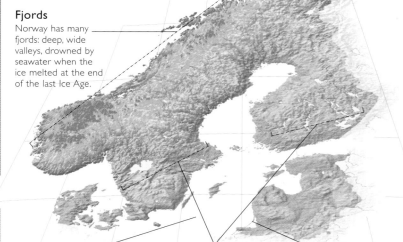

Fjords
Norway has many fjords: deep, wide valleys, drowned by seawater when the ice melted at the end of the last Ice Age.

Baltic Sea (D 7)
Ships from Finland, Sweden and the Baltic states use the Baltic Sea as their route to the north Atlantic Ocean. In winter, much of the sea is frozen.

Glacial lakes
Finland and Sweden have many thousands of lakes. During the last Ice Age, glaciers scoured hollows which filled with water when the ice melted.

Courland Spit (D 7)
This wide sandspit runs f 100 km along the Baltic c of Lithuania and the Russ enclave of Kaliningrad. It encloses a huge lagoon

POPULATION

The population is distributed mainly along the warmer and flatter southern and coastal areas. Population totals and densities are low for all of the countries, and Iceland has the lowest population density in Europe, with just three people per sq km. Many Scandinavians have holiday homes on the islands, along the lake shores, or in coastal areas.

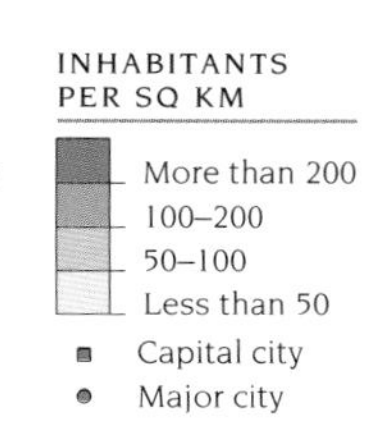

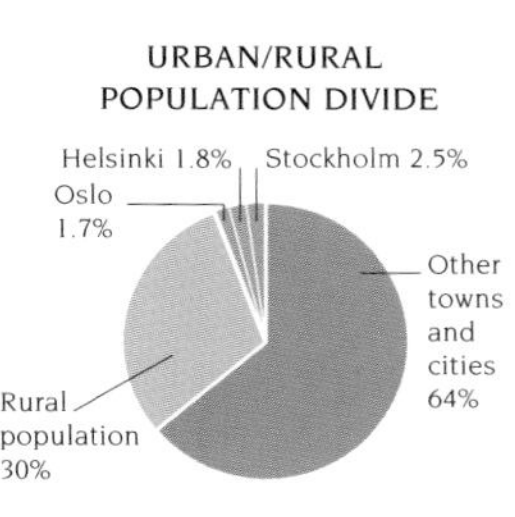

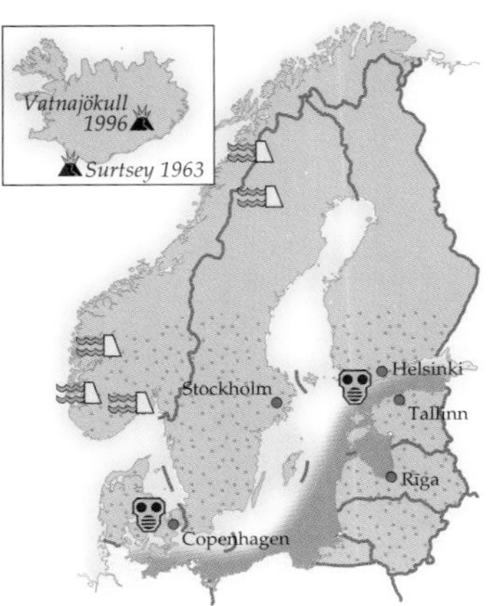

EUROPE
Northern Europe
NORTH AMERICA
ASIA
AFRICA
SOUTH AMERICA
AUSTRALASIA AND OCEANIA
ANTARCTICA

ENVIRONMENTAL ISSUES

Northern Europe has been badly affected by industrial pollution from other parts of Europe. Polluted air moves north, and mixes with the rain to create acid rain. This poisons forests and lakes, destroying the plants and animals living in them. In Norway and Sweden, electricity is produced by dams that obtain power from the plentiful water supply. Hydroelectric power is a clean, alternative energy source.

Vatnajökull 1996
Surtsey 1963
Stockholm
Helsinki
Tallinn
Riga
Copenhagen

ENVIRONMENTAL ISSUES

- Major dams
- Urban air pollution
- Volcanic eruption
- Affected by acid rain
- Sea pollution
- Major industrial centre

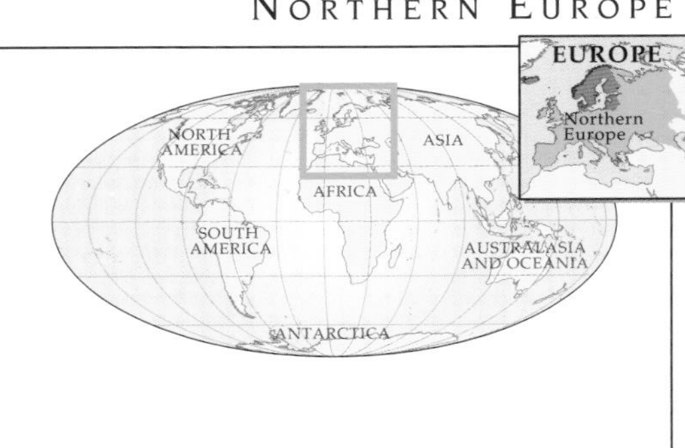

CLIMATE

Warm ocean currents flowing north along the coasts of Norway and Iceland make the climate mild and wet. Away from the sea, the climate is generally colder, and drier.

January

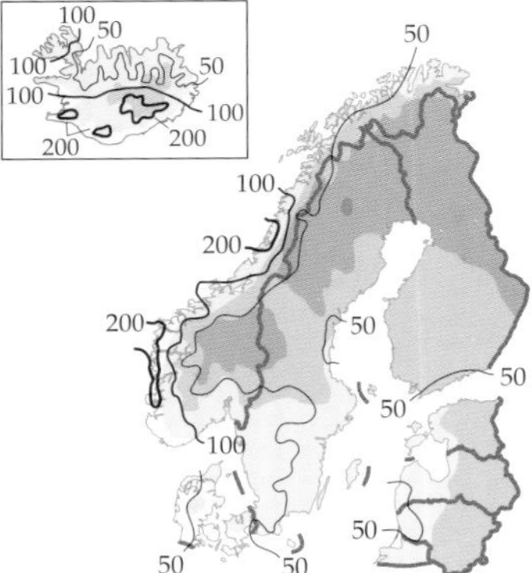

100
50
200
100
50
200
100
50
200
50
100
50
100
50
50
50

July

50
100
50
50
100
50
100
200
100
100
100
100
100
100
100

TEMPERATURE AND PRECIPITATION

- More than 15°C
- 10 to 15°C
- 5 to 10°C
- 0 to 5°C
- 0 to -5°C
- -5 to -10°C
- -10 to -15°C
- Less than -15°C
- 100 Precipitation (mm)

ICELAND
Norwegian Sea
Arctic Circle
REYKJAVÍK
ATLANTIC OCEAN
SCALE BAR
0 km 100 200
0 miles 100 200
LAND HEIGHT
2000–4000 m
1000–2000 m
500–1000 m
250–500 m
100–250 m
0–100 m
SEA DEPTH
0–50 m
50–100 m
100–250 m
250–500 m
500–1000 m
1000–2000 m
Below 2000 m
CITIES AND TOWNS
Over 500,000 people
100,000–500,000
50,000–100,000
Less than 50,000
Barents Sea
North Cape (Nordkapp)
Lapland
RUSSIAN FEDERATION
Norwegian Sea
NORWAY
SWEDEN
FINLAND
Gulf of Bothnia
OSLO
STOCKHOLM
HELSINKI
TALLINN
ESTONIA
LATVIA
RIGA
LITHUANIA
VILNIUS
Kaliningrad
KALININGRAD (part of Russian Federation)
BELARUS
RUSS. FED.
Gulf of Finland
Gulf of Riga
Baltic Sea
North Sea
Skagerrak
Kattegat
DENMARK
COPENHAGEN (KØBENHAVN)
GERMANY
POLAND
Lake Ladoga
Bergen
Stavanger
Trondheim
Gothenburg (Göteborg)
Malmö
Tampere
Turku (Åbo)
Oulu
Uppsala
Göteborg
Aarhus
Odense
Aalborg
Kaunas
Klaipėda
Tartu

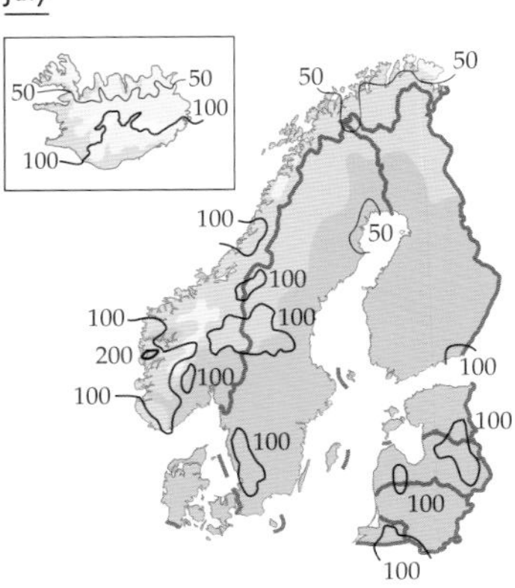

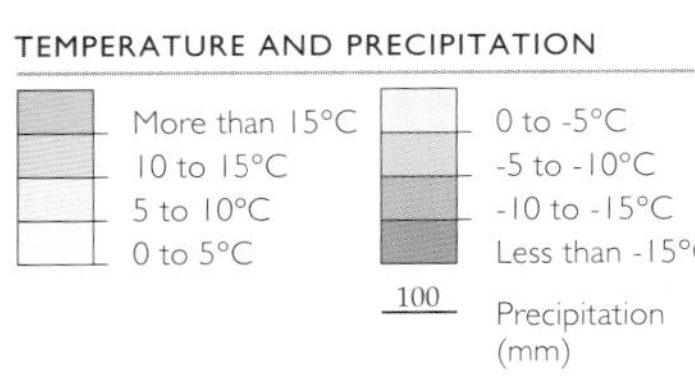

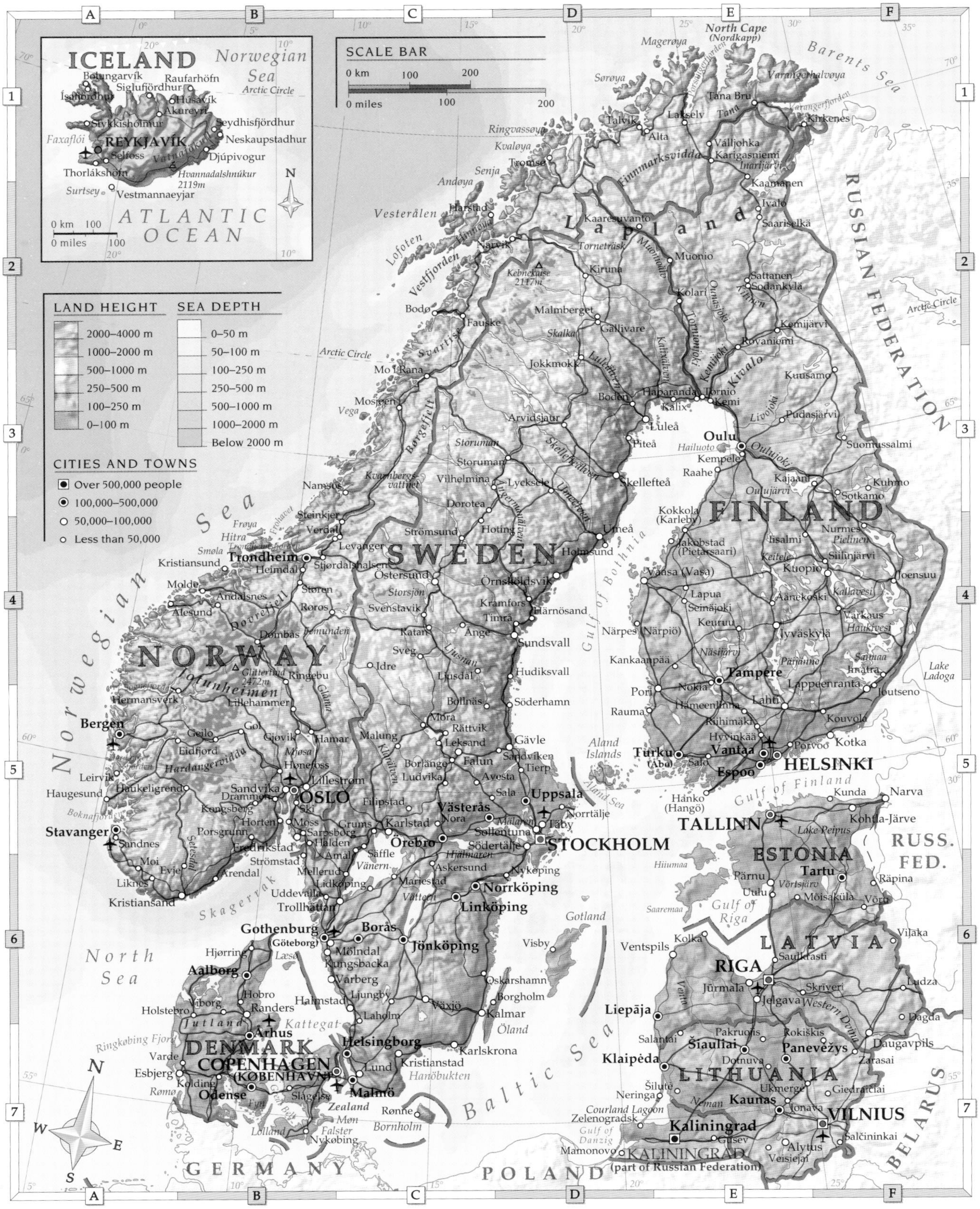

The Low Countries

BELGIUM, LUXEMBOURG, NETHERLANDS

Belgium, Luxembourg and the Netherlands are called the Low Countries because most of their land is flat and low-lying. Much of the Netherlands lies below sea level, and over hundreds of years the Dutch have built dykes and dams to prevent flooding, and have pumped water off large areas of land to reclaim them from the sea. The Low Countries are Europe's most densely populated countries, but most of their people have a high living standard.

ENVIRONMENTAL ISSUES

Huge land reclamation projects in the Netherlands, such as the IJsselmeer project, have created some new land for agricultural use, and also for houses, roads and open spaces. Heavy industry has caused serious air pollution in cities such as Amsterdam and Rotterdam, and added to Europe's acid rain problem.

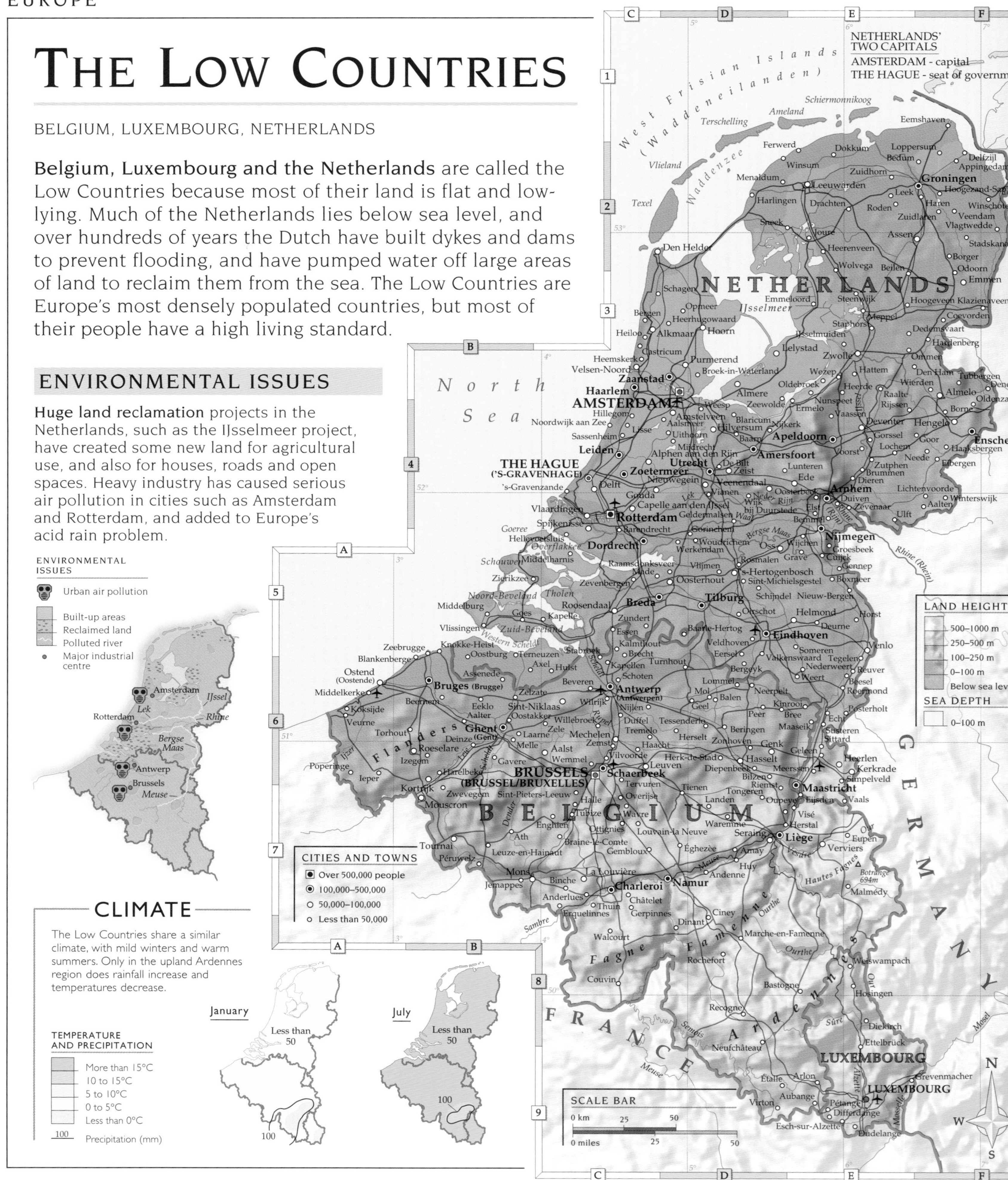

CLIMATE

The Low Countries share a similar climate, with mild winters and warm summers. Only in the upland Ardennes region does rainfall increase and temperatures decrease.

EUROPE
Low Countries
NORTH AMERICA
SOUTH AMERICA
AFRICA
ASIA
AUSTRALASIA AND OCEANIA
ANTARCTICA

POPULATION

More than 25 million people live in the Low Countries and nine out of every ten people live in a town or city. The largest urban area – known as the *Randstad Holland* – is in the Netherlands. It runs in an unbroken line from Rotterdam in the south, to Amsterdam in the west. Even most rural areas in the Low Countries are densely populated.

INHABITANTS PER SQ KM

- More than 200
- 100–200
- 50–100
- 0–50
- Capital city
- Major city

URBAN/RURAL POPULATION DIVIDE

Amsterdam 2.8%
Brussels 3.9%
Rotterdam 2.3%
Rural population 8%
Other towns and cities 83%

FARMING AND LAND USE

The Low Countries' fertile soils and flat plains provide excellent conditions for farming. The main crops grown are barley, potatoes, and flax for making linen. In the Netherlands, much farmland is used for dairy-farming. The country is also famous for growing flowers, which are exported around the world. Flowers and vegetables are grown either in open fields or in enormous greenhouses, which allow production all year round.

LAND USE

Forest 16%
Pasture 26%
Cropland 29%
Other (including urban) 29%

FARMING AND LAND USE

- Cattle
- Pigs
- Cereals
- Flax
- Flowers
- Market gardening
- Sugar beet
- Pasture
- Cropland
- Forest
- Wetland
- Major conurbation

THE LANDSCAPE

The Low Countries are largely flat and low-lying. The ancient hills of the Ardennes, in the far southeast, are the only higher region. They rise to heights of more than 500 m. Two major rivers – the Meuse and the Rhine – flow across the Low Countries to their mouths in the North Sea. At the coast, the River Rhine deposits large quantities of sediment to form a delta.

Polders

In the Netherlands, land has been reclaimed from the sea since the Middle Ages by building dykes and drainage ditches. These areas of land are called polders. They are very fertile.

The River Rhine (E4)

The River Rhine erodes and carries large amounts of sediment along its course. When it reaches the Netherlands it divides into three rivers. As they approach the North Sea, the rivers slow down, depositing the sediment to form a delta.

Low-lying Netherlands

Over two-thirds of the Netherlands lies at or below sea level. This makes flooding a constant threat in coastal areas.

Flanders (B6)

The plains of Flanders in western Belgium have fertile soils which were deposited by glaciers during the last Ice Age. They provide excellent land for growing crops.

Heathlands

The heathlands on the Dutch-Belgian border have thin, sandy soils. The only plants which grow well here are heathers and gorse.

The Ardennes (D8)

The hills of the Ardennes were formed over 300 million years ago. They have many deep valleys, which have been eroded by rivers like the Meuse.

INDUSTRY

The Low Countries are an important centre for the hi-tech and electronics industries. Good transport links to the rest of Europe allow them to sell their products in other countries. The built-up area stretching from Amsterdam in the Netherlands to Antwerp in Belgium has the greatest number of factories. Luxembourg is also an important banking centre; many international banks have their headquarters in its capital city.

STRUCTURE OF INDUSTRY

Primary 3%
Services 68%
Manufacturing 29%

INDUSTRY

- Aerospace
- Chemicals
- Engineering
- Pharmaceuticals
- Textiles
- Finance
- Hi-tech industry
- Tourism
- Major industrial centre / area
- Major road

THE BRITISH ISLES

UNITED KINGDOM, IRELAND

The British Isles lie off the northwest coast of mainland Europe. They are made up of two large islands and over 5,000 smaller ones. Politically, the region is divided into two countries: the United Kingdom – England, Wales, Scotland and Northern Ireland – and Ireland. Geographically, the British Isles are divided between highlands to the north and west, and lowlands to the south and east.

THE LANDSCAPE

Low rolling hills, high moorlands, and small fields with high hedges are all typical of the British Isles. Ireland is known as the Emerald Isle, because heavy rainfall gives it a lush, green appearance. Scotland and Wales are mountainous; the rocks forming the mountains there are some of the oldest in the world.

Indented coastlines
The west coast of the British Isles faces the Atlantic Ocean, and over 3,000 km of open sea to the North American continent. Storms and high waves constantly batter the hard, rocky coastline, giving it a jagged outline.

Ben Nevis (C4)
This mountain is the highest point in the British Isles. It is 1,343 m above sea level.

The Lake District (D5)
The Lake District National Park has England's highest peak, Scafell Pike, at 978 m (E4), its deepest lake, Wast Water (80 m), and its largest lake, Windermere (16 km long).

The Pennines (D6)
The Pennines are a chain of high hills, topped by moorland. They run for over 400 km, and are known as the 'backbone of England'.

The Burren (A6)
The Burren is a large area of limestone rock in the west of Ireland. Its flat surfaces are known as limestone 'pavements'. There are also many caves and sinkholes in the area.

Rias
Rias are river valleys that have been drowned by rising sea levels. The southern coast of southwest England has many good examples.

The Fens (E6)
This is the flattest area in England. Much of the land here has been reclaimed from the sea.

FARMING AND LAND USE

The English lowlands and the wide, flat stretches of land in East Anglia are the agricultural heartland of the United Kingdom. The country is no longer self-sufficient in food, but wheat, potatoes and other vegetables, and fruits, are widely grown. In Ireland, and in central and southern England, dairy and beef cattle feed off grassy pastures. In the hilly and mountainous areas, sheep farming is more usual.

INDUSTRY

The United Kingdom's traditional industries, such as coal mining, iron and steel-making, and textiles, have declined in recent years. Today, newer industries make cars, chemicals, electronic and hi-tech goods. Service industries, especially banking and insurance, have grown in importance. The country's most valuable natural resource is its large North Sea oil and gas fields.

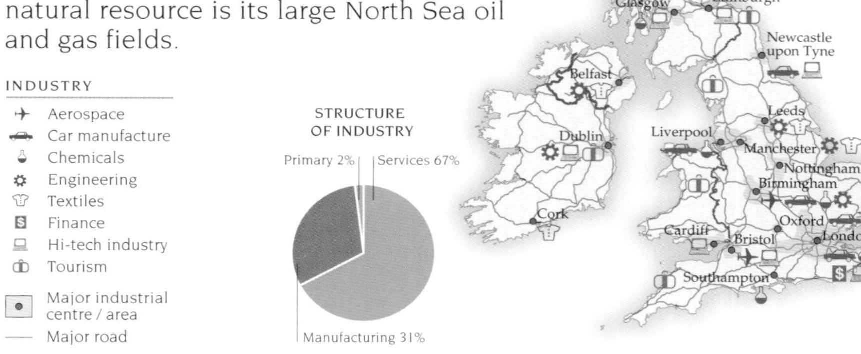

POPULATION

The United Kingdom is densely populated, with most of the people living in urban areas. The southeast is the most crowded part of the country. The Scottish Highlands are less populated today than they were 200 years ago. Ireland is still mainly rural, with many Irish people making their living from farming.

ENVIRONMENTAL ISSUES

Air pollution is becoming a serious problem in many British cities, as the number of vehicles using the roads increases. The seas around the British Isles have been polluted by sewage and industrial waste. In recent years, several major oil spills have occurred off the coast of the United Kingdom.

ENVIRONMENTAL ISSUES

- Major oil spill
- Urban air pollution
- Sea pollution
- Polluted rivers
- Major industrial centre

CLIMATE

The British Isles' climate is moderated by the warm Atlantic ocean current called the Gulf Stream. The west is generally wetter than the east, and the south warmer than the north.

FRANCE

ANDORRA, MONACO, FRANCE

France has helped to shape the history and culture of Europe for centuries. Today, as a founder-member of the European Union, France is a keen supporter of the eventual political and economic integration of Europe's different countries. France is Western Europe's leading farming nation, and one of the world's top industrial powers. Its cultural attractions and scenery draw tourists from around the world.

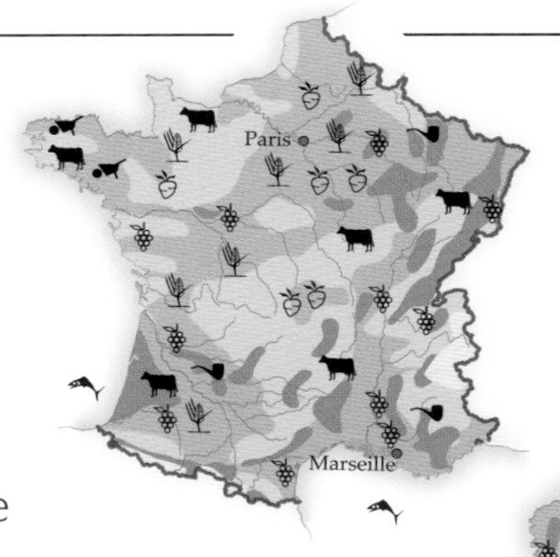

FARMING AND LAND USE

France is able to produce a variety of crops because of its rich soils and mild climate. Wheat is grown in many parts of the north, along with potatoes and other vegetables. Fields of maize and sunflowers and fruit orchards, are found in the south, while grapes for the famous wine industry are grown across the country. Beef and dairy cattle are grazed on low-lying pasture.

THE LANDSCAPE

The north and west of France is made up of mainly flat, grassy plains or low hills. Wooded mountains line the country's borders in the south and east, and much of central France is taken up by the Massif Central, an enormous plateau, cut by deep river valleys and scattered with extinct volcanoes. Three major rivers, the Loire, Seine and Garonne drain the lowland basins.

Paris Basin
The Paris Basin is a saucer-shaped hollow made up of layers of hard and soft rock, covered with very fertile soils. It runs across about 100,000 sq km of northern France.

Alps (E5)
The western end of the European Alpine mountain chain stretches into southeast France. The French Alps can be crossed by several passes, which give access to Italy and Switzerland.

Normandy
The coast of Normandy is lined with high chalk cliffs.

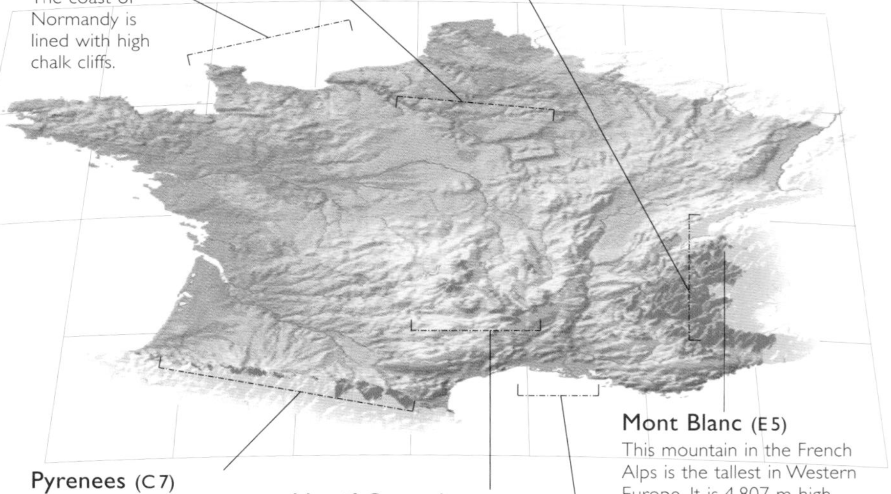

Pyrenees (C7)
These mountains form a natural barrier between France and Spain. Several of their peaks reach heights of over 3,000 m. The Pyrenees are difficult to cross, due to their height, and because they have few low passes.

Massif Central (D5)
This vast granite plateau was formed over 200 million years ago. Volcanic activity here only stopped within the last 10,000 years and the region's rounded hills are the worn down remains of volcanic mountains.

Camargue (D7)
The Camargue is an area of marshes, pastures, sand dunes and salt flats at the mouth of the River Rhône. Rare animal and plant species are found there.

Mont Blanc (E5)
This mountain in the French Alps is the tallest in Western Europe. It is 4,807 m high.

INDUSTRY

France is one of the world's top manufacturing nations, with a variety of both traditional and hi-tech industries. Cars, machinery and electronic products are exported worldwide, along with luxury goods such as perfumes, fashions and fine wines. Fossil fuels provide some energy, but France is currently the world's second-biggest producer of nuclear power.

Lille, Amiens, le Havre, Rouen, Caen, Brest, Reims, Metz, Paris, Strasbourg, Rennes, le Mans, Angers, Orléans, Mulhouse, Nantes, Tours, Bourges, Limoges, Clermont-Ferrand, Lyon, St-Etienne, Bordeaux, Grenoble, Toulouse, Marseille, Nice, Toulon

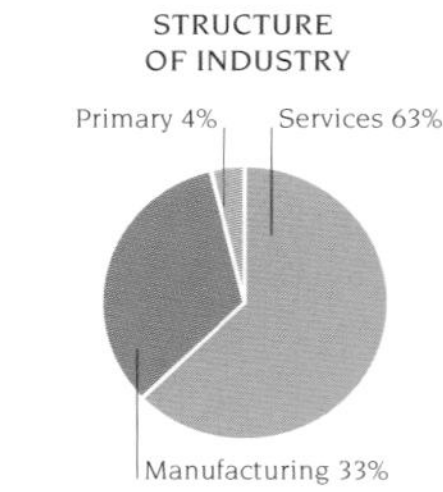

POPULATION

In the past 50 years, most people have moved from the countryside into urban areas. Paris and its suburbs, the industrial cities, and the Côte d'Azur in the southeast are the most economically developed parts of France and now have the biggest populations.

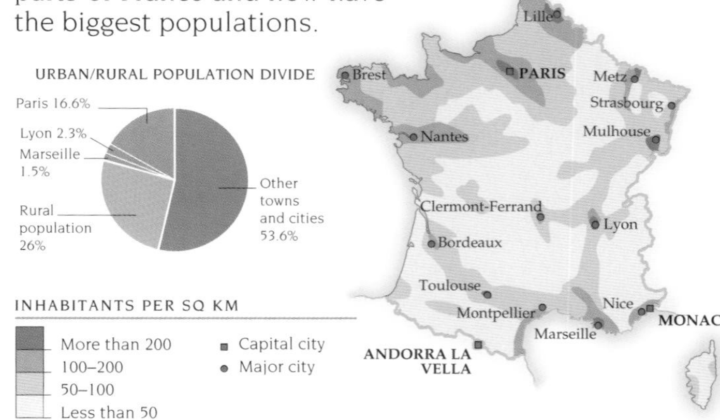

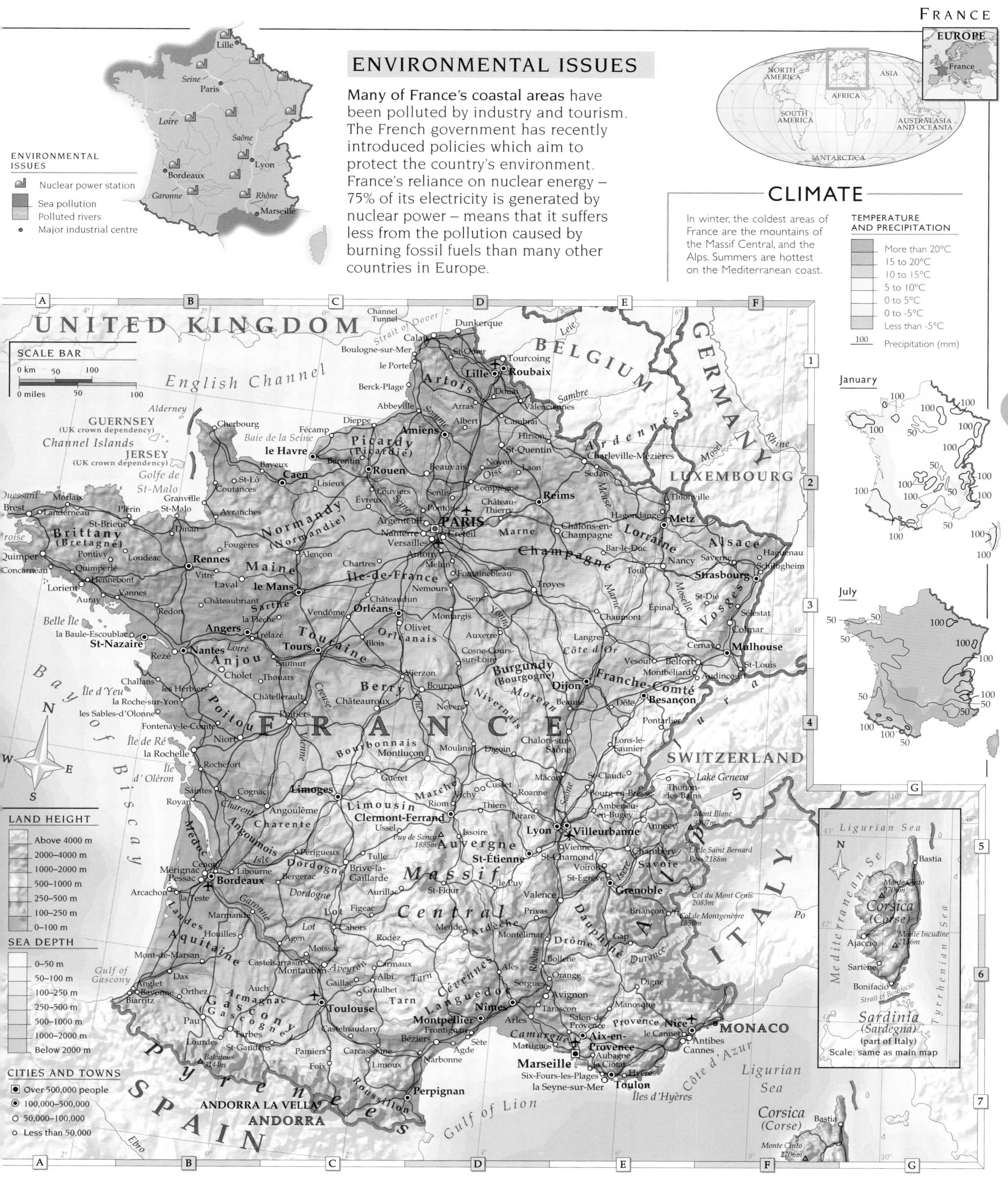
EUROPE
France
NORTH AMERICA
ASIA
AFRICA
SOUTH AMERICA
AUSTRALASIA AND OCEANIA
ANTARCTICA
ENVIRONMENTAL ISSUES
Many of France's coastal areas have been polluted by industry and tourism. The French government has recently introduced policies which aim to protect the country's environment. France's reliance on nuclear energy – 75% of its electricity is generated by nuclear power – means that it suffers less from the pollution caused by burning fossil fuels than many other countries in Europe.
ENVIRONMENTAL ISSUES
Nuclear power station
Sea pollution
Polluted rivers
Major industrial centre
Lille
Seine
Paris
Loire
Saône
Lyon
Bordeaux
Garonne
Rhône
Marseille
CLIMATE
In winter, the coldest areas of France are the mountains of the Massif Central, and the Alps. Summers are hottest on the Mediterranean coast.
TEMPERATURE AND PRECIPITATION
More than 20°C
15 to 20°C
10 to 15°C
5 to 10°C
0 to 5°C
0 to -5°C
Less than -5°C
Precipitation (mm)
January
July
SCALE BAR
0 km 50 100
0 miles 50 100
LAND HEIGHT
Above 4000 m
2000–4000 m
1000–2000 m
500–1000 m
250–500 m
100–250 m
0–100 m
SEA DEPTH
0–50 m
50–100 m
100–250 m
250–500 m
500–1000 m
1000–2000 m
Below 2000 m
CITIES AND TOWNS
Over 500,000 people
100,000–500,000
50,000–100,000
Less than 50,000
UNITED KINGDOM
BELGIUM
GERMANY
LUXEMBOURG
SWITZERLAND
ITALY
SPAIN
ANDORRA
ANDORRA LA VELLA
MONACO
FRANCE
English Channel
Bay of Biscay
Gulf of Lion
Ligurian Sea
PARIS
Lyon
Marseille
Toulouse
Bordeaux
Nantes
Lille
Strasbourg
Nice
Massif Central
Alps
Pyrenees
Corsica (Corse)
Sardinia (Sardegna) (part of Italy)
Scale: same as main map

SPAIN AND PORTUGAL

PORTUGAL, SPAIN

Spain and Portugal occupy the Iberian Peninsula, which is cut off from the rest of Europe by the Pyrenees. Over the centuries, Iberia has been invaded and settled by many different peoples. The Moors, who arrived from North Africa in the 8th century, ruled much of Spain for almost 800 years and their influence can still be seen in Spanish culture. Portugal is one of the poorest countries in western Europe, but Spain's economy is rapidly expanding.

FARMING AND LAND USE

Cereals, especially wheat and barley, are Iberia's chief crops. In the dry south of Spain, the land is irrigated to grow citrus fruits, especially oranges, and vegetables. In both countries, olive trees and vineyards occupy large areas of land; olive oil and wine are important exports. Cork oak trees from Iberia's forests supply 80% of the world's cork.

FARMING AND LAND USE

- Fishing
- Sheep
- Cereals
- Citrus fruit
- Market gardening
- Olive oil
- Vineyards
- Cork
- Pasture
- Cropland
- Forest
- Mountain region
- Major conurbation

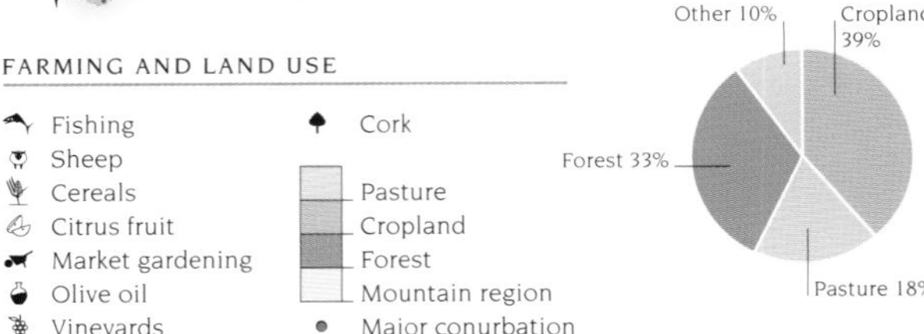

INDUSTRY

Madrid, Barcelona and the northern ports are Spain's industrial centres. Here, iron ore from Spanish mines is used to make steel, and factories produce cars, machinery and chemicals. Portugal exports textiles, clothing and footwear, along with fish such as sardines and tuna, caught off the Atlantic coast. In both countries, tourism is very important to the economy.

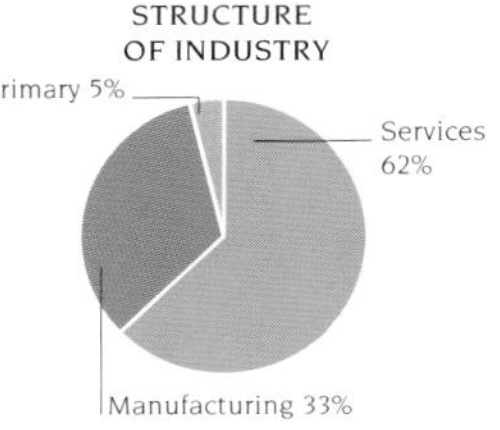

INDUSTRY

- Car manufacture
- Chemicals
- Engineering
- Fish processing
- Shipbuilding
- Steel
- Textiles
- Mining
- Publishing
- Tourism
- Major industrial centre / area
- Major road

THE LANDSCAPE

Most of inland Spain is taken up by the Meseta, a dry, almost treeless plateau surrounded by steep mountain ranges. The only lowlands, apart from narrow strips along the Mediterranean coast, are the valleys of the Ebro, Tagus, Guadiana and Guadalquivir rivers. Portugal's coast is lined by wide plains. Inland, the River Tagus divides the country in two. To the north the land is hilly and wooded; to the south it is low-lying and drier.

Westward-flowing rivers
The Duero, Tagus and Guadalquivir rivers flow across the Meseta on their courses to the Atlantic Ocean.

River Ebro (E2)
The River Ebro carries vital irrigation water to Spain's northeastern plains before flowing into the Mediterranean Sea.

Cordillera Cantábrica (C1)
These rugged, forested mountains rise on Spain's Atlantic coast. They form the northern edge of the Meseta.

The Pyrenees (F2)
These high mountains form a natural boundary with France.

River Duero (D2)

River Tagus (B4)

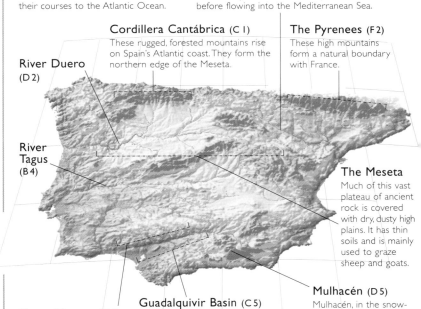

The Meseta
Much of this vast plateau of ancient rock is covered with dry, dusty high plains. It has thin soils and is mainly used to graze sheep and goats.

Sierra Morena (C5)
The southern end of the Meseta is marked by this low range of mountains.

Guadalquivir Basin (C5)
The River Guadalquivir has deposited layers of rich soil called alluvium on its flood plain, making this one of Spain's most fertile regions.

Mulhacén (D5)
Mulhacén, in the snow-capped Sierra Nevada range in southern Spain, is 3,481 m high. It is Iberia's tallest mountain.

POPULATION

In the first half of the 20th century, most Spaniards lived in villages or small towns, scattered around the country. Today, tourism and industry have drawn most of the population to the cities and coastal areas. Most Portuguese still live in rural areas along the coast or in the river valleys, but the cities are growing fast.

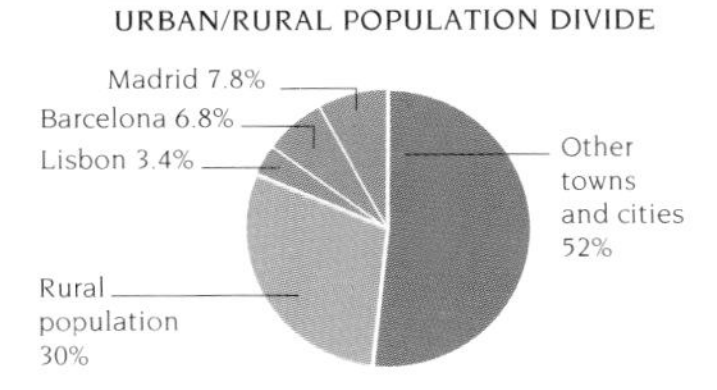

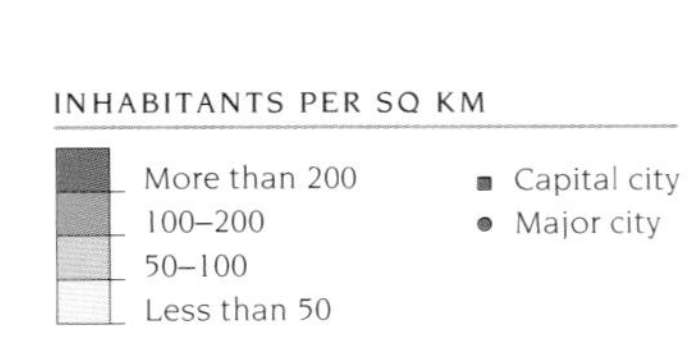

ENVIRONMENTAL ISSUES
Soil erosion – where the top layer of soil has been worn away by wind and rain – has affected much of the Iberian Peninsula. This is caused by farming, combined with drought and deforestation. In Spain, a national tree-planting scheme has been started to combat this problem. Industrial and tourist development along the Mediterranean coast of Spain, and in the Balearic Islands, has damaged natural habitats on both land and sea.
ENVIRONMENTAL ISSUES
Major oil spill
Overbuilding
Soil degradation
Severe soil degradation
Polluted rivers
Cabo Fisterra 2003
Costa Brava
Douro
Ebro
Guadiana
Guadalquivir
Segura
Majorca
Ibiza
Costa Blanca
Costa del Sol
CLIMATE
Northern Spain is wetter and cooler than the south. On the central plateau, summers are very hot and dry, and winters often freezing. The north of Portugal is cooled by winds blowing off the Atlantic Ocean. The south is warmer, with dry, mild winters.
TEMPERATURE AND PRECIPITATION
More than 25°C
20 to 25°C
15 to 20°C
10 to 15°C
5 to 10°C
0 to 5°C
0 to -5°C
-5 to -10°C
Less than -10°C
100 Precipitation (mm)
January
July
EUROPE
NORTH AMERICA
SOUTH AMERICA
AFRICA
ASIA
AUSTRALASIA AND OCEANIA
ANTARCTICA
Spain and Portugal
Bay of Biscay
Costa Verde
FRANCE
ANDORRA
Gulf of Lion
Pyrenees
Cordillera Cantábrica
Sistema Ibérico
Sistema Central
Sierra de Gredos
Sierra de Guadarrama
Sierra Morena
Sistemas Béticos
Sierra Nevada
Serra da Estrela
SPAIN
PORTUGAL
Galicia
Asturias
Cantabria
The Basque Country (País Vasco)
Navarra
La Rioja
Castilla-León
Aragón
Cataluña
Catalonia
Extremadura
Castilla-La Mancha
País Valenciano
Murcia
Andalusia (Andalucía)
Algarve
MADRID
LISBON (LISBOA)
A Coruña (La Coruña)
Gijón (Xixón)
Oviedo
Santander
Bilbao
Donostia-San Sebastián
Vitoria-Gasteiz
Pamplona (Iruña)
Logroño
Burgos
León
Valladolid
Salamanca
Zaragoza
Lleida (Lérida)
Barcelona
L'Hospitalet de Llobregat
Sabadell
Terrassa
Tarragona
Getafe
Castelló de la Plana
Valencia
Albacete
Alicante (Alacant)
Elche (Elx)
Murcia
Cartagena
Córdoba
Jaén
Granada
Seville (Sevilla)
Huelva
Cádiz
Málaga
Algeciras
Badajoz
Oporto (Porto)
Vila Nova de Gaia
Matosinhos
Vigo
Ourense (Orense)
Santiago de Compostela
Balearic Islands (Islas Baleares)
Majorca (Mallorca)
Minorca (Menorca)
Ibiza (Eivissa)
Formentera
Cabrera
Palma de Mallorca
Mahón
Gulf of Valencia
Costa del Azahar
Costa Blanca
Costa Brava
Costa del Sol
Mediterranean Sea
Gulf of Cadiz (Golfo de Cádiz)
Strait of Gibraltar
Baía de Setúbal
GIBRALTAR (UK dependent territory)
Ceuta (part of Spain)
MOROCCO
ALGERIA
Monte Perdido 3348m
Alto da Torre 1993m
Javalambre 2020m
Mulhacén 3481m
Cabo Fisterra
Cabo de São Vicente
LAND HEIGHT
2000–4000 m
1000–2000 m
500–1000 m
250–500 m
100–250 m
0–100 m
SEA DEPTH
0–250 m
250–500 m
500–1000 m
1000–2000 m
2000–3000 m
3000–4000 m
Below 4000 m
CITIES AND TOWNS
Over 500,000 people
100,000–500,000
50,000–100,000
Less than 50,000
SCALE BAR
0 km 50 100
0 miles 50 100
N
E
S
W

Germany and the Alpine States

AUSTRIA, GERMANY, LIECHTENSTEIN, SLOVENIA, SWITZERLAND

Germany lies at the heart of Europe and is the biggest industrial power in the continent. In 1945, Germany was divided into two separate countries, East and West Germany, which were reunited in 1990. To the south, the snow-capped peaks of the Alps, Europe's highest mountains, tower over the Alpine states – Switzerland, Austria, Liechtenstein and the former Yugoslavian state of Slovenia.

Industry

Germany is a leading manufacturer of cars, chemicals, machinery and transport equipment. Switzerland and Liechtenstein, with few raw materials, make high-value products such as watches and pharmaceuticals, and provide services such as banking. The Alpine states are a popular tourist location all year round.

INDUSTRY

- Car manufacture
- Chemicals
- Engineering
- Iron & steel
- Shipbuilding
- Pharmaceuticals
- Finance
- Hi-tech industry
- Tourism
- Major industrial centre / area
- Major road

STRUCTURE OF INDUSTRY

Primary 1%
Services 62%
Manufacturing 37%

Kiel, Rostock, Hamburg, Bremen, Hannover, Berlin, Dortmund, Ruhr Valley, Düsseldorf, Halle, Kassel, Liepzig, Dresden, Cologne, Frankfurt am Main, Saarbrücken, Heidelberg, Nuremberg, Stuttgart, Munich, Linz, Salzburg, Vienna, Zürich, Bern, Vaduz, Innsbruck, Donawitz, Graz, Klagenfurt, Geneva, Ljubljana, Novo Mesto

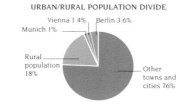

Farming and Land Use

Germany produces three-quarters of its own food. Crop farming is widespread, with cereals and root crops grown in flat, fertile areas. Cattle and pig farming supplies meat and dairy products. Across the Alps, the mountains limit farming, although vines are grown on the warmer, south-facing slopes. The rich pastures of the lower slopes are used to graze beef and dairy cattle.

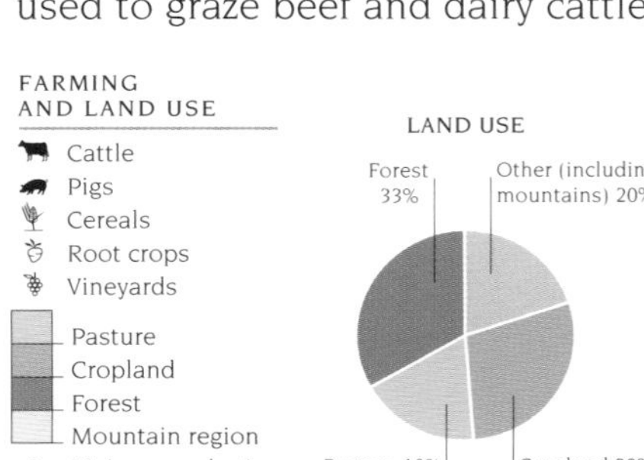

Bremen, Berlin, Dortmund, Liepzig, Nuremberg, Stuttgart, Munich, Vienna, Bern, Zürich, Innsbruck, Ljubljana

Population

Western and central Germany are the most densely populated areas in this region – particularly in and around the Rhine and Ruhr valleys, where there are many industries. In the south, the steep slopes of the Alps and permanent snow cover on the higher peaks means that most large towns and cities are in scattered lowland areas.

Hamburg, BERLIN, Dortmund, Essen, Leipzig, Dresden, Cologne, Frankfurt am Main, Nuremburg, Stuttgart, Munich, Linz, VIENNA, Zürich, Graz, BERN, LJUBLJANA

INHABITANTS PER SQ KM

- More than 200
- 100–200
- 50–100
- Less than 50
- Capital city
- Major city

URBAN/RURAL POPULATION DIVIDE

Vienna 1.4%
Berlin 3.6%
Munich 1%
Rural population 18%
Other towns and cities 76%

The Landscape

To the north, flat plains and heathlands surround the North Sea coast. Further south are Germany's central uplands, which are lower and older than the jagged peaks of the Alps, which began to form about 65 million years ago. From its source in the Black Forest, the River Danube flows eastward across Germany and Austria on its course to the Black Sea. The other major river, the Rhine, flows northward.

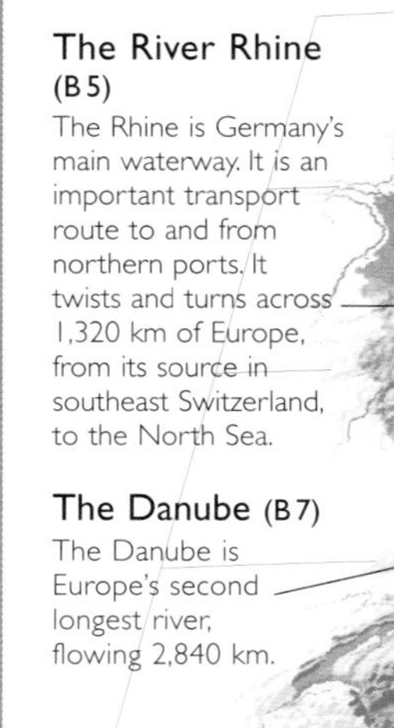

The River Rhine (B5)
The Rhine is Germany's main waterway. It is an important transport route to and from northern ports. It twists and turns across 1,320 km of Europe, from its source in southeast Switzerland, to the North Sea.

The Danube (B7)
The Danube is Europe's second longest river, flowing 2,840 km.

Lake Constance (B7)
Lake Constance covers 540 sq km and is Germany's largest lake, although its waters are shared by Austria and Switzerland.

The Harz mountains (C4)
These rugged, wooded mountains are much older than the Alps. They were formed over 300 million years ago.

Karst region (E8)
Most of the water in this limestone region of Slovenia flows underground, through huge caves and caverns.

The Alps (C8)
The Alps were formed when the African Plate collided with the Eurasian Plate, pushing up and crushing huge amounts of rock, to form mountains.

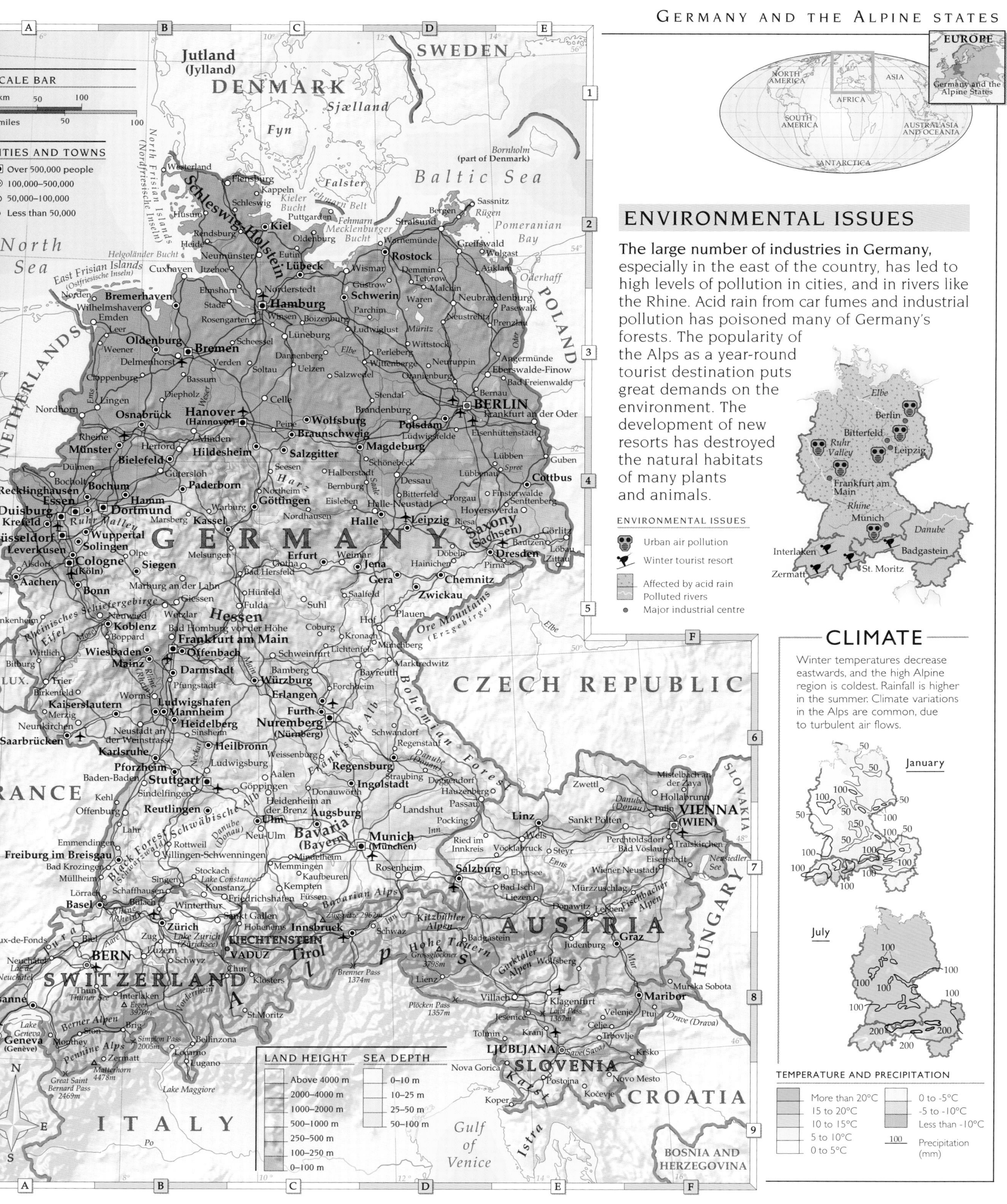

ENVIRONMENTAL ISSUES

The large number of industries in Germany, especially in the east of the country, has led to high levels of pollution in cities, and in rivers like the Rhine. Acid rain from car fumes and industrial pollution has poisoned many of Germany's forests. The popularity of the Alps as a year-round tourist destination puts great demands on the environment. The development of new resorts has destroyed the natural habitats of many plants and animals.

CLIMATE

Winter temperatures decrease eastwards, and the high Alpine region is coldest. Rainfall is higher in the summer. Climate variations in the Alps are common, due to turbulent air flows.

ITALY

ITALY, SAN MARINO, VATICAN CITY

Italy has played an important role in Europe since the Romans based their mighty empire here over 2,000 years ago. The famous boot shape divides into two very different halves. Northern Italy has a varied range of industries and agriculture. Beautiful cities like Venice, Florence, and Rome draw tourists from all over the world. Southern Italy is poorer and less developed than the north, with a hotter, drier climate and less productive land.

THE LANDSCAPE

Italy is a peninsula jutting south from mainland Europe into the Mediterranean Sea. In northern and central Italy the land is mainly mountainous. Most of the flat land is in the Po Valley and along the eastern coast. Italy lies within an earthquake zone, which makes the land unstable, and there are also a number of active volcanoes.

Po Valley (C 2)
The basin of the River Po has the best soils in Italy. Rich alluvium is washed from the mountains by the river to form a wide plain.

Italian lakes
Great lakes like Garda (B3) and Como (B2) fill several south-facing valleys once occupied by glaciers.

The Dolomites (D 2)
These high mountains are part of the same range as the Alps. They were formed 65 million years ago.

The Apennines (C 4)
This mountain range forms the 'backbone' of Italy, dividing the rocky west coast from the flatter, sandy east coast.

Earthquakes
The southern Apennines, as well as coastal areas of southwestern Italy, often experience earthquakes and mudslides.

Tyrrhenian Sea (C 6)
This sea, which divides the Italian mainland from Sardinia, is gradually filling with sediment from the rivers which flow into it.

Sardinia
The island of Sardinia is made from very old rocks which were thrust up to form mountains.

Sicily
Sicily is the largest island in the Mediterranean. It has a famous active volcano called Mount Etna, and often experiences earthquakes

Gulf of Taranto (F 7)
During earthquakes, great blocks of land have broken away and sunk into the sea, forming the Gulf's square shape.

FARMING AND LAND USE

The Po Valley is a broad, flat plain in the north of Italy. It contains the most fertile land in the country, and wheat and rice are the main cereal crops grown here. Grapes for wine are grown everywhere in Italy. In much of the south, the land must be irrigated to support crops. Where there is enough water, citrus fruits, olives, and many kinds of tomatoes are grown.

LAND USE

Cropland 41%, Pasture 15%, Forest 23%, Other 21%

FARMING AND LAND USE

Cattle, Pigs, Sheep, Cereals, Citrus fruits, Olive oil, Rice, Vineyards
Pasture, Cropland, Forest, Mountain region, Major conurbation

INDUSTRY

Italian industry is located mainly in the north. Design is extremely important to Italians and they are proud of the elegant designs of their furniture, clothes and shoes. Though many firms are small, they are very efficient. Italy has few mineral resources so it needs to import raw materials to make cars, engines and other hi-tech products.

INDUSTRY

Car manufacture, Chemicals, Iron & steel, Textiles, Finance, Hi-tech industry, Tourism
Major industrial centre / area, Major road

STRUCTURE OF INDUSTRY

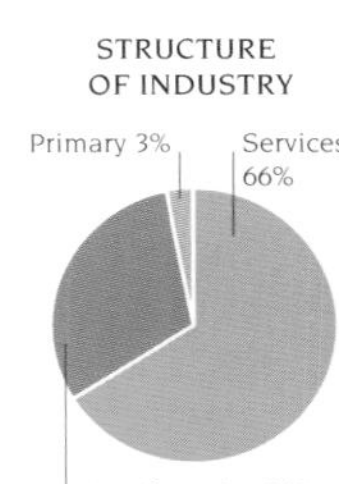

POPULATION

Most of Italy's population lives in the north, mainly in and around the Po Valley, which is home to over 25 million people. Most people here have a high standard of living. Southern Italy is much more rural; towns are smaller and life is often much harder.

URBAN/RURAL POPULATION DIVIDE

Milan 1.5%, Rome 2.8%, Naples 1.2%, Rural population 31%, Other towns and cities 63.5%

INHABITANTS PER SQ KM

More than 200, 100–200, 50–100, 0–50
Capital city, Major city

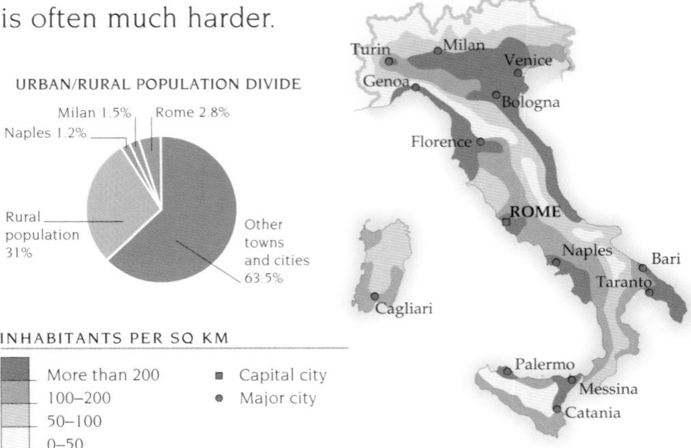

EUROPE
Italy
NORTH AMERICA
SOUTH AMERICA
AFRICA
ASIA
AUSTRALASIA AND OCEANIA
ANTARCTICA
ENVIRONMENTAL ISSUES
Sewage and chemical by-products from industry have polluted the Mediterranean and Adriatic seas. In many northern cities, severe air pollution is a health hazard. Southern Italy is subject to natural dangers like earthquakes and mudslides.
ENVIRONMENTAL ISSUES
Catastrophic earthquakes
Urban air pollution
Acid rain
Sea pollution
Major industrial centre
Turin
Milan
Genoa
Gemona del Friuli 1976
Ancona 1972
Tuscania 1971
L'Aquila 1980
Rome
Isernia 1984
Naples
Irpino 1980
Palermo
Belice 1968
Sicily
Siracusa 1990
CLIMATE
The Alpine north has cold winters, often with snow. Further south, temperatures are higher. Sicily has Italy's highest temperatures, due to warm African winds.
January
July
Less than 50
TEMPERATURE AND PRECIPITATION
More than 25°C
20 to 25°C
15 to 20°C
10 to 15°C
5 to 10°C
0 to 5°C
0 to -5°C
-5 to -10°C
Less than -10°C
100 Precipitation (mm)
SCALE BAR
0 km 40 80
0 miles 40 80
CITIES AND TOWNS
Over 500,000 people
100,000–500,000
50,000–100,000
Less than 50,000
LAND HEIGHT
Above 4000m
2000–4000 m
1000–2000 m
500–1000 m
250–500 m
100–250 m
0–100 m
SEA DEPTH
0–50 m
50–100 m
100–250 m
250–500 m
500–1000 m
1000–2000 m
Below 2000 m
GERMANY
SWITZERLAND
LIECHTENSTEIN
AUSTRIA
SLOVENIA
CROATIA
TUNISIA
MALTA
SAN MARINO
VATICAN CITY
ROME (ROMA)
Milan (Milano)
Turin (Torino)
Naples (Napoli)
Florence (Firenze)
Venice (Venezia)
Genoa (Genova)
Lake Constance
Lake Geneva
Lake Maggiore
Lake Como
Lake Garda
Lago Trasimeno
Mont Blanc 4807m
Great Saint Bernard Pass 2469m
Gran Paradiso 4061m
Bremner Pass 1374m
Dolomites
Lombardy (Lombardia)
Piedmont (Piemonte)
Tuscany (Toscana)
Campania
Apulia (Puglia)
Marche
Umbria
Abruzzo
Molise
Basilicata
Calabria
La Sila
Appennino Ligure
Ligurian Sea
Gulf of Genoa
Gulf of Venice
Adriatic Sea
Tyrrhenian Sea
Ionian Sea
Mediterranean Sea
Gulf of Taranto
Gulf of Gaeta
Gulf of Salerno
Strait of Bonifacio
Strait of Sicily
Strait of Messina
Strait of Otranto
Malta Channel
Corsica (Corse) (part of France)
Sardinia (Sardegna)
Punta La Marmora 1834m
Sicily (Sicilia)
Monte Etna 3340m
Vesuvio 1277m
Aeolian Islands
Stromboli
Lipari
Vulcano
Ustica
Egadi Is.
Pantelleria
Pelagie
Ponziane Is.
Capri
Elba
Archipelago Toscano
Istra
Dalmatia
Bolzano
Trento
Verona
Vicenza
Padua (Padova)
Mestre
Trieste
Bergamo
Brescia
Monza
Bologna
Modena
Parma
Reggio nell' Emilia
Ferrara
Ravenna
Rimini
Forlì
Prato
Pisa
Livorno
La Spezia
Piacenza
Perugia
Terni
Ancona
Pescara
Foggia
Bari
Taranto
Lecce
Brindisi
Salerno
Torre del Greco
Cosenza
Catanzaro
Reggio di Calabria
Messina
Catania
Siracusa
Palermo
Sassari
Cagliari
Trapani
Marsala
Agrigento
Caltanissetta
Ragusa

CENTRAL EUROPE

CZECH REPUBLIC, HUNGARY, POLAND, SLOVAKIA

Central Europe has been invaded many times throughout history. The countries have changed shape frequently as their borders have shifted backwards and forwards. From the end of the Second World War until 1989, they were ruled by communist governments, which were supported by the Soviet Union. In 1993, the state of Czechoslovakia voted to split into two separate nations, called the Czech Republic and Slovakia.

FARMING AND LAND USE

Central Europe's main crops are cereals such as maize, wheat and rye, along with sugar beet and potatoes. In Hungary, sweet peppers grow, helped by the warm summers and mild winters. They are used to make paprika. Grapes are also grown, to make wine. Large areas of the plains of Hungary and Poland are used for rearing pigs and cattle. Trees for timber grow in the mountains of Slovakia and the Czech Republic.

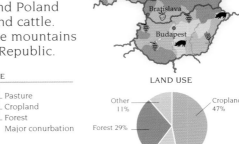

FARMING AND LAND USE

Cattle
Pigs
Cereals
Root crops
Potatoes
Timber
Vineyards
Pasture
Cropland
Forest
Major conurbation

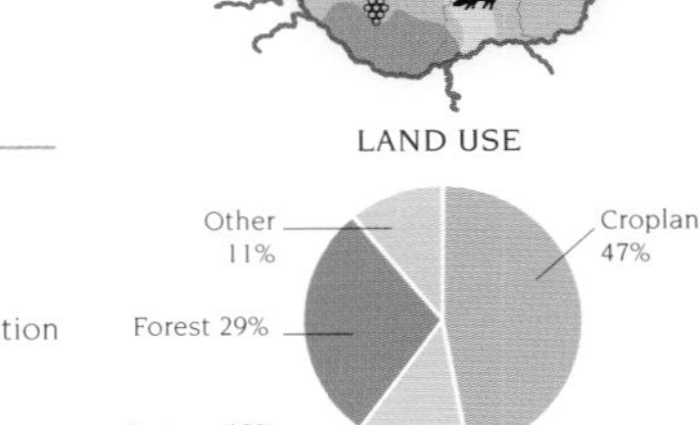

INDUSTRY

Brown coal, or lignite, is central Europe's main fuel, and one of Poland's major exports. A variety of minerals are mined in the mountains of the Czech Republic and Slovakia. Hungary has a wide range of industries producing vehicles, metals, and chemicals, as well as textiles and electrical goods. The Czech Republic is famous for its breweries and glass-making.

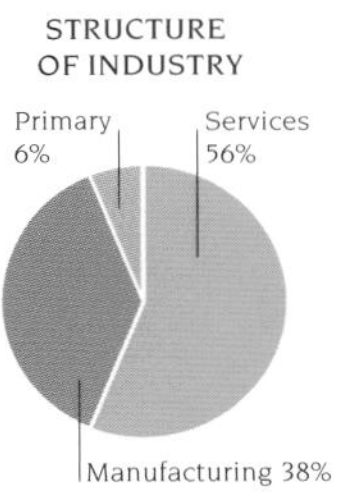

THE LANDSCAPE

The high Carpathian Mountains sweep across northern Slovakia. The lower Sudeten Mountains lie on the border of the Czech Republic and Poland. Together, these mountains form a barrier which divides the Great Hungarian Plain and the River Danube basin in the south from Poland and the vast rolling lowlands of the North European Plain.

Pomerania (C2)
This is a sandy coastal area with lakes formed by glaciers. It stretches west from the River Vistula to just beyond the German border.

River Vistula (F4)
Poland's largest river is the Vistula. It flows northwards, passing through the capital, Warsaw, on its way to the Baltic Sea.

North European Plain

Hot springs
The Sudeten mountains (C5) are famous for their hot mineral springs. These occur where water heated deep within the Earth's crust finds its way to the surface along fractures in the rock.

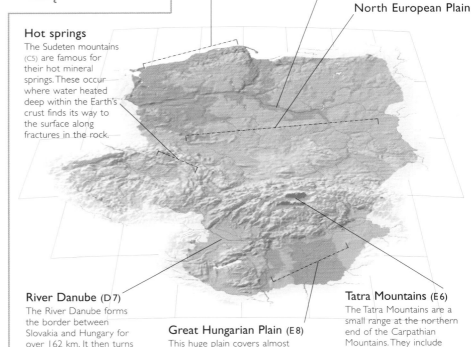

River Danube (D7)
The River Danube forms the border between Slovakia and Hungary for over 162 km. It then turns south to flow across the Great Hungarian Plain.

Great Hungarian Plain (E8)
This huge plain covers almost half of Hungary's land area. It is a mixture of farmland and steppe.

Tatra Mountains (E6)
The Tatra Mountains are a small range at the northern end of the Carpathian Mountains. They include Gerlachovsky Stít, which is Central Europe's highest point at 2,655 m.

ENVIRONMENTAL ISSUES

The growth of heavy industries that took place under communist rule has caused terrible environmental pollution in some places. Hungary's oil and Poland's brown coal have a high sulphur content. Burning these fuels to produce electricity causes air pollution, and the sulphur dioxide produced combines with moisture in the air, leading to acid rain.

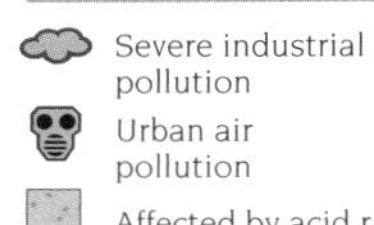

POPULATION

Most people in central Europe live in low-lying areas, for example, along the River Vistula in Poland, and in the lowlands of the Czech Republic. In mountainous Slovakia, many people still live in rural towns and villages. The industrial areas and capital cities have the highest population densities.

CLIMATE

The Carpathian Mountains are both the coldest and the wettest part of central Europe. Temperatures plunge below zero across the whole region during winter. In summer, eastern Hungary is the hottest place.

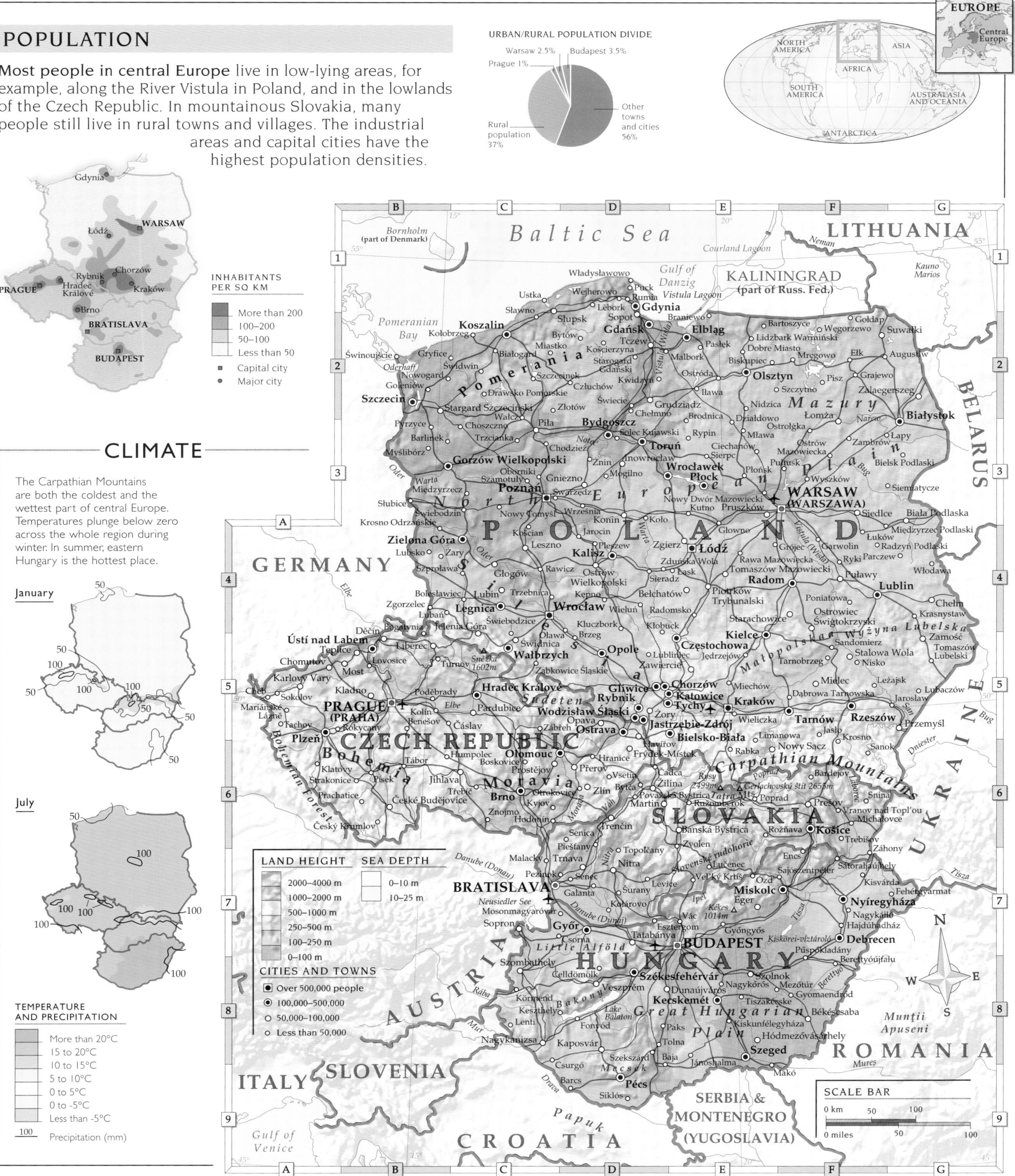

Southeast Europe

ALBANIA, BOSNIA AND HERZEGOVINA, BULGARIA, CROATIA, GREECE, MACEDONIA, SERBIA & MONTENEGRO (YUGOSLAVIA)

Southeast Europe extends inland from the coasts of the Aegean, Adriatic and Black seas. Ancient Greece was the birthplace of European civilization. Albania and Bulgaria were ruled by communists for over 50 years, until the early 1990s. The rest of the region was part of a communist union of states called Yugoslavia. The collapse of this union in 1991 led to a civil war, after which five separate countries emerged.

THE LANDSCAPE

Southeast Europe is largely mountainous, with ranges running from northwest to southeast. The Dinaric Alps run parallel to the Dalmatian coast, and the Pindus Mountains continue this line into Greece. In the Aegean Sea, the drowned peaks of an old mountain chain form thousands of islands.

Earthquakes
Bulgaria, Greece, and Macedonia lie in earthquake zones. Major earthquakes have hit the Ionian Islands in 1953, and Macedonia in 1963.

Great Hungarian Plain (D 1)
The Vojvodina region of Serbia and Montenegro is the southern part of the Great Hungarian Plain. The plain is flat and fertile soils allow grain crops like corn and wheat to be grown.

Dinaric Alps (C 2)

Balkan Mountains (F 3)
The mountains form a spur running east to west through Bulgaria and separate the two main rivers, the Danube and the Maritsa.

Dalmatian coast (B 2)
The Dalmatian coast has many long, narrow islands near the shore. These were formed as the Adriatic Sea flooded the river valleys which ran parallel to the coast.

Greek Islands

The Peloponnese (E 6)
The Peloponnese is a mountainous peninsula linked to the Greek mainland only by a narrow strip of land called an isthmus. Here, it is the Isthmus of Corinth.

Greek Islands
There are two groups of Greek Islands, the Ionian Islands to the west of mainland Greece, and the more numerous islands to the east in the Aegean Sea.

STRUCTURE OF INDUSTRY

Primary 16%
Services 52%
Manufacturing 32%

FARMING AND LAND USE

Cereals like wheat, and fruits, vegetables and grapes are grown in the fertile north of the region. The band of mountains across southeast Europe is used mainly for grazing sheep and goats. Further south, and in coastal areas, the warm Mediterranean climate is ideal for growing grapes, olives and tobacco.

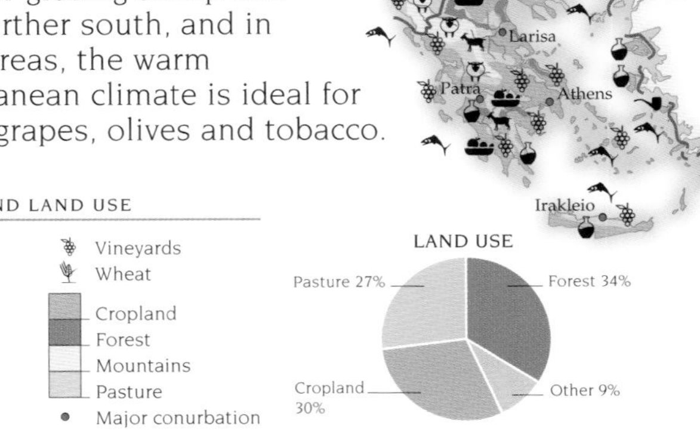

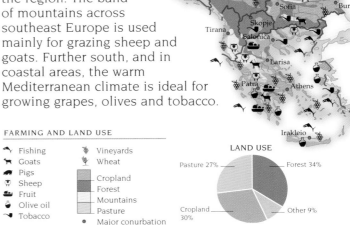

FARMING AND LAND USE

- Fishing
- Goats
- Pigs
- Sheep
- Fruit
- Olive oil
- Tobacco
- Vineyards
- Wheat
- Cropland
- Forest
- Mountains
- Pasture
- Major conurbation

INDUSTRY

Mainland Greece and the many islands in the Aegean Sea are centres of a thriving tourist trade, while tourism on the Black Sea coast continues to grow. The Dalmatian coast had a small, but growing tourist industry, until the civil war in former Yugoslavia disrupted that, and other industries. Heavy industries like chemicals, engineering and shipbuilding remain an important source of income in Bulgaria.

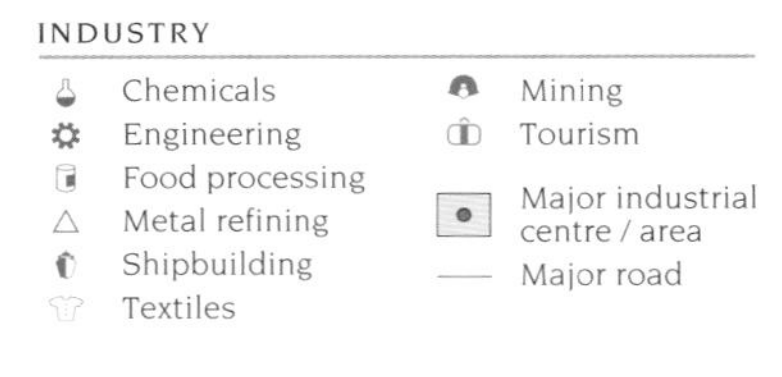

INDUSTRY

- Chemicals
- Engineering
- Food processing
- Metal refining
- Shipbuilding
- Textiles
- Mining
- Tourism
- Major industrial centre / area
- Major road

POPULATION

Greece's population is mostly urban; over 50% live in the capital, Athens and in Salonica. In Bulgaria, most people live in cities. About half of Albania's and Macedonia's people are still rural. Since the civil war, the different ethnic groups in Bosnia and Herzegovina, Serbia and Montenegro and Croatia have lived apart from one another.

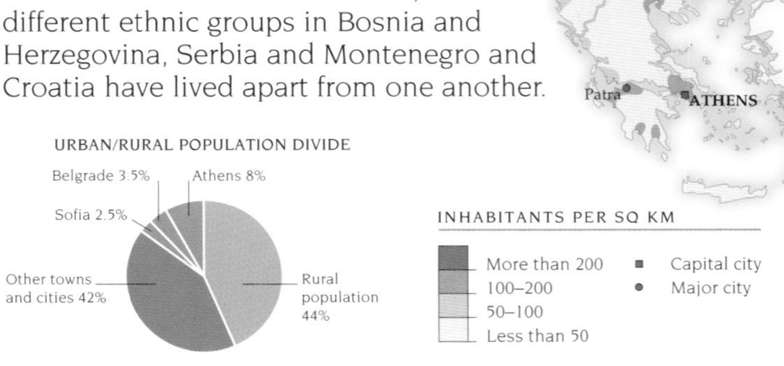

URBAN/RURAL POPULATION DIVIDE

Belgrade 3.5%
Athens 8%
Sofia 2.5%
Other towns and cities 42%
Rural population 44%

INHABITANTS PER SQ KM

- More than 200
- 100–200
- 50–100
- Less than 50
- Capital city
- Major city

CLIMATE
Southeastern Europe's climate varies from north to south. Continental climates are found in the north; winters are cold and dry, while towards the south, winters are milder and summers much hotter. Europe's wettest place is found in the mountains in Bosnia and Herzegovina.
January
July
TEMPERATURE AND PRECIPITATION
More than 25°C
20 to 25°C
15 to 20°C
10 to 15°C
5 to 10°C
0 to 5°C
0 to -5°C
Less than -5°C
100 Precipitation (mm)
EUROPE
Southeast Europe
NORTH AMERICA
SOUTH AMERICA
AFRICA
ASIA
AUSTRALASIA AND OCEANIA
ANTARCTICA
SCALE BAR
0 km 50 100
0 miles 50 100
N
S
E
W
CITIES AND TOWNS
Over 500,000 people
100,000–500,000
50,000–100,000
Less than 50,000
AUSTRIA
HUNGARY
SLOVENIA
CROATIA
BOSNIA AND HERZEGOVINA
SERBIA & MONTENEGRO (YUGOSLAVIA)
ROMANIA
MOLDOVA
UKRAINE
BULGARIA
ALBANIA
MACEDONIA
GREECE
TURKEY
SAN MARINO
ZAGREB
SARAJEVO
BELGRADE (BEOGRAD)
SOFIA (SOFIYA)
SKOPJE
TIRANA (TIRANË)
ATHENS (ATHINA)
Adriatic Sea
Black Sea
Aegean Sea
Ionian Sea
Sea of Crete (Kritikó Pélagos)
Mediterranean Sea
Sea of Marmara
Thracian Sea
Mirtoan Sea
Strait of Otranto
Ionian Islands (Iónia Nisiá)
Cyclades (Kykládes)
Dodecanese (Dodekánisa)
Northern Sporades
Dinaric Alps
Balkan Mountains
Rhodope Mountains
Pindus Mountains
Danubian Plain
Great Hungarian Plain
Dalmatia
Istra
Crete (Kriti)
Rhodes (Rodos)
Euboea (Evvoia)
Limnos
Lesbos
Chios
Danube
Sava
Drava
Tisza
Morava
Mureș
Ialomița
Vardar
Maritsa
Subotica
Osijek
Novi Sad
Zemun
Pančevo
Kikinda
Zrenjanin
Vršac
Rijeka
Pula
Split
Zadar
Dubrovnik
Banja Luka
Mostar
Tuzla
Zenica
Niš
Priština
Podgorica
Nikšić
Kragujevac
Kraljevo
Ruse
Varna
Burgas
Dobrich
Shumen
Razgrad
Pleven
Plovdiv
Stara Zagora
Sliven
Pernik
Vidin
Kozloduy
Shkodër
Durrës
Vlorë
Bitola
Prilep
Kumanovo
Salonica (Thessaloniki)
Larisa
Volos
Patra
Piraeus (Peiraias)
Irakleio
Chania
Mount Olympus 2917m
Musala 2925m
LAND HEIGHT
2000–4000 m
1000–2000 m
500–1000 m
250–500 m
100–250 m
0–100 m
SEA DEPTH
0–50 m
50–100 m
100–250 m
250–500 m
500–1000 m
1000–2000 m
Below 2000 m
ENVIRONMENTAL ISSUES
Emissions from industry and traffic fumes have polluted the air in Athens and Zagreb. In Athens, smog caused by vehicle exhausts can become so severe on some days that the use of cars is banned. Earthquakes are common; Macedonia's capital city, Skopje, was badly hit in 1963, and Bulgaria's run-down Kozloduy nuclear power station lies within the earthquake zone.
Zagreb
Danube
Kozloduy
Skopje 1963
Salonica 1978
Athens
ENVIRONMENTAL ISSUES
Catastrophic earthquake
Unstable nuclear reactor
Urban air pollution
Sea pollution
Polluted river
Major town

Eastern Europe

BELARUS, MOLDOVA, ROMANIA, UKRAINE

Much of Eastern Europe, which extends north from the River Danube and the Black Sea, is covered by open grasslands called steppe. Ukraine's excellent farmland and large mineral reserves make it one of the strongest new countries to emerge from the former Soviet Union. Moldova and Belarus were also part of the USSR, until they became independent in 1991. Romania was a strict communist regime from 1945 until 1989.

POPULATION

Most Romanians live in Bucharest, the capital, or in other cities and towns. In Ukraine, two-thirds of the population lives in cities in the Donbass industrial area. Most of Belarus's people are city dwellers. Moldova is the most rural country in Eastern Europe; half its people live in the countryside and make their living from farming.

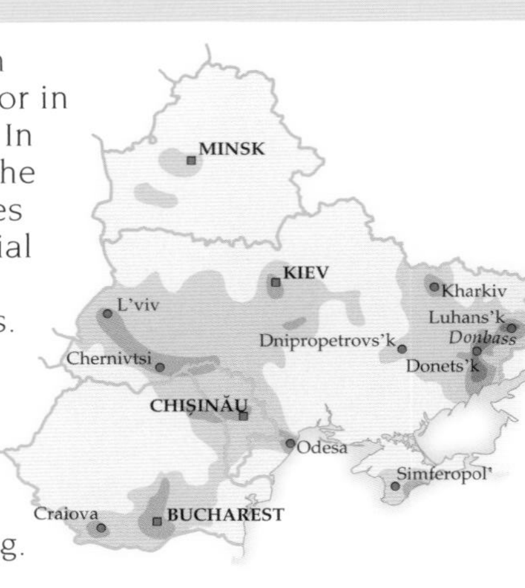

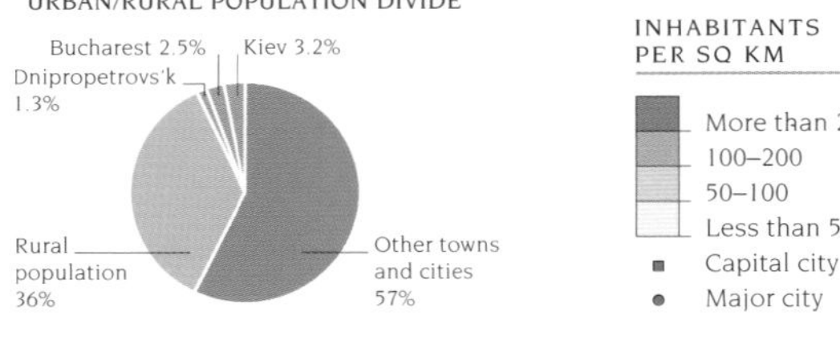

INDUSTRY

In Ukraine, most industry is based around the country's mineral reserves. The Donbass region has Europe's largest coalfield and is an important centre for iron and steel production. Belarus's main industries are chemicals, machine building and food-processing. Romania's manufacturing industries are growing, with the help of foreign investment.

STRUCTURE OF INDUSTRY

Primary 20%
Manufacturing 47%
Services 33%

INDUSTRY

Car manufacture
Chemicals
Engineering
Food processing
Iron & steel
Textiles
Coal
Mining
Oil and gas
Tourism
Major industrial centre / area
Major road

THE LANDSCAPE

Flat or rolling grasslands, marshes and river flood plains cover almost all of Ukraine and Belarus. The Carpathian Mountains cross the southwestern corner of Ukraine and continue in a large arc-shaped chain of high peaks at the heart of Romania. Along the southern part of this chain, the Carpathians are called the Transylvanian Alps.

Pripet Marshes (C 3)
The Pripet Marshes in Belarus and Ukraine form the largest area of marshland in Europe.

The steppes
The steppes are great, wide grasslands which are found across eastern Europe and central Asia. Over 70% of the Ukrainian landscape is steppe. Little rain falls throughout the steppes.

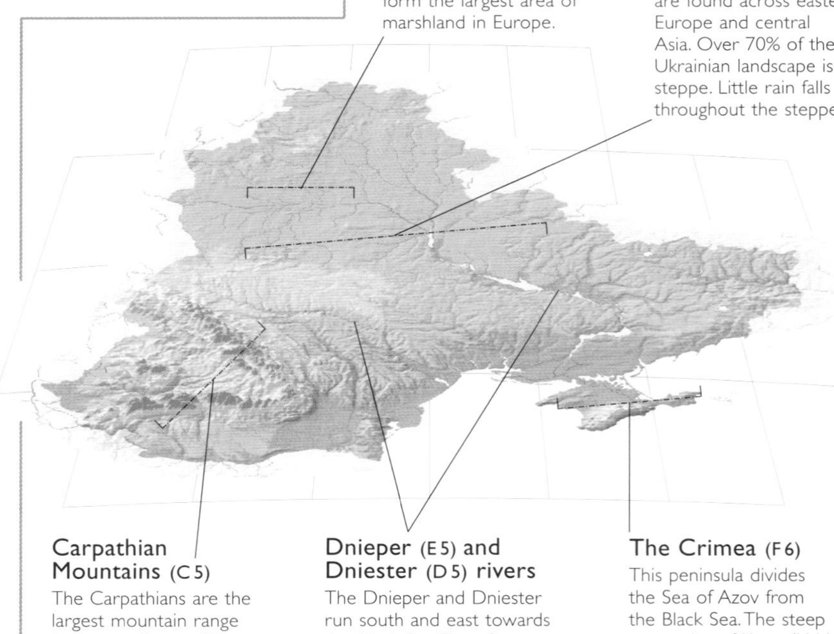

Carpathian Mountains (C 5)
The Carpathians are the largest mountain range in Eastern Europe. They are a rich source of timber and minerals.

Dnieper (E 5) and Dniester (D 5) rivers
The Dnieper and Dniester run south and east towards the Black Sea. They flow slowly across huge areas of low-lying land.

The Crimea (F 6)
This peninsula divides the Sea of Azov from the Black Sea. The steep mountains of Kryms'ki Hory run along the southeastern coast of the Crimea.

FARMING AND LAND USE

The black soils found across much of Ukraine are very fertile and the country is a big producer of cereals, sugar beet, and sunflowers, which are grown for their oil. In Moldova and southern Romania, the warm summers are ideal for growing grapes for wine, along with sunflowers and a variety of vegetables. Cattle and pigs are farmed throughout Eastern Europe.

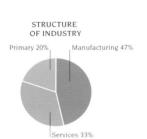

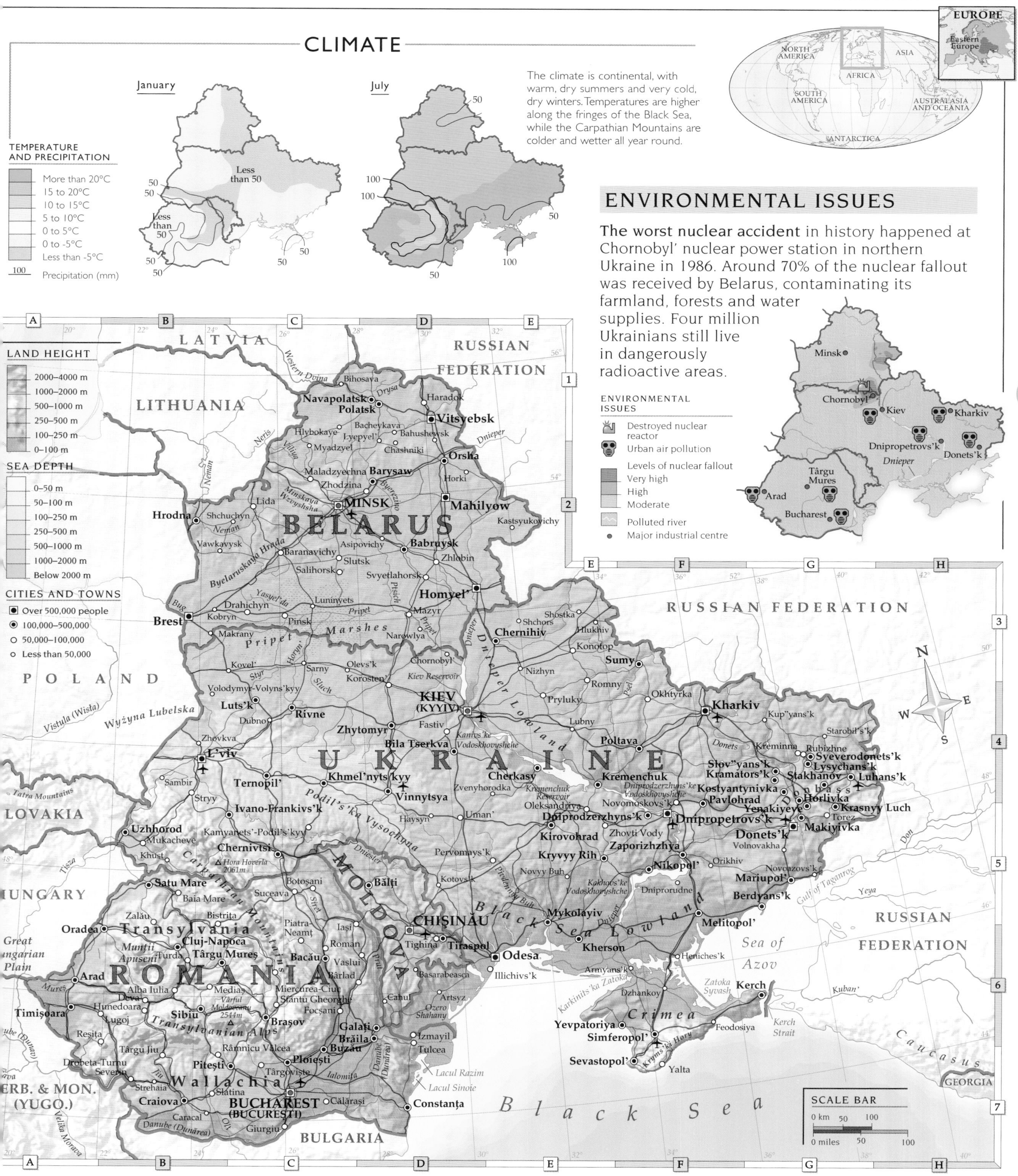
EUROPE
Eastern Europe
NORTH AMERICA
SOUTH AMERICA
AFRICA
ASIA
AUSTRALASIA AND OCEANIA
ANTARCTICA
CLIMATE
January
July
TEMPERATURE AND PRECIPITATION
More than 20°C
15 to 20°C
10 to 15°C
5 to 10°C
0 to 5°C
0 to -5°C
Less than -5°C
100 Precipitation (mm)
Less than 50
The climate is continental, with warm, dry summers and very cold, dry winters. Temperatures are higher along the fringes of the Black Sea, while the Carpathian Mountains are colder and wetter all year round.
ENVIRONMENTAL ISSUES
The worst nuclear accident in history happened at Chornobyl' nuclear power station in northern Ukraine in 1986. Around 70% of the nuclear fallout was received by Belarus, contaminating its farmland, forests and water supplies. Four million Ukrainians still live in dangerously radioactive areas.
ENVIRONMENTAL ISSUES
Destroyed nuclear reactor
Urban air pollution
Levels of nuclear fallout
Very high
High
Moderate
Polluted river
Major industrial centre
Minsk
Chornobyl'
Kiev
Kharkiv
Dnipropetrovs'k
Donets'k
Dnieper
Târgu Mures
Arad
Bucharest
LAND HEIGHT
2000–4000 m
1000–2000 m
500–1000 m
250–500 m
100–250 m
0–100 m
SEA DEPTH
0–50 m
50–100 m
100–250 m
250–500 m
500–1000 m
1000–2000 m
Below 2000 m
CITIES AND TOWNS
Over 500,000 people
100,000–500,000
50,000–100,000
Less than 50,000
LATVIA
LITHUANIA
RUSSIAN FEDERATION
BELARUS
POLAND
UKRAINE
MOLDOVA
ROMANIA
HUNGARY
SLOVAKIA
SERB. & MON. (YUGO.)
BULGARIA
GEORGIA
MINSK
KIEV (KYYIV)
CHIŞINĂU
BUCHAREST (BUCUREŞTI)
Black Sea
Sea of Azov
Crimea
Carpathian Mountains
Transylvania
Wallachia
Transylvanian Alps
Pripet Marshes
Dnieper Lowland
Black Sea Lowland
Great Hungarian Plain
Caucasus
SCALE BAR
0 km 50 100
0 miles 50 100

EUROPEAN RUSSIA

RUSSIAN FEDERATION

European Russia is separated from the Asiatic part of the Russian Federation by the Ural Mountains. It is home to two-thirds of the country's population. Russia was the largest and most powerful republic of the communist Soviet Union, which collapsed in 1991. Though new businesses were set up when communism ended, many old state industries closed down, causing unemployment and further hardship for many people.

POPULATION

Three-quarters of European Russia's people live in towns and cities, most in a broad band stretching south from Saint Petersburg to Moscow, and eastwards to the Urals. The capital, Moscow, and Saint Petersburg are very crowded cities. Living conditions there are cramped, with two families often sharing one flat. The southeast is also heavily populated. Over 12 million people live in the cities and towns which line the banks of the River Volga.

INHABITANTS PER SQ KM

- More than 100
- 50–100
- 10–50
- Less than 10
- Capital city
- Major city

INDUSTRY

European Russia is rich in natural resources. Minerals are mined on the Kola Peninsula, and in the Urals, while dense forests are felled and processed in many of the larger northern cities. The Volga basin is one of Europe's largest sources of oil and gas. Moscow, and the cities near the Volga are centres of skilled labour for a wide range of manufacturing industries like cars, chemicals and heavy engineering and steel production.

INDUSTRY

- Car manufacture
- Chemicals
- Engineering
- Iron & steel
- Textiles
- Mining
- Oil & gas
- Timber processing
- Major industrial centre/area
- Major road

THE LANDSCAPE

European Russia lies on the North European Plain, a huge, rolling lowland with wide river basins. The northern half of the plain, which was once covered by glaciers, has many lakes and swamps. The River Volga drains much of the plain as it flows south to the Caspian Sea. The Caucasus and Ural mountains form natural boundaries in the south and east.

Northern European Russia (C3)
Northern European Russia reaches into the Arctic Circle. It is a region of pine and birch forests, marshes and tundra. There are also tens of thousands of lakes, including the biggest in Europe, Ladoga, which covers about 17,700 sq km.

Ural Mountains (E5)
The Ural Mountains run from north to south, stretching almost 4,020 km.

Lake Ladoga (B4)

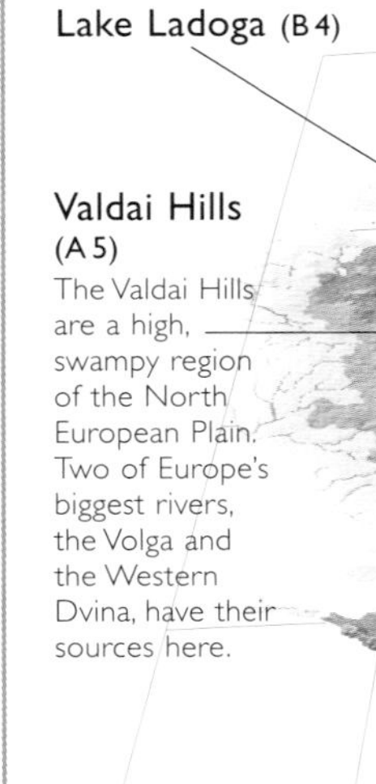

Valdai Hills (A5)
The Valdai Hills are a high, swampy region of the North European Plain. Two of Europe's biggest rivers, the Volga and the Western Dvina, have their sources here.

The North European Plain (C4)
The North European Plain sweeps west from the Ural Mountains, all the way to the River Rhine in Germany. In European Russia it includes a number of hill ranges, such as the Volga Uplands and the Central Russian Upland.

River Volga (C7)
The River Volga flows for 3,688 km, making it Europe's longest river and Russia's most important inland waterway. It is used for transport and to generate hydro-electric power.

Caspian Sea (C9)

Caucasus (A9)
This massive barrier of mountains stretches from the Black Sea to the Caspian Sea. It includes El'brus, the highest peak in Europe, at 5,642 m.

FARMING AND LAND USE

Russia's best farmland lies within this region. Big crops of wheat, barley and oats, potatoes and sunflowers are produced in the fertile black soil which forms a thick band across the country to the south of Moscow. The far north is cold and frozen, with bare mountains and tundra making cultivation impossible. Further south there are extensive forests, and rough pastures used for herding and hunting.

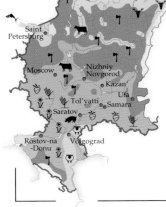

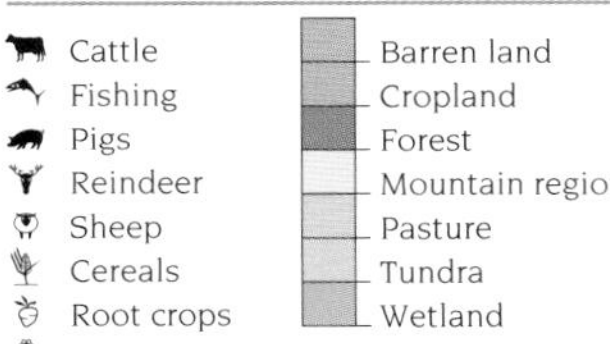

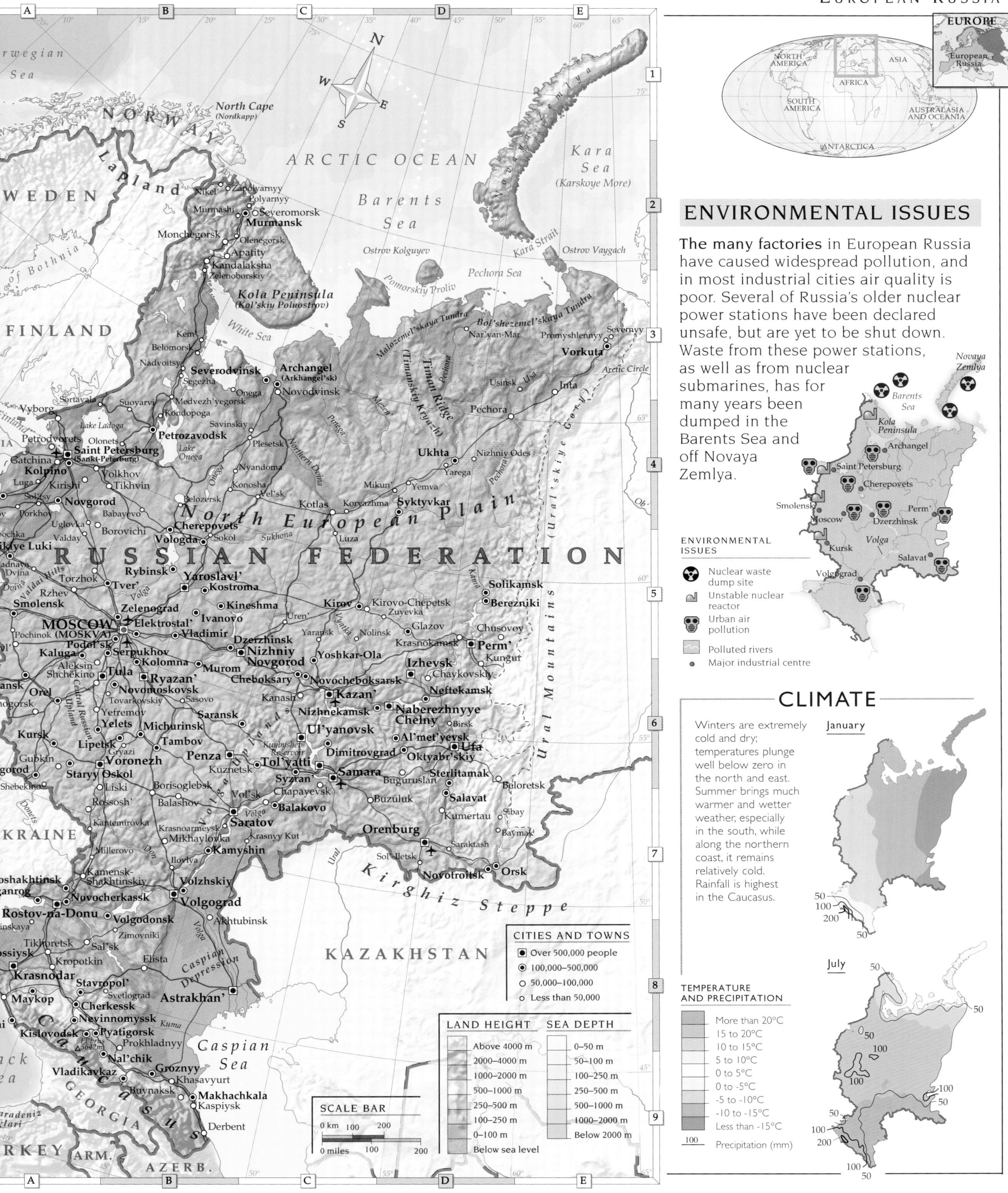
ENVIRONMENTAL ISSUES
The many factories in European Russia have caused widespread pollution, and in most industrial cities air quality is poor. Several of Russia's older nuclear power stations have been declared unsafe, but are yet to be shut down. Waste from these power stations, as well as from nuclear submarines, has for many years been dumped in the Barents Sea and off Novaya Zemlya.
ENVIRONMENTAL ISSUES
Nuclear waste dump site
Unstable nuclear reactor
Urban air pollution
Polluted rivers
Major industrial centre
CLIMATE
Winters are extremely cold and dry; temperatures plunge well below zero in the north and east. Summer brings much warmer and wetter weather, especially in the south, while along the northern coast, it remains relatively cold. Rainfall is highest in the Caucasus.
January
July
TEMPERATURE AND PRECIPITATION
More than 20°C
15 to 20°C
10 to 15°C
5 to 10°C
0 to 5°C
0 to -5°C
-5 to -10°C
-10 to -15°C
Less than -15°C
Precipitation (mm)
CITIES AND TOWNS
Over 500,000 people
100,000–500,000
50,000–100,000
Less than 50,000
LAND HEIGHT
Above 4000 m
2000–4000 m
1000–2000 m
500–1000 m
250–500 m
100–250 m
0–100 m
Below sea level
SEA DEPTH
0–50 m
50–100 m
100–250 m
250–500 m
500–1000 m
1000–2000 m
Below 2000 m
SCALE BAR
ARCTIC OCEAN
Barents Sea
Kara Sea
RUSSIAN FEDERATION
North European Plain
KAZAKHSTAN
Kirghiz Steppe
Caspian Sea
MOSCOW (MOSKVA)
Saint Petersburg
Ural Mountains

THE MEDITERRANEAN

The Mediterranean Sea separates Europe from Africa. It stretches more than 4,000 km from east to west and is almost completely enclosed by land. Many great civilizations, including the Greek and Roman empires grew up around the Mediterranean. It has been a crossroads of international trade routes for many centuries. More than 100 million people live in the 28 countries which border the sea and their numbers are increased by the large crowds of tourists who regularly visit the area.

ENVIRONMENTAL ISSUES

Sea pollution is widespread in the Mediterranean, especially near the large coastal resorts where raw sewage and industrial effluent is pumped out to sea and often ends up on the beaches. Oil refining and oil spills have also furthered pollution.

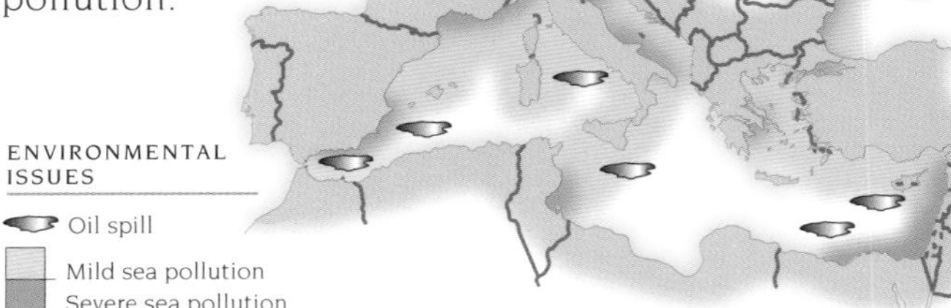

SCALE BAR
0 km 100 200
0 miles 100 200

LAND HEIGHT
Above 4000 m
2000–4000 m
1000–2000 m
500–1000 m
250–500 m
100–250 m
0–100 m
Below sea level

SEA DEPTH
0–250 m
250–500 m
500–1000 m
1000–2000 m
2000–3000 m
3000–4000 m
Below 4000 m

CITIES AND TOWNS
Over 500,000 people
100,000–500,000
50,000–100,000
Less than 50,000

MALTA

CYPRUS

TURKISH REPUBLIC OF NORTHERN CYPRUS (recognized only by Turkey)

THE LANDSCAPE

The Mediterranean Sea would be an enormous lake if it were not for the Strait of Gibraltar, a narrow opening only 13 km wide, which joins it to the Atlantic Ocean. The Mediterranean lies over the boundary of two continental plates. Where they meet, earthquakes and volcanoes are common.

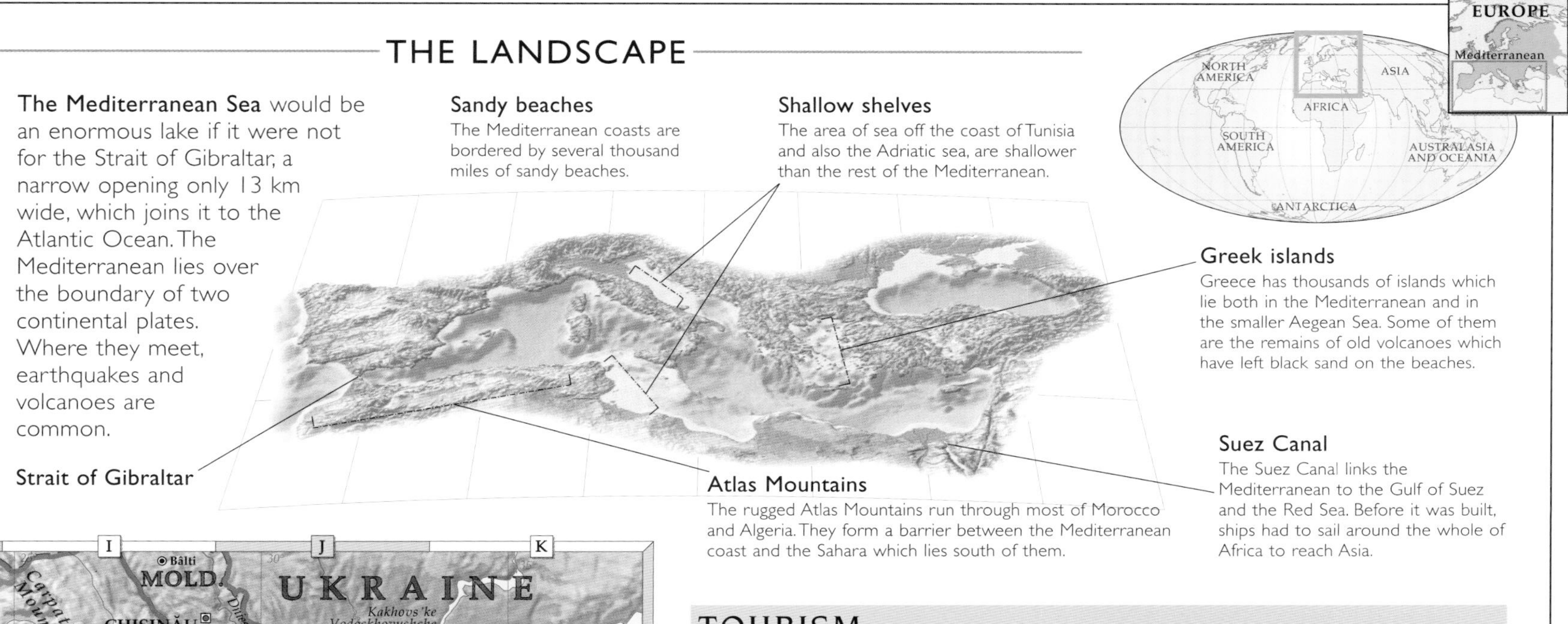

Sandy beaches
The Mediterranean coasts are bordered by several thousand miles of sandy beaches.

Shallow shelves
The area of sea off the coast of Tunisia and also the Adriatic sea, are shallower than the rest of the Mediterranean.

Greek islands
Greece has thousands of islands which lie both in the Mediterranean and in the smaller Aegean Sea. Some of them are the remains of old volcanoes which have left black sand on the beaches.

Strait of Gibraltar

Atlas Mountains
The rugged Atlas Mountains run through most of Morocco and Algeria. They form a barrier between the Mediterranean coast and the Sahara which lies south of them.

Suez Canal
The Suez Canal links the Mediterranean to the Gulf of Suez and the Red Sea. Before it was built, ships had to sail around the whole of Africa to reach Asia.

TOURISM

The tourist industry in and around the Mediterranean is one of the most highly developed in the world. More than half the world's income from tourism is generated here. Resorts have grown up along the northwest coast of Africa, and in Egypt, in southern Spain, France, Italy, Greece and Turkey. Tourism brings huge economic benefits, but the ever-increasing number of visitors has also damaged the environment.

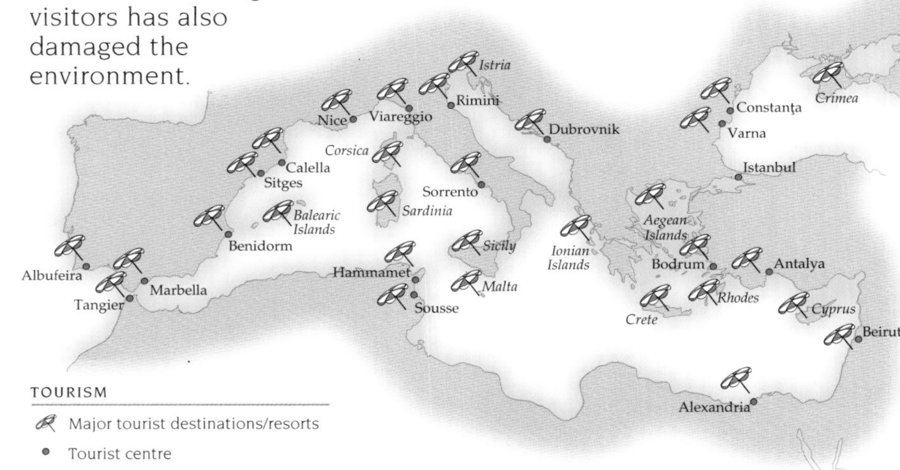

INDUSTRY

The Mediterranean has a large fishing industry, although most of the fishing is small-scale. Tuna and sardines are caught throughout the region and mussels are farmed off the coast of Italy. Fish canning and packing takes place at most of the larger ports. Small oil and gas reserves are extracted off the coast of North Africa and near Greece, Spain and Italy.

Genoa
Marseille
Livorno
Constanţa
Barcelona
Rome
Istanbul
Valencia
Naples
Izmir
Palermo
Piraeus
Málaga
Tunis
Antalya
Algiers
Oran
Sfax
Valletta
Tripoli
Beruit
Benghazi
Alexandria
Tel Aviv-Yafo
Port Said
Cairo

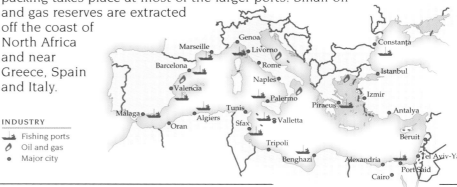

INDUSTRY
Fishing ports
Oil and gas
Major city

Continental Asia

6,500 km
9,700 km

Asia is the world's largest continent, and has the greatest range of physical extremes. Some of the highest, lowest, and coldest places on Earth are found in Asia: Mount Everest in the Himalayas is the highest, the Dead Sea in the west is the lowest, and the frozen wastes of northern Siberia are among the coldest. More people live in Asia than on any other continent – 1.29 billion of them in China, and 1.04 billion in India.

Cross-section through Asia

The Gulf
Arabian Peninsula
Iranian Plateau
Himalayas
Plateau of Tibet
Mouth of the Ganges
Yellow River
Taiwan
W — 7,800 km — E

The Arabian Peninsula and the mountainous Iranian Plateau are divided by The Gulf, fed by the Tigris and Euphrates rivers. Further east, the land begins to rise, the mountains spreading north to the Plateau of Tibet, and south to the Himalayas. The plains to the south of the Himalayas are drained by the Indus and Ganges, and to the east of the Plateau of Tibet by the Yellow River.

Physical Asia

Northern Asia is made up of old mountains and ancient, stable plateaus. The jagged Himalayan mountains dominate the central part of the continent, along with the Plateau of Tibet, which stretches north into China. In Southeast Asia, there are many islands. Volcanoes and earthquakes are common, and some of the islands are volcanically-formed.

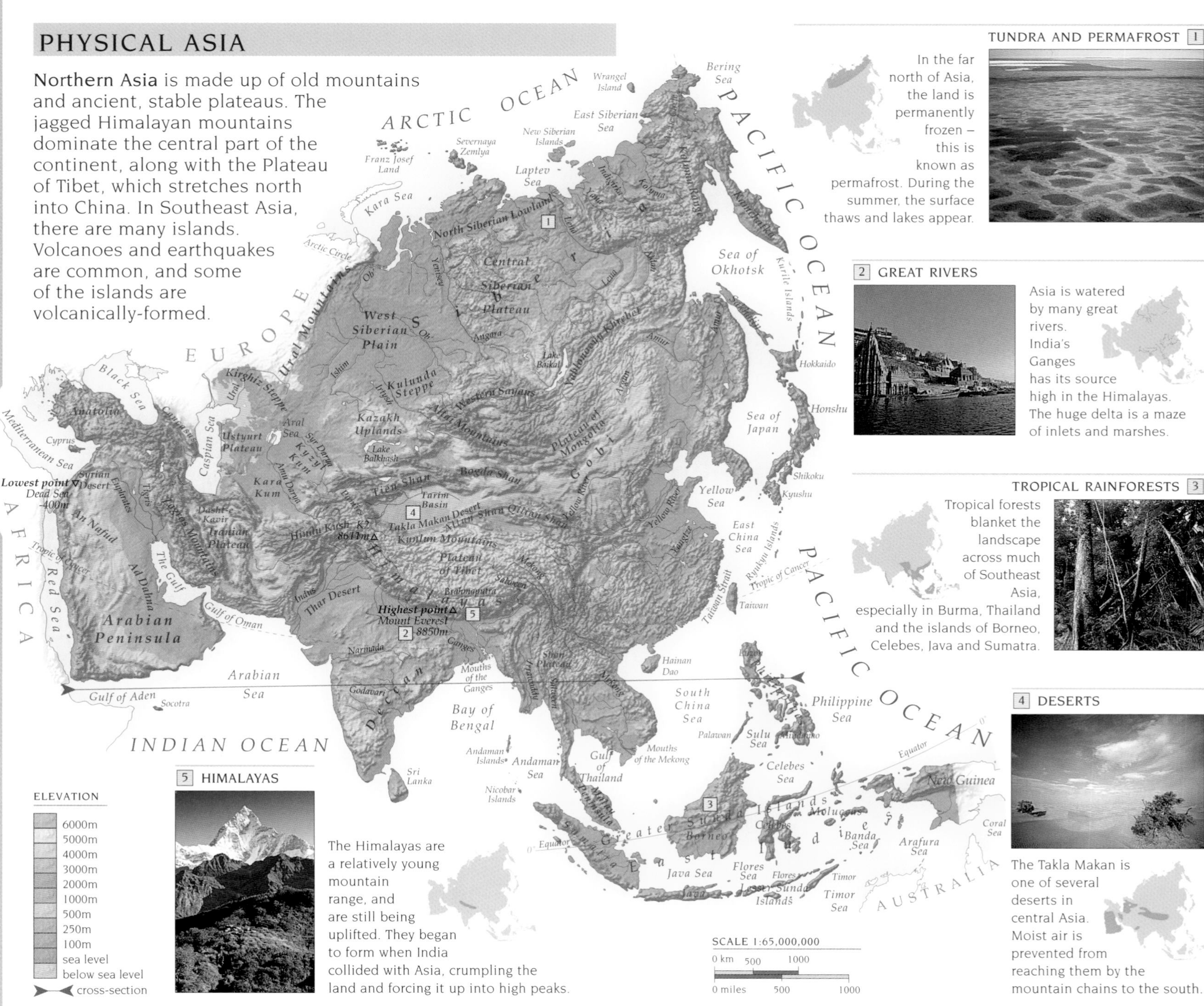

1 Tundra and permafrost

In the far north of Asia, the land is permanently frozen – this is known as permafrost. During the summer, the surface thaws and lakes appear.

2 Great rivers

Asia is watered by many great rivers. India's Ganges has its source high in the Himalayas. The huge delta is a maze of inlets and marshes.

3 Tropical rainforests

Tropical forests blanket the landscape across much of Southeast Asia, especially in Burma, Thailand and the islands of Borneo, Celebes, Java and Sumatra.

4 Deserts

The Takla Makan is one of several deserts in central Asia. Moist air is prevented from reaching them by the mountain chains to the south.

5 Himalayas

The Himalayas are a relatively young mountain range, and are still being uplifted. They began to form when India collided with Asia, crumpling the land and forcing it up into high peaks.

POLITICAL ASIA

Asia is a continent of many contrasts: in its lands, its peoples and its traditions. The break up of the Soviet Union, which once stretched south from Russia to Iran, produced the new central Asian republics of Kazakhstan, Kyrgyzstan, Tajikistan, Turkmenistan and Uzbekistan. The countries in southwest Asia are mainly Muslim, but are divided by religious differences and conflicts. India is the world's largest democracy, while China is a communist power with restricted access to the rest of the world.

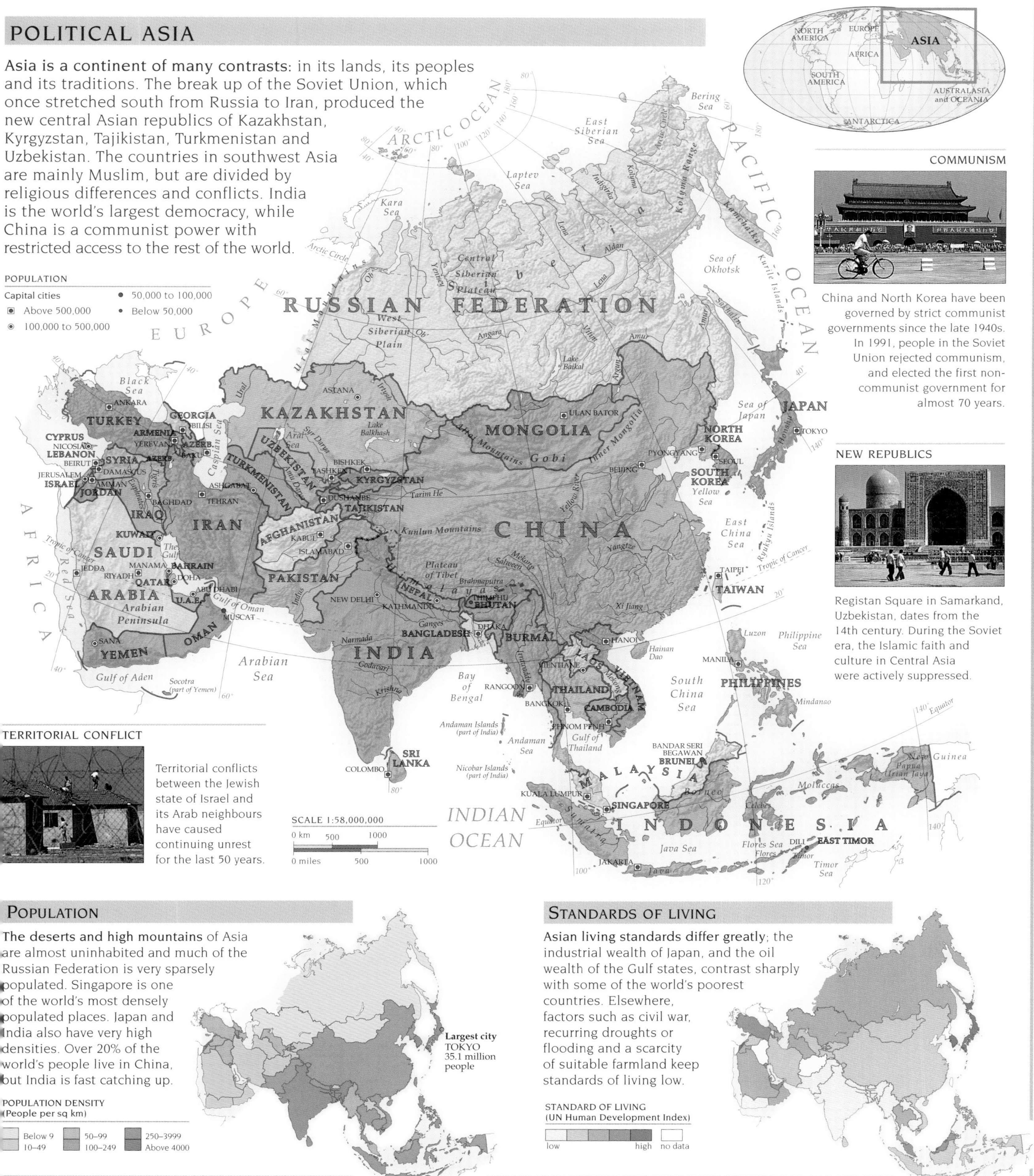

China and North Korea have been governed by strict communist governments since the late 1940s. In 1991, people in the Soviet Union rejected communism, and elected the first non-communist government for almost 70 years.

NEW REPUBLICS

Registan Square in Samarkand, Uzbekistan, dates from the 14th century. During the Soviet era, the Islamic faith and culture in Central Asia were actively suppressed.

TERRITORIAL CONFLICT

Territorial conflicts between the Jewish state of Israel and its Arab neighbours have caused continuing unrest for the last 50 years.

POPULATION

The deserts and high mountains of Asia are almost uninhabited and much of the Russian Federation is very sparsely populated. Singapore is one of the world's most densely populated places. Japan and India also have very high densities. Over 20% of the world's people live in China, but India is fast catching up.

STANDARDS OF LIVING

Asian living standards differ greatly; the industrial wealth of Japan, and the oil wealth of the Gulf states, contrast sharply with some of the world's poorest countries. Elsewhere, factors such as civil war, recurring droughts or flooding and a scarcity of suitable farmland keep standards of living low.

ASIAN GEOGRAPHY

Asia's forbidding mountain ranges, barren deserts and fertile plains have affected the way in which people settled the continent. Intensive agriculture is found in the more fertile areas, and the largest concentrations of people grew up near fertile land, and close to great rivers. Asia's mineral wealth has brought people to the more inhospitable parts of the continent; the deserts of southwest Asia for oil, and frozen Siberia for oil, gas, and minerals.

INDUSTRY

Many people in Asia still rely on agriculture as a source of income, and some countries have very few industries. Heavy industry dominates eastern China and Russia, but Japan is the most industrially productive country. In recent years, booming 'tiger' economies have developed in countries such as Taiwan, which border the Pacific Ocean.

GNP per capita (US$)

- Below 1999
- 2000-4999
- 5000-9999
- 10,000-19,999
- 20,000-24,999
- Above 25,000
- Industrial centre

INDUSTRY

- Aerospace
- Brewing
- Car/vehicle manufacture
- Cement
- Chemicals
- Coal
- Electronics
- Engineering
- Finance
- Food processing
- Hi-tech industry
- Iron & steel
- Mining
- Oil & gas
- Pharmaceuticals
- Printing & publishing
- Shipbuilding
- Textiles
- Timber processing

MINERAL RESOURCES

Over half of the world's oil and gas reserves are in Asia, most importantly around The Gulf, and in western Siberia. Coal in Siberia and China has provided power for steel industries. Metallic minerals are also abundant: tin in Southeast Asia, and platinum and nickel in Siberia.

MINERAL RESOURCES

- Chromium
- Tin
- Nickel
- Iron
- Platinum
- Gold
- Lead
- Oil/gas field
- Coal field

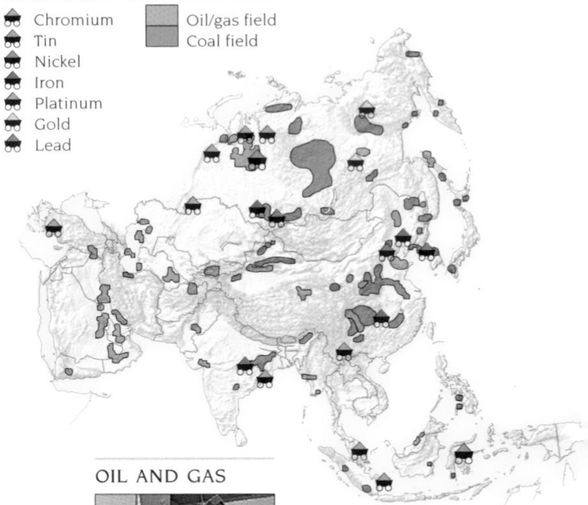

OIL AND GAS

The discovery of oil in The Gulf has generated enormous wealth, and produced rapid industrial and social change in countries such as Saudi Arabia, U.A.E. and Kuwait which control the oil supplies.

HI-TECH INDUSTRIES

Japan is a world-leading producer of electronic and hi-tech goods like computers, cameras and hi-fi equipment. Taiwan, South Korea and Singapore also produce electronic goods.

FINANCE

Mumbai is India's leading industrial city, and has a thriving stock market. Modern office blocks stand close to sprawling slums.

INDUSTRIAL COMPLEXES

Noril'sk is one of several Soviet-era industrial complexes built in Russia. It is a processing centre for the rich mineral reserves found nearby.

TRADITIONAL INDUSTRIES

Traditional industries and methods of working are still important to less industrialized nations. Here in Vietnam, sea water has been evaporated by the sun, and the salt is collected for market.

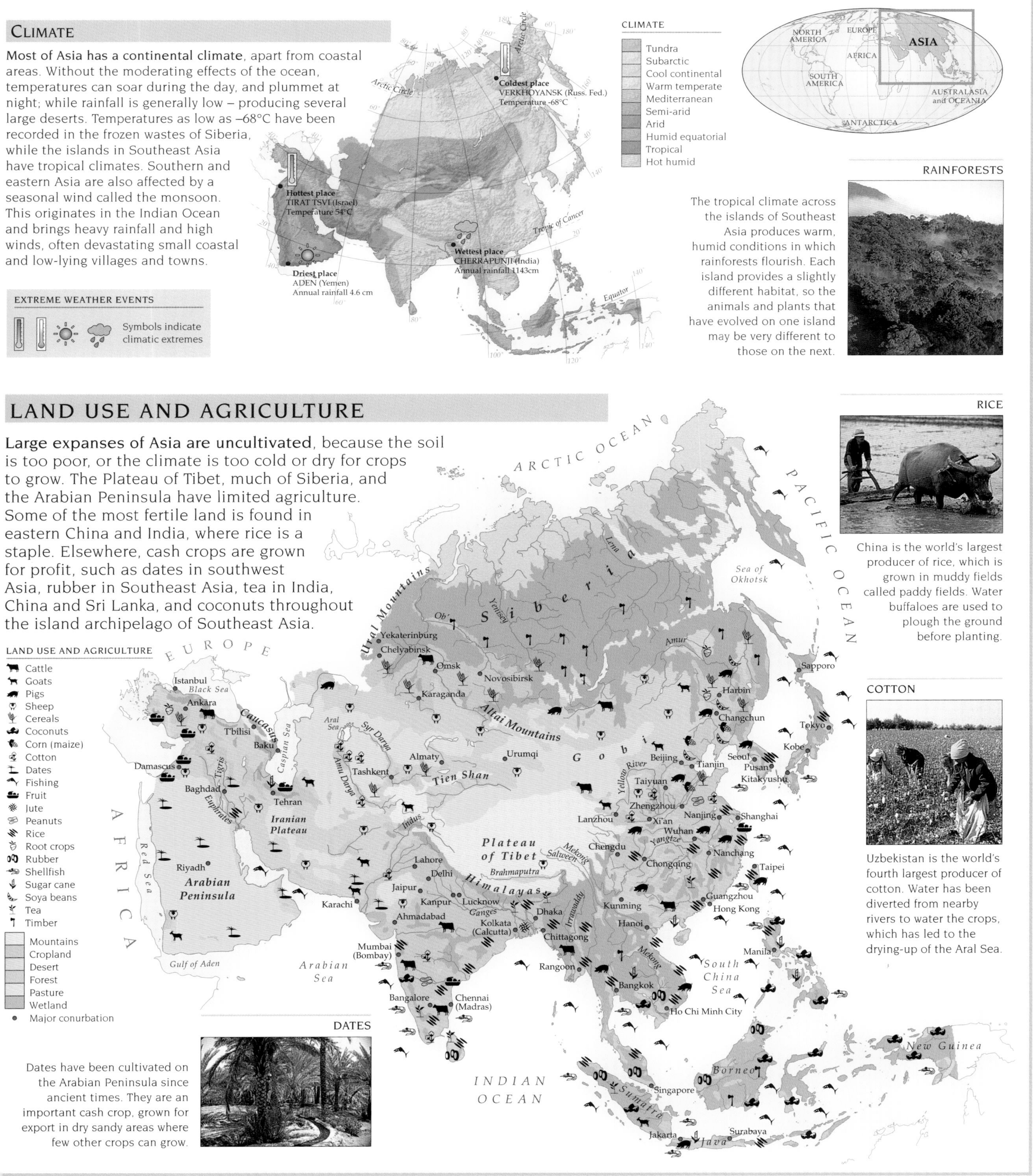

CLIMATE

Most of Asia has a continental climate, apart from coastal areas. Without the moderating effects of the ocean, temperatures can soar during the day, and plummet at night; while rainfall is generally low – producing several large deserts. Temperatures as low as –68°C have been recorded in the frozen wastes of Siberia, while the islands in Southeast Asia have tropical climates. Southern and eastern Asia are also affected by a seasonal wind called the monsoon. This originates in the Indian Ocean and brings heavy rainfall and high winds, often devastating small coastal and low-lying villages and towns.

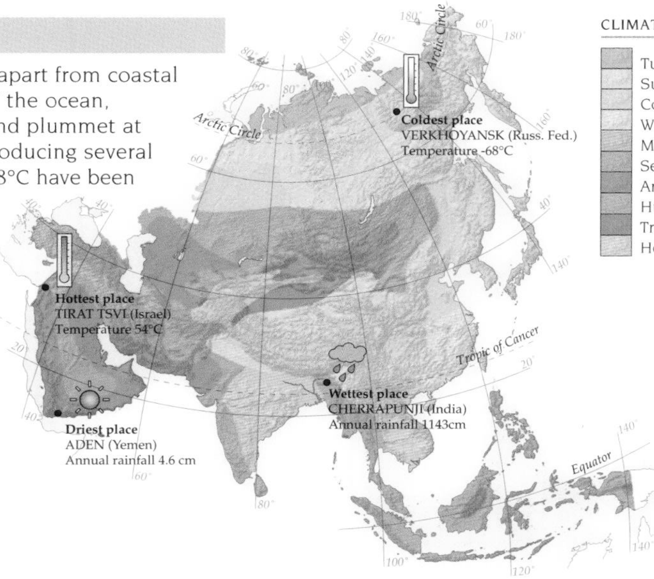

EXTREME WEATHER EVENTS

Symbols indicate climatic extremes

CLIMATE

- Tundra
- Subarctic
- Cool continental
- Warm temperate
- Mediterranean
- Semi-arid
- Arid
- Humid equatorial
- Tropical
- Hot humid

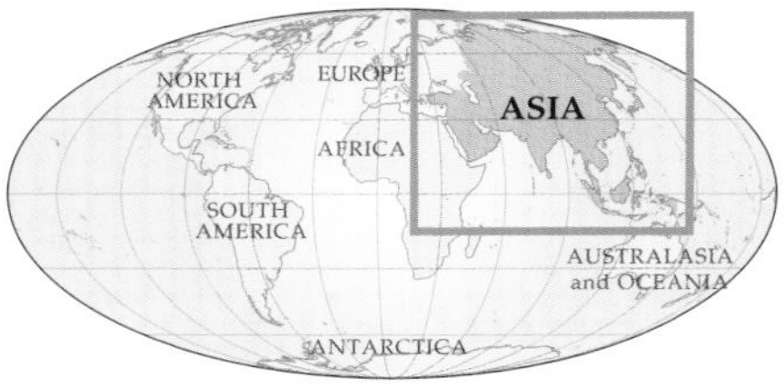

RAINFORESTS

The tropical climate across the islands of Southeast Asia produces warm, humid conditions in which rainforests flourish. Each island provides a slightly different habitat, so the animals and plants that have evolved on one island may be very different to those on the next.

LAND USE AND AGRICULTURE

Large expanses of Asia are uncultivated, because the soil is too poor, or the climate is too cold or dry for crops to grow. The Plateau of Tibet, much of Siberia, and the Arabian Peninsula have limited agriculture. Some of the most fertile land is found in eastern China and India, where rice is a staple. Elsewhere, cash crops are grown for profit, such as dates in southwest Asia, rubber in Southeast Asia, tea in India, China and Sri Lanka, and coconuts throughout the island archipelago of Southeast Asia.

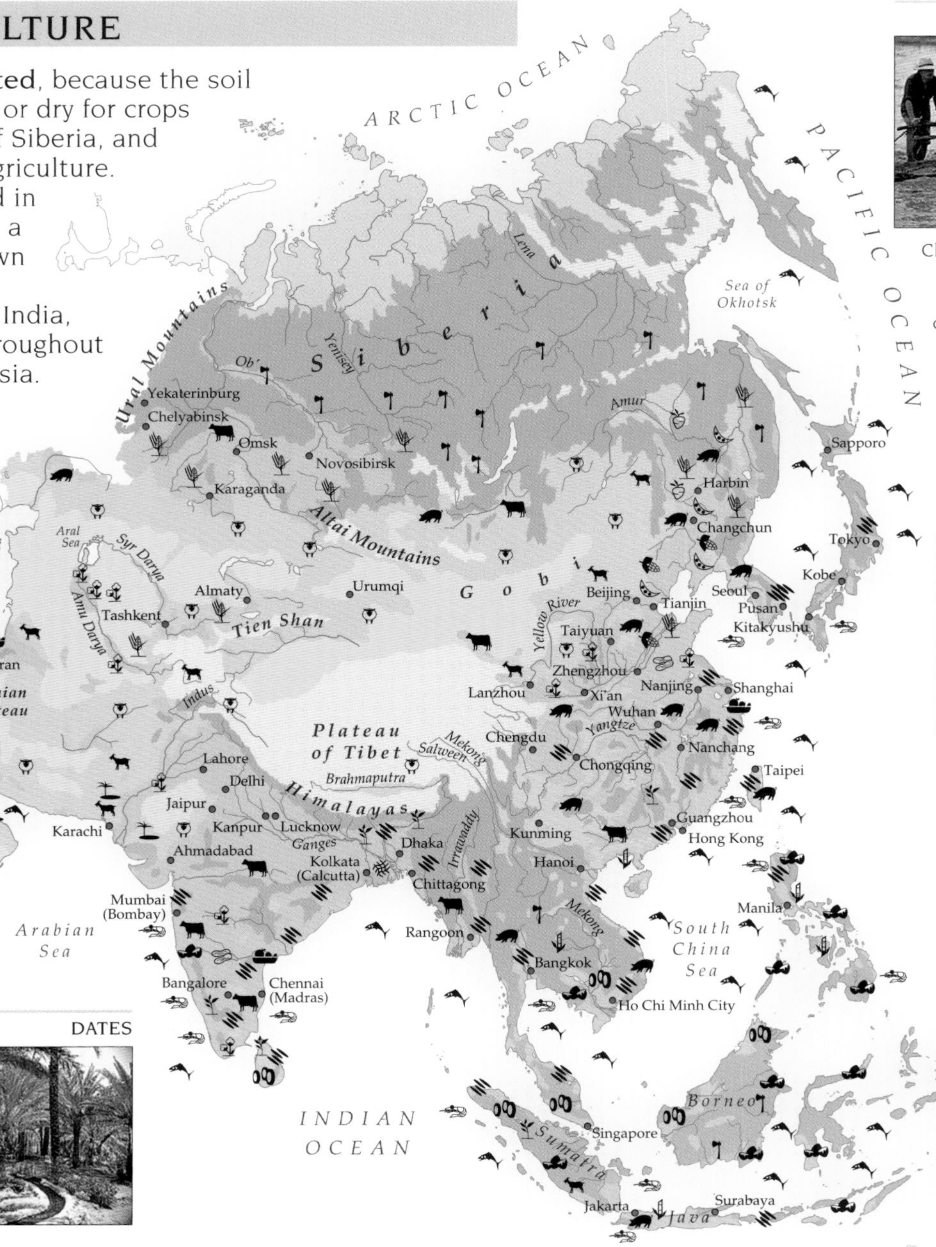

LAND USE AND AGRICULTURE

- Cattle
- Goats
- Pigs
- Sheep
- Cereals
- Coconuts
- Corn (maize)
- Cotton
- Dates
- Fishing
- Fruit
- Jute
- Peanuts
- Rice
- Root crops
- Rubber
- Shellfish
- Sugar cane
- Soya beans
- Tea
- Timber
- Mountains
- Cropland
- Desert
- Forest
- Pasture
- Wetland
- Major conurbation

RICE

China is the world's largest producer of rice, which is grown in muddy fields called paddy fields. Water buffaloes are used to plough the ground before planting.

COTTON

Uzbekistan is the world's fourth largest producer of cotton. Water has been diverted from nearby rivers to water the crops, which has led to the drying-up of the Aral Sea.

DATES

Dates have been cultivated on the Arabian Peninsula since ancient times. They are an important cash crop, grown for export in dry sandy areas where few other crops can grow.

Russia and Kazakhstan

Russia lies partly in Europe, but mostly in Asia. The land to the east of the Ural Mountains is called Siberia. This immense stretch of grasslands, thick, evergreen forest and tundra is crossed by giant rivers. Vast areas of Siberia are almost untouched by human activity, yet in the industrial regions set up under communism (1922–1991), air, water and soil are heavily polluted with harmful substances. Along with the former Soviet state of Kazakhstan, Siberia is rich in a huge variety of minerals.

INDUSTRY

The discovery of gold in the 19th century opened Siberia up to economic and industrial development. Later, vast reserves of oil, coal and gas were found, especially in the west, which is now the main centre for oil extraction. Gold and diamonds are mined in the east. In Kazakhstan, mining and other industries are growing, with the help of foreign investors.

THE LANDSCAPE

East of the Ural Mountains lies the West Siberian Plain – the world's biggest area of flat ground. The plain gradually rises to the Central Siberian Plateau, and then again to highlands in the southeast. Great coniferous forests called *taiga* stretch across most of this land. The far north of Siberia extends into the Arctic Circle. There, the landscape is made up of frozen plains called tundra. Much of Kazakhstan is covered by huge rolling grasslands, or steppe; in the south are arid sandy deserts.

Tundra and *taiga*
Stubby birch trees, dwarf bushes, moss and lichen huddle close to the ground in the frozen tundra wastes of northern Russia. They lie between the permanent ice and snow of the Arctic, and the thick *taiga* forests which cover an area greater than the Amazon rainforest.

The Caspian Sea (A5)
The Caspian Sea covers 371,000 sq km and is the world's largest expanse of inland water. It is fed by the Volga and Ural rivers, which flow in from the plains of the north.

West Siberian Plain (D4)
This vast, flat expanse is covered with a network of marshes and streams. The Ob' river, which winds its way north across the plains, is frozen for up to half the year.

Lake Baikal (F5)
Lake Baikal is the deepest lake in the world, and the largest freshwater one – it is more than 1.6 km deep, and covers 32,500 sq km. It is fed by 336 rivers and contains around 20% of all the fresh water in the world.

CLIMATE

Russia and Kazakhstan have strongly continental climates, and their distance away from seas and oceans means that temperatures fluctuate wildly, both daily and seasonally. Temperatures in eastern Siberia have been known to reach -68°C.

TEMPERATURE AND PRECIPITATION

- More than 30°C
- 25 to 30°C
- 20 to 25°C
- 15 to 20°C
- 10 to 15°C
- 5 to 10°C
- 0 to 5°C
- 0 to -5°C
- -5 to -10°C
- -10 to -15°C
- Less than -15°C
- 100 Precipitation (mm)

January

July

FARMING AND LAND USE

Siberia's harsh climate has restricted farming to the south, where there are a few areas warm enough to grow cereal crops, such as wheat and oats, and to raise cattle on the small pockets of pasture. The rest of the region is used for hunting, herding reindeer, and forestry – the *taiga* forests contain the world's biggest timber reserves. In Kazakhstan, big herds of cattle, goats and sheep are raised for wool and meat, and wheat is cultivated in the fertile north.

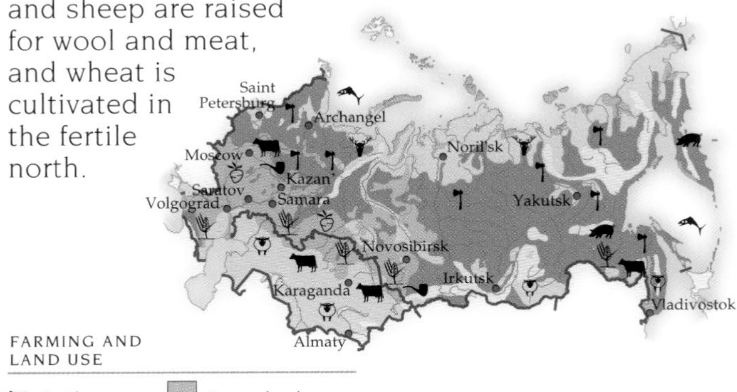

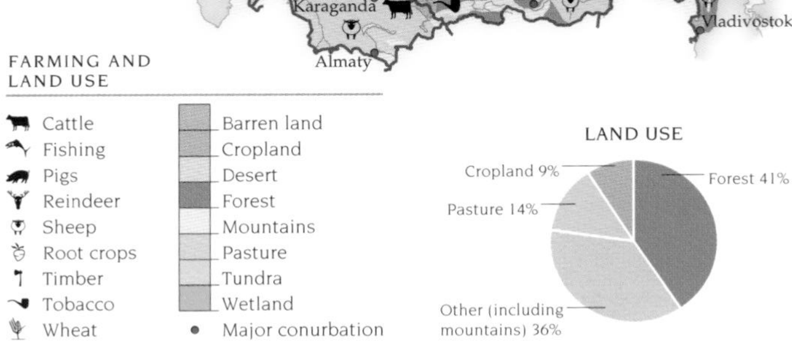

LAND USE

- Forest 41%
- Cropland 9%
- Pasture 14%
- Other (including mountains) 36%

POPULATION

Siberia has some of the world's largest areas of uninhabited land – the bitingly cold climate and harsh living conditions have kept the population small. The industrial cities in the west hold the most people. Despite its huge size, Kazakhstan has only 16 million people; most of whom live in urban areas.

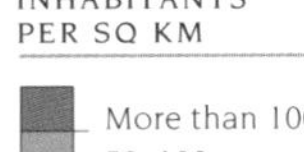

INHABITANTS PER SQ KM

- More than 100
- 50–100
- 10–50
- Less than 10
- Capital city
- Major city

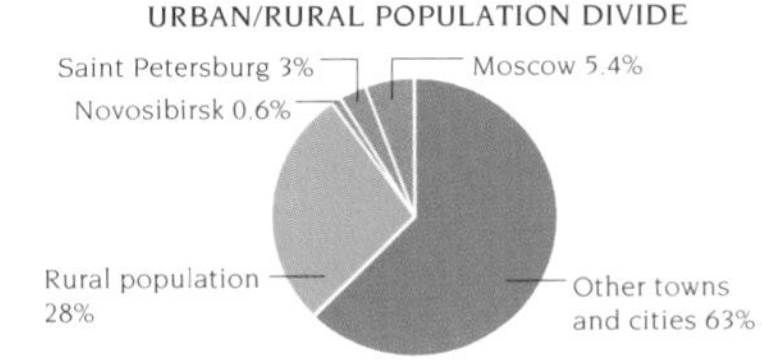

ENVIRONMENTAL ISSUES

Decades of industrial development during the communist regime brought new industries to undeveloped parts of the region, like Siberia. This industrial development has now led to environmental degradation on a massive scale and river, air and land pollution in Russia is among the worst in the world.

TURKEY AND THE CAUCASUS

ARMENIA, AZERBAIJAN, GEORGIA, TURKEY

Turkey and the Caucasus lie partly in Europe, partly in Asia. Turkey has a long Islamic tradition, and although the country is now a secular (non-religious) one, most Turks are Muslims. Turkey is becoming more industrialized, although half its workforce is still employed in agriculture. The ancient countries of the Caucasus were under Russian rule for 70 years, until 1991. They are home to more than 50 different ethnic groups.

INDUSTRY

Turkey has a wide range of industries, including tourism and growing trade links with Europe. Azerbaijan has large oil reserves and is able to export oil. The other states use imported fuel and hydro-electric power generated by their rushing rivers. Georgia produces industrial machinery and chemicals. Armenia's economy is recovering from civil war and earthquake damage.

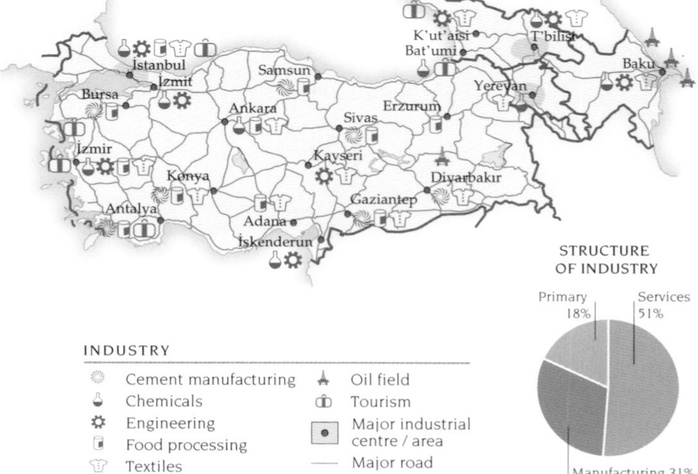

FARMING AND LAND USE

With its warm climate and good soils, Turkey is able to produce all of its own food. Cattle and goats are kept on the central plateau. Along the Mediterranean coast, farmers grow olives, figs, grapes and peaches. Hazelnuts are cultivated along the shores of the Black Sea. Across the Caucasus, the limited fertile land is used to grow wine grapes, tobacco and cotton.

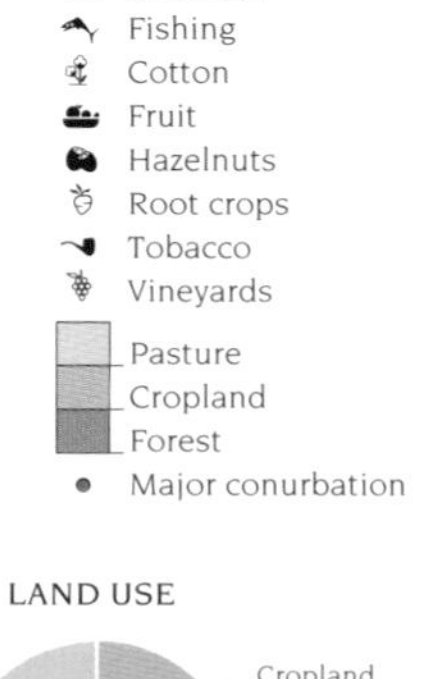

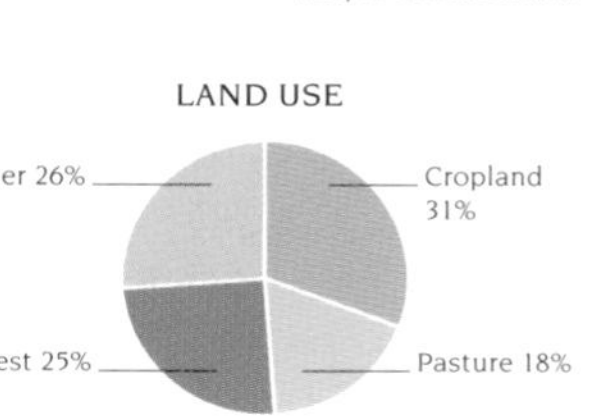

THE LANDSCAPE

A huge semi-arid plateau called Anatolia runs across the centre of Turkey. It is rimmed by several mountain ranges along the Black Sea coast, and the steep Taurus Mountains in the south. A narrow strip of lowland separates the Caucasus and the Lesser Caucasus mountains in the northeast.

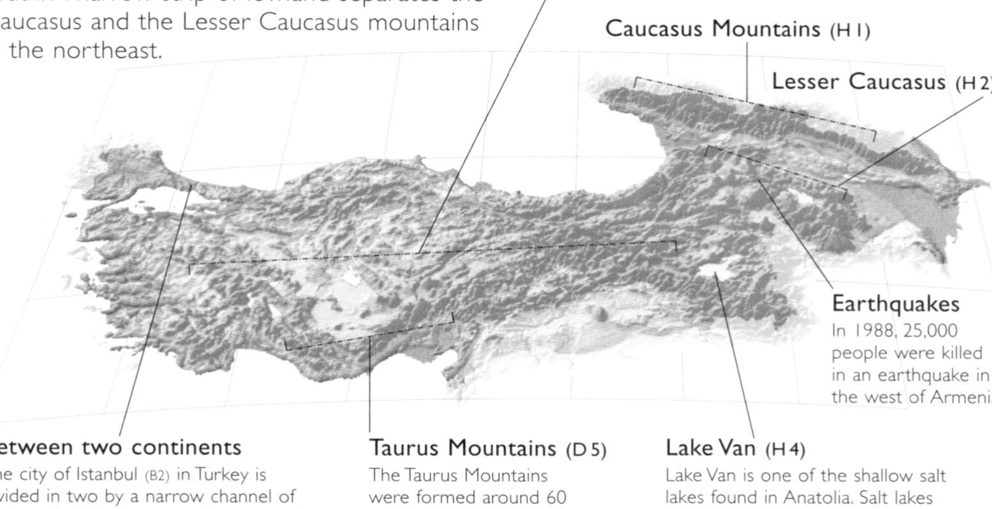

Anatolia
Anatolia has large areas of soft limestone rock. Over a long period of time, layers of rock have been worn away by water to produce strange landscapes with caves, and tall, isolated rock pinnacles.

Caucasus Mountains (H1)

Lesser Caucasus (H2)

Earthquakes
In 1988, 25,000 people were killed in an earthquake in the west of Armenia.

Between two continents
The city of Istanbul (B2) in Turkey is divided in two by a narrow channel of water called the Bosporus. One part of the city is in Europe, the other in Asia. The two parts are linked by bridges.

Taurus Mountains (D5)
The Taurus Mountains were formed around 60 to 65 million years ago. Weathering has formed caves and deep gorges.

Lake Van (H4)
Lake Van is one of the shallow salt lakes found in Anatolia. Salt lakes develop in hot, dry areas where large quantities of water evaporate, leaving behind salty deposits.

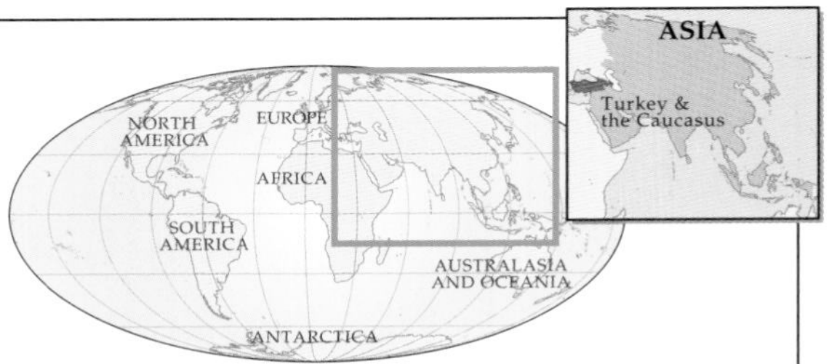

POPULATION

Over 65% of Turks live in large towns or cities, mostly in the western half of the country. The eastern and southeastern parts of Anatolia are home to the Kurdish people. The Caucasian republics became more industrialized under Russian rule, and today, over half of their people live in urban places.

INHABITANTS PER SQ KM

- More than 200
- 100–200
- 50–100
- Less than 50
- Capital city
- Major city

URBAN/RURAL POPULATION DIVIDE

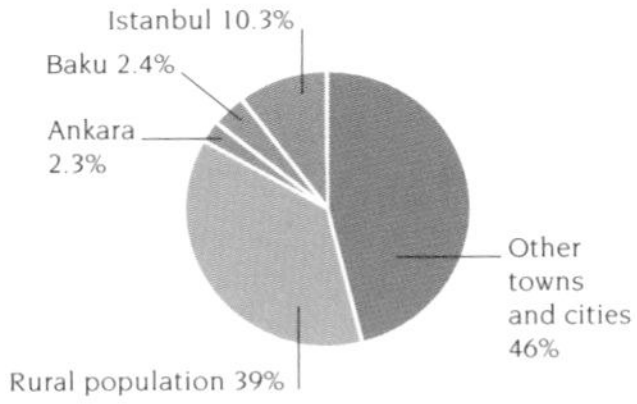

ENVIRONMENTAL ISSUES

Turkey has built many large dams to use water from rivers – especially the Euphrates – to irrigate its farmland. Syria and Iraq, which lie downstream, have opposed the dams, because they will have less water flowing into their countries. The safety of old-style nuclear plants such as Metsamor in Armenia has caused concern.

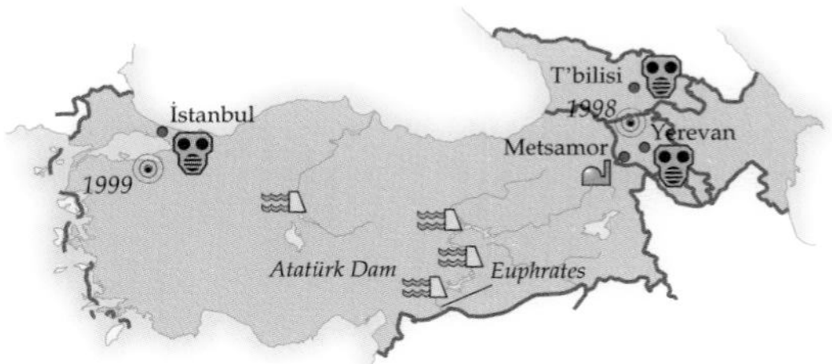

ENVIRONMENTAL ISSUES

- Earthquake zone
- Major dam
- Unstable nuclear power station
- Urban air pollution
- Major industrial centre

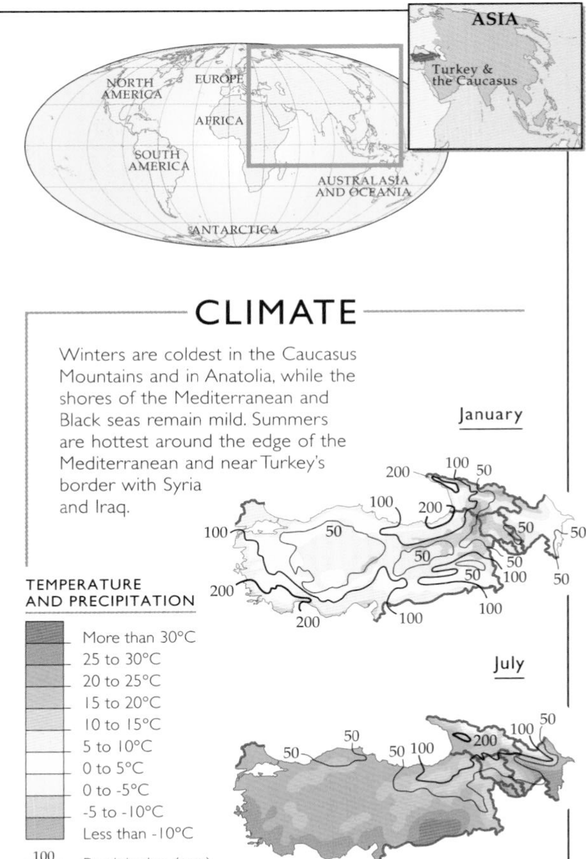

CLIMATE

Winters are coldest in the Caucasus Mountains and in Anatolia, while the shores of the Mediterranean and Black seas remain mild. Summers are hottest around the edge of the Mediterranean and near Turkey's border with Syria and Iraq.

January

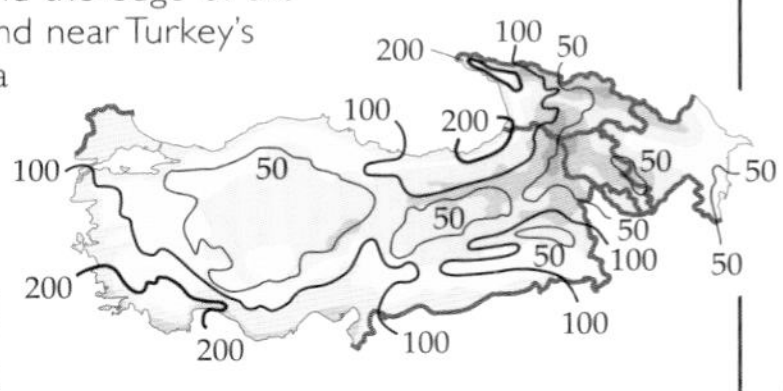

July

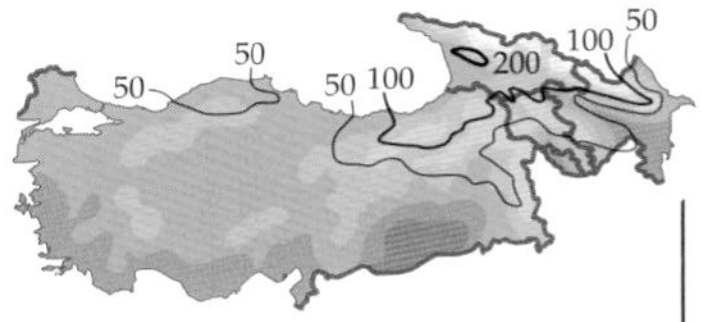

TEMPERATURE AND PRECIPITATION

- More than 30°C
- 25 to 30°C
- 20 to 25°C
- 15 to 20°C
- 10 to 15°C
- 5 to 10°C
- 0 to 5°C
- 0 to -5°C
- -5 to -10°C
- Less than -10°C
- 100 Precipitation (mm)

Southwest Asia

BAHRAIN, IRAN, IRAQ, ISRAEL, JORDAN, KUWAIT, LEBANON, OMAN, QATAR, SAUDI ARABIA, SYRIA, UNITED ARAB EMIRATES, YEMEN

Most of southwest Asia is barren desert, yet the world's first cities developed here, over 5,000 years ago. It was also the birthplace of three major religions: Islam, Judaism and Christianity. In recent years, the discovery of oil has brought great wealth to much of the region, but it has been torn by civil wars, and conflict between neighbouring countries. Most people here are Muslims, although Israel is the world's only Jewish state.

ENVIRONMENTAL ISSUES

Water shortages are common because of the hot, dry climate and the lack of rivers. Desalination plants convert sea water into fresh water, and are found along the Red Sea and Gulf coasts. Lack of water also makes the risk of desertification greater. Iran has had many catastrophic earthquakes; in 1978 an earthquake killed 25,000 people.

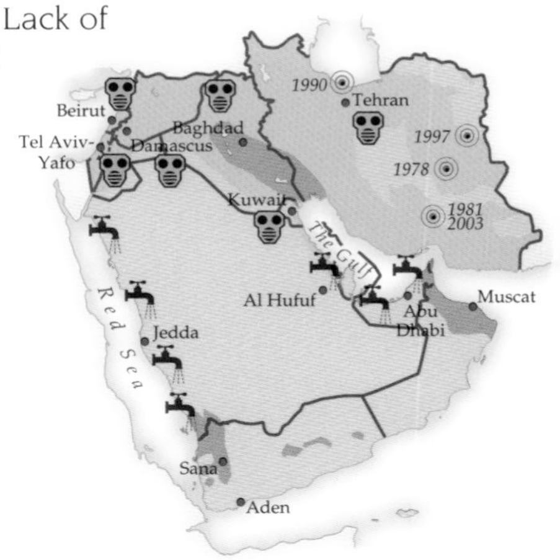

ENVIRONMENTAL ISSUES

- Area with many desalination plants
- Catastrophic earthquake
- Urban air pollution
- Existing desert
- Risk of desertification
- Major industrial centre

INDUSTRY

Oil has made the previously poor Arab states very wealthy. Oil and natural gas continue to be the main source of income for many of the countries here, although other industries are being developed to support their economies when these resources run out. Iran is famous for its carpets, which are woven from wool or silk.

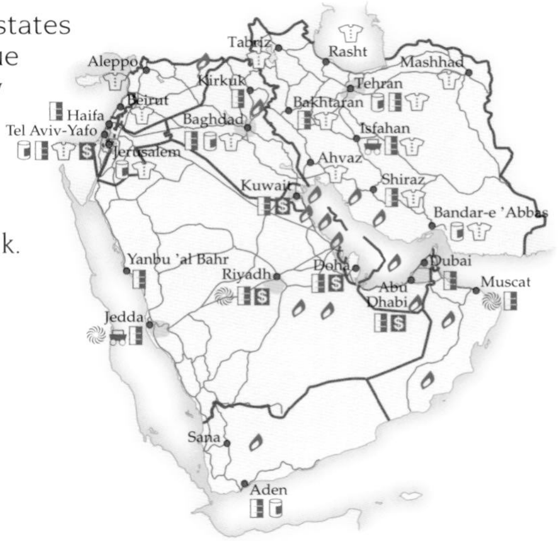

INDUSTRY

- Cement manufacturing
- Food processing
- Iron and steel
- Oil refining
- Textiles
- Oil and gas
- Finance
- Major industrial centre / area
- Major road

STRUCTURE OF INDUSTRY

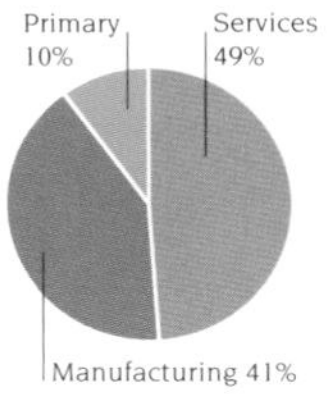

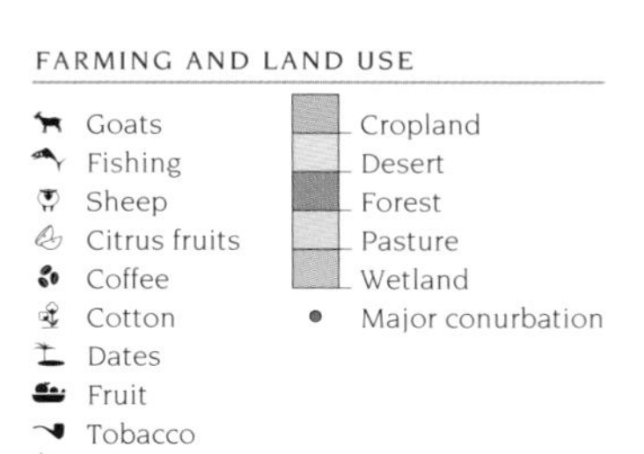

THE LANDSCAPE

Great desert plateaus, both sandy and rocky, cover much of southwest Asia. On the enormous Arabian Peninsula, which covers an area almost the size of India, narrow, sandy plains along the Red Sea and south coast rise to dry mountains. In the centre is a vast, high plateau that slopes gently down to the flat shores of the Gulf. The mountainous areas of Iran experience frequent earthquakes.

Wadis

Valleys or riverbeds, called *wadis*, are found in the Saudi Arabian desert. Usually they are dry, but after heavy rains, they are briefly filled by fast flowing rivers.

Oases

Oases are areas within a desert where water is available for plants, and human use. They are usually formed when a fault, or split, in the rock allows water to come to the surface. Oases can be no bigger than a few palm trees, or cover several hundred sq km.

Syrian Desert (B 2)

The Syrian Desert extends from the Jordan valley in the west, to the fertile plains of the Tigris and Euphrates rivers in the east. It is mainly a rocky desert, as the sand has been swept away by winds and occasional heavy rainstorms.

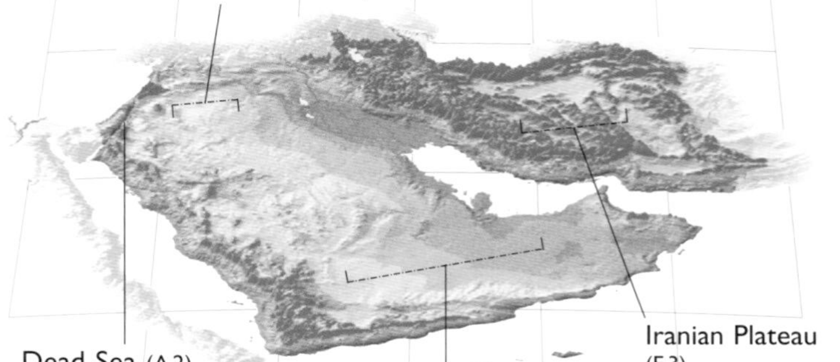

Dead Sea (A 2)

This large lake on the border between Israel and Jordan is the lowest point on the Earth's surface – its shores lie 392 m below sea level. It is also the world's saltiest body of water, and can support no life forms.

Ar Rub' al Khali (D 5)

The Ar Rub' al Khali desert, also known as the 'Empty Quarter', is the largest uninterrupted stretch of sand on Earth. It covers some 650,000 sq km and is one of the world's driest and most hostile deserts.

Iranian Plateau (E 3)

Central Iran is taken up by a vast, semi-arid plateau, which rises steeply from the coastal lowlands bordering the Gulf. It is ringed by the high Zagros and Elburz mountains.

FARMING AND LAND USE

The best farmland is found along the Mediterranean coast, and in the fertile valleys of the Tigris, Euphrates and Jordan rivers. Wheat is the main cereal crop, and cotton, dates, citrus and orchard fruits are grown for export. Elsewhere, modern irrigation techniques have created patches of fertile land in the desert. Dates, wheat and coffee are cultivated in the oases and along the Gulf coast.

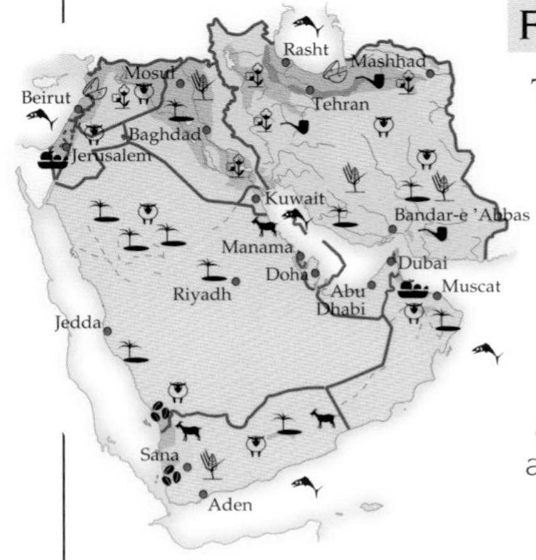

LAND USE

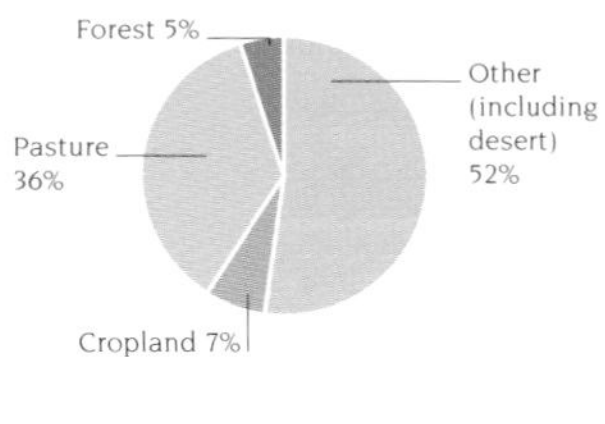

FARMING AND LAND USE

- Goats
- Fishing
- Sheep
- Citrus fruits
- Coffee
- Cotton
- Dates
- Fruit
- Tobacco
- Wheat
- Cropland
- Desert
- Forest
- Pasture
- Wetland
- Major conurbation

POPULATION

Desert has kept much of the population clustered along the coastal areas and rivers, or around the oases. Most people live in the cities, some of which are the fastest growing in the world. Oman and Yemen have mainly rural populations, and in Saudi Arabia, small groups of Bedouin tribespeople roam the desert with their animals.

CLIMATE

Most of the region receives very little rain, apart from a few isolated pockets. During July, temperatures soar, but in January temperatures are much cooler, especially in the north.

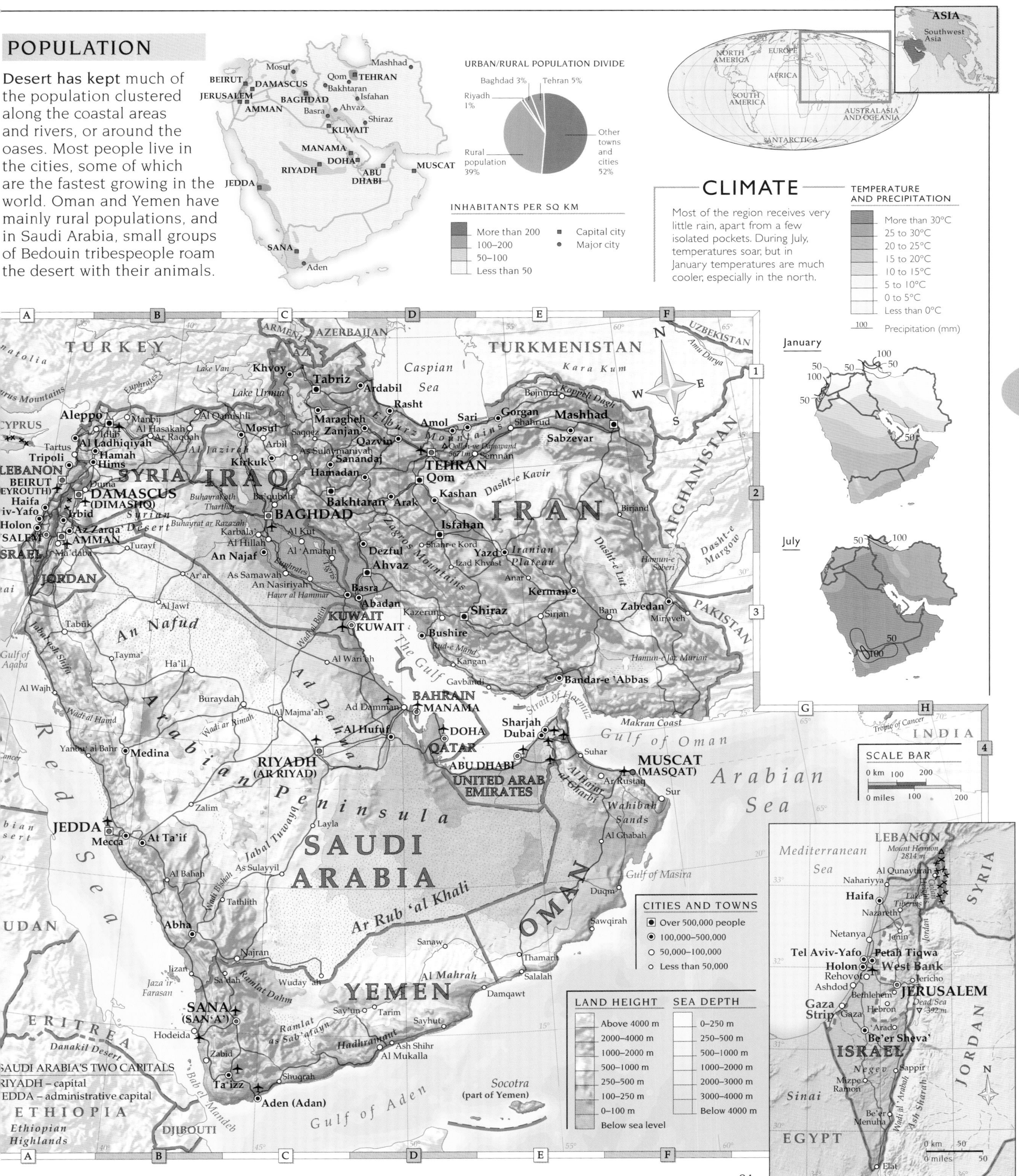

Central Asia

AFGHANISTAN, KYRGYZSTAN, TAJIKISTAN, TURKMENISTAN, UZBEKISTAN

Central Asia is a land of hot, dry deserts and high, rugged mountains. It lies on the ancient Silk Road, an important trade route between China and Europe for over 400 years, until the 15th century. All of the countries here, apart from Afghanistan, were part of the Soviet Union from the 1920s, until 1991, when they gained independence. Since then, their people have re-established their local languages and Islamic faith, all of which were restricted under Russian rule.

INDUSTRY

Fossil fuels, especially coal, natural gas and oil, are extracted and processed throughout Central Asia. Agriculture supplies the raw materials for many industries, including food and textile processing, and the manufacture of leather goods and clothing. The region is famous for its colourful traditional carpets, hand-woven from the wool of the Karakul sheep. The Fergana Valley, southeast of Tashkent, is the main industrial area.

Nukus, Urganch, Türkmenbaşy, Türkmenabat, Aşgabat, Mary, Buxoro, Samarqand, Tashkent, Muragap, Bishkek, Farg'ona, Dushanbe, Herat, Kabul

INDUSTRY
- Chemicals
- Engineering
- Food processing
- Textiles
- Mining
- Oil and gas
- Major industrial centre / area
- Major road

STRUCTURE OF INDUSTRY

Primary 16%, Manufacturing 58%, Services 26%

POPULATION

The peoples of Central Asia are mostly rural farmers, living in the river valleys and in oases. There are few large cities. A few still lead a traditional nomadic lifestyle, moving from place to place with their animals, in search of new pastures. Large areas of Afghanistan, the western deserts and the mountain regions in the east, are virtually uninhabited.

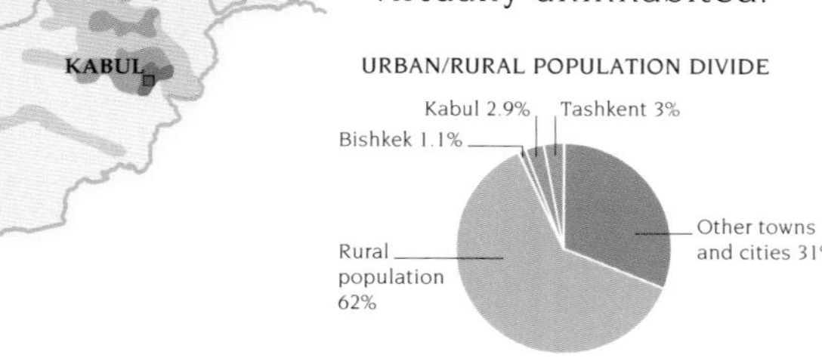

INHABITANTS PER SQ KM
- More than 100
- 50–100
- 10–50
- Less than 10
- Capital city
- Major city

URBAN/RURAL POPULATION DIVIDE

Kabul 2.9%, Tashkent 3%, Bishkek 1.1%, Other towns and cities 31%, Rural population 62%

FARMING AND LAND USE

Farming is concentrated around the fertile river valleys in the east, like the Fergana Valley. A variety of cereals, and fruits, including peaches, melons and apricots, are grown. In drier areas, animal breeding is important, with goats, sheep and cattle supplying wool, meat and hides. Big crops of cotton, which is a major export, are produced on land irrigated by the Amu Darya river.

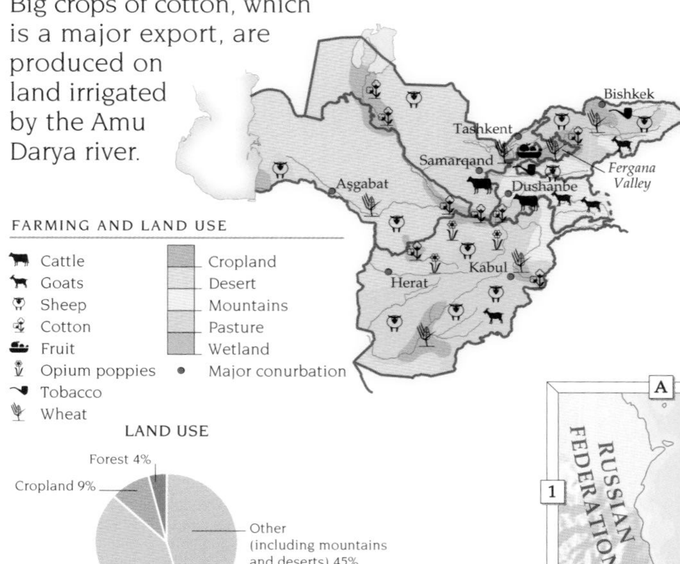

LAND USE

Forest 4%, Cropland 9%, Pasture 41%, Other (including mountains and deserts) 45%

THE LANDSCAPE

Two of the world's great deserts, the Garagum and the Kyzyl Kum, cover much of the western portion of Central Asia. In the east, a belt of high mountain ranges – the Hindu Kush, the Tien Shan and the Pamirs – tower above the land. Few rivers cross the deserts, apart from the Amu Darya, which flows from the Pamirs to the shrinking Aral Sea.

The Aral Sea (D 1)
The Aral Sea was once the fourth largest lake in the world, but it has shrunk by 40% since 1960. Diversion of its water for irrigation has made the lake shallower, so its waters evaporate faster.

Garagum (D 3)
The sandy desert of the Kara Kum occupies over 70% of Turkmenistan. Its surface consists of wind-sculpted dunes and depressions. Human settlement is limited to the desert's fringes.

Tien Shan (H 2)

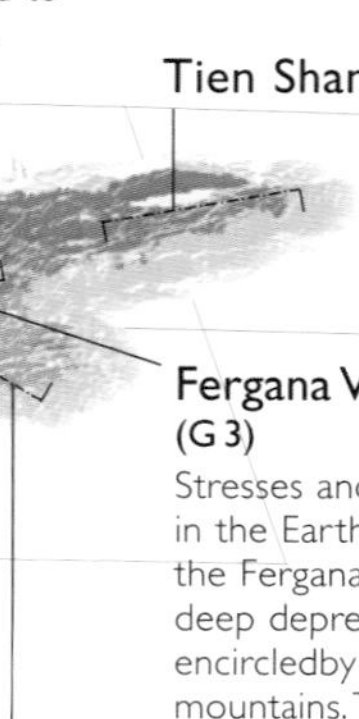

Fergana Valley (G 3)
Stresses and strains in the Earth created the Fergana Valley, a deep depression encircledby high mountains. The valley's fertile soils are irrigated by water from the Syr Darya river, and underground sources.

Amu Darya river (E 3)

Hindu Kush (G 4)

Pamirs (G 4)
The Pamirs lie mainly in Tajikistan. Their highest point, at 7,495 m, is Communism Peak, so named because it was the highest peak in the former Soviet Union.

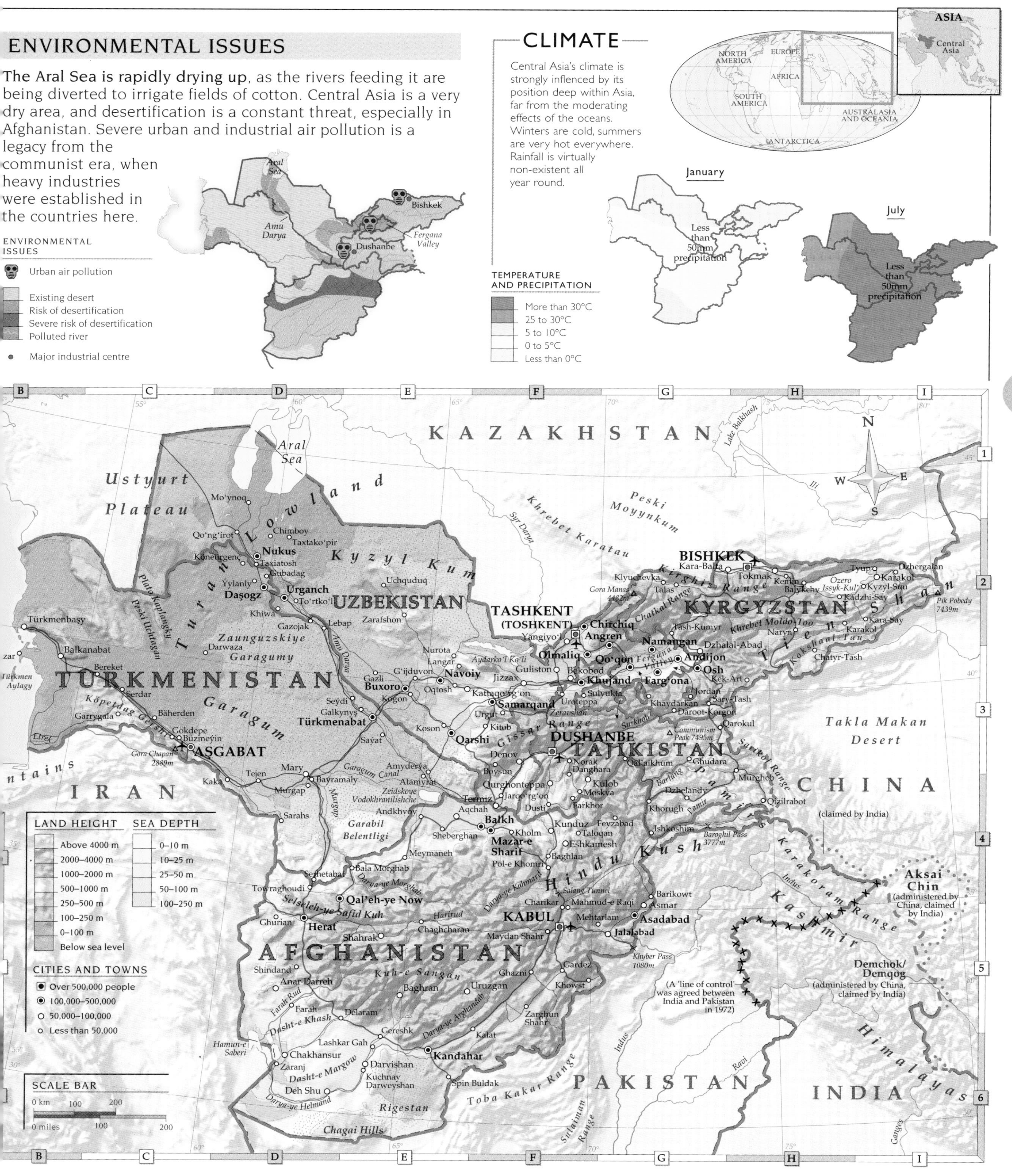
ENVIRONMENTAL ISSUES
The Aral Sea is rapidly drying up, as the rivers feeding it are being diverted to irrigate fields of cotton. Central Asia is a very dry area, and desertification is a constant threat, especially in Afghanistan. Severe urban and industrial air pollution is a legacy from the communist era, when heavy industries were established in the countries here.
ENVIRONMENTAL ISSUES
Urban air pollution
Existing desert
Risk of desertification
Severe risk of desertification
Polluted river
Major industrial centre
Aral Sea
Amu Darya
Bishkek
Dushanbe
Fergana Valley
CLIMATE
Central Asia's climate is strongly inflenced by its position deep within Asia, far from the moderating effects of the oceans. Winters are cold, summers are very hot everywhere. Rainfall is virtually non-existent all year round.
TEMPERATURE AND PRECIPITATION
More than 30°C
25 to 30°C
5 to 10°C
0 to 5°C
Less than 0°C
January
Less than 50mm precipitation
July
Less than 50mm precipitation
ASIA
Central Asia
NORTH AMERICA
EUROPE
AFRICA
SOUTH AMERICA
AUSTRALASIA AND OCEANIA
ANTARCTICA
KAZAKHSTAN
UZBEKISTAN
TURKMENISTAN
KYRGYZSTAN
TAJIKISTAN
AFGHANISTAN
IRAN
PAKISTAN
INDIA
CHINA
BISHKEK
TASHKENT (TOSHKENT)
DUSHANBE
ASGABAT
KABUL
Aral Sea
Ustyurt Plateau
Turan Lowland
Kyzyl Kum
Zaunguzskiye Garagumy
Garagum
Takla Makan Desert
Hindu Kush
Pamirs
Tien Shan
Karakoram Range
Himalayas
Kashmir
Aksai Chin (administered by China, claimed by India)
Demchok/ Demqog (administered by China, claimed by India)
(A 'line of control' was agreed between India and Pakistan in 1972)
(claimed by India)
Gora Chapan 2889m
Communism Peak 7495m
Pik Pobedy 7439m
Gora Manas 4482m
Baroghil Pass 3777m
Khyber Pass 1080m
Salang Tunnel
Nukus
Urganch
Daşogz
Türkmenbaşy
Balkanabat
Türkmenabat
Mary
Buxoro
Navoiy
Samarqand
Qarshi
Termiz
Namangan
Andijon
Osh
Farg'ona
Khujand
Chirchiq
Angren
Olmaliq
Qo'qon
Balkh
Mazar-e Sharif
Herat
Qal'eh-ye Now
Kandahar
Asadabad
Jalalabad
Rigestan
Chagai Hills
Dasht-e Margow
Dasht-e Khash
Kuh-e Sangan
Toba Kakar Range
Sulaiman Range
LAND HEIGHT
Above 4000 m
2000–4000 m
1000–2000 m
500–1000 m
250–500 m
100–250 m
0–100 m
Below sea level
SEA DEPTH
0–10 m
10–25 m
25–50 m
50–100 m
100–250 m
CITIES AND TOWNS
Over 500,000 people
100,000–500,000
50,000–100,000
Less than 50,000
SCALE BAR
0 km 100 200
0 miles 100 200
N
S
E
W

JAPAN AND KOREA

JAPAN, NORTH KOREA, SOUTH KOREA

Japan is a curved chain of over 4,000 islands in the Pacific Ocean. To the west, Korea juts out from northern China. Japan has few natural resources but it has become one of the world's most successful industrial nations due to investment in new technology and a highly efficient workforce. North Korea is a communist state with limited contact with the outside world, while South Korea is a democracy with major international trade links.

THE LANDSCAPE

Most of Japan is covered by forested mountains and hills, among which are many short, fast-flowing rivers and small lakes. Only about a quarter of the land is suitable for building and farming and new land has been created by cutting back hillsides and reclaiming land from the sea. North and South Korea are mostly mountainous, with some coastal plains.

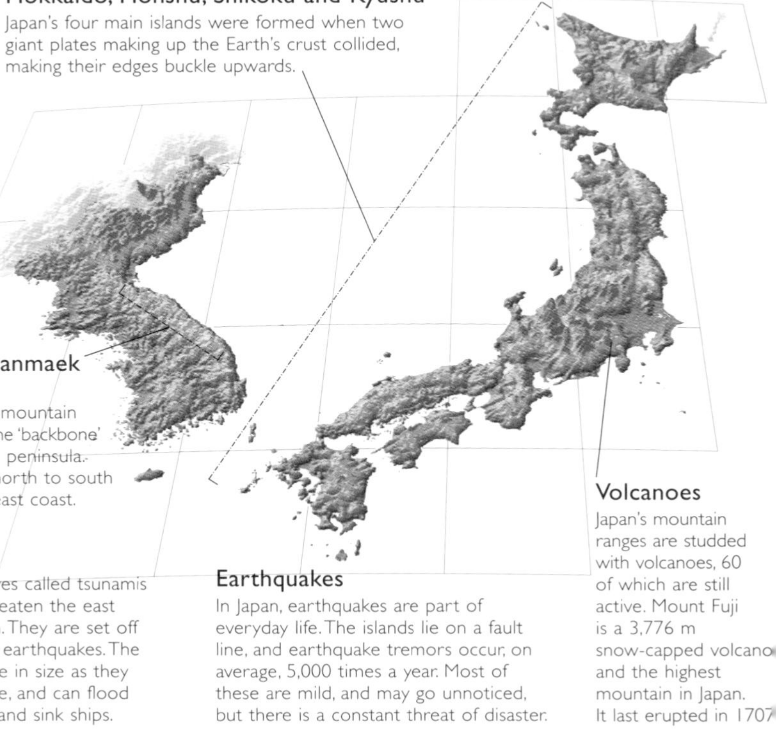

Hokkaido, Honshu, Shikoku and Kyushu
Japan's four main islands were formed when two giant plates making up the Earth's crust collided, making their edges buckle upwards.

T'aebaek-sanmaek (C 5)
This wooded mountain range forms the 'backbone' of the Korean peninsula. It runs from north to south close to the east coast.

Tsunamis
Huge sea waves called tsunamis frequently threaten the east coast of Japan. They are set off by submarine earthquakes. The waves increase in size as they near the shore, and can flood coastal areas and sink ships.

Earthquakes
In Japan, earthquakes are part of everyday life. The islands lie on a fault line, and earthquake tremors occur, on average, 5,000 times a year. Most of these are mild, and may go unnoticed, but there is a constant threat of disaster.

Volcanoes
Japan's mountain ranges are studded with volcanoes, 60 of which are still active. Mount Fuji is a 3,776 m snow-capped volcano and the highest mountain in Japan. It last erupted in 1707.

FARMING AND LAND USE

Modern farming methods allow Japan to grow much of its own food, despite a shortage of farmland. Rice is the main crop grown throughout the region. Japan has a large fishing fleet; the Japanese eat more fish than any other nation. In North Korea, farming is controlled by the government.

Sapporo, Sendai, Pyongyang, Seoul, Tokyo, Yokohama, Nagoya, Kobe, Osaka, Pusan, Hiroshima, Kwangju, Fukuoka

FARMING AND LAND USE

- Cattle
- Fishing
- Pigs
- Fruit
- Rice
- Soya beans
- Tea
- Tobacco
- Cropland
- Forest
- Pasture
- Major conurbation

LAND USE

Pasture 1%
Cropland 14%
Other (including mountains) 30%
Forest 55%

POPULATION

Most of Japan's 128 million people live in crowded cities on the coasts of the four main islands. The Kanto Plain around Tokyo is Japan's biggest area of flat land, and the most populous part of the country. In South Korea, a quarter of the population lives in the capital, Seoul. Most North Koreans live on the coastal plains.

Sapporo, Sendai, Hamhung, PYONGYANG, SEOUL, Nagaoka, TOKYO, Yokohama, Nagoya, Taejon, Taegu, Pusan, Kwangju, Kobe, Osaka, Hiroshima, Fukuoka, Kagoshima

URBAN/RURAL POPULATION DIVIDE

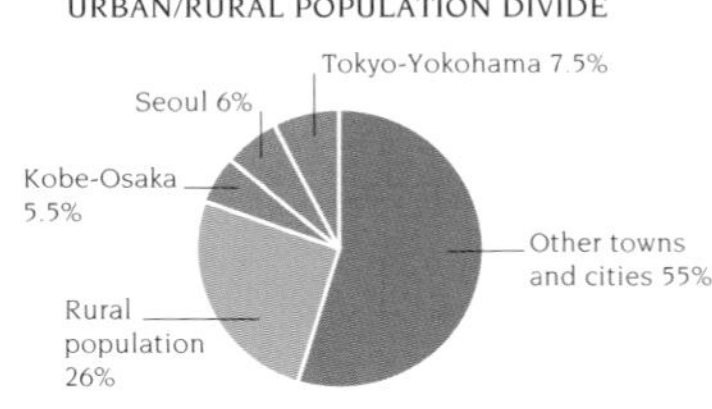

INHABITANTS PER SQ KM

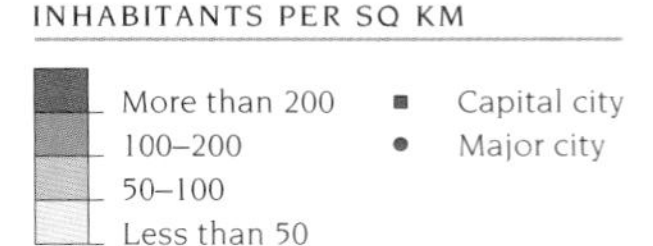

INDUSTRY

Japan is a world leader in hi-tech electronic goods like computers, televisions and cameras, as well as cars. South Korea also has a thriving economy. It produces ships, cars, hi-tech goods, shoes and clothes for worldwide export. Both countries have to import most of their raw materials and energy. North Korea has little trade with other countries, but it is rich in minerals such as coal and silver.

Kushiro, Sapporo, Hachinohe, Ch'ongjin, Sendai, Nagaoka, Hitachi, Pyongyang, Toyama, Tokyo, Yokohama, Seoul, Inch'on, Kyoto, Nagoya, Pusan, Kobe, Osaka, Hiroshima, Kwangju, Kitakyushu, Fukuoka

STRUCTURE OF INDUSTRY

Primary 3%
Services 57%
Manufacturing 40%

INDUSTRY

- Car manufacture
- Chemicals
- Engineering
- Food processing
- Iron & steel
- Shipbuilding
- Textiles
- Mining
- Finance
- Hi-tech
- Research & Development
- Major industrial centre / area
- Major road

ENVIRONMENTAL ISSUES
Industrial pollution from Korea and China has produced acid rain, and pollution in Japanese cities has led to people wearing masks to filter the air. Russia regularly dumps nuclear waste into the Sea of Japan. In 1995, an earthquake caused great destruction to the city of Kobe.
Sea of Japan
Seoul
Tokyo
Kobe 1995
Osaka
ENVIRONMENTAL ISSUES
Catastrophic earthquake
Nuclear waste dump site
Urban air pollution
Affected by acid rain
Major industrial area
CLIMATE
Korea has hot summers and dry, very cold winters, especially in the north, where snow is common. In Japan, winters are less cold than on the Asian mainland; summers are hot, wet and humid.
January
Less than 50
200
50
100
July
TEMPERATURE AND PRECIPITATION
More than 20°C
15 to 20°C
10 to 15°C
5 to 10°C
0 to 5°C
0 to -5°C
Less than -5°C
Precipitation (mm)
ASIA
Japan and Korea
NORTH AMERICA
EUROPE
AFRICA
SOUTH AMERICA
AUSTRALASIA AND OCEANIA
ANTARCTICA
SCALE BAR
NORTH KOREA
SOUTH KOREA
CHINA
RUSS. FED.
PYONGYANG
SEOUL (SOUL)
Sea of Japan
East Korea Bay
(North and South Korea have been divided by a ceasefire agreement since 1953)
Liancourt Rocks (claimed by Japan and South Korea)
Korea Strait
Cheju Strait
East China Sea
Yellow Sea
Ryukyu Islands (part of Japan)
Philippine Sea
JAPAN
Hokkaido
Honshu
Shikoku
Kyushu
Sea of Okhotsk
La Perouse Strait
Kurile Islands (administered by Russian Federation, claimed by Japan)
PACIFIC OCEAN
TOKYO
Sapporo
Sendai
Nagoya
Kyoto
Osaka
Kobe
Hiroshima
Fukuoka
Kitakyushu
Yokohama
Kawasaki
Chiba
Kagoshima
Kumamoto
Hakodate
Aomori
Niigata
Kanazawa
Okayama
Matsuyama
Kochi
Nagasaki
Mount Fuji 3776m
Kanto Plain
Oki-shoto
Izu-shoto
LAND HEIGHT
2000–4000 m
1000–2000 m
500–1000 m
250–500 m
100–250 m
0–100 m
SEA DEPTH
0–250 m
250–500 m
500–1000 m
1000–2000 m
2000–3000 m
3000–4000 m
Below 4000 m
CITIES AND TOWNS
Over 500,000 people
100,000–500,000
50,000–100,000
Less than 50,000

East Asia

CHINA, MONGOLIA, TAIWAN

China is the world's third largest country and its most populous – over one billion people live there. Under its communist government, which came to power in 1949, China has become a major industrial nation, but most of its people still live and work on the land, as they have for thousands of years. Taiwan also has a booming economy and exports its products around the world. Mongolia is a vast, remote country with a small population, many of whom are nomads.

FARMING AND LAND USE

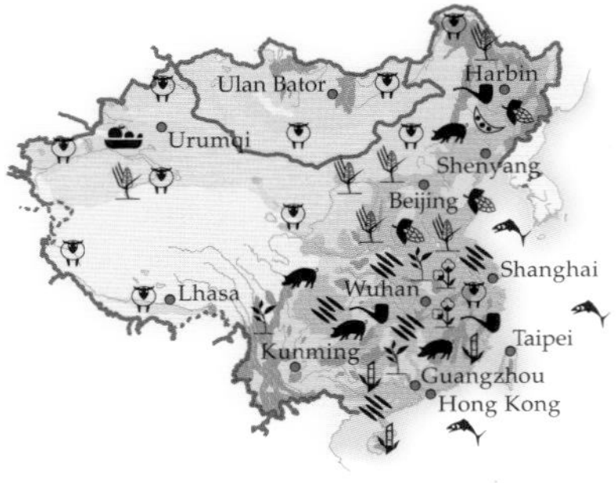

Despite its size, about 90% of China is unsuitable for farming. Either the soils and climate are poor, or the landscape is too mountainous. In the north and west, most farmers make their living by herding animals. On the fertile eastern plains, soya beans, wheat, corn and cotton are grown. Further south, rice becomes the main crop, and pigs are raised in large numbers.

FARMING AND LAND USE

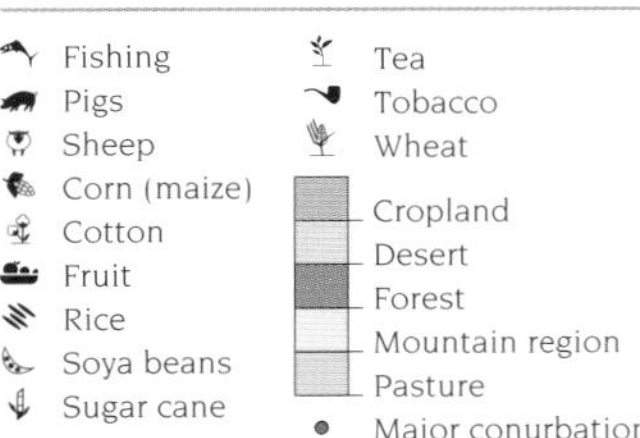

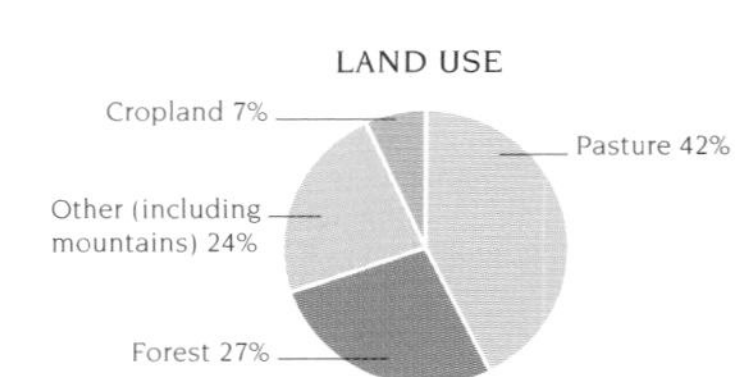

INDUSTRY

Chemicals, iron and steel, engineering and textiles are the main industries in China's east coast cities, and in industrial centres like Shenyang. Shanghai, Hong Kong and Beijing are also important financial centres. In the interior, large deposits of coal support the heavy industries in major cities such as Chengdu and Wuhan. Taiwan specializes in textiles and shoe manufacture, along with electronic goods. Mongolia's economy is mainly agricultural.

INDUSTRY

- Car manufacture
- Chemicals
- Electronics
- Electronic goods
- Engineering
- Food processing
- Iron & steel
- Shipbuiding
- Textiles
- Coal
- Mining
- Finance
- Major industrial centre / area
- Major road

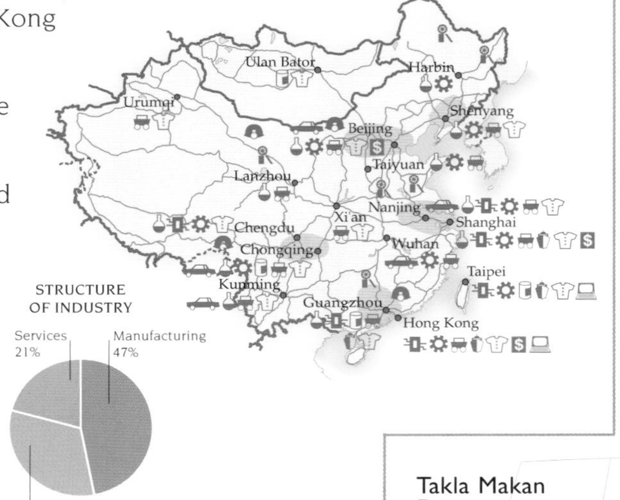

POPULATION

Most of China's people live in the eastern part of the country, where the climate, landscape and soils are most favourable. Urban areas there house over 250 million people, but almost 75% of the population lives in villages and farm the land. Taiwan's lowlands are very densely populated. In Mongolia, about 50% of the people live in the countryside.

ULAN BATOR, Harbin, Jinzhou, BEIJING, Tianjin, Xuzhou, Shanghai, Chengdu, Wuhan, Chongqing, Changsha, TAIPEI, Guangzhou, Hong Kong

URBAN/RURAL POPULATION DIVIDE

- Shanghai 1%
- Other towns and cities 27%
- Rural population 72%

INHABITANTS PER SQ KM

- More than 200
- 100–200
- 50–100
- Less than 50
- Capital city
- Major city

THE LANDSCAPE

China's landscape divides into three areas. The vast Plateau of Tibet in the southwest is the highest and largest plateau on Earth. It contains both dry deserts and pockets of pasture surrounded by high mountains. Northwest China has dry highlands. The great plains of eastern China were formed from soils deposited by rivers like the Yellow River over thousands of years. Most of Mongolia is dry, grassland steppe and cold, arid desert.

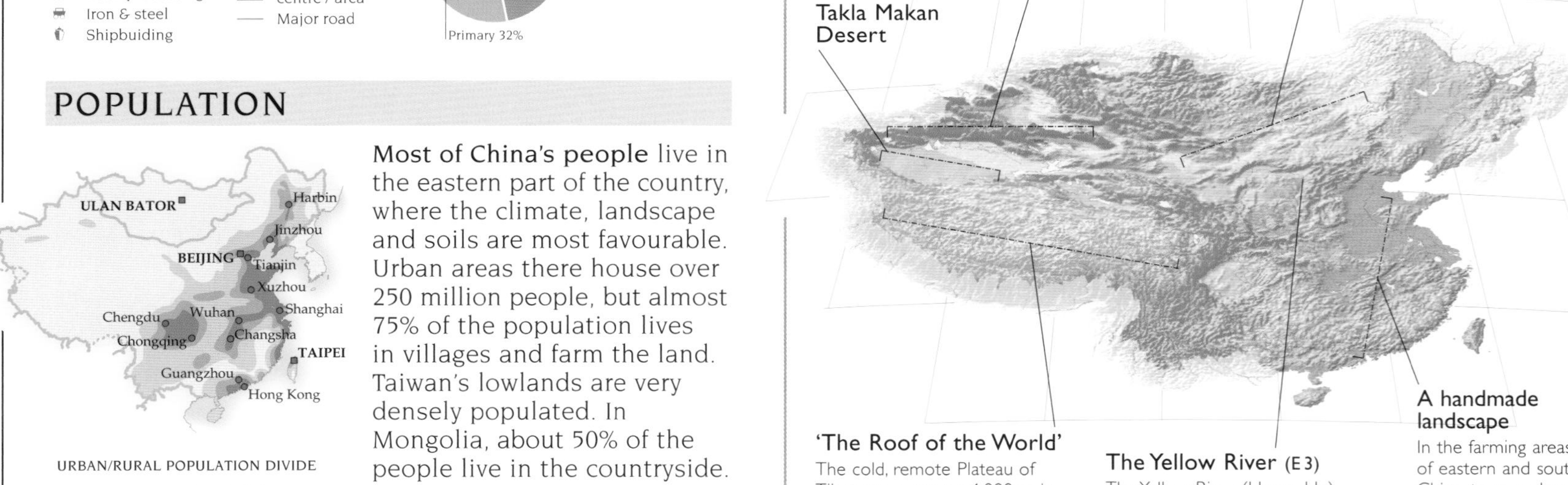

Takla Makan Desert

Tien Shan mountains (B2)

The Tien Shan, or 'Heavenly Mountains' reach heights of 7,435 m. They surround fields of permanent ice and spectacular glaciers.

Gobi (E2) and Takla Makan (B3) deserts

The arid landscapes of the Gobi and Takla Makan deserts are made up of bare rock surfaces and huge areas of shifting sand dunes. They are hot in summer, but unlike most other deserts, are extremely cold in winter.

'The Roof of the World'

The cold, remote Plateau of Tibet (C4) averages 4,000 m in height. Many of China's great rivers have their sources here. The world's highest human settlement, a town called Wenquan, is found in the east of the plateau. It lies 5,099 m above sea level.

The Yellow River (E3)

The Yellow River (Huang He) is the world's muddiest river, carrying hundreds of lorry loads of sediment to the sea every minute. The river has burst its banks many times throughout history, causing enormous damage and claiming millions of human lives.

A handmade landscape

In the farming areas of eastern and southern China, terraces have been carved into the hillsides to make them flat enough to grow rice and other crops. This method of farming has been used for over 7,000 years.

ENVIRONMENTAL ISSUES

The Three Gorges hydro-electric scheme on the Yangtze River will be the world's largest. Nearly 563 km of canyon will be flooded, and 1.3 million people forced to move. Earthquakes are common in the area and 100 million people downstream will be threatened if the dam breaks. In eastern China, many cities are affected by industrial pollution.

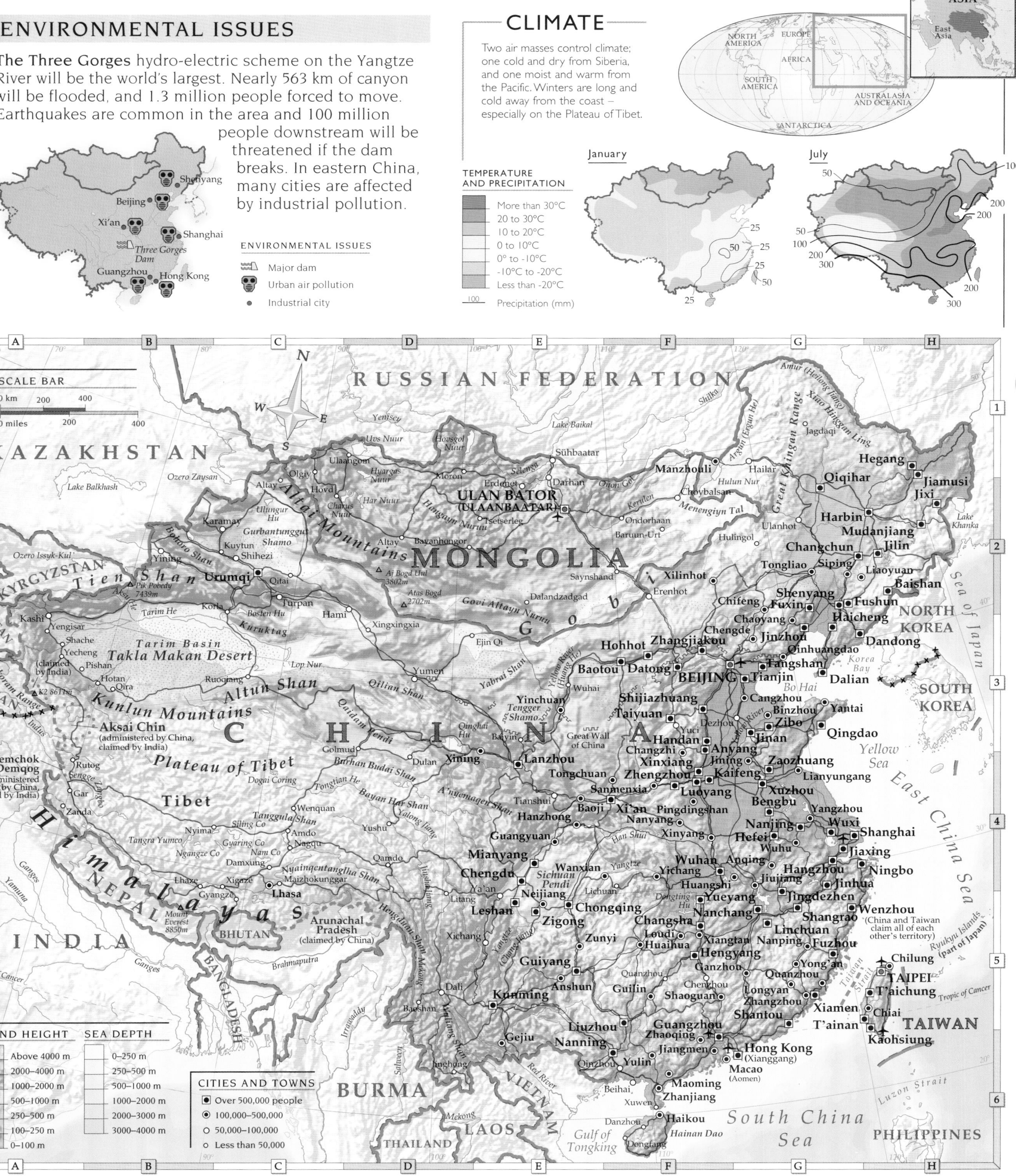

South Asia

BANGLADESH, BHUTAN, INDIA, NEPAL, PAKISTAN, SRI LANKA

South Asia is a land of many contrasts. Its landscape ranges from the mighty peaks of the Himalayas in the north, through vast plains and arid desert, to tropical forests and palm-fringed beaches in the south. More than one-fifth of the world's people live here, and a long history of foreign invasions has left a mosaic of hugely different cultures, religions and traditions, and thousands of languages and dialects.

FARMING AND LAND USE

Over 60% of the population is involved in agriculture, but most farms are small, and produce only enough food to feed one family. Grains are the staple food crops – rice in the wetter parts of the east and west, corn and millet on the Deccan plateau, and wheat in the north. Groundnuts are widely grown as a source of cooking oil. Cash crops include tea, which is grown on plantations, and jute.

FARMING AND LAND USE

- Cattle
- Fishing
- Goats
- Cereals
- Groundnuts
- Jute
- Rice
- Tea
- Cropland
- Desert
- Forest
- Pasture
- Wetland
- Major conurbation

LAND USE

Pasture 5%
Forest 21%
Cropland 50%
Other 24%

INDUSTRY

Industry has expanded in India in recent years, and in the cities a variety of goods are produced and processed, including cars, aeroplanes, chemicals, food and drink. Service industries such as tourism and banking are also growing. Elsewhere, small-scale cottage industries serve the needs of local people, but many products, mainly silk and cotton textiles, clothing, leather and jewellery, are also exported.

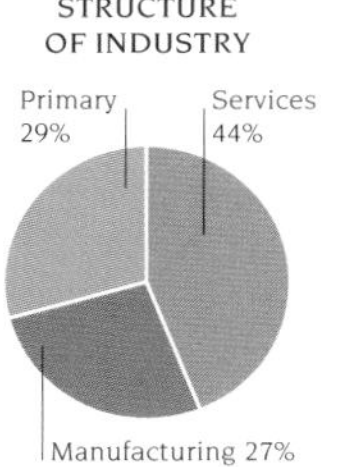

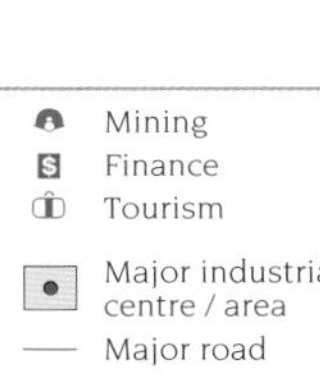

STRUCTURE OF INDUSTRY

Primary 29%
Services 44%
Manufacturing 27%

INDUSTRY

- Aerospace
- Car manufacture
- Chemicals
- Electronics
- Engineering
- Food processing
- Iron and steel
- Textiles
- Mining
- Finance
- Tourism
- Major industrial centre / area
- Major road

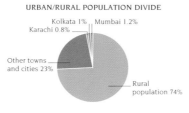

POPULATION

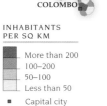

Most of South Asia's people live in villages scattered across the fertile river floodplains, in mountain valleys or along the coasts, but increasing numbers are migrating to the cities in search of work. Overcrowding is a serious problem in both rural and urban areas; in many cities, thousands of people are forced to live in slums, or on the streets.

INHABITANTS PER SQ KM

- More than 200
- 100–200
- 50–100
- Less than 50
- Capital city
- Major city

URBAN/RURAL POPULATION DIVIDE

Kolkata 1%
Mumbai 1.2%
Karachi 0.8%
Other towns and cities 23%
Rural population 74%

THE LANDSCAPE

A massive, towering wall of snow-capped mountains stretches in an arc across the north, isolating South Asia from the rest of the continent. The huge floodplains and deltas of the Indus, Ganges and Brahmaputra rivers separate the mountains from the rest of the peninsula: a great rolling plateau, bordered on either side by coastal hills called the Eastern and Western Ghats.

Himalayas (E 2)
The Himalayas are the highest mountain system in the world. They were formed about 40 million years ago when two of the Earth's plates collided, thrusting up huge masses of land.

Mount Everest (F 3)
The northern ranges of the Himalayas average 7,000 m in height. They include the highest point on Earth, Mount Everest on the Nepal–China border, which soars to 8,850 m.

Thar Desert (C 3)
The border between India and Pakistan runs through the arid, sandy Thar Desert.

Western Ghats (C 5)
The Western Ghats run continuously along the Arabian Sea coast, while the lower Eastern Ghats are interrupted by rivers that follow the gentle slope of the Deccan plateau and flow across broad lowlands into the Bay of Bengal. This is one of the wettest regions in the world.

Eastern Ghats (E 5)

Deccan plateau (D 5)
This giant plateau makes up most of central and southern India. Its volcanic rock has been deeply cut by rivers such as the Krishna, creating stepped valleys called *traps*.

Bangladesh (G 3)
Much of Bangladesh lies in an enormous delta formed by the Brahmaputra and Ganges rivers. During the summer monsoon, the rivers become swollen by the torrential rains – and meltwater from the Himalayas – and the delta floods. Over the years, millions of people have drowned or been made homeless by heavy flooding.

LAND HEIGHT
Above 4000 m
2000–4000 m
1000–2000 m
500–1000 m
250–500 m
100–250 m
0–100 m
SEA DEPTH
0–250 m
250–500 m
500–1000 m
1000–2000 m
2000–3000 m
3000–4000 m
Below 4000 m
CITIES AND TOWNS
Over 500,000 people
100,000–500,000
50,000–100,000
Less than 50,000
(claimed by India)
(A "line of control" was agreed between India and Pakistan in 1972)
Aksai Chin
(administered by China, claimed by India)
Demchok/ Demqog
(administered by China, claimed by India)
Arunachal Pradesh
(claimed by China)
ASIA
South Asia
NORTH AMERICA
EUROPE
AFRICA
SOUTH AMERICA
AUSTRALASIA AND OCEANIA
ANTARCTICA
AFGHANISTAN
PAKISTAN
INDIA
CHINA
NEPAL
BHUTAN
BANGLADESH
BURMA
SRI LANKA
MALDIVES
Hindu Kush
Karakoram Range
K2 8611m
Himalayas
Annapurna 8091m
Mount Everest 8850m
Kula Kangri 7554m
Khyber Pass 1080m
Mingaora
Mardan
Wah
Srinagar
ISLAMABAD
Peshawar
Rawalpindi
Jammu and Kashmir
Jhelum
Jammu
Gujrat
Sargodha
Gujranwala
Faisalabad
Lahore
Amritsar
Jalandhar
Ludhiana
Chandigarh
Punjab
Okara
Sahiwal
Multan
Bathinda
Karnal
Chaman
Quetta
Dera Ghazi Khan
Sibi
Kalat
Chagai Hills
Darya-ye Helmand
Toba Kakar Range
Sulaiman Range
Baluchistan
Bahawalpur
Rahimyar Khan
Jacobabad
Shikarpur
Larkana
Sukkur
Khairpur
Central Makran Range
Turbat
Gwadar
Pasni
Nawabshah
Hyderabad
Mirpur Khas
Karachi
Sind
Sujawal
Mouths of the Indus
Thar Desert
Jaisalmer
Jodhpur
Ajmer
Bikaner
Beawar
Pali
Rajasthan
Kota
Udaipur
Palanpur
Rann of Kachchh
Gulf of Kachchh
Gandhidham
Gujarat
Ahmadabad
Surendranagar
Jamnagar
Rajkot
Porbandar
Vadodara
Bhavnagar
Bharuch
Surat
Gulf of Khambhat
Daman
Haryana
Delhi
NEW DELHI
Meerut
Faridabad
Alwar
Jaipur
Agra
Bareilly
Budaun
Etawah
Uttar Pradesh
Lucknow
Gwalior
Jhansi
Shivpuri
Kanpur
Allahabad
Salyan
Pokhara
KATHMANDU
Lalitpur
Bhaktapur
Bahraich
Gorakhpur
Faizabad
Mau
Jaunpur
Varanasi
Gaya
Chhapra
Patna
Bihar
Biratnagar
Birhar Sharif
Darjiling
Gangtok
THIMPHU
Shiliguri
Bongaigaon
Koch Bihar
Assam
Guwahati
Shillong
Dibrugarh
Jorhat
Kohima
Imphal
Silchar
Sylhet
Saidpur
Rangpur
Dinajpur
Bhagalpur
Rajshahi
Pabna
Brahmanbaria
Comilla
Jessore
DHAKA
Barisal
Chittagong
Khulna
Tropic of Cancer
Brahmaputra
Ganges
Yamuna
Indus
Sutlej
Ravi
Irrawaddy
Madhya Pradesh
Sagar
Ratlam
Godhra
Vindhya Range
Bhopal
Murwara
Jabalpur
Chota Nagpur
Ranchi
Dhanbad
Asansol
Bankura
Jamshedpur
West Bengal
Haora
Kolkata (Calcutta)
Kharagpur
Raulakela
Mouths of the Ganges
Indore
Khandwa
Satpura Range
Bilaspur
Gondia
Raipur
Durg
Nagpur
Sambalpur
Baleshwar
Bhusawal
Amravati
Mahanadi
Cuttack
Bhubaneshwar
Puri
Orissa
Brahmapur
Manmad
Nashik
Kalyan
Aurangabad
Maharashtra
Chandrapur
Nanded
Jagdalpur
Mumbai (Bombay)
Ahmadnagar
Nizamabad
Karimnagar
Pune
Solapur
Warangal
Godavari
Gulbarga
Secunderabad
Hyderabad
Sangli
Deccan
Kolhapur
Belgaum
Mahbubnagar
Raichur
Krishna
Vijayawada
Rajahmundry
Kakinada
Srikakulam
Vizianagaram
Visakhapatnam
Eastern Ghats
Western Ghats
Machilipatnam
Chirala
Ongole
Kavali
Nellore
Andhra Pradesh
Panaji
Gadag
Hubli
Kurnool
Nandyal
Anantapur
Davangere
Shimoga
Bhadravati
Karnataka
Cuddapah
Udupi
Tumkur
Bangalore
Mangalore
Mandya
Vellore
Mysore
Krishnagiri
Chennai (Madras)
Kanchipuram
Pondicherry
Neyveli
Salem
Erode
Cannanore
Calicut
Coimbatore
Tamil Nadu
Tiruchchirappalli
Trichur
Dindigul
Ernakulam
Kerala
Madurai
Cochin
Alleppey
Rajapalaiyam
Tuticorin
Quilon
Trivandrum
Nagercoil
Palk Strait
Jaffna
Mannar
Vavuniya
Trincomalee
Anuradhapura
Puttalam
Batticaloa
Matale
Kandy
Negombo
COLOMBO
Sri Jayawardanapura
Ratnapura
Galle
Matara
Gulf of Mannar
Arabian Sea
Bay of Bengal
INDIAN OCEAN
Amindivi Islands
Kavaratti
Laccadive Islands (Lakshadweep)
Nine Degree Channel
Minicoy Island
Eight Degree Channel
Faadhippolhu Atoll
MALE'
Hadhdhunmathi Atoll
North Andaman
Andaman Islands (part of India)
Middle Andaman
Port Blair
South Andaman
Little Andaman
Ten Degree Channel
Car Nicobar
Nicobar Islands (part of India)
Camorta
Katchall Island
Little Nicobar
Great Nicobar
Indira Point
Bananga
Andaman Sea
SCALE: same as main map
SCALE BAR
0 km 100 200
0 miles 100 200
N
S
E
W
CLIMATE
Climate is strongly influenced by the annual monsoon between July and September which brings hot, humid conditions and extremely high levels of rainfall to much of the region.
Less than 25
More than 25
January
July
TEMPERATURE AND PRECIPITATION
More than 30°C
25 to 30°C
20 to 25°C
15 to 20°C
10 to 15°C
5 to 10°C
0 to 5°C
0 to -5°C
-5 to -10°C
Less than -10°C
Precipitation (mm)
ENVIRONMENTAL ISSUES
Deforestation is a problem in the tropical south, as well as in the Himalayas, where trees are being felled for fuelwood, causing soil erosion. Many of the large cities suffer from poor air quality.
Lahore
New Delhi
Karachi
Indus
Ganges
Kolkata
Mumbai
Godavari
Krishna
ENVIRONMENTAL ISSUES
Severe fuelwood shortage
Urban air pollution
Major industrial centre
Existing desert
Risk of desertification
Severe risk of desertification
Deforested area
Remaining tropical forest
Polluted rivers

Southeast Asia

BRUNEI, BURMA, CAMBODIA, EAST TIMOR, INDONESIA, LAOS, MALAYSIA, PHILIPPINES, SINGAPORE, THAILAND, VIETNAM

Southeast Asia is made up of a mainland area and many thousands of tropical islands. The region has great natural wealth – from precious stones to oil – and has recently experienced fast industrial growth. Some countries here, especially Singapore and Malaysia, have become prosperous, but Laos and Cambodia remain poor, and are still recovering from years of terrible warfare.

ENVIRONMENTAL ISSUES

In Burma, Malaysia and across Indonesia, ancient rainforests are being cut down faster than they can grow back. The fantastic biodiversity of the forests, with their thousands of unique species of plants and animals, is severely threatened. Forest burning has recently caused terrible smog in Indonesia.

ENVIRONMENTAL ISSUES

- Urban air pollution
- Deforested area
- Remaining tropical forest
- Major industrial centre

POPULATION

On the mainland, the population is concentrated in the river valleys, plateaus or plains. Upland areas are inhabited by small groups of hill peoples. Most people still live in rural areas, but the cities are growing fast. In Indonesia and the Philippines, the population is unevenly distributed. Some islands, such as Java, are densely settled; others are barely occupied.

INHABITANTS PER SQ KM

- More than 200
- 100–200
- 50–100
- Less than 50
- Capital city
- Major city

URBAN/RURAL POPULATION DIVIDE

Bangkok 1.8%
Rural population 28.2%
Other towns and cities 70%

INDUSTRY

Industries based on the processing of raw materials, like metallic minerals, timber, oil and gas and agricultural produce, are important here, but manufacturing has grown dramatically in recent years. Many foreign firms, attracted by low labour costs, have invested in the region. Malaysia and Singapore are major producers of electronic goods like disk drives for computers.

STRUCTURE OF INDUSTRY

Primary 19%
Services 45%
Manufacturing 36%

INDUSTRY

- Chemicals
- Engineering
- Food processing
- Textiles
- Mining
- Oil and gas
- Timber
- Hi-tech
- Tourism
- Major industrial centre / area
- Major road

THE LANDSCAPE

On the mainland, a belt of mountain ranges, cloaked in thick forest, runs north–south. The mountains are cut through by the wide valleys of five great rivers. On their route to the sea, these rivers have deposited sediment, forming immense, fertile flood plains and deltas. To the southeast of the mainland lies a huge arc of over 20,000 mountainous, volcanic islands.

Borneo (D7)

Borneo is the world's third-largest island, with a total area of 757,050 sq km. Lying on the Equator and in the path of two monsoons, the island is hot, and one of the wettest places on Earth. The landscape contains thickly-forested central highlands and swampy lowlands.

Mekong river (C4)

The mighty Mekong river flows through southern China and Burma and forms much of the border between Laos and Thailand. It then travels through Cambodia before ending in a vast delta on the southern coast of Vietnam, that is one of the world's most productive rice-growing areas.

Philippines (E4)

The Philippines' 7,000 islands are mountainous and volcanic with narrow coastal plains.

Papua (Irian Jaya) (I7)

Papua is a province of Indonesia. Its dense rainforests are some of the last unexplored areas on Earth and are inhabited by many rare plant and animal species.

Volcanoes

Indonesia is the most active volcanic region in the world; Java alone has over 50 active volcanoes out of the country's total of more than 220.

Indonesia (C7)

Indonesia is an archipelago of 13,677 islands, scattered over almost 5,000 km. The islands lie on the boundary between two of the Earth's tectonic plates and frequently experience earthquakes.

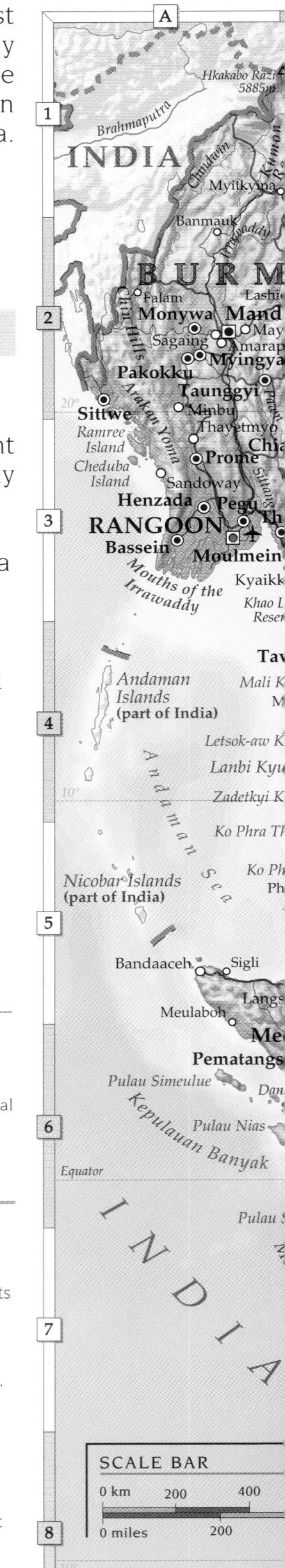

FARMING AND LAND USE

The staple crop here is rice, which grows in low-lying flooded fields called paddies, or on terraces cut into the hillsides. Sugar cane, coconuts, bananas and pineapples are widely grown as cash crops, and Malaysia produces 25% of the world's rubber. Freshwater and marine fish are caught in large quantities; fish is one of the main foods in this region.

CLIMATE

Southeast Asia's climate is strongly affected by the monsoon, which brings warm, humid air and high rainfall to mainland Southeast Asia during July, and to maritime southeast Asia during January.

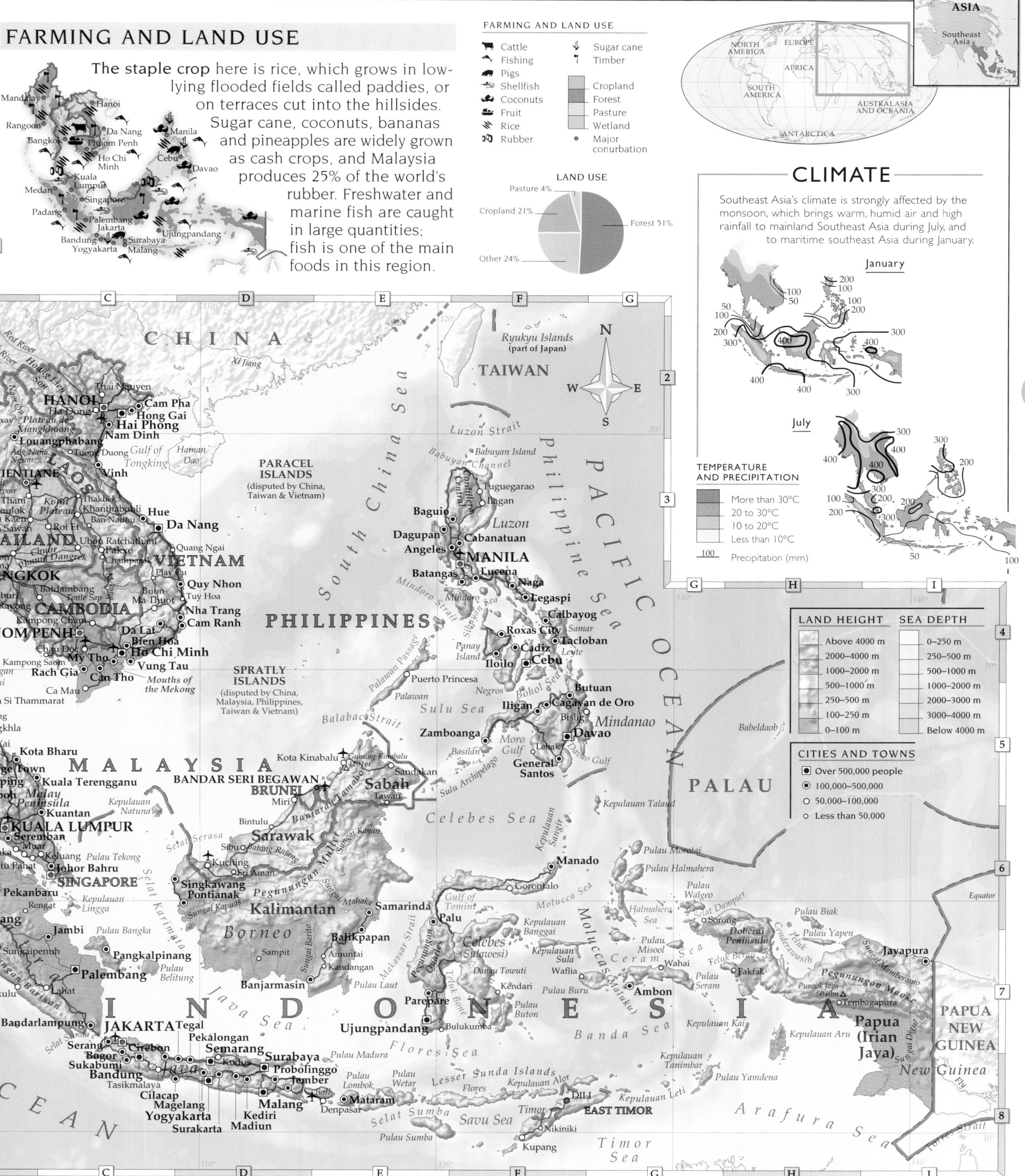

CONTINENTAL NORTH AMERICA

North America is the world's third largest continent, stretching from icy Greenland to the tropical Caribbean. The first people came from Asia more than 20,000 years ago. Their descendants spread across the continent, ate fish, meat, and wild and cultivated plants, and developed a wide variety of cultures and languages. About 500 years ago, immigrants from Europe, Africa, and Asia began to arrive in North America, bringing their own languages and cultures.

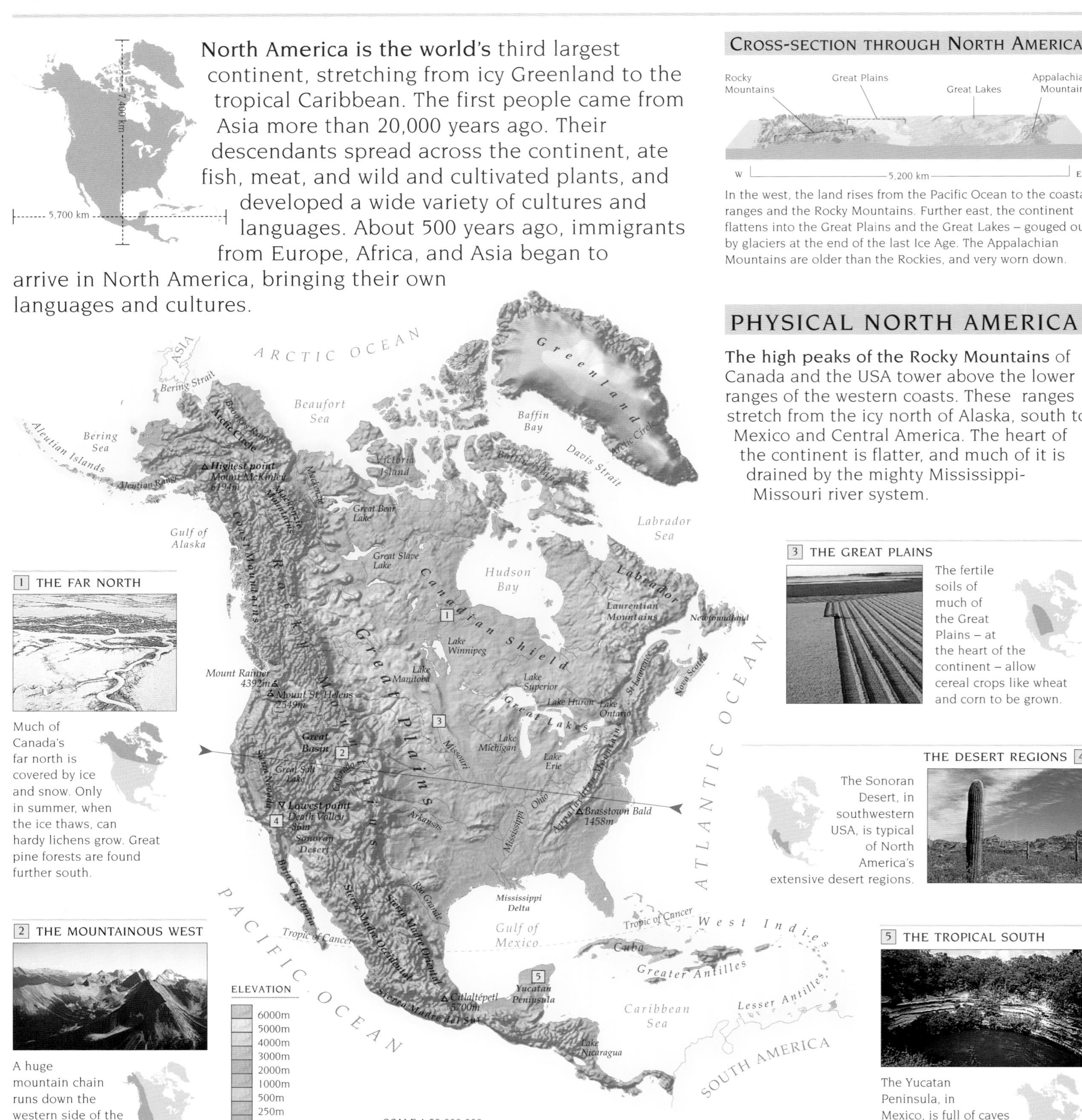

CROSS-SECTION THROUGH NORTH AMERICA

In the west, the land rises from the Pacific Ocean to the coastal ranges and the Rocky Mountains. Further east, the continent flattens into the Great Plains and the Great Lakes – gouged out by glaciers at the end of the last Ice Age. The Appalachian Mountains are older than the Rockies, and very worn down.

PHYSICAL NORTH AMERICA

The high peaks of the Rocky Mountains of Canada and the USA tower above the lower ranges of the western coasts. These ranges stretch from the icy north of Alaska, south to Mexico and Central America. The heart of the continent is flatter, and much of it is drained by the mighty Mississippi-Missouri river system.

1 THE FAR NORTH

Much of Canada's far north is covered by ice and snow. Only in summer, when the ice thaws, can hardy lichens grow. Great pine forests are found further south.

2 THE MOUNTAINOUS WEST

A huge mountain chain runs down the western side of the continent. These mountains are young, and are still being formed.

3 THE GREAT PLAINS

The fertile soils of much of the Great Plains – at the heart of the continent – allow cereal crops like wheat and corn to be grown.

THE DESERT REGIONS 4

The Sonoran Desert, in southwestern USA, is typical of North America's extensive desert regions.

5 THE TROPICAL SOUTH

The Yucatan Peninsula, in Mexico, is full of caves and sinkholes because the humid tropical climate accelerates erosion.

POLITICAL NORTH AMERICA

The USA, Canada and Mexico are all federal countries. This means that political power is shared between the national government and the state or provincial governments. Canada and the USA are democracies with a long history of freedom and equal rights. Governments in the countries south of the USA have been less stable, often ruled by dictators or harsh regimes. Many people have suffered for their political beliefs. Until about 20 years ago many of the Caribbean islands were ruled by European countries as colonies.

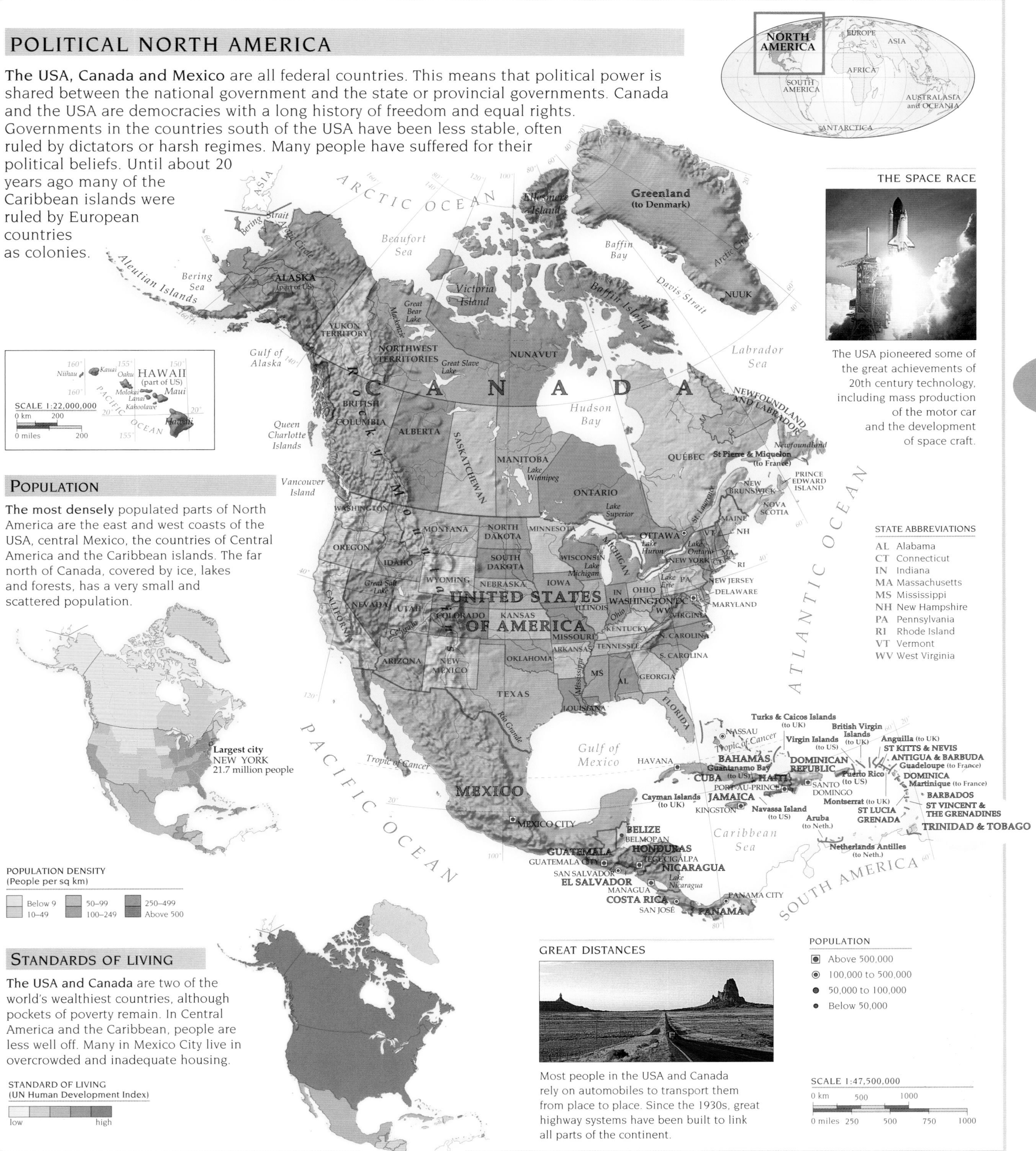

THE SPACE RACE

The USA pioneered some of the great achievements of 20th century technology, including mass production of the motor car and the development of space craft.

POPULATION

The most densely populated parts of North America are the east and west coasts of the USA, central Mexico, the countries of Central America and the Caribbean islands. The far north of Canada, covered by ice, lakes and forests, has a very small and scattered population.

STANDARDS OF LIVING

The USA and Canada are two of the world's wealthiest countries, although pockets of poverty remain. In Central America and the Caribbean, people are less well off. Many in Mexico City live in overcrowded and inadequate housing.

GREAT DISTANCES

Most people in the USA and Canada rely on automobiles to transport them from place to place. Since the 1930s, great highway systems have been built to link all parts of the continent.

NORTH AMERICAN GEOGRAPHY

Canada and the USA are among the world's wealthiest countries. They have rich natural resources, good farmland and thriving, varied industries. The range of different industries in Mexico is growing, but other Central American countries and the Caribbean islands rely on one or two important cash crops and tourism for most of their incomes. They have a lower standard of living than Canada and the USA.

INDUSTRY

The USA and Canada have an extremely wide range of industries, from mining and the processing of farm produce, to heavy and light manufacturing and service industries like banking. A variety of goods are produced, including aeroplanes, cars and computers. Oil exports and machine assembly are Mexico's main industries. In Central America and the Caribbean nations, most industry is based on agricultural produce.

INDUSTRY

- Aerospace
- Brewing
- Car/vehicle manufacture
- Chemicals
- Coal
- Defence
- Engineering
- Film industry
- Finance
- Food processing
- Hi-tech industry
- Iron & steel
- Oil & gas
- Pharmaceuticals
- Printing & publishing
- Research & development
- Shipbuilding
- Textiles
- Timber processing

GNP per capita (US$)

- Below 1999
- 2000-4999
- 5000-9999
- 10,000-19,999
- 20,000-24,999
- Above 25,000
- Industrial centre

MANUFACTURING

Mexico has many car assembly plants, like this Volkswagen plant. Labour costs in Mexico are low, making it cheap to assemble cars here.

MINERAL RESOURCES

North America still has large amounts of mineral resources. Canada has important nickel reserves, Mexico is renowned for its silver, and bauxite – used to make aluminum – is found in Jamaica. Oil and gas are plentiful, particularly in the arctic northwest by the Beaufort Sea, and further south by the Gulf of Mexico.

MINERAL RESOURCES

- Bauxite
- Copper
- Iron
- Nickel
- Phosphates
- Silver
- Uranium
- Oil/gas field
- Coal field

TIMBER PROCESSING

Huge tracts of forest are found toward the north of the continent; over 40% of Canada is covered by forest. Timber is processed to make paper in cities such as Portland and Vancouver.

HI-TECH INDUSTRY

The Santa Clara Valley, just south of San Francisco is also known as Silicon Valley, because of the number of firms producing computer hardware and software and micro-electronics which have set up in the area.

FOOD PROCESSING

Jamaica has been famous for its rum since the 16th century. Syrup is extracted from sugar cane which is then fermented to make rum.

CLIMATE

Much of northern Canada lies within the Arctic Circle and is permanently covered by ice or the sparse vegetation known as tundra. Southern Canada and much of central USA have a continental climate, with hot summers and cold winters. The southern parts of the USA, Central America and the Caribbean have a hot, humid tropical climate. The Caribbean and the eastern and central states of the USA often experience hurricane-force winds, waterspouts and tornadoes.

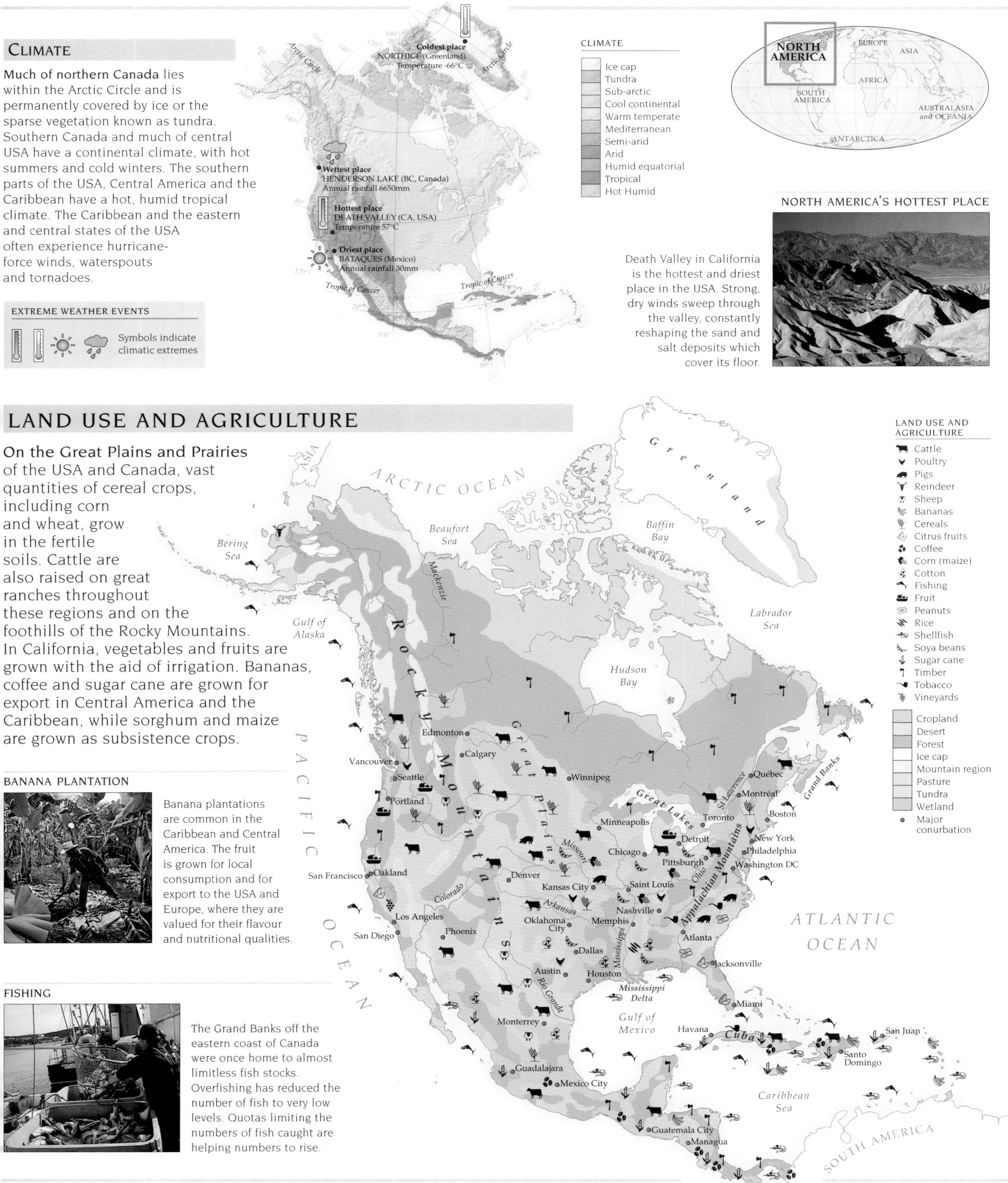

NORTH AMERICA'S HOTTEST PLACE

Death Valley in California is the hottest and driest place in the USA. Strong, dry winds sweep through the valley, constantly reshaping the sand and salt deposits which cover its floor.

LAND USE AND AGRICULTURE

On the Great Plains and Prairies of the USA and Canada, vast quantities of cereal crops, including corn and wheat, grow in the fertile soils. Cattle are also raised on great ranches throughout these regions and on the foothills of the Rocky Mountains. In California, vegetables and fruits are grown with the aid of irrigation. Bananas, coffee and sugar cane are grown for export in Central America and the Caribbean, while sorghum and maize are grown as subsistence crops.

BANANA PLANTATION

Banana plantations are common in the Caribbean and Central America. The fruit is grown for local consumption and for export to the USA and Europe, where they are valued for their flavour and nutritional qualities.

FISHING

The Grand Banks off the eastern coast of Canada were once home to almost limitless fish stocks. Overfishing has reduced the number of fish to very low levels. Quotas limiting the numbers of fish caught are helping numbers to rise.

WESTERN CANADA & ALASKA

ALBERTA, BRITISH COLUMBIA, MANITOBA, NORTHWEST TERRITORIES, NUNAVUT, SASKATCHEWAN, YUKON TERRITORY, ALASKA

The first inhabitants of western Canada were the First Nations. Then came the Inuit. By the late 1800s, the Canadian Pacific Railway was completed and European settlers moved west, turning most of the prairie into grain farms. North of the prairies lie the vast, sparsely populated territories. Alaska, part of the USA, has huge oil reserves amidst spectacular wilderness.

POPULATION

Most of western Canada's people live near the Canada/US border, taking advantage of the warmer climate and convenient transport routes. Further north, the population is sparse, with only a few people – mainly the Inuit – per 100 sq km. In Alaska, most people live in the city of Anchorage and in the southern regions.

URBAN/RURAL POPULATION DIVIDE

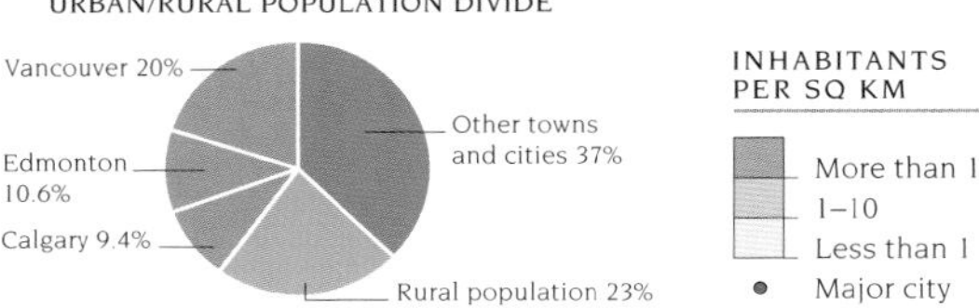

INHABITANTS PER SQ KM

- More than 10
- 1–10
- Less than 1
- Major city

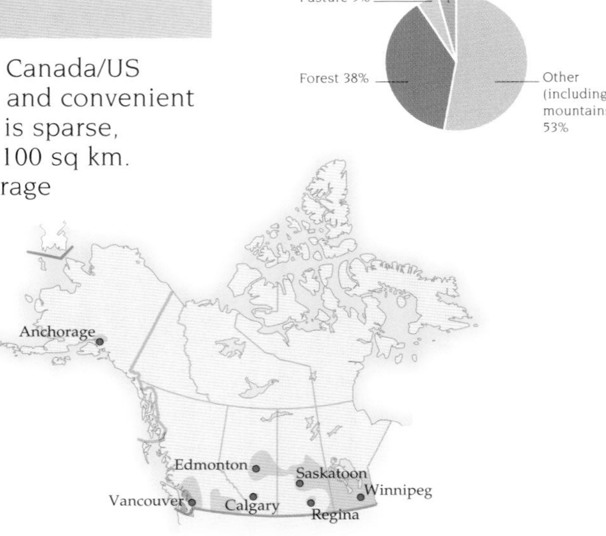

ENVIRONMENTAL ISSUES

Across the north of the region, the ground is permanently frozen. This is called permafrost. Building on this frozen surface is very difficult, because the heat from houses or roads can cause the ground to melt, and subside. The Trans-Alaskan Pipeline, which brings oil from Prudhoe Bay to Valdez, was built above ground to prevent the permafrost melting.

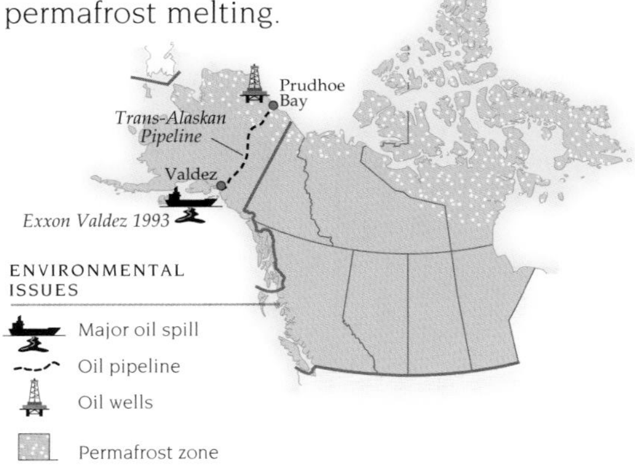

FARMING AND LAND USE

More than 20% of the world's wheat is grown in Canada's prairie provinces: Manitoba, Alberta and Saskatchewan. Beef cattle graze on the ranches of Alberta and British Columbia. Fruits, especially apples, flourish in the sheltered southern valleys of British Columbia, and Pacific salmon and herring are caught off the west coast. Much of the region is heavily forested.

LAND USE

- Pasture 5%
- Cropland 4%
- Forest 38%
- Other (including mountains) 53%

FARMING AND LAND USE

- Cattle
- Fishing
- Cereals
- Fruit
- Timber
- Major conurbation
- Pasture
- Cropland
- Forest
- Mountain region
- Barren
- Tundra

THE LANDSCAPE

The prairie provinces are mostly flat. Occasionally, the level plains are broken up by river valleys such as the Qu'Appelle in Saskatchewan. In the west, the jagged peaks and steep passes of the Rocky Mountains are covered in snow for months on end. West of the Rockies and the Coast Mountains, the land descends sharply to the British Columbia coast. Alaska is mountainous, and scattered with plains and many lakes left by glaciers.

The Arctic
Most of Canada's northern islands are within of the Arctic Circle. They are covered by ice all year round.

Glacial lakes
The plains are covered by thousands of lakes, many of which are vast. They are the remains of great glacial lakes left after the last Ice Age.

Alaska's mountains
The ten highest mountains in the USA are all in Alaska. Mount McKinley (Denali) (D4) is the highest at 6,194 m.

Mount Logan (E5)
Mount Logan is Canada's tallest peak. It rises 5,959 m.

Islands and inlets (E 6)
The British Columbia coast is peppered with islands and fjord-like inlets, created by the force of the Pacific Ocean.

River valleys
Prairie river valleys such as the Qu'Appelle (H7) (French for 'who calls') were cut by glacial meltwater thousands of years ago.

Bering Sea
Near Islands
Attu Island
Rat Islands
Amchitka Island
Aleutian Islands
Andreanof Islands
Atka
Pribilof Islands
Umnak Island
Unalaska Island
Dutch Harb
Unimak Island
Belkof
Limit of winter pa

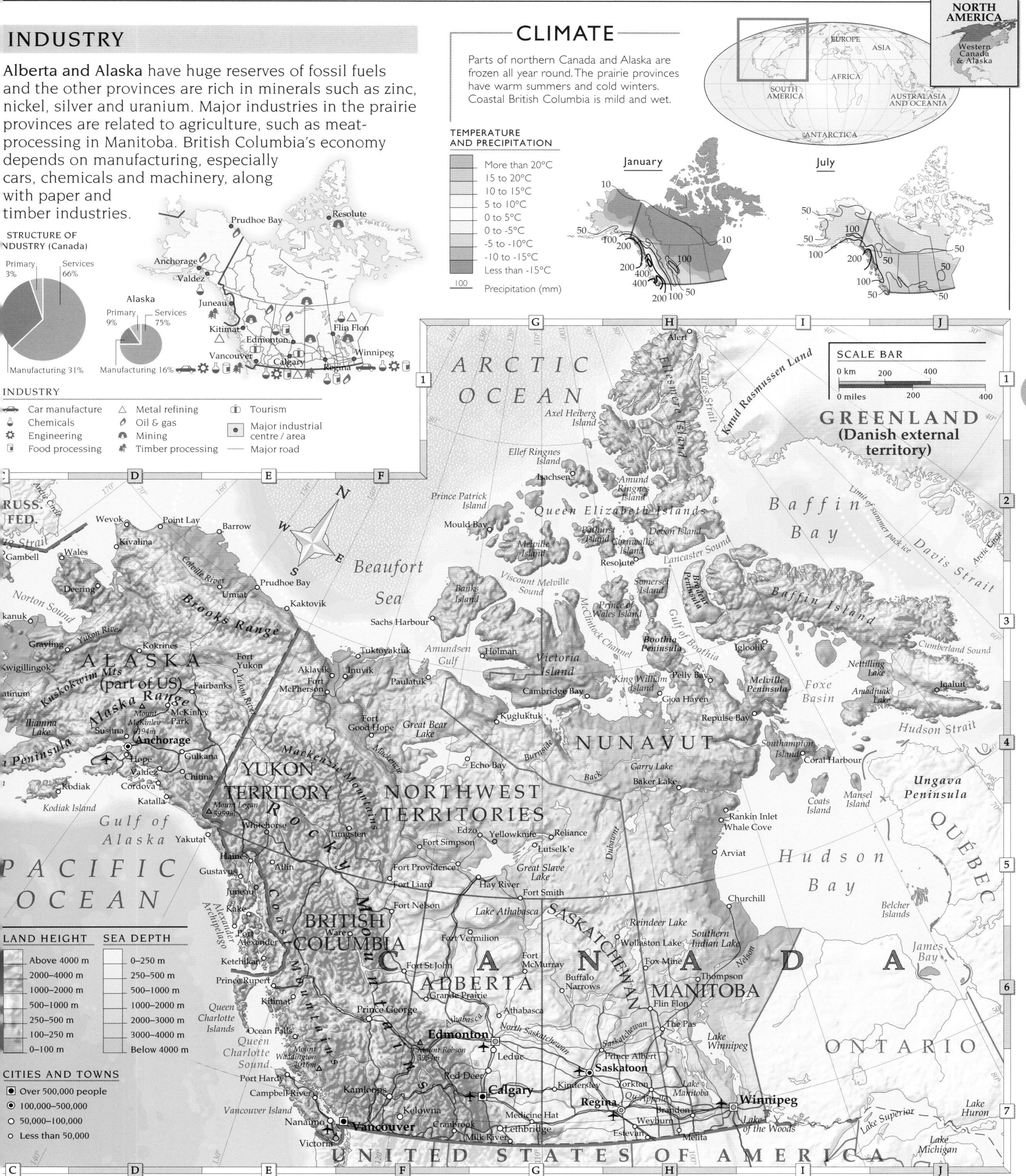
INDUSTRY
Alberta and Alaska have huge reserves of fossil fuels and the other provinces are rich in minerals such as zinc, nickel, silver and uranium. Major industries in the prairie provinces are related to agriculture, such as meat-processing in Manitoba. British Columbia's economy depends on manufacturing, especially cars, chemicals and machinery, along with paper and timber industries.
STRUCTURE OF INDUSTRY (Canada)
Primary 3%
Services 66%
Manufacturing 31%
Alaska
Primary 9%
Services 75%
Manufacturing 16%
Prudhoe Bay
Resolute
Anchorage
Valdez
Juneau
Kitimat
Edmonton
Flin Flon
Vancouver
Calgary
Winnipeg
Regina
INDUSTRY
Car manufacture
Chemicals
Engineering
Food processing
Metal refining
Oil & gas
Mining
Timber processing
Tourism
Major industrial centre / area
Major road
CLIMATE
Parts of northern Canada and Alaska are frozen all year round. The prairie provinces have warm summers and cold winters. Coastal British Columbia is mild and wet.
TEMPERATURE AND PRECIPITATION
More than 20°C
15 to 20°C
10 to 15°C
5 to 10°C
0 to 5°C
0 to -5°C
-5 to -10°C
-10 to -15°C
Less than -15°C
Precipitation (mm)
January
July
NORTH AMERICA
Western Canada & Alaska
EUROPE
ASIA
AFRICA
SOUTH AMERICA
AUSTRALASIA AND OCEANIA
ANTARCTICA
SCALE BAR
0 km 200 400
0 miles 200 400
ARCTIC OCEAN
GREENLAND (Danish external territory)
Baffin Bay
Davis Strait
Beaufort Sea
Queen Elizabeth Islands
ALASKA (part of US)
Brooks Range
Alaska Range
Gulf of Alaska
PACIFIC OCEAN
YUKON TERRITORY
NORTHWEST TERRITORIES
NUNAVUT
BRITISH COLUMBIA
ALBERTA
SASKATCHEWAN
MANITOBA
ONTARIO
QUÉBEC
CANADA
Hudson Bay
Hudson Strait
Ungava Peninsula
Baffin Island
Victoria Island
Great Bear Lake
Great Slave Lake
Lake Athabasca
Lake Winnipeg
Rocky Mountains
Coast Mountains
Mackenzie Mountains
UNITED STATES OF AMERICA
LAND HEIGHT
Above 4000 m
2000–4000 m
1000–2000 m
500–1000 m
250–500 m
100–250 m
0–100 m
SEA DEPTH
0–250 m
250–500 m
500–1000 m
1000–2000 m
2000–3000 m
3000–4000 m
Below 4000 m
CITIES AND TOWNS
Over 500,000 people
100,000–500,000
50,000–100,000
Less than 50,000

EASTERN CANADA

NEW BRUNSWICK, NEWFOUNDLAND AND LABRADOR, NOVA SCOTIA, ONTARIO, PRINCE EDWARD ISLAND, QUÉBEC

The first European settlements grew up in the Atlantic provinces, and along the St. Lawrence River, where Québec City and Montréal were founded. People gradually migrated further west along the St. Lawrence River and the Great Lakes, establishing other cities including Toronto. Although the majority of Canadians speak English, people in Québec speak mainly French, and both English and French are official languages in Canada.

FARMING AND LAND USE

The best farmland lies on the flat, fertile plains close to the St. Lawrence River and on the strip of land between lakes Erie and Ontario. It is used to grow fruits such as grapes, cherries and peaches, and to raise cattle. Nova Scotia has fruit farms, and the rich red soils of Prince Edward Island produce a big crop of potatoes. The vast forests that grow across the north are a major source of timber.

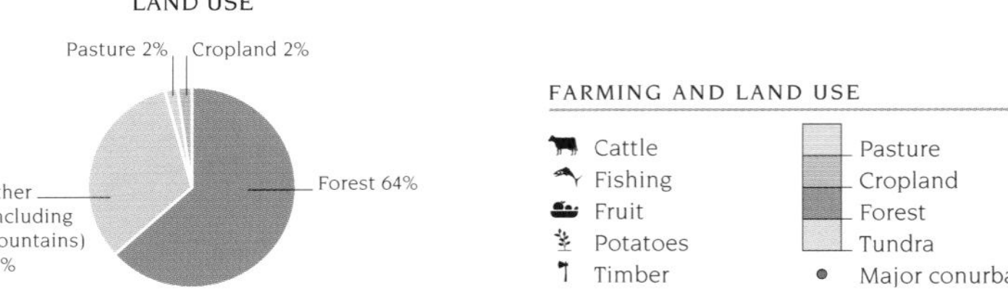

INDUSTRY

In the Atlantic provinces the traditional fishing industry has declined, causing unemployment. However, Newfoundland has a thriving food processing industry. Ontario and Québec have a wide range of industries, including the generation of hydro-electricity, mining, and chemicals, car manufacture and fruit canning in the great cities. Large amounts of wood pulp and paper are also produced.

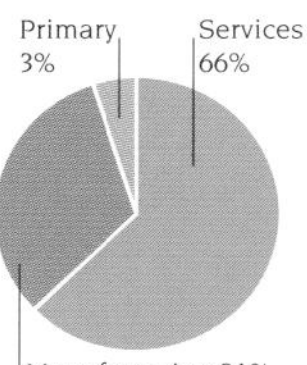

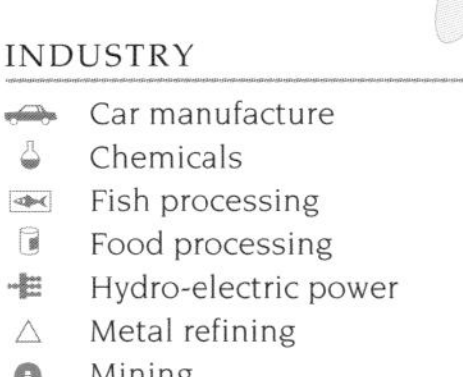

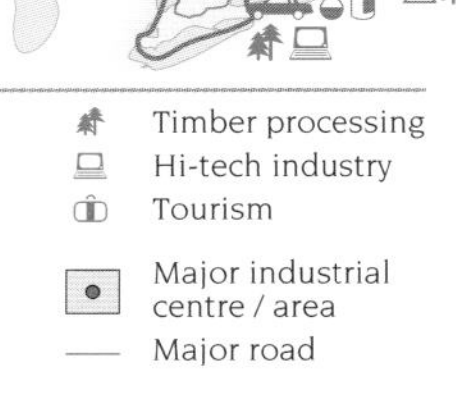

ENVIRONMENTAL ISSUES

Acid rain caused by emissions from factories in the USA and along the St. Lawrence River destroys forests and kills marine life. Massive hydro-electric power projects in James Bay on Hudson Bay have flooded huge areas of land, affecting the environment and the local Cree people. Overfishing in the Atlantic has led to limits being set on the number of fish that can be caught.

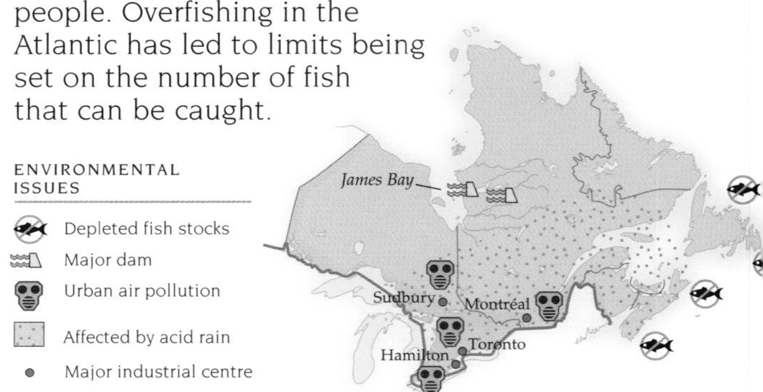

THE LANDSCAPE

A huge, ancient mass of rock called the Canadian Shield lies beneath much of eastern Canada. It is covered by low hills, rocky outcrops, thousands of lakes and huge areas of forest. Much of the Canadian Shield is permanently frozen. The St. Lawrence River flows out of Lake Ontario and on into the Atlantic Ocean. It is surrounded by rolling hills and flat areas of very fertile farmland.

Scoured by ice

About 20,000 years ago, Labrador and northern Québec were completely covered by ice. The glaciers scraped hollows in the rock beneath. When the ice melted, lakes were left in the hollows that remained.

Lake Superior (B5)

Lake Superior is the largest freshwater lake in the world. It covers an area of 83,270 sq km and lies between Canada and the USA.

St. Lawrence River (E5)

The St. Lawrence River is 1,197 km long. Parts of it have become silted up, causing it to be 'braided' into many different channels. Between December and mid-April the river freezes over.

Highlands

The highlands of New Brunswick, Nova Scotia and Newfoundland are the most northerly part of the Appalachian mountain chain.

The Bay of Fundy (F5)

This bay has the world's highest tides. It is shaped like a funnel, and as the Atlantic flows into it, the ever narrowing shores cause the water level to rise 6–15 m at every high tide.

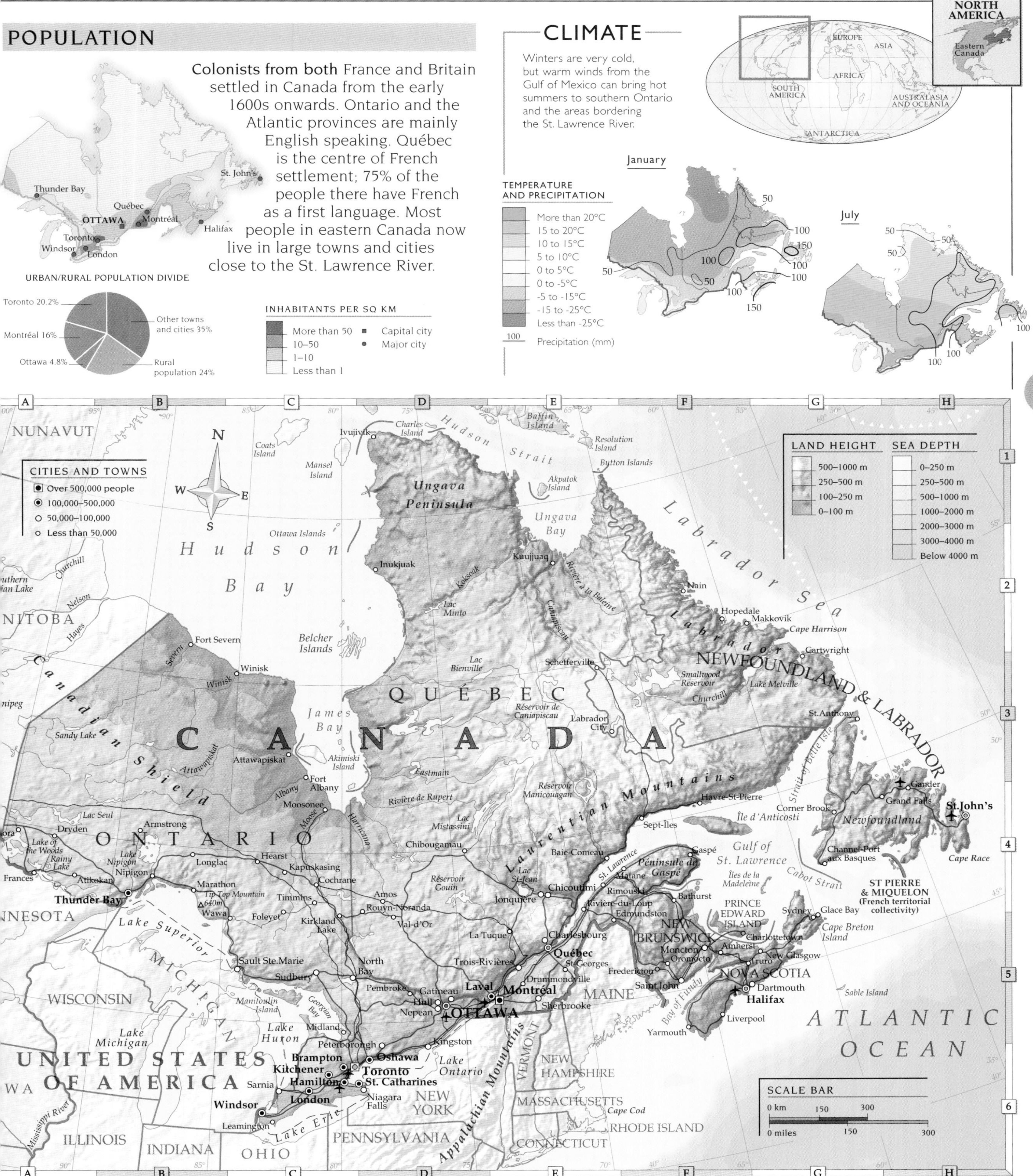
POPULATION
Colonists from both France and Britain settled in Canada from the early 1600s onwards. Ontario and the Atlantic provinces are mainly English speaking. Québec is the centre of French settlement; 75% of the people there have French as a first language. Most people in eastern Canada now live in large towns and cities close to the St. Lawrence River.
Thunder Bay
Québec
OTTAWA
Montréal
Toronto
Windsor
London
St. John's
Halifax
URBAN/RURAL POPULATION DIVIDE
Toronto 20.2%
Montréal 16%
Ottawa 4.8%
Other towns and cities 35%
Rural population 24%
INHABITANTS PER SQ KM
More than 50
10–50
1–10
Less than 1
Capital city
Major city
CLIMATE
Winters are very cold, but warm winds from the Gulf of Mexico can bring hot summers to southern Ontario and the areas bordering the St. Lawrence River.
NORTH AMERICA
Eastern Canada
EUROPE
ASIA
AFRICA
SOUTH AMERICA
AUSTRALASIA AND OCEANIA
ANTARCTICA
TEMPERATURE AND PRECIPITATION
More than 20°C
15 to 20°C
10 to 15°C
5 to 10°C
0 to 5°C
0 to -5°C
-5 to -15°C
-15 to -25°C
Less than -25°C
Precipitation (mm)
January
July
CITIES AND TOWNS
Over 500,000 people
100,000–500,000
50,000–100,000
Less than 50,000
LAND HEIGHT
500–1000 m
250–500 m
100–250 m
0–100 m
SEA DEPTH
0–250 m
250–500 m
500–1000 m
1000–2000 m
2000–3000 m
3000–4000 m
Below 4000 m
SCALE BAR
0 km 150 300
0 miles 150 300
NUNAVUT
Hudson Bay
Hudson Strait
Labrador Sea
Ungava Peninsula
Ungava Bay
QUÉBEC
CANADA
Canadian Shield
ONTARIO
James Bay
Laurentian Mountains
NEWFOUNDLAND & LABRADOR
Newfoundland
Gulf of St. Lawrence
NEW BRUNSWICK
PRINCE EDWARD ISLAND
NOVA SCOTIA
ST PIERRE & MIQUELON (French territorial collectivity)
ATLANTIC OCEAN
UNITED STATES OF AMERICA
Appalachian Mountains
Lake Superior
Lake Michigan
Lake Huron
Lake Ontario
Lake Erie
MAINE
VERMONT
NEW HAMPSHIRE
MASSACHUSETTS
RHODE ISLAND
CONNECTICUT
NEW YORK
PENNSYLVANIA
OHIO
INDIANA
ILLINOIS
WISCONSIN
MICHIGAN
MINNESOTA
Thunder Bay
Sudbury
Sault Ste.Marie
OTTAWA
Montréal
Laval
Québec
Toronto
Hamilton
Kitchener
London
Windsor
St. Catharines
Oshawa
Brampton
Kingston
Halifax
St.John's
Saint John
Moncton
Fredericton
Charlottetown
Sept-Îles
Chicoutimi
Sherbrooke
Trois-Rivières
Gatineau
Schefferville
Labrador City
Nain
Hopedale
Gander
Corner Brook
Sable Island
Cape Race
Cape Breton Island
Bay of Fundy
Cabot Strait

EASTERN USA

The east coast of the USA was settled by European colonists from the 17th century onwards. When the USA became independent in 1776, people gradually spread westwards towards the Mississippi River, and down towards the southern states. In the late 19th and early 20th centuries, thousands of immigrants from all over the world passed through New York on their way to new lives elsewhere in the USA. Today, the eastern USA contains some of the world's most developed and powerful cities.

POPULATION

The northeastern and Great Lakes states are the most populous parts of North America, with people taking advantage of the good transport routes and the availability of jobs. Some of the USA's biggest cities, like New York, are found here, yet in New England many towns have less than 30,000 people. In recent years, many have migrated to the 'Sunbelt' states of the south – especially to Florida.

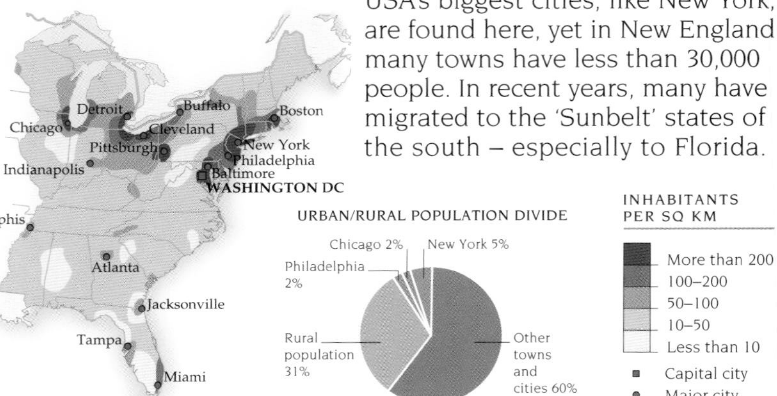

INDUSTRY

The northeast is the USA's industrial heartland. The Great Lakes states are the centre of car manufacturing, but service industries are also developing. Hi-tech industries such as computers and electronics are found around Boston and in New Jersey. New York is the USA's financial capital. Further south, states like North Carolina are centres for research and development and Florida has a successful tourist industry.

STRUCTURE OF INDUSTRY

Primary 5%
Services 63%
Manufacturing 32%

INDUSTRY

- Car manufacture
- Chemicals
- Engineering
- Food processing
- Iron & steel
- Textiles
- Coal
- Finance
- Hi-tech industry
- Research & Development
- Tourism
- Major industrial centre / area
- Major road

THE LANDSCAPE

The Atlantic and Gulf coasts are bordered in the south by a wide and mainly low-lying plain, with many swampy areas. Towards the north, the plain gradually falls away, forming salt marshes, lagoons and offshore sandbars. Inland, the plain is overlooked by the rounded peaks of the Appalachian Mountains. West of the mountains is the vast Mississippi Basin.

Great Lakes

The five Great Lakes were formed during the last Ice Age and contain 20% of the world's fresh water. The area around the lakes is rich in natural resources, including coal, iron, copper and timber.

Appalachian Mountains (E4)

The forest-covered Appalachians are one of the oldest mountain chains in the world. Over a period of about 400 million years they have been lowered and rounded by erosion. Their eastern side has been worn down to a plain called a piedmont, or 'mountain foot'.

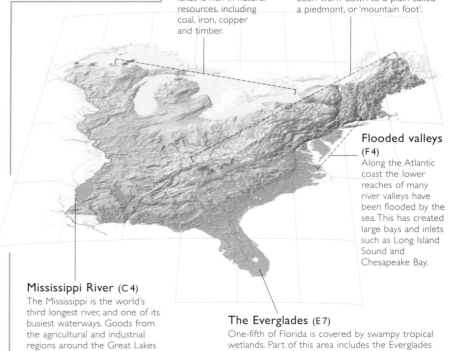

Flooded valleys (F4)

Along the Atlantic coast the lower reaches of many river valleys have been flooded by the sea. This has created large bays and inlets such as Long Island Sound and Chesapeake Bay.

Mississippi River (C4)

The Mississippi is the world's third longest river, and one of its busiest waterways. Goods from the agricultural and industrial regions around the Great Lakes are transported by barge down to the Gulf of Mexico.

The Everglades (E7)

One-fifth of Florida is covered by swampy tropical wetlands. Part of this area includes the Everglades National Park, which is home to many wild animals and plants, including some endangered species.

FARMING AND LAND USE

Dairy, livestock and fruit farming are important in New York, Pennsylvania and the Great Lakes states. North Carolina is the USA's biggest tobacco grower. The southeastern states once grew most of the world's cotton; today soya beans and peanuts are the most important crops. Fish are caught in the states bordering the Gulf of Mexico, and Florida is famous for its citrus fruits.

LAND USE

Other (including urban) 12%
Forest 39%
Pasture 25%
Cropland 24%

FARMING AND LAND USE

- Cattle
- Fishing
- Pigs
- Poultry
- Cereals
- Cotton
- Fruit
- Peanuts
- Soya beans
- Tobacco
- Cropland
- Forest
- Pasture
- Wetland
- Major conurbation

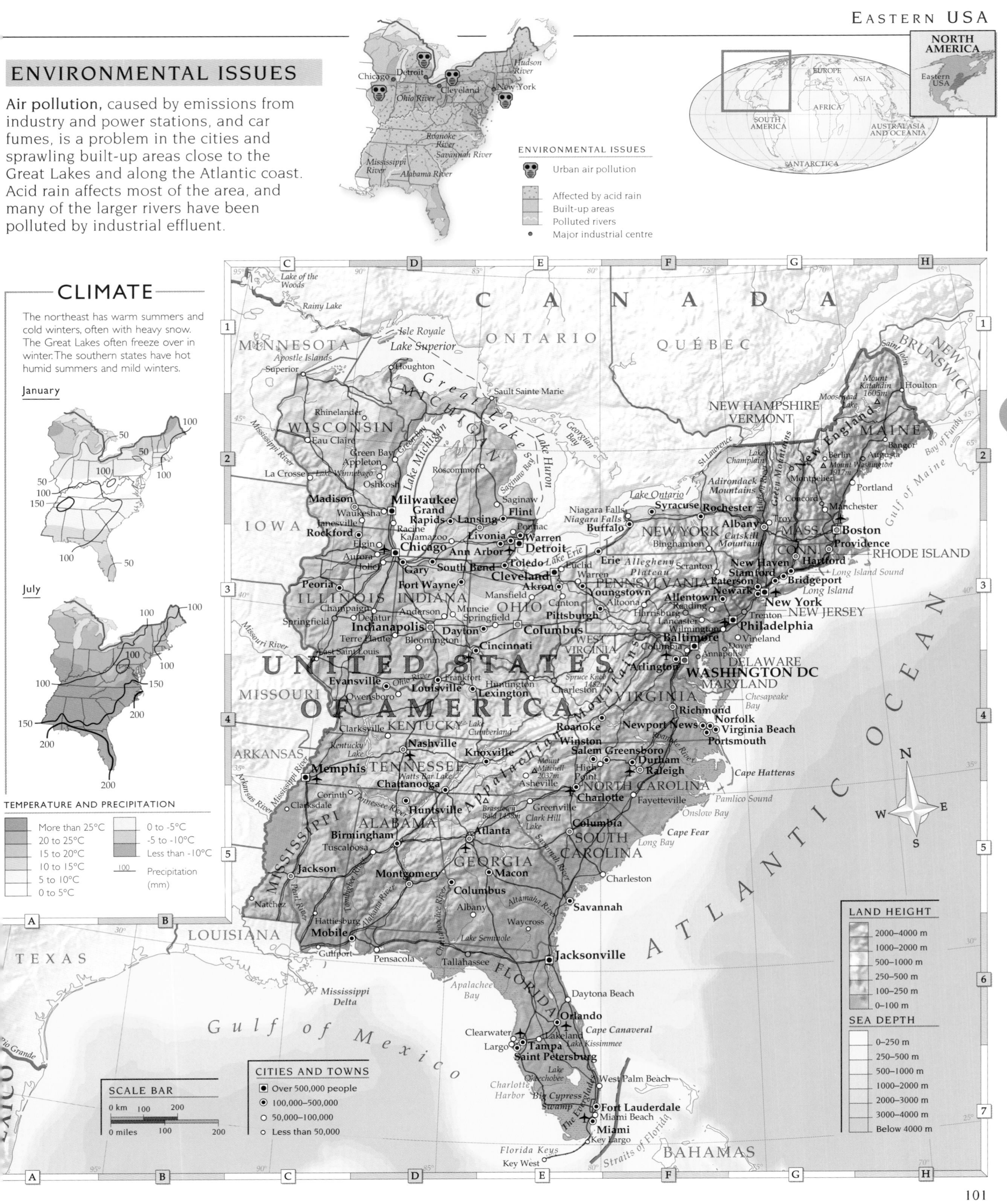
ENVIRONMENTAL ISSUES
Air pollution, caused by emissions from industry and power stations, and car fumes, is a problem in the cities and sprawling built-up areas close to the Great Lakes and along the Atlantic coast. Acid rain affects most of the area, and many of the larger rivers have been polluted by industrial effluent.
Chicago
Detroit
Cleveland
Hudson River
New York
Ohio River
Roanoke River
Savannah River
Mississippi River
Alabama River
ENVIRONMENTAL ISSUES
Urban air pollution
Affected by acid rain
Built-up areas
Polluted rivers
Major industrial centre
NORTH AMERICA
Eastern USA
EUROPE
ASIA
AFRICA
SOUTH AMERICA
AUSTRALASIA AND OCEANIA
ANTARCTICA
CLIMATE
The northeast has warm summers and cold winters, often with heavy snow. The Great Lakes often freeze over in winter. The southern states have hot humid summers and mild winters.
January
July
TEMPERATURE AND PRECIPITATION
More than 25°C
20 to 25°C
15 to 20°C
10 to 15°C
5 to 10°C
0 to 5°C
0 to -5°C
-5 to -10°C
Less than -10°C
Precipitation (mm)
CANADA
ONTARIO
QUÉBEC
NEW BRUNSWICK
MINNESOTA
WISCONSIN
MICHIGAN
IOWA
ILLINOIS
INDIANA
OHIO
MISSOURI
KENTUCKY
TENNESSEE
ARKANSAS
MISSISSIPPI
ALABAMA
GEORGIA
LOUISIANA
TEXAS
FLORIDA
SOUTH CAROLINA
NORTH CAROLINA
VIRGINIA
WEST VIRGINIA
MARYLAND
DELAWARE
NEW JERSEY
PENNSYLVANIA
NEW YORK
MASS.
CONN.
RHODE ISLAND
NEW HAMPSHIRE
VERMONT
MAINE
UNITED STATES OF AMERICA
WASHINGTON DC
Chicago
Detroit
Cleveland
Columbus
Indianapolis
Memphis
Nashville
Atlanta
Jacksonville
Philadelphia
New York
Boston
Baltimore
Charlotte
Miami
Gulf of Mexico
ATLANTIC OCEAN
BAHAMAS
Great Lakes
Lake Superior
Lake Michigan
Lake Huron
Lake Erie
Lake Ontario
Appalachian Mountains
LAND HEIGHT
2000–4000 m
1000–2000 m
500–1000 m
250–500 m
100–250 m
0–100 m
SEA DEPTH
0–250 m
250–500 m
500–1000 m
1000–2000 m
2000–3000 m
3000–4000 m
Below 4000 m
CITIES AND TOWNS
Over 500,000 people
100,000–500,000
50,000–100,000
Less than 50,000
SCALE BAR
0 km 100 200
0 miles 100 200

Western USA

Western USA stretches from the Mississippi Basin across the Great Plains to the mighty Rocky Mountains and the Pacific Ocean. Its dramatic scenery varies from vast evergreen forests and lush valleys in the north, to the huge farming and cattle-ranching prairies of the Midwest and the deserts of the southwest, where temperatures soar over 40°C in summer. The western states have a very racially mixed population. Many people have ancestors from Europe, Africa and Asia, and the southwest is home to communities of native Americans such as the Navajo.

Farming and Land Use

Huge cereal farms and cattle ranches take up most of the Great Plains. More maize and wheat is produced here than anywhere else in the world. Fruit is grown in the sheltered valleys of Oregon and Washington, and in California, where the fertile but dry land is irrigated almost all year round to produce the country's biggest crop of citrus and other fruits.

LAND USE

Pasture 45%, Cropland 29%, Forest 15%, Other 11%

FARMING AND LAND USE

- Cattle
- Fishing
- Pigs
- Poultry
- Shellfish
- Cereals
- Cotton
- Fruit
- Soya beans
- Timber
- Cropland
- Desert
- Forest
- Pasture
- Wetland
- Major conurbation

Industry

Western USA is a major agricultural producer, although its cities have a variety of manufacturing and service industries. Washington has an important aerospace industry, and its forests, along with those in Oregon, supply most of the USA's timber. Oklahoma and Texas have big oil and gas fields, and minerals are mined in Montana and Wyoming. 'Silicon Valley' in California is a world centre for micro-electronics.

INDUSTRY

- Aerospace industry
- Car manufacture
- Chemicals
- Engineering
- Food processing
- Textiles
- Mining
- Oil & gas
- Timber processing
- Hi-tech industry
- Research & development
- Tourism
- Major industrial centre / area
- Major road

STRUCTURE OF INDUSTRY

Primary 7%, Services 65%, Manufacturing 28%

The Landscape

The Great Plains sweep west from the Mississippi River flood plain. At the western edge of the plains the land rises, becoming the Rocky Mountains. Within this chain there are many high plateaus and basins. Further west are the Sierra Nevada, the Cascade Range, and finally the Coast Ranges, which run along the Pacific seaboard.

Cascade Range (B 2)
These mountains run from Washington through Oregon and south into California. They include a chain of volcanoes, one of which, Mount Saint Helens, last erupted in 1980.

Death Valley (C 3)
Death Valley in California lies 86 m below sea level. It is the lowest point in the western hemisphere, and one of the hottest places on Earth.

Rocky Mountains (D 3)
The Rockies stretch in an almost unbroken chain from Alaska to New Mexico. Some of North America's highest peaks are found here, as well as many active volcanoes.

Badlands (E 2)
About 5,200 sq km of South Dakota is covered by 'badlands'. These are created in dry areas with little or no vegetation; occasional heavy rainstorms wear away the exposed rock to create deep gullies and sharp pinnacles.

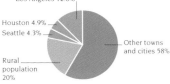

Earthquakes
The San Andreas Fault is a break in the Earth's crust that runs for 1,050 km through California. A sudden movement of land along the fault causes earthquakes, such as the one in 1994 which caused much damage in Los Angeles.

Grand Canyon (C 4)
The Grand Canyon in Arizona is a spectacular gorge cut by the Colorado River. The canyon is about 446 km long, between 8–29 km wide and up to 1,829 m deep.

Great Plains (E 3)
The landscape of the Great Plains is largely treeless farmland. The region was once natural grassland or prairie, grazed by huge herds of buffalo. Being far from any oceans, summers here are very hot and winters freezing.

Population

California has more people than any other US state. Immigrants from Asia and Latin America, especially Mexico, make up a large, and growing, part of its population. Outside the big cities, most of the other western states are sparsely populated, and people depend on cars to cover the huge distances between places.

INHABITANTS PER SQ KM

- More than 200
- 100–200
- 50–100
- 10–50
- Less than 10
- Major city

URBAN/RURAL POPULATION DIVIDE

Los Angeles 12.8%, Houston 4.9%, Seattle 4.3%, Rural population 20%, Other towns and cities 58%

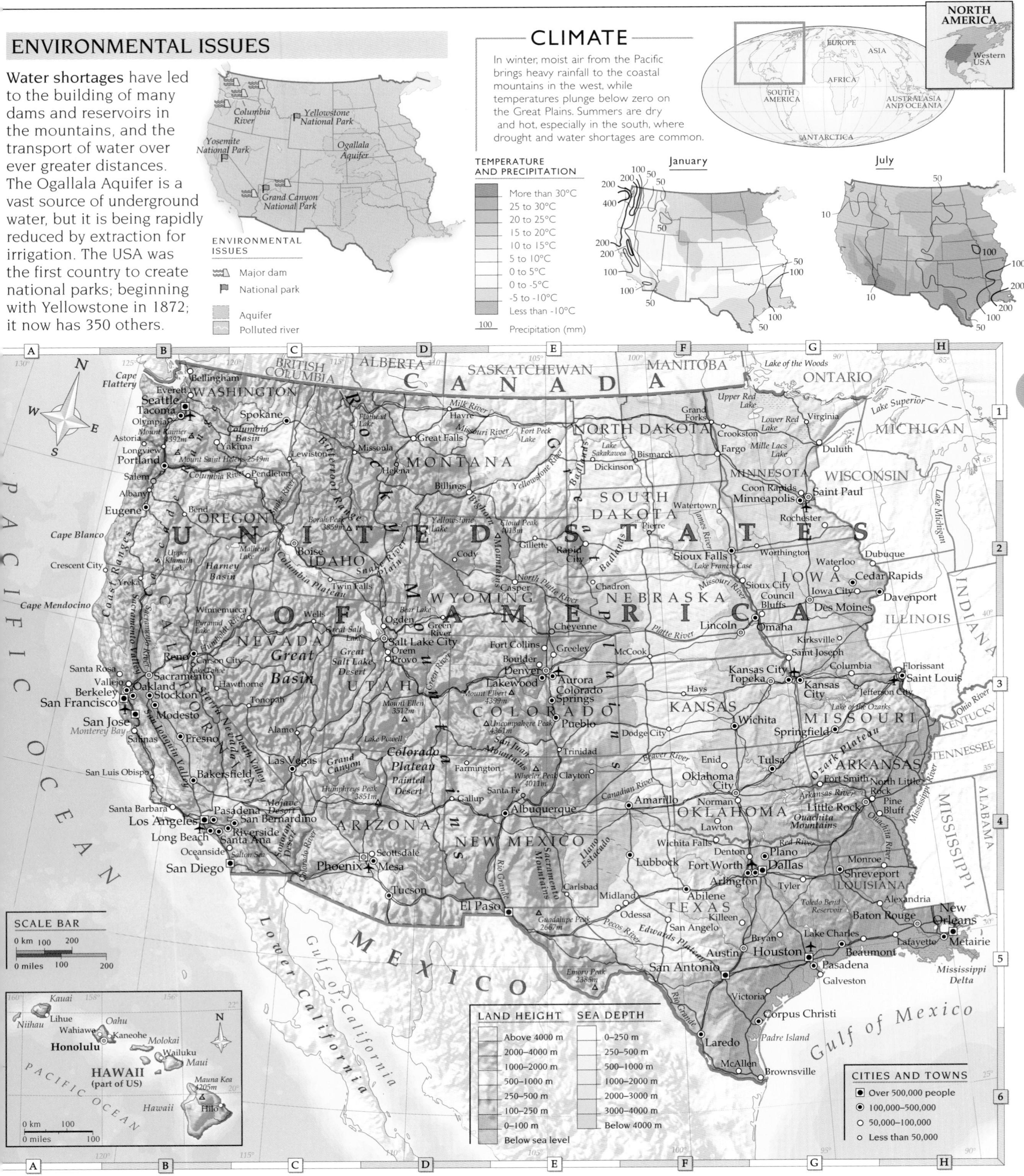
ENVIRONMENTAL ISSUES
Water shortages have led to the building of many dams and reservoirs in the mountains, and the transport of water over ever greater distances. The Ogallala Aquifer is a vast source of underground water, but it is being rapidly reduced by extraction for irrigation. The USA was the first country to create national parks; beginning with Yellowstone in 1872; it now has 350 others.
Columbia River
Yellowstone National Park
Yosemite National Park
Ogallala Aquifer
Grand Canyon National Park
ENVIRONMENTAL ISSUES
Major dam
National park
Aquifer
Polluted river
CLIMATE
In winter, moist air from the Pacific brings heavy rainfall to the coastal mountains in the west, while temperatures plunge below zero on the Great Plains. Summers are dry and hot, especially in the south, where drought and water shortages are common.
NORTH AMERICA
Western USA
EUROPE
ASIA
AFRICA
SOUTH AMERICA
AUSTRALASIA AND OCEANIA
ANTARCTICA
TEMPERATURE AND PRECIPITATION
More than 30°C
25 to 30°C
20 to 25°C
15 to 20°C
10 to 15°C
5 to 10°C
0 to 5°C
0 to -5°C
-5 to -10°C
Less than -10°C
100 Precipitation (mm)
January
July
CANADA
BRITISH COLUMBIA
ALBERTA
SASKATCHEWAN
MANITOBA
ONTARIO
UNITED STATES OF AMERICA
WASHINGTON
OREGON
IDAHO
MONTANA
NORTH DAKOTA
SOUTH DAKOTA
MINNESOTA
WISCONSIN
MICHIGAN
IOWA
NEBRASKA
WYOMING
NEVADA
UTAH
COLORADO
KANSAS
MISSOURI
ILLINOIS
INDIANA
KENTUCKY
TENNESSEE
CALIFORNIA
ARIZONA
NEW MEXICO
OKLAHOMA
ARKANSAS
MISSISSIPPI
ALABAMA
LOUISIANA
TEXAS
MEXICO
PACIFIC OCEAN
Gulf of Mexico
Gulf of California
Lower California
Rocky Mountains
Great Plains
Great Basin
Colorado Plateau
Seattle
Tacoma
Portland
Spokane
Boise
Salt Lake City
Denver
Sacramento
San Francisco
San Jose
Los Angeles
San Diego
Las Vegas
Phoenix
Tucson
Albuquerque
El Paso
Oklahoma City
Dallas
Fort Worth
Houston
San Antonio
Austin
Kansas City
Omaha
Minneapolis
Saint Paul
Saint Louis
Des Moines
New Orleans
SCALE BAR
0 km 100 200
0 miles 100 200
HAWAII (part of US)
Kauai
Niihau
Oahu
Molokai
Maui
Hawaii
Honolulu
Hilo
Mauna Kea 4205m
PACIFIC OCEAN
LAND HEIGHT
Above 4000 m
2000–4000 m
1000–2000 m
500–1000 m
250–500 m
100–250 m
0–100 m
Below sea level
SEA DEPTH
0–250 m
250–500 m
500–1000 m
1000–2000 m
2000–3000 m
3000–4000 m
Below 4000 m
CITIES AND TOWNS
Over 500,000 people
100,000–500,000
50,000–100,000
Less than 50,000

MEXICO

Mexico is a large country with a rich mixture of traditions and cultures. The ancient civilization of the Aztecs which flourished here was crushed by Spanish invaders in the 16th century. Spain ruled Mexico until its independence in 1836 and today, the country has the world's largest and fastest growing Spanish-speaking population. Mexico is mostly dry and mountainous, and farm land is limited, so the country has to import most of the basic foods it needs to feed its people.

FARMING AND LAND USE

Most of the land suitable for farming is planted with corn – a big part of the Mexican diet. Along the Gulf coast coffee, sugar cane and cotton are grown on plantations for export. Parts of the dry north are irrigated to grow cotton, but most of the land is taken up by large cattle ranches. Fishing, especially for shellfish such as lobster and shrimp is important in coastal areas.

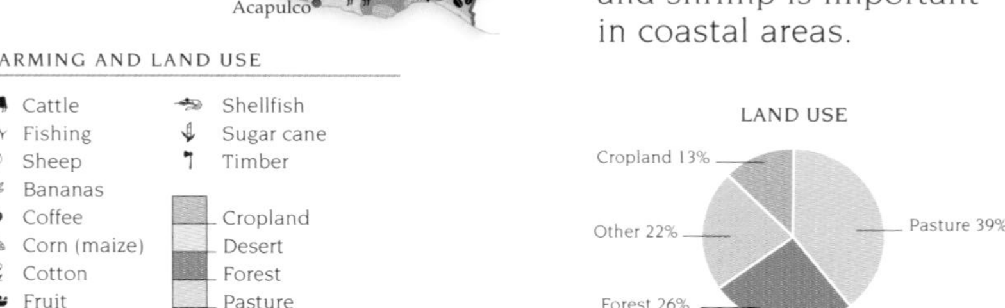

THE LANDSCAPE

Much of Mexico is made up of a high plateau. The climate there is very dry and varies between true desert in the north, and semi-desert further south. The plateau is separated from the coastal plains by two long, rugged mountain chains: the Eastern Sierra Madre and the Western Sierra Madre. Towards the south, the mountain ranges join, meeting in the region of high volcanic peaks that surround Mexico City.

The Rio Grande (D 2)
This river flows from Colorado in the USA and forms much of Mexico's northern border. It crosses a vast arid area on its way to the Gulf of Mexico.

Earthquakes and volcanoes
Volcanic activity is common in Mexico. Popocatépetl (F5) and Volcán El Chichónal (G5) have erupted recently, and Mexico City was hit by a devastating earthquake in 1985

Eastern Sierra Madre (D 5).

Yucatan Peninsula (H 4)
The Yucatan Peninsula is a low, wide tableland, formed by layers of limestone. Limestone absorbs water, so there are few rivers on the peninsula, and the tropical rainforests found there are fed mainly by streams and underground water.

Lower California (B 3)
This long and very dry peninsula, separates the Gulf of California from the Pacific Ocean. The Gulf was formed after the last Ice Age, when the sea rose to flood a major rift valley.

Western Sierra Madre (C 3).

POPULATION

Most of the north is sparsely populated due to the hot, dry climate and lack of cultivable farm land. As people have migrated from the countryside in search of work, the cities have grown dramatically; almost 75% of Mexicans now live in urban areas. Mexico City is home to almost a quarter of the population and is one of the world's largest cities.

INHABITANTS PER SQ KM
- More than 200
- 100–200
- 50–100
- Less than 50
- Capital city
- Major city

URBAN/RURAL POPULATION DIVIDE
- Mexico City 21.6%
- Guadalajara 2.4%
- Monterrey 2%
- Rural population 26%
- Other towns and cities 48%

ENVIRONMENTAL ISSUES

Fast, unplanned growth has led to poor sanitation and water supplies in Mexico City, while the wall of mountains which surround the city traps pollution from cars and factories, giving it some of the world's worst air pollution. Much of Mexico's tropical rainforest has been felled, leading to increased soil erosion. Land clearance further north is also causing desertification.

ENVIRONMENTAL ISSUES

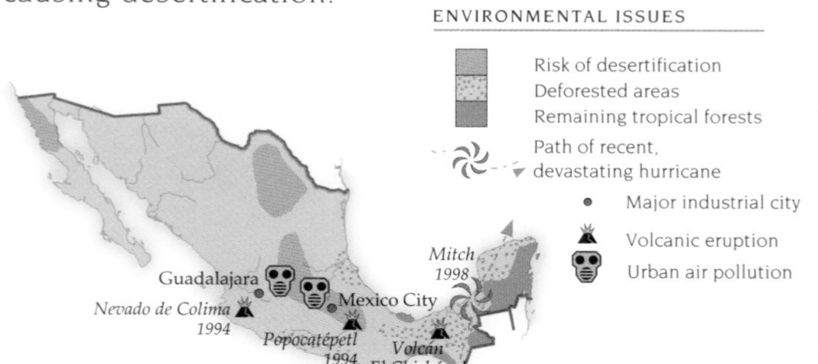

INDUSTRY

Oil and gas on the Gulf coast are the biggest source of income. Mexico is also rich in other minerals; it is the world's top silver producer. Manufacturing is centred around Mexico City and along the US border, where mainly foreign owned factories assemble products for export. Tourism is increasing throughout Mexico.

STRUCTURE OF INDUSTRY

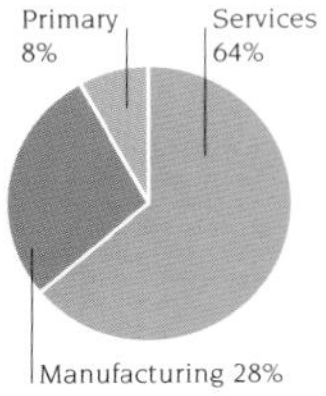

INDUSTRY

- Car manufacture
- Electronics
- Engineering
- Food processing
- Iron & steel
- Oil refining
- Textiles
- Mining
- Oil and gas
- Tourism
- Major industrial centre / area
- Major road

CLIMATE

Northern Mexico and the peninsula of Lower California are dry, hot and largely desert. Towards the south, rainfall increases, especially in July. Moist, warm conditions allow rainforests to grow.

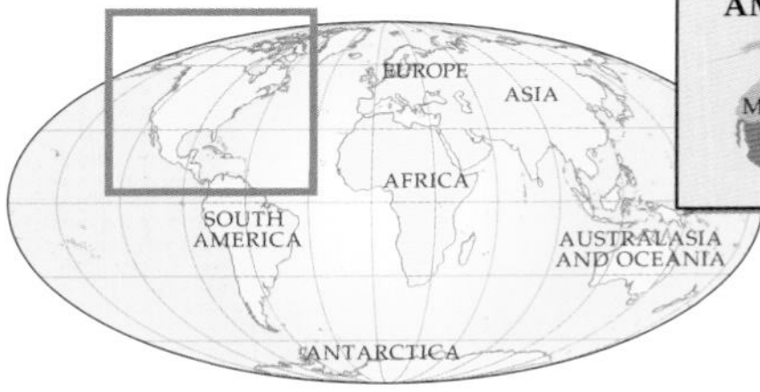

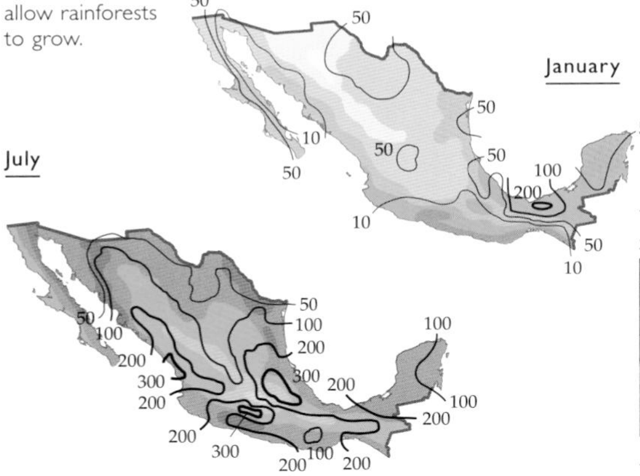

TEMPERATURE AND PRECIPITATION

- More than 30°C
- 25 to 30°C
- 20 to 25°C
- 15 to 20°C
- 10 to 15°C
- 5 to 10°C
- Less than 5°C
- 100 Precipitation (mm)

CENTRAL AMERICA

BELIZE, COSTA RICA, EL SALVADOR, GUATEMALA, HONDURAS, NICARAGUA, PANAMA

Central America lies on a narrow bridge of land which links North and South America. All the countries here, except Belize, were once governed by Spain. Today, most of their people are *mestizos* – a mix of the original Maya Indian inhabitants and Spanish settlers. The hot, steamy climate is ideal for growing tropical crops, such as coffee and bananas, which are exported worldwide.

FARMING AND LAND USE

About half of all the agricultural products grown here are exported. The Pacific coast has fertile, well-watered land suitable for growing cotton and sugar cane. In the central highlands are big coffee plantations, and ranches where beef cattle are raised. Bananas grow well along the humid Caribbean coastal plain, and shrimp and lobster are caught offshore.

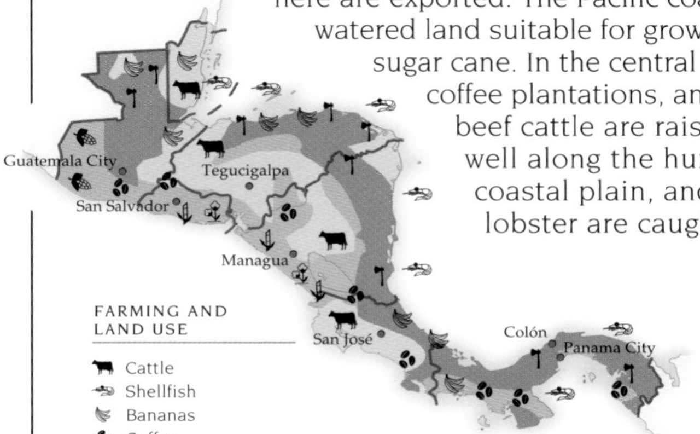

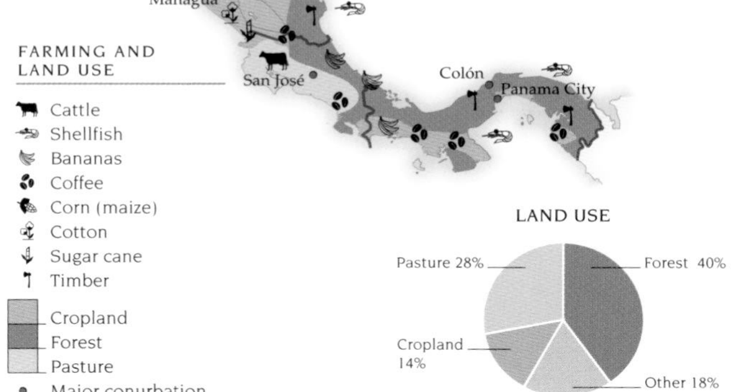

Guatemala City
San Salvador
Tegucigalpa
Managua
San José
Colón
Panama City

FARMING AND LAND USE

- Cattle
- Shellfish
- Bananas
- Coffee
- Corn (maize)
- Cotton
- Sugar cane
- Timber
- Cropland
- Forest
- Pasture
- Major conurbation

LAND USE

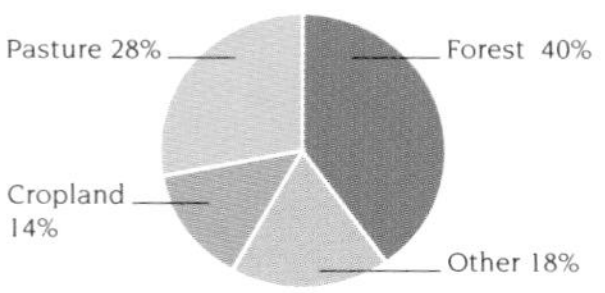

Pasture 28%
Forest 40%
Cropland 14%
Other 18%

ENVIRONMENTAL ISSUES

Central America's rainforests are rapidly being cut down for timber and to make way for farmland and land for building. Over half of Guatemala's forests have been felled, mostly in the last 30 years. The situation is also bleak in Honduras, Costa Rica and Nicaragua. Central America has a line of volcanoes running through the region which are still active.

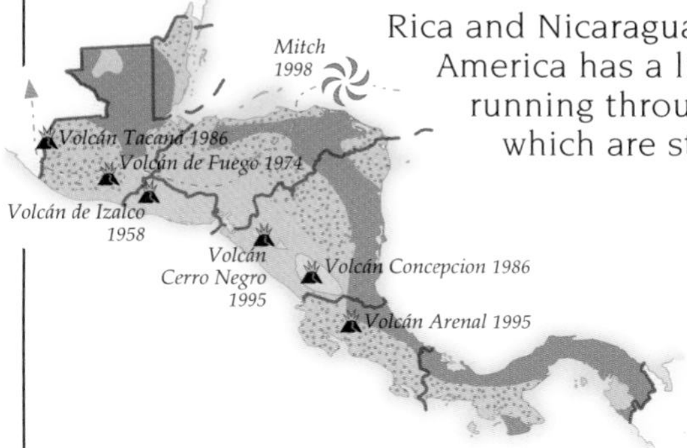

Mitch 1998
Volcán Tacaná 1986
Volcán de Fuego 1974
Volcán de Izalco 1958
Volcán Cerro Negro 1995
Volcán Concepcion 1986
Volcán Arenal 1995

ENVIRONMENTAL ISSUES

- Volcanic eruption
- Deforested areas
- Remaining forests
- Path of recent, devastating hurricane

POPULATION

Central America's people live mainly in the valleys of the central highlands or along the Pacific coastal plains. Despite the threat of volcanic eruptions and earthquakes, towns and cities developed in these areas because of the fertile volcanic soils found there. Just over half the population still live in rural areas, mostly in small villages or remote settlements, but the cities have expanded rapidly and overcrowding has become a serious problem.

BELMOPAN
GUATEMALA CITY
TEGUCIGALPA
SAN SALVADOR
MANAGUA
SAN JOSÉ
PANAMA CITY

INHABITANTS PER SQ KM

- More than 50
- 25–50
- Less than 25
- Capital city

URBAN/RURAL POPULATION DIVIDE

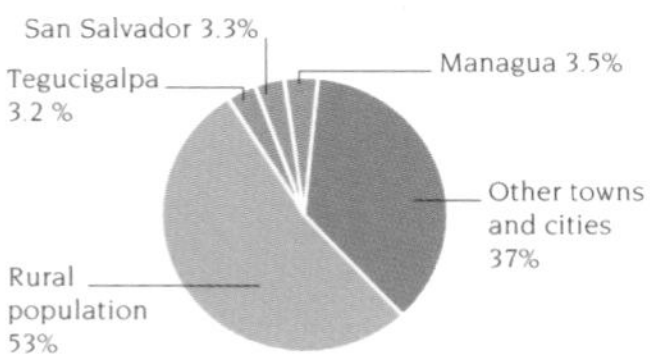

San Salvador 3.3%
Tegucigalpa 3.2 %
Managua 3.5%
Other towns and cities 37%
Rural population 53%

THE LANDSCAPE

The Sierra Madre in the north and the Cordillera Central to the south form a mountainous ridge that stretches down most of Central America. Along the Pacific coast north of Panama is a belt of more than 40 active volcanoes. The mountains are broken by valleys and basins with large, fertile areas of rich, volcanic soil.

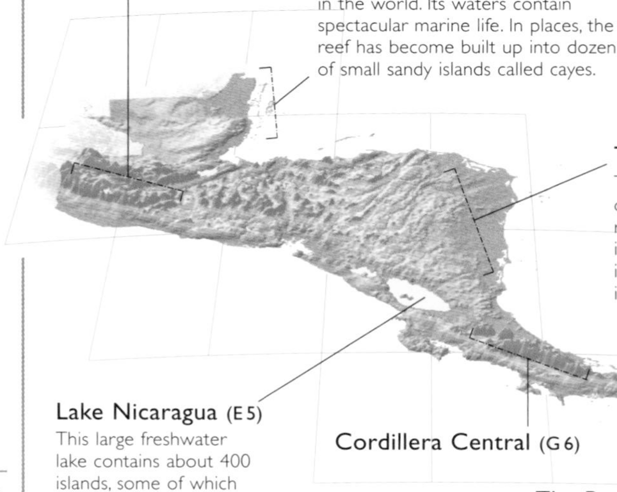

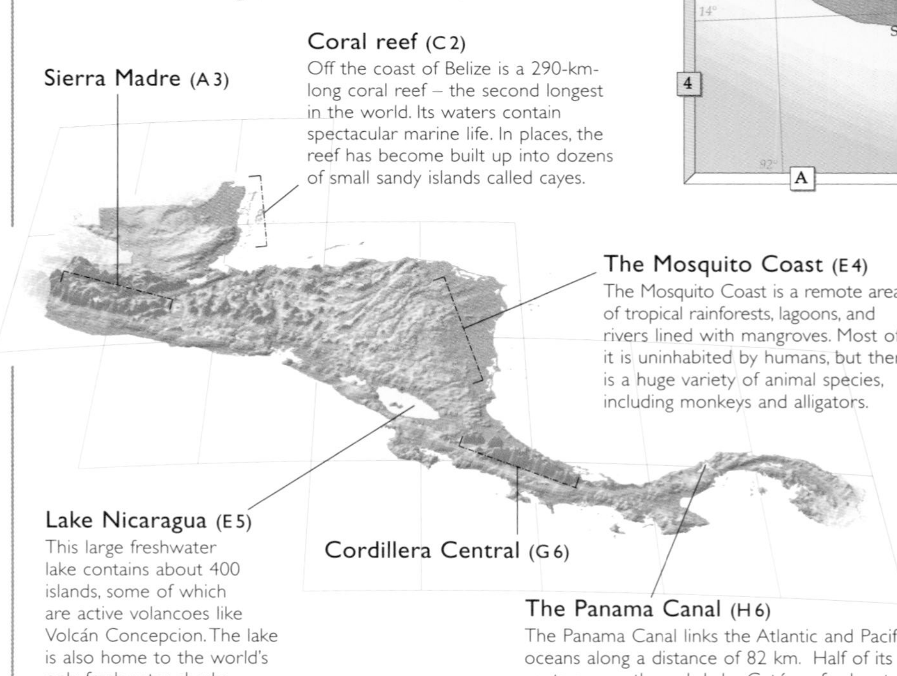

Sierra Madre (A 3)

Coral reef (C 2)
Off the coast of Belize is a 290-km-long coral reef – the second longest in the world. Its waters contain spectacular marine life. In places, the reef has become built up into dozens of small sandy islands called cayes.

The Mosquito Coast (E 4)
The Mosquito Coast is a remote area of tropical rainforests, lagoons, and rivers lined with mangroves. Most of it is uninhabited by humans, but there is a huge variety of animal species, including monkeys and alligators.

Lake Nicaragua (E 5)
This large freshwater lake contains about 400 islands, some of which are active volancoes like Volcán Concepcion. The lake is also home to the world's only freshwater sharks.

Cordillera Central (G 6)

The Panama Canal (H 6)
The Panama Canal links the Atlantic and Pacific oceans along a distance of 82 km. Half of its route passes through Lake Gatún, a freshwater lake which acts as a reservoir for the canal, providing water to operate the locks.

A
1
2
3
4
MEXICO
Barillas
Jacaltenango
Chajul
Huehuetenango
Volcán Tacaná 4093m
Santa Cruz del Quiché
San Marcos
Quezalten
GUATEMALA
Champerico

CLIMATE

Temperatures are high all year round, although in January the Caribbean side of Central America is is cooler and wetter than the Pacific side. Summers are generally much wetter, especially in the Sierra Madre in Guatemala and on the Pacific coasts of Costa Rica and Panama.

INDUSTRY

Coffee, fish, and timber processing, fruit exporting and textile-weaving are typical of the small-scale industries found in Central America. Most industries are based in the capital cities and larger towns. In Panama, many people work at the Panama Canal, which is one of the world's busiest shipping routes. The country is also a major financial centre, with many banking and insurance companies.

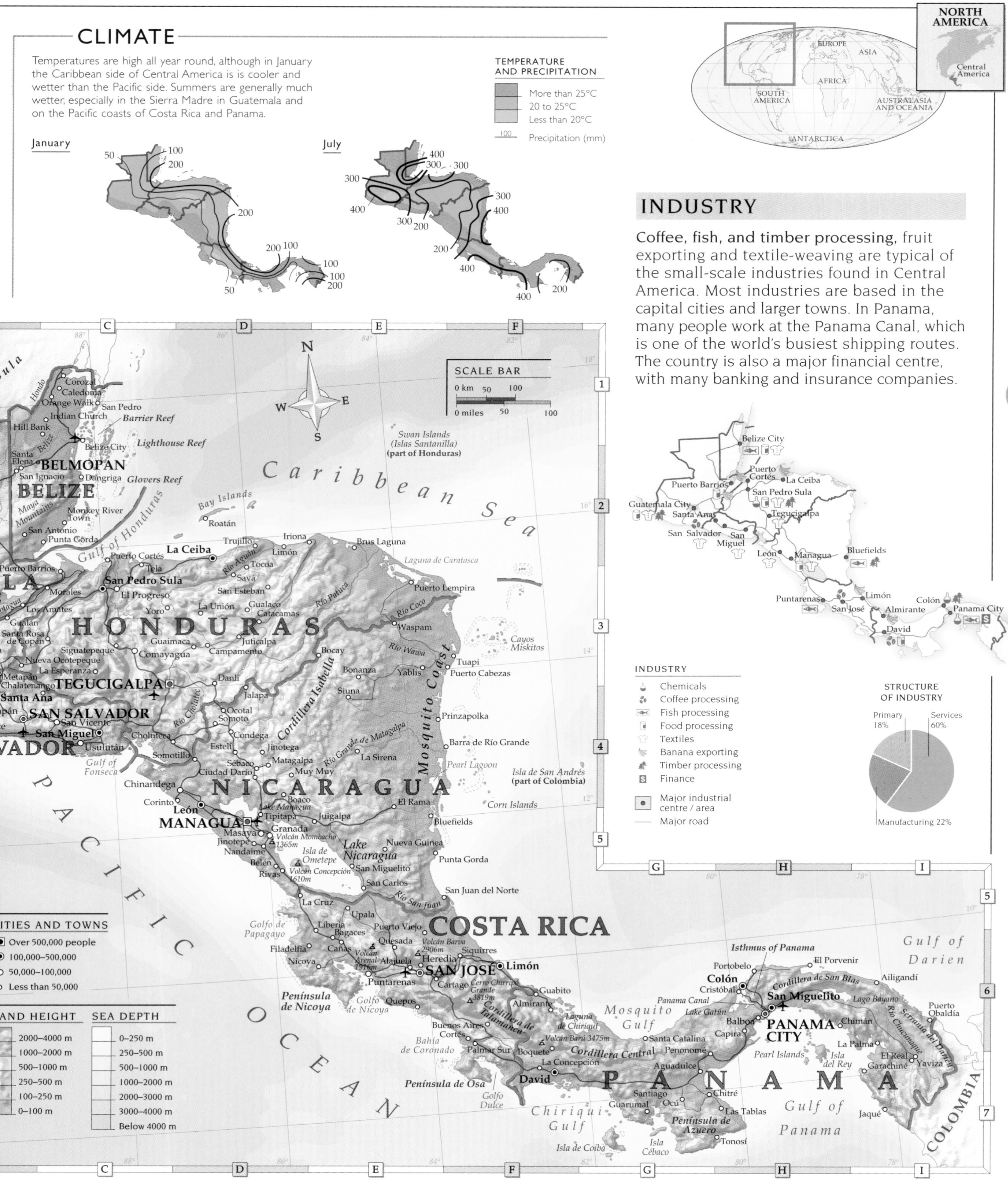

THE CARIBBEAN

The Caribbean Sea is enclosed by an arc of many hundreds of islands, islets and offshore reefs which reach from Florida in the USA round to Venezuela in South America. From 1492, Spain, France, Britain and the Netherlands claimed the islands as colonies. Most of the islands' original inhabitants were wiped out by disease and a wide mixture of peoples – of African, Asian and European descent – now make up the population. The islands are prone to earthquakes, hurricanes and volcanic eruptions.

THE LANDSCAPE

The islands are formed from two main mountain chains: the Greater Antilles, which are part of a chain running from west to east, and the Lesser Antilles, which run from north to south. The mountains are now almost submerged under the Atlantic Ocean and Caribbean Sea. Only the higher peaks reach above sea level to form islands.

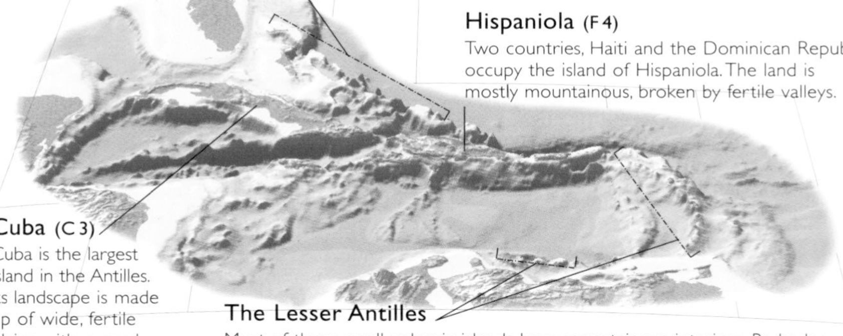

The Bahamas
The Bahamas are low-lying, islands formed from limestone rock. Their coastlines are fringed by coral reefs, lagoons and mangrove swamps. Some of the bigger islands are covered by forests.

Hispaniola (F 4)
Two countries, Haiti and the Dominican Republic occupy the island of Hispaniola. The land is mostly mountainous, broken by fertile valleys.

Cuba (C 3)
Cuba is the largest island in the Antilles. Its landscape is made up of wide, fertile plains with rugged hills and mountains in the southeast.

The Lesser Antilles
Most of these small volcanic islands have mountainous interiors. Barbados and Antigua and Barbuda are flatter, with some higher volcanic areas. Monserrat was evacuated in 1997, following volcanic eruptions on the island.

ENVIRONMENTAL ISSUES

The islands of the Caribbean are often under threat from hurricane storm systems which sweep in from the Atlantic Ocean between May and October. The winds can reach speeds of up to 250 km per hour, devastating everything that lies in their path and causing severe flooding. The storms themselves are enormous; a hurricane can extend outwards for 650 km from its calm centre, which is known as the 'eye'.

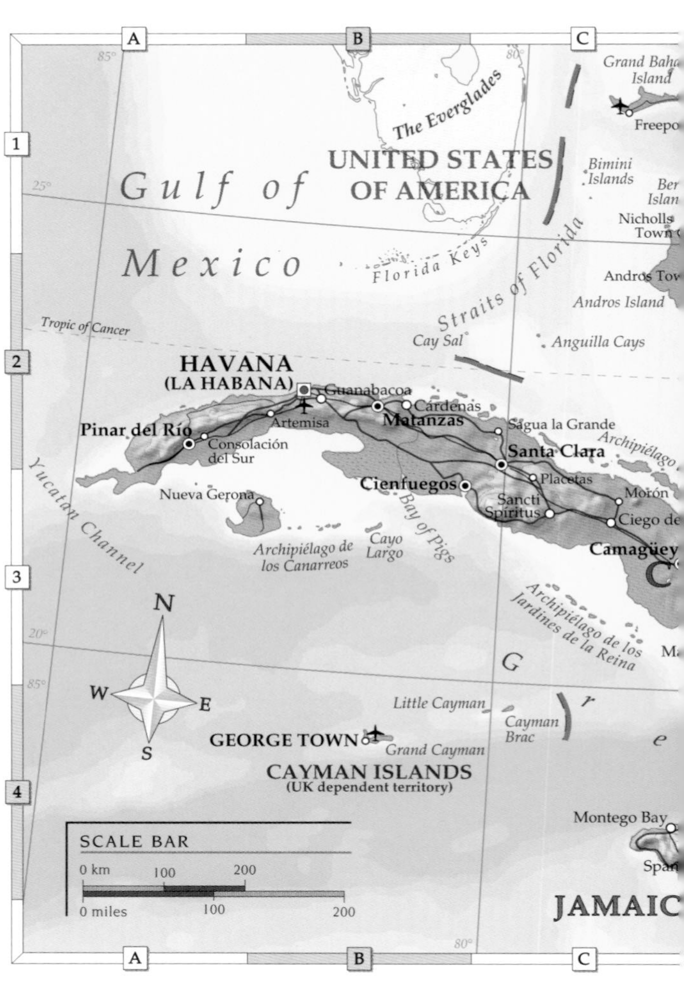

FARMING AND LAND USE

Agriculture is an important source of income, with over half of all produce exported. Many islands have fertile, well-watered land and large areas are set aside for commercial crops such as sugar cane, tobacco and coffee. Some islands rely heavily on a single crop; in Dominica, bananas provide over half the country's income. Cuba is one of the world's biggest sugar producers.

TOURISM

Tourism is thriving in the Caribbean, often bringing more income to the region than other, traditional industries. Long sandy beaches, clear, warm waters and the climate are the main attractions. In Cuba and the Dominican Republic, tourism is expanding at some of the fastest rates in North America. As hotel complexes and new roads and airports are developed, the environment is often damaged. Local people who work in the industry often receive little of the extra cash brought in by the tourists.

TOURISM
Major tourist destinations
Bahamas
Cuba
Jamaica
Puerto Rico
Virgin Islands
Antigua & Barbuda
Dominican Republic
Guadeloupe
St Lucia
Barbados
Grenada
Aruba
Trinidad & Tobago

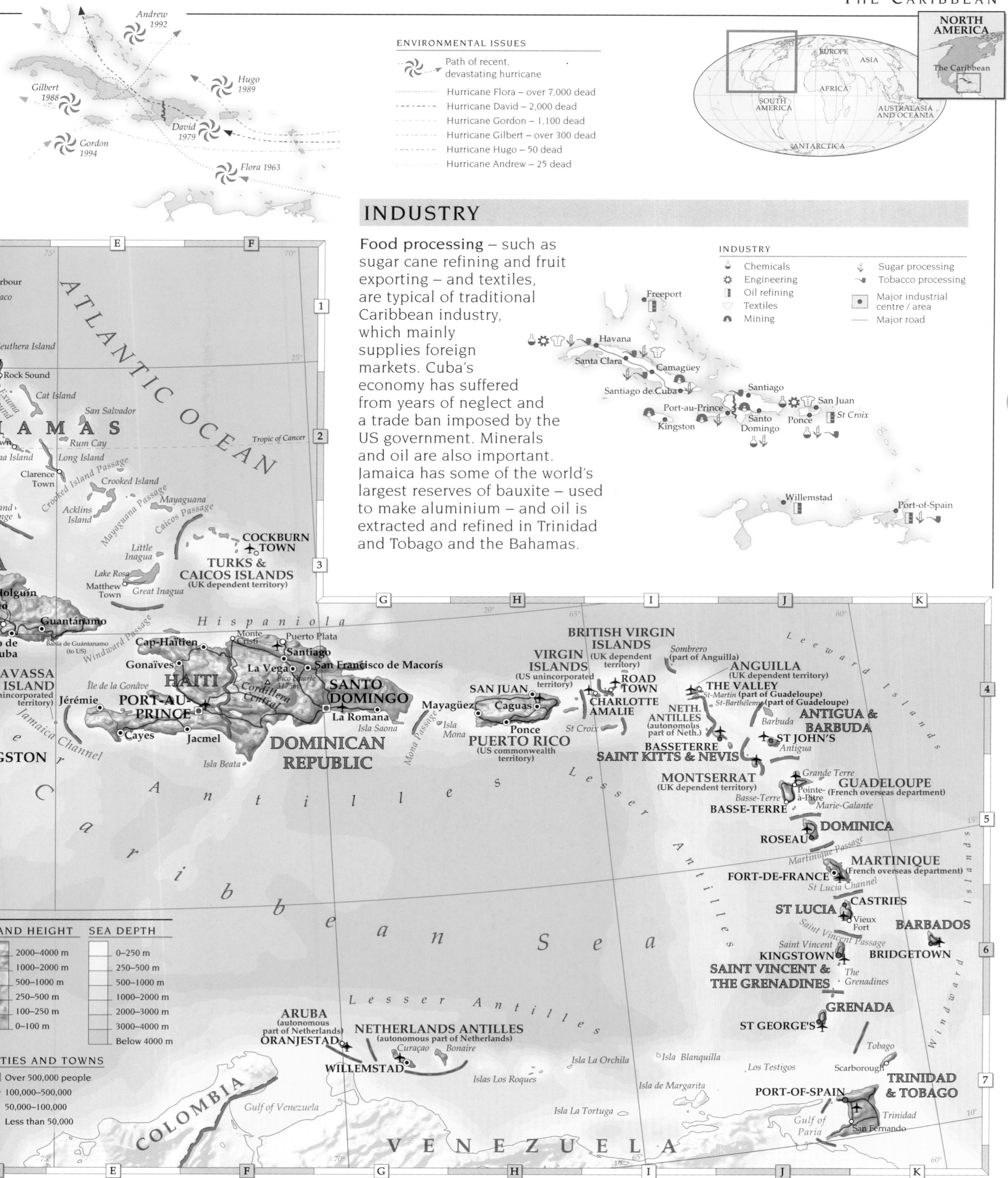

INDUSTRY

Food processing – such as sugar cane refining and fruit exporting – and textiles, are typical of traditional Caribbean industry, which mainly supplies foreign markets. Cuba's economy has suffered from years of neglect and a trade ban imposed by the US government. Minerals and oil are also important. Jamaica has some of the world's largest reserves of bauxite – used to make aluminium – and oil is extracted and refined in Trinidad and Tobago and the Bahamas.

Continental South America

The towering peaks of the Andes stand high above the western side of South America. They act as a barrier to the sparsely inhabited interior of the continent which includes the dense rainforest of the Amazon Basin – one of the Earth's last great wildernesses. Most people live on South America's coastal fringes. Brazil is both the largest country, and the most populous. Over half the continent's land area and half its people are found there.

Cross-section across South America

The high peaks of the Andes rise up from a narrow strip of land bordering the Pacific Ocean. East of the Andes, the land flattens into a broad, shallow basin into which the Amazon River flows. To the north are the older Guiana Highlands where rock has been eroded to form flat-topped 'table' mountains.

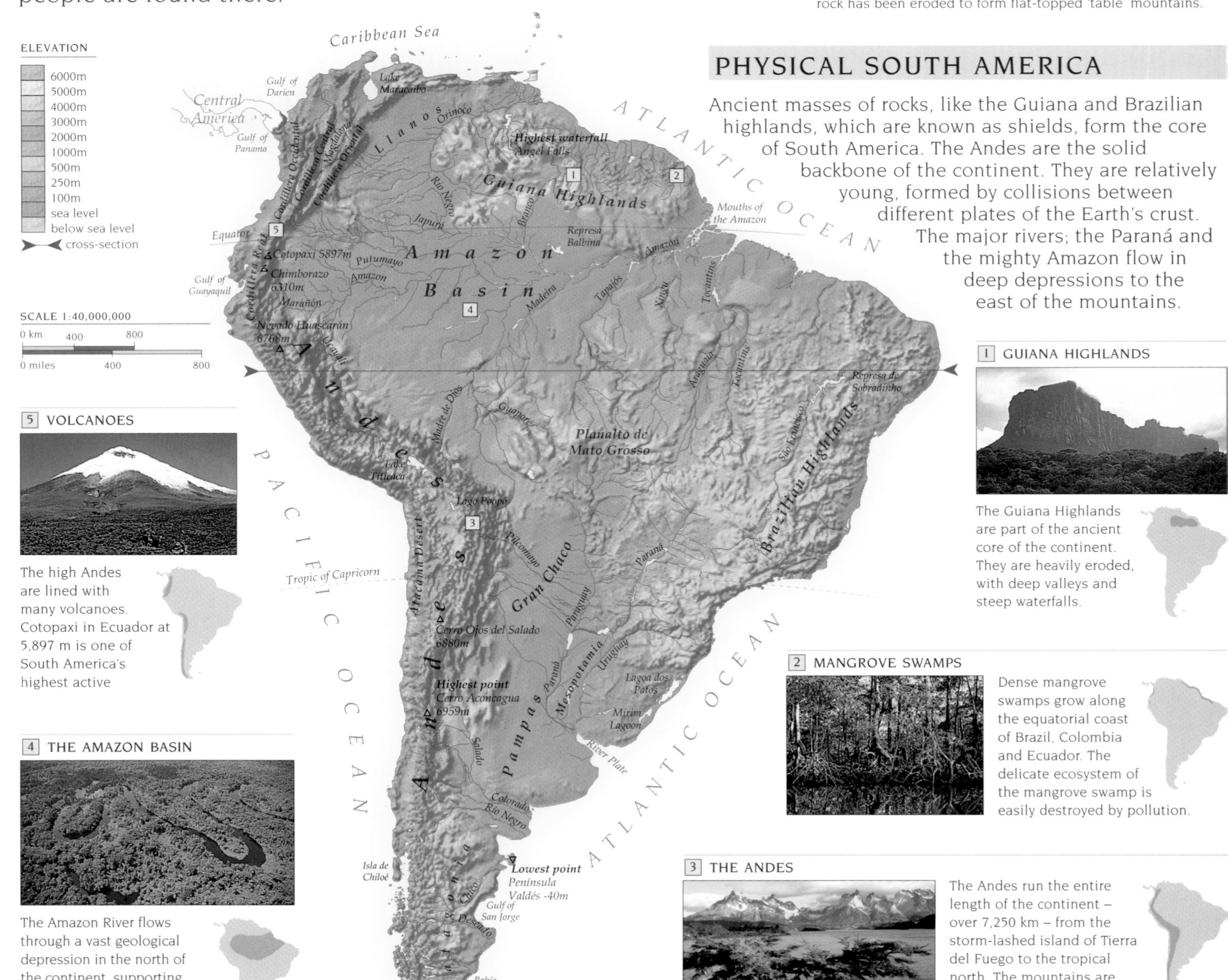

Physical South America

Ancient masses of rocks, like the Guiana and Brazilian highlands, which are known as shields, form the core of South America. The Andes are the solid backbone of the continent. They are relatively young, formed by collisions between different plates of the Earth's crust. The major rivers; the Paraná and the mighty Amazon flow in deep depressions to the east of the mountains.

1 Guiana Highlands

The Guiana Highlands are part of the ancient core of the continent. They are heavily eroded, with deep valleys and steep waterfalls.

2 Mangrove Swamps

Dense mangrove swamps grow along the equatorial coast of Brazil, Colombia and Ecuador. The delicate ecosystem of the mangrove swamp is easily destroyed by pollution.

3 The Andes

The Andes run the entire length of the continent – over 7,250 km – from the storm-lashed island of Tierra del Fuego to the tropical north. The mountains are on a volcanically active zone, and earthquakes are common.

5 Volcanoes

The high Andes are lined with many volcanoes. Cotopaxi in Ecuador at 5,897 m is one of South America's highest active

4 The Amazon Basin

The Amazon River flows through a vast geological depression in the north of the continent, supporting thousands of square kilometres of tropical rainforest.

POLITICAL SOUTH AMERICA

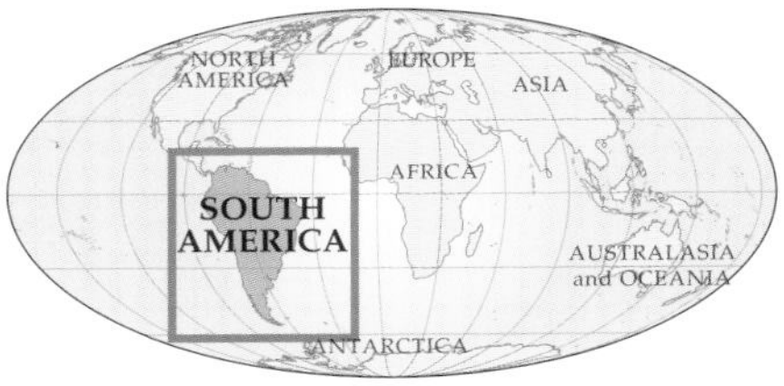

In the 17th century, explorers from Spain and Portugal claimed most of South America for their rulers in Europe. Their influences are still strong today: Brazilians speak Portuguese, while much of the rest of the continent is Spanish-speaking. The small nations of the north, Surinam and Guyana, were Dutch and British colonies and French Guiana is a French overseas department. The mix of peoples is mainly European, native American and African. Some native peoples still live in the dense Amazon rainforest.

SCALE 1:35,000,000

0 km 400 800

0 miles 400 800

BORDER DISPUTES

Many of South America's borders have been, or remain, disputed. Bolivia is landlocked as a result of a dispute with Chile in 1883, when it lost its lands bordering the Pacific Ocean.

TRANSPORT LINKS

The Pan American Highway is a vital transport link, running from the far south of the continent, northwards along the Pacific coast. Its route takes it through sparsely populated areas like the Atacama Desert.

URBAN GROWTH

Urban growth has transformed São Paulo into a major population and industrial centre. Its rapid growth has created many problems, like traffic congestion, overcrowding, and inadequate sewerage.

POPULATION

Capital cities
- Above 500,000
- 100,000 to 500,000
- 50,000 to 100,000
- Below 50,000

Other cities
- Above 500,000
- 50,000 to 100,000

POPULATION

Many South American countries have a similar pattern of population distribution. The largest numbers of people are found near the coasts. Migration to the coastal cities has led to rocketing population figures, and growing social problems. São Paulo is now the world's third largest city after Mexico City and Tokyo; its outskirts are fringed with sprawling, shantytown suburbs – known as *favelas*.

Largest city
SÃO PAULO
19.9 million people

POPULATION DENSITY
(People per sq km)

Below 5 | 5–9 | 10–14 | 15–19 | 20–29 | Above 29

STANDARDS OF LIVING

There are many inequalities in living standards across South America. Argentina's economy has suffered during the regional recession but living standards are still above those of Guyana and Bolivia, which have weak economies, and are heavily reliant upon trade in raw materials. The booming black market drug trade increases crime and corruption.

STANDARD OF LIVING
(UN Human Development Index)

low — high | no data

South American Geography

Agriculture is still the most common form of employment in South America. Cattle and cash crops of coffee, cocoa and, in some places, coca for cocaine, provide the main sources of income. Brazil has the greatest range of industries, followed by Argentina, Venezuela and Chile. The large coastal cities such as Rio de Janeiro, Lima and Buenos Aires are where most of the jobs are found. This encourages people to migrate from the country to the city, in search of employment.

Mineral resources

South America's mineral resources are highly localized. Few countries have both fossil fuels and metallic ores. The richest oilfields are in the north, especially in Venezuela. Coal, however, is scarce. When the Andes formed, heat helped create the many metallic minerals which are mined today.

MINERAL RESOURCES

- Bauxite
- Copper
- Iron
- Lead
- Silver
- Tin
- Oil/Gas field
- Coal field

Copper mines

Metallic mineral reserves are abundant in the Andes. Chuquicamata, northern Chile, is one of the world's largest copper mines.

Industry

Brazil is the continent's leading industrial producer and São Paulo the major industrial city. Manufactured products include iron and steel, automobiles, chemicals, textiles, and meat and leather products from the continent's vast cattle herds. In the mountains of Bolivia and Colombia, coca plants are grown to make cocaine, which has created a black market for this illegal drug.

Oil and gas

Under the waters of Lake Maracaibo, Venezuela, lie some of South America's biggest oil reserves. Oil exploitation has brought great wealth to Venezuela. The money has helped the country to build new roads and develop other industries.

Industrial centre

São Paulo, Brazil, is the largest city in South America and a leading industrial centre. A wide range of goods is manufactured here, including automobiles, chemicals, textiles and electronic products. São Paulo is also a leading financial centre Hundreds of people flock to the city daily in search of work.

Trade and exports

The Chilean port of Valparaíso ships many different products out of South America. Trade is growing with Japan and other countries around the Pacific Ocean.

GNP per capita (US$)

- Below 999
- 999-1999
- 2000-2999
- 3000-3999
- 4000-4999
- Above 5000
- Industrial centre

ECONOMIC ACTIVITY

- Aerospace
- Brewing
- Car/vehicle manufacture
- Chemicals
- Coal
- Electronics
- Engineering
- Finance
- Fish processing
- Food processing
- Hi-tech industry
- Iron & steel
- Metal refining
- Narcotics
- Oil and gas
- Pharmaceuticals
- Printing & publishing
- Shipbuilding
- Textiles
- Timber processing
- Tobacco processing

CLIMATE

South America has four main climatic regions; tropical, arid, temperate, and the cold climate of the far south. The Amazon Basin, covered by massive rain forests, and the Guiana Highlands have a humid, tropical climate which allows vegetation to flourish. West of the Andes the climate tends to be very dry. Moist air flowing west from the Atlantic Ocean is prevented from reaching the shores of the Pacific Ocean by the Andes and rain falls before it can pass over the mountains. This creates arid deserts like the Atacama.

EXTREME WEATHER EVENTS

Symbols indicate climatic extremes

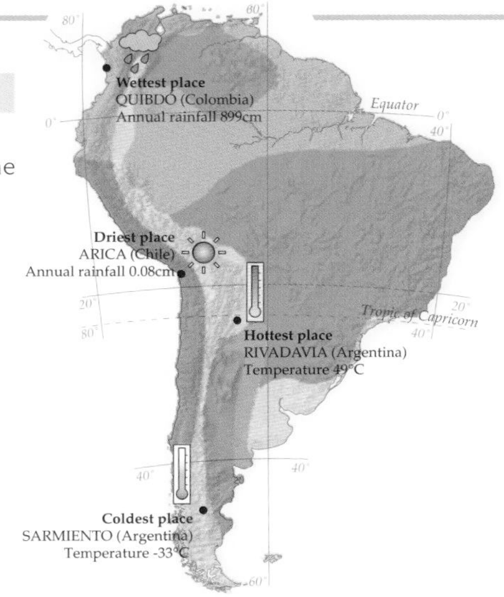

CLIMATE

- Subarctic
- Cool continental
- Warm temperate
- Semi-arid
- Arid
- Temperate
- Tropical
- Humid equatorial

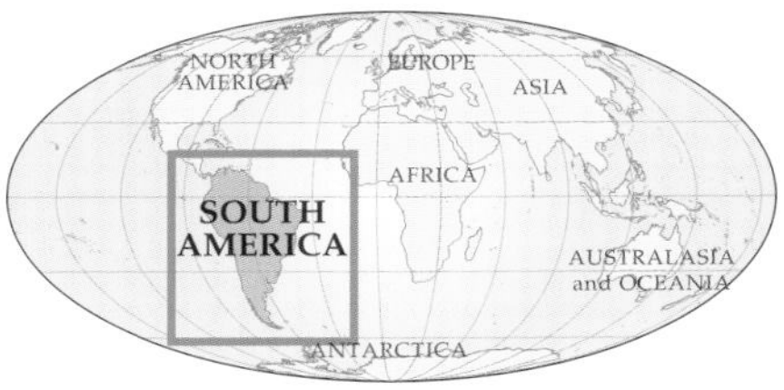

PATAGONIAN ICEFIELDS

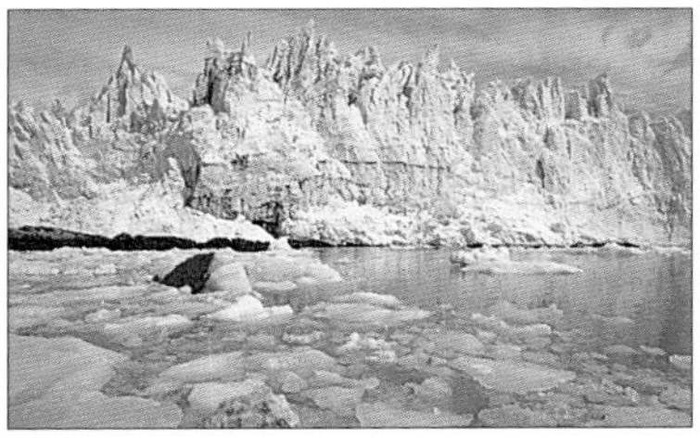

Towards the south of the continent, the climate becomes very cold. Large expanses of ice, forming glaciers are found in southern Patagonia and on islands such as Tierra del Fuego at the tip of South America.

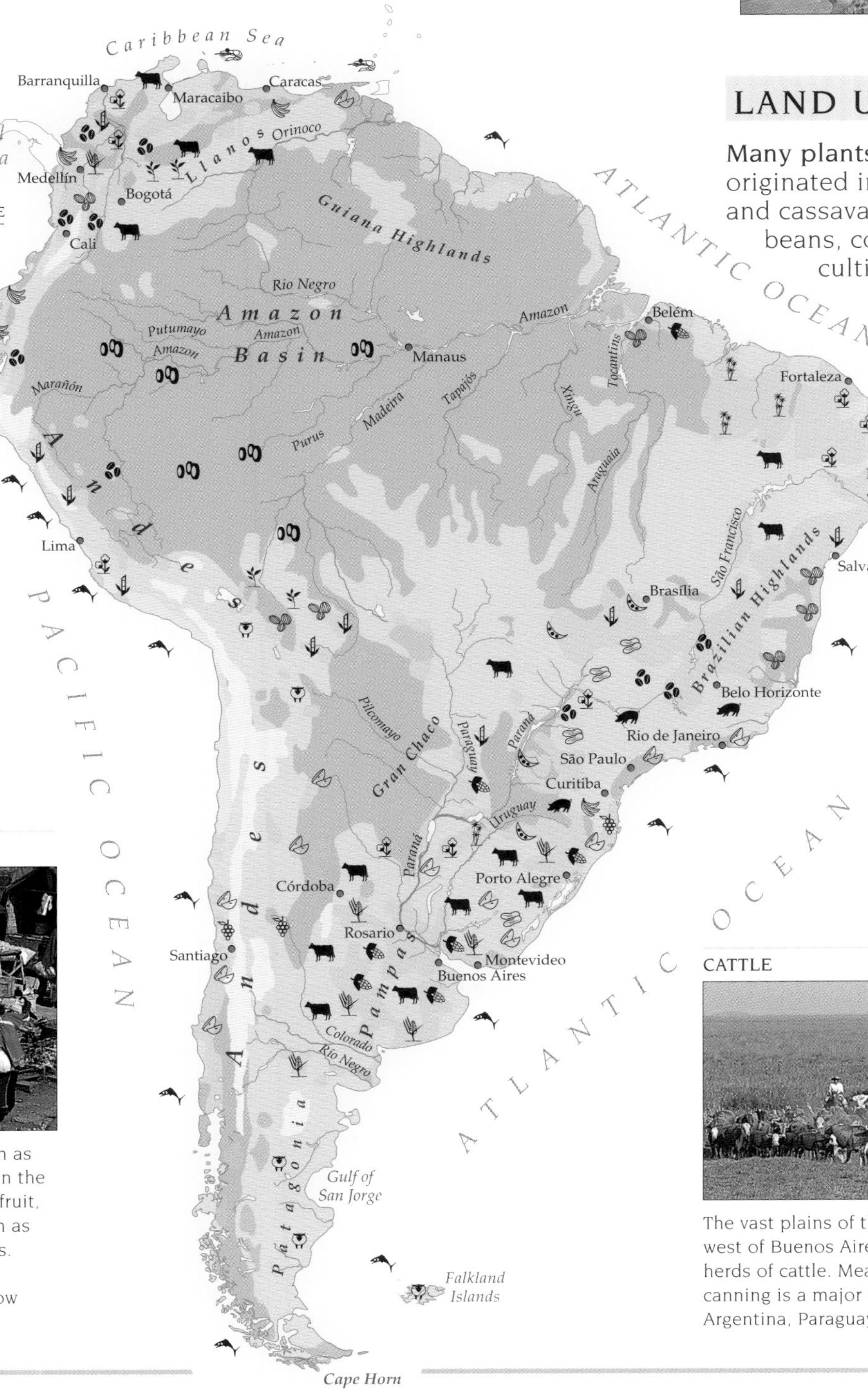

LAND USE AND AGRICULTURE

- Cattle
- Pigs
- Sheep
- Bananas
- Corn (Maize)
- Citrus fruits
- Coca
- Cocoa
- Cotton
- Coffee
- Fishing
- Oil palms
- Peanuts
- Rubber
- Shellfish
- Soya beans
- Sugar cane
- Vineyards
- Wheat

- Barren land
- Cropland
- Desert
- Forest
- Mountain region
- Pasture
- Wetland
- Major conurbation

LAND USE AND AGRICULTURE

Many plants now found throughout the world originated in South America, like the tomato, potato and cassava. Today, coffee, cocoa, rubber, soya beans, corn (maize), and sugar cane are widely cultivated, and grapes are grown in sheltered valleys in the Andes. Much of the Amazon Basin is covered by dense rainforest and is unsuitable for cultivation, although some farmers practise 'slash and burn' techniques to make land for crops and cattle farming, which destroy ancient forest.

COFFEE

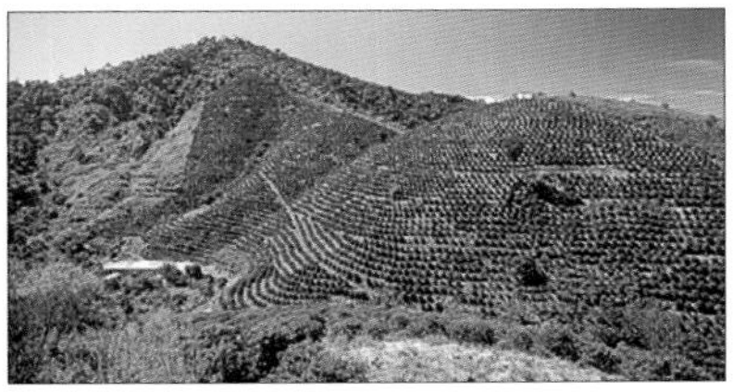

South America, and Brazil in particular, is a major producer of coffee. The plants thrive in the rich red soils of southern Brazil and are grown on huge plantations on the mountain slopes.

LOCAL MARKETS

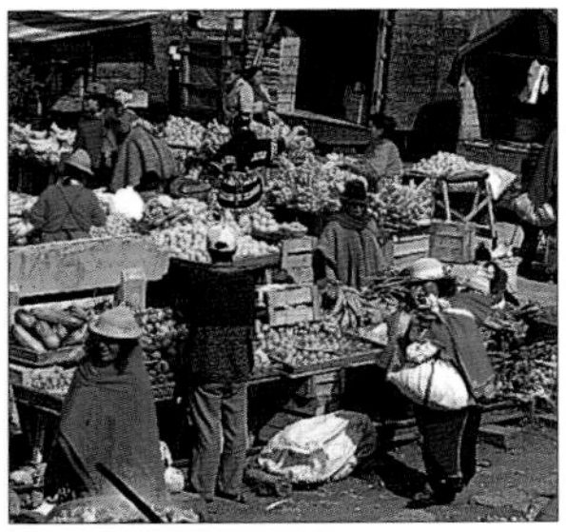

At traditional markets such as this one in Ecuador, high in the Andes, local people trade fruit, vegetables and goods such as clothing, rugs and blankets. Some goods produced by Ecuadorean Indians are now exported world wide.

CATTLE

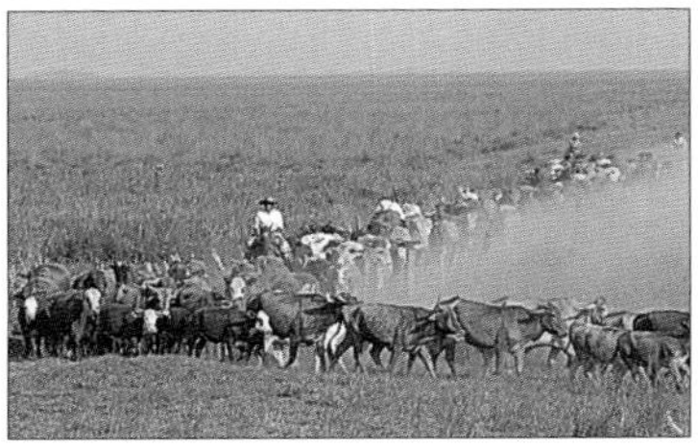

The vast plains of the Pampas, to the west of Buenos Aires, support large herds of cattle. Meat processing and canning is a major industry in Argentina, Paraguay and Uruguay.

NARCOTICS

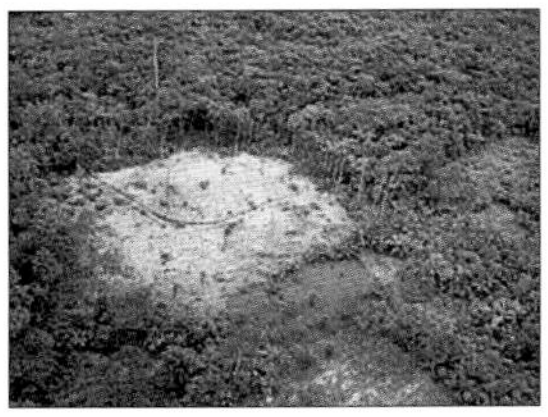

Coca, grown in forest clearings in remote mountain areas, is used to make the drug cocaine. Government troops burn any coca plants they discover to discourage production.

NORTHERN SOUTH AMERICA

BRAZIL, COLOMBIA, ECUADOR, GUYANA, PERU, SURINAM, VENEZUELA

High mountains, steamy rain forests and hot, grassy plains cover much of northern South America. From the 16th century, after the conquest of the Incas, the western countries were ruled by Spain, while Brazil was governed by Portugal, Guyana by Britain, and Surinam by the Dutch. The more recent history of some of these countries has included periods of civil war and military rule. Most are still troubled by widespread poverty.

FARMING AND LAND USE

The variety of climates means a wide range of crops including sugar cane, cocoa and bananas can be grown for export. Coffee is the most important cash crop; Brazil is the world's leading coffee grower. Cattle are farmed on the plains of Colombia, Venezuela and southern Brazil. Much of the good farmland is owned by a few rich landowners, and many peasant farmers do not have enough land to make a living.

FARMING AND LAND USE

- Cattle
- Fishing
- Goats
- Sheep
- Bananas
- Cocoa
- Cotton
- Coffee
- Rubber
- Sugar cane
- Timber
- Cropland
- Forest
- Mountain region
- Pasture
- Wetland
- Major conurbation

LAND USE

Cropland 6%, Other (including mountains) 15%, Pasture 23%, Forest 56%

INDUSTRY

Important oil reserves are found in Venezuela and parts of the Amazon Basin; Venezuela is one of the world's top oil producers. Brazil's cities have a wide range of industries including chemicals, clothes and shoes, and textiles. Metallic minerals, particularly iron ore, are mined throughout the area and specially-built industrial centres like Ciudad Guayana have been developed to refine them.

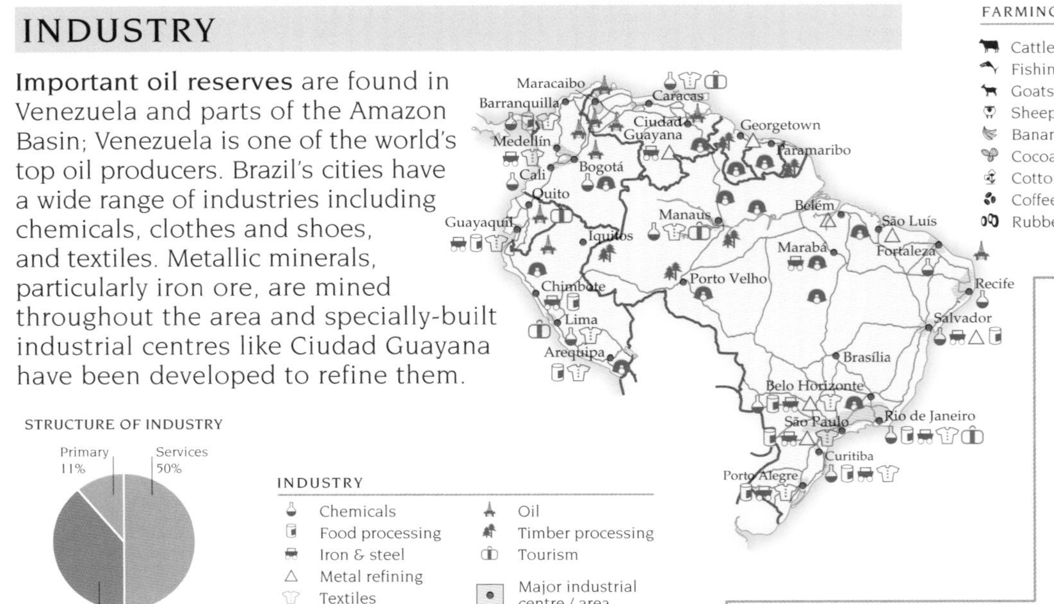

THE LANDSCAPE

The Andes run down the western side of South America. There are many volcanoes among their peaks, and earthquakes are common. The tropical rainforests surrounding the River Amazon take up most of western Brazil. Huge, dry, flat grasslands called *llanos* cover central Venezuela and part of eastern Colombia.

Angel Falls (D 2)
Venezuela's Angel Falls is the world's highest waterfall. Twenty times as high as Niagara Falls, it drops 980 m from a spectacular plateau deep in the Guiana Highlands.

River Amazon (D 4)
The Amazon is the longest river in South America, and the second longest in the world. It flows over 6,439 km from the Peruvian Andes to the coast of Brazil. One-fifth of the world's fresh water is carried by the river.

Andes (B 5)
The snow-capped Andes are the longest mountain range on Earth. They stretch 7,250 km down the whole length of South America.

Lake Titicaca (C 6)
South America's largest lake is the highest navigable lake in the world at 12,500 ft above sea level. It lies across the border between Peru and Bolivia.

Pantanal (E 6)
This is the largest area of wetlands in the world. It spreads across 130,000 sq km of Brazil. Many hundreds of plant and animal species are found here.

Amazon rainforest (D 4)
The enormous rainforest surrounding the River Amazon and its tributaries covers 6,500,000 sq km, an area almost as big as Australia. It is estimated that at least half of all known living species are found in the forest.

POPULATION

Most of the population lives in urban areas. Many cities are extremely overcrowded, with poor housing. São Paulo in Brazil is one of the world's fastest-growing cities. The rainforests of the interior and high Andes are sparsely populated. The few native American peoples live in remote areas.

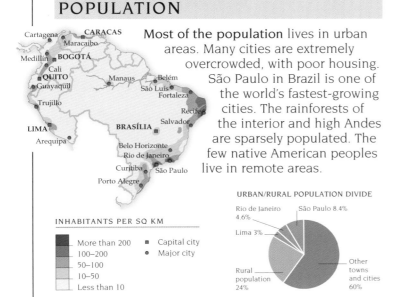

INHABITANTS PER SQ KM

- More than 200
- 100–200
- 50–100
- 10–50
- Less than 10
- Capital city
- Major city

URBAN/RURAL POPULATION DIVIDE

Rio de Janeiro 4.6%, São Paulo 8.4%, Lima 3%, Rural population 24%, Other towns and cities 60%

SOUTH AMERICA
Northern South America
NORTH AMERICA
EUROPE
ASIA
AFRICA
AUSTRALASIA AND OCEANIA
ANTARCTICA
SCALE BAR
0 km 200 400
0 miles 200 400
CITIES AND TOWNS
Over 500,000 people
100,000–500,000
50,000–100,000
Less than 50,000
LAND HEIGHT
Above 4000 m
2000–4000 m
1000–2000 m
500–1000 m
250–500 m
100–250 m
0–100 m
SEA DEPTH
0–250 m
250–500 m
500–1000 m
1000–2000 m
2000–3000 m
3000–4000 m
Below 4000 m
Caribbean Sea
Lesser Antilles
TRINIDAD & TOBAGO
CARACAS
VENEZUELA
COLOMBIA
BOGOTÁ
QUITO
ECUADOR
PERU
LIMA
GUYANA
GEORGETOWN
SURINAM
PARAMARIBO
FRENCH GUIANA
(French overseas department)
CAYENNE
BRAZIL
BRASÍLIA
BOLIVIA
PARAGUAY
ARGENTINA
CHILE
URUGUAY
Amazon Basin
Guiana Highlands
Brazilian Highlands
Andes
Mato Grosso
Gran Chaco
Atacama Desert
PACIFIC OCEAN
ATLANTIC OCEAN
Equator
Tropic of Capricorn
Galapagos Islands
(Archipiélago de Colón)
(part of Ecuador)
Manaus
Belém
Fortaleza
Recife
Salvador
Belo Horizonte
Rio de Janeiro
São Paulo
Curitiba
Porto Alegre
Medellín
Cali
Guayaquil
Trujillo
Arequipa
Cusco
Lake Titicaca
ENVIRONMENTAL ISSUES
The destruction of the Amazon rainforest, which is being reduced by 4 sq km every hour, is the most important environmental issue in this region. This is seriously threatening one of the world's most valuable resources, and wiping out entire species. In 1992, the United Nations held its first Earth Summit in Rio de Janeiro, Brazil, to help highlight this problem.
Colombia all forests destroyed by 2000
Amazon Basin 8 million hectares of forest destroyed every year
Ecuador 50% of forests destroyed by 2000
Atlantic coastal forests 5% of forest remaining
ENVIRONMENTAL ISSUES
Deforested areas
Remaining forests
CLIMATE
Lowland areas are hot and humid all year round. The highlands are cooler, and the higher peaks of the Andes are permanently covered by snow.
TEMPERATURE AND PRECIPITATION
More than 30°C
20 to 30°C
10 to 20°C
0 to 10°C
Less than 0°
Precipitation (mm)
January
July

Southern South America

ARGENTINA, BOLIVIA, CHILE, PARAGUAY, URUGUAY

The southern half of South America forms a long, narrow cone, with landscapes ranging from barren desert in the west, to frozen glaciers in the far south. The whole area was governed by Spain until the early 19th century, and Spanish is still the main language spoken, although the few remaining native American groups use their own languages. Most people now live in vast cities such as Buenos Aires and Santiago.

POPULATION

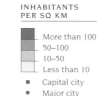

Since the 1950s, there has been a tremendous move from the countryside to the cities, and in Argentina, Chile and Uruguay more than 80% of the people are now city dwellers. The capital cities of all these countries have grown hugely – Buenos Aires now holds a third of Argentina's population, and more than half of Uruguay's people live in the capital, Montevideo.

LA PAZ
SUCRE
ASUNCIÓN
Córdoba
SANTIAGO
BUENOS AIRES
MONTEVIDEO

INHABITANTS PER SQ KM

- More than 100
- 50–100
- 10–50
- Less than 10
- Capital city
- Major city

URBAN/RURAL POPULATION DIVIDE

Buenos Aires 22%
Santiago 9%
Montevideo 2%
Rural population 18%
Other towns and cities 49%

INDUSTRY

Rich deposits of minerals – especially copper – in the Andes have led to the development of large metal refining industries in Chile. The capital cities, Buenos Aires and Santiago, are home to the widest range of industries and Argentina is an important producer of processed foods like canned beef. There are fewer industries in the south, although oil and gas are extracted in southern Argentina and Chile.

La Paz
Santa Cruz
Sucre
Chuquicamata
Antofagasta
San Salvador de Jujuy
Asunción
Resistencia
Córdoba
Valparaíso
Santiago
Mendoza
Rosario
Buenos Aires
Montevideo
Concepción
Valdivia
Neuquén
Bahía Blanca
Comodoro Rivadavia
Punta Arenas
Río Grande

INDUSTRY

- Car manufacture
- Chemicals
- Food processing
- Metal refining
- Textiles
- Oil and gas
- Timber processing
- Major industrial centre / area
- Major road

STRUCTURE OF INDUSTRY

Primary 6%
Services 64%
Manufacturing 30%

ENVIRONMENTAL ISSUES

Many of southern South America's rivers are polluted, particularly close to Buenos Aires. The Itaipú Dam on the Paraná River is the world's largest hydro-electric power project. Deforestation is a persistent problem. In Bolivia, forests are being cut down at a record rate of 200,000 hectares a year. Air quality in Buenos Aires and Santiago is poor, especially in Santiago which is surrounded by mountains, making it difficult for pollution to escape.

ENVIRONMENTAL ISSUES

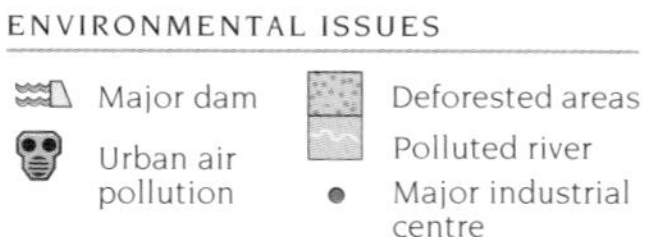

THE LANDSCAPE

Southern South America's landscape varies from tropical forest and dry desert in the north, to sub-Arctic conditions in the south. The towering Andes divide Chile from Argentina. East of the Andes lie forests and rolling grasslands. To the west is a thin coastal strip. The wet, windswept, freezing southern tip of the continent has volcanoes alongside glaciers and fjords.

Gran Chaco (C 3)
This huge stretch of forest and grassland runs from Bolivia, through Paraguay and into Argentina. The south and east provide grazing for cattle.

The Paraná River (C4)
South America's second longest river is the Paraná. It stretches 4,200 km from the Brazilian Highlands, finally flowing into the River Plate near Buenos Aires in Argentina.

Iguazu Falls (D4)
The Iguazu River drops 80 m over the Iguazu Falls. When the river is at its fullest, the water flowing over the falls could fill six Olympic swimming pools every second.

Atacama Desert (A 3)
The Atacama Desert in northern Chile is the driest place on Earth. In some parts, rain has not fallen for hundreds of years.

The Pampas (B5)
The grassy plains in central Argentina – known as the Pampas – cover 650,000 sq km. The western part is semi-desert, but the east gets plenty of rain.

Chile
The far south of Chile has a dramatic landscape of fjords, lakes, jagged mountain peaks and spectacular glaciers.

Patagonia (B8)
The high, windswept plateau of Patagonia covers 770,000 sq km of southern Argentina. The south is dry and freezing cold, with very little vegetation.

CLIMATE

Temperature patterns are similar in January and July; warmer to the north and east, colder to the south and west, although January is much warmer than July. Temperatures are always low high in the Andes.

FARMING AND LAND USE

The enormous grasslands to the east of the Andes provide good grazing for cattle and sheep, and Argentina is one of the world's leading suppliers of meat, milk and hides. The country is also an important grower of wheat and fruit. Chile is the world's top producer of fishmeal, and grows grapes for its successful wine industry, and for eating. The illegal growing of coca, used to make the drug cocaine, is a major source of income in Bolivia.

Continental Africa

Africa is the second largest continent in the world. Its dramatic landscapes include arid deserts, humid rainforests, and the valleys of the east African rift – the place where humans first evolved. Today, there are 53 separate countries in Africa, and its people speak a rich variety of languages. The world's highest temperatures have been recorded in Africa's deserts.

7,260 km
7,623 km

Cross-section through Africa

Niger Delta
Congo Basin
Great Rift Valley
Lake Victoria
Ethiopian Highlands
Horn of Africa
W — 5,200 km — E

In the west, the Niger River flows into the Atlantic Ocean through the swampy Niger Delta. Further east is the immense Congo Basin, where the Congo River winds its way through thick rainforests. In the east is the Great Rift Valley, and the Ethiopian Highlands. The Horn of Africa is Africa's most easterly point.

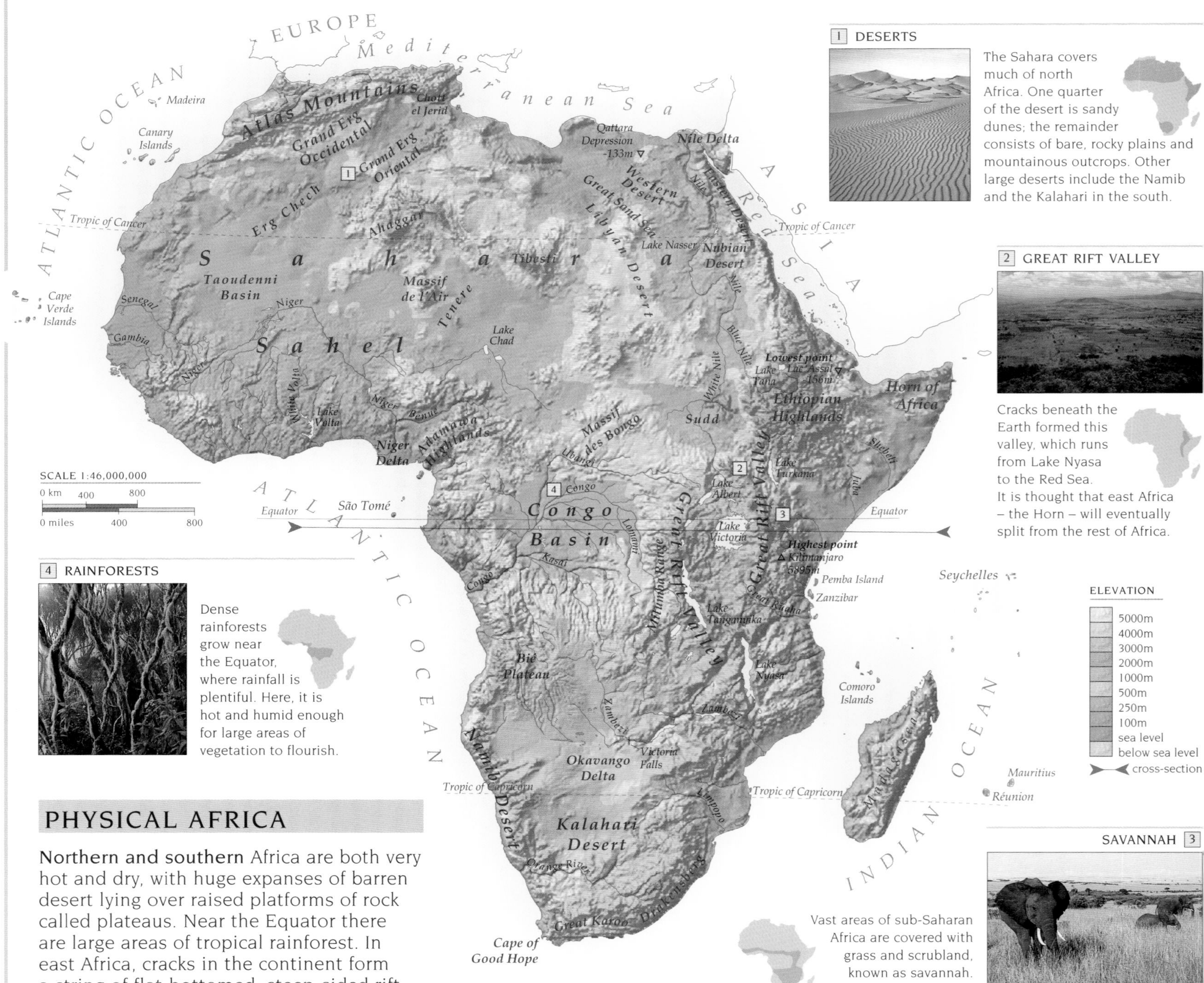

1 Deserts

The Sahara covers much of north Africa. One quarter of the desert is sandy dunes; the remainder consists of bare, rocky plains and mountainous outcrops. Other large deserts include the Namib and the Kalahari in the south.

2 Great Rift Valley

Cracks beneath the Earth formed this valley, which runs from Lake Nyasa to the Red Sea. It is thought that east Africa – the Horn – will eventually split from the rest of Africa.

4 Rainforests

Dense rainforests grow near the Equator, where rainfall is plentiful. Here, it is hot and humid enough for large areas of vegetation to flourish.

Savannah 3

Vast areas of sub-Saharan Africa are covered with grass and scrubland, known as savannah. Many of Africa's largest animals, such as elephants, live here.

Physical Africa

Northern and southern Africa are both very hot and dry, with huge expanses of barren desert lying over raised platforms of rock called plateaus. Near the Equator there are large areas of tropical rainforest. In east Africa, cracks in the continent form a string of flat-bottomed, steep-sided rift valleys, many of which contain vast lakes.

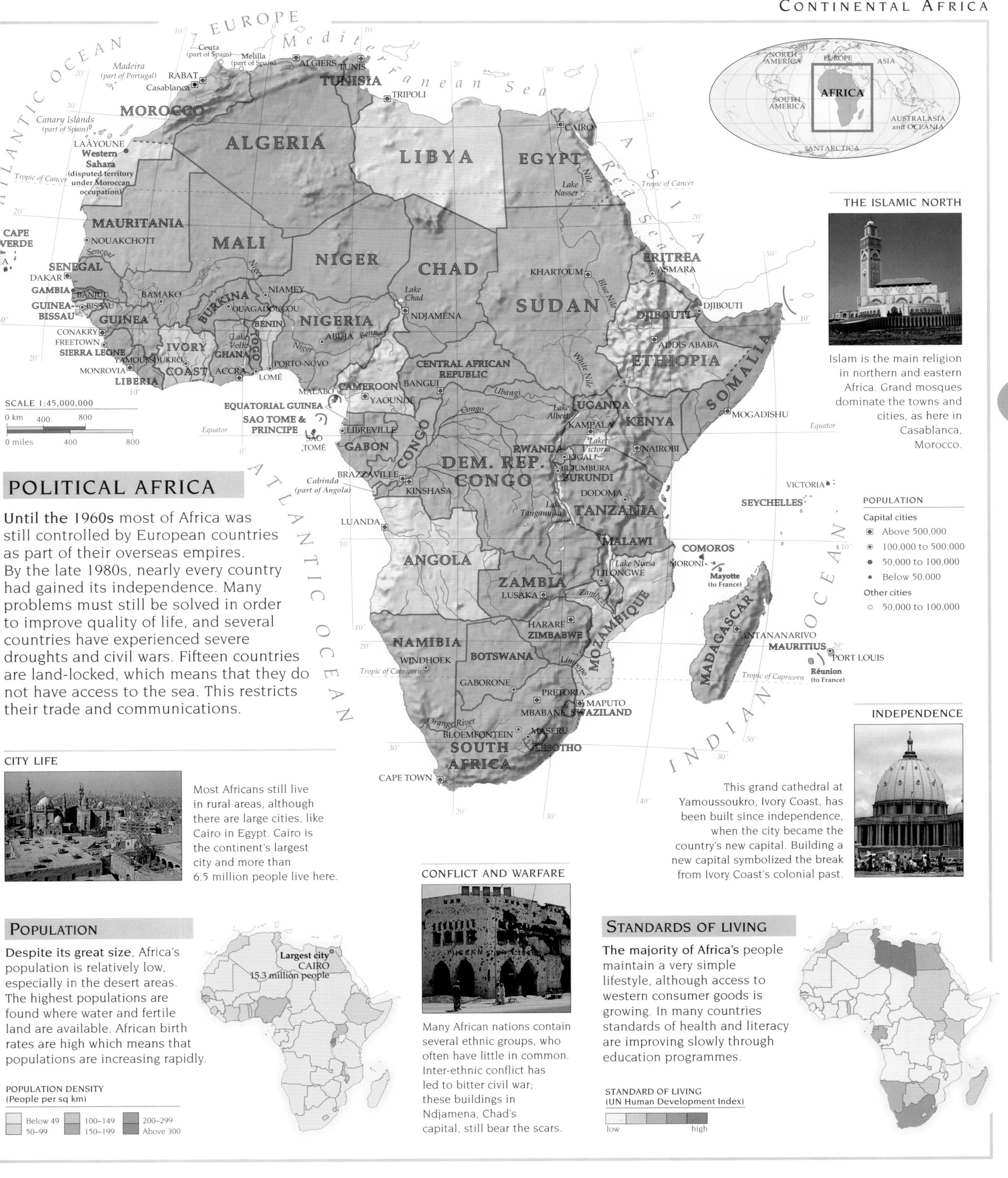

POLITICAL AFRICA

Until the 1960s most of Africa was still controlled by European countries as part of their overseas empires. By the late 1980s, nearly every country had gained its independence. Many problems must still be solved in order to improve quality of life, and several countries have experienced severe droughts and civil wars. Fifteen countries are land-locked, which means that they do not have access to the sea. This restricts their trade and communications.

THE ISLAMIC NORTH

Islam is the main religion in northern and eastern Africa. Grand mosques dominate the towns and cities, as here in Casablanca, Morocco.

CITY LIFE

Most Africans still live in rural areas, although there are large cities, like Cairo in Egypt. Cairo is the continent's largest city and more than 6.5 million people live here.

INDEPENDENCE

This grand cathedral at Yamoussoukro, Ivory Coast, has been built since independence, when the city became the country's new capital. Building a new capital symbolized the break from Ivory Coast's colonial past.

POPULATION

Despite its great size, Africa's population is relatively low, especially in the desert areas. The highest populations are found where water and fertile land are available. African birth rates are high which means that populations are increasing rapidly.

CONFLICT AND WARFARE

Many African nations contain several ethnic groups, who often have little in common. Inter-ethnic conflict has led to bitter civil war; these buildings in Ndjamena, Chad's capital, still bear the scars.

STANDARDS OF LIVING

The majority of Africa's people maintain a very simple lifestyle, although access to western consumer goods is growing. In many countries standards of health and literacy are improving slowly through education programmes.

AFRICAN GEOGRAPHY

Africa's massive reserves of minerals, including oil, gold, copper and diamonds, are amongst the largest in the world. Mining is a very important industry for many countries, and has provided money for growth and development. Africa's wide range of environments means that many different types of crops can be grown. Rubber, bananas and oil palms are grown for export in the tropics, and east Africa is especially famous for its tea and coffee.

INDUSTRY

Most African industries are based on processing raw materials such as food crops or mineral ores. Some African countries depend on one product or crop for most of their income, but in many larger cities different industries are developing. Northern Africa, Nigeria, and South Africa have the widest range of industries.

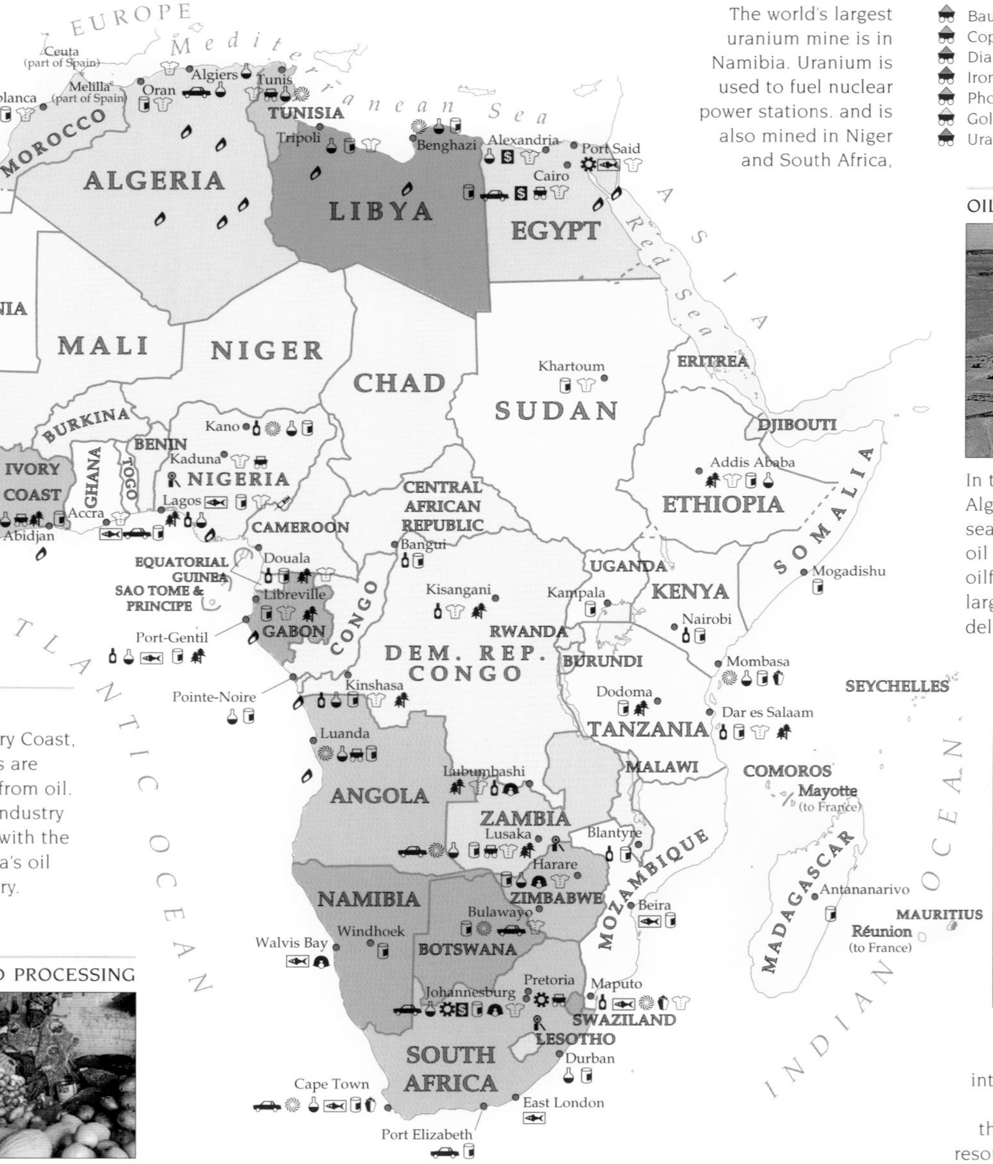

CHEMICALS

In Abidjan, Ivory Coast, petrochemicals are manufactured from oil. The chemical industry has expanded with the growth of Africa's oil and gas industry.

FOOD PROCESSING

Fruit and vegetables are sold in Africa's numerous local markets, as here in Dakar, Senegal. Many crops are grown specially for canning and export overseas and are known as 'cash crops.'

MINERAL RESOURCES

The southern countries, in particular South Africa, have large reserves of diamonds, gold, uranium and copper. The large copper deposits in Dem. Rep. Congo and Zambia are known as the 'copper belt'. Oil and gas are extracted in Algeria, Angola, Egypt, Libya, and Nigeria.

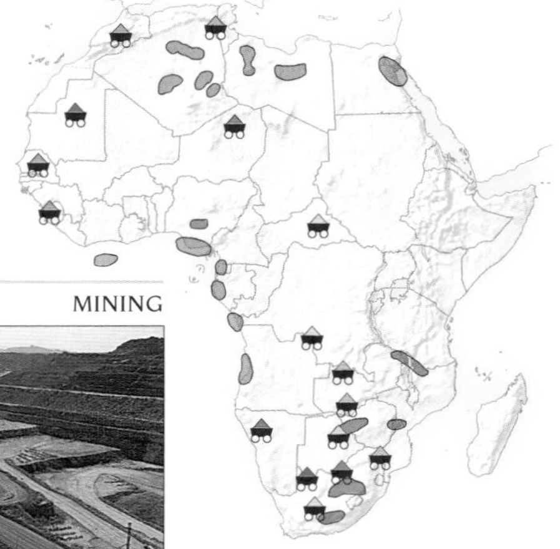

MINING

The world's largest uranium mine is in Namibia. Uranium is used to fuel nuclear power stations, and is also mined in Niger and South Africa.

OIL AND GAS

In the desert wastes of Algeria, a drilling rig searches for new sources of oil in the rich north African oilfields. There are several large oil fields in the Niger delta, and north Africa.

FINANCE AND TRADE

Johannesburg, in South Africa, is home to many international banks. Wealth has been generated from the country's large mineral resources, such as diamonds.

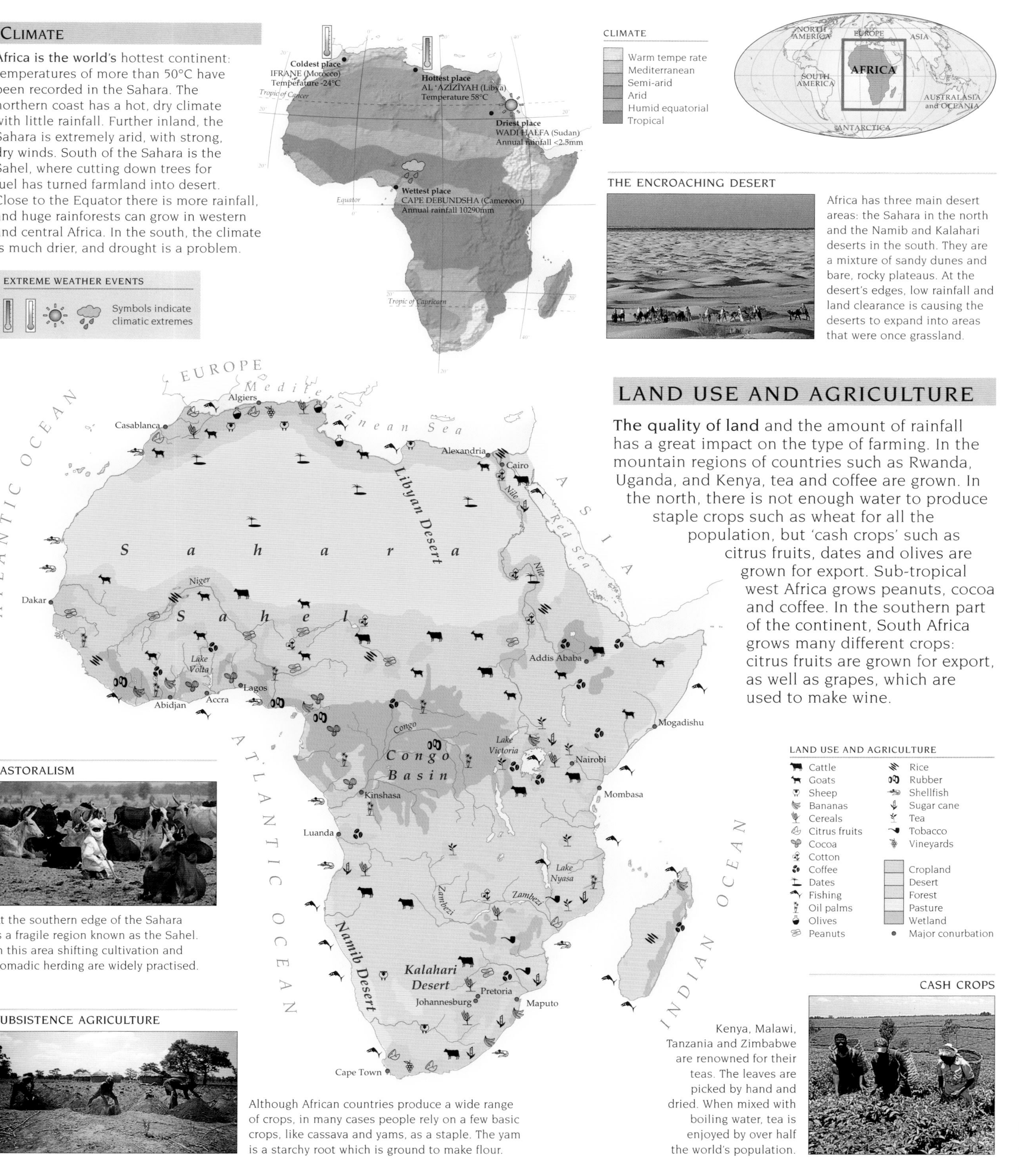

CLIMATE

Africa is the world's hottest continent: temperatures of more than 50°C have been recorded in the Sahara. The northern coast has a hot, dry climate with little rainfall. Further inland, the Sahara is extremely arid, with strong, dry winds. South of the Sahara is the Sahel, where cutting down trees for fuel has turned farmland into desert. Close to the Equator there is more rainfall, and huge rainforests can grow in western and central Africa. In the south, the climate is much drier, and drought is a problem.

EXTREME WEATHER EVENTS

Symbols indicate climatic extremes

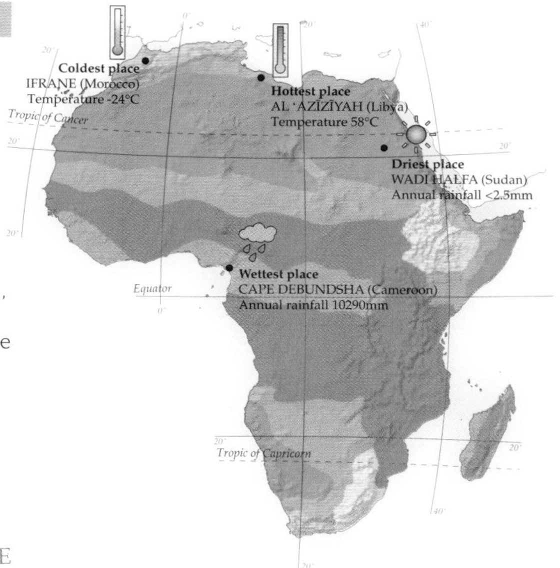

CLIMATE

- Warm tempe rate
- Mediterranean
- Semi-arid
- Arid
- Humid equatorial
- Tropical

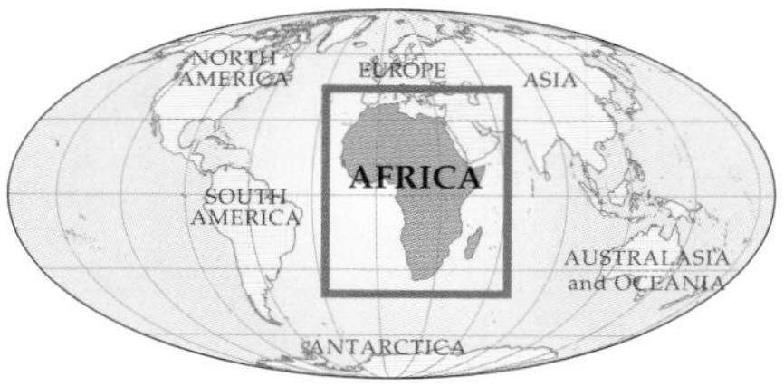

THE ENCROACHING DESERT

Africa has three main desert areas: the Sahara in the north and the Namib and Kalahari deserts in the south. They are a mixture of sandy dunes and bare, rocky plateaus. At the desert's edges, low rainfall and land clearance is causing the deserts to expand into areas that were once grassland.

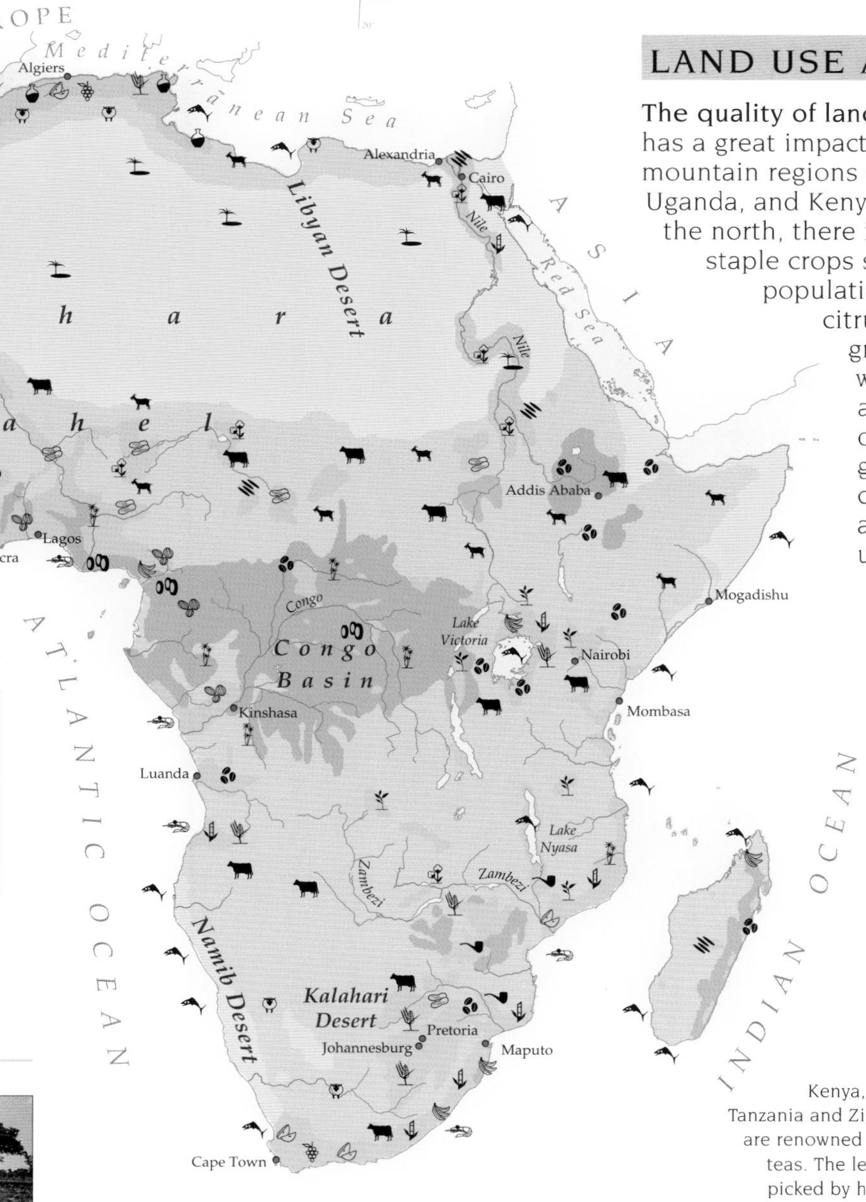

LAND USE AND AGRICULTURE

The quality of land and the amount of rainfall has a great impact on the type of farming. In the mountain regions of countries such as Rwanda, Uganda, and Kenya, tea and coffee are grown. In the north, there is not enough water to produce staple crops such as wheat for all the population, but 'cash crops' such as citrus fruits, dates and olives are grown for export. Sub-tropical west Africa grows peanuts, cocoa and coffee. In the southern part of the continent, South Africa grows many different crops: citrus fruits are grown for export, as well as grapes, which are used to make wine.

LAND USE AND AGRICULTURE

- Cattle
- Goats
- Sheep
- Bananas
- Cereals
- Citrus fruits
- Cocoa
- Cotton
- Coffee
- Dates
- Fishing
- Oil palms
- Olives
- Peanuts
- Rice
- Rubber
- Shellfish
- Sugar cane
- Tea
- Tobacco
- Vineyards
- Cropland
- Desert
- Forest
- Pasture
- Wetland
- Major conurbation

PASTORALISM

At the southern edge of the Sahara is a fragile region known as the Sahel. In this area shifting cultivation and nomadic herding are widely practised.

SUBSISTENCE AGRICULTURE

Although African countries produce a wide range of crops, in many cases people rely on a few basic crops, like cassava and yams, as a staple. The yam is a starchy root which is ground to make flour.

CASH CROPS

Kenya, Malawi, Tanzania and Zimbabwe are renowned for their teas. The leaves are picked by hand and dried. When mixed with boiling water, tea is enjoyed by over half the world's population.

NORTH AFRICA

ALGERIA, EGYPT, LIBYA, MOROCCO, TUNISIA.

Sandwiched between the Mediterranean and the Sahara, North Africa has a history dating back to the dawn of civilization. 6,000 years ago, settlements were established along the banks of the River Nile, and since that time, waves of settlers, including Romans, Arabs and Turks have brought a mix of different cultures to the area. In the 19th century, Spain, France and Britain claimed colonies in the region, but today North Africa is independent, although Western Sahara is occupied by Morocco.

FARMING AND LAND USE

Most farming in North Africa is restricted to the fertile Mediterranean coastal strip, and the banks of the Nile where it relies heavily on irrigation. In spite of these seemingly inhospitable conditions, the region is a major producer of dates, which grow in desert oases, and of cork, made from the bark of the cork oak tree. A wide variety of other crops is also grown, including grapes, olives and cotton.

CLIMATE

Most of north Africa is desert, and the climate is harsh. Rainfall is scarce, and drought is common. Temperatures are freezing at night, scorching by day and have been known to climb to over 50°C.

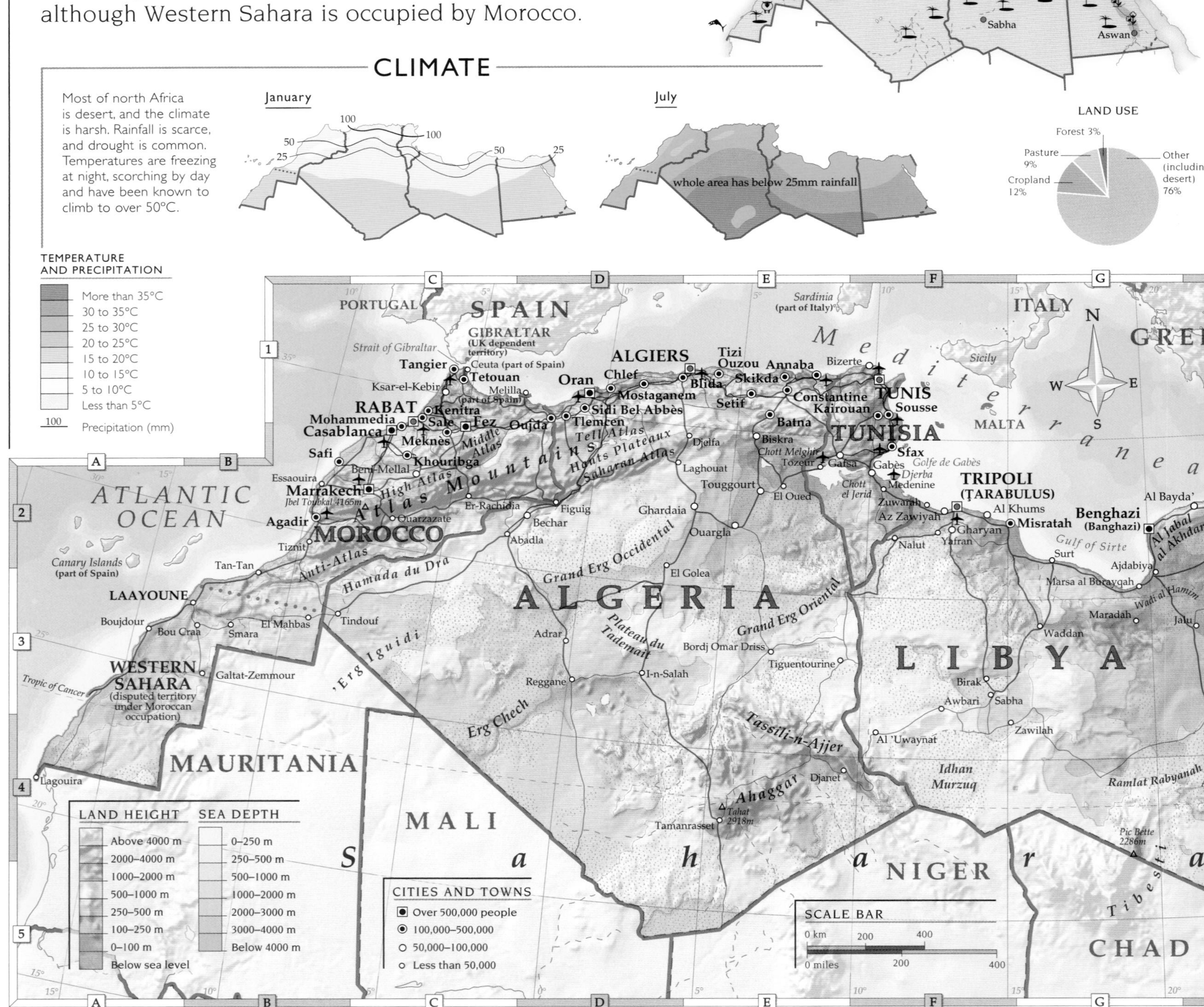

POPULATION

The majority of the population, and all of the big towns and cities, are found on the coastal plains, or along the banks of the Nile – about 99% of Egyptians live along the river. Egypt's capital, Cairo, is Africa's largest city, with over six million people. Western Sahara, and the southern portions of Egypt, Algeria and Libya are sparsely populated by Tuareg nomads who roam the Sahara.

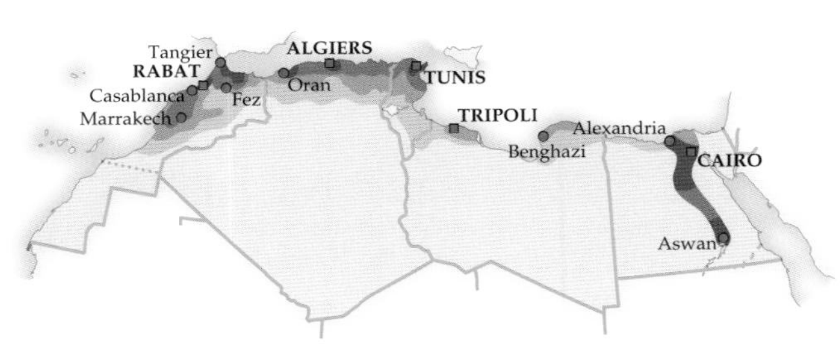

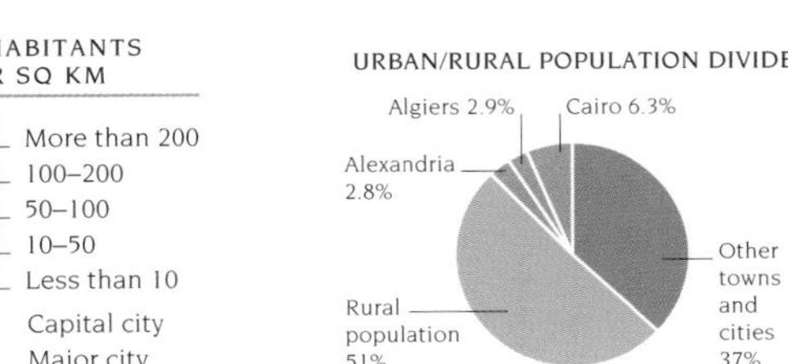

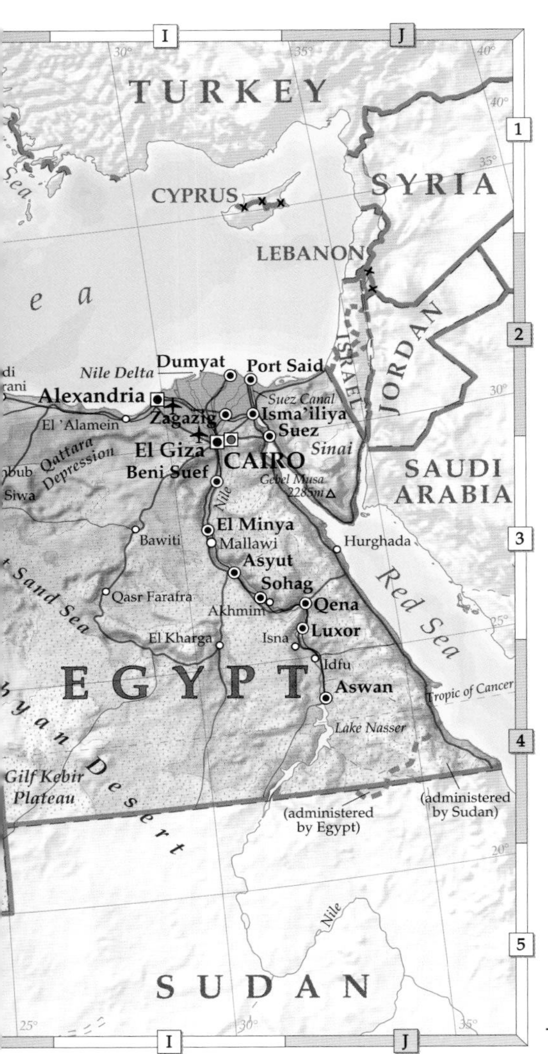

THE LANDSCAPE

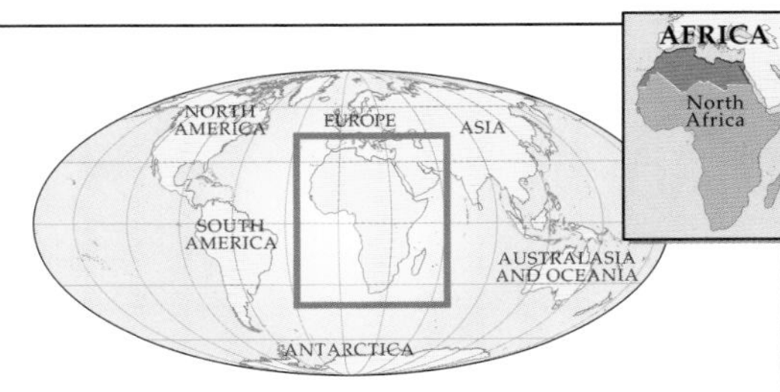

The parched rocks and endless sandy expanses of the Sahara occupy much of North Africa. The only major river here is the Nile, with a delta that extends into the Mediterranean Sea. The old, eroded Atlas Mountains are the highest mountain range.

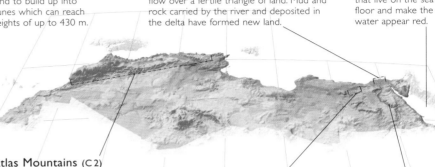

Sand dunes
Winds blowing across the Sahara cause the sand to build up into dunes which can reach heights of up to 430 m.

Nile Delta (I 2)
As the River Nile nears the Mediterranean, it separates into many small streams, which flow over a fertile triangle of land. Mud and rock carried by the river and deposited in the delta have formed new land.

Red Sea (J 3)
The Red Sea gets its name from red algae that live on the sea floor and make the water appear red.

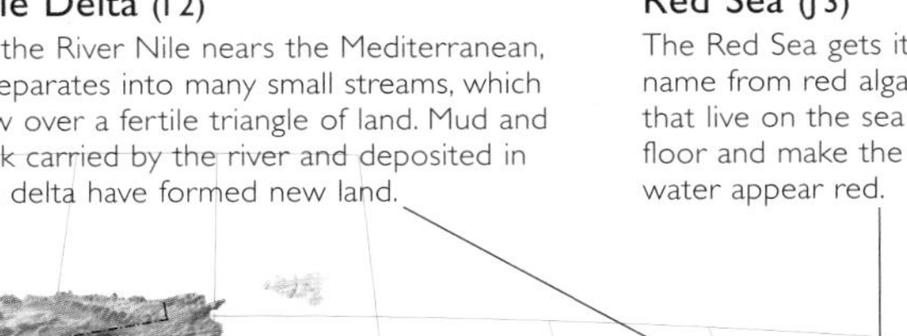

Atlas Mountains (C 2)
The Atlas Mountains are made up of a number of different ranges – the Anti-Atlas, High Atlas, Middle Atlas, Tell Atlas and Saharan Atlas. They stretch some 2,250 km from the north of Tunisia to the Atlantic coast of Morocco.

Qattara Depression (I 3)
In the northwest of Egypt is a huge desert depression 320 km long and 120 km wide. Its floor, part of which is 134 m below sea level, is covered with sand, brackish ponds and salt marshes.

The River Nile (I 3)
The world's longest river flows 6,695 km to the Mediterranean Sea. The system of rivers and lakes that flow into the Nile drain some 2,850,000 sq km – about 10% of the entire African continent.

INDUSTRY

Oil and natural gas have brought wealth to the area, particularly to Libya, which has enough oil reserves to last well into the 21st. century. Textile manufacture is widespread – North Africa is famous for its exotic cloths and rugs. Several large chemical refineries and steel plants have been established along the coast, especially in the major industrial cities like Alexandria and Cairo in Egypt.

STRUCTURE OF INDUSTRY

Primary 16%
Services 49%
Manufacturing 35%

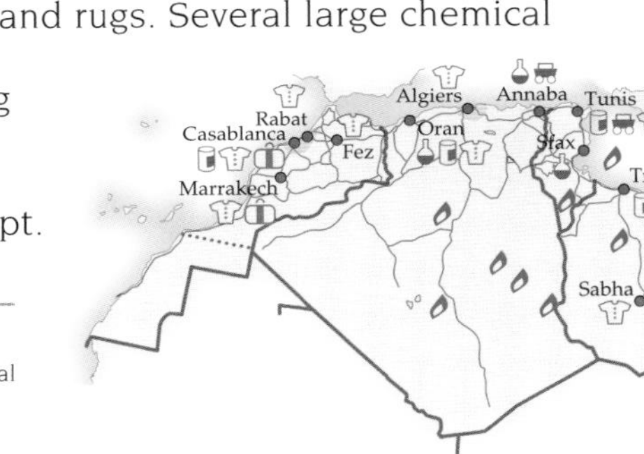

INDUSTRY

- Chemicals
- Food processing
- Iron and steel
- Textiles
- Oil and gas
- Tourism
- Major industrial centre / area
- Major road

ENVIRONMENTAL ISSUES

Droughts, overgrazing and the stripping of vegetation for fuelwood and animal fodder have caused the Sahara to expand northwards. This has reduced the already limited amount of land available for farming. The risk of desertification is acute in many coastal areas. North Africa is very dry, and there are severe droughts periodically. Many of the larger cities like Alexandria and Cairo have very poor air quality.

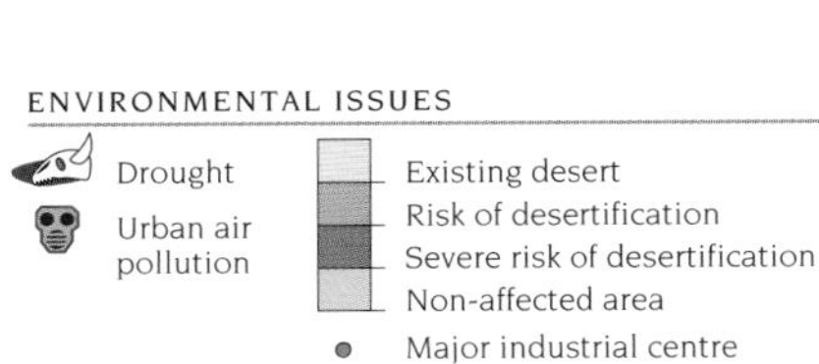

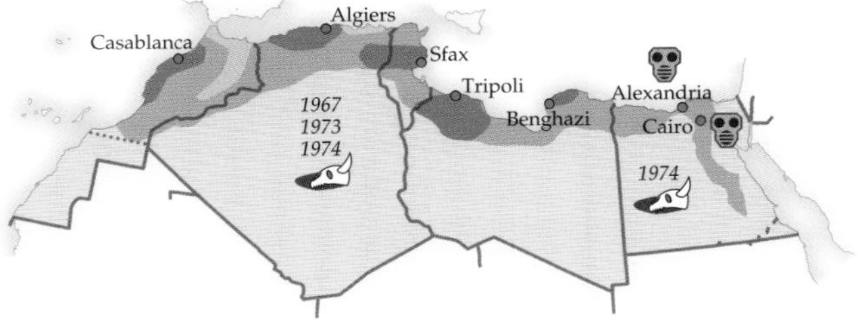

West Africa

BENIN, BURKINA, CAMEROON, CENTRAL AFRICAN REPUBLIC, CHAD, EQUATORIAL GUINEA, GAMBIA, GHANA, GUINEA, GUINEA-BISSAU, IVORY COAST, LIBERIA, MALI, MAURITANIA, NIGER, NIGERIA, SAO TOME & PRINCIPE, SENEGAL, SIERRA LEONE, TOGO

West Africa's varied climate and agricultural and mineral wealth have provided the foundation for some of Africa's greatest civilizations, like those of the Malinke and Asante people. The area remains ethnically and culturally diverse today, as well as densely populated; Nigeria is by far the most populous country in Africa. Since independence from European colonial powers in the 1960s, political instability has been a feature of many countries here.

INDUSTRY

Agricultural products still form the basis of most economies in West Africa. Food processing is widespread – oil palms and groundnuts are processed for their valuable vegetable oils. Oil and gas are found off the coast of Ivory Coast and around the Niger delta, where a large chemical industry has developed.

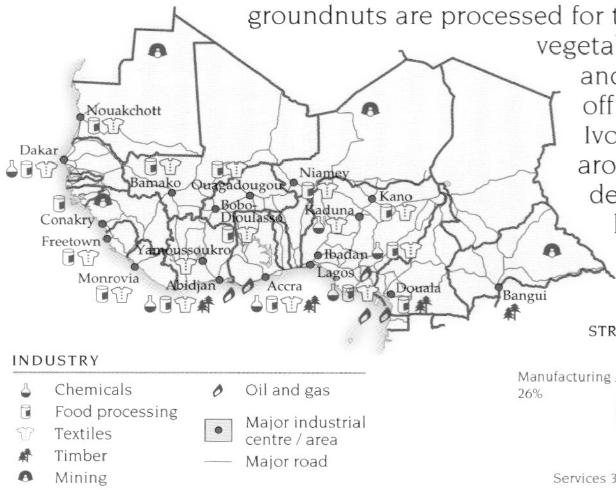

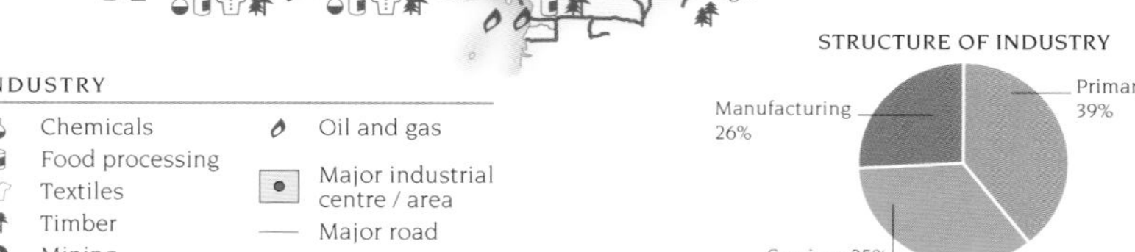

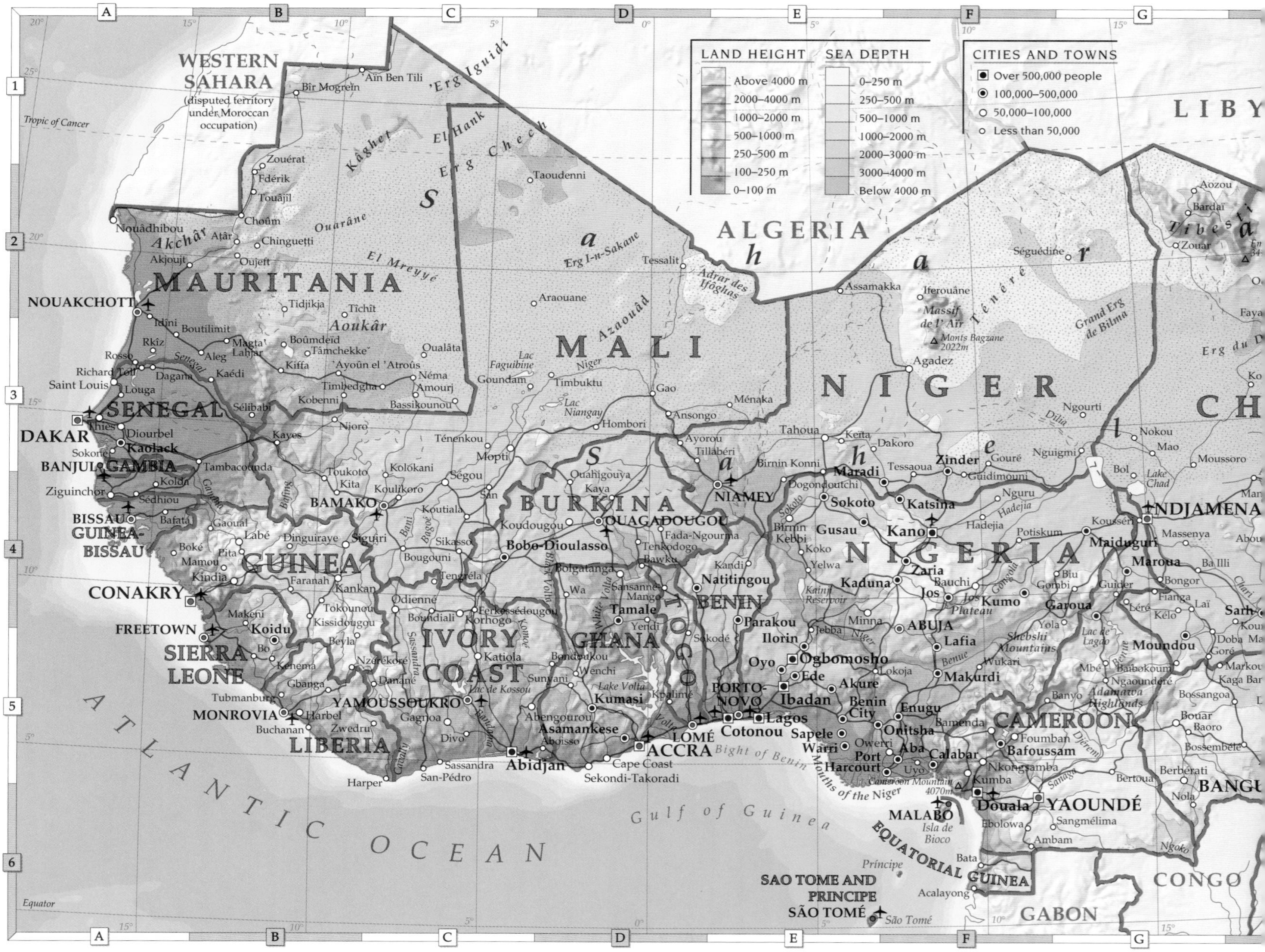

LAND HEIGHT
Above 4000 m
2000–4000 m
1000–2000 m
500–1000 m
250–500 m
100–250 m
0–100 m

SEA DEPTH
0–250 m
250–500 m
500–1000 m
1000–2000 m
2000–3000 m
3000–4000 m
Below 4000 m

CITIES AND TOWNS
Over 500,000 people
100,000–500,000
50,000–100,000
Less than 50,000

FARMING AND LAND USE

Well-watered land along the coast allows a wide variety of crops to be grown, including cocoa and oil palms, both of which provide important cash crops. In the drier north, goats and sheep are grazed, and subsistence crops such as yams, millet and cassava are grown.

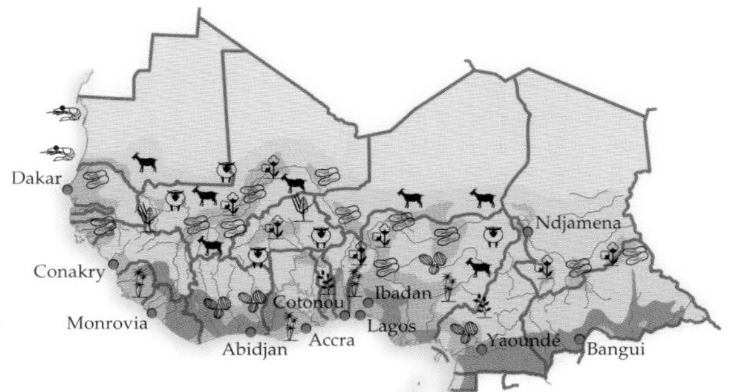
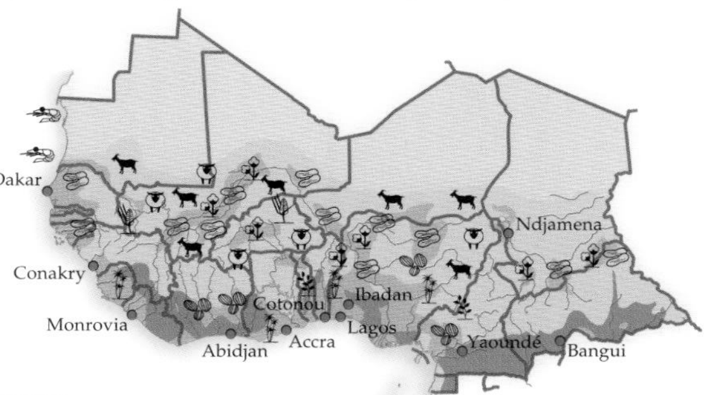
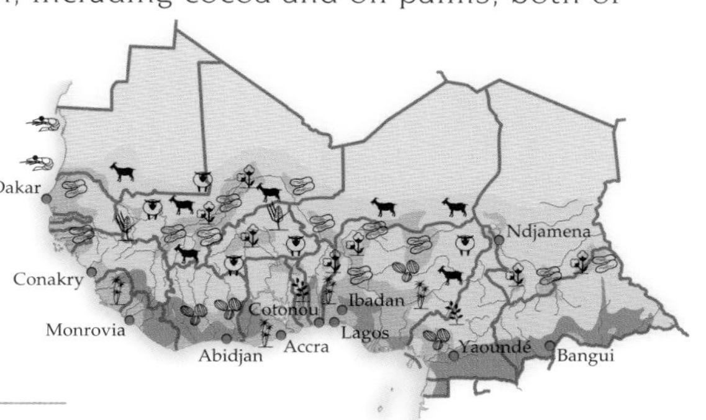
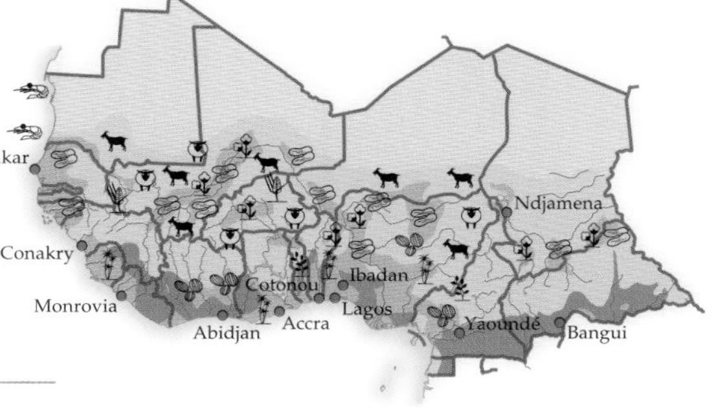

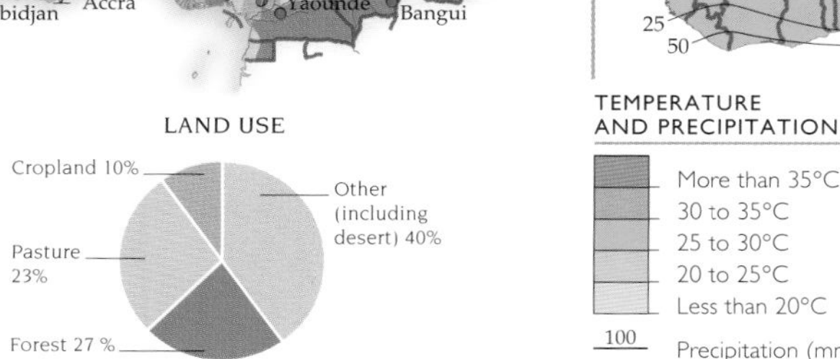

CLIMATE

The climate differs immensely from the hot desert north, through to the tropical rainforest south. July is the wet season, and rainfall is heavy in the south, while the desert areas remain dry throughout the year.

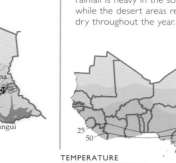

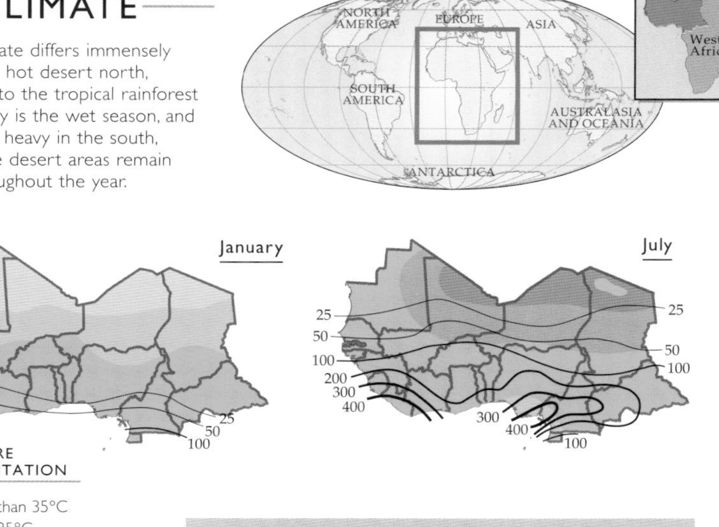

ENVIRONMENTAL ISSUES

Persistent droughts are the main concerns in the north of the region. The problem is made worse by a shortage of wood needed for fuel, which leads to the cutting down of any available trees for fuelwood. In the tropical south, the timber industry is destroying much of the ancient forest.

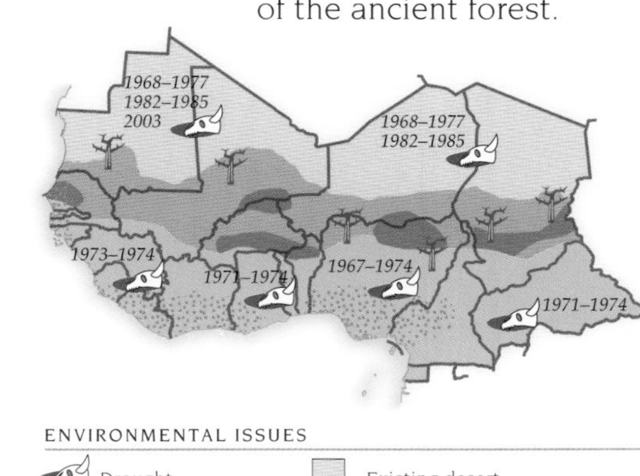

POPULATION

Most of the population lives in the southern coastal regions. In the drier north, settlement becomes more sporadic, and nomadic tribespeople are best suited to live in the desert north. Nigeria is the most populated country in Africa and Lagos is one of the continent's larger cities, although West Africa's population remains mainly rural.

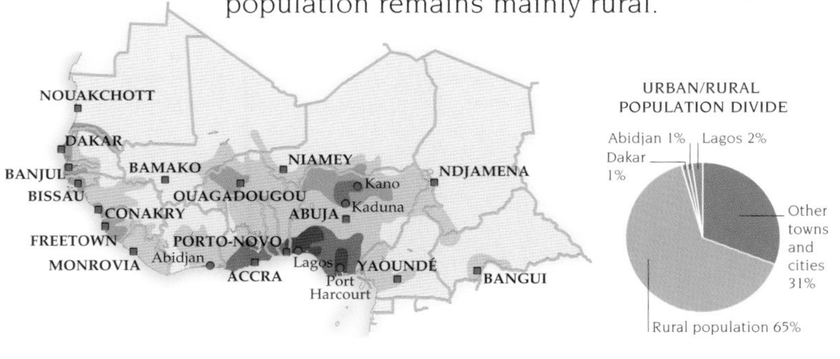

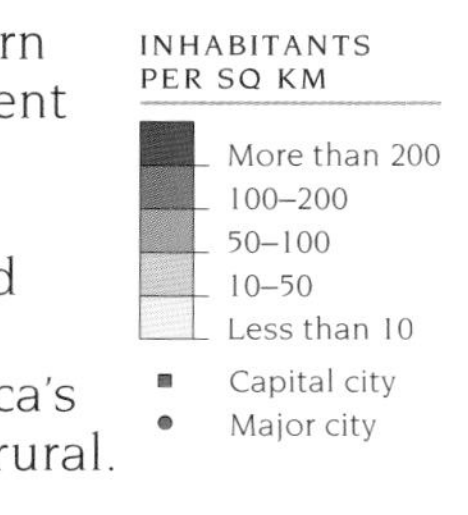

THE LANDSCAPE

Large differences in rainfall from north to south have led to a varied landscape. The wet coastal regions contain tropical rainforest. To the north, savannah grasslands, arid Sahel scrubland and barren desert lie in successive bands. The Niger is one of the larger rivers and is unusual because it has two deltas; one at the sea, and one inland.

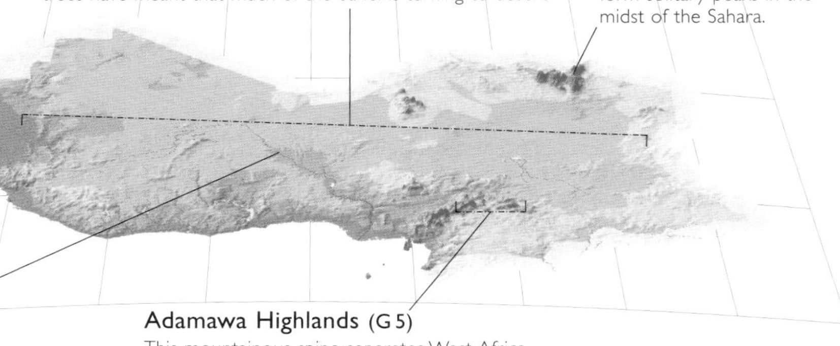

Sahel (E 3)
The band of semi-desert stretching from Senegal to Sudan along the southern boundary of the Sahara is called the Sahel. Frequent droughts in recent years, and excessive cutting of trees have meant that much of the Sahel is turning to desert.

Tibesti mountains (G 2)
These mountains in north-western Chad are a chain of extinct volcanoes which now form solitary peaks in the midst of the Sahara.

River Niger (D 3)
The River Niger is West Africa's longest river. When it reaches the sea, it flows through a vast delta of mud flats and mangrove swamps. Great oil deposits have been found here.

Adamawa Highlands (G 5)
This mountainous spine separates West Africa from the vast Congo Basin to the southeast.

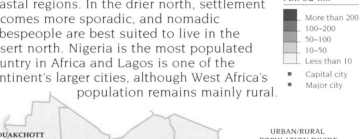

East Africa

BURUNDI, DJIBOUTI, ERITREA, ETHIOPIA, KENYA, RWANDA, SOMALIA, SUDAN, TANZANIA, UGANDA

Much of East Africa is covered by long grass, scrub and scattered trees, called savannah. This land is grazed by both domestic animals and a great variety of wild animals including lions, giraffes and elephants. The east of the region is known as the Horn of Africa, because it is shaped like an animal horn. Along with Sudan, the countries there have recently been devastated by civil wars, and periods of drought and famine. In contrast, Kenya in the south is one of Africa's more stable and wealthy countries.

Farming and Land Use

Much of the north and east is too dry for farming, but in Sudan, cotton is grown on land irrigated by the River Nile. The Lake Victoria basin and rich volcanic soils of the highlands in Kenya, Uganda and Tanzania support staple food crops, and those grown for export, such as tea and coffee. Kenya also grows high-quality vegetables, like mangetout, and exports them by air to supermarkets abroad. Sheep, goats and cattle are herded on the savannah.

Khartoum, Addis Ababa, Mogadishu, Kampala, Nairobi, Mombasa, Dar es Salaam

LAND USE

Cropland 9%, Pasture 40%, Other 26%, Forest 25%

FARMING AND LAND USE

- Cattle
- Fishing
- Goats
- Sheep
- Bananas
- Coffee
- Cotton
- Dates
- Market gardening
- Sugar cane
- Sisal
- Tea
- Cropland
- Desert
- Forest
- Pasture
- Wetland
- Major conurbation

Industry

East Africa has few mineral resources, and industry is mainly based on processing raw materials. Coffee, tea, sugar cane and sisal, are harvested and processed before being exported. Textile production is widespread, but is only on a small scale. Tourism is increasingly important in Kenya and Tanzania; each year, many thousands of people visit the wildlife reserves there.

Port Sudan, Khartoum, Asmara, Addis Ababa, Dire Dawa, Mogadishu, Kampala, Kigali, Nairobi, Bujumbura, Arusha, Mombasa, Dodoma, Dar es Salaam

INDUSTRY

- Cement manufacturing
- Chemicals
- Food processing
- Textiles
- Tourism
- Major industrial centre / area
- Major road

STRUCTURE OF INDUSTRY

Primary 15%, Services 46%, Manufacturing 39%

Environmental Issues

Rapid population growth has created a need for increasing amounts of land for farming. This, as well as the need for fuelwood, has led to tree cover being stripped, allowing the soil to be washed or blown away. Over the past 30 years, eastern Africa has been stricken by many catastrophic droughts which have made desertification worse, and brought much human suffering.

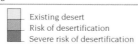

1973, 1980, 1985–1986, 1989; 1973–1975, 1980, 1985, 1989; 1973–1975, 1980, 1986–1987, 1989; 1986; 1972–1974; 1973–1975, 1980, 1985, 1987, 1989; 1973–1974, 1991–1992

ENVIRONMENTAL ISSUES

- Drought
- Severe fuelwood shortage
- Existing desert
- Risk of desertification
- Severe risk of desertification

The Landscape

The south of East Africa is savannah grassland, broken by the rugged mountains – some of them active volcanoes – and large fresh and saltwater lakes that make up part of the Great Rift Valley. The River Nile has its source here, flowing through lakes Victoria, Kyoga and Albert as it takes much-needed water to the arid desert areas in the north.

Great Rift Valley (D 6) (D 4)
The Great Rift Valley is like a deep scar running 7, 000 km from north to south through East Africa. It has been formed by the movements of two of the Earth's plates over millions of years. If these movements continue, East Africa may eventually become an island, separated by the ocean from the rest of the continent.

Sudd (B 4)
The north of Sudan is rocky desert, but in the south, the waters of the White Nile run into a swampy area called the Sudd where much of its water disperses and evaporates.

River Juba (E 5)
This river rises in the highlands of Ethiopia and flows some 1,200 km southwards to the Indian Ocean. It, and the River Shebeli, which joins it about 30 km from the coast, are the only permanent rivers in Somalia.

Lake Victoria (C 5)
Lake Victoria is Africa's largest lake and the second largest freshwater lake in the world. It lies on the Equator, between Kenya, Tanzania and Uganda, and covers 69,500 sq km. Its only outlet is the River Nile in the north.

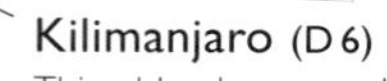

Kilimanjaro (D 6)
This old volcano, made up of alternating layers of lava and ash, is Africa's highest mountain, rising to 5,895 m. Although it lies only three degrees from the Equator, its peak is permanently covered with snow.

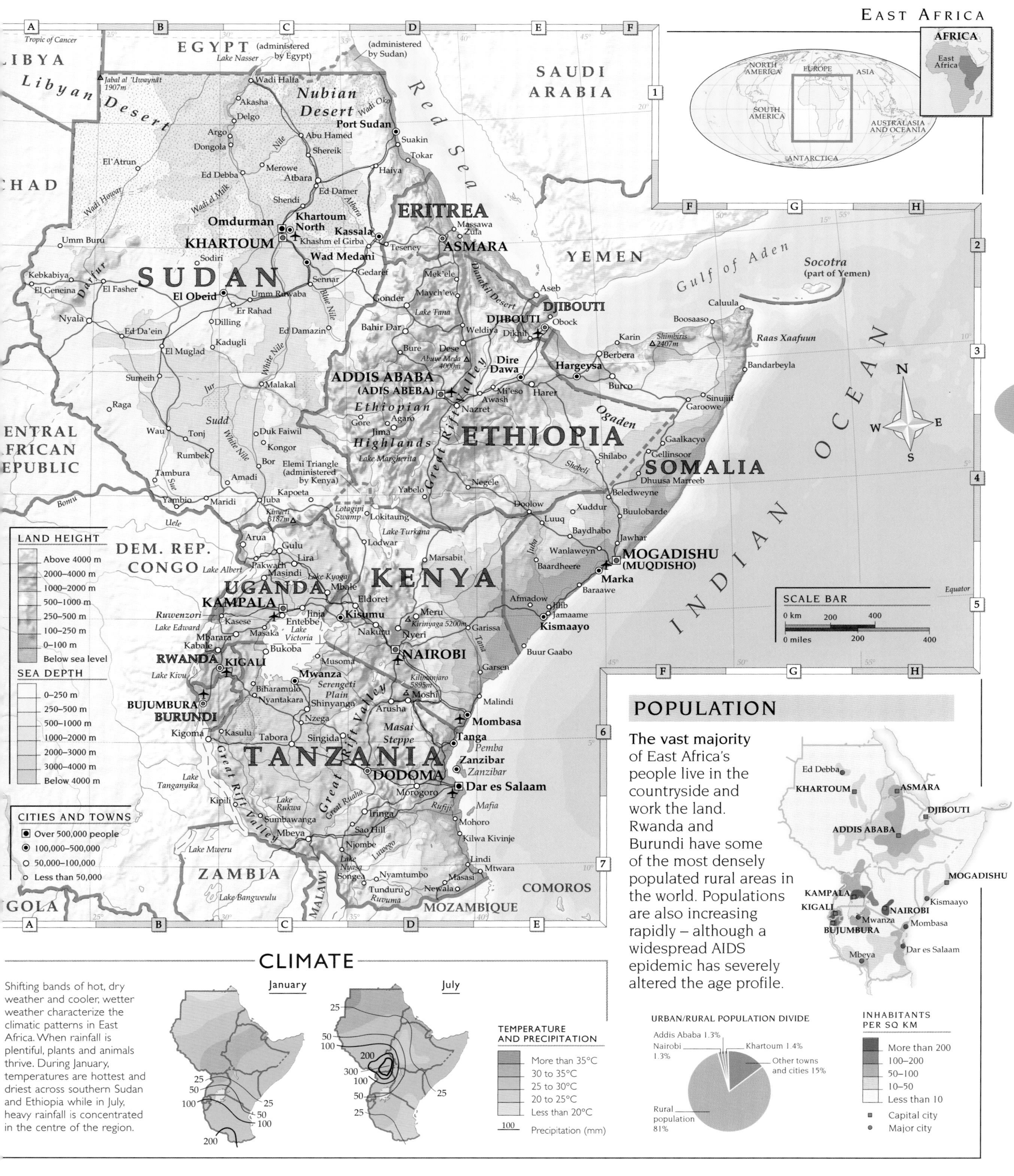
AFRICA
East Africa
NORTH AMERICA
EUROPE
ASIA
SOUTH AMERICA
AUSTRALASIA AND OCEANIA
ANTARCTICA
EGYPT (administered by Egypt)
(administered by Sudan)
Lake Nasser
LIBYA
Libyan Desert
Tropic of Cancer
Jabal al 'Uwaynāt 1907m
Wadi Halfa
Nubian Desert
Red Sea
SAUDI ARABIA
Akasha
Delgo
Argo
Dongola
Abu Hamed
Port Sudan
Suakin
Tokar
Shereik
El'Atrun
Merowe
Ed Debba
Atbara
Haiya
CHAD
Wadi Howar
Wadi el Milk
Shendi
Ed Damer
Omdurman
Khartoum North
KHARTOUM
Kassala
Khashm el Girba
Teseney
ERITREA
Massawa
Zula
ASMARA
Umm Buru
Sodiri
Wad Medani
YEMEN
Gulf of Aden
Socotra (part of Yemen)
SUDAN
Kebkabiya
El Geneina
Darfur
El Fasher
El Obeid
Umm Ruwaba
Sennar
Gedaref
Mek'ele
Maych'ew
Danakil Desert
Aseb
DJIBOUTI
Obock
Dikhil
Er Rahad
Gonder
Lake Tana
Dilling
Bahir Dar
Weldiya
Nyala
Ed Da'ein
Ed Damazin
Kadugli
El Muglad
Bure
Dese
Abune Meda 4000m
Dire Dawa
Hargeysa
Berbera
Karin
Shimbiris 2407m
Boosaaso
Caluula
Raas Xaafuun
Bandarbeyla
Burco
Sumeih
Malakal
ADDIS ABABA (ADIS ABEBA)
Mi'eso
Harer
Awash
Nazret
Sinujiif
Garoowe
Ogaden
Raga
Jur
Ethiopian Highlands
Gore
Agaro
Jima
Great Rift Valley
ETHIOPIA
Gaalkacyo
Gellinsoor
CENTRAL AFRICAN REPUBLIC
Wau
Tonj
Sudd
Duk Faiwil
Kongor
Bor
White Nile
Rumbek
Elemi Triangle (administered by Kenya)
Lake Margherita
Shilabo
Shebeli
SOMALIA
Dhuusa Marreeb
Tambura
Amadi
Negele
Yabelo
Beledweyne
Bomu
Yambio
Maridi
Juba
Kapoeta
Lotagipi Swamp
Lokitaung
Doolow
Xuddur
Buulobarde
Kinyeti 3187m
Luuq
Uele
Lake Turkana
Baydhabo
Jawhar
Lodwar
DEM. REP. CONGO
Arua
Gulu
Wanlaweyn
MOGADISHU (MUQDISHO)
Lake Albert
Pakwach
Lira
Marsabit
Baardheere
Masindi
Marka
UGANDA
Lake Kyoga
Mbale
KENYA
Baraawe
KAMPALA
Eldoret
Afmadow
Ruwenzori
Jinja
Kisumu
Meru
Jamaame
Kasese
Entebbe
Kirinyaga 5200m
Garissa
Kismaayo
Lake Edward
Masaka
Lake Victoria
Nakuru
Nyeri
Mbarara
Kabale
Bukoba
NAIROBI
Tana
Buur Gaabo
RWANDA
KIGALI
Musoma
Lake Kivu
Garsen
Mwanza
Kilimanjaro 5895m
Biharamulo
Serengeti Plain
Moshi
Nyantakara
Shinyanga
Arusha
Malindi
BUJUMBURA
BURUNDI
Nzega
Mombasa
Kigoma
Kasulu
Tabora
Singida
Masai Steppe
Tanga
Pemba
TANZANIA
Zanzibar
DODOMA
Lake Tanganyika
Morogoro
Dar es Salaam
Kipili
Lake Rukwa
Great Ruaha
Iringa
Rufiji
Mafia
Sumbawanga
Sao Hill
Mohoro
Mbeya
Njombe
Kilwa Kivinje
Lake Mweru
Luwego
Lake Nyasa
Lindi
Mtwara
ZAMBIA
MALAWI
Songea
Nyamtumbo
Masasi
Newala
Tunduru
Ruvuma
COMOROS
Lake Bangweulu
ANGOLA
MOZAMBIQUE
INDIAN OCEAN
Equator
N
S
E
W
SCALE BAR
0 km 200 400
0 miles 200 400
LAND HEIGHT
Above 4000 m
2000–4000 m
1000–2000 m
500–1000 m
250–500 m
100–250 m
0–100 m
Below sea level
SEA DEPTH
0–250 m
250–500 m
500–1000 m
1000–2000 m
2000–3000 m
3000–4000 m
Below 4000 m
CITIES AND TOWNS
Over 500,000 people
100,000–500,000
50,000–100,000
Less than 50,000
CLIMATE
Shifting bands of hot, dry weather and cooler, wetter weather characterize the climatic patterns in East Africa. When rainfall is plentiful, plants and animals thrive. During January, temperatures are hottest and driest across southern Sudan and Ethiopia while in July, heavy rainfall is concentrated in the centre of the region.
January
July
TEMPERATURE AND PRECIPITATION
More than 35°C
30 to 35°C
25 to 30°C
20 to 25°C
Less than 20°C
100 Precipitation (mm)
POPULATION
The vast majority of East Africa's people live in the countryside and work the land. Rwanda and Burundi have some of the most densely populated rural areas in the world. Populations are also increasing rapidly – although a widespread AIDS epidemic has severely altered the age profile.
Ed Debba
KHARTOUM
ASMARA
DJIBOUTI
ADDIS ABABA
MOGADISHU
KAMPALA
KIGALI
NAIROBI
Kismaayo
Mwanza
Mombasa
BUJUMBURA
Dar es Salaam
Mbeya
URBAN/RURAL POPULATION DIVIDE
Addis Ababa 1.3%
Nairobi 1.3%
Khartoum 1.4%
Other towns and cities 15%
Rural population 81%
INHABITANTS PER SQ KM
More than 200
100–200
50–100
10–50
Less than 10
Capital city
Major city

Southern Africa

ANGOLA, BOTSWANA, COMOROS, CONGO, DEM. REP. CONGO, GABON, LESOTHO, MADAGASCAR, MALAWI, MOZAMBIQUE, NAMIBIA, SOUTH AFRICA, SWAZILAND, ZAMBIA, ZIMBABWE

Southern Africa contains the richest deposits of valuable minerals on the continent. South Africa is the wealthiest and most industrialized country in the region. Most of the surrounding countries rely on it for trade and work. Racial segregation under apartheid operated from 1948 until 1994, when South Africa held its first multiracial elections.

FARMING AND LAND USE

Most of southern Africa's farmers grow just enough food to feed their families, though much of the farmland is in the hands of a few wealthy landowners. In the tropical north, oil palms and rubber are grown on large commercial plantations. Fruits are cultivated in the south, and tea and coffee are important in the east. Cattle farming is widespread across the dry grasslands.

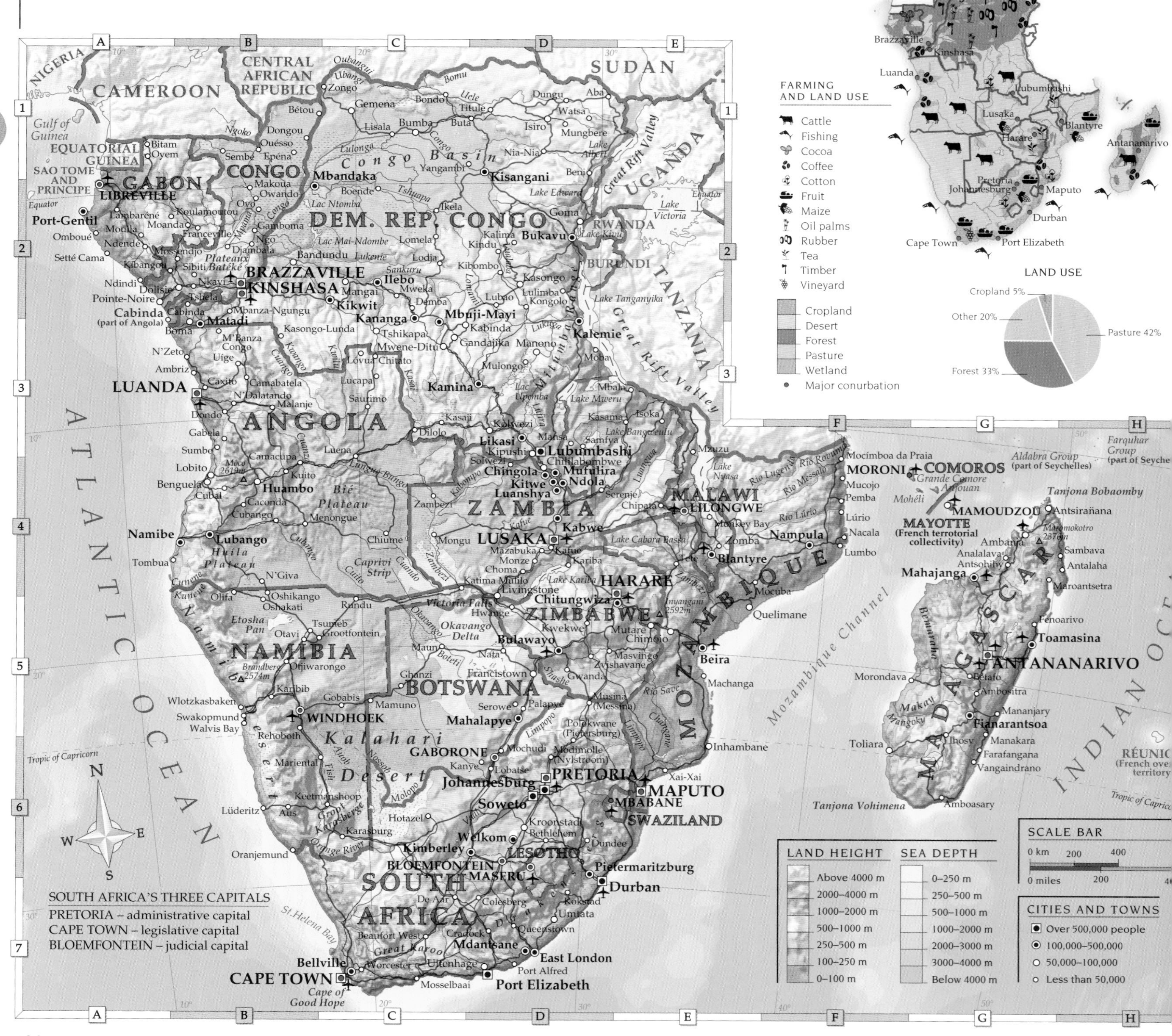

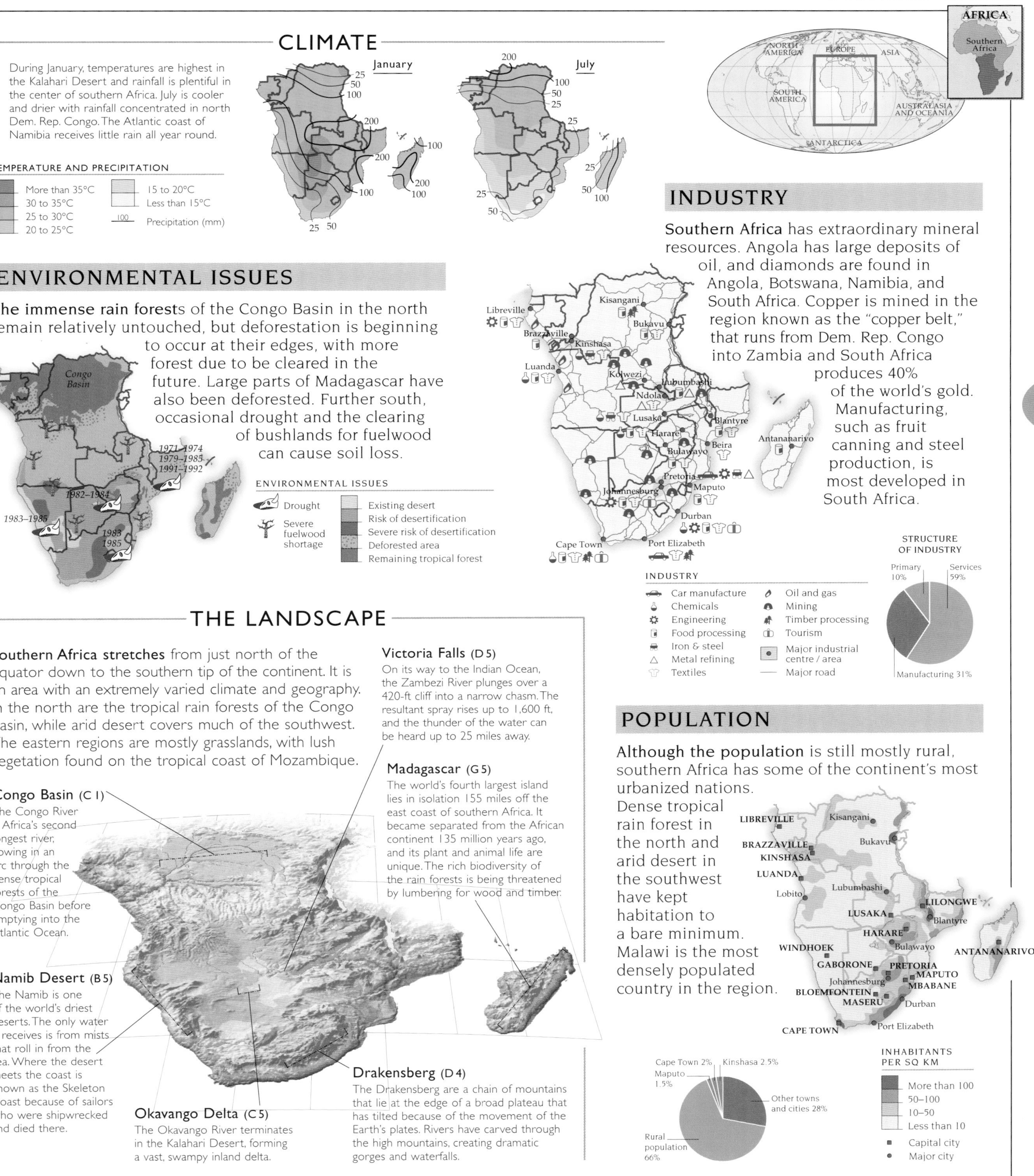

CLIMATE

During January, temperatures are highest in the Kalahari Desert and rainfall is plentiful in the center of southern Africa. July is cooler and drier with rainfall concentrated in north Dem. Rep. Congo. The Atlantic coast of Namibia receives little rain all year round.

ENVIRONMENTAL ISSUES

The immense rain forests of the Congo Basin in the north remain relatively untouched, but deforestation is beginning to occur at their edges, with more forest due to be cleared in the future. Large parts of Madagascar have also been deforested. Further south, occasional drought and the clearing of bushlands for fuelwood can cause soil loss.

INDUSTRY

Southern Africa has extraordinary mineral resources. Angola has large deposits of oil, and diamonds are found in Angola, Botswana, Namibia, and South Africa. Copper is mined in the region known as the "copper belt," that runs from Dem. Rep. Congo into Zambia and South Africa produces 40% of the world's gold. Manufacturing, such as fruit canning and steel production, is most developed in South Africa.

THE LANDSCAPE

Southern Africa stretches from just north of the equator down to the southern tip of the continent. It is an area with an extremely varied climate and geography. In the north are the tropical rain forests of the Congo Basin, while arid desert covers much of the southwest. The eastern regions are mostly grasslands, with lush vegetation found on the tropical coast of Mozambique.

Congo Basin (C 1)
The Congo River is Africa's second longest river, flowing in an arc through the dense tropical forests of the Congo Basin before emptying into the Atlantic Ocean.

Namib Desert (B 5)
The Namib is one of the world's driest deserts. The only water it receives is from mists that roll in from the sea. Where the desert meets the coast is known as the Skeleton Coast because of sailors who were shipwrecked and died there.

Okavango Delta (C 5)
The Okavango River terminates in the Kalahari Desert, forming a vast, swampy inland delta.

Victoria Falls (D 5)
On its way to the Indian Ocean, the Zambezi River plunges over a 420-ft cliff into a narrow chasm. The resultant spray rises up to 1,600 ft, and the thunder of the water can be heard up to 25 miles away.

Madagascar (G 5)
The world's fourth largest island lies in isolation 155 miles off the east coast of southern Africa. It became separated from the African continent 135 million years ago, and its plant and animal life are unique. The rich biodiversity of the rain forests is being threatened by lumbering for wood and timber.

Drakensberg (D 4)
The Drakensberg are a chain of mountains that lie at the edge of a broad plateau that has tilted because of the movement of the Earth's plates. Rivers have carved through the high mountains, creating dramatic gorges and waterfalls.

POPULATION

Although the population is still mostly rural, southern Africa has some of the continent's most urbanized nations. Dense tropical rain forest in the north and arid desert in the southwest have kept habitation to a bare minimum. Malawi is the most densely populated country in the region.

AUSTRALASIA & OCEANIA

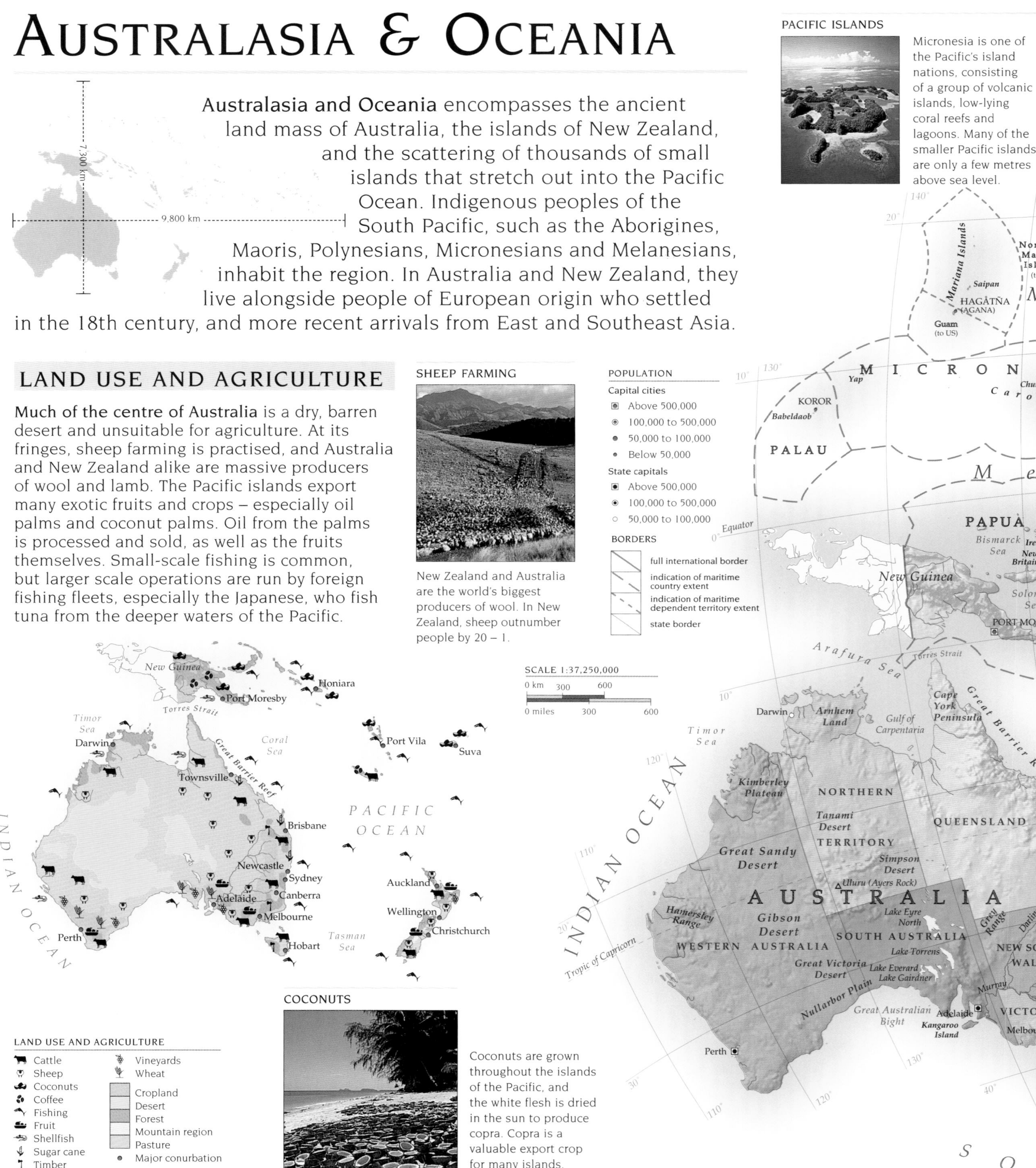

Australasia and Oceania encompasses the ancient land mass of Australia, the islands of New Zealand, and the scattering of thousands of small islands that stretch out into the Pacific Ocean. Indigenous peoples of the South Pacific, such as the Aborigines, Maoris, Polynesians, Micronesians and Melanesians, inhabit the region. In Australia and New Zealand, they live alongside people of European origin who settled in the 18th century, and more recent arrivals from East and Southeast Asia.

PACIFIC ISLANDS

Micronesia is one of the Pacific's island nations, consisting of a group of volcanic islands, low-lying coral reefs and lagoons. Many of the smaller Pacific islands are only a few metres above sea level.

LAND USE AND AGRICULTURE

Much of the centre of Australia is a dry, barren desert and unsuitable for agriculture. At its fringes, sheep farming is practised, and Australia and New Zealand alike are massive producers of wool and lamb. The Pacific islands export many exotic fruits and crops – especially oil palms and coconut palms. Oil from the palms is processed and sold, as well as the fruits themselves. Small-scale fishing is common, but larger scale operations are run by foreign fishing fleets, especially the Japanese, who fish tuna from the deeper waters of the Pacific.

SHEEP FARMING

New Zealand and Australia are the world's biggest producers of wool. In New Zealand, sheep outnumber people by 20 – 1.

POPULATION

Capital cities
- Above 500,000
- 100,000 to 500,000
- 50,000 to 100,000
- Below 50,000

State capitals
- Above 500,000
- 100,000 to 500,000
- 50,000 to 100,000

BORDERS
- full international border
- indication of maritime country extent
- indication of maritime dependent territory extent
- state border

SCALE 1:37,250,000
0 km 300 600
0 miles 300 600

LAND USE AND AGRICULTURE
- Cattle
- Sheep
- Coconuts
- Coffee
- Fishing
- Fruit
- Shellfish
- Sugar cane
- Timber
- Vineyards
- Wheat
- Cropland
- Desert
- Forest
- Mountain region
- Pasture
- Major conurbation

COCONUTS

Coconuts are grown throughout the islands of the Pacific, and the white flesh is dried in the sun to produce copra. Copra is a valuable export crop for many islands.

MINERAL RESOURCES

Mineral resources are not widespread, but where they are found, it is in great abundance. Most of the small Pacific islands have no mineral resources, but Australia has enormous reserves of bauxite and iron ore, and also sizeable reserves of gold and zinc. Copper is found in Papua New Guinea, and New Caledonia has large nickel reserves. There are ample supplies of fossil fuels and although coal is plentiful in eastern Australia, oil and gas are found only in isolated pockets around Australia's coast.

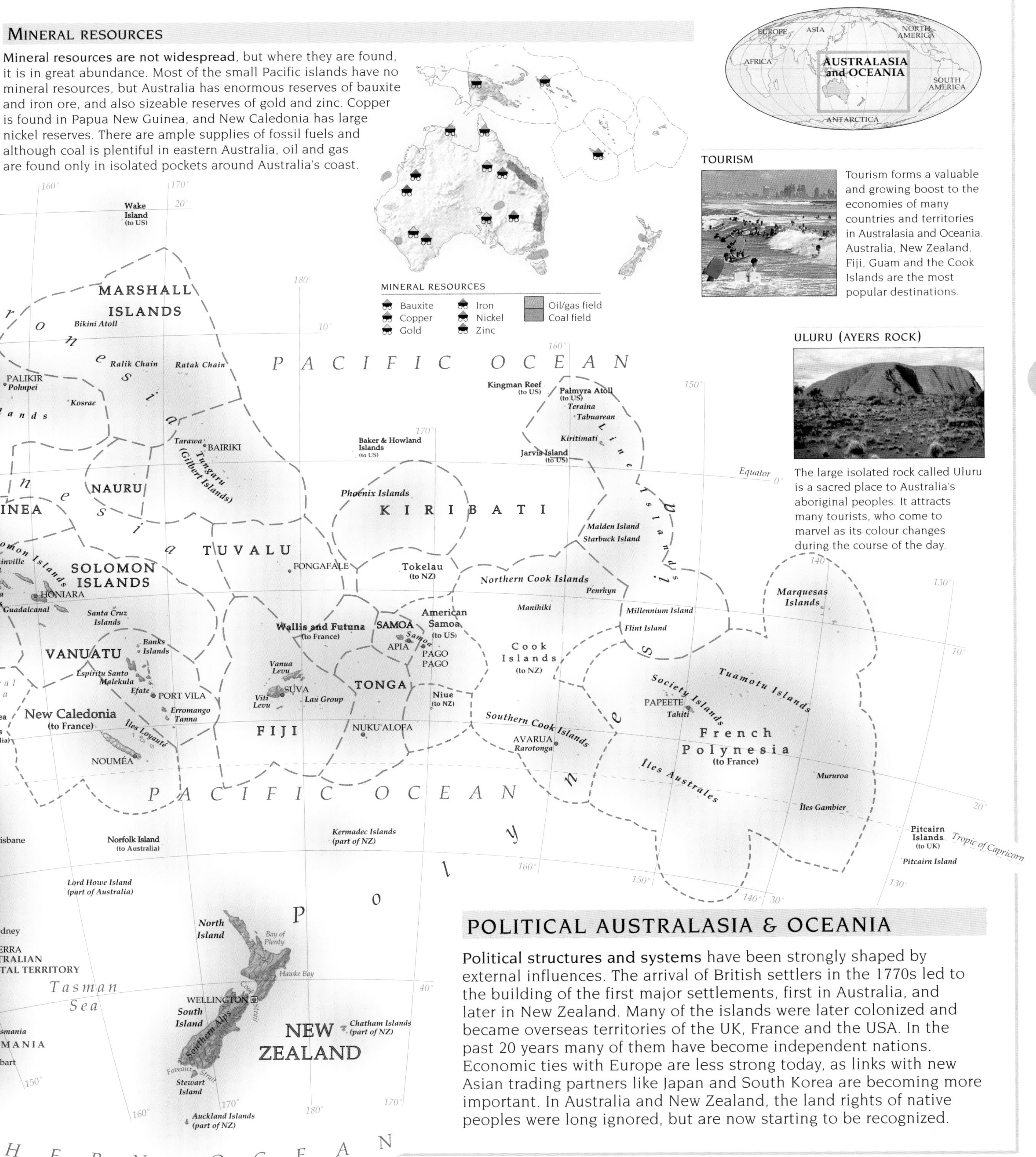

TOURISM

Tourism forms a valuable and growing boost to the economies of many countries and territories in Australasia and Oceania. Australia, New Zealand, Fiji, Guam and the Cook Islands are the most popular destinations.

ULURU (AYERS ROCK)

The large isolated rock called Uluru is a sacred place to Australia's aboriginal peoples. It attracts many tourists, who come to marvel as its colour changes during the course of the day.

POLITICAL AUSTRALASIA & OCEANIA

Political structures and systems have been strongly shaped by external influences. The arrival of British settlers in the 1770s led to the building of the first major settlements, first in Australia, and later in New Zealand. Many of the islands were later colonized and became overseas territories of the UK, France and the USA. In the past 20 years many of them have become independent nations. Economic ties with Europe are less strong today, as links with new Asian trading partners like Japan and South Korea are becoming more important. In Australia and New Zealand, the land rights of native peoples were long ignored, but are now starting to be recognized.

AUSTRALIA

Australia is the world's sixth-largest country, and also the smallest, flattest continent, with the lowest rainfall. Most Australians are of European, mainly British, origin but in the past 50 years almost five million settlers from more than 200 countries have made Australia their home. The Aboriginal peoples, now only a tiny minority, were the first inhabitants. Recently, there have been several moves to restore their ancient lands.

FARMING AND LAND USE

Darwin
Townsville
Brisbane
Sydney
Canberra
Melbourne
Adelaide
Perth
Hobart

Away from the coasts, much of the land is too dry for agriculture. Fields of sugar cane grow close to the east coast, and grapes for the thriving wine industry are cultivated in the south and west, along with wheat. Vast numbers of cattle and sheep are raised for their meat and wool – both of which are major exports. They are grazed in the desert, on huge farms called 'stations', and in more fertile areas.

FARMING AND LAND USE

- Cattle
- Fishing
- Sheep
- Wheat
- Sugar cane
- Timber
- Vineyards
- Cropland
- Desert
- Forest
- Pasture
- Major conurbation

LAND USE

Cropland 6%
Other (including desert) 21%
Forest 19%
Pasture 54%

INDUSTRY

Australia has one of the world's biggest mining industries. Bauxite, coal, copper, gold and iron ore are mined and exported, especially to Japan. In the cities, service industries, particularly tourism, are growing fast; Australia's sunshine and dramatic scenery are attracting an increasing number of overseas visitors.

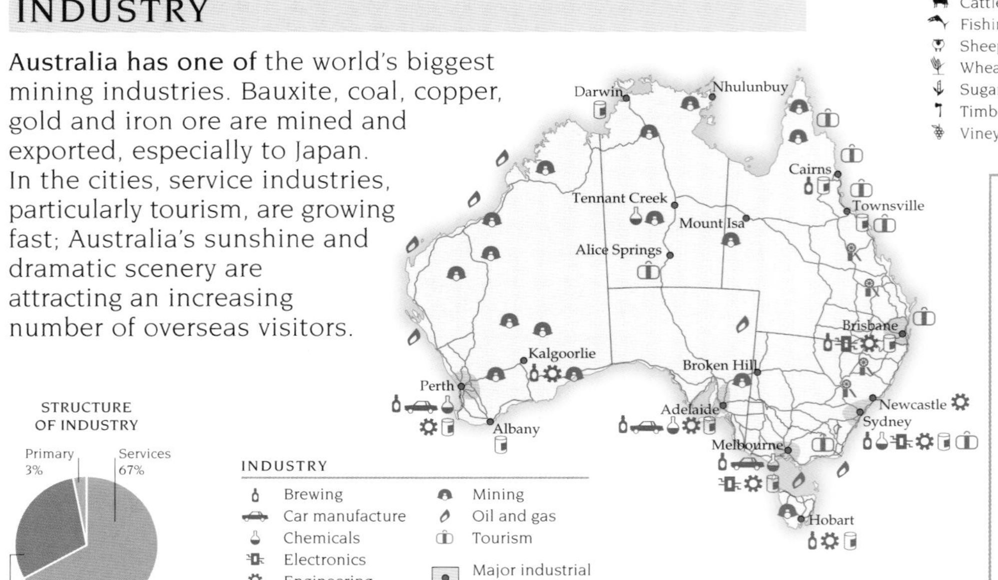

THE LANDSCAPE

Most of Australia is dry, flat and barren; all of the wetter, fertile land is found along its coastline. Huge sun-baked deserts, fringed by semi-arid plains of scrub and grassland cover most of the west and centre of the country. In the east, the land rises to the highlands of the Great Dividing Range, which run the whole length of the east coast. The tropical north coast has rainforests and mangrove swamps.

Blue Mountains (G6)
The Blue Mountains lie towards the southern end of the Great Dividing Range. They get their name from the blue haze of oil droplets given off by the eucalyptus trees covering their slopes.

Great Barrier Reef (G2)
This spectacular coral reef, which stretches for over 2,000 km off the coast of Queensland, is the largest living structure on Earth. The reef has built up over millions of years and its waters are home to thousands of different species of coral and marine animals.

Uluru (Ayers Rock) (D4)
Uluru is an enormous block of red sandstone, standing almost in the middle of Australia. It is the world's biggest free-standing rock – 9.4 km around the base, and 867 m high. It is the summit of a sandstone hill that is buried beneath the sands of the desert.

Simpson Desert (E4)
The Simpson Desert covers around 130,000 sq km. It contains long, parallel lines of sand dunes and is scattered with large salt pans and salt lakes, which were created when old rivers evaporated. They are now fed by the seasonal rains.

Murray River (F5)
Together with its tributaries, the Murray River is Australia's main river system. It winds slowly westwards for more than 2,500 km from the Great Dividing Range to the Indian Ocean. It is fed by snow from mountains in the far southeast.

Great Dividing Range (H5)
These highlands separate the desert regions from the fertile eastern plains. Rivers and streams have eroded them, creating deep valleys and gorges.

POPULATION

Despite its vast size, Australia is sparsely populated. The desert 'outback', which covers most of the interior, is too dry and barren to support many people. About 70% of the population live in the cities and towns on the east and southeast coasts, and around Perth in the west.

Darwin
Cairns
Mount Isa
Townsville
Alice Springs
Brisbane
Perth
Newcastle
Sydney
Adelaide
Melbourne
CANBERRA
Hobart

INHABITANTS PER SQ KM

- More than 50
- 10–50
- 1–10
- Less than 1
- Capital city
- Major city

URBAN/RURAL POPULATION DIVIDE

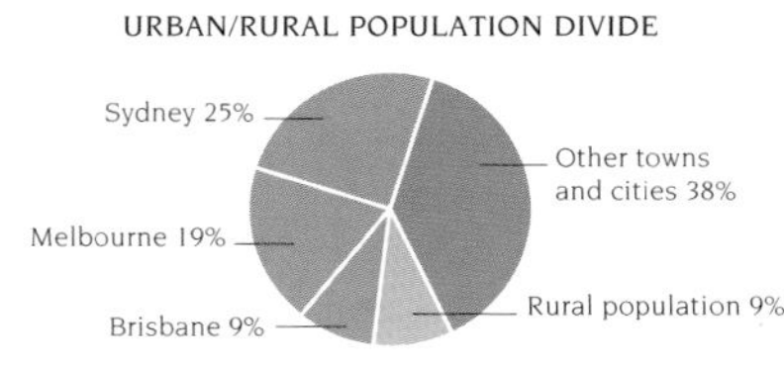

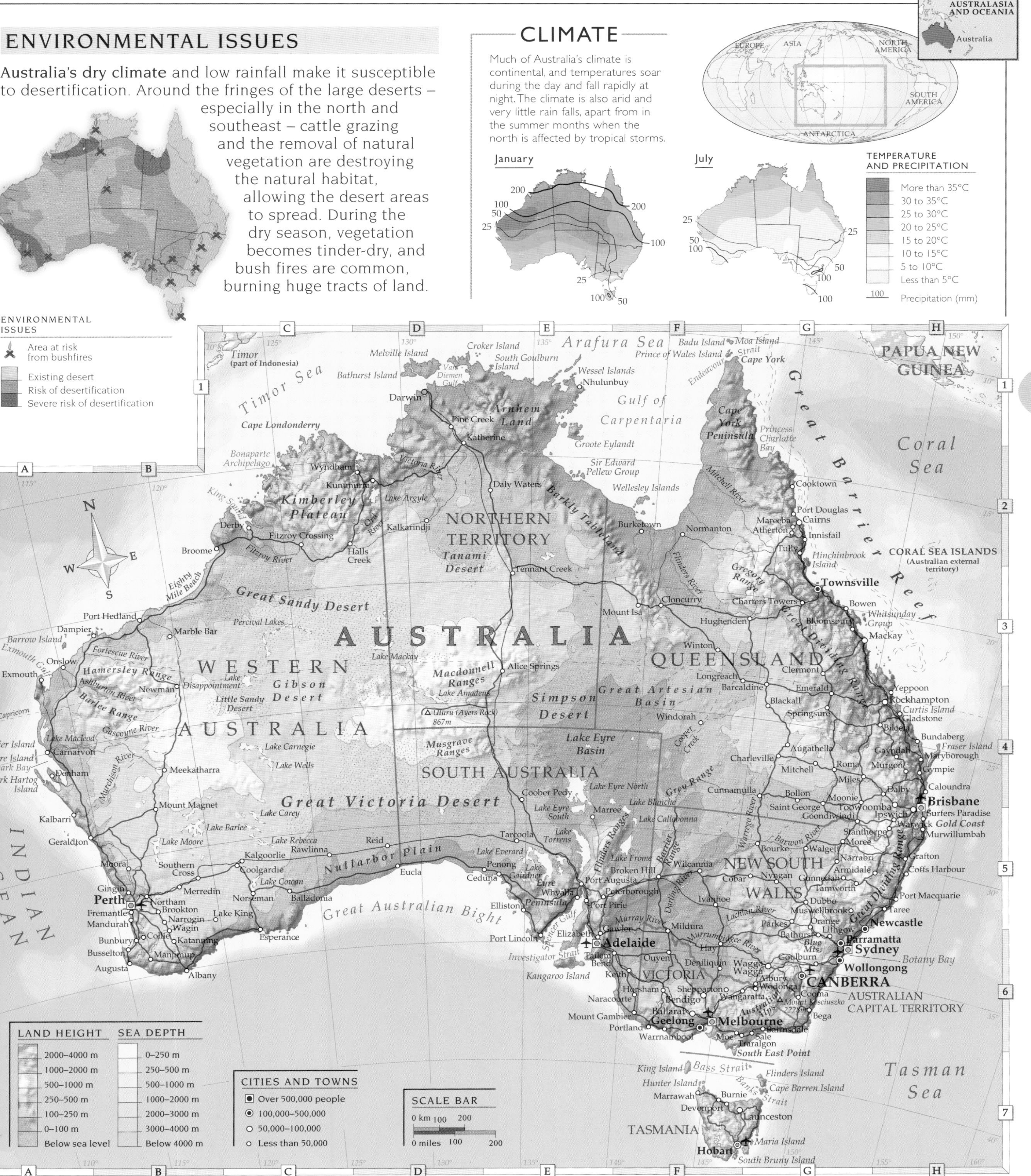
AUSTRALASIA AND OCEANIA
Australia
ENVIRONMENTAL ISSUES
Australia's dry climate and low rainfall make it susceptible to desertification. Around the fringes of the large deserts – especially in the north and southeast – cattle grazing and the removal of natural vegetation are destroying the natural habitat, allowing the desert areas to spread. During the dry season, vegetation becomes tinder-dry, and bush fires are common, burning huge tracts of land.
ENVIRONMENTAL ISSUES
Area at risk from bushfires
Existing desert
Risk of desertification
Severe risk of desertification
CLIMATE
Much of Australia's climate is continental, and temperatures soar during the day and fall rapidly at night. The climate is also arid and very little rain falls, apart from in the summer months when the north is affected by tropical storms.
EUROPE
ASIA
NORTH AMERICA
SOUTH AMERICA
ANTARCTICA
January
July
TEMPERATURE AND PRECIPITATION
More than 35°C
30 to 35°C
25 to 30°C
20 to 25°C
15 to 20°C
10 to 15°C
5 to 10°C
Less than 5°C
Precipitation (mm)
AUSTRALIA
WESTERN AUSTRALIA
NORTHERN TERRITORY
SOUTH AUSTRALIA
QUEENSLAND
NEW SOUTH WALES
VICTORIA
TASMANIA
AUSTRALIAN CAPITAL TERRITORY
PAPUA NEW GUINEA
CORAL SEA ISLANDS (Australian external territory)
Timor (part of Indonesia)
Timor Sea
Arafura Sea
Gulf of Carpentaria
Coral Sea
Tasman Sea
Great Australian Bight
INDIAN OCEAN
Great Barrier Reef
Great Sandy Desert
Gibson Desert
Great Victoria Desert
Simpson Desert
Tanami Desert
Nullarbor Plain
Great Artesian Basin
Lake Eyre Basin
Kimberley Plateau
Barkly Tableland
Great Dividing Range
Macdonnell Ranges
Musgrave Ranges
Uluru (Ayers Rock) 867m
Mount Kosciuszko 2228m
Cape York Peninsula
Arnhem Land
CANBERRA
Sydney
Melbourne
Brisbane
Perth
Adelaide
Darwin
Hobart
Alice Springs
Townsville
Cairns
Newcastle
Wollongong
Geelong
Launceston
Bass Strait
LAND HEIGHT
2000–4000 m
1000–2000 m
500–1000 m
250–500 m
100–250 m
0–100 m
Below sea level
SEA DEPTH
0–250 m
250–500 m
500–1000 m
1000–2000 m
2000–3000 m
3000–4000 m
Below 4000 m
CITIES AND TOWNS
Over 500,000 people
100,000–500,000
50,000–100,000
Less than 50,000
SCALE BAR
0 km 100 200
0 miles 100 200

New Zealand

New Zealand is one of the most remote populated places in the world. The first people to settle on the islands were the Maori, a Polynesian people. When European settlers arrived during the 19th century, the Maori became a minority, and now only make up about 9% of the population. With a small population and rich natural resources, New Zealand's people have high living standards. The country's magnificent rugged scenery is popular with tourists.

Environmental Issues

New Zealand is one of the world's least polluted countries – largely due to its low population and lack of heavy industries, although air quality is occasionally poor in Auckland and Christchurch. Environment-friendly geothermal energy is tapped to make electricity in the volcanic region of North Island. Recently, logging companies have begun to exploit the rich forest reserves, although this has been widely opposed.

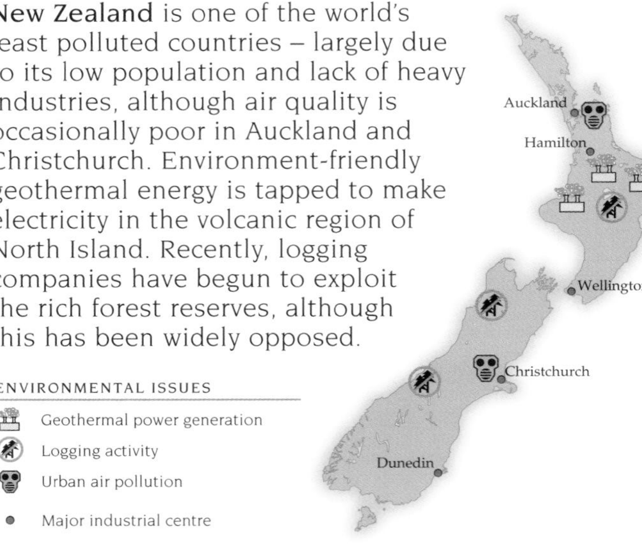

ENVIRONMENTAL ISSUES
- Geothermal power generation
- Logging activity
- Urban air pollution
- Major industrial centre

Industry

Hi-tech industries such as electronics and computing are growing in the major cities of Auckland and Wellington, although agricultural products such as meat, wool and milk are still among New Zealand's major exports, and large pine forests supply wood for paper pulp and timber. The exciting scenery and varied climate draw tourists from all over the world, especially for walking and adventure holidays.

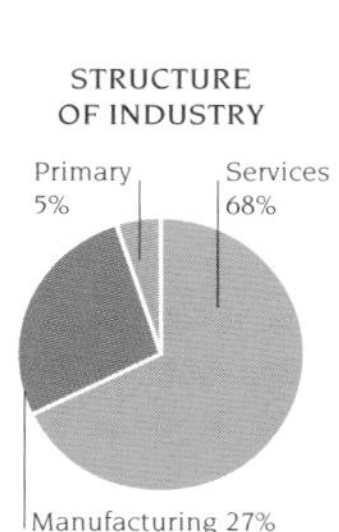

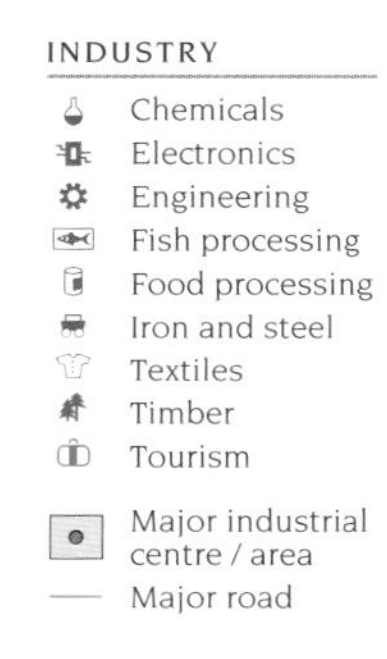

Population

Most of the population is descended from European settlers, although immigrants from Asia and from the Pacific islands are increasing. More than one-third of New Zealand's 4 million people live in Auckland on North Island, which also has the largest Polynesian population of any city in the Pacific. Elsewhere, the population is clustered along the coasts, where the land is lower.

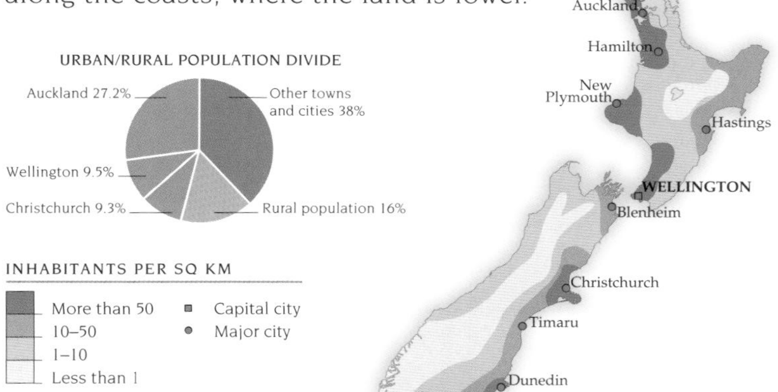

The Landscape

Two large, mountainous islands form New Zealand's main land areas. A large crack or fault – the Alpine Fault, in the west of South Island – is the boundary between two plates in the Earth's crust. Land either side of the fault tends to move, causing earthquakes. Volcanoes, many of them still active, are also found, on both islands. South Island has many high peaks, several more than 3,000 m high.

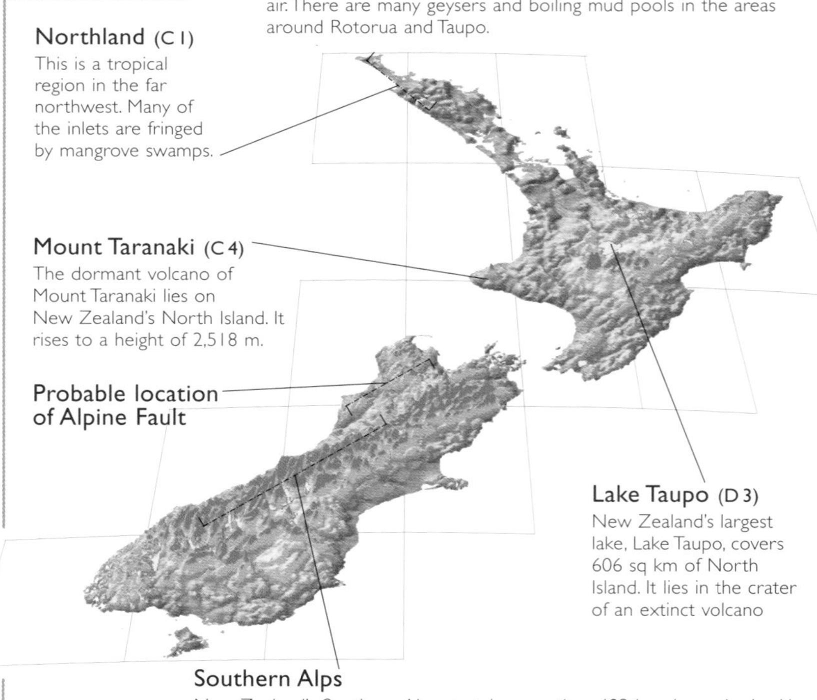

Geysers and boiling mud
Geysers occur when hot volcanic rocks come into contact with underground water. The water boils and turns to steam forcing the water above it to burst through the Earth's surface into the air. There are many geysers and boiling mud pools in the areas around Rotorua and Taupo.

Northland (C 1)
This is a tropical region in the far northwest. Many of the inlets are fringed by mangrove swamps.

Mount Taranaki (C 4)
The dormant volcano of Mount Taranaki lies on New Zealand's North Island. It rises to a height of 2,518 m.

Probable location of Alpine Fault

Lake Taupo (D 3)
New Zealand's largest lake, Lake Taupo, covers 606 sq km of North Island. It lies in the crater of an extinct volcano

Southern Alps
New Zealand's Southern Alps stretch more than 483 km down the backbone of South Island. They were formed by the collision of the Indo-Australian and Pacific plates. Heavy snowfalls here, brought by westerly winds, feed the Fox Glacier which moves at a speed of 0.5–4.5 m a day.

FARMING AND LAND USE

Large areas of rich, sweet grasslands have made New Zealand one of the world's top areas for rearing sheep. There are almost 20 sheep for every person, grazing alongside about six million cattle. Fruits, including apples, strawberries, oranges, peaches, and the famous kiwi fruit, are cultivated, particularly on South Island, and are exported throughout the world. Fish caught off the Pacific coast are another important source of income.

CLIMATE

North Island has a generally warm climate which becomes tropical – hotter and more humid – towards the far north. South Island is cooler and wetter. There may be heavy snowfall in winter, particularly in the highlands, and many mountains are permanently snow-capped

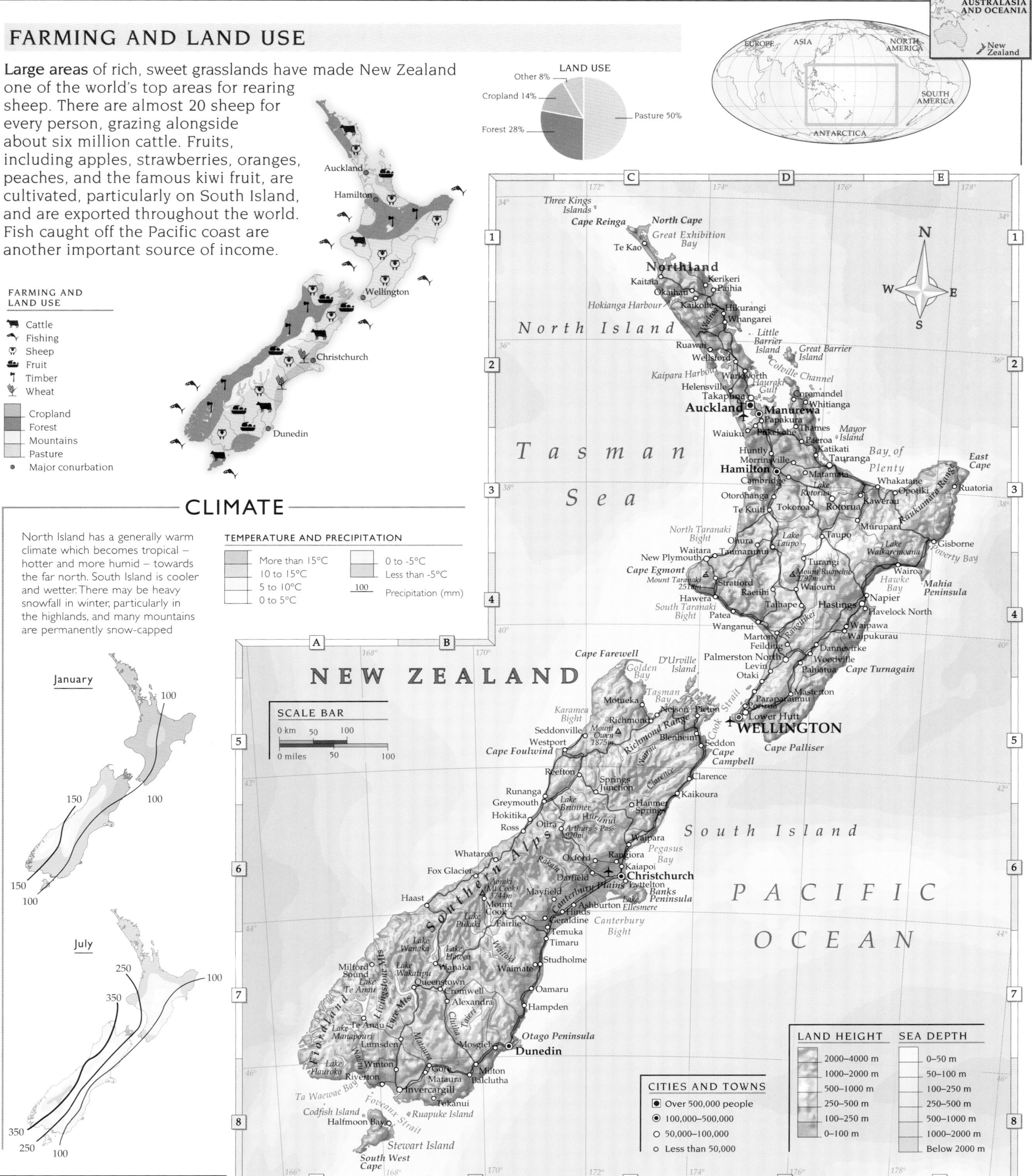

Southwest Pacific

The many thousands of islands in the Pacific Ocean are scattered across an enormous area. The original inhabitants, the Polynesians, Melanesians and Micronesians, settled the islands following the last Ice Age. In the 1700s Europeans arrived. They colonized all of the Pacific islands, introducing their culture, languages and religion. Today, many, though not all, of the islands have become independent. Their economies are simple, based largely on fishing and agriculture. Many are increasingly relying on their beautiful scenery and tropical climates to attract tourists and give a valuable boost to their economies.

INDUSTRY

Today, the main industry for many of the Pacific islands is tourism. Food processing and small-scale textile industries are also common on many islands.

INDUSTRY
- Brewing
- Food processing
- Textiles
- Timber processing
- Mining
- Tourism
- Major industrial centre
- Major road

Mount Hagen
Madang
Lae
Rabaul
Port Moresby
Honiara
Port Vila
Suva
Nouméa

LANDSCAPE

Most of the Pacific islands are extremely small, the largest land mass is the half of the island of New Guinea occupied by Papua New Guinea. The edges of the Indo-Australian and Pacific plates meet on the western edge of the area, leading to much volcanic and earthquake activity. Many of the islands are coral atolls, originally formed by volcanic activity, and some are no more than a few metres above sea level.

New Guinea (A 2)
A mountainous spine runs through the centre of the island, separating the northern coast from the dense forests and mangroves found in the south.

Pacific Ocean
The Pacific Ocean is the Earth's oldest and deepest ocean. Its name means peaceful, though it is far from being so; the highest wave ever recorded on open ocean – 34 m – occurred during a hurricane in the Pacific.

Kavachi
Kavachi is a submarine volcano lying off the coast of New Georgia, in the Solomon Islands. It still erupts every few years.

Ring of Fire
The 'Ring of Fire' is the term used to describe the string of volcanoes which surround the entire Pacific Ocean and erupt frequently because of intense stress and movement from within the Earth. The ring crosses the south Pacific, running between Vanuatu and New Caledonia, along the edge of the Solomon Islands, and between New Britain and New Guinea.

Sea trenches
Deep trenches mark the sea floor boundary where the Indo-Australian plate 'dives' under the Pacific plate.

Coral atolls
Volcanic activity in the Pacific has led to the creation of many islands. These islands become fringed with a ring of coral. When the islands subside beneath the sea once again, only the circle of coral is left, forming an atoll.

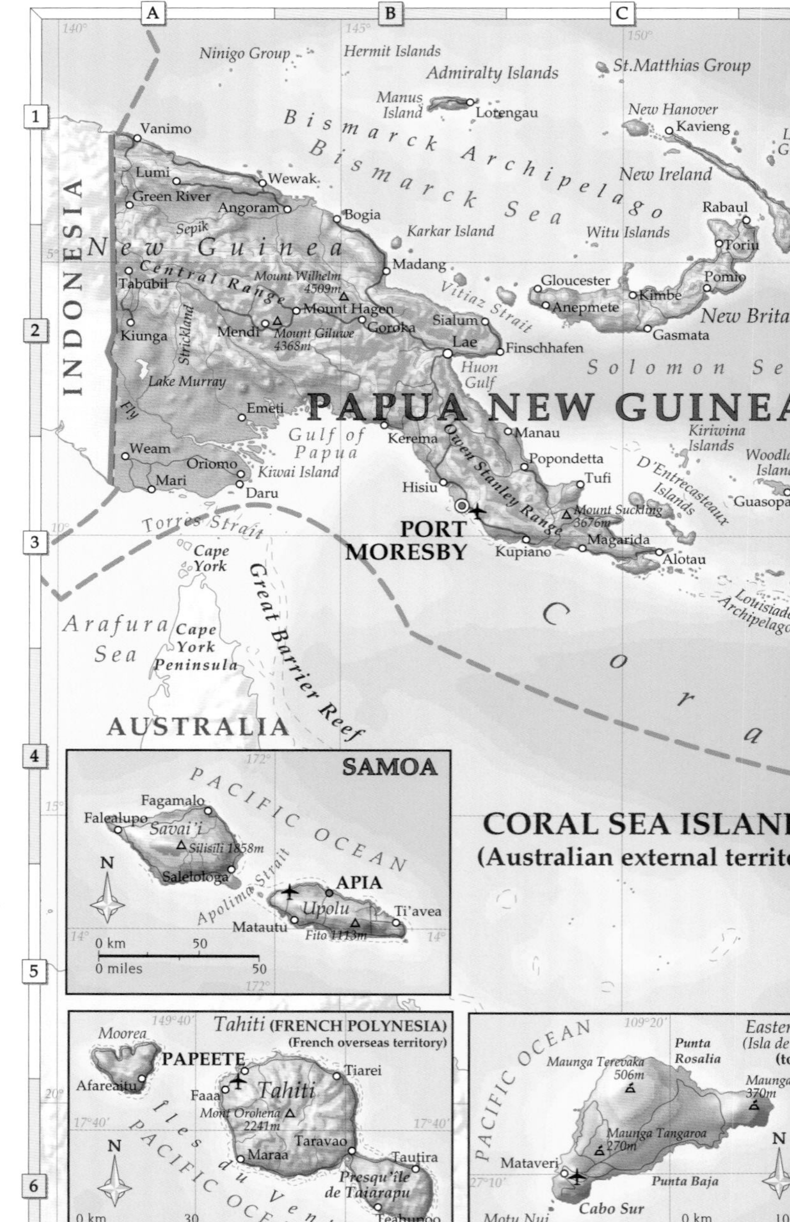

FARMING AND LAND USE

Most farming that takes place on the Pacific islands is at a subsistence level, and many people keep pigs and chickens. A few crops are grown for export, especially oil palms, and coconuts, which are dried in the sun to produce copra. Many islanders make their living from the rich fishing grounds of the Pacific. The thick forests of Papua New Guinea are increasingly cut down for timber.

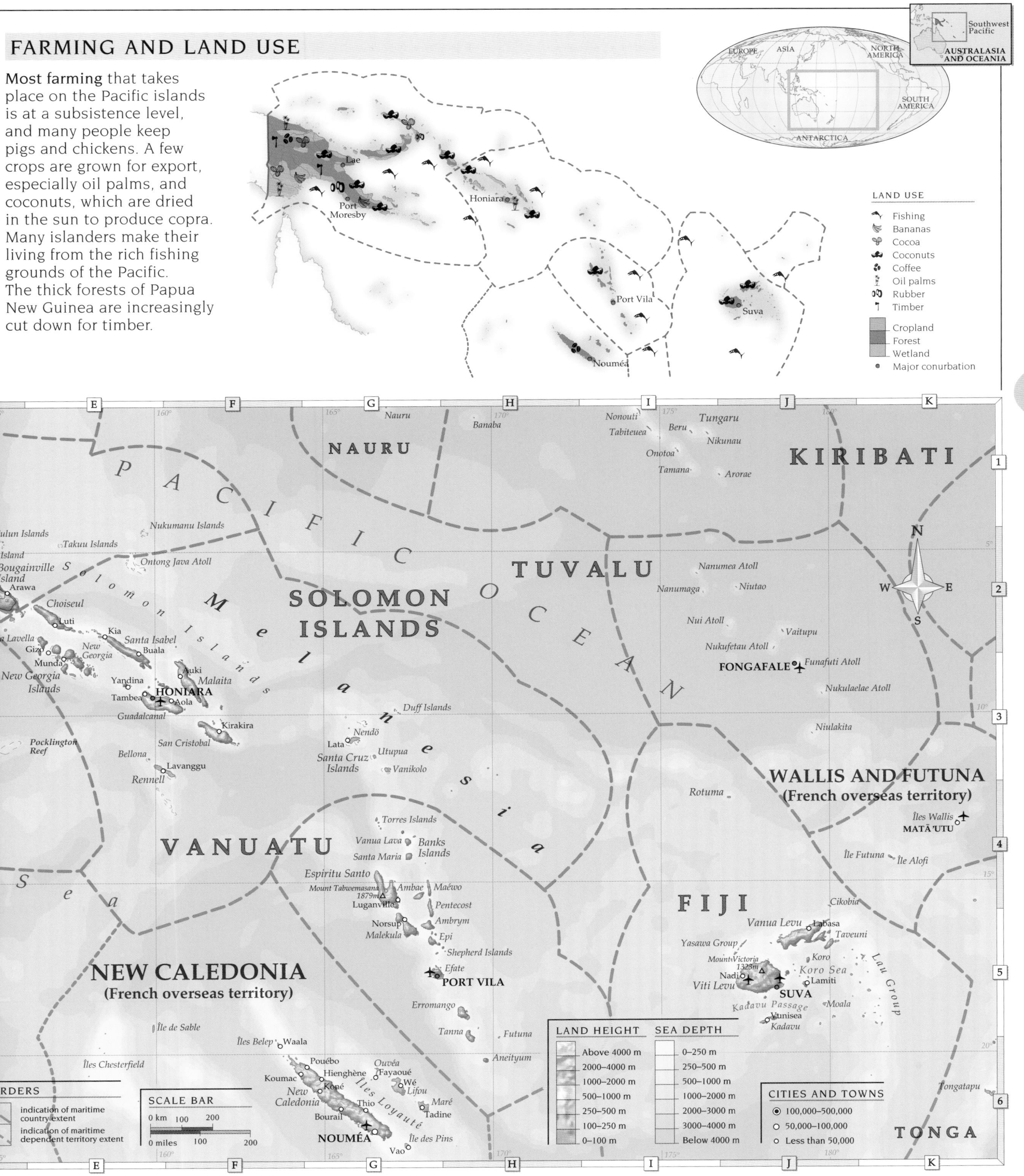

ANTARCTICA

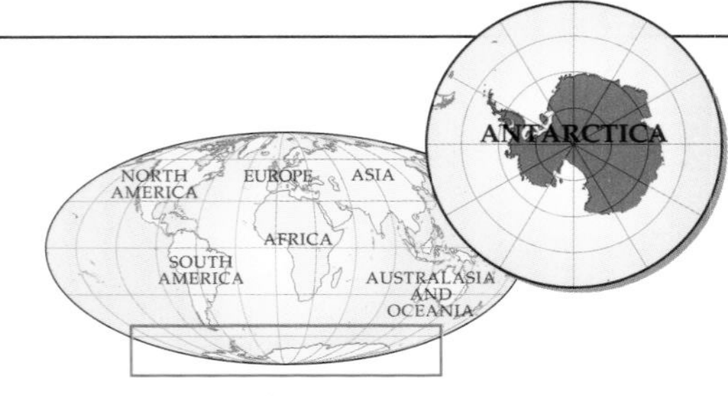

The continent of Antarctica has no permanent human population and very few animals can survive on the frozen land, although the surrounding seas teem with fish and mammals. Even in the summer the temperature is rarely above freezing and the sea-ice only partly melts; in winter, temperatures plummet to –80°C. The only people who live in Antarctica are teams of scientists who study the wildlife and monitor the ice for changes in the Earth's atmosphere.

THE LANDSCAPE

Antarctica is the world's most southerly continent. It is also the world's coldest continent and its highest, mainly due to the great ice sheet – up to 2 km thick in parts – which lies over the mountains of the Antarctic Peninsula and the plateau of Greater Antarctica.

Frozen seas
During the cold winter months, the seas surrounding Antarctica freeze, almost doubling the size of the continent.

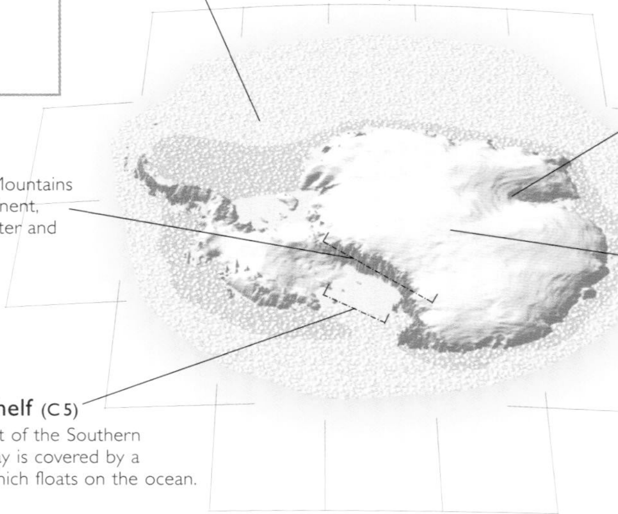

Lambert Glacier (E4)
The Lambert Glacier is the world's largest series of glaciers. It is 80 km wide at the coast and reaches more than 300 km inland.

Transantarctic Mountains (C5)
The Transantarctic Mountains run across the continent, splitting it into Greater and Lesser Antarctica.

Ice sheet
A massive sheet of ice, about 4,800 m thick at its deepest point, covers almost the entire area of Antarctica. It contains most of the fresh water on Earth. The weight of the ice pushes the land down below sea level.

The Ross Ice Shelf (C5)
The Ross Sea is part of the Southern Ocean. This deep bay is covered by a thick sheet of ice which floats on the ocean.

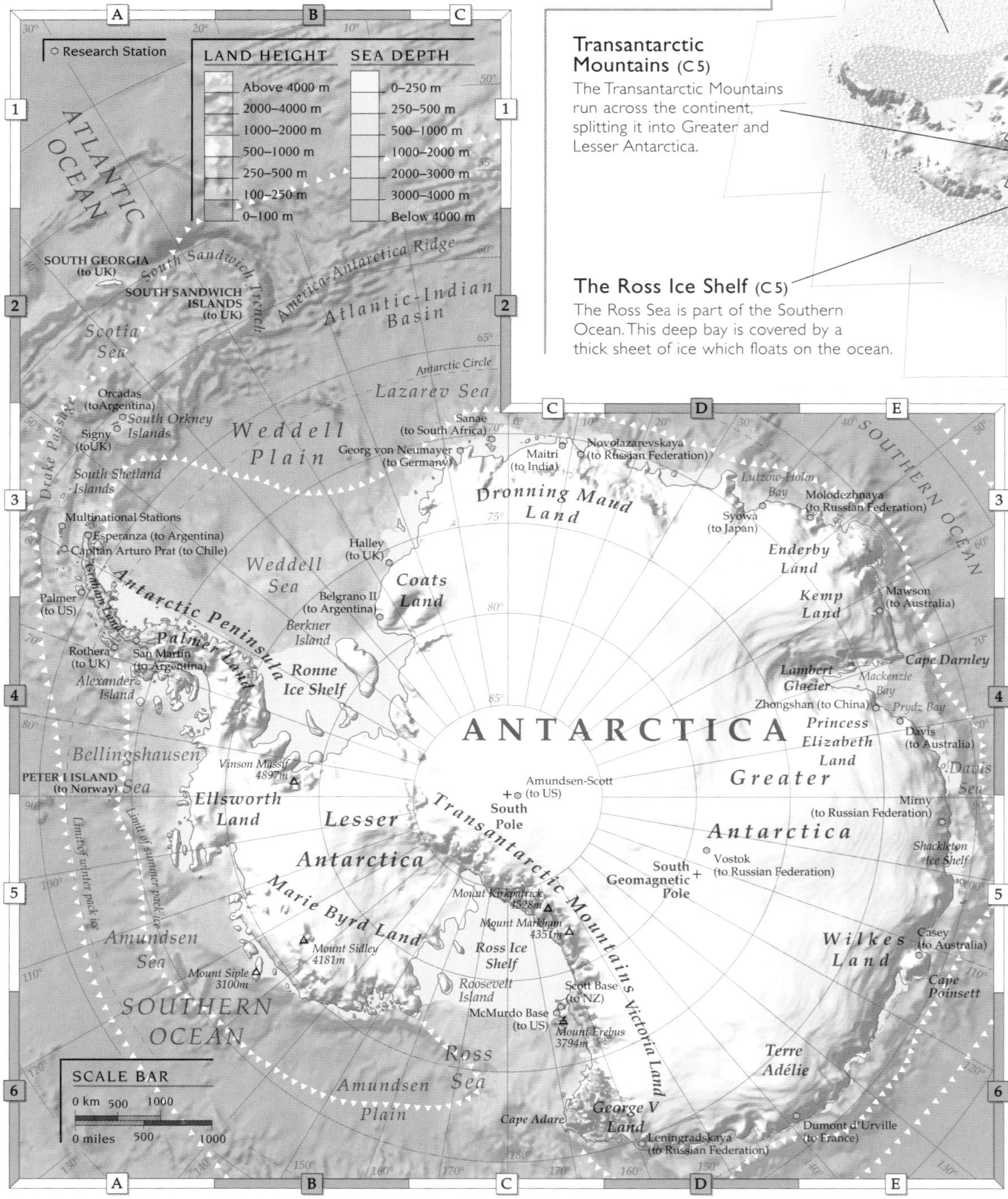

○ Research Station

LAND HEIGHT	SEA DEPTH
Above 4000 m	0–250 m
2000–4000 m	250–500 m
1000–2000 m	500–1000 m
500–1000 m	1000–2000 m
250–500 m	2000–3000 m
100–250 m	3000–4000 m
0–100 m	Below 4000 m

SCALE BAR
0 km 500 1000
0 miles 500 1000

RESOURCES

The mountains of Antarctica have rich mineral reserves. Gold, iron and coal are found, and there is natural gas in the surrounding seas. The unique and abundant marine wildlife is Antarctica's greatest resource. Colonies of penguins breed on the ice sheet, and whales, seals and many bird and fish species thrive in the icy waters.

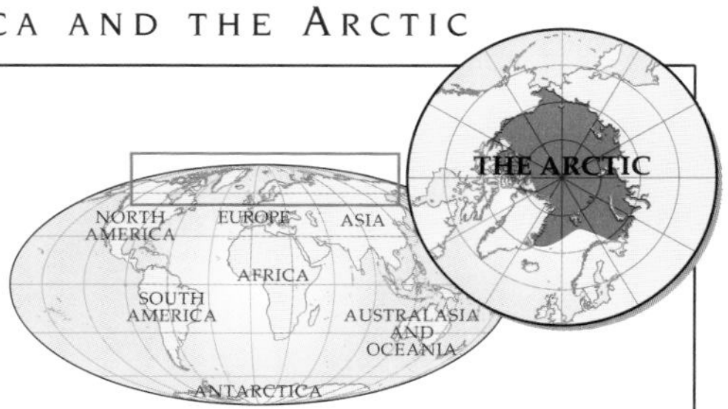

THE ARCTIC

The ice-covered Arctic Ocean is encircled by the most northerly parts of Europe, North America and Asia. Very few people live in the often freezing conditions. Those who do, including the Sami of northern Scandinavia, the Siberian Yugyt and Nenet people and the Canadian Inuit, were nomads who lived by hunting and herding. Some live like this today, but many have now settled in small towns.

THE LANDSCAPE

The Arctic Ocean is the smallest ocean in the world, covering a total area of 15,100,000 sq km. The ocean is divided into two large basins, divided by three great underwater mountain ranges including the Lomonosov Ridge which is more than 3,000 m high on average.

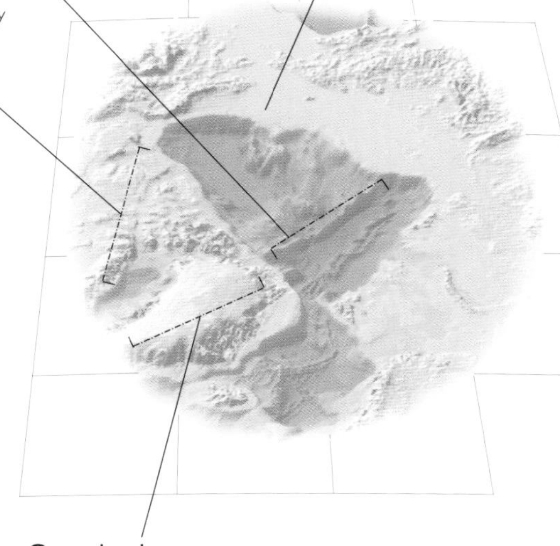

Lomonosov Ridge (C4)

Arctic islands (A4)
In the far north of Canada, there are many thousands of islands including Baffin Island and Victoria Island. Many of them are almost entirely surrounded by pack-ice.

Pack-ice
Much of the Arctic Ocean is permanently covered by pack-ice. When the ice breaks up, it forms enormous floating ice-masses called icebergs.

Greenland (A3)
Greenland is the world's largest island. It is covered by a huge ice sheet, more than 1,683,400 sq km across. The weight of the ice has pushed most of the land below sea level.

Sastrugi
Snow, blown by strong winds can scratch deep patterns in the snow. These patterns are known as sastrugi and line up with the direction of the wind.

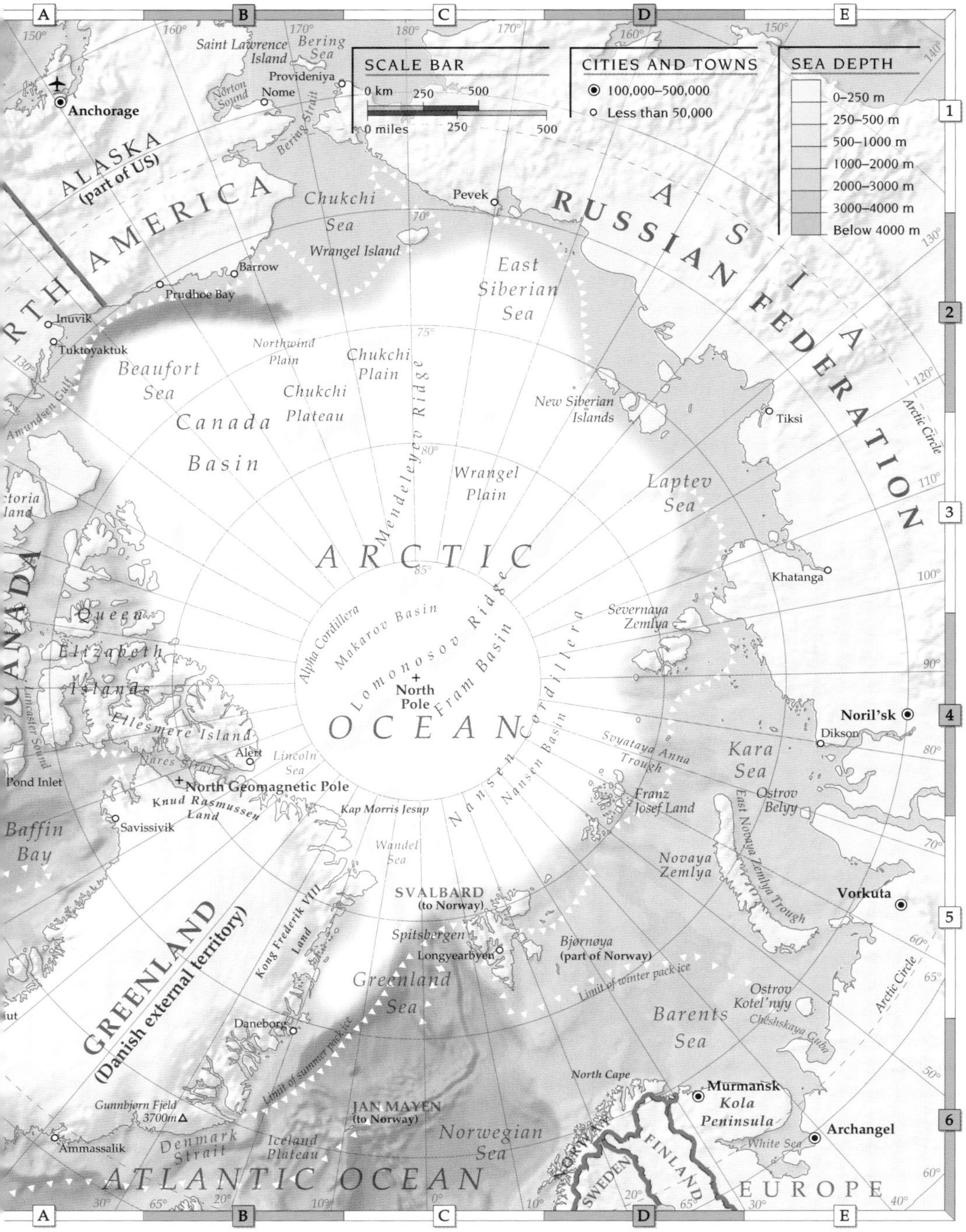

SCALE BAR
0 km 250 500
0 miles 250 500

CITIES AND TOWNS
◉ 100,000–500,000
○ Less than 50,000

SEA DEPTH
0–250 m
250–500 m
500–1000 m
1000–2000 m
2000–3000 m
3000–4000 m
Below 4000 m

RESOURCES

Coal, oil and gas are found beneath the Arctic Ocean and in Canada, Alaska and Russia. Fears about damage to the environment and the cost of extracting these resources have restricted the quantities removed. Overfishing has reduced fish stocks to very low levels. Quotas have been put in place to allow them to revive.

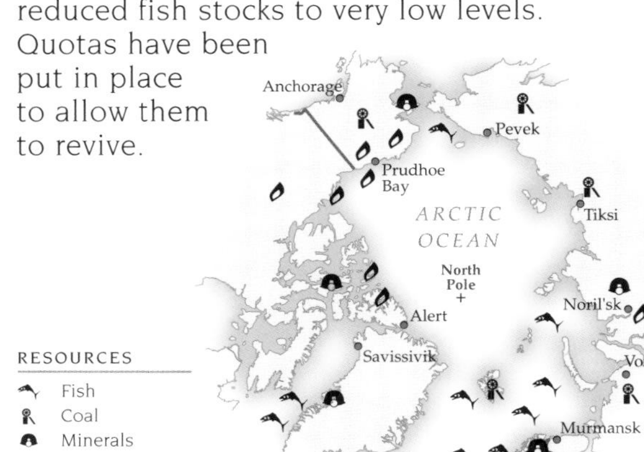

RESOURCES
Fish
Coal
Minerals
Oil and gas
Major town/city

GLOSSARY

This glossary defines certain geographical and technical terms used in this Atlas.

Acid rain Rain, sleet, snow or mist which has absorbed waste gases from fossil-fuelled power stations and vehicle exhausts, becoming acidic and poisonous.

Alluvium Material deposited by a river, such as silt, sand and mud.

Archipelago A group, or chain, of islands.

Atoll A circular or horseshoe-shaped coral reef enclosing a shallow area of water (lagoon).

Aquifer A body of rock that can absorb water. It may be a source of water for wells or springs.

Bar, coastal An offshore strip of sand or shingle, either above or below the water.

Biodiversity The quantity of different animal or plant species in a given area.

Birth rate The number of live births per 1000 individuals annually within a population.

Cash crop Agricultural produce grown for sale, often for foreign export, rather than to be consumed by the country or area where it was grown.

Climate The long term trends in weather conditions for an area.

Coniferous forest A type of forest containing trees or shrubs, like pines and firs, which have needles instead of leaves. They are found in temperate zones.

Continental plates The huge interlocking plates which make up the Earth's surface. A plate boundary is an area where two plates meet, and is the point at which earthquakes occur most frequently.

Conurbation A large urban area created by the merging of several towns.

Coral reef An underwater barrier created by colonies of coral polyps. The polyps secrete a protective skeleton of calcium carbonate, and reefs develop as live polyps build on the skeletons of dead generations.

Core The layers of liquid rock and solid iron at the centre of the Earth.

Crust The hard, thin outer shell of the Earth. The crust floats on the mantle, which is softer, but more dense.

Deciduous forest A type of broadleaf forest found in temperate regions.

Deforestation Cutting down trees or forest for timber or farmland. It can lead to soil erosion, flooding and landslides.

Delta A low-lying, fan-shaped area at a river mouth, formed by the deposition of successive layers of sediment. Slowing as it enters the sea, a river deposits sediment and may, as a result, split into many smaller channels called distributaries.

Deposition The laying down of material broken down by erosion or weathering and transported by the wind, water or gravity.

Desertification The spread of desert conditions into a region which was not previously a desert.

Drainage basin The land drained by a river and its tributaries.

Drought A long period of continuously low rainfall.

Earthquake A trembling or shaking of the ground caused by the sudden movement of rocks in the Earth's crust – and sometimes deeper than the crust. Earthquakes occur most frequently along continental plate boundaries.

Economy The organization of a country's finances, exports, imports, industry, agriculture and services.

Ecosytem A community of species dependent on each other and on the habitat in which they live.

Equator The 0° line of latitude. Equatorial climates are hot and there is plenty of rain.

Erosion The wearing down of the land surface by running water, waves, moving ice, wind and weather.

Estuary The mouth of a river, where the salt water from the sea meets the fresh water of the river.

Fault A crack or fracture in the Earth along which there has been movement of the rock masses relative to one another.

Fjord A coastal valley which was sculpted by glacial action.

Flood plain The broad, flat part of a river valley, next to the river itself, formed by sediment deposited during flooding.

Geyser A fountain of hot water or steam that erupts periodically as a result of underground streams coming into contact with hot rocks.

GDP Gross Domestic Product. The total value of goods and services produced by a country, excluding income from foreign countries.

GIS Geographical Information System. A computerized system for the collection, storage and retrieval of geographical data.

Glacier A huge mass of ice made up of compacted and frozen snow which moves slowly, eroding and depositing rock.

Glaciation The moulding of the land by a glacier or ice sheet.

GNP Gross National Product. The total value of goods and services produced by a country.

Groundwater Water that has seeped into the pores, cavities and cracks of rocks or into soil and water held in an aquifer or permeable rock.

Gully A deep, narrow chasm eroded in the landscape by a fast-flowing stream.

Heavy industry Industry that uses large amounts of energy and raw materials to produce heavy goods, such as machinery, ships, or locomotives.

Humidity The moisture content of the air.

Hurricane Violent tropical storms, also known as cyclones in the Indian Ocean and typhoons in the Pacific Ocean.

Hydroelectric power Energy produced by harnessing the rapid movement of water down steep mountain slopes to drive turbines to generate electricity.

Ice Age Periods of time in the past when much of the Earth's surface was covered by massive ice sheets. The most recent Ice Age began two million years ago and ended 10,000 years ago.

Iceberg A floating mass of ice that has broken off from a glacier or ice sheet.

Ice sheet A massive area of ice, thousands of metres thick.

Irrigation The artificial supply of water to dry areas – mainly for agricultural use. Water is carried or pumped to the area through pipes or ditches.

Lagoon A shallow stretch of coastal saltwater behind a partial barrier such as a sandbank or coral reef.

Latitude The distance north or south of the Equator, measured in degrees, and shown on a globe as imaginary circles running around the Earth parallel to the Equator.

Lava The molten rock, magma, which erupts onto the Earth's surface through a volcano, or through a fault or crack in the Earth's crust. Lava refers to the rock both in its liquid and its later, solidified form.

Load The material that is carried by a river or stream.

Longitude The distance, measured in degrees, east or west of the Prime Meridian.

Limestone A type of rock, formed by sediment, through which water can pass.

Magma Underground, molten rock, which is very hot and highly charged with gas. It originates in the Earth's lower crust or mantle.

Mantle The layer of the Earth's interior between the crust and the core. It is about 2,900 km thick.

Map projection A mathematical formula that is used to show the curved surface of the Earth on a flat map.

Market gardening The intensive growing of fruit and vegetables close to large local markets.

Meander A loop-like bend in a river. As a river nears the sea, it tends to wind more and more. The bigger the river and the shallower its slope, the more likely it is that meanders will form.

Mediterranean climate A temperate climate of hot, dry summers and warm, damp winters.

Meltwater Water which has melted from glaciers or ice sheets.

Mestizo A person of mixed native American and European origin.

Mineral A chemical compound that occurs naturally in the Earth.

Monsoon Winds that change direction according to the seasons. They are most common in South and East Asia, where they blow from the southwest in summer, bringing heavy rainfall, and the northeast in winter.

Moraine Sand and gravel that have been deposited by a glacier or ice sheet.

Nomads (nomadic) Wandering communities who move around in search of suitable pasture for their herds of animals.

Oasis A fertile area in a desert, usually watered by an underground aquifer.

Pack ice Ice masses more than three metres thick which form on the sea surface and are not attached to a landmass.

Pacific Rim The name given to the economically dynamic countries bordering the Pacific Ocean.

Peat Decomposed vegetation found in bogs. It can be dried and used as fuel.

Per capita A latin term meaning 'for each person'.

Plantation A large farm on which only one crop is usually grown, e.g. bananas or coffee.

Plain A flat, level region of land, often relatively low-lying.

Plateau A large area of high, flat land. When surrounded by steep slopes it is called a tableland.

Peninsula A thin strip of land surrounded on three of its sides by water. Large examples include Italy, Florida and Korea.

Permafrost Permanently frozen ground, in which temperatures have remained below 0°C for more than two years.

Precipitation The fall of moisture from the atmosphere onto the surface of the Earth, as dew, hail, rain, sleet or snow.

Prairie A Spanish-American term for grassy plains, with few or no trees.

Prime Meridian 0° longitude. Also known as the Greenwich Meridian because it runs through Greenwich in England.

Rainforest Dense forests in tropical zones with high rainfall, temperature and humidity.

Rainshadow An area downwind from high terrain which has little or no rainfall because it has fallen upon the high relief.

Remote-sensing A way of obtaining information about the environment by using unmanned equipment, such as a satellite, which relays the information to a point where it is collected.

Ria A flooded V-shaped river valley or estuary flooded by a rise in sea level or sinking land.

Rift valley A long, narrow depression in the Earth's crust, formed by the sinking of rocks between two faults.

Savannah Open grassland, where an annual dry season prevents the growth of most trees. They lie between the tropical rainforest and hot desert regions.

Scale The relationship between distance on a map and on the Earth's surface

Sediment Grains of rock transported and deposited by rivers, sea, ice or wind.

Semi-arid Areas between deserts and better-watered areas, where there is sufficient moisture to support a little more vegetation than in a true desert.

Service industry An industry that supplies services, such as banking, rather than producing manufactured goods.

Shanty town An area in or around a city where people live in temporary shacks, usually without basic facilities such as running water.

Silt Small particles, finer than sand, often carried by water and deposited on riverbanks, at river mouths and harbours.

Soil A thin layer of rock particles mixed with the remains of dead plants and animals. Soil occurs naturally on the surface of the Earth and provides a medium for plants to grow.

Soil erosion The wearing away of soil more quickly than it is replaced by natural processes. Over-grazing and the clearing of land for farming speeds up the process.

Sorghum A type of grass found in South America, similar to sugar cane.

Spit A narrow bank of shingle or sand extending out from the sea shore. Spits are made out of material transported along the coast by currents, wind and waves.

Staple crop The main food crop grown in a region, for example rice in Southeast Asia.

Steppe Large areas of dry grassland in the northern hemisphere – particularly found in southeast Europe and central Asia.

Subsistence farming A method of farming where enough food is produced to feed farmers and their families but not providing any extra to generate an income.

Taiga A Russian name given to the belt of coniferous forest found in Russia, which borders tundra in the north and mixed forests and grasslands in the south.

Temperate The mild, variable climate found in areas between the tropics and cold polar regions.

Terrace Steps cut into steep slopes to create flat surfaces for cultivating crops.

Tropics An area between the Equator and the Tropic of Cancer and Tropic of Capricorn that has heavy rainfall, high temperatures, and lacks any clear seasonal variation.

Tundra The land area lying in the very cold northern regions of Europe, Asia and Canada, where winters are long and cold and the ground beneath the surface is permanently frozen.

U-shaped valley A river valley that has been deepened and widened by a glacier. They are flat-bottomed and steep-sided, and usually much deeper than river valleys.

V-shaped valley A typical valley eroded by a river in its upper course.

Volcano An opening or vent in the Earth's crust where magma erupts. Volcanos are caused by the movement of the Earth's plates. When the plates collide or spread apart, magma is forced to the surface, at or near the place where the plates meet.

Watershed The dividing line between one drainage basin and another.

INDEX

A

Aachen 59 A5 W Germany
Aalborg 49 B6 N Denmark
Aalen 59 C6 S Germany
Aalsmeer 50 D4 C Netherlands
Aalst 50 C6 C Belgium
Aalten 50 F4 E Netherlands
Aalter 50 B6 NW Belgium
Äänekoski 49 E4 C Finland
Aare 59 B8 〰 W Switzerland
Aba 128 E1 NE Dem Rep Congo
Aba 124 F5 S Nigeria
Abadan 81 D3 SW Iran
Abadla 122 C2 W Algeria
Abakan 76 E5 S Russ. Fed.
Abashiri 85 G1 NE Japan
Abbeville 55 D1 N France
Abbeydorney 31 B6 SW Ireland
Abbeyleix 31 D5 C Ireland
Abéché 124 H3 SE Chad
Abengourou 124 D5 E Ivory Coast
Aberaeron 39 C5 SW Wales, UK
Abercarn 39 E6 S Wales, UK
Abercraf 39 D6 C Wales, UK
Aberdare 39 E6 S Wales, UK
Aberdaron 39 B3 NW Wales, UK
Aberdeen 33 F4 NE Scotland, UK
Aberdeen 28 ◈ Unitary auth., NE Scotland, UK
Aberdeenshire 28 ◈ Unitary auth., NE Scotland, UK
Aberdyfi 39 C4 NW Wales, UK
Aberfeldy 33 D4 C Scotland, UK
Aberffraw 39 C2 NW Wales, UK
Abergavenny 39 F6 SE Wales, UK
Abergele 39 D1 N Wales, UK
Abergynolwyn 39 D3 NW Wales, UK
Aberkenfig 39 D7 S Wales, UK
Aberporth 39 B5 W Wales, UK
Abersoch 39 B3 NW Wales, UK
Abersychan 39 E6 SE Wales, UK
Abertillery 39 E6 SE Wales, UK
Aberystwyth 39 C4 W Wales, UK
Abha 81 B6 SW Saudi Arabia
Abidjan 124 C5 S Ivory Coast
Abilene 103 F5 Texas, USA
Abingdon 37 E3 S England, UK
Åbo see Turku
Aboisso 124 D5 SE Ivory Coast
Abou-Déïa 124 H4 SE Chad
Abrantes 57 B4 C Portugal
Abruzzese, Appennino 61 D5 ⛰ C Italy
Abu Dhabi 81 E4 ● C United Arab Emirates
Abu Hamed 127 C1 N Sudan
Abuja 124 F4 ● C Nigeria
Abunã, Rio 115 D5 〰 Bolivia/Brazil
Abuye Meda 127 D3 ▲ C Ethiopia
Acalayong 124 F6 SW Equatorial Guinea
Acaponeta 105 D4 C Mexico
Acapulco 105 F6 S Mexico
Accra 124 D5 ● SE Ghana
Accrington 35 C4 NW England, UK
Achacachi 117 A2 W Bolivia
Achill Head 31 A3 Headland, W Ireland
Achill Sound 31 B3 W Ireland
Acklins Island 109 E3 Island, SE Bahamas
Aconcagua, Cerro 117 A5 ▲ W Argentina
A Coruña 57 B1 NW Spain
Acre 115 C5 ◈ State, W Brazil
Adamawa Highlands 124 G5 Plateau, NW Cameroon
Adana 79 D5 S Turkey
Adapazarı 79 B2 NW Turkey
Adare, Cape 138 C6 Headland, Antarctica
Ad Dahna' 81 C4 Desert, E Saudi Arabia
Ad Damman 81 D4 NE Saudi Arabia
Addis Ababa 127 D3 ● C Ethiopia
Adelaide 133 E6 S Australia
Aden 81 C7 SW Yemen
Aden, Gulf of 127 F2 Gulf, NW Arabian Sea
Adige 61 C2 〰 N Italy
Adirondack Mountains 101 F2 ⛰ New York, USA
Adis Abeba see Addis Ababa
Adıyaman 79 E4 SE Turkey
Admiralty Islands 137 B1 Island group, N PNG
Adra 57 E6 S Spain
Adrar 122 D3 C Algeria
Adriatic Sea 70 F2 Sea, N Mediterranean Sea
Adycha 76 G3 〰 NE Russ. Fed.
Aegean Sea 65 F5 Sea, NE Mediterranean Sea
Aeolian Islands 61 D7 Island group, S Italy
Afareaitu 137 A5 W French Polynesia
Afghanistan 83 D5 ◆ Islamic state, C Asia
Afmadow 127 E5 S Somalia
Africa 118 Continent
Africa, Horn of 118 Physical region, Ethiopia/Somalia
Afyon 79 B3 W Turkey
Agadez 124 F3 C Niger
Agadir 122 B2 SW Morocco
Agana see Hagåtña
Agaro 127 D4 W Ethiopia
Agathonísi 65 F6 Island, Dodecanese, Greece
Agde 55 D6 S France
Agen 55 C6 SW France
Agialousa 70 D6 NE Cyprus
Ágios Nikólaos 65 F7 Crete, Greece
Agra 89 D3 N India
Ağri 79 G3 NE Turkey
Agrigento 61 C8 Sicily, Italy
Agropoli 61 D6 S Italy
Aguadulce 107 G7 S Panama
Aguán, Río 107 D2 〰 N Honduras
Agua Prieta 105 C2 NW Mexico
Aguascalientes 105 E4 C Mexico
Aguilas 57 E5 SE Spain
Aguililla 105 E5 SW Mexico
Ahaggar 122 E4 High plateau region, SE Algeria
Ahmadabad 89 C4 W India
Ahmadnagar 89 D5 W India
Ahuachapán 107 B4 W El Salvador
Ahvaz 81 D3 SW Iran
Ailigandí 107 I6 NE Panama
Ailsa Craig 33 C6 Island, SW Scotland, UK
'Aïn Ben Tili 124 C1 N Mauritania
Aiquile 117 B2 C Bolivia
Airdrie 33 D6 S Scotland, UK
Aire 35 D4 〰 N England, UK
Aïr, Massif de l' 124 F2 ⛰ NC Niger
Aix-en-Provence 55 E6 SE France
Ajaccio 55 G6 Corsica, France
Aj Bogd Uul 87 D2 ▲ SW Mongolia
Ajdabiya 122 G2 NE Libya
Ajmer 89 D3 N India
Akasha 127 C1 N Sudan
Akchâr 124 A2 Desert, W Mauritania
Akhalts'ikhe 79 G2 SW Georgia
Akhdar, Al Jabal al 122 G2 Hill range, NE Libya
Akhisar 79 A3 W Turkey
Akhmim 122 I3 C Egypt
Akhtubinsk 69 B7 SW Russ. Fed.
Akimiski Island 99 C3 Island, NW Terr., C Canada
Akita 85 F3 C Japan
Akjoujt 124 B2 W Mauritania
Akkeshi 85 H1 NE Japan
Aklavik 97 E3 NW Terr., NW Canada
Akmola see Astana
Akpatok Island 99 E1 Island, Québec, E Canada
Akron 101 E3 Ohio, USA
Akrotiri Sovereign Base Area 70 C6 Air base, S Cyprus
Aksai Chin 87 B3 Disputed region, China/India
Aksaray 79 D4 C Turkey
Akşehir 79 C4 W Turkey
Aksu He 87 B2 〰 China/Kyrgyzstan
Aktau 76 A5 W Kazakhstan
Aktobe 76 B4 NW Kazakhstan
Akure 124 E5 SW Nigeria
Akureyri 49 A1 N Iceland
Alabama 101 D5 ◈ State, S USA
Alabama River 101 D6 〰 Alabama, USA
Alaca 79 D3 N Turkey
Alacant see Alicante
Alagoas 115 H5 ◈ State, E Brazil
Alajuela 107 E6 C Costa Rica
Alakanuk 97 C3 Alaska, USA
Al 'Amarah 81 C3 E Iraq
Alamo 103 C3 Nevada, USA
Aland Islands 49 D5 Island group, Finland
Aland Sea 49 D5 Sea waterway, Finland/Sweden
Alanya 79 C5 S Turkey
Al 'Aqabah 70 K6 SW Jordan
A Laracha 57 B1 NW Spain
Alaşehir 79 A4 W Turkey
Alaska 97 D3 ◈ State, NW USA
Alaska, Gulf of 97 D5 Gulf, Canada/USA
Alaska Peninsula 97 C4 Peninsula, Alaska, USA
Alaska Range 97 D4 ⛰ Alaska, USA
Alaw, Llyn 39 B1 ◎ NW Wales, UK
Alazeya 76 H2 〰 NE Russ. Fed.
Albacete 57 E4 C Spain
Al Bahah 81 B5 SW Saudi Arabia
Alba Iulia 67 B6 W Romania
Albania 65 C3 ◆ Republic, SE Europe
Albany 133 B6 Western Australia
Albany 101 E6 Georgia, USA
Albany 101 G3 New York, USA
Albany 103 B2 Oregon, USA
Albany 99 C4 〰 Ontario, S Canada
Al Bayda' 122 H2 NE Libya
Albergaria-a-Velha 57 B3 N Portugal
Albert 55 D1 N France
Alberta 97 F6 ◈ Province, SW Canada
Albert, Lake 127 B5 ◎ Dem. Rep. Congo/Uganda
Albi 55 D6 S France
Albuquerque 103 E4 New Mexico, USA
Albury 133 G6 NSW, SE Australia
Alcácer do Sal 57 B4 W Portugal
Alcalá de Henares 57 D3 C Spain
Alcamo 61 C8 Sicily, Italy
Alcañiz 57 F3 NE Spain
Alcántara, Embalse de 57 B4 ▣ W Spain
Alcoi see Alcoy
Alcoy 57 F4 E Spain
Aldabra Group 128 G3 Island group, SW Seychelles
Aldan 76 G3 〰 NE Russ. Fed.
Alde 37 H2 〰 E England, UK
Aldeburgh 37 H2 E England, UK
Alderney 37 H5 Island, Channel Islands
Aldershot 37 F4 S England, UK
Aleg 124 B3 SW Mauritania
Aleksin 69 A5 W Russ. Fed.
Alençon 55 C3 N France
Aleppo 81 B1 NW Syria
Alert 97 H1 Ellesmere Island, Nunavut, N Canada
Alès 55 D6 S France
Alessandria 61 B2 N Italy
Ålesund 49 A4 S Norway
Aleutian Basin 15 Undersea feature, S Bering Sea
Aleutian Islands 97 A3 Island group, Alaska, USA
Aleutian Trench 15 Undersea feature, S Bering Sea
Alexander Island 138 A4 Island, Antarctica
Alexandra 135 B7 South Island, NZ
Alexandria 122 I2 N Egypt
Alexandria 103 H5 Louisiana, USA
Alexandroúpoli 65 F4 NE Greece
Alfeiós 65 D6 〰 S Greece
Alfreton 35 E5 C England, UK
Alga 76 B4 NW Kazakhstan
Algarve 57 B5 Cultural region, S Portugal
Algeciras 57 C6 SW Spain
Algemesí 57 F4 E Spain
Algeria 122 C3 ◆ Republic, N Africa
Al Ghabah 81 F5 C Oman
Alghero 61 A5 Sardinia, Italy
Algiers 122 E1 ● N Algeria
Al Hajar al Gharbi 81 E4 ⛰ N Oman
Al Hasakah 81 B1 NE Syria
Al Hillah 81 C2 C Iraq
Al Hufuf 81 D4 NE Saudi Arabia
Aliákmonas 65 E4 〰 N Greece
Alíartos 65 E5 C Greece
Ali-Bayramli 79 J2 SE Azerbaijan
Alicante 57 F5 SE Spain
Alice Springs 133 E3 Northern Territory, C Australia
Alindao 124 H5 S CAR
Al Jaghbub 122 H3 NE Libya
Al Jawf 81 B3 NW Saudi Arabia
Al Jazirah 81 B2 Physical region, Iraq/Syria
Al Khufrah 122 H4 SE Libya
Al Khums 122 F2 NW Libya
Alkmaar 50 C3 NW Netherlands
Al Kut 81 C2 E Iraq
Al Ladhiqiyah 81 A2 W Syria
Allahabad 89 E3 N India
Allegheny Plateau 101 F3 ⛰ NE USA
Allen, Lough 31 D3 ◎ NW Ireland
Allentown 101 G3 Pennsylvania, USA
Alleppey 89 D7 SW India
Alloa 33 D5 C Scotland, UK
Alma-Ata see Almaty
Almada 57 A4 W Portugal
Al Mahrah 81 D6 ⛰ E Yemen
Al Majma'ah 81 C4 C Saudi Arabia
Almansa 57 F4 C Spain
Almaty 76 C6 SE Kazakhstan
Almelo 50 F3 E Netherlands
Almendra, Embalse de 57 C3 Reservoir, NW Spain
Almendralejo 57 C4 W Spain
Almere 50 D3 C Netherlands
Almería 57 E6 S Spain
Al'met'yevsk 69 D6 W Russ. Fed.
Almirante 107 F6 NW Panama
Al Mukalla 81 D7 SE Yemen
Alnwick 35 D1 N England, UK
Alofi, Île 137 K4 Island, S Wallis and Futuna
Alónnisos 65 E5 Island, Vóreioi Sporádes, Greece
Álora 57 D6 S Spain
Alor, Kepulauan 91 F8 Island group, E Indonesia
Alotau 137 C3 SE PNG
Alpha Cordillera 139 B4 Undersea feature, Arctic Ocean
Alphen aan den Rijn 50 C4 C Netherlands
Alps 44 ⛰ C Europe
Al Qamishli 81 B1 NE Syria
Al Qunaytirah 81 H5 SW Syria
Alsace 55 F2 Cultural region, NE France
Alsager 35 D5 W England, UK
Alsdorf 59 A5 W Germany
Alta 49 D1 N Norway
Altai Mountains 87 C2 ⛰ Asia/Europe
Altamaha River 101 E5 〰 Georgia, USA
Altamira 115 F4 NE Brazil
Altamura 61 E6 SE Italy
Altar, Desierto de 105 A1 Desert, Mexico/USA
Altay 87 C2 NW China
Altay 87 D2 W Mongolia
Alton 37 F4 S England, UK
Altoona 101 F3 Pennsylvania, USA
Altun Shan 87 C3 ⛰ NW China
Al 'Uwaynat 122 F4 SW Libya
Alvarado 105 G5 E Mexico
Al Wajh 81 A4 NW Saudi Arabia
Alwar 89 D3 N India
Al Wari'ah 81 C3 N Saudi Arabia
Alwen, Llyn 39 D2 ◎ N Wales, UK
Alytus 49 E7 S Lithuania
Alzette 50 E9 〰 S Luxembourg
Amadeus, Lake 133 D4 Seasonal lake, Northern Territory, C Australia
Amadi 127 C4 SW Sudan
Amadjuak Lake 97 I3 ◎ Baffin Island, Nunavut, N Canada
Amakusa-nada 85 C8 Gulf, SW Japan
Åmål 49 C5 S Sweden
Amami-gunto 85 A7 Island group, SW Japan
Amami-o-shima 85 A7 Island, S Japan
Amantea 61 E7 SW Italy
Amapá 115 F3 ◈ State, NE Brazil
Amarapura 91 A2 C Burma
Amarillo 103 F4 Texas, USA
Amay 50 D7 E Belgium
Amazon 115 F3 〰 Brazil/Peru
Amazonas 115 C4 ◈ State, N Brazil
Amazon Basin 115 E4 Basin, N South America
Amazon, Mouths of the 115 G3 Delta, NE Brazil
Ambae 137 G4 Island, C Vanuatu
Ambam 124 F6 S Cameroon
Ambanja 128 G4 N Madagascar
Ambarchik 76 H2 NE Russ. Fed.
Ambergris Cays 40 Island group, S Turks and Caicos Islands
Ambérieu-en-Bugey 55 E5 E France
Amble 35 D2 N England, UK
Amboasary 128 G6 S Madagascar
Ambon 91 G7 E Indonesia
Ambositra 128 G5 SE Madagascar
Ambriz 128 B3 NW Angola
Ambrym 137 G5 Island, C Vanuatu
Amdo 87 C4 W China
Ameland 50 D1 Island, Waddeneilanden, N Netherlands
America-Antarctica Ridge 138 B2 Undersea feature, S Atlantic Ocean
American Samoa 131 US ◇ W Polynesia
Amersfoort 50 D4 C Netherlands
Amga 76 G4 〰 NE Russ. Fed.
Amherst 99 F5 Nova Scotia, SE Canada
Amiens 55 D1 N France
Amindivi Islands 89 C7 Island group, Laccadive Islands, India
Amlwch 39 C1 NW Wales, UK
Amman 81 A2 ● NW Jordan
Ammanford 39 D6 S Wales, UK
Ammassalik 139 A6 S Greenland
Ammochostos see Famagusta
Amol 81 D1 N Iran
Amorgós 65 F6 Island, Cyclades, Greece
Amos 99 D4 Québec, SE Canada
Amourj 124 C3 SE Mauritania
Ampato, Nevado 115 B6 ▲ S Peru
Amposta 57 F3 NE Spain
Amravati 89 D4 C India
Amritsar 89 D2 N India
Amstelveen 50 D4 C Netherlands
Amsterdam 50 C4 ● C Netherlands
Am Timan 124 H4 SE Chad
Amu Darya 83 D3 〰 C Asia
Amyderya 83 E4 NE Turkmenistan
Amund Ringnes Island 97 H2 Island, Sverdrup Islands, Nunavut, N Canada
Amundsen Gulf 97 F3 Gulf, NW Terr., N Canada
Amundsen Plain 138 B6 Undersea feature, S Pacific Ocean
Amundsen-Scott 138 C4 US research station, Antarctica
Amundsen Sea 138 A5 Sea, S Pacific Ocean
Amuntai 91 E7 C Indonesia
Amur 76 H5 〰 China/Russ. Fed.
Anabar 76 F3 〰 NE Russ. Fed.
Anadyr' 76 H2 〰 NE Russ. Fed.
Anadyr, Gulf of 76 I1 Gulf, NE Russ. Fed.
Anáfi 65 F6 Island, Cyclades, Greece
Analalava 128 G4 NW Madagascar
Anamur 79 C5 S Turkey
Anantapur 89 D6 S India
Anápolis 115 G6 C Brazil
Anar 81 E3 C Iran
Anar Darreh 83 D5 W Afghanistan
Anatolia 79 C4 Plateau, C Turkey
Añatuya 117 B4 N Argentina
Anchorage 97 D4 Alaska, USA
Ancona 61 D4 C Italy
Ancud 117 A7 S Chile
Åndalsnes 49 B4 S Norway
Andalucia see Andalusia
Andalusia 57 D5 Cultural region, S Spain
Andaman Islands 89 H4 Island group, India, NE Indian Ocean
Andaman Sea 89 H5 Sea, NE Indian Ocean
Andenne 50 D7 SE Belgium
Anderlues 50 C7 S Belgium
Anderson 101 D3 Indiana, USA
Andhra Pradesh 89 E6 Cultural region, E India
Andijon 83 G3 E Uzbekistan
Andkhvoy 83 E4 N Afghanistan
Andong 85 C6 E South Korea
Andorra 55 C7 ◆ Monarchy, SW Europe
Andorra la Vella 55 B7 ● C Andorra
Andover 37 E4 S England, UK
Andøya 49 C2 Island, C Norway
Andria 61 E6 SE Italy
Ándros 65 F5 Island, Cyclades, Greece
Andros Island 109 C2 Island, NW Bahamas
Andros Town 109 D2 NW Bahamas
Anegada 40 Island, NE British Virgin Islands
Aneityum 137 H6 Island, S Vanuatu
Anepmete 137 C2 E PNG
Angara 76 E4 〰 C Russ. Fed.
Angarsk 76 F5 S Russ. Fed.
Ånge 49 C4 C Sweden
Ángel de la Guarda, Isla 105 B2 Island, NW Mexico
Angeles 91 F3 Luzon, N Philippines
Angel Falls 115 D2 Waterfall, E Venezuela
Ångermanälven 49 D3 〰 N Sweden
Angermünde 59 E3 NE Germany
Angers 55 C3 NW France
Angle 39 A6 SW Wales, UK
Anglesey 39 C1 Island, NW Wales, UK
Anglet 55 B6 SW France
Ang Nam Ngum 91 B3 ◎ C Laos
Angola 128 B3 ◆ Republic, SW Africa
Angola Basin 15 Undersea feature, E Atlantic Ocean
Angoram 137 B1 NW PNG
Angostura, Presa de la 105 H6 ▣ SE Mexico
Angoulême 55 C5 W France
Angoumois 55 C5 Cultural region, W France
Angren 83 G3 E Uzbekistan
Anguilla 109 J4 UK ◇ E West Indies
Anguilla Cays 109 C2 Islets, SW Bahamas
Angus 28 ◈ Unitary auth., E Scotland, UK
Anjou 55 C3 Cultural region, NW France
Anjouan 128 G4 Island, SE Comoros
Anju 85 A5 W North Korea
Ankara 79 C3 ● C Turkey
Anklam 59 D2 NE Germany
Annaba 122 E1 NE Algeria
An Nafud 81 B3 Desert, NW Saudi Arabia
An Najaf 81 C3 S Iraq
Annalee 31 D3 〰 N Ireland
Annalong 31 F3 S Northern Ireland, UK
Annan 33 E7 S Scotland, UK
Annapolis 101 F4 Maryland, USA
Annapurna 89 F2 ▲ C Nepal
Ann Arbor 101 E3 Michigan, USA
An Nasiriyah 81 C3 SE Iraq
Annecy 55 E5 E France
Anqing 87 G4 E China
Anshun 87 E5 S China
Ansongo 124 D3 E Mali
Antakya 79 E5 S Turkey
Antalaha 128 H4 NE Madagascar
Antalya 79 B5 SW Turkey
Antalya, Gulf of 79 B5 Gulf, SW Turkey
Antananarivo 128 G5 ● C Madagascar
Antarctica 138 C4 Continent
Antarctic Peninsula 138 A4 Peninsula, Antarctica
Antequera 57 D5 S Spain
Antibes 55 F6 SE France
Anticosti, Île d' 99 F4 Island, Québec, E Canada
Antigua 109 J5 Island, S Antigua and Barbuda, Leeward Islands
Antigua and Barbuda 109 J4 ◆ Commonwealth Republic, E West Indies
Antikythira 65 E7 Island, S Greece
Antofagasta 117 A3 N Chile
Antony 55 D2 N France
Antrim 31 E2 NE Northern Ireland, UK
Antrim 29 ◈ District, NE Northern Ireland, UK
Antrim Mountains 31 E1 ⛰ NE Northern Ireland, UK
Antsirañana 128 G4 N Madagascar
Antsohihy 128 G4 NW Madagascar
Antwerp 50 C6 N Belgium
Antwerpen see Antwerp
Anuradhapura 89 E7 C Sri Lanka
Anyang 87 F3 C China
A'nyêmaqên Shan 87 D4 ⛰ C China
Anzio 61 C5 C Italy
Aola 137 F3 C Solomon Islands
Aomori 85 G3 C Japan
Aoraki 135 B6 South Island, NZ
Aosta 61 A2 NW Italy
Aoukâr 124 B2 Plateau, C Mauritania
Aouk, Bahr 124 H4 〰 CAR/Chad
Aozou 124 G2 N Chad
Apalachee Bay 101 D6 Bay, SE USA
Apaporis, Río 115 C3 〰 Brazil/Colombia
Apatity 69 B2 NW Russ. Fed.
Apeldoorn 50 E4 E Netherlands
Apennines 61 C3 ⛰ Italy
Apia 137 B5 ● SE Samoa
Apolima Strait 137 A5 Strait, C Pacific Ocean
Apostle Islands 101 C1 Island group, Wisconsin, USA
Appalachian Mountains 101 E4 ⛰ E USA
Appingedam 50 F2 NE Netherlands
Appleton 101 D2 Wisconsin, USA
Apulia 61 F6 Cultural region, SE Italy
Apuseni, Munții 67 A6 ⛰ W Romania
Aqaba, Gulf of 81 A3 Gulf, NE Red Sea
Aqchah 83 F4 N Afghanistan
Aquitaine 55 B6 Cultural region, SW France
'Arabah, Wadi al 81 H7 Dry watercourse, Israel/Jordan
Arabian Basin 15 Undersea feature, N Arabian Sea
Arabian Peninsula 81 C4 Peninsula, SW Asia
Arabian Sea 72 Sea, NW Indian Ocean
Aracaju 115 I5 E Brazil
'Arad 81 H6 S Israel
Arad 67 A6 W Romania
Arafura Sea 91 H8 Sea, W Pacific Ocean
Aragón 57 E3 Autonomous community, E Spain
Araguaia, Río 115 F5 〰 C Brazil
Araguari 115 G7 SE Brazil
Arak 81 D2 W Iran
Arakan Yoma 91 A2 ⛰ W Burma
Aral Sea 83 D1 Inland sea, Kazakhstan/Uzbekistan
Aral'sk 76 B5 SW Kazakhstan
Aranda de Duero 57 D2 N Spain
Aran Fawddwy 39 D3 ▲ NW Wales, UK
Aran Island 31 C2 Island, NW Ireland
Aran Islands 31 B4 Island group, W Ireland
Aranjuez 57 D3 C Spain
Araouane 124 D2 N Mali
'Ar'ar 81 B3 NW Saudi Arabia
Ararat, Mount 79 G3 ▲ E Turkey
Aras 79 I3 〰 SW Asia
Arawa 137 D2 Bougainville Island, NE PNG
Arbil 81 C2 N Iraq
Arbroath 33 E5 E Scotland, UK
Arcachon 55 B5 SW France
Archangel 69 C3 NW Russ. Fed.
Archidona 57 D5 S Spain
Arch Islands 40 Island group, SW Falkland Islands
Arco 61 C2 N Italy
Arctic Ocean 139 C3 Ocean
Arda 65 F3 〰 Bulgaria/Greece
Ardabil 81 D1 NW Iran
Ardara 31 C2 N Ireland
Ardas 65 F3 〰 Bulgaria/Greece
Ardèche 55 D6 Cultural region, E France
Ardee 31 E3 NE Ireland
Ardennes 50 D8 Physical region, Belgium/France
Ardglass 31 F3 E Northern Ireland, UK
Ardgroom 31 B7 S Ireland
Ardmore 31 D6 S Ireland
Ardnamurchan, Point of 33 B4 Headland, N Scotland, UK
Ardrahan 31 C4 W Ireland
Ards 29 ◈ District, E Northern Ireland, UK
Ards Peninsula 31 F2 Peninsula, E Northern Ireland, UK
Arenal, Volcán 107 E6 🌋 NW Costa Rica
Arendal 49 B6 S Norway
Arenig Fawr 39 D2 ▲ NW Wales, UK
Arenys de Mar 57 G2 NE Spain
Areópoli 65 E6 S Greece
Arequipa 115 C6 SE Peru
Arezzo 61 C4 C Italy
Argenteuil 55 D2 N France
Argentina 117 A6 ◆ Republic, S South America
Argentine Basin 14 Undersea basin, SW Atlantic Ocean
Arghandab, Darya-ye 83 E5 〰 SE Afghanistan
Argo 127 C1 N Sudan
Argun 87 F1 〰 China/Russ. Fed.
Argyle, Lake 133 D2 Salt lake, Western Australia
Argyll and Bute 28 ◈ Unitary auth., W Scotland, UK
Århus 49 B7 C Denmark
Arica 117 A2 N Chile
Arizona 103 C4 ◈ State, SW USA
Arkansas 101 C4 ◈ State, S USA
Arkansas River 101 C5 〰 C USA
Arkhangel'sk see Archangel
Arklow 31 E5 SE Ireland
Arles 55 E6 SE France
Arlington 103 G4 Texas, USA
Arlington 101 F4 Virginia, USA
Arlon 50 E9 SE Belgium
Armagh 31 E3 S Northern Ireland, UK
Armagh 29 ◈ District, S Northern Ireland, UK
Armagnac 55 C6 Cultural region, S France
Armenia 115 B2 W Colombia
Armenia 79 H2 ◆ Republic, SW Asia
Armidale 133 H5 NSW, SE Australia
Armstrong 99 B4 Ontario, S Canada
Armyans'k 67 F6 S Ukraine
Arnedo 57 E2 N Spain
Arnhem 50 E4 SE Netherlands
Arnhem Land 133 E1 Physical region, Northern Territory, N Australia
Arno 61 C3 〰 C Italy
Arnold 35 E5 C England, UK
Arorae 137 J1 Atoll, Tungaru, W Kiribati
Arran, Isle of 33 C6 Island, SW Scotland, UK
Ar Raqqah 81 B2 N Syria
Arras 55 D1 N France
Arriaga 105 G5 SE Mexico
Ar Riyad see Riyadh
Arrow, Lough 31 C3 ◎ N Ireland
Ar Rub 'al Khali 81 D6 Desert, SW Asia
Ar Rustaq 81 F4 N Oman
Árta 65 D5 W Greece
Artashat 79 H3 S Armenia
Artemisa 109 B2 W Cuba
Arthurs's Pass 135 C6 Pass, South Island, NZ
Artigas 117 C5 N Uruguay
Art'ik 79 H2 W Armenia

◈ Administrative region ◆ Country ● Country capital ◇ Dependent territory ○ Dependent territory capital ⛰ Mountain range ▲ Mountain 🌋 Volcano 〰 River ◎ Lake ▣ Reservoir

Artois 55 D1 Cultural region, N France
Artsyz 67 D6 SW Ukraine
Artvin 79 G2 NE Turkey
Arua 127 C5 NW Uganda
Aruba 109 G7 Dutch ◇ S West Indies
Aru, Kepulauan 91 H7 Island group, E Indonesia
Arunachal Pradesh 89 F2 Cultural region, NE India
Arusha 127 D6 N Tanzania
Arviat 97 H5 Nunavut, C Canada
Arvidsjaur 49 D3 N Sweden
Arys' 76 C6 S Kazakhstan
Asadabad 83 G5 E Afghanistan
Asahi-dake 85 G1 ▲ N Japan
Asahikawa 85 F1 N Japan
Asamankese 124 D5 SE Ghana
Asansol 89 F4 NE India
Ascension Island 40 St.Helena ◇ C Atlantic Ocean
Ascoli Piceno 61 D4 C Italy
Aseb 127 E3 SE Eritrea
A Serra de Outes 57 B1 NW Spain
Aşgabat 83 C3 ● C Turkmenistan
Ashbourne 31 E4 E Ireland
Ashburton 135 C6 South Island, NZ
Ashburton River 133 B4 ~ Western Australia
Ashby de la Zouch 35 E6 C England, UK
Ashdod 81 G6 W Israel
Asheville 101 E4 North Carolina, USA
Ashford 37 G4 SE England, UK
Ashington 35 D2 N England, UK
Ash Sharah 81 H7 ⛰ W Jordan
Ash Shihr 81 D7 SE Yemen
Asia 72 Continent
Asinara 61 A5 Island, W Italy
Asipovichy 67 D2 C Belarus
Aşkale 79 F3 NE Turkey
Askersund 49 C6 C Sweden
Asmar 83 G5 E Afghanistan
Asmara 127 D2 ● C Eritrea
Assad, Lake 79 E5 ▣ N Syria
Assam 89 G3 Cultural region, NE India
Assamakka 124 E2 NW Niger
As Samawah 81 C3 S Iraq
Assen 50 F2 NE Netherlands
Assenede 50 B6 NW Belgium
As Sulaymaniyah 81 C2 NE Iraq
As Sulayyil 81 C5 S Saudi Arabia
Astana 76 C5 ● NE Kazakhstan
Asti 61 B2 NW Italy
Astorga 57 C2 N Spain
Astoria 103 B1 Oregon, USA
Astrakhan' 69 B8 SW Russ. Fed.
Asturias 57 C1 Cultural region, NW Spain
Astypálaia 65 F6 Island, Cyclades, Greece
Asunción 117 C4 ● S Paraguay
Aswan 122 J4 SE Egypt
Asyut 122 I3 C Egypt
Atacama Desert 117 A3 Desert, N Chile
Atamyrat 83 E4 E Turkmenistan
Atâr 124 B2 W Mauritania
Atas Bogd 87 D2 ▲ SW Mongolia
Atatürk Baraji 79 F4 ▣ S Turkey
Atbara 127 C2 NE Sudan
Atbara 127 D2 ~ Eritrea/Sudan
Atbasar 76 C5 N Kazakhstan
Ath 50 C7 SW Belgium
Athabasca 97 G6 Alberta, SW Canada
Athabasca 97 F6 ~ Alberta, SW Canada
Athabasca, Lake 97 G5 ◎ Alberta/Saskatchewan, SW Canada
Athboy 31 E4 E Ireland
Athens 65 E5 ● C Greece
Atherton 133 G2 Queensland, NE Australia
Athina see Athens
Athlone 31 D4 C Ireland
Ati 124 H3 C Chad
Atikokan 99 A4 Ontario, S Canada
Atka 76 H3 E Russ. Fed.
Atka 97 A3 Atka Island, Alaska, USA
Atlanta 101 E5 Georgia, USA
Atlantic Ocean 14 Ocean
Atlas Mountains 122 C2 ⛰ NW Africa
Atlasovo 76 I3 E Russ. Fed.
Atlin 97 E5 British Columbia, W Canada
At Ta'if 81 B5 W Saudi Arabia
Attawapiskat 99 C3 Ontario, C Canada
Attawapiskat 99 C3 ~ Ontario, S Canada
Attu Island 97 A2 Island, Aleutian Islands, Alaska, USA
Atyrau 76 B4 W Kazakhstan
Aubagne 55 E7 SE France
Aubange 50 E9 SE Belgium
Auch 55 C6 S France
Auckland 135 D2 North Island, NZ
Audincourt 55 F3 E France
Augathella 133 G4 Queensland, E Australia
Augsburg 59 C7 S Germany
Augusta 133 B6 Western Australia
Augusta 101 H2 Maine, USA
Augustów 63 G2 NE Poland
Auki 137 F3 Malaita, N Solomon Islands
Auob 128 C6 ~ Namibia/South Africa
Aurangabad 89 D5 C India
Auray 55 B3 NW France
Aurès, Massif de l' 70 D4 ⛰ NE Algeria
Aurillac 55 D5 C France
Aurora 103 E3 Colorado, USA
Aurora 101 D3 Illinois, USA
Aus 128 B6 SW Namibia
Austin 103 F5 Texas, USA
Australes, Îles 131 Island group, SW French Polynesia
Australia 133 D3 ◆ Commonwealth Republic
Australian Alps 133 G6 ⛰ SE Australia
Australian Capital Territory 133 G6 Territory, SE Australia
Austria 59 E8 ◆ Republic, C Europe
Auvergne 55 D5 Cultural region, C France
Auxerre 55 D3 C France
Avarua 131 ○ Rarotonga, S Cook Islands
Aveiro 57 B3 W Portugal
Avellino 61 D6 S Italy
Avesta 49 C5 C Sweden
Aveyron 55 C6 ~ S France
Avezzano 61 D5 C Italy
Aviemore 33 D4 N Scotland, UK
Avignon 55 E6 SE France
Ávila 57 D3 C Spain
Avilés 57 C1 NW Spain
Avon 37 E4 ~ C England, UK
Avon 37 D4 ~ SW England, UK
Avonmouth 37 D4 SW England, UK
Avranches 55 B2 N France
Awaji-shima 85 E6 Island, SW Japan
Awash 127 E3 C Ethiopia
Awbari 122 F3 SW Libya
Awe, Loch 33 C5 ◎ W Scotland, UK
Axe 37 D5 ~ SW England, UK
Axel 50 B6 SW Netherlands
Axel Heiberg Island 97 G1 Island, Nunavut, N Canada
Ayacucho 115 C6 S Peru
Ayagoz 76 D6 E Kazakhstan
Ayamonte 57 B5 S Spain
Aydarko'l Ko'li 83 F3 ◎ C Uzbekistan
Aydın 79 A4 SW Turkey
Ayers Rock see Uluru
Aylesbury 37 F3 SE England, UK
Ayorou 124 D3 W Niger
'Ayoûn el 'Atroûs 124 B3 SE Mauritania
Ayr 33 D6 W Scotland, UK
Ayr 33 D6 ~ W Scotland, UK
Ayre, Point of 35 A3 Headland, N Isle of Man
Ayr, Point of 39 E1 Headland, N Wales, UK
Aytos 65 F3 E Bulgaria
Ayvalık 79 A3 W Turkey
Azahar, Costa del 57 F4 Coastal region, E Spain
Azaouâd 124 D2 Desert, C Mali
Azerbaijan 79 I2 ◆ Republic, SW Asia
Azoum, Bahr 124 H4 Seasonal river, SE Chad
Azov 76 A4 SW Russ. Fed.
Azov, Sea of 67 F6 Sea, NE Black Sea
Azuaga 57 C5 W Spain
Azuero, Península de 107 G7 Peninsula, S Panama
Azul 117 C6 E Argentina
Az Zarqa' 81 A2 NW Jordan
Az Zawiyah 122 F2 NW Libya

B

Baardheere 127 E5 SW Somalia
Baarle-Hertog 50 D5 N Belgium
Baarn 50 D4 C Netherlands
Babayevo 69 B4 NW Russ. Fed.
Babeldaob 91 H5 Island, N Palau
Bab el Mandeb 81 B7 Strait, Gulf of Aden/Red Sea
Babruysk 67 D3 E Belarus
Babuyan Channel 91 F3 Channel, N Philippines
Babuyan Island 91 F3 Island, N Philippines
Bacabal 115 G4 E Brazil
Bacău 67 C6 NE Romania
Bacheykava 67 D2 N Belarus
Back 97 G4 ~ Nunavut, N Canada
Bacton 37 H1 E England, UK
Badajoz 57 B4 W Spain
Baden-Baden 59 B6 SW Germany
Bad Freienwalde 59 E3 NE Germany
Badgastein 59 D8 NW Austria
Bad Hersfeld 59 C5 C Germany
Bad Homburg vor der Höhe 59 B5 W Germany
Bad Ischl 59 E7 N Austria
Bad Krozingen 59 B7 SW Germany
Badlands 103 E2 Physical region, North Dakota, USA
Badu Island 133 F1 Island, Queensland, NE Australia
Bad Vöslau 59 F7 NE Austria
Bafatá 124 A4 C Guinea-Bissau
Baffin Bay 97 I2 Bay, Canada/Greenland
Baffin Island 97 I3 Island, Nunavut, NE Canada
Bafing 124 B4 ~ W Africa
Bafoussam 124 F5 W Cameroon
Bafra 79 D2 N Turkey
Bagaces 107 E5 NW Costa Rica
Bagé 115 F9 S Brazil
Baghdad 81 C2 ● C Iraq
Baghlan 83 F4 NE Afghanistan
Baghran 83 E5 S Afghanistan
Bagoé 124 C4 ~ Ivory Coast/Mali
Baguio 91 F3 Luzon, N Philippines
Bagzane, Monts 124 F3 ▲ N Niger
Bahamas 109 D2 ◆ Commonwealth Republic, N West Indies
Bahawalpur 89 C2 E Pakistan
Bäherden 83 C3 C Turkmenistan
Bahia 115 G5 ◐ State, E Brazil
Bahía Blanca 117 B6 E Argentina
Bahir Dar 127 D3 NW Ethiopia
Bahraich 89 E3 N India
Bahrain 81 D4 ◆ Monarchy, SW Asia
Bahushewsk 67 D2 NE Belarus
Baia Mare 67 B5 NW Romania
Baïbokoum 124 G5 SW Chad
Baie-Comeau 99 F4 Québec, SE Canada
Baikal, Lake 76 F5 ◎ S Russ. Fed.
Bailén 57 D5 S Spain
Ba Illi 124 G4 SW Chad
Bairiki 131 ● Tarawa, NW Kiribati
Bairnsdale 133 G6 Victoria, SE Australia
Baishan 87 H2 NE China
Baiyin 87 E3 N China
Baja 63 E8 S Hungary
Baja, Punta 137 C6 Headland, Easter Island, Chile
Bajram Curri 65 D3 N Albania
Bakala 124 H5 C CAR
Baker & Howland Islands 131 US ◇ C Pacific Ocean
Baker Lake 97 H4 Nunavut, N Canada
Bakersfield 103 B4 California, USA
Bakhtaran 81 C2 W Iran
Baki see Baku
Bakony 63 D8 ⛰ W Hungary
Baku 79 J2 ● E Azerbaijan
Bala 39 D3 NW Wales, UK
Balabac Strait 91 E5 Strait, Malaysia/Philippines
Balaguer 57 G2 NE Spain
Balaitous 55 B7 ▲ France/Spain
Balakovo 69 C7 W Russ. Fed.
Bala Lake 39 D3 ◎ NW Wales, UK
Bala Morghab 83 E4 NW Afghanistan
Balashov 69 B6 W Russ. Fed.
Balaton, Lake 63 D8 ◎ Hungary
Balbina, Represa 115 E3 ▣ NW Brazil
Balboa 107 H6 C Panama
Balbriggan 31 E4 E Ireland
Balcarce 117 C6 E Argentina
Balclutha 135 B8 South Island, NZ
Baleares, Islas see Balearic Islands
Balearic Islands 57 G4 Island group, Spain
Baleine, Rivière à la 99 E2 ~ Québec, E Canada
Balen 50 D6 N Belgium
Baleshwar 89 F4 E India
Bali 91 E8 Island, C Indonesia
Balıkesir 79 A3 W Turkey
Balikpapan 91 E7 C Indonesia
Balkanabat 83 B3 W Turkmenistan
Balkan Mountains 65 E3 ⛰ Bulgaria/Serbia and Montenegro (Yugoslavia)
Balkh 83 F4 N Afghanistan
Balkhash 76 C6 SE Kazakhstan
Balkhash, Lake 76 C6 ◎ SE Kazakhstan
Balladonia 133 C5 Western Australia
Ballaghmore 31 D5 C Ireland
Ballantrae 33 C7 W Scotland, UK
Ballarat 133 F6 Victoria, SE Australia
Ballater 33 E4 NE Scotland, UK
Ballina 31 C3 W Ireland
Ballinasloe 31 C4 W Ireland
Ballindine 31 C4 NW Ireland
Ballinhassig 31 C7 S Ireland
Ballinskelligs 31 A6 SW Ireland
Ballinskelligs Bay 31 A7 Inlet, SW Ireland
Ballinspittle 31 C7 S Ireland
Ballintra 31 D2 NW Ireland
Ballybofey 31 D2 NW Ireland
Ballybunnion 31 B5 SW Ireland
Ballycastle 31 E1 N Northern Ireland, UK
Ballyclare 31 F2 E Northern Ireland, UK
Ballyconneely 31 B4 W Ireland
Ballycotton 31 C7 S Ireland
Ballycroy 31 B3 NW Ireland
Ballydehob 31 B7 S Ireland
Ballydonegan 31 A7 S Ireland
Ballyduff 31 B5 SW Ireland
Ballyferriter 31 A6 SW Ireland
Ballyhaunis 31 C3 W Ireland
Ballyhoura Mountains 31 C6 ⛰ S Ireland
Ballymena 31 E2 NE Northern Ireland, UK
Ballymena 29 ◐ District, NE Northern Ireland, UK
Ballymoe 31 C4 W Ireland
Ballymoney 31 E1 NE Northern Ireland, UK
Ballymoney 29 ◐ District, N Northern Ireland, UK
Ballynafid 31 D4 C Ireland
Ballyshannon 31 C2 NW Ireland
Ballywalter 31 F2 E Northern Ireland, UK
Balrath 31 E4 E Ireland
Balsas 115 G4 E Brazil
Balsas, Río 105 E5 ~ S Mexico
Baltasound 33 B5 NE Scotland, UK
Bălţi 67 D5 N Moldova
Baltic Sea 49 D7 Sea, N Europe
Baltimore 31 B7 S Ireland
Baltimore 101 F4 Maryland, USA
Baltinglass 31 E5 E Ireland
Baluchistan 89 B3 Cultural region, SW Pakistan
Balykchy 83 H2 NE Kyrgyzstan
Bam 81 F3 SE Iran
Bamako 124 C4 ● SW Mali
Bambari 124 H5 C CAR
Bambarra 40 N Turks and Caicos Islands
Bamberg 59 C5 SE Germany
Bamburgh 35 D1 N England, UK
Bamenda 124 F5 W Cameroon
Banaba 137 H1 Island, W Kiribati
Bananga 89 H6 Nicobar Islands, India
Banbridge 31 E3 SE Northern Ireland, UK
Banbridge 29 ◐ District, SE Northern Ireland, UK
Banbury 37 E3 S England, UK
Banchory 33 F4 NE Scotland, UK
Bandaaceh 91 A5 Sumatra, W Indonesia
Bandama 124 C5 ~ S Ivory Coast
Bandarbeyla 127 G3 NE Somalia
Bandar-e 'Abbas 81 E4 S Iran
Bandarlampung 91 B7 Sumatra, W Indonesia
Bandar Seri Begawan 91 D5 ● N Brunei
Banda Sea 91 G7 Sea, E Indonesia
Bandırma 79 A2 NW Turkey
Bandon 31 B7 ~ S Ireland
Bandundu 128 B2 W Dem. Rep. Congo
Bandung 91 C8 Java, C Indonesia
Banff 33 E3 NE Scotland, UK
Bangalore 89 D6 S India
Bangassou 124 I5 SE CAR
Banggai, Kepulauan 91 F6 Island group, C Indonesia
Banghazi see Benghazi
Bangka, Pulau 91 C7 Island, W Indonesia
Bangkok 91 B4 ● C Thailand
Bangladesh 89 G3 ◆ Republic, S Asia
Bangor 31 F2 E Northern Ireland, UK
Bangor 39 C2 NW Wales, UK
Bangor 101 H2 Maine, USA
Bangui 124 H5 ● SW CAR
Bangweulu, Lake 128 D3 ◎ N Zambia
Bani 124 C4 ~ S Mali
Banja Luka 65 C2 NW Bosnia and Herzegovina
Banjarmasin 91 E7 C Indonesia
Banjul 124 A3 ● W Gambia
Banks Island 97 F3 Island, NW Terr., NW Canada
Banks Islands 137 G4 Island group, N Vanuatu
Banks Peninsula 135 C6 Peninsula, South Island, NZ
Banks Strait 133 G7 Strait, SW Tasman Sea
Bankura 89 F4 NE India
Banmauk 91 A2 N Burma
Bann 31 E2 ~ N Northern Ireland, UK
Ban Nadou 91 C3 S Laos
Bansha 31 C6 S Ireland
Banská Bystrica 63 E6 C Slovakia
Banteer 31 C6 S Ireland
Bantry 31 B7 SW Ireland
Bantry Bay 31 B7 Bay, SW Ireland
Banyak, Kepulauan 91 A6 Island group, NW Indonesia
Banyo 124 F5 NW Cameroon
Banyoles 57 H2 NE Spain
Baoji 87 E4 C China
Baoro 124 G5 W CAR
Baoshan 87 D5 SW China
Baotou 87 F3 N China
Ba'qubah 81 C2 C Iraq
Baraawe 127 E5 S Somalia
Baranavichy 67 C3 SW Belarus
Barbados 109 K6 ◆ Commonwealth Republic, SE West Indies
Barbastro 57 F2 NE Spain
Barbate de Franco 57 C6 S Spain
Barbuda 109 J4 Island, N Antigua and Barbuda
Barcaldine 133 G3 Queensland, E Australia
Barcelona 57 G2 E Spain
Barcelona 115 D1 NE Venezuela
Barcs 63 D9 SW Hungary
Bardaï 124 G2 N Chad
Bardejov 63 F6 NE Slovakia
Bardsey Island 39 B3 Island, NW Wales, UK
Bardsey Sound 39 B3 Sound, NW Wales, UK
Bareilly 89 E3 N India
Barendrecht 50 C4 SW Netherlands
Barentin 55 C2 N France
Barents Sea 69 C2 Sea, Arctic Ocean
Bargoed 39 E6 S Wales, UK
Bari 61 E6 SE Italy
Barikowt 83 G4 NE Afghanistan
Barillas 107 A2 NW Guatemala
Barinas 115 C2 W Venezuela
Barisal 89 G4 S Bangladesh
Barisan, Pegunungan 91 B7 ⛰ Sumatra, W Indonesia
Barito, Sungai 91 E7 ~ Borneo, C Indonesia
Barking and Dagenham 29 ◐ London borough, SE England, UK
Barkly Tableland 133 E2 Plateau, Northern Territory/Queensland, N Australia
Bârlad 67 C6 E Romania
Bar-le-Duc 55 E2 NE France
Barlee, Lake 133 B5 ◎ Western Australia
Barlee Range 133 B4 ⛰ Western Australia
Barletta 61 E5 SE Italy
Barlinek 63 C3 W Poland
Barmouth 39 C3 NW Wales, UK
Barmouth Bay 39 C3 Bay, NW Wales, UK
Barnard Castle 35 D3 N England, UK
Barnaul 76 D5 C Russ. Fed.
Barnet 29 ◐ London borough, SE England, UK
Barnsley 35 D5 N England, UK
Barnsley 29 ◐ Unitary auth., N England, UK
Barnstaple 37 B4 SW England, UK
Barnstaple Bay 37 B4 Bay, SW England, UK
Baroghil Pass 83 G4 Pass, Afghanistan/Pakistan
Barquisimeto 115 C1 NW Venezuela
Barra 33 A4 Island, NW Scotland, UK
Barra de Río Grande 107 E4 E Nicaragua
Barranca 115 B5 W Peru
Barrancabermeja 115 B2 N Colombia
Barranquilla 115 B1 N Colombia
Barreiro 57 A4 W Portugal
Barrier Range 133 F5 Hill range, NSW, SE Australia
Barrier Reef 107 C1 Reef, E Belize
Barrow 97 E2 Alaska, USA
Barrow 31 D6 ~ SE Ireland
Barrow-in-Furness 35 C4 NW England, UK
Barrow Island 133 A3 Island, Western Australia
Barry 39 E7 S Wales, UK
Bartang 83 G4 ~ SE Tajikistan
Bartın 79 C2 N Turkey
Barton-upon-Humber 35 F4 N England, UK
Bartoszyce 63 E2 N Poland
Baruun-Urt 87 F2 E Mongolia
Barú, Volcán 107 F6 ✲ W Panama
Barva, Volcán 107 E6 ✲ NW Costa Rica
Barwon River 133 G5 ~ NSW, SE Australia
Barysaw 67 D2 NE Belarus
Basarabeasca 67 D6 SE Moldova
Basel 59 B7 NW Switzerland
Basilan 91 F5 Island, SW Philippines
Basildon 37 G3 E England, UK
Basingstoke 37 E4 S England, UK
Basque Country, The 57 E1 Cultural region, N Spain
Basra 81 D3 SE Iraq
Bassano del Grappa 61 C2 NE Italy
Bassein 91 A3 SW Burma
Bassenthwaite Lake 35 C3 ◎ NW England, UK
Basse-Terre 109 J5 ○ Basse Terre, SW Guadeloupe
Basseterre 109 J4 ● Saint Kitts, Saint Kitts and Nevis
Bassikounou 124 C3 SE Mauritania
Bass Strait 133 F7 Strait, SE Australia
Bassum 59 B3 NW Germany
Bastia 55 G5 Corsica, France
Bastogne 50 E8 SE Belgium
Bata 124 F6 NW Equatorial Guinea
Batangas 91 F4 Luzon, N Philippines
Batdambang 91 C4 NW Cambodia
Batéké, Plateaux 128 B2 Plateau, S. Congo
Bath 37 D4 SW England, UK
Bath and North East Somerset 29 ◐ Unitary auth., W England, UK
Bathinda 89 D2 NW India
Bathurst 133 G6 NSW, SE Australia
Bathurst 99 F4 New Brunswick, SE Canada
Bathurst Island 133 C1 Island, Northern Territory, N Australia
Bathurst Island 97 G2 Island, Parry Islands, Nunavut, N Canada
Batin, Wadi al 81 C3 Dry watercourse, SW Asia
Batman 79 G4 SE Turkey
Batna 122 E1 NE Algeria
Baton Rouge 101 H5 Louisiana, USA
Batticaloa 89 E8 E Sri Lanka
Battipaglia 61 D6 S Italy
Bat'umi 79 G2 W Georgia
Batu Pahat 91 C6 Peninsular Malaysia
Bauchi 124 F4 NE Nigeria
Bautzen 59 E4 E Germany
Bavaria 59 C7 Cultural region, SE Germany
Bavarian Alps 59 C7 ⛰ Austria/Germany
Bavispe, Río 105 C2 ~ NW Mexico
Bawiti 122 I3 N Egypt
Bawku 124 D4 N Ghana
Bayamo 109 D3 E Cuba
Bayan Har Shan 87 D4 ⛰ C China
Bayanhongor 87 D2 C Mongolia
Bayano, Lago 107 H6 ◎ E Panama
Baydhabo 127 E5 SW Somalia
Bayern see Bavaria
Bayeux 55 C2 N France
Bay Islands 107 D2 Island group, N Honduras
Baymak 69 D7 W Russ. Fed.
Bayonne 55 B6 SW France
Baýramaly 83 D4 S Turkmenistan
Bayreuth 59 C5 SE Germany
Baza 57 E5 S Spain
Beachy Head 37 G5 Headland, SE England, UK
Beacon Hill 39 E4 Hill, E Wales, UK
Beagle Channel 117 B9 Channel, Argentina/Chile
Bear Lake 103 D2 ◎ NW USA
Beas de Segura 57 E5 S Spain
Beata, Isla 109 F5 Island, SW Dominican Republic
Beaufort Sea 97 F2 Sea, Arctic Ocean
Beaufort West 128 C7 SW South Africa
Beauly 33 D3 N Scotland, UK
Beaumaris 39 C1 NW Wales, UK
Beaumont 103 G5 Texas, USA
Beaune 55 E4 C France
Beauvais 55 D2 N France
Beaver River 103 F4 ~
Beaver Settlement 40 Beaver Island, W Falkland Islands
Beawar 89 D3 N India
Beccles 37 H2 E England, UK
Béchar 122 D2 W Algeria
Beddgelert 39 C2 NW Wales, UK
Bedford 37 F2 E England, UK
Bedford Level 37 F2 Physical region, E England, UK
Bedfordshire 29 ◐ County, E England, UK
Bedum 50 F2 NE Netherlands
Bedworth 35 E6 C England, UK
Beef Island 40 Island E British Virgin Islands
Be'er Menuha 81 H7 S Israel
Beernem 50 B6 NW Belgium
Be'ér Sheva' 81 G6 S Israel
Beesel 50 E6 SE Netherlands
Beeston 35 E6 C England, UK
Bega 133 G6 NSW, SE Australia
Beihai 87 F6 S China
Beijing 87 F3 ● E China
Beilen 50 E3 NE Netherlands
Beinn Dearg 33 D3 ▲ N Scotland, UK
Beira 128 E5 C Mozambique
Beirut 81 A2 ● W Lebanon
Beja 57 B5 SE Portugal
Béjar 57 C3 N Spain
Békéscsaba 63 F8 SE Hungary
Bekobod 83 F3 E Uzbekistan
Belarus 67 C2 ◆ Republic, E Europe
Bełchatów 63 E4 C Poland
Belcher Islands 99 C2 Island group, Nunavut, SE Canada
Beledweyne 127 F4 C Somalia
Belém 115 G3 N Brazil
Belén 107 D5 SW Nicaragua
Belep, Îles 137 F6 Island group, W New Caledonia
Belfast 31 F2 Political division capital, E Northern Ireland, UK
Belfast 29 District, E Northern Ireland, UK
Belfort 55 F3 E France
Belgaum 89 D6 W India
Belgium 50 B7 ◆ Monarchy, NW Europe
Belgorod 69 A6 W Russ. Fed.
Belgrade 65 D2 ● N Serbia and Montenegro (Yugoslavia)
Belgrano II 138 B4 Argentinian research station, Antarctica
Belitung, Pulau 91 C7 Island, W Indonesia
Belize 107 B2 ◆ Commonwealth Republic, Central America
Belize 107 B1 ~ Belize/Guatemala
Belize City 107 C1 NE Belize
Belkofski 97 B4 Alaska, USA
Bellananagh 31 D3 N Ireland
Bellavary 31 B3 NW Ireland
Belle Île 55 A3 Island, NW France
Belle Isle, Strait of 99 G3 Strait, Newfoundland, E Canada
Bellingham 103 B1 Washington, USA
Bellingshausen Sea 138 A4 Sea, Antarctica
Bellinzona 59 B8 S Switzerland
Bello 115 B2 W Colombia
Bellona 137 E3 Island, S Solomon Islands
Bellville 128 C7 SW South Africa
Belmopan 107 B2 ● C Belize
Belmullet 31 B3 W Ireland
Belo Horizonte 115 G7 SE Brazil
Belomorsk 69 B3 NW Russ. Fed.
Beloretsk 69 D6 W Russ. Fed.
Belorussia see Belarus
Belozersk 69 B4 NW Russ. Fed.
Belper 35 E5 C England, UK
Belturbet 31 D3 N Ireland
Belukha, Gora 76 D5 ▲ Kazakhstan/Russ. Fed.
Belyy, Ostrov 76 D2 Island, N Russ. Fed.
Bemaraha 128 G5 ⛰ W Madagascar
Bemmel 50 E4 SE Netherlands
Benavente 57 C2 N Spain
Benbecula 33 A3 Island, NW Scotland, UK
Bend 103 B2 Oregon, USA
Bendigo 133 F6 Victoria, SE Australia
Benešov 63 B5 W Czech Republic
Benevento 61 D6 S Italy
Bengbu 87 G4 E China
Benghazi 122 G2 NE Libya
Bengkulu 91 B7 Sumatra, W Indonesia
Benguela 128 B4 W Angola
Ben Hope 33 D2 ▲ N Scotland, UK
Beni 128 D1 NE Dem. Rep. Congo
Benidorm 57 F4 SE Spain
Beni-Mellal 122 C2 C Morocco
Benin 124 D4 ◆ Republic, W Africa
Benin, Bight of 124 E5 Gulf, W Africa
Benin City 124 E5 SW Nigeria
Beni, Río 117 A2 ~ N Bolivia
Beni Suef 122 I3 N Egypt
Ben Klibreck 33 C2 ▲ N Scotland, UK
Ben Lawers 33 D5 ▲ C Scotland, UK
Benllech 39 C1 NW Wales, UK
Ben Lui 33 C5 ▲ C Scotland, UK
Ben Macdui 33 E4 ▲ C Scotland, UK
Ben More 33 D5 ▲ C Scotland, UK
Ben More 33 B5 ▲ W Scotland, UK
Ben More Assynt 33 D2 ▲ N Scotland, UK
Ben Nevis 33 C4 ▲ N Scotland, UK
Benue 124 F5 ~ Cameroon/Nigeria
Beograd see Belgrade
Berat 65 D4 C Albania
Berau, Teluk 91 H7 Bay, E Indonesia
Berbera 127 F3 NW Somalia
Berbérati 124 G5 SW CAR
Berck-Plage 55 D1 N France
Berdyans'k 67 G6 SE Ukraine
Berettyó 63 F8 ~ Hungary/Romania

◐ Administrative region ◆ Country ● Country capital ◇ Dependent territory ○ Dependent territory capital ⛰ Mountain range ▲ Mountain ✲ Volcano ~ River ◎ Lake ▣ Reservoir

Berettyóújfalu 63 F7 E Hungary
Bereket 83 C3 W Turkmenistan
Berezniki 69 D5 NW Russ. Fed.
Berga 57 G2 NE Spain
Bergamo 61 B2 N Italy
Bergen 59 D2 NE Germany
Bergen 50 C3 NW Netherlands
Bergen 49 A5 S Norway
Bergerac 55 C5 SW France
Bergeyk 50 D6 S Netherlands
Bergse Maas 50 D5 ≈ S Netherlands
Beringen 50 D6 NE Belgium
Bering Sea 97 A2 *Sea*, N Pacific Ocean
Bering Strait 97 C2 *Strait*, Bering Sea/Chukchi Sea
Berja 57 E6 S Spain
Berkeley 103 B3 California, USA
Berkhamsted 37 F3 SE England, UK
Berkner Island 138 B4 *Island*, Antarctica
Berlin 59 D3 ● NE Germany
Berlin 101 G2 New Hampshire, USA
Bermejo, Río 117 B3 ≈ N Argentina
Bermeo 57 E1 N Spain
Bermuda 40 *UK* ◇ NW Atlantic Ocean
Bern 59 A8 ● W Switzerland
Bernau 59 D3 NE Germany
Bernburg 59 D4 C Germany
Berner Alpen 59 A8 ⛰ SW Switzerland
Berneray 33 A4 *Island*, NW Scotland, UK
Bernier Island 133 A4 *Island*, Western Australia
Berry 55 D3 *Cultural region*, C France
Berry Islands 109 C1 *Island group*, N Bahamas
Bertoua 124 G5 E Cameroon
Berwick-upon-Tweed 35 D1 N England, UK
Besançon 55 E4 E France
Bessbrook 31 E3 S Northern Ireland, UK
Betafo 128 G5 C Madagascar
Betanzos 57 B1 NW Spain
Bethel 40 E Montserrat
Bethesda 39 C2 NW Wales, UK
Bethlehem 128 D6 C South Africa
Bethlehem 81 H6 C West Bank
Béticos, Sistemas 57 D5 ⛰ S Spain
Bétou 128 C1 N. Congo
Bette, Pic 122 G4 ▲ S Libya
Betws-y-Coed 39 D2 N Wales, UK
Beulah 39 D5 C Wales, UK
Beveren 50 C6 N Belgium
Beverley 35 F4 E England, UK
Bexhill 37 G4 SE England, UK
Bexley 29 ◐ *London borough*, SE England, UK
Beyla 124 C4 SE Guinea
Beyrouth *see* Beirut
Beyşehir Gölü 79 B4 ◎ C Turkey
Béziers 55 D6 S France
Bhadravati 89 D6 SW India
Bhagalpur 89 F3 NE India
Bhaktapur 89 F3 C Nepal
Bharuch 89 C4 W India
Bhavnagar 89 C4 W India
Bhopal 89 D4 C India
Bhubaneshwar 89 F4 E India
Bhusawal 89 D4 C India
Bhutan 89 G3 ◆ *Monarchy*, S Asia
Biak, Pulau 91 H6 *Island*, E Indonesia
Biała Podlaska 63 G3 E Poland
Białogard 63 C2 NW Poland
Białystok 63 G2 E Poland
Biarritz 55 B6 SW France
Bicester 37 E3 C England, UK
Bideford 37 B4 SW England, UK
Biel 59 A8 W Switzerland
Bielefeld 59 B4 NW Germany
Bielsko-Biała 63 E5 S Poland
Bielsk Podlaski 63 G3 E Poland
Biên Hoa 91 C4 S Vietnam
Bienville, Lac 99 D3 ◎ Québec, C Canada
Bié Plateau 128 C4 *Plateau*, C Angola
Bigbury Bay 37 B6 *Bay*, SW England, UK
Big Cypress Swamp 101 E7 *Wetland*, SE USA
Biggleswade 37 F2 C England, UK
Big Point 40 *Headland*, N Tristan da Cunha
Bihać 65 B2 NW Bosnia and Herzegovina
Bihar 89 F3 *Cultural region*, N India
Biharamulo 127 C6 NW Tanzania
Bihosava 67 C1 NW Belarus
Bijelo Polje 65 D3 SW Serbia and Montenegro (Yugoslavia)
Bikaner 89 D3 NW India
Bikin 76 H5 SE Russ. Fed.
Bilaspur 89 E4 C India
Biläsuvar 79 I3 SE Azerbaijan
Bila Tserkva 67 D4 N Ukraine
Bilauktaung Range 91 B4 ⛰ Burma/Thailand
Bilbao 57 E1 N Spain
Bilecik 79 B3 NW Turkey
Billingham 35 E3 N England, UK
Billings 103 D2 Montana, USA
Bilma, Grand Erg de 124 G2 *Desert*, NE Niger
Biloela 133 H4 Queensland, E Australia
Biltine 124 H3 E Chad
Bilzen 50 D6 NE Belgium
Bimini Islands 109 C1 *Island group*, W Bahamas
Binche 50 C7 S Belgium
Binghamton 101 G3 New York, USA
Bingöl 79 F3 E Turkey
Bintulu 91 D6 East Malaysia
Binzhou 87 G3 E China
Bío Bío, Río 117 A6 ≈ C Chile
Bioco, Isla de 124 F6 *Island*, NW Equatorial Guinea
Birak 122 F3 C Libya
Birao 124 I4 NE CAR
Biratnagar 89 F3 SE Nepal
Birdhill 31 C5 S Ireland
Birhar Sharif 89 F3 N India
Birjand 81 F2 E Iran
Birkenfeld 59 A6 SW Germany
Birkenhead 35 C5 NW England, UK
Birmingham 35 D6 C England, UK
Birmingham 101 D5 Alabama, USA
Birmingham 29 ◐ *Unitary auth.*, C England, UK
Bîr Mogreïn 124 B1 N Mauritania
Birnin Kebbi 124 E4 NW Nigeria
Birnin Konni 124 E3 SW Niger
Birobidzhan 76 H5 SE Russ. Fed.
Birr 31 D4 C Ireland
Birsk 69 D6 W Russ. Fed.
Birżebbuġa 70 B6 SE Malta
Biscay, Bay of 55 B4 *Bay*, France/Spain
Bishah, Wadi 81 B5 *Dry watercourse*, C Saudi Arabia
Bishkek 83 H2 ● N Kyrgyzstan
Bishop Auckland 35 D3 N England, UK
Biskra 122 E1 NE Algeria
Biskupiec 63 F2 N Poland
Bislig 91 G5 S Philippines
Bismarck 103 F1 North Dakota, USA
Bismarck Archipelago 137 B1 *Island group*, NE PNG
Bismarck Sea 137 B1 *Sea*, W Pacific Ocean
Bissau 124 A4 ● W Guinea-Bissau
Bistrița 67 B6 N Romania
Bitam 128 A1 N Gabon
Bitburg 59 A5 SW Germany
Bitlis 79 G4 SE Turkey
Bitola 65 D4 S FYR Macedonia
Bitonto 61 E6 SE Italy
Bitterfeld 59 D4 E Germany
Bitterroot Range 103 C1 ⛰ NW USA
Biu 124 G4 E Nigeria
Biwa-ko 85 E6 ◎ Honshu, SW Japan
Bizerte 122 F1 N Tunisia
Bjørnøya 139 D5 *Island*, N Norway
Blackall 133 G4 Queensland, E Australia
Blackburn 35 C4 NW England, UK
Blackburn with Darwen 29 ◐ *Unitary auth.*, NW England, UK
Black Drin 65 D3 ≈ Albania/FYR Macedonia
Black Forest 59 B7 ⛰ SW Germany
Black Mountains 39 E5 ⛰ SE Wales, UK
Blackpool 35 C4 NW England, UK
Blackpool 29 ◐ *Unitary auth.*, NW England, UK
Black River 91 B2 ≈ China/Vietnam
Black Sea 44 *Sea*, Asia/Europe
Black Sea Lowland 67 E6 *Depression*, SE Europe
Blacksod Bay 31 A3 *Inlet*, W Ireland
Black Volta 124 D4 ≈ W Africa
Blackwater 31 E6 SE Ireland
Blackwater 31 D6 ≈ S Ireland
Blackwater 31 E2 ≈ Ireland/Northern Ireland, UK
Blaenau Ffestiniog 39 D2 NW Wales, UK
Blaenau Gwent 29 ◐ *Unitary auth.*, SE Wales, UK
Blaenavon 39 E6 SE Wales, UK
Blagoevgrad 65 E3 W Bulgaria
Blagoveshchensk 76 H5 SE Russ. Fed.
Blairgowrie 33 E5 C Scotland, UK
Blakeney Point 37 G1 *Headland*, E England, UK
Blanca, Bahía 117 B6 *Bay*, E Argentina
Blanca, Costa 57 F5 *Physical region*, SE Spain
Blanche, Lake 133 F4 ◎ S Australia
Blanc, Mont 55 F5 ▲ France/Italy
Blanco, Cape 103 A2 *Headland*, Oregon, USA
Blandford Forum 37 D5 S England, UK
Blanes 57 H2 NE Spain
Blankenberge 50 B5 NW Belgium
Blankenheim 59 A5 W Germany
Blanquilla, Isla 109 I7 *Island*, N Venezuela
Blantyre 128 E4 S Malawi
Blaricum 50 D4 C Netherlands
Bleaker Island 40 *Island*, SE Falkland Islands
Blenheim 135 C5 South Island, NZ
Blenheim Reef 40 *Reef*, N British Indian Ocean Territory
Blida 122 D1 N Algeria
Bloemfontein 128 D6 ● C South Africa
Blois 55 C3 C France
Bloody Foreland 31 C1 *Headland*, NW Ireland
Bloomington 101 D4 Indiana, USA
Bloomsbury 133 G3 Queensland, NE Australia
Bluefields 107 E4 SE Nicaragua
Blue Hills 40 NW Turks and Caicos Islands
Blue Mountains 133 G6 ⛰ NSW, SE Australia
Blue Nile 127 C3 ≈ Ethiopia/Sudan
Bluff Cove 40 Falkland Islands
Blumenau 115 F8 S Brazil
Blyth 35 D2 N England, UK
Bo 124 B5 S Sierra Leone
Boaco 107 D4 S Nicaragua
Boa Vista 115 E3 NW Brazil
Boabomby, Tanjona 128 G4 *Headland*, N Madagascar
Bobo-Dioulasso 124 C4 SW Burkina
Bocay 107 D3 N Nicaragua
Bocholt 59 A4 W Germany
Bochum 59 A4 W Germany
Bodaybo 76 F4 E Russ. Fed.
Boddam Island 40 *Island*, N British Indian Ocean Territory
Bodden Town 40 SW Cayman Islands
Boden 49 D3 N Sweden
Bodmin 37 B5 SW England, UK
Bodmin Moor 37 B5 *Moorland*, SW England, UK
Bodø 49 C2 C Norway
Bodrum 79 A4 SW Turkey
Boende 128 C2 C Dem. Rep. Congo
Bofin, Lough 31 D3 ◎ N Ireland
Bogatynia 63 B4 SW Poland
Boğazlıyan 79 D3 C Turkey
Boggeragh Mountains 31 C6 ⛰ S Ireland
Bogia 137 B1 N PNG
Bognor Regis 37 F5 SE England, UK
Bogor 91 C8 Java, C Indonesia
Bogotá 115 B2 ● C Colombia
Bo Hai 87 G3 *Gulf*, NE China
Bohemia 63 B6 *Cultural region*, W Czech Republic
Bohemian Forest 59 D6 ⛰ C Europe
Bohol Sea 91 F5 *Sea*, S Philippines
Bohoro Shan 87 B2 ⛰ NW China
Boise 103 C2 Idaho, USA
Boizenburg 59 C3 N Germany
Bojnürd 81 E1 N Iran
Boké 124 A4 W Guinea
Boknafjorden 49 A5 *Fjord*, S Norway
Bol 124 G3 W Chad
Bolesławiec 63 C4 SW Poland
Bolgatanga 124 D4 N Ghana
Bolivia 117 A2 ◆ *Republic*, W South America
Bollene 55 E6 SE France
Bollnäs 49 C5 C Sweden
Bollon 133 G4 Queensland, C Australia
Bologna 61 C3 N Italy
Bol'shevik, Ostrov 76 F2 *Island*, Severnaya Zemlya, N Russ. Fed.
Bol'shezemel'skaya Tundra 69 E3 *Physical region*, NW Russ. Fed.
Bol'shoy Lyakhovskiy, Ostrov 76 G2 *Island*, NE Russ. Fed.
Bolton 35 C4 NW England, UK
Bolton 28 ◐ *Unitary auth.*, NW England, UK
Bolu 79 C2 NW Turkey
Bolungarvík 49 A1 NW Iceland
Bolus Head 31 A6 *Headland*, SW Ireland
Bolzano 61 C1 N Italy
Boma 128 B3 W Dem. Rep. Congo
Bombay *see* Mumbai
Bomu 128 C1 ≈ CAR/Dem. Rep. Congo
Bonaire 109 H7 *Island*, E Netherlands Antilles
Bonanza 107 E3 NE Nicaragua
Bonaparte Archipelago 133 B2 *Island group*, Western Australia
Bon, Cap 70 E4 *Headland*, N Tunisia
Bondo 128 C1 N Dem. Rep. Congo
Bondoukou 124 D5 E Ivory Coast
Bone, Teluk 91 F7 *Bay*, Celebes, C Indonesia
Bongaigaon 89 G3 NE India
Bongo, Massif des 124 H4 ⛰ NE CAR
Bongor 124 G4 SW Chad
Bonifacio 55 G6 Corsica, France
Bonifacio, Strait of 61 A5 *Strait*, C Mediterranean Sea
Bonin Trench 15 *Undersea feature*, NW Pacific Ocean
Bonn 59 A5 W Germany
Bonvilston 39 E7 S Wales, UK
Booby Point 40 *Headland*, W Cayman Islands
Boosaaso 127 F3 N Somalia
Boothia, Gulf of 97 H3 *Gulf*, Nunavut, NE Canada
Boothia Peninsula 97 H3 *Peninsula*, Nunavut, NE Canada
Boppard 59 B5 W Germany
Boquete 107 F6 W Panama
Boquillas 105 D2 NE Mexico
Bor 127 C4 S Sudan
Bor 65 D2 E Serbia and Montenegro (Yugoslavia)
Borah Peak 103 C2 ▲ Idaho, USA
Borås 49 C6 S Sweden
Bordeaux 55 B5 SW France
Bordj Omar Driss 122 E3 E Algeria
Bordon 37 F4 S England, UK
Børgefjelt 49 C3 ⛰ C Norway
Borger 50 F2 NE Netherlands
Borgholm 49 C6 S Sweden
Borisoglebsk 69 B6 W Russ. Fed.
Borlänge 49 C5 C Sweden
Borne 50 F4 E Netherlands
Borneo 91 D7 *Island*, Brunei/Indonesia/Malaysia
Bornholm 49 C7 *Island*, E Denmark
Borovichi 69 A4 W Russ. Fed.
Borrisokane 31 C5 S Ireland
Borth 39 C4 W Wales, UK
Bosanski Novi 65 B1 NW Bosnia and Herzegovina
Boskovice 63 C6 SE Czech Republic
Bosna 65 C2 ≈ N Bosnia and Herzegovina
Bosna i Hercegovina, Federacija 65 C2 ◐ *Republic*, Bosnia and Herzegovina, SE Europe
Bosnia and Herzegovina 65 ◆ *Republic*, SE Europe
Boso-hanto 85 G6 *Peninsula*, Honshu, S Japan
Bosporus 78 B2 *Strait*, NW Turkey
Bossangoa 124 H5 C CAR
Bossembélé 124 H5 C CAR
Bosten Hu 87 C3 ◎ NW China
Boston 35 F5 E England, UK
Boston 101 H3 Massachusetts, USA
Botany Bay 133 H6 *Inlet*, NSW, SE Australia
Boteti 128 C5 ≈ N Botswana
Bothnia, Gulf of 49 D4 *Gulf*, N Baltic Sea
Botoşani 67 C5 NE Romania
Botrange 50 E7 ▲ E Belgium
Botswana 128 C5 ◆ *Republic*, S Africa
Bottle Creek 40 N Turks and Caicos Islands
Bouar 124 G5 W CAR
Bou Craa 122 B3 NW Western Sahara
Bougainville Island 137 D2 *Island*, NE PNG
Bougaroun, Cap 70 D4 *Headland*, NE Algeria
Bougouni 124 C4 SW Mali
Boujdour 122 A3 W Western Sahara
Boulder 103 E3 Colorado, USA
Boulogne-sur-Mer 55 D1 N France
Boûmdeïd 124 B3 S Mauritania
Boundiali 124 C4 N Ivory Coast
Bourail 137 G6 C New Caledonia
Bourbonnais 55 D4 *Cultural region*, C France
Bourg-en-Bresse 55 E4 E France
Bourges 55 D4 C France
Bourgogne *see* Burgundy
Bourke 133 G5 NSW, SE Australia
Bournemouth 37 E5 S England, UK
Bournemouth 29 ◐ *Unitary auth.*, S England, UK
Boutilimit 124 A3 SW Mauritania
Bowen 133 G3 Queensland, NE Australia
Bowland, Forest of 35 C4 *Forest*, N England, UK
Boxmeer 50 E5 SE Netherlands
Boyle 31 C3 C Ireland
Boyne 31 E4 ≈ E Ireland
Boysun 83 F3 S Uzbekistan
Bozüyük 79 B3 NW Turkey
Brač 65 B3 *Island*, S Croatia
Bracknell Forest 29 ◐ *Unitary auth.*, SE England, UK
Bradford 35 D4 N England, UK
Bradford 29 ◐ *Unitary auth.*, N England, UK
Brae 33 A6 NE Scotland, UK
Braemar 33 E4 NE Scotland, UK
Braga 57 B2 NW Portugal
Bragança 57 C2 NE Portugal
Brahmanbaria 89 G3 E Bangladesh
Brahmapur 89 F5 E India
Brahmaputra 89 H3 ≈ S Asia
Braich y Pwll 39 B3 *Headland*, NW Wales, UK
Brăila 67 D7 E Romania
Braine-le-Comte 50 C7 SW Belgium
Braintree 37 G3 SE England, UK
Brampton 99 D6 Ontario, S Canada
Brampton 35 C2 NW England, UK
Brandberg 128 B5 ▲ NW Namibia
Brandenburg 59 D3 NE Germany
Brandon 97 H7 Manitoba, S Canada
Brandon 31 A6 SW Ireland
Brandon Bay 31 A6 *Bay*, SW Ireland
Brandon Mountain 31 A6 ▲ SW Ireland
Braniewo 63 E2 N Poland
Brasília 115 G6 ● C Brazil
Braşov 67 C6 C Romania
Brasstown Bald 101 E5 ▲ Georgia, USA
Bratislava 63 D7 ● SW Slovakia
Bratsk 76 F5 C Russ. Fed.
Braunschweig 59 C4 N Germany
Brava, Costa 57 H2 *Coastal region*, NE Spain
Bravo, Río 105 D2 ≈ Mexico/USA
Bray 31 E4 E Ireland
Brazil 115 C4 ◆ *Federal Republic*, South America
Brazil Basin 14 *Undersea feature*, W Atlantic Ocean
Brazilian Highlands 115 G6 ⛰ E Brazil
Brazzaville 128 B2 ● S Congo
Brechin 33 E4 E Scotland, UK
Brecht 50 C5 N Belgium
Brecon 39 E5 E Wales, UK
Brecon Beacons 39 D6 ⛰ S Wales, UK
Breda 50 D5 S Netherlands
Bree 50 D6 NE Belgium
Bregalnica 65 E3 ≈ E FYR Macedonia
Bremen 59 B3 NW Germany
Bremerhaven 59 B3 NW Germany
Brenig, Llyn 39 D2 ◎ N Wales, UK
Brenner Pass 59 C8 *Pass*, Austria/Italy
Brent 29 ◐ *London borough*, SE England, UK
Brentwood 37 G3 E England, UK
Brescia 61 C2 N Italy
Bressanone 61 C1 N Italy
Bressay 33 B6 *Island*, NE Scotland, UK
Brest 67 B3 SW Belarus
Brest 55 A2 NW France
Bretagne *see* Brittany
Bria 124 H5 C CAR
Briançon 55 F5 SE France
Bride 35 A3 N Isle of Man
Bridgend 39 D7 S Wales, UK
Bridgend 29 ◐ *Unitary auth.*, S Wales, UK
Bridgeport 101 G3 Connecticut, USA
Bridgetown 109 K6 ● SW Barbados
Bridgetown 31 E6 SE Ireland
Bridgwater 37 D4 SW England, UK
Bridgwater Bay 37 C4 *Bay*, SW England, UK
Bridlington 35 F4 E England, UK
Bridlington Bay 35 F4 *Bay*, E England, UK
Bridport 37 D5 S England, UK
Brig 59 B8 SW Switzerland
Brigg 35 F5 N England, UK
Brighton 37 F5 SE England, UK
Brighton and Hove 29 ◐ *Unitary auth.*, SE England, UK
Brindisi 61 F6 SE Italy
Brisbane 133 H4 Queensland, E Australia
Bristol 37 D4 SW England, UK
Bristol 29 ◐ *Unitary auth.*, SW England, UK
Bristol Bay 97 C4 *Bay*, Alaska, USA
Bristol Channel 37 C4 *Inlet*, England/Wales, UK
Britain 27 *Island*, UK
British Columbia 97 E5 ◐ *Province*, SW Canada
British Indian Ocean Territory 40 *UK* ◇ C Indian Ocean
British Isles 44 *Island group*, Ireland/United Kingdom
British Virgin Islands 40 *UK* ◇ E West Indies
Briton Ferry 39 D6 S Wales, UK
Brittany 55 B2 *Cultural region*, NW France
Brive-la-Gaillarde 55 C5 C France
Brixham 37 C5 SW England, UK
Brno 63 C6 SE Czech Republic
Broad Bay 33 C2 *Bay*, NW Scotland, UK
Broadford 33 C4 N Scotland, UK
Broad Haven 31 B2 *Inlet*, NW Ireland
Broad Law 33 E6 ▲ S Scotland, UK
Broad Sound 39 A6 *Sound*, SW Wales, UK
Broadstairs 37 H4 SE England, UK
Broads, The 37 H2 *Wetland*, E England, UK
Brodeur Peninsula 97 H3 *Peninsula*, Baffin Island, Nunavut, NE Canada
Brodick 33 C6 W Scotland, UK
Brodnica 63 E2 N Poland
Broek-in-Waterland 50 D3 C Netherlands
Broken Hill 133 F5 NSW, SE Australia
Bromley 37 F4 SE England, UK
Bromley 29 ◐ *London borough*, SE England, UK
Bromsgrove 35 D7 W England, UK
Brooks Range 97 D3 ⛰ Alaska, USA
Brookton 133 B5 Western Australia
Broome 133 C2 Western Australia
Brora 33 D3 N Scotland, UK
Brora 33 D2 ≈ N Scotland, UK
Brough 35 D3 NW England, UK
Brownsville 103 G6 Texas, USA
Bruges 50 B6 NW Belgium
Brugge *see* Bruges
Brummen 50 E4 E Netherlands
Brunei 91 D5 ◆ *Monarchy*, SE Asia
Brunner, Lake 135 C6 ◎ South Island, NZ
Brus Laguna 107 E2 E Honduras
Brussel *see* Brussels
Brussels 50 C6 ● C Belgium
Bruxelles *see* Brussels
Bryan 103 G5 Texas, USA
Bryansk 69 A6 W Russ. Fed.
Brynamman 39 D6 S Wales, UK
Bryn Du 39 D5 *Hill*, E Wales, UK
Brynmawr 39 E6 SE Wales, UK
Brzeg 63 D4 SW Poland
Buala 137 E2 E Solomon Islands
Bucaramanga 115 C2 N Colombia
Buchanan 124 B5 SW Liberia
Buchan Ness 33 F3 *Headland*, NE Scotland, UK
Bucharest 67 C7 ● S Romania
Buckie 33 E3 NE Scotland, UK
Buckinghamshire 29 ◐ *County*, SE England, UK
Buckley 39 E2 N Wales, UK
Bucureşti *see* Bucharest
Budapest 63 E7 ● N Hungary
Budaun 89 E3 N India
Bude 37 B5 SW England, UK
Bude Bay 37 B5 *Bay*, SW England, UK
Buenaventura 115 B3 W Colombia
Buena Vista 117 B2 C Bolivia
Buena Vista 40 S Gibraltar
Buenos Aires 117 C5 ● E Argentina
Buenos Aires 107 F6 SE Costa Rica
Buenos Aires, Lago 117 A8 ◎ Argentina/Chile
Buffalo 101 F3 New York, USA
Buffalo Narrows 97 G6 Saskatchewan, C Canada
Bug 67 B3 ≈ E Europe
Buguruslan 69 D6 W Russ. Fed.
Builth Wells 39 E5 E Wales, UK
Bujalance 57 D5 S Spain
Bujanovac 65 D3 SE Serbia and Montenegro (Yugoslavia)
Bujumbura 127 B6 ● W Burundi
Buka Island 137 D2 *Island*, NE PNG
Bukavu 128 D2 E Dem. Rep. Congo
Bukoba 127 C5 NW Tanzania
Bülach 59 B7 NW Switzerland
Bulawayo 128 D5 SW Zimbabwe
Bulgaria 65 E3 ◆ *Republic*, SE Europe
Bulukumba 91 E7 Celebes, C Indonesia
Bumba 128 C1 N Dem. Rep. Congo
Bunbury 133 B6 Western Australia
Bunclody 31 E5 SE Ireland
Buncrana 31 D1 NW Ireland
Bundaberg 133 H4 Queensland, E Australia
Bungo-suido 85 D7 *Strait*, SW Japan
Bunmahon 31 D6 S Ireland
Bunratty 31 C5 W Ireland
Bünyan 79 D3 C Turkey
Buon Ma Thuot 91 C4 S Vietnam
Buraydah 81 C4 N Saudi Arabia
Burco 127 F3 NW Somalia
Burdur 79 B4 SW Turkey
Burdur Gölü 79 B4 *Salt lake*, SW Turkey
Bure 127 D3 NW Ethiopia
Bure 37 H1 ≈ E England, UK
Burgas 65 G3 E Bulgaria
Burgaski Zaliv 79 A1 *Gulf*, E Bulgaria
Burgess Hill 37 F4 SE England, UK
Burgos 57 D2 N Spain
Burgundy 55 E4 *Cultural region*, E France
Burhan Budai Shan 87 D4 ⛰ C China
Burjassot 57 F4 E Spain
Burketown 133 F2 Queensland, NE Australia
Burkina 124 C4 ◆ *Republic*, W Africa
Burkina Faso *see* Burkina
Burma 91 A2 ◆ *military dictatorship*, SE Asia
Burnham-on-Crouch 37 G3 SE England, UK
Burnham-on-Sea 37 D4 SW England, UK
Burnie 133 F7 Tasmania, SE Australia
Burnley 35 D4 NW England, UK
Burnside 97 G4 ≈ Nunavut, NW Canada
Burren 31 B5 *Physical region*, W Ireland
Burriana 57 F3 E Spain
Burry Port 39 C6 S Wales, UK
Bursa 79 B3 NW Turkey
Burton upon Trent 35 D6 C England, UK
Burundi 127 B6 ◆ *Republic*, C Africa
Buru, Pulau 91 F7 *Island*, E Indonesia
Bury 35 D4 NW England, UK
Bury 28 ◐ *Unitary auth.*, NW England, UK
Bury St Edmunds 37 G2 E England, UK
Bushire 81 D3 S Iran
Bushmills 31 E1 N Northern Ireland, UK
Busselton 133 B6 Western Australia
Buta 128 D1 N Dem. Rep. Congo
Bute, Island of 33 C6 *Island*, SW Scotland, UK
Buton, Pulau 91 F7 *Island*, C Indonesia
Buttevant 31 C6 S Ireland
Button Islands 99 E1 *Island group*, Québec, NE Canada
Butuan 91 F5 S Philippines
Buulobarde 127 F4 C Somalia
Buur Gaabo 127 E5 S Somalia
Buxoro 83 E3 C Uzbekistan
Buxton 35 D5 C England, UK
Buynaksk 69 B9 SW Russ. Fed.
Büyükmenderes Nehri 79 A4 ≈ SW Turkey
Buzău 67 C7 SE Romania
Büzmeýin 83 C3 C Turkmenistan
Buzuluk 69 C6 W Russ. Fed.
Bydgoszcz 63 D3 W Poland
Byelaruskaya Hrada 67 C3 *Ridge*, N Belarus
Byerezino 67 D2 ≈ C Belarus
Bylchau 39 D2 N Wales, UK
Bytča 63 D6 NW Slovakia
Bytów 63 D2 NW Poland

C

Caazapá 117 C4 S Paraguay
Cabañaquinta 57 C1 N Spain
Cabanatuan 91 F3 N Philippines
Cabinda 128 B2 NW Angola
Cabinda 128 B3 *Province*, NW Angola
Cabora Bassa, Lake 128 E4 ⊡ NW Mozambique
Caborca 105 B2 NW Mexico
Cabot Strait 99 G4 *Strait*, E Canada
Cabrera 57 G4 *Island*, Balearic Islands, Spain
Cáceres 57 C4 W Spain
Cachimbo, Serra do 115 E4 ⛰ C Brazil
Caconda 128 B4 C Angola
Čadca 63 D6 N Slovakia
Cader Idris 39 C3 ▲ NW Wales, UK
Cadiz 91 F4 C Philippines
Cádiz 57 C6 SW Spain
Cádiz, Golfo de *see* Cadiz, Gulf of
Cadiz, Gulf of 57 B6 *Gulf*, Portugal/Spain
Caen 55 C2 N France
Caergwrle 39 E2 N Wales, UK
Caernarfon 39 C2 NW Wales, UK
Caernarfon Bay 39 B2 *Bay*, NW Wales, UK
Caerphilly 39 E7 S Wales, UK
Caerphilly 29 ◐ *Unitary auth.*, S Wales, UK
Caersws 39 E4 C Wales, UK
Caerwent 39 F6 SE Wales, UK
Cafayate 117 B4 N Argentina
Cagayan de Oro 91 F5 Mindanao, S Philippines
Cagliari 61 A6 Sardinia, Italy
Caguas 109 I4 E Puerto Rico
Caha Mountains 31 B7 ⛰ SW Ireland

CAR Central African Republic **FYR** Former Yugoslavian Rebublic **NSW** New South Wales **NZ** New Zealand **PNG** Papua New Guinea **Russ. Fed.** Russian Federation **UAE** United Arab Emirates **UK** United Kingdom **USA** United States of America

Caher 31 D6 S Ireland
Caherciveen 31 A6 SW Ireland
Cahore Point 31 E5 Headland, SE Ireland
Cahors 55 C6 S France
Cahul 67 D6 S Moldova
Caicos Bank 40 Undersea feature, N Caribbean Sea
Caicos Passage 40 Strait, Bahamas/Turks and Caicos Islands
Cairngorm Mountains 33 E4 ⛰ C Scotland, UK
Cairns 133 G2 Queensland, NE Australia
Cairo 122 I2 ● N Egypt
Cajamarca 115 B5 NW Peru
Calabar 124 F5 S Nigeria
Calahorra 57 E2 N Spain
Calais 55 D1 N France
Calama 117 A3 N Chile
Călăraşi 67 C7 SE Romania
Calatayud 57 E3 NE Spain
Calbayog 91 F4 Samar, C Philippines
Calcutta see Kolkata
Caldas da Rainha 57 A4 W Portugal
Caldera 117 A4 N Chile
Calderdale 29 ◐ Unitary auth., N England, UK
Caldey Island 39 B6 Island, SW Wales, UK
Caldicot 39 F7 SE Wales, UK
Caledonia 107 C1 N Belize
Caleta Olivia 117 B8 SE Argentina
Calf of Man 35 A4 Island, SW Isle of Man
Calgary 97 G7 Alberta, SW Canada
Cali 115 B3 W Colombia
Calicut 89 D7 SW India
California 103 B3 ◐ State, W USA
California, Gulf of 105 B2 Gulf, NE Mexico
Callabonna, Lake 133 F5 ◎ S Australia
Callan 31 D5 S Ireland
Callander 33 D5 C Scotland, UK
Callao 115 B5 W Peru
Callosa de Segura 57 F5 E Spain
Calne 37 E4 S England, UK
Caloundra 133 H4 Queensland, E Australia
Caltanissetta 61 D8 Sicily, Italy
Caluula 127 G3 NE Somalia
Cam 37 F2 〰 E England, UK
Camabatela 128 B3 NW Angola
Camacupa 128 B4 C Angola
Camagüey 109 D3 C Cuba
Camagüey, Archipiélago de 109 D3 Island group, C Cuba
Camargue 55 E6 Physical region, SE France
Ca Mau 91 C5 S Vietnam
Cambodia 91 C4 ◆ Republic, SE Asia
Cambrai 55 D1 N France
Cambrian Mountains 39 D4 ⛰ C Wales, UK
Cambridge 135 D3 North Island, NZ
Cambridge 37 G2 E England, UK
Cambridge Bay 97 G4 Victoria Island, Nunavut, NW Canada
Cambridgeshire 29 ◐ County, E England, UK
Camden 29 ◐ London borough, SE England, UK
Cameroon 124 F5 ◆ Republic, W Africa
Cameroon Mountain 124 E5 ※ SW Cameroon
Camocim 115 H4 E Brazil
Camorta 89 H6 Island, Nicobar Islands, India
Campamento 107 D3 C Honduras
Campbell, Cape 135 D5 Headland, South Island, NZ
Campbell Plateau 15 Undersea feature, SW Pacific Ocean
Campbell River 97 E7 Vancouver Island, British Columbia, SW Canada
Campbeltown 33 C6 W Scotland, UK
Campeche 105 H4 SE Mexico
Campeche, Bay of 105 G4 Bay, E Mexico
Câm Pha 91 C2 N Vietnam
Campina Grande 115 I5 E Brazil
Campinas 115 G7 S Brazil
Campobasso 61 D5 C Italy
Campo de Criptana 57 D4 C Spain
Campo Grande 115 F7 SW Brazil
Campos 115 H7 SE Brazil
Cam Ranh 91 D4 S Vietnam
Canada 93 ◆ Commonwealth Republic, N North America
Canada Basin 139 B3 Undersea feature, Arctic Ocean
Canadian River 103 F4 〰 SW USA
Canadian Shield 99 B3 Physical region, Canada
Çanakkale 79 A2 W Turkey
Cananea 105 B2 NW Mexico
Canarreos, Archipiélago de los 109 B3 Island group, W Cuba
Canary Islands 122 A2 Island group, Spain, NE Atlantic Ocean
Cañas 107 E5 NW Costa Rica
Canaveral, Cape 101 E6 Headland, SE USA
Canavieiras 115 H6 E Brazil
Canberra 133 G6 ● Australian Capital Territory, SE Australia
Cancún 105 I4 SE Mexico
Cangzhou 87 G3 E China
Caniapiscau 99 E2 〰 Québec, E Canada
Caniapiscau, Réservoir de 99 E3 ▣ Québec, C Canada
Canik Dağları 79 E2 ⛰ N Turkey
Çankırı 79 C2 N Turkey
Canna 33 B4 Island, NW Scotland, UK
Cannanore 89 D7 SW India
Cannes 55 F6 SE France
Cannock 35 D6 C England, UK
Canoas 115 F9 S Brazil
Cantabria 57 D1 Cultural region, N Spain
Cantábrica, Cordillera 57 C1 ⛰ N Spain
Canterbury 37 H4 SE England, UK
Canterbury Bight 135 C6 Bight, South Island, NZ
Canterbury Plains 135 C6 Plain, South Island, NZ
Can Tho 91 C4 S Vietnam
Canton 101 E3 Ohio, USA
Cape Barren Island 133 G7 Island, Tasmania, SE Australia
Cape Breton Island 99 G5 Island, Nova Scotia, SE Canada
Cape Coast 124 D5 S Ghana
Cape Cod 99 E6 Bay, Massachusetts, USA
Capel Curig 39 D2 N Wales, UK
Capelle aan den IJssel 50 C4 SW Netherlands
Cape Town 128 C7 ● SW South Africa
Cape Verde 119 ◆ Republic, E Atlantic Ocean
Cape York Peninsula 133 F1 Peninsula, Queensland, N Australia
Cap-Haïtien 109 F4 N Haiti
Capira 107 H6 C Panama
Capitán Arturo Prat 138 A3 Chilean research station, South Shetland Islands, Antarctica
Capitán Pablo Lagerenza 117 C3 N Paraguay
Capri 61 D6 S Italy
Caprivi Strip 128 C4 Cultural region, NE Namibia
Caquetá, Río 115 B3 〰 Brazil/Colombia
Caracal 67 B7 S Romania
Caracaraí 115 E3 W Brazil
Caracas 115 D1 ● N Venezuela
Caratasca, Laguna de 107 E2 Lagoon, NE Honduras
Carbonia 61 A6 Sardinia, Italy
Carcassonne 55 D6 S France
Cárdenas 109 C2 W Cuba
Cardiff 39 E7 National region capital, S Wales, UK
Cardiff 29 ◐ Unitary auth., S Wales, UK
Cardigan 39 B5 SW Wales, UK
Cardigan Bay 39 C4 Bay, W Wales, UK
Carey, Lake 133 C5 ◎ Western Australia
Caribbean Sea 109 F6 Sea, W Atlantic Ocean
Carlisle 35 C2 NW England, UK
Carlow 31 E5 SE Ireland
Carlow 29 ◐ County, SE Ireland
Carloway 33 B2 NW Scotland, UK
Carlsbad 103 E5 New Mexico, USA
Carmarthen 39 C6 SW Wales, UK
Carmarthen Bay 39 B6 Inlet, SW Wales, UK
Carmarthenshire 29 ◐ Unitary auth., S Wales, UK
Carmaux 55 D6 S France
Carmel Head 39 B1 Headland, NW Wales, UK
Carmelita 107 B1 N Guatemala
Carmen 105 H5 SE Mexico
Carmona 57 C5 S Spain
Carna 31 B4 W Ireland
Carnarvon 133 A4 Western Australia
Carndonagh 31 D1 NW Ireland
Carnedd Llywelyn 39 D2 ▲ NW Wales, UK
Carnegie, Lake 133 C4 Salt lake, Western Australia
Carn Eige 33 C4 ▲ N Scotland, UK
Car Nicobar 89 H5 Island, Nicobar Islands, India
Carnlough 31 F2 E Northern Ireland, UK
Carno 39 D4 C Wales, UK
Carnoustie 33 E5 E Scotland, UK
Carolina 115 G4 E Brazil
Carpathian Mountains 63 F6 ⛰ E Europe
Carpentaria, Gulf of 133 E1 Gulf, N Australia
Carpi 61 C3 N Italy
Carrara 61 B3 C Italy
Carrauntoohil 31 A6 ▲ SW Ireland
Carrickfergus 31 F2 NE Northern Ireland, UK
Carrickfergus 29 ◐ District, E Northern Ireland, UK
Carrickmacross 31 E3 N Ireland
Carrick-on-Shannon 31 D3 NW Ireland
Carrowmore Lake 31 B3 ◎ NW Ireland
Carson City 103 B3 Nevada, USA
Cartagena 115 B1 NW Colombia
Cartagena 57 F5 SE Spain
Cartago 107 E6 C Costa Rica
Cartwright 99 G3 Newfoundland, E Canada
Casablanca 122 C1 NW Morocco
Cascade Range 103 B2 ⛰ NW USA
Cascais 57 A4 C Portugal
Caserta 61 D5 S Italy
Casey 138 E5 Australian research station, Antarctica
Cashel 31 D5 S Ireland
Čáslav 63 C5 C Czech Republic
Casper 103 E2 Wyoming, USA
Caspian Depression 69 B8 Depression, Kazakhstan/Russ. Fed.
Caspian Sea 72 Inland sea, Asia/Europe
Casteggio 61 B2 N Italy
Castelló de la Plana 57 F3 E Spain
Castelnaudary 55 C6 S France
Castelo Branco 57 B4 C Portugal
Castelsarrasin 55 C6 S France
Castelvetrano 61 C8 Sicily, Italy
Castilla-La Mancha 57 E4 Cultural region, NE Spain
Castilla-León 57 C2 Cultural region, NW Spain
Castle Acre 37 G1 E England, UK
Castlebar 31 B3 W Ireland
Castlebay 33 A4 NW Scotland, UK
Castlebellingham 31 E3 NE Ireland
Castleblayney 31 E3 N Ireland
Castlebridge 31 E6 SE Ireland
Castlecomer 31 D5 SE Ireland
Castlecove 31 A6 SW Ireland
Castledawson 31 E2 C Northern Ireland, UK
Castlederg 31 D2 W Northern Ireland, UK
Castle Douglas 33 D7 S Scotland, UK
Castleford 35 E4 N England, UK
Castleisland 31 B6 SW Ireland
Castlemartyr 31 C6 S Ireland
Castlereagh 29 ◐ District, E Northern Ireland, UK
Castletown 35 A4 SE Isle of Man
Castletown Bearhaven 31 B7 SW Ireland
Castletownroche 31 C6 S Ireland
Castricum 50 C3 W Netherlands
Castries 109 K6 ● N Saint Lucia
Castro 117 A7 W Chile
Castrovillari 61 E7 SW Italy
Castuera 57 C4 W Spain
Catacamas 107 D3 C Honduras
Catalan Bay 40 Bay, E Gibraltar
Catalonia 57 G2 Cultural region, N Spain
Cataluña see Catalonia
Catania 61 D8 Sicily, Italy
Catanzaro 61 E7 SW Italy
Catarroja 57 F4 E Spain
Caterham 37 G4 SE England, UK
Cat Island 109 E2 Island, C Bahamas
Catskill Mountains 101 F3 ⛰ New York, USA
Catterick 35 D3 N England, UK
Caucasus 79 G1 ⛰ Georgia/Russ. Fed.
Cavally 124 C5 〰 Ivory Coast/Liberia
Cavan 31 D3 N Ireland
Cavan 29 ◐ County, N Ireland
Cave Point 40 Headland, S Tristan da Cunha
Caviana de Fora, Ilha 115 G3 Island, N Brazil
Caxito 128 B3 NW Angola
Cayenne 115 F2 ○ NE French Guiana
Cayes 109 E4 SW Haiti
Cayman Brac 40 Island, E Cayman Islands
Cayman Islands 40 UK ◇ W West Indies
Cay Sal 109 C2 Islet, SW Bahamas
Cazorla 57 E5 S Spain
Ceará 115 H4 ◐ State, C Brazil
Cébaco, Isla 107 G7 Island, SW Panama
Cebu 91 F4 Cebu, C Philippines
Cecina 61 B4 C Italy
Cedar Rapids 103 G2 Iowa, USA
Cedros, Isla 105 A3 Island, W Mexico
Ceduna 133 E5 S Australia
Cefalù 61 D8 Sicily, Italy
Celbridge 31 E4 E Ireland
Celebes 91 E7 Island, C Indonesia
Celebes Sea 91 E6 Sea, Indonesia/Philippines
Celje 59 E8 C Slovenia
Celldömölk 63 D8 W Hungary
Celle 59 C3 N Germany
Celtic Sea 53 B8 Sea, SW British Isles
Cemaes 39 C1 NW Wales, UK
Cemaes Head 39 B5 Headland, SW Wales, UK
Cenderawasih, Teluk 91 H7 Bay, E Indonesia
Cenon 55 B5 SW France
Central African Republic 124 H5 ◆ Republic, C Africa
Central, Cordillera 109 F4 ⛰ C Dominican Republic
Central, Cordillera 107 G6 ⛰ C Panama
Central, Cordillera 91 F3 ⛰ N Philippines
Central Makran Range 89 B3 ⛰ W Pakistan
Central Pacific Basin 15 Undersea feature, C Pacific Ocean
Central Range 137 A2 ⛰ NW PNG
Central Russian Upland 69 A6 ⛰ C Russ. Fed.
Central Siberian Plateau 76 E3 ⛰ N Russ. Fed.
Central, Sistema 57 D3 ⛰ C Spain
Centre Hills 40 ⛰ C Montserrat
Ceram Sea 91 G7 Sea, E Indonesia
Ceredigion 29 ◐ Unitary auth., W Wales, UK
Cerignola 61 E5 SE Italy
Çerkeş 79 C2 N Turkey
Cernay 55 F3 NE France
Cerrigydrudion 39 D2 N Wales, UK
Cerro de Pasco 115 B5 C Peru
Cervera 57 G2 NE Spain
Cesena 61 C3 N Italy
České Budějovice 63 B6 SW Czech Republic
Český Krumlov 63 B6 SW Czech Republic
Ceuta 57 C6 Spain, N Africa
Cévennes 55 D6 ⛰ S France
Ceyhan 79 D5 S Turkey
Ceylanpınar 79 F5 SE Turkey
Chachapoyas 115 A4 NW Peru
Chad 124 G3 ◆ Republic, C Africa
Chad, Lake 124 G3 ◎ C Africa
Chadron 103 E2 Nebraska, USA
Chagai Hills 89 B2 ⛰ Afghanistan/Pakistan
Chaghcharan 83 E5 C Afghanistan
Chagos Archipelago 40 Island group, British Indian Ocean Territory
Chajul 107 A3 W Guatemala
Chakhansur 83 D6 SW Afghanistan
Chalatenango 107 B3 N El Salvador
Chálki 65 G6 Island, Dodecanese, Greece
Chalkída 65 E5 E Greece
Chalkidikí 65 E4 Peninsula, NE Greece
Challans 55 B4 NW France
Châlons-en-Champagne 55 E2 NE France
Chalon-sur-Saône 55 E4 C France
Chaman 89 B2 SW Pakistan
Chambéry 55 E5 E France
Champagne 55 E2 Cultural region, N France
Champaign 101 D3 Illinois, USA
Champasak 91 C3 S Laos
Champerico 107 A3 SW Guatemala
Champlain, Lake 101 F2 ◎ Canada/USA
Champotón 105 H4 SE Mexico
Chañaral 117 A4 N Chile
Chances Peak 40 ▲ S Montserrat
Chandigarh 89 D2 N India
Chandrapur 89 E5 C India
Changane 128 E5 〰 S Mozambique
Changchun 87 G2 NE China
Chang Jiang see Yangtze
Changsha 87 F5 S China
Changyon 85 A5 SW North Korea
Changzhi 87 F4 C China
Chaniá 65 E7 Crete, Greece
Chañi, Nevado de 117 A3 ▲ NW Argentina
Channel Islands 37 G6 Island group, S English Channel
Channel-Port aux Basques 99 G4 Newfoundland, SE Canada
Channel Tunnel 53 F8 Tunnel, France/UK
Chantada 57 B2 NW Spain
Chaoyang 87 G3 NE China
Chapala, Lago de 105 E5 ◎ C Mexico
Chapan, Gora 83 C3 ▲ C Turkmenistan
Chapayevsk 69 C6 W Russ. Fed.
Chard 37 D5 SW England, UK
Charente 55 C5 Cultural region, W France
Charente 55 C5 〰 W France
Chari 124 H4 〰 CAR/Chad
Charikar 83 F5 NE Afghanistan
Charleroi 50 C7 S Belgium
Charlesbourg 99 E5 Québec, SE Canada
Charles Island 99 D1 Island, Québec, NE Canada
Charleston 101 F5 South Carolina, USA
Charleston 101 E4 West Virginia, USA
Charlestown 31 C3 NW Ireland
Charleville 133 G4 Queensland, E Australia
Charleville-Mézières 55 E2 N France
Charlotte 101 E5 North Carolina, USA
Charlotte Amalie 109 I4 ○ Saint Thomas, N Virgin Islands (US)
Charlotte Harbor 101 E7 Inlet, SE USA
Charlottetown 99 G5 Prince Edward Island, SE Canada
Charters Towers 133 G3 Queensland, NE Australia
Chartres 55 D3 C France
Charus Nuur 87 C2 ◎ NW Mongolia
Chashniki 67 D2 N Belarus
Châteaubriant 55 B3 NW France
Châteaudun 55 D3 C France
Châteauroux 55 D4 C France
Château-Thierry 55 D2 N France
Châtelet 50 C7 S Belgium
Châtellerault 55 C4 W France
Chatham 37 G4 SE England, UK
Chatkal Range 83 G2 ⛰ Kyrgyzstan/Uzbekistan
Chattahoochee River 101 D6 〰 SE USA
Chattanooga 101 D5 Tennessee, USA
Chatyr-Tash 83 H3 C Kyrgyzstan
Chau Doc 91 C4 S Vietnam
Chaumont 55 E3 N France
Chaves 57 B2 N Portugal
Chaykovskiy 69 D6 NW Russ. Fed.
Cheb 63 A5 W Czech Republic
Cheboksary 69 C6 W Russ. Fed.
Chech, Erg 124 C1 Desert, Algeria/Mali
Cheduba Island 91 A3 Island, W Burma
Cheju-do 85 B8 Island, S South Korea
Cheju Strait 85 B7 Strait, S South Korea
Chelkar 76 B5 W Kazakhstan
Chełm 63 G4 SE Poland
Chełmno 63 D2 N Poland
Chelmsford 37 G3 E England, UK
Cheltenham 37 D3 C England, UK
Chelyabinsk 76 C4 C Russ. Fed.
Chemnitz 59 D5 E Germany
Chengde 87 G3 E China
Chengdu 87 E4 C China
Chennai 89 E6 S India
Chenzhou 87 F5 S China
Chepstow 39 F6 SE Wales, UK
Cher 55 D4 〰 C France
Cherbourg 55 B1 N France
Cherepovets 69 B4 NW Russ. Fed.
Chergui, Chott ech 70 B5 Salt lake, NW Algeria
Cherkasy 67 E4 C Ukraine
Cherkessk 69 A8 SW Russ. Fed.
Chernihiv 67 E3 NE Ukraine
Chernivtsi 67 C5 W Ukraine
Cherskiy 76 H2 NE Russ. Fed.
Cherskogo, Khrebet 76 G3 ⛰ NE Russ. Fed.
Chesapeake Bay 101 G4 Inlet, NE USA
Chesham 37 F3 C England, UK
Cheshire 29 ◐ County, C England, UK
Chëshskaya Guba 139 E6 Bay, NW Russ. Fed.
Chester 35 C5 C England, UK
Chesterfield 35 E5 C England, UK
Chesterfield, Îles 137 E6 Island group, NW New Caledonia
Chester-le-Street 35 D2 N England, UK
Chetumal 105 I4 SE Mexico
Cheviot Hills 35 C2 Hill range, England/Scotland, UK
Cheviot, The 35 D1 ▲ NE England, UK
Cheyenne 103 E3 Wyoming, USA
Chhapra 89 F3 N India
Chiai 87 H5 C Taiwan
Chiang Mai 91 B3 NW Thailand
Chiapa de Corzo 105 H5 SE Mexico
Chiba 85 G5 S Japan
Chibougamau 99 D4 Québec, SE Canada
Chicago 101 D3 Illinois, USA
Chichester 37 F5 SE England, UK
Chiclayo 115 B5 NW Peru
Chico, Río 117 B7 〰 SE Argentina
Chico, Río 117 A8 〰 S Argentina
Chicoutimi 99 E4 Québec, SE Canada
Chieti 61 D5 C Italy
Chifeng 87 G2 N China
Chihuahua 105 D2 NW Mexico
Chile 117 A4 ◆ Republic, SW South America
Chile Chico 117 A8 W Chile
Chililabombwe 128 D4 C Zambia
Chillán 117 A6 C Chile
Chiloé, Isla de 117 A7 Island, W Chile
Chilpancingo 105 F5 S Mexico
Chiltern Hills 37 F3 Hill range, S England, UK
Chilung 87 H5 N Taiwan
Chimán 107 H6 E Panama
Chimbote 115 B5 W Peru
Chimboy 83 D2 NW Uzbekistan
Chimoio 128 E5 C Mozambique
China 87 C3 ◆ Republic, E Asia
Chinandega 107 C4 NW Nicaragua
Chin-do 85 B7 Island, SW South Korea
Chindwin 91 A1 〰 N Burma
Chingola 128 D4 C Zambia
Chinguetti 124 B2 C Mauritania
Chin Hills 91 A2 ⛰ W Burma
Chioggia 61 D2 NE Italy
Chíos 65 F5 E Greece
Chíos 65 F5 Island, E Greece
Chipata 128 E4 E Zambia
Chippenham 37 D4 S England, UK
Chiquimula 107 B3 SE Guatemala
Chirala 89 E6 E India
Chirchiq 83 F2 E Uzbekistan
Chiriquí Gulf 107 F7 Gulf, SW Panama
Chiriquí, Laguna de 107 F6 Lagoon, NW Panama
Chirk 39 E2 NE Wales, UK
Chirripó Grande, Cerro 107 F6 ▲ SE Costa Rica
Chisec 107 B2 C Guatemala
Chişinău 67 D6 ● C Moldova
Chita 76 G5 S Russ. Fed.
Chitato 128 C3 NE Angola
Chitina 97 D4 Alaska, USA
Chitose 85 G2 NE Japan
Chitré 107 G7 S Panama
Chittagong 89 H4 SE Bangladesh
Chitungwiza 128 E5 NE Zimbabwe
Chiume 128 C4 E Angola
Chlef 122 D1 NW Algeria
Chodzież 63 C3 NW Poland
Choele Choel 117 B6 C Argentina
Choiseul 137 E2 Island, NW Solomon Islands
Cholet 55 B4 NW France
Choluteca 107 C4 S Honduras
Choluteca, Río 107 D4 〰 SW Honduras
Choma 128 D4 S Zambia
Chomutov 63 A5 NW Czech Republic
Ch'onan 85 B6 W South Korea
Ch'ongjin 85 C3 NE North Korea
Chongju 85 A5 W North Korea
Chongqing 87 E5 C China
Chonos, Archipiélago de los 117 A7 Island group, S Chile
Chorley 35 C4 NW England, UK
Chornobyl' 67 D3 N Ukraine
Chorzów 63 E5 S Poland
Ch'osan 85 A4 N North Korea
Choshi 85 G5 S Japan
Choszczno 63 C3 W Poland
Chota Nagpur 89 E4 Plateau, N India
Choûm 124 B2 C Mauritania
Choybalsan 87 F2 E Mongolia
Christchurch 135 C6 South Island, NZ
Christchurch 37 E5 S England, UK
Chubut, Río 117 B7 〰 SE Argentina
Chucunaque, Río 107 I6 〰 E Panama
Chugoku-sanchi 85 D6 ⛰ Honshu, SW Japan
Chukchi Plain 139 C2 Undersea feature, Arctic Ocean
Chukchi Plateau 139 B2 Undersea feature, Arctic Ocean
Chukchi Sea 76 H1 Sea, Arctic Ocean
Chukot Range 76 H1 ⛰ NE Russ. Fed.
Chulucanas 115 A4 NW Peru
Chulym 76 E5 〰 C Russ. Fed.
Ch'unch'on 85 B5 N South Korea
Ch'ungju 85 B6 C South Korea
Chunya 76 F4 〰 C Russ. Fed.
Chuquicamata 117 A3 N Chile
Chur 59 C8 E Switzerland
Churchill 97 H5 Manitoba, C Canada
Churchill 99 A2 〰 C Canada
Churchill 99 F3 〰 Newfoundland, E Canada
Church Stoke 39 E4 C Wales, UK
Church Stretton 35 C6 W England, UK
Churchtown 31 E6 SE Ireland
Chusovoy 69 D5 NW Russ. Fed.
Chuy 117 D5 E Uruguay
Cide 79 C2 N Turkey
Ciechanów 63 E3 C Poland
Ciego de Ávila 109 D3 C Cuba
Cienfuegos 109 C3 C Cuba
Cieza 57 E5 SE Spain
Cihanbeyli 79 C4 C Turkey
Cikobia 137 I3 Island, N Fiji
Cilacap 91 D8 Java, C Indonesia
Cincinnati 101 E4 Ohio, USA
Ciney 50 D8 SE Belgium
Cinto, Monte 55 F7 ▲ Corsica, France
Cipolletti 117 B6 C Argentina
Cirebon 91 C8 Java, S Indonesia
Cirencester 37 E3 C England, UK
Cirò Marina 61 E7 S Italy
Ciudad Bolívar 115 D2 E Venezuela
Ciudad Camargo 105 D3 N Mexico
Ciudad Darío 107 D4 W Nicaragua
Ciudad del Este 117 C4 SE Paraguay
Ciudad Guayana 115 D2 NE Venezuela
Ciudad Guzmán 105 D5 SW Mexico
Ciudad Hidalgo 105 H6 SE Mexico
Ciudad Juárez 105 C1 N Mexico
Ciudad Lerdo 105 D3 C Mexico
Ciudad Madero 105 F4 C Mexico
Ciudad Mante 105 F4 C Mexico
Ciudad Miguel Alemán 105 E3 C Mexico
Ciudad Obregón 105 C3 NW Mexico
Ciudad Real 57 D4 C Spain
Ciudad-Rodrigo 57 C3 N Spain
Ciudad Valles 105 F4 C Mexico
Ciudad Victoria 105 F3 C Mexico
Ciutadella de Menorca 57 H3 Minorca, Spain
Civitanova Marche 61 D4 C Italy
Civitavecchia 61 C5 C Italy
Clackmannanshire 28 ◐ Unitary auth., C Scotland, UK
Clacton-on-Sea 37 H3 E England, UK
Claerwen Reservoir 39 D4 ▣ E Wales, UK
Clare 29 ◐ County, W Ireland
Clare 31 C4 〰 W Ireland
Clarecastle 31 C5 W Ireland
Claregalway 31 C4 W Ireland
Clare Island 31 A3 Island, W Ireland
Claremorris 31 C3 W Ireland
Clarence 135 C5 South Island, NZ
Clarence 135 C5 〰 South Island, NZ
Clarence Town 109 E2 Long Island, C Bahamas
Clarión, Isla 105 A5 Island, W Mexico
Clark Hill Lake 101 E5 ▣ SE USA
Clarksdale 101 C5 Mississippi, USA
Clarksville 101 D4 Tennessee, USA
Clayton 103 E4 New Mexico, USA
Clear Island 31 B7 Island, S Ireland
Clearwater 101 E7 Florida, USA
Cleethorpes 35 F4 E England, UK
Clermont 133 G3 Queensland, E Australia
Clermont-Ferrand 55 D5 C France
Clevedon 37 D4 SW England, UK
Cleveland 101 E3 Ohio, USA
Clew Bay 31 B3 Inlet, W Ireland
Clifden 31 B4 W Ireland
Clisham 33 B2 ▲ NW Scotland, UK
Clitheroe 35 C4 NW England, UK
Cloghan 31 D4 C Ireland
Cloncurry 133 F3 Queensland, C Australia
Clondalkin 31 E4 E Ireland
Clones 31 D3 N Ireland
Clonmel 31 D6 S Ireland
Cloonboo 31 C4 W Ireland
Cloppenburg 59 B3 NW Germany
Cloud Peak 103 E2 ▲ Wyoming, USA
Clovelly 37 B4 SW England, UK
Cluj-Napoca 67 B6 NW Romania
Clutha 135 B7 〰 South Island, NZ
Clwyd 39 E2 〰 N Wales, UK
Clwydian Range 39 E2 ⛰ N Wales, UK
Clydach 39 D6 S Wales, UK
Clydach Vale 39 E6 S Wales, UK
Clyde 33 E6 〰 W Scotland, UK
Clydebank 33 D5 W Scotland, UK
Clyde, Firth of 33 C6 Inlet, S Scotland, UK
Clyro 39 E5 C Wales, UK
Clywedog, Llyn 39 D4 ▣ E Wales, UK
Coari 115 D4 N Brazil
Coast Mountains 97 E5 ⛰ Canada/USA
Coatbridge 33 D6 S Scotland, UK
Coats Island 97 I4 Island, Nunavut, NE Canada
Coats Land 138 B3 Physical region, Antarctica
Coatzacoalcos 105 G5 E Mexico
Cobán 107 B3 C Guatemala
Cobar 133 G5 NSW, SE Australia
Cobija 117 A1 NW Bolivia
Coburg 59 C5 SE Germany
Cochabamba 117 B2 C Bolivia

◐ Administrative region ◆ Country ● Country capital ◇ Dependent territory ○ Dependent territory capital ⛰ Mountain range ▲ Mountain ※ Volcano 〰 River ◎ Lake ▣ Reservoir

Cochin 89 D7 SW India
Cochrane 99 C4 Ontario, S Canada
Cochrane 117 A8 S Chile
Cockburn Harbour 40 South Caicos, S Turks and Caicos Islands
Cockburn Town 109 F3 E Bahamas
Cockburn Town 40 ○ Grand Turk Island, Turks and Caicos Islands
Cockermouth 35 B3 NW England, UK
Coco, Río 107 E3 ~ Honduras/Nicaragua
Cocos Basin 15 *Undersea feature,* E Indian Ocean
Codfish Island 135 A8 *Island,* SW NZ
Cody 103 D2 Wyoming, USA
Coedpoeth 39 E2 NE Wales, UK
Coevorden 50 F3 NE Netherlands
Coffs Harbour 133 H5 NSW, SE Australia
Cognac 55 C4 W France
Coiba, Isla de 107 F7 *Island,* SW Panama
Coihaique 117 A7 S Chile
Coimbatore 89 D7 S India
Coimbra 57 B3 W Portugal
Coín 57 D6 S Spain
Colchester 37 G3 E England, UK
Coldstream 33 F6 SE Scotland, UK
Coleraine 31 E1 N Northern Ireland, UK
Coleraine 29 ◐ *District,* N Northern Ireland, UK
Colesberg 128 D7 C South Africa
Colima 105 D5 S Mexico
Coll 33 B4 *Island,* W Scotland, UK
Collie 133 B6 Western Australia
Collon 31 E3 NE Ireland
Collooney 31 C3 NW Ireland
Colmar 55 F3 NE France
Colne 35 D4 NW England, UK
Cologne 59 A5 W Germany
Colombia 115 B3 ◆ *Republic,* N South America
Colombo 89 E8 ● W Sri Lanka
Colón 107 H6 C Panama
Colón, Archipiélago de *see* Galapagos Islands
Colonsay 33 B5 *Island,* W Scotland, UK
Colorado 103 E3 ◐ *State,* C USA
Colorado Plateau 103 D4 *Plateau,* W USA
Colorado, Río 117 B6 ~ E Argentina
Colorado River 103 C4 ~ Mexico/USA
Colorado Springs 103 E3 Colorado, USA
Columbia 101 F4 Maryland, USA
Columbia 103 G3 Missouri, USA
Columbia 101 E5 South Carolina, USA
Columbia Basin 103 B1 *Basin,* Washington, USA
Columbia Plateau 103 C2 *Plateau,* NW USA
Columbia River 103 B1 ~ Canada/USA
Columbus 101 D5 Georgia, USA
Columbus 101 E3 Ohio, USA
Colville Channel 135 D2 *Channel,* North Island, NZ
Colville River 97 D2 ~ Alaska, USA
Colwyn Bay 39 D1 N Wales, UK
Comacchio 61 C3 N Italy
Comalcalco 105 G5 SE Mexico
Comarapa 117 B2 C Bolivia
Comayagua 107 C3 W Honduras
Comeragh Mountains 31 D6 ▲ S Ireland
Comilla 89 G4 E Bangladesh
Comino 70 B6 *Island,* C Malta
Comitán 105 H5 SE Mexico
Communism Peak 83 G3 ▲ E Tajikistan
Como 61 B2 N Italy
Comodoro Rivadavia 117 B7 SE Argentina
Como, Lake 61 B2 ◎ Italy
Comoros 128 G4 ◆ *Republic,* W Indian Ocean
Compiègne 55 D2 N France
Conakry 124 B4 ● SW Guinea
Concarneau 55 A3 NW France
Concepción 117 B2 E Bolivia
Concepción 117 A6 C Chile
Concepción 117 C3 C Paraguay
Concepción, Volcán 107 D5 ▲ SW Nicaragua
Conchos, Río 105 D2 ~ NW Mexico
Concord 101 G2 New Hampshire, USA
Concordia 117 C5 E Argentina
Condega 107 D4 NW Nicaragua
Congleton 35 D5 W England, UK
Congo 128 B2 ◆ *Republic,* C Africa
Congo 128 B2 ~ C Africa
Congo Basin 128 C1 *Drainage basin,* W Dem. Rep. Congo
Congo, Dem. Rep. 128 C2 ◆ *Republic,* C Africa
Connah's Quay 39 E2 N Wales, UK
Connaught 31 B3 *Cultural region,* W Ireland
Connecticut 101 G3 ◐ *State,* NE USA
Connemara 31 B4 *Physical region,* W Ireland
Conn, Lough 31 B3 ◎ W Ireland
Consett 35 D2 N England, UK
Consolación del Sur 109 B2 W Cuba
Constance, Lake 59 B7 ◎ C Europe
Constanța 67 D7 SE Romania
Constantine 122 E1 NE Algeria
Conwy 39 D1 N Wales, UK
Conwy 29 ◐ *Unitary auth.,* N Wales, UK
Conwy 39 D2 ~ N Wales, UK
Coober Pedy 133 E4 S Australia
Cook Islands 131 *NZ* ◇ S Pacific Ocean
Cookstown 31 E2 C Northern Ireland, UK
Cookstown 29 ◐ *District,* C Northern Ireland, UK
Cook Strait 135 D5 *Strait,* NZ
Cooktown 133 G2 Queensland, NE Australia
Coolgardie 133 C5 Western Australia
Cooma 133 G6 NSW, SE Australia
Coon Rapids 103 G2 Minnesota, USA
Cooper Creek 133 F4 *Seasonal river,* Queensland/S Australia
Cooper Island 40 *Island,* SE British Virgin Islands
Copacabana 117 A2 W Bolivia
Copenhagen 49 B7 ● E Denmark
Copiapó 117 A4 N Chile
Coquimbo 117 A5 N Chile
Coral Harbour 97 I4 Southampton Island, Nunavut, NE Canada
Coral Sea 137 C4 *Sea,* SW Pacific Ocean
Coral Sea Islands 137 B4 *Australian* ◇ SW Pacific Ocean
Corby 37 F2 C England, UK
Corcovado, Golfo 117 A7 *Gulf,* S Chile
Córdoba 117 B5 C Argentina
Córdoba 105 F5 E Mexico
Córdoba 57 D5 SW Spain
Cordova 97 D4 Alaska, USA
Corfu 65 C5 *Island,* Ionian Islands, Greece
Coria 57 C3 W Spain
Corinth 65 E5 S Greece
Corinth 101 D5 Mississippi, USA
Corinth, Gulf of 65 E5 *Gulf,* C Greece
Corinth, Isthmus of 65 D5 *Isthmus,* S Greece
Corinto 107 C4 NW Nicaragua
Cork 31 C6 S Ireland
Cork 29 ◐ *County,* SW Ireland
Çorlu 79 A2 NW Turkey
Corner Brook 99 G4 Newfoundland, E Canada
Corn Islands 107 F4 *Island group,* SE Nicaragua
Cornwall 29 ◐ *County,* SW England, UK
Cornwall, Cape 37 A6 *Headland,* SW England, UK
Cornwallis Island 97 G2 *Island,* Parry Islands, Nunavut, N Canada
Coro 115 C1 NW Venezuela
Corocoro 117 A2 W Bolivia
Coromandel 135 D2 North Island, NZ
Coronado, Bahía de 107 E6 *Bay,* S Costa Rica
Coronel Dorrego 117 B6 E Argentina
Corozal 107 C1 N Belize
Corpus Christi 103 G5 Texas, USA
Corrib, Lough 31 B4 ◎ W Ireland
Corrientes 117 C4 NE Argentina
Corris 39 D3 NW Wales, UK
Corsham 37 D4 S England, UK
Corsica 55 F7 *Island* France, C Mediterranean Sea
Cortegana 57 B5 S Spain
Cortés 107 F6 SE Costa Rica
Cortina d'Ampezzo 61 D2 NE Italy
Coruche 57 B4 C Portugal
Çoruh Nehri 79 F2 ~ Georgia/Turkey
Çorum 79 D2 N Turkey
Corwen 39 E2 N Wales, UK
Cosenza 61 E7 SW Italy
Cosne-Cours-sur-Loire 55 D3 C France
Costa Rica 107 E5 ◆ *Republic,* Central America
Cotagaita 117 B3 S Bolivia
Côte d'Or 55 E3 *Cultural region,* C France
Cotonou 124 E5 S Benin
Cotswold Hills 37 D3 *Hill range,* S England, UK
Cottbus 59 E4 E Germany
Council Bluffs 103 G2 Iowa, USA
Courland Lagoon 49 D7 *Lagoon,* Lithuania/Russ. Fed.
Courtown 31 E5 SE Ireland
Coutances 55 B2 N France
Couvin 50 C8 S Belgium
Coventry 35 E6 C England, UK
Coventry 29 ◐ *Unitary auth.,* C England, UK
Covilhã 57 B3 E Portugal
Cowan, Lake 133 C5 ◎ Western Australia
Cowbridge 39 E7 S Wales, UK
Cozumel, Isla 105 I4 *Island,* SE Mexico
Cradock 128 D7 S South Africa
Crai 39 D6 C Wales, UK
Craigavon 31 E2 C Northern Ireland, UK
Craigavon 29 ◐ *District,* C Northern Ireland, UK
Craiova 67 B7 SW Romania
Cranbrook 97 F7 British Columbia, SW Canada
Cranleigh 37 F4 SE England, UK
Craughwell 31 C4 W Ireland
Craven Arms 35 C6 W England, UK
Crawley 37 F4 SE England, UK
Creegh 31 B5 W Ireland
Cremona 61 B3 N Italy
Cres 65 B2 *Island,* W Croatia
Crescent City 103 B2 California, USA
Crete 65 F7 *Island,* Greece
Créteil 55 D2 N France
Crete, Sea of 65 F6 *Sea,* Greece, Aegean Sea
Creuse 55 C4 ~ C France
Crewe 35 C5 C England, UK
Criccieth 39 C2 NW Wales, UK
Crickhowell 39 E6 C Wales, UK
Crieff 33 D5 C Scotland, UK
Crimea 67 F6 *Peninsula,* SE Ukraine
Cristóbal 107 H6 C Panama
Crna Reka 65 D4 ~ S FYR Macedonia
Croagh Patrick 31 B3 ▲ W Ireland
Croatia 65 B1 ◆ *Republic,* SE Europe
Croker Island 133 D1 *Island,* Northern Territory, N Australia
Cromarty 33 D3 N Scotland, UK
Cromer 37 H1 E England, UK
Cromwell 135 B7 South Island, NZ
Crooked Island 109 E2 *Island,* SE Bahamas
Crooked Island Passage 109 E2 *Channel,* SE Bahamas
Crookston 103 F1 Minnesota, USA
Croom 31 C5 SW Ireland
Crosby 35 C5 NW England, UK
Cross Fell 35 C3 ▲ N England, UK
Cross Hands 39 C6 S Wales, UK
Crossmaglen 31 E3 S Northern Ireland, UK
Crotone 61 E7 SW Italy
Croydon 37 F4 SE England, UK
Croydon 29 ◐ *London borough,* SE England, UK
Crozet Islands 15 *Island group,* French Southern and Antarctic Territories
Crusheen 31 C5 W Ireland
Crymych 39 B5 SW Wales, UK
Csorna 63 D7 NW Hungary
Csurgó 63 D8 SW Hungary
Cuando 128 C4 ~ S Africa
Cuango 128 B3 ~ Angola/Dem. Rep. Congo
Cuanza 128 B3 ~ C Angola
Cuauhtémoc 105 C2 N Mexico
Cuautla 105 F5 S Mexico
Cuba 109 D3 ◆ *Republic,* W West Indies
Cubal 128 B4 W Angola
Cubango 128 B4 SW Angola
Cubango 128 B4 ~ S Africa
Cúcuta 115 C2 N Colombia
Cuddapah 89 E6 S India
Cudjoehead 40 NW Montserrat
Cuenca 115 B4 S Ecuador
Cuenca 57 E3 C Spain
Cuernavaca 105 F5 S Mexico
Cuiabá 115 E6 SW Brazil
Cuijck 50 E5 SE Netherlands
Cuito 128 C4 ~ SE Angola
Culiacán 105 C3 C Mexico
Cullera 57 F4 E Spain
Cullybackey 31 E2 NE Northern Ireland, UK
Cumberland, Lake 101 E4 ▣ Kentucky, USA
Cumberland Sound 97 J3 *Inlet,* Baffin Island, Nunavut, NE Canada
Cumbernauld 33 D5 S Scotland, UK
Cumbria 29 ◐ *County,* NW England, UK
Cumbrian Mountains 35 C3 ▲ NW England, UK
Cumnock 33 D6 W Scotland, UK
Cumpas 105 C2 NW Mexico
Cunene 128 B4 ~ Angola/Namibia
Cuneo 61 A3 NW Italy
Cunnamulla 133 G4 Queensland, E Australia
Curaçao 109 H7 *Island,* Netherlands Antilles
Curicó 117 A6 C Chile
Curitiba 115 F8 S Brazil
Curtis Island 133 H4 *Island,* Queensland, SE Australia
Cusco 115 C6 C Peru
Cushcamcarragh 31 B3 ▲ NW Ireland
Cushendall 31 E1 N Northern Ireland, UK
Cusset 55 D4 C France
Cuttack 89 F4 E India
Cuxhaven 59 B2 NW Germany
Cwmbran 39 F6 S Wales, UK
Cyclades 65 F6 *Island group,* SE Greece
Cynwyl Elfed 39 C6 S Wales, UK
Cyprus 70 C5 ◆ *Republic,* E Mediterranean Sea
Czech Republic 63 B6 ◆ *Republic,* C Europe
Częstochowa 63 E5 S Poland
Człuchów 63 D2 NW Poland

D

Dąbrowa Tarnowska 63 F5 SE Poland
Dagana 124 A3 N Senegal
Dagda 49 F6 SE Latvia
Dagupan 91 F3 N Philippines
Dahm, Ramlat 81 C6 *Desert,* NW Yemen
Daimiel 57 D4 C Spain
Dakar 124 A3 ● W Senegal
Dakoro 124 E3 S Niger
Dalaman 79 A5 SW Turkey
Dalandzadgad 87 E2 S Mongolia
Da Lat 91 C4 S Vietnam
Dalby 133 H4 Queensland, E Australia
Dale 39 A6 SW Wales, UK
Dali 87 D5 SW China
Dalian 87 G3 NE China
Dalkeith 33 E5 SE Scotland, UK
Dallas 103 G4 Texas, USA
Dalmatia 65 B2 *Cultural region,* S Croatia
Daly Waters 133 E2 Northern Territory, N Australia
Daman 89 C4 W India
Damara 124 H5 S CAR
Damascus 81 A2 ● SW Syria
Damavand, Qolleh-ye 81 D2 ▲ N Iran
Dampier 133 B3 Western Australia
Dampier, Selat 91 G6 *Strait,* E Indonesia
Damqawt 81 E6 E Yemen
Damxung 87 C4 W China
Danakil Desert 127 E3 *Desert,* E Africa
Danané 124 C5 W Ivory Coast
Da Nang 91 C3 C Vietnam
Dandong 87 G3 NE China
Daneborg 139 B6 N Greenland
Danger Island 40 *Island,* W British Indian Ocean Territory
Danghara 83 F4 SW Tajikistan
Dangriga 107 C2 E Belize
Danlí 107 D3 S Honduras
Dannenberg 59 C3 N Germany
Dannevirke 135 D4 North Island, NZ
Danube 44 ~ C Europe
Danubian Plain 65 E2 *Plain,* N Bulgaria
Danzhou 87 F6 S China
Danzig, Gulf of 63 D1 *Gulf,* N Poland
Dardanelles 79 A3 *Strait,* Sea of Marmara/Mediterranean Sea
Dar es Salaam 127 D6 E Tanzania
Darfield 135 C6 South Island, NZ
Darfur 127 B3 *Cultural region,* W Sudan
Darhan 87 E2 N Mongolia
Darien, Gulf of 115 B2 *Gulf,* S Caribbean Sea
Darién, Serranía del 107 I6 ▲ Colombia/Panama
Darjiling 89 G3 NE India
Darling River 133 F5 ~ NSW, SE Australia
Darlington 35 D3 N England, UK
Darlington 28 ◐ *Unitary auth.,* N England, UK
Darmstadt 59 B5 SW Germany
Darnah 122 H2 NE Libya
Darnley, Cape 138 E4 *Headland,* Antarctica
Daroca 57 E3 NE Spain
Daroot-Korgon 83 G3 SW Kyrgyzstan
Dart 37 C5 ~ SW England, UK
Dartmoor 37 B5 *Moorland,* SW England, UK
Dartmouth 99 G5 Nova Scotia, SE Canada
Dartmouth 37 C5 SW England, UK
Daru 137 A3 SW PNG
Darvishan 83 E6 S Afghanistan
Darwaza 83 C3 C Turkmenistan
Darwin 133 D1 Northern Territory, N Australia
Darwin 40 Falkland Islands
Darwin, Isla 115 A6 *Island,* Galapagos Islands, Ecuador
Daşogz 83 D2 N Turkmenistan
Datong 87 F3 C China
Daugavpils 49 F7 SE Latvia
Dauphiné 55 E6 *Cultural region,* E France
Davangere 89 D6 W India
Davao 91 F5 Mindanao, S Philippines
Davao Gulf 91 G5 *Gulf,* S Philippines
Davenport 103 H2 Iowa, USA
Daventry 37 E2 C England, UK
David 107 F7 W Panama
Davis 138 E4 *Australian research station,* Antarctica
Davis Sea 138 E4 *Sea,* Antarctica
Davis Strait 97 J2 *Strait,* Baffin Bay/Labrador Sea
Dawlish 37 C5 SW England, UK
Dawros Head 31 C2 *Headland,* N Ireland
Dax 55 B6 SW France
Dayton 101 E3 Ohio, USA
Daytona Beach 101 E6 Florida, USA
De Aar 128 C7 C South Africa
Dead Sea 81 H6 *Salt lake,* Israel/Jordan
Deal 37 H4 SE England, UK
Dean, Forest of 37 D3 *Forest,* C England, UK
Deán Funes 117 B5 C Argentina
Death Valley 103 C4 *Valley,* California, USA
De Bilt 50 D4 C Netherlands
Debrecen 63 F7 E Hungary
Decatur 101 D3 Illinois, USA
Deccan 89 D5 *Plateau,* C India
Děčín 63 B5 NW Czech Republic
Dedemsvaart 50 E3 E Netherlands
Dee 39 F2 ~ England/Wales, UK
Dee 33 D7 ~ S Scotland, UK
Dee 33 E4 ~ NE Scotland, UK
Deering 97 D3 Alaska, USA
Deggendorf 59 D6 SE Germany
Deh Shu 83 D6 S Afghanistan
Deinze 50 B6 NW Belgium
Dékoa 124 H5 C CAR
Delaram 83 E5 SW Afghanistan
Delaware 101 G4 ◐ *State,* NE USA
Delft 50 C4 W Netherlands
Delfzijl 50 F2 NE Netherlands
Delgo 127 C1 N Sudan
Delhi 89 D3 N India
Delicias 105 D2 N Mexico
Delmenhorst 59 B3 NW Germany
Del Norte 105 C2 California, USA
Demba 128 C2 C Dem. Rep. Congo
Dembia 124 I5 SE CAR
Demchok 89 E2 *Disputed region,* China/India
Demmin 59 D2 NE Germany
Demqog 87 A4 *Disputed region,* China/India
Denali *see* McKinley, Mount
Denbigh 39 E2 NE Wales, UK
Denbighshire 29 ◐ *Unitary auth.,* N Wales, UK
Dender 50 B7 ~ W Belgium
Denekamp 50 F3 E Netherlands
Den Ham 50 F3 E Netherlands
Denham 133 A4 Western Australia
Den Helder 50 C2 NW Netherlands
Dénia 57 F4 E Spain
Deniliquin 133 F6 NSW, SE Australia
Denizli 79 B4 SW Turkey
Denmark 49 B7 ◆ *Monarchy,* N Europe
Denov 83 F3 S Uzbekistan
Denpasar 91 E8 Bali, C Indonesia
Denton 103 G4 Texas, USA
D'Entrecasteaux Islands 137 C3 *Island group,* SE PNG
Denver 103 E3 Colorado, USA
Dera Ghazi Khan 89 C2 C Pakistan
Đeravica 65 D3 ▲ S Serbia and Montenegro (Yugoslavia)
Derbent 69 B9 SW Russ. Fed.
Derby 133 C2 Western Australia
Derby 35 E6 C England, UK
Derby 29 ◐ *Unitary auth.,* C England, UK
Derbyshire 29 ◐ *County,* C England, UK
Derg 31 D2 ~ Ireland/Northern Ireland, UK
Derg, Lough 31 C5 ◎ W Ireland
Déroute, Passage de la 37 G5 *Strait,* Channel Islands/France
Derreendarragh 31 B6 SW Ireland
Derwent 35 E3 ~ N England, UK
Dese 127 E3 N Ethiopia
Deseado, Río 117 B8 ~ S Argentina
Des Moines 103 G2 Iowa, USA
Desna 69 A6 ~ Russian Federation/Ukraine
Dessau 59 D4 E Germany
Detroit 101 E3 Michigan, USA
Deurne 50 E5 SE Netherlands
Deva 67 B6 W Romania
Deventer 50 E4 E Netherlands
Deveron 33 E3 ~ NE Scotland, UK
Devil's Bridge 39 D4 W Wales, UK
Devizes 37 E4 S England, UK
Devon 29 ◐ *County,* SW England, UK
Devon Island 97 H2 *Island,* Parry Islands, Nunavut, NE Canada
Devonport 133 F7 Tasmania, SE Australia
Devrek 79 C2 N Turkey
Dewsbury 35 D4 N England, UK
Dezful 81 D2 SW Iran
Dezhou 87 G3 E China
Değirmenlik *see* Kythrea
Dhaka 89 G4 ● C Bangladesh
Dhanbad 89 F4 NE India
Dhekelia Sovereign Base Area 70 D6 *Air base,* SE Cyprus
Dhuusa Marreeb 127 F4 C Somalia
Diamantina, Chapada 115 H5 ▲ E Brazil
Diana's Peak 40 ▲ C Saint Helena
Dibrugarh 89 H3 NE India
Dickinson 103 E1 North Dakota, USA
Didcot 37 E3 C England, UK
Didymóteicho 65 F3 NE Greece
Diego Garcia 40 *Island,* S British Indian Ocean Territory
Diekirch 50 E8 C Luxembourg
Diepenbeek 50 D6 NE Belgium
Diepholz 59 B3 NW Germany
Dieppe 55 C1 N France
Dieren 50 E4 E Netherlands
Differdange 50 E9 SW Luxembourg
Digne 55 E6 SE France
Digoin 55 E4 C France
Digul, Sungai 91 I7 ~ E Indonesia
Dijon 55 E4 C France
Dikhil 127 E3 SW Djibouti
Dikson 76 E2 N Russ. Fed.
Díkti 65 F7 ▲ Crete, Greece
Dili 91 F8 ● N East Timor
Dilia 124 G3 ~ SE Niger
Dilling 127 C3 C Sudan
Dilolo 128 C3 S Dem. Rep. Congo
Dimashq *see* Damascus
Dimitrovgrad 65 F3 S Bulgaria
Dimitrovgrad 69 C6 W Russ. Fed.
Dimovo 65 E2 NW Bulgaria
Dinajpur 89 G3 NW Bangladesh
Dinan 55 B2 NW France
Dinant 50 D8 S Belgium
Dinar 79 B4 SW Turkey
Dinaric Alps 65 C2 ▲ Bosnia and Herzegovina/Croatia
Dindigul 89 D7 SE India
Dingle 31 A6 SW Ireland
Dingle Bay 31 A6 *Bay,* SW Ireland
Dinguiraye 124 B4 N Guinea
Dingwall 33 D3 N Scotland, UK
Diourbel 124 A3 W Senegal
Dire Dawa 127 E3 E Ethiopia
Dirk Hartog Island 133 A4 *Island,* Western Australia
Disappointment, Lake 133 B3 *Salt lake,* Western Australia
Diss 37 H2 E England, UK
Divinópolis 115 G7 SE Brazil
Divo 124 C5 S Ivory Coast
Diyarbakır 79 F4 SE Turkey
Djambala 128 B2 C Congo
Djanet 122 E4 SE Algeria
Djelfa 122 E1 N Algeria
Djéma 124 I5 E CAR
Djerba 122 F2 *Island,* E Tunisia
Djérem 124 G5 ~ C Cameroon
Djibouti 127 E3 ● E Djibouti
Djibouti 127 E3 ◆ *Republic,* E Africa
Djourab, Erg du 124 H3 *Dunes,* N Chad
Djúpivogur 49 B1 SE Iceland
Dnieper 44 ~ E Europe
Dnieper Lowland 67 E4 *Lowlands,* Belarus/Ukraine
Dniester 67 D5 ~ Moldova/Ukraine
Dniprodzerzhyns'k 67 F5 E Ukraine
Dniprodzerzhyns'ke Vodoskhovyshche 67 F5 ▣ C Ukraine
Dnipropetrovs'k 67 F5 E Ukraine
Dniprorudne 67 F5 SE Ukraine
Doba 124 G4 S Chad
Döbeln 59 D4 E Germany
Doberai Peninsula 91 G7 *Peninsula,* E Indonesia
Dobre Miasto 63 E2 N Poland
Dobrich 65 G2 NE Bulgaria
Dodecanese 65 F6 *Island group,* SE Greece
Dodekánisa *see* Dodecanese
Dodge City 103 F3 Kansas, USA
Dodman Point 37 B6 *Headland,* SW England, UK
Dodoma 127 D6 ● C Tanzania
Dogai Coring 87 C4 ◎ W China
Dogo 85 D6 *Island,* Oki-shoto, SW Japan
Dogondoutchi 124 E3 SW Niger
Doğubayazıt 79 H3 E Turkey
Doğu Karadeniz Dağları 79 F2 ▲ NE Turkey
Doha 81 D4 ● C Qatar
Dokkum 50 E2 N Netherlands
Dôle 55 E4 E France
Dolgarrog 39 D2 N Wales, UK
Dolgellau 39 D3 NW Wales, UK
Dolisie 128 B2 S Congo
Dolomites 61 C2 ▲ Italy
Dolores 117 C6 E Argentina
Dolores 107 B2 N Guatemala
Dolores 117 C5 SW Uruguay
Dolores Hidalgo 105 E4 C Mexico
Dolphin, Cape 40 *Headland,* Falkland Islands
Dolwyddelan 39 D2 N Wales, UK
Dombås 49 B4 S Norway
Domeyko 117 A4 N Chile
Dominica 109 K5 ◆ *Republic,* E West Indies
Dominican Republic 109 F5 ◆ *Republic,* C West Indies
Don 69 B7 ~ SW Russ. Fed.
Don 35 E5 ~ N England, UK
Don 33 F4 ~ NE Scotland, UK
Donaghadee 31 F2 E Northern Ireland, UK
Donau *see* Danube
Donauwörth 59 C6 S Germany
Donawitz 59 E7 SE Austria
Donbass 67 G5 *Industrial region,* Russ. Fed./Ukraine
Don Benito 57 C4 W Spain
Doncaster 35 E5 N England, UK
Doncaster 29 ◐ *Unitary auth.,* N England, UK
Dondo 128 B3 NW Angola
Donegal 31 D2 NW Ireland
Donegal 29 ◐ *County,* NW Ireland
Donegal Bay 31 C2 *Bay,* NW Ireland
Donets 69 A7 ~ Russ. Fed./Ukraine
Donets'k 67 G5 E Ukraine
Dongfang 87 F6 S China
Dongola 127 C1 N Sudan
Dongou 128 B1 NE Congo
Dongting Hu 87 F5 ◎ S China
Donostia-San Sebastián 57 E1 N Spain
Doolow 127 E4 SE Ethiopia
Dorchester 37 D5 S England, UK
Dordogne 55 C5 *Cultural region,* SW France
Dordogne 55 C5 ~ W France
Dordrecht 50 C5 SW Netherlands
Dornoch 33 D3 N Scotland, UK
Dorotea 49 C3 N Sweden
Dorre Island 133 A4 *Island,* W Australia
Dorset 29 ◐ *County,* S England, UK
Dortmund 59 B4 W Germany
Dos Hermanas 57 C5 S Spain
Dotnuva 49 E7 C Lithuania
Douai 55 D1 N France
Douala 124 F5 W Cameroon
Douglas 40 Falkland Islands
Douglas 31 C6 S Ireland
Douglas 35 A4 ○ E Isle of Man
Douro 57 B3 ~ Portugal/Spain
Dover 37 H4 SE England, UK
Dover 101 G4 Delaware, USA
Dover, Strait of 37 H5 *Strait,* France/UK
Dovrefjell 49 B4 *Plateau,* S Norway
Down 29 ◐ *District,* SE Northern Ireland, UK
Downham Market 37 G2 E England, UK
Downpatrick 31 F3 SE Northern Ireland, UK
Dozen 85 D6 *Island,* Oki-shoto, SW Japan
Drachten 50 E2 N Netherlands
Dra, Hamada du 122 C2 *Plateau,* W Algeria
Drahichyn 67 C3 SW Belarus
Drakensberg 128 D7 ▲ Lesotho/South Africa
Drake Passage 117 B9 *Passage,* Atlantic Ocean/Pacific Ocean
Dráma 65 E4 NE Greece
Drammen 49 B5 S Norway
Drau *see* Drava
Drava 63 C9 ~ C Europe
Drave *see* Drava
Drawsko Pomorskie 63 C2 NW Poland
Dresden 59 D5 E Germany
Driffield 35 F4 E England, UK
Drina 65 D2 ~ Bosnia and Herzegovina/Serbia and Montenegro (Yugoslavia)
Drinit, Lumi i 65 D3 ~ NW Albania
Drobeta-Turnu Severin 67 B7 SW Romania
Drogheda 31 E4 NE Ireland
Droichead Nua 31 E4 E Ireland
Droitwich 35 D7 W England, UK

CAR Central African Republic **FYR** Former Yugoslavian Rebublic **NSW** New South Wales **NZ** New Zealand **PNG** Papua New Guinea **Russ. Fed.** Russian Federation **UAE** United Arab Emirates **UK** United Kingdom **USA** United States of America

Drôme 55 E6 *Cultural region,* SE France
Dronfield 35 E5 C England, UK
Dronning Maud Land 138 C3 *Physical region,* Antarctica
Drumahoe 31 D2 NW Northern Ireland, UK
Drumbilla 31 E3 NE Ireland
Drumcliff 31 C3 N Ireland
Drummondville 99 E5 Québec, SE Canada
Druridge Bay 35 D2 *Bay,* N England, UK
Dryden 99 A4 Ontario, C Canada
Drygarn Fawr 39 D5 ▲ E Wales, UK
Drysa 67 D1 ≈ N Belarus
Duarte, Pico 109 G4 ▲ C Dominican Republic
Dubai 81 E4 NE UAE
Dubawnt 97 G5 ≈ NW Terr., NW Canada
Dubbo 133 G5 NSW, SE Australia
Dublin 31 E3 ● E Ireland
Dublin 29 ◐ *County,* E Ireland
Dubno 67 C4 NW Ukraine
Dubrovnik 65 C3 SE Croatia
Dubuque 103 G2 Iowa, USA
Dudelange 50 E9 S Luxembourg
Dudley 35 D6 C England, UK
Dudley 29 ◐ *Unitary auth.,* C England, UK
Duero 57 D2 ≈ Portugal/Spain
Duffel 50 C6 C Belgium
Duff Islands 137 G3 *Island group,* E Solomon Islands
Dugi Otok 65 B2 *Island,* W Croatia
Duisburg 59 A4 W Germany
Duiven 50 E4 E Netherlands
Duk Faiwil 127 C4 SE Sudan
Dulan 87 D4 C China
Dulce, Golfo 107 F7 *Gulf,* S Costa Rica
Dülmen 59 B4 W Germany
Dulovo 65 F2 NE Bulgaria
Duluth 103 G1 Minnesota, USA
Duma 81 A2 SW Syria
Dumbarton 33 D5 W Scotland, UK
Dumfries 33 E7 S Scotland, UK
Dumfries and Galloway 29 ◐ *Unitary auth.,* SW Scotland, UK
Dumont d'Urville 138 E6 *French research station,* Antarctica
Dumyât 122 I2 N Egypt
Duna *see* Danube
Dunaj *see* Danube
Dunany Point 31 E3 *Headland,* NE Ireland
Dunărea *see* Danube
Dunaújváros 63 E8 C Hungary
Dunav *see* Danube
Duncansby Head 33 E2 *Headland,* N Scotland, UK
Dundalk 31 E3 NE Ireland
Dundee 128 D6 E South Africa
Dundee 33 E5 E Scotland, UK
Dundee 28 ◐ *Unitary auth.,* E Scotland, UK
Dundrum 31 C5 S Ireland
Dundrum Bay 31 F3 *Inlet,* NW Irish Sea
Dunedin 135 B7 South Island, NZ
Dunfanaghy 31 D1 NW Ireland
Dunfermline 33 E5 C Scotland, UK
Dungannon 31 E2 Dungannon, C Northern Ireland, UK
Dungannon 29 ◐ *District,* C Northern Ireland, UK
Dungarvan 31 D6 S Ireland
Dungeness 37 H4 *Headland,* SE England, UK
Dungiven 31 E2 N Northern Ireland, UK
Dunglow 31 C2 NW Ireland
Dungu 128 D1 NE Dem. Rep. Congo
Dunkerque 55 D1 N France
Dunkery Beacon 37 B4 ▲ SW England, UK
Dún Laoghaire 31 E4 E Ireland
Dunleer 31 E3 NE Ireland
Dunmore 31 C4 W Ireland
Dunmurry 31 F2 E Northern Ireland, UK
Dunnet Head 33 D2 *Headland,* N Scotland, UK
Duns 33 F6 SE Scotland, UK
Dunshaughlin 31 E4 E Ireland
Dunstable 37 F3 E England, UK
Duqm 81 F5 E Oman
Durance 55 E6 ≈ SE France
Durango 105 D4 W Mexico
Durban 128 D7 E South Africa
Durg 89 E4 C India
Durham 35 D2 N England, UK
Durham 101 F4 North Carolina, USA
Durham 29 ◐ *County,* N England, UK
Durness 33 D2 N Scotland, UK
Durrës 65 C4 W Albania
Durrow 31 D5 C Ireland
Dursey Head 31 A7 *Headland,* S Ireland
D'Urville Island 135 C4 *Island,* C NZ
Dushanbe 83 F3 ● W Tajikistan
Düsseldorf 59 A4 W Germany
Dusti 83 F4 SW Tajikistan
Dutch Harbor 97 B4 Unalaska Island, Alaska, USA
Dyfi 39 D4 ≈ W Wales, UK
Dzerzhinsk 69 B5 W Russ. Fed.
Dzhalal-Abad 83 G3 W Kyrgyzstan
Dzhankoy 67 F6 S Ukraine
Dzhelandy 83 G4 SE Tajikistan
Dzhergalan 83 I2 NE Kyrgyzstan
Dzhugdzhur, Khrebet 76 H4 ▲▲ E Russ. Fed.
Dzhusaly 76 B5 SW Kazakhstan
Działdowo 63 E3 C Poland

E

Eagle Islands 40 *Island group,* W British Indian Ocean Territory
Ealing 29 ◐ *London borough,* SE England, UK
Earn 33 D5 ≈ N Scotland, UK
Easky 31 C3 N Ireland
East Anglia 37 G2 *Physical region,* E England, UK
East Ayrshire 28 ◐ *Unitary auth.,* SW Scotland, UK
Eastbourne 37 G5 SE England, UK
East Caicos 40 *Island,* E Turks and Caicos Islands
East Cape 135 E3 *Headland,* North Island, NZ
East China Sea 72 *Sea,* W Pacific Ocean
East Dereham 37 G1 E England, UK
East Dunbartonshire 28 ◐ *Unitary auth.,* C Scotland, UK
East End 40 W Cayman Islands
Easter Island 137 D5 *Island,* Chile, E Pacific Ocean
Eastern Ghats 89 E5 ▲▲ SE India
Eastern Sayans 76 E5 ▲▲ Mongolia/Russ. Fed.
East Falkland 40 *Island,* E Falkland Islands
East Frisian Islands 59 A2 *Island group,* NW Germany
East Grinstead 37 G4 SE England, UK
East Kilbride 33 D6 S Scotland, UK
East Korea Bay 85 B5 *Bay,* E North Korea
Eastleigh 37 E4 S England, UK
East London 128 D7 S South Africa
East Lothian 28 *Cultural region* SE Scotland, UK
Eastmain 99 D4 ≈ Québec, C Canada
East Novaya Zemlya Trough 139 E5 *Undersea feature,* W Kara Sea
East Pacific Rise 14 *Undersea feature,* E Pacific Ocean
East Renfrewshire 28 ◐ *Unitary auth.,* C Scotland, UK
East Riding of Yorkshire 29 ◐ *Unitary auth.,* N England, UK
East Saint Louis 101 C4 Illinois, USA
East Siberian Sea 139 C2 *Sea,* Arctic Ocean
East Sussex 29 ◐ *County,* SE England, UK
East Timor 91 G8 ◆ *Country,* SE Asia
Eau Claire 101 C2 Wisconsin, USA
Ebbw Vale 39 E6 SE Wales, UK
Ebensee 59 E7 N Austria
Eberswalde-Finow 59 D3 E Germany
Ebetsu 85 F2 NE Japan
Ebolowa 124 F6 S Cameroon
Ebro 57 E2 ≈ NE Spain
Echo Bay 97 G4 NW Terr., NW Canada
Echt 50 E6 SE Netherlands
Ecija 57 C5 SW Spain
Ecuador 115 B3 ◆ *Republic,* NW South America
Eday 33 E1 *Island,* NE Scotland, UK
Ed Da'ein 127 B3 W Sudan
Ed Damazin 127 C3 E Sudan
Ed Damer 127 C2 NE Sudan
Ed Debba 127 C2 N Sudan
Eddrachillis Bay 33 C2 *Bay,* NW Scotland, UK
Eddystone Rocks 37 B6 *Rocks,* SW England, UK
Ede 50 E4 C Netherlands
Ede 124 E5 SW Nigeria
Eden 35 C2 ≈ NW England, UK
Edgeworthstown 31 D4 C Ireland
Edinburgh 40 ○ NW Tristan da Cunha
Edinburgh 33 E5 *National region capital,* S Scotland, UK
Edinburgh 28 ◐ *Unitary auth.,* E Scotland, UK
Edirne 79 A2 NW Turkey
Edmonton 97 G6 Alberta, SW Canada
Edmundston 99 F5 New Brunswick, SE Canada
Edolo 61 C2 N Italy
Edremit 79 A3 NW Turkey
Edward, Lake 128 D2 ◎ Dem. Rep. Congo/Uganda
Edwards Plateau 103 F5 *Plain,* Texas, USA
Edzo 97 F5 NW Terr., NW Canada
Eeklo 50 B6 NW Belgium
Eemshaven 50 F1 NE Netherlands
Eersel 50 D5 S Netherlands
Efate 137 H5 *Island,* C Vanuatu
Efstratios, Agios 65 F5 *Island,* Vóreion Aigaíon, E Greece
Egadi Island 61 B8 *Island group,* S Italy
Eger 63 F7 NE Hungary
Éghezée 50 D7 C Belgium
Eglwyswrw 39 B5 SW Wales, UK
Egmont, Cape 135 C4 *Headland,* North Island, NZ
Egmont, Mount *see* Taranaki, Mount
Egmont Islands 40 *Island group,* W British Indian Ocean Territory
Egypt 122 I4 ◆ *Republic,* NE Africa
Eibar 57 E1 N Spain
Eibergen 50 F4 E Netherlands
Eidfjord 49 A5 S Norway
Eifel 59 A5 *Plateau,* W Germany
Eiger 59 B8 ▲ C Switzerland
Eigg 33 B4 *Island,* W Scotland, UK
Eight Degree Channel 89 C8 *Channel,* India/Maldives
Eighty Mile Beach 133 B3 *Beach,* Western Australia
Eijsden 50 E7 SE Netherlands
Eilean Siar 28 ◐ *Unitary auth.,* NW Scotland, UK
Eindhoven 50 D5 S Netherlands
Eisenhüttenstadt 59 E4 E Germany
Eisenstadt 59 F7 E Austria
Eisleben 59 C4 C Germany
Eivissa *see* Ibiza
Ejea de los Caballeros 57 E2 NE Spain
Ejin Qi 87 E3 N China
El 'Alamein 122 I2 N Egypt
Elat 81 G7 S Israel
El'Atrun 127 B2 NW Sudan
Elâzığ 79 F3 E Turkey
Elba 61 B4 *Island,* Archipelago Toscano, C Italy
Elbe 59 C3 ≈ Czech Republic/Germany
Elbert, Mount 103 D3 ▲ Colorado, USA
Elbląg 63 E2 N Poland
El'brus 69 A8 ▲ SW Russ. Fed.
El Burgo de Osma 57 E2 C Spain
Elburz Mountains 81 D2 ▲▲ N Iran
El Calafate 117 A8 S Argentina
Elche 57 F5 E Spain
El Chichónal, Volcán 105 G5 ※ SE Mexico
Elda 57 F4 E Spain
Eldorado 117 D4 NE Argentina
El Dorado 105 C4 C Mexico
Eldoret 127 D5 W Kenya
Elektrostal' 69 B5 W Russ. Fed.
Elemi Triangle 127 C4 *Disputed region,* Kenya/Sudan
Eleuthera Island 109 D1 *Island,* N Bahamas
El Fasher 127 B3 W Sudan
El Geneina 127 A3 W Sudan
Elgin 33 E3 NE Scotland, UK
Elgin 101 D3 Illinois, USA
El Giza 122 I2 N Egypt
El Goléa 122 D2 C Algeria
El Hank 124 C1 *Cliff,* N Mauritania
Elista 69 B8 SW Russ. Fed.
Elizabeth 133 E6 S Australia
Ełk 63 F2 NE Poland
El Kharga 122 I3 C Egypt
Ellef Ringnes Island 97 G2 *Island,* Nunavut, N Canada
Ellen, Mount 103 D3 ▲ Utah, USA
Ellesmere Island 97 H1 *Island,* Queen Elizabeth Islands, Nunavut, N Canada
Ellesmere, Lake 135 C6 ◎ South Island, NZ
Ellesmere Port 35 C5 C England, UK
Elliston 133 E5 S Australia
Ellon 33 F3 NE Scotland, UK
Ellsworth Land 138 A5 *Physical region,* Antarctica
El Mahbas 122 B3 SW Western Sahara
El Minya 122 I3 C Egypt
El Mreyyé 124 C2 *Desert,* E Mauritania
Elmshorn 59 C2 N Germany
El Muglad 127 B3 C Sudan
El Obeid 127 C3 C Sudan
El Oued 122 E2 NE Algeria
El Paso 103 E5 Texas, USA
El Porvenir 107 H6 N Panama
El Progreso 107 C3 NW Honduras
El Puerto de Santa María 57 C6 S Spain
El Rama 107 E4 SE Nicaragua
El Real 107 I6 SE Panama
El Salvador 107 B4 ◆ *Republic,* Central America
El Sáuz 105 C2 N Mexico
Elst 50 E4 E Netherlands
El Sueco 105 C2 N Mexico
El Tigre 115 D2 W Colombia
Elvas 57 B4 C Portugal
El Vendrell 57 G3 NE Spain
Elx *see* Elche
Ely 37 G2 E England, UK
Ely 39 E7 S Wales, UK
Ely 39 E7 ≈ SE Wales, UK
Emba 76 B5 W Kazakhstan
Emden 59 B3 NW Germany
Emerald 133 G4 Queensland, E Australia
Emeti 137 A2 SW PNG
Emi Koussi 124 H2 ▲ N Chad
Emmeloord 50 E3 N Netherlands
Emmen 50 F3 NE Netherlands
Emmendingen 59 B7 SW Germany
Emory Peak 103 E5 ▲ Texas, USA
Empalme 105 B3 NW Mexico
Emperor Seamounts 15 *Undersea feature,* NW Pacific Ocean
Ems 59 B3 ≈ NW Germany
Enard Bay 33 C2 *Bay,* NW Scotland, UK
Encarnación 117 C4 S Paraguay
Encs 63 F6 NE Hungary
Endeavour Strait 133 F1 *Strait,* Queensland, NE Australia
Enderby Land 138 D3 *Physical region,* Antarctica
Enfield 29 ◐ *London borough,* SE England, UK
Enghien 50 C7 SW Belgium
England 29 *National region,* England, UK
English Channel 53 E8 *Channel,* NW Europe
Enguri 79 G1 ≈ NW Georgia
Enid 103 F4 Oklahoma, USA
Ennedi 124 H2 *Plateau,* E Chad
Ennis 31 C5 W Ireland
Enniscorthy 31 E5 SE Ireland
Enniskillen 31 D3 SW Northern Ireland, UK
Ennistimon 31 B5 W Ireland
Enns 59 E7 ≈ C Austria
Enschede 50 F4 E Netherlands
Ensenada 105 A1 NW Mexico
Entebbe 127 C5 S Uganda
Entroncamento 57 B4 C Portugal
Enugu 124 F5 S Nigeria
Epéna 128 B1 NE Congo
Epi 137 H5 *Island,* C Vanuatu
Épinal 55 F3 NE France
Epping 37 G3 SE England, UK
Equatorial Guinea 124 F6 ◆ *Republic,* C Africa
Erciş 79 G3 E Turkey
Erdenet 87 E2 N Mongolia
Erdi 124 H2 *Plateau,* NE Chad
Erebus, Mount 138 C6 ※ Ross Island, Antarctica
Ereğli 79 D4 S Turkey
Erenhot 87 F2 NE China
Erfurt 59 C5 C Germany
Ergene Nehri 79 A2 ≈ NW Turkey
Ergun He *see* Argun
Eriboll, Loch 33 D2 *Inlet,* NW Scotland, UK
Ericht, Loch 33 D4 ◎ C Scotland, UK
Erie 101 F3 Pennsylvania, USA
Erie, Lake 101 E3 ◎ Canada/USA
Eriskay 33 A4 *Island,* NW Scotland, UK
Eritrea 127 D2 ◆ *Transitional government,* E Africa
Erlangen 59 C6 S Germany
Ermelo 50 E3 C Netherlands
Ermióni 65 E6 S Greece
Ernakulam 89 D7 SW India
Erne 31 D3 ≈ Ireland/Northern Ireland, UK
Erode 89 D7 SE India
Erquelinnes 50 C7 S Belgium
Er-Rachidia 122 C2 E Morocco
Er Rahad 127 C3 C Sudan
Erriga Mountain 31 C1 ▲ N Ireland
Erris Head 31 A3 *Headland,* W Ireland
Erromango 137 G5 *Island,* S Vanuatu
Erzgebirge *see* Ore Mountains
Erzincan 79 F3 E Turkey
Erzurum 79 G3 NE Turkey
Esbjerg 49 A7 W Denmark
Esch-sur-Alzette 50 E9 S Luxembourg
Escuinapa 105 D4 C Mexico
Escuintla 107 A3 S Guatemala
Escuintla 105 H6 SE Mexico
Esha Ness 33 A6 *Headland,* NE Scotland, UK
Eshkamesh 83 F4 NE Afghanistan
Esk 35 E3 ≈ N England, UK
Esk 33 E6 ≈ England/Scotland, UK
Eskişehir 79 B3 W Turkey
Esmeraldas 115 B3 N Ecuador
Esperance 133 C5 Western Australia
Esperanza 105 C3 NW Mexico
Esperanza 138 A5 *Argentinian research station,* Antarctica
Espírito Santo 115 G7 ◐ *State,* E Brazil
Espiritu Santo 137 G4 *Island,* W Vanuatu
Espoo 49 E5 S Finland
Esquel 117 A7 SW Argentina
Essaouira 122 B2 W Morocco
Essen 50 C5 N Belgium
Essen 59 A4 W Germany
Essex 29 ◐ *County,* E England, UK
Estacado, Llano 103 E4 *Plain,* SW USA
Estados, Isla de los 117 B9 *Island,* S Argentina
Estância 115 I5 E Brazil
Estelí 107 D4 NW Nicaragua
Estella-Lizarra 57 E2 N Spain
Estepona 57 C6 S Spain
Estevan 97 H7 Saskatchewan, S Canada
Estonia 49 F6 ◆ *Republic,* NE Europe
Estrela, Serra da 57 B3 ▲▲ C Portugal
Estremoz 57 B4 S Portugal
Esztergom 63 D7 N Hungary
Étalle 50 D9 SE Belgium
Etawah 89 E3 N India
Ethiopia 127 D4 ◆ *Republic,* E Africa
Ethiopian Highlands 127 D4 *Plateau,* N Ethiopia
Etna, Monte 61 D8 ※ Sicily, Italy
Etosha Pan 128 B5 *Salt lake,* N Namibia
Etrek 83 B3 ≈ Iran/Turkmenistan
Ettelbrück 50 E8 C Luxembourg
Euboea 65 E5 *Island,* C Greece
Eucla 133 D5 Western Australia
Euclid 101 E3 Ohio, USA
Eugene 103 B2 Oregon, USA
Eupen 50 E7 E Belgium
Euphrates 81 C3 ≈ SW Asia
Europa Point 40 *Headland,* S Gibraltar
Europe 44 *Continent*
Eutin 59 C2 N Germany
Evansville 101 D4 Indiana, USA
Everard, Lake 133 D5 *Salt lake,* S Australia
Everest, Mount 87 B5 ▲ China/Nepal
Everett 103 B1 Washington, USA
Everglades, The 101 E7 *Wetland,* SE USA
Evesham 35 D7 C England, UK
Evje 49 B6 S Norway
Évora 57 B4 C Portugal
Évreux 55 D2 N France
Évros 65 F4 ≈ SE Europe
Evvoia *see* Euboea
Exe 37 C4 ≈ SW England, UK
Exeter 37 C5 SW England, UK
Exmoor 37 C4 *Moorland,* SW England, UK
Exmouth 133 A3 Western Australia
Exmouth 37 C5 SW England, UK
Exmouth Gulf 133 A3 *Gulf,* Western Australia
Extremadura 57 C4 *Cultural region,* W Spain
Exuma Cays 109 D2 *Islets,* C Bahamas
Exuma Sound 109 D2 *Sound,* C Bahamas
Eyemouth 33 F6 SE Scotland, UK
Eye Peninsula 33 B2 *Peninsula,* NW Scotland, UK
Eyre Basin, Lake 133 E4 *Salt lake,* S Australia
Eyre Mountains 135 B7 ▲▲ South Island, NZ
Eyre North, Lake 133 E4 *Salt lake,* S Australia
Eyre Peninsula 133 E5 *Peninsula,* S Australia
Eyre South, Lake 133 E5 *Salt lake,* S Australia

F

Faaa 137 A6 W French Polynesia
Faadhippolhu Atoll 89 C8 Atoll, N Maldives
Fada 124 H2 E Chad
Fada-Ngourma 124 D4 E Burkina
Faenza 61 C3 N Italy
Fagamalo 137 A4 N Samoa
Fagne 50 C8 *Hill range,* S Belgium
Faguibine, Lac 124 C3 ◎ NW Mali
Fairbanks 97 D4 Alaska, USA
Fairbourne 39 C3 NW Wales, UK
Fair Isle 33 A7 *Island,* NE Scotland, UK
Fairlie 135 B6 South Island, NZ
Faisalabad 89 D2 NE Pakistan
Faizabad 89 E3 N India
Fakenham 37 G1 E England, UK
Fakfak 91 H7 E Indonesia
Falam 91 A2 W Burma
Falconara Marittima 61 D4 C Italy
Falealupo 137 A4 NW Samoa
Falkirk 33 D5 C Scotland, UK
Falkirk 28 ◐ *Unitary auth.,* C Scotland, UK
Falkland Islands 40 *UK* ◇ SW Atlantic Ocean
Falkland Sound 40 *Strait,* C Falkland Islands
Falmouth 37 A6 SW England, UK
Falster 49 B7 *Island,* SE Denmark
Falun 49 C5 C Sweden
Famagusta 70 D6 E Cyprus
Famagusta Bay 70 D6 *Bay,* E Cyprus
Famenne 50 D8 *Physical region,* SE Belgium
Fan Brycheiniog 39 D6 ▲ E Wales, UK
Fannich, Loch 33 C3 ◎ NW Scotland, UK
Fano 61 D3 C Italy
Farafangana 128 G6 SE Madagascar
Farah 83 D5 W Afghanistan
Farah Rud 83 D5 ≈ W Afghanistan
Faranah 124 B4 S Guinea
Farasan, Jaza'ir 81 B6 *Island group,* SW Saudi Arabia
Fareham 37 E5 S England, UK
Farewell, Cape 135 C4 *Headland,* South Island, NZ
Fargo 103 F1 North Dakota, USA
Farg'ona 83 G3 E Uzbekistan
Faridabad 89 D3 N India Asia
Farkhor 83 F4 SW Tajikistan
Farmington 103 D4 New Mexico, USA
Farnborough 37 F4 S England, UK
Farne Islands 35 D1 *Island group,* N England, UK
Farnham 37 F4 S England, UK
Faro 57 B5 S Portugal
Farquhar Group 128 H3 *Island group,* S Seychelles
Farranfore 31 B6 SW Ireland
Fastiv 67 D4 NW Ukraine
Fastnet Rock 31 B7 *Island,* SW Ireland
Fauske 49 C2 C Norway
Faversham 37 G4 SE England, UK
Faxaflói 49 A1 *Bay,* W Iceland
Faya 124 H2 N Chad
Fayaoué 137 G6 C New Caledonia
Fayetteville 101 F5 North Carolina, USA
Fdérik 124 B1 NW Mauritania
Feale 31 B6 ≈ SW Ireland
Fear, Cape 101 F5 *Headland,* Bald Head Island, North Carolina, USA
Fécamp 55 C1 N France
Fehérgyarmat 63 G7 E Hungary
Fehmarn 59 C2 *Island,* N Germany
Fehmarn Belt 59 C2 *Strait,* Denmark/Germany
Feijó 115 C5 W Brazil
Feilding 135 D4 North Island, NZ
Feira de Santana 115 H5 E Brazil
Felanitx 57 H4 Majorca, Spain
Felipe Carrillo Puerto 105 I4 SE Mexico
Felixstowe 37 H3 E England, UK
Femunden 49 B4 ◎ S Norway
Fenoarivo 128 G5 E Madagascar
Fens, The 37 G1 *Wetland,* E England, UK
Feodosiya 67 F6 S Ukraine
Ferbane 31 D4 C Ireland
Fergana Valley 83 G3 *Basin,* Tajikistan/Uzbekistan
Ferkessédougou 124 C4 N Ivory Coast
Fermanagh 29 ◐ *District,* SW Northern Ireland, UK
Fermo 61 D4 C Italy
Fermoy 31 C6 SW Ireland
Ferrara 61 C3 N Italy
Ferrol 57 B1 NW Spain
Ferwerd 50 E2 N Netherlands
Fethiye 79 B5 SW Turkey
Fetlar 33 B6 *Island,* NE Scotland, UK
Feyzabad 83 G4 NE Afghanistan
Fez 122 C1 N Morocco
Ffestiniog 39 D2 NW Wales, UK
Fianarantsoa 128 G5 C Madagascar
Fianga 124 G4 SW Chad
Fier 65 D4 SW Albania
Fife 28 ◐ *Unitary auth.,* E Scotland, UK
Figeac 55 D5 S France
Figueira da Foz 57 A3 W Portugal
Figueres 57 H2 E Spain
Figuig 122 D2 E Morocco
Fiji 137 I5 ◆ *Republic,* SW Pacific Ocean
Filadelfia 107 D6 W Costa Rica
Filey 35 F3 N England, UK
Filey Bay 35 F3 *Bay,* N England, UK
Filipstad 49 C5 C Sweden
Finale Ligure 61 B3 NW Italy
Findhorn 33 E3 ≈ N Scotland, UK
Finike 79 B5 SW Turkey
Finland 49 E4 ◆ *Republic,* N Europe
Finland, Gulf of 49 E5 *Gulf,* E Baltic Sea
Finnmarksvidda 49 D1 *Physical region,* N Norway
Finschhafen 137 C2 C PNG
Finsterwalde 59 D4 E Germany
Fiordland 135 A7 *Physical region,* South Island, NZ
Firenze *see* Florence
Fischbacher Alpen 59 F7 ▲▲ E Austria
Fish 128 C6 ≈ S Namibia
Fishguard 39 B5 SW Wales, UK
Fishguard Bay 39 A5 *Bay,* SW Wales, UK
Fisterra, Cabo 57 A1 *Headland,* NW Spain
Fitful Head 33 A7 *Headland,* NE Scotland, UK
Fito 137 B5 ▲ C Samoa
Fitzroy Crossing 133 C2 Western Australia
Fitzroy River 133 C2 ≈ Western Australia
Flamborough Head 35 F4 *Headland,* E England, UK
Fläming 63 A3 *Hill range,* NE Germany
Flanders 50 A6 *Cultural region,* Belgium/France
Flannan Isles 33 A2 *Island group,* NW Scotland, UK
Flathead Lake 103 D1 ◎ Montana, USA
Flattery, Cape 103 B1 *Headland,* Washington, USA
Flatts Village 40 C Bermuda
Fleetwood 35 C4 NW England, UK
Flensburg 59 C2 N Germany
Flinders Island 133 G7 *Island,* Tasmania, SE Australia
Flinders Ranges 133 F5 ▲▲ S Australia
Flinders River 133 F3 ≈ Queensland, N Australia
Flin Flon 97 H6 Manitoba, C Canada
Flint 39 E1 NE Wales, UK
Flint 101 E3 Michigan, USA
Flint Island 131 *Island,* Line Islands, E Kiribati
Flintshire 29 ◐ *Unitary auth.,* N Wales, UK
Flitwick 37 F3 C England, UK
Florence 61 D3 C Italy
Florencia 115 B3 S Colombia
Flores 107 B1 N Guatemala
Flores 91 F8 *Island,* Nusa Tenggara, C Indonesia
Flores Sea 91 E8 *Sea,* C Indonesia
Floriano 115 H4 E Brazil
Florianópolis 115 G8 S Brazil
Florida 117 C5 S Uruguay
Florida 101 E6 ◐ *State,* SE USA
Florida Keys 101 E7 *Island group,* SE USA
Florida, Straits of 101 F7 *Strait,* Atlantic Ocean/Gulf of Mexico
Florissant 103 H3 Missouri, USA
Fly 137 A2 ≈ Indonesia/PNG
Foča 65 C2 SE Bosnia and Herzegovina
Focşani 67 C6 E Romania
Foggia 61 E5 SE Italy
Foix 55 C7 S France
Foleyet 99 C5 Ontario, S Canada
Foligno 61 D4 C Italy
Folkestone 37 H4 SE England, UK
Fongafale 137 J3 ● Funafuti Atoll, SE Tuvalu
Fonseca, Gulf of 107 C4 *Gulf,* C Central America
Fontainebleau 55 D3 N France
Fontenay-le-Comte 55 C4 NW France
Fonyód 63 D8 W Hungary
Forchheim 59 C6 SE Germany
Forfar 33 E4 E Scotland, UK
Forli 61 C3 N Italy
Formby 35 C5 NW England, UK
Formentera 57 G4 *Island,* Balearic Islands, Spain
Formosa 117 C4 NE Argentina
Formosa, Serra 115 F5 ▲▲ C Brazil
Forres 33 E3 NE Scotland, UK
Fort Albany 99 C4 Ontario, C Canada
Fortaleza 117 B1 N Bolivia
Fortaleza 115 H4 NE Brazil
Fort Augustus 33 D4 N Scotland, UK
Fort Collins 103 E3 Colorado, USA
Fort-de-France 109 K5 ○ W Martinique
Fortescue River 133 B3 ≈ Western Australia
Fort Frances 99 A4 Ontario, S Canada
Fort Good Hope 97 F4 NW Terr., NW Canada
Forth 33 E6 C Scotland, UK
Forth 33 D5 ≈ C Scotland, UK
Forth, Firth of 33 E5 *Estuary,* E Scotland, UK
Fort Lauderdale 101 F7 Florida, USA

◐ Administrative region ◆ Country ● Country capital ◇ Dependent territory ○ Dependent territory capital ▲▲ Mountain range ▲ Mountain ※ Volcano ≈ River ◎ Lake ⊡ Reservoir

Fort Liard 97 F5 NW Terr., W Canada
Fort McMurray 97 G6 Alberta, C Canada
Fort McPherson 97 E4 NW Terr., NW Canada
Fort Nelson 97 F5 British Columbia, W Canada
Fort Peck Lake 103 E1 ⊠ Montana, USA
Fort Providence 97 F5 NW Terr., W Canada
Fort St.John 97 F6 British Columbia, W Canada
Fort Severn 99 B2 Ontario, C Canada
Fort-Shevchenko 76 A5 W Kazakhstan
Fort Simpson 97 F5 NW Terr., W Canada
Fort Smith 97 G5 NW Terr., W Canada
Fort Smith 103 G4 Arkansas, USA
Fort Vermilion 97 F6 Alberta, W Canada
Fort Wayne 101 E3 Indiana, USA
Fort William 33 C4 N Scotland, UK
Fort Worth 103 G4 Texas, USA
Fort Yukon 97 E3 Alaska, USA
Fougères 55 C2 NW France
Foula 33 A6 Island, NE Scotland, UK
Foulness Island 37 H3 Island, SE England, UK
Foulwind, Cape 135 B5 Headland, South Island, NZ
Fouman 124 F5 NW Cameroon
Foveaux Strait 135 A8 Strait, S NZ
Fowey 37 B5 ≈ SW England, UK
Fox Bay East 40 Falkland Islands
Fox Bay West 40 Falkland Islands
Foxe Basin 97 I3 Sea, Nunavut, N Canada
Foxford 31 C3 NW Ireland
Fox Glacier 135 B6 South Island, NZ
Fox Mine 97 H6 Manitoba, C Canada
Fox Point 40 Headland, Falkland Islands
Foyle 31 D2 ≈ Ireland/Northern Ireland, UK
Foyle, Lough 31 D1 Inlet, N Ireland
Foynes 31 B5 SW Ireland
Fraga 57 F2 NE Spain
Fram Basin 139 C4 Undersea feature, Arctic Ocean
France 55 C4 ◆ Republic, W Europe
Franceville 128 B2 E Gabon
Franche-Comté 55 E4 Cultural region, E France
Francis Case, Lake 103 F2 ⊠ South Dakota, USA
Francisco Escárcega 105 H5 SE Mexico
Francistown 128 D5 North East, NE Botswana
Frankfort 101 E4 Kentucky, USA
Frankfurt am Main 59 B5 SW Germany
Frankfurt an der Oder 59 E4 E Germany
Fränkische Alb 59 C6 ⛰ S Germany
Franz Josef Land 76 D1 Island group, N Russ. Fed.
Fraserburgh 33 F3 NE Scotland, UK
Fraser Island 133 H4 Island, Queensland, E Australia
Fray Bentos 117 C5 W Uruguay
Fredericton 99 F5 New Brunswick, SE Canada
Fredrikstad 49 B5 S Norway
Freeport 109 D1 N Bahamas
Freetown 124 B4 ● W Sierra Leone
Freiburg im Breisgau 59 B7 SW Germany
Fremantle 133 B5 Western Australia
French Guiana 115 F2 French ◇ N South America
French Polynesia 131 French ◇ S Pacific Ocean
Fresnillo 105 E4 C Mexico
Fresno 103 B3 California, USA
Frías 117 B4 N Argentina
Friedrichshafen 59 B7 S Germany
Frohavet 49 B4 Sound, C Norway
Frome 37 D4 SW England, UK
Frome 37 D5 ≈ S England, UK
Frome, Lake 133 F5 Salt lake, S Australia
Frongoch 39 D2 NW Wales, UK
Frontera 105 H5 SE Mexico
Frontignan 55 D6 S France
Frøya 49 B4 Island, W Norway
Frýdek-Místek 63 D6 SE Czech Republic
Fuengirola 57 D6 S Spain
Fuerte Olimpo 117 C3 NE Paraguay
Fuji, Mount 85 F6 ▲ Honshu, SE Japan
Fukui 85 F6 SW Japan
Fukuoka 85 D7 SW Japan
Fukushima 85 G4 C Japan
Fulda 59 C5 C Germany
Funafuti Atoll 137 J3 Atoll, C Tuvalu
Fundy, Bay of 99 F5 Bay, Canada/USA
Fürth 59 C6 S Germany
Furukawa 85 G4 C Japan
Fushun 87 G2 NE China
Füssen 59 C7 S Germany
Futuna 137 H5 Island, S Vanuatu
Futuna, Île 137 J4 Island, S Wallis and Futuna
Fuxin 87 G2 NE China
Fuzhou 87 G5 SE China
Fyn 49 B7 Island, C Denmark
Fyne, Loch 33 C5 Inlet, W Scotland, UK

G

Gaalkacyo 127 F4 C Somalia
Gabela 128 B3 W Angola
Gabès 122 F2 E Tunisia
Gabès, Golfe de 122 F2 Gulf, E Tunisia
Gabon 128 A1 ◆ Republic, C Africa
Gaborone 128 D6 ● SE Botswana
Gabrovo 65 F3 C Bulgaria
Gadag 89 D6 W India
Gaeta 61 D5 C Italy
Gaeta, Gulf of 61 C5 Gulf, C Italy
Gafsa 122 E2 W Tunisia
Gagnoa 124 C5 C Ivory Coast
Gagra 79 F1 NW Georgia
Gaillac 55 C6 S France
Gainsborough 35 E5 E England, UK
Gairdner, Lake 133 E5 Salt lake, S Australia
Galán, Cerro 117 A4 ▲ NW Argentina
Galanta 63 D7 SW Slovakia
Galapagos Islands 115 A7 Island group, Ecuador
Galashiels 33 E6 SE Scotland, UK
Galaţi 67 D7 E Romania
Galicia 57 B1 Cultural region, NW Spain
Galkynyş 83 E3 NE Turkmenistan
Galle 89 E8 SW Sri Lanka
Gallipoli 61 F6 SE Italy
Gällivare 49 D2 N Sweden
Galloway, Mull of 33 C7 Headland, S Scotland, UK
Gallup 103 D4 New Mexico, USA
Galtat-Zemmour 122 B3 C Western Sahara
Galty Mountains 31 C6 ⛰ S Ireland
Galveston 103 G5 Texas, USA
Galway 31 C4 W Ireland
Galway 29 ◐ County, W Ireland
Galway Bay 31 B4 Bay, W Ireland
Gambell 97 C2 Saint Lawrence Island, Alaska, USA
Gambia 124 A3 ◆ Republic, W Africa
Gambia 124 B3 ≈ W Africa
Gambier, Îles 131 Island group, E French Polynesia
Gamboma 128 B2 E.Congo
Gäncä 79 H2 W Azerbaijan
Gandajika 128 C3 S Dem. Rep. Congo
Gander 99 H4 Newfoundland, SE Canada
Gandhidham 89 C4 W India
Gandía 57 F4 E Spain
Ganges 89 G3 ≈ Bangladesh/India
Ganges, Mouths of the 89 G4 Delta, Bangladesh/India
Gangtok 89 G3 N India
Ganzhou 87 G5 S China
Gao 124 D3 E Mali
Gaoual 124 B4 N Guinea
Gap 55 E6 SE France
Gar 87 A4 W China
Garabil Belentligi 83 D4 ⛰ S Turkmenistan
Garachiné 107 I7 SE Panama
Garagum 83 D3 Desert, C Turkmenistan
Garagum Canal 83 E4 Canal, C Turkmenistan
Gara, Lough 31 C3 ◎ N Ireland
Garda, Lake 61 C2 ◎ Italy
Gardez 83 F5 E Afghanistan
Garforth 35 E4 N England, UK
Garissa 127 E5 E Kenya
Garonne 55 C5 ≈ S France
Garoowe 127 F3 N Somalia
Garoua 124 G4 N Cameroon
Garrison 31 D2 W Northern Ireland, UK
Garron Point 31 F2 Headland, E Northern Ireland, UK
Garrygala 83 C3 W Turkmenistan
Garry Lake 97 H4 ◎ Nunavut, N Canada
Garsen 127 E6 S Kenya
Garth 33 A6 NE Scotland, UK
Garwolin 63 F4 E Poland
Gary 101 D3 Indiana, USA
Gascogne see Gascony
Gascony 55 C6 Cultural region, France
Gascony, Gulf of 55 B6 Gulf, France/Spain
Gascoyne River 133 B4 ≈ Western Australia
Gasmata 137 C2 E PNG
Gaspé 99 F4 Québec, SE Canada
Gaspé, Péninsule de 99 F4 Peninsula, Québec, SE Canada
Gatchina 69 A4 NW Russ. Fed.
Gateshead 35 D2 NE England, UK
Gateshead 28 ◐ Unitary auth., NE England, UK
Gatineau 99 D5 Québec, SE Canada
Gatún, Lago 107 G6 ⊠ C Panama
Gavbandi 81 E4 S Iran
Gavere 50 B6 NW Belgium
Gävle 49 D5 C Sweden
Gawler 133 E6 S Australia
Gaya 89 F3 N India
Gayndah 133 H4 Queensland, E Australia
Gaza 81 G6 NE Gaza Strip
Gaza Strip 81 G6 Disputed region, SW Asia
Gaziantep 79 E4 S Turkey
Gazimağusa see Famagusta
Gazli 83 E3 C Uzbekistan
Gazojak 83 D2 NE Turkmenistan
Gbanga 124 B5 N Liberia
Gdańsk 63 D2 N Poland
Gdynia 63 D1 N Poland
Gedaref 127 D2 E Sudan
Gediz 79 B3 W Turkey
Gediz Nehri 79 A3 ≈ W Turkey
Geel 50 D6 N Belgium
Geelong 133 F6 Victoria, SE Australia
Geilo 49 B5 S Norway
Gejiu 87 E6 S China
Gela 61 D8 Sicily, Italy
Geldermalsen 50 D4 C Netherlands
Geleen 50 E6 SE Netherlands
Gellinsoor 127 F4 NE Somalia
Gembloux 50 C7 SE Belgium
Gemena 128 C1 NW Dem. Rep. Congo
Gemona del Friuli 61 D2 NE Italy
General Alvear 117 B5 W Argentina
General Eugenio A.Garay 117 B3 S Paraguay
General Santos 91 F5 S Philippines
Geneva 59 A8 SW Switzerland
Geneva, Lake 59 A8 ◎ France/Switzerland
Genève see Geneva
Genk 50 D6 NE Belgium
Gennep 50 E5 SE Netherlands
Genoa 61 B3 NW Italy
Genoa, Gulf of 61 B3 Gulf, NW Italy
Genova see Genoa
Gent see Ghent
George Island 40 Island, S Falkland Islands
Georgetown 40 ○ NW Ascension Island
George Town 109 D2 C Bahamas
George Town 40 ○ SW Cayman Islands
Georgetown 115 E2 ● N Guyana
George Town 91 B5 Peninsular, Malaysia
George V Land 138 C6 Physical region, Antarctica
Georgia 79 G1 ◆ Republic, SW Asia
Georgia 101 E5 ◐ State, SE USA
Georgian Bay 99 C5 Lake bay, Ontario, S Canada
Georg von Neumayer 138 B3 German research station, Antarctica
Gera 59 D5 E Germany
Geraldine 135 C6 South Island, NZ
Geraldton 133 B5 Western Australia
Gerede 79 C2 N Turkey
Gereshk 83 E6 SW Afghanistan
Gerlachovský štít 63 E6 ▲ N Slovakia
Germany 59 B5 ◆ Federal Republic, N Europe
Gerona see Girona
Gerpinnes 50 C7 S Belgium
Gerze 79 D2 N Turkey
Getafe 57 D3 C Spain
Gevaş 79 G4 SE Turkey
Ghana 124 D5 ◆ Republic, W Africa
Ghanzi 128 C5 W Botswana
Ghardaïa 122 E2 N Algeria
Gharyan 122 F2 NW Libya
Ghazni 83 F5 E Afghanistan
Ghent 50 B6 NW Belgium
Ghudara 83 G3 SE Tajikistan
Ghurian 83 D5 W Afghanistan
Giannitsá 65 E4 N Greece
Gibbs Hill 40 Hill, S Bermuda
Gibraltar 40 UK ◇ SW Europe
Gibraltar, Bay of 40 Bay, W Gibraltar
Gibraltar Harbour 40 W Gibraltar
Gibraltar, Strait of 40 Strait, Atlantic Ocean/Mediterranean Sea
Gibson Desert 133 C4 Desert, Western Australia
Giedraičiai 49 F7 E Lithuania
Giessen 59 B5 W Germany
Giffnock 33 D6 C Scotland, UK
Gifu 85 F6 SW Japan
Giganta, Sierra de la 105 B3 ⛰ W Mexico
Gigha Island 33 B6 Island, SW Scotland, UK
G'ijduvon 83 E3 C Uzbekistan
Gijón 57 C1 NW Spain
Gilf Kebir Plateau 122 H4 Plateau, SW Egypt
Gilford 31 E3 SE Northern Ireland, UK
Gillette 103 E2 Wyoming, USA
Gillingham 37 G4 SE England, UK
Gill Point 40 Headland, E Saint Helena
Giluwe, Mount 137 B2 ▲ W PNG
Gilwern 39 E6 SE Wales, UK
Ginger Island 40 Island, SE British Virgin Islands
Gingin 133 B5 Western Australia
Giresun 79 E2 NE Turkey
Girne see Kyrenia
Girona 57 H2 NE Spain
Girvan 33 D6 W Scotland, UK
Gisborne 135 E3 North Island, NZ
Gissar Range 83 F3 ⛰ Tajikistan/Uzbekistan
Giulianova 61 D4 C Italy
Giurgiu 67 C7 S Romania
Gizo 137 E2 NW Solomon Islands
Gjirokastër 65 D4 S Albania
Gjoa Haven 97 H3 King William Island, Nunavut, NW Canada
Gjøvik 49 B5 S Norway
Glace Bay 99 G5 Cape Breton Island, Nova Scotia, SE Canada
Gladstone 133 H4 Queensland, E Australia
Glåma 49 B5 ≈ SE Norway
Glasgow 33 D6 S Scotland, UK
Glasgow 28 ◐ Unitary auth., C Scotland, UK
Glaslyn 39 C2 ≈ NW Wales, UK
Glastonbury 37 D4 SW England, UK
Glazov 69 D5 NW Russ. Fed.
Glenamoy 31 B3 NW Ireland
Glen Coe 33 C4 Valley, N Scotland, UK
Glengad Head 31 D1 Headland, N Ireland
Glengarriff 31 B7 S Ireland
Glenluce 33 D7 SW Scotland, UK
Glen Mor 33 D4 Valley, NW Scotland, UK
Glenrothes 33 E5 E Scotland, UK
Glenties 31 C2 NW Ireland
Glin 31 B5 SW Ireland
Glittertind 49 B4 ▲ S Norway
Gliwice 63 D5 S Poland
Głogów 63 C4 W Poland
Glossop 35 D5 C England, UK
Gloucester 137 C2 E PNG
Gloucester 37 D3 C England, UK
Gloucestershire 29 ◐ County, C England, UK
Glovers Reef 107 C2 Reef, E Belize
Głowno 63 E3 C Poland
Glyn-Neath 39 D6 S Wales, UK
Gniezno 63 D3 C Poland
Gobabis 128 C5 E Namibia
Gobi 87 E3 Desert, China/Mongolia
Gobo 85 E7 SW Japan
Godalming 37 F4 SE England, UK
Godavari 89 E5 ≈ C India
Godhra 89 D4 W India
Godoy Cruz 117 A5 W Argentina
Goeree 50 B5 Island, SW Netherlands
Goes 50 B5 SW Netherlands
Goginan 39 D4 W Wales, UK
Goiânia 115 G6 C Brazil
Goiás 115 F6 ◐ State, C Brazil
Gojome 85 F3 NW Japan
Gökdepe 83 C3 C Turkmenistan
Göksun 79 E4 C Turkey
Gol 49 B5 S Norway
Golan Heights 81 H5 ⛰ SW Syria
Gołdap 63 F2 NE Poland
Gold Coast 133 H5 Cultural region, Queensland, E Australia
Golden Bay 135 C4 Bay, South Island, NZ
Goleniów 63 B2 NW Poland
Golmud 87 D3 C China
Goma 128 D2 NE Dem. Rep. Congo
Gombi 124 G4 E Nigeria
Gómez Palacio 105 D3 C Mexico
Gonaïves 109 F4 N Haiti
Gonâve, Île de la 109 E4 Island, C Haiti
Gonder 127 D3 NW Ethiopia
Gondia 89 E4 C India
Gongola 124 F4 ≈ E Nigeria
Good Hope, Cape of 128 B7 Headland, SW South Africa
Goodwick 39 A5 SW Wales, UK
Goole 35 E4 E England, UK
Goondiwindi 133 G5 Queensland, E Australia
Goor 50 F4 E Netherlands
Goose Green 40 East Falkland, Falkland Islands
Göppingen 59 C6 SW Germany
Gorakhpur 89 F3 N India
Goré 124 G5 S Chad
Gore 127 D4 W Ethiopia
Gore 135 B8 South Island, NZ
Gorey 31 E5 SE Ireland
Gorey 37 H6 Jersey, Channel Islands
Gorgan 81 E1 N Iran
Gori 79 H1 C Georgia
Gorinchem 50 D5 C Netherlands
Goris 79 I3 SE Armenia
Görlitz 59 E4 E Germany
Goroka 137 B2 C PNG
Gorontalo 91 F6 Celebes, C Indonesia
Gorseinon 39 C6 S Wales, UK
Gorssel 50 E4 E Netherlands
Gort 31 C5 W Ireland
Gorzów Wielkopolski 63 C3 W Poland
Goshogawara 85 F3 C Japan
Gosport 37 E5 S England, UK
Göteborg see Gothenburg
Gotha 59 C5 C Germany
Gothenburg 49 B6 S Sweden
Gotland 49 D6 Island, SE Sweden
Goto-retto 85 C8 Island group, SW Japan
Gotsu 85 D6 SW Japan
Göttingen 59 C4 C Germany
Gouda 50 C4 C Netherlands
Gouin, Réservoir 99 D4 ⊠ Québec, SE Canada
Goulburn 133 G6 NSW, SE Australia
Goundam 124 D3 NW Mali
Gouré 124 F3 SE Niger
Governador Valadares 115 H7 SE Brazil
Govi Altayn Nuruu 87 E2 ⛰ S Mongolia
Gower 39 C7 Peninsula, S Wales, UK
Gowran 31 D5 SE Ireland
Goya 117 C4 NE Argentina
Goz Beïda 124 H4 SE Chad
Gozo 70 A6 Island, N Malta
Gradačac 65 C2 N Bosnia and Herzegovina
Gradas, Serra dos 115 F5 ⛰ C Brazil
Grafton 133 H5 NSW, SE Australia
Graham Land 138 A4 Physical region, Antarctica
Grajewo 63 F2 NE Poland
Grampian Mountains 33 D4 ⛰ C Scotland, UK
Granada 107 D5 SW Nicaragua
Granada 57 D5 S Spain
Gran Chaco 117 B3 Lowland plain, South America
Grand Bahama Island 109 C1 Island, N Bahamas
Grand Caicos 40 Island, C Turks and Caicos Islands
Grand Canal 31 C4 Canal, C Ireland
Grand Canyon 103 C4 Canyon, Arizona, USA
Grand Cayman 40 Island, SW Cayman Islands
Grande, Bahía 117 B8 Bay, S Argentina
Grande Comore 128 G4 Island, NW Comoros
Grande de Matagalpa, Río 107 E4 ≈ C Nicaragua
Grande Prairie 97 F6 Alberta, W Canada
Grand Erg Occidental 122 D2 Desert, W Algeria
Grand Erg Oriental 122 E3 Desert, Algeria/Tunisia
Grande, Rio 101 F5 ≈ Mexico/USA
Grande Terre 109 K5 Island, E West Indies
Grand Falls 99 H4 Newfoundland, SE Canada
Grand Forks 103 F1 North Dakota, USA
Grand Rapids 101 D3 Michigan, USA
Grand Turk Island 40 Island, SE Turks and Caicos Islands
Grand Union Canal 37 E2 Canal, SE England, UK
Grange 31 C2 N Ireland
Grangemouth 33 D5 C Scotland, UK
Gran Paradiso 61 A2 ▲ NW Italy
Grantham 35 E6 E England, UK
Grantown-on-Spey 33 E3 N Scotland, UK
Granville 55 B2 N France
Graulhet 55 C6 S France
Grave 50 E5 SE Netherlands
Gravesend 37 G4 SE England, UK
Grayling 97 C3 Alaska, USA
Graz 59 E8 SE Austria
Great Abaco 109 D1 Island, N Bahamas
Great Artesian Basin 133 F4 Lowlands, Queensland, C Australia
Great Australian Bight 133 D5 Bight, S Australia
Great Barrier Island 135 D2 Island, N NZ
Great Barrier Reef 133 G2 Reef, Queensland, NE Australia
Great Basin 103 C3 Basin, W USA
Great Bear Lake 97 F4 ◎ NW Terr., NW Canada
Great Belt 49 B7 Sea waterway, Denmark
Great Camanoe 40 Island, N British Virgin Islands
Great Chagos Bank 40 Undersea feature, C Indian Ocean
Great Dividing Range 130 ⛰ NE Australia
Greater Antarctica 138 D4 Physical region, Antarctica
Greater Antilles 109 E5 Island group, West Indies
Great Exhibition Bay 135 C1 Inlet, North Island, NZ
Great Exuma Island 109 D2 Island, C Bahamas
Great Falls 103 D1 Montana, USA
Great Harbour 40 W British Virgin Islands
Great Hungarian Plain 63 D8 Plain, SE Europe
Great Inagua 109 F3 Island, S Bahamas
Great Karoo 128 C7 Plateau region, S South Africa
Great Khingan Range 87 G1 ⛰ NE China
Great Lakes 101 E2 Lakes, Canada/USA
Great Malvern 35 D7 W England, UK
Great Nicobar 89 H6 Island, Nicobar Islands, India
Great Ormes Head 39 D1 Headland, N Wales, UK
Great Ouse 35 F6 ≈ E England, UK
Great Rift Valley 117 Depression, Asia/Africa
Great Ruaha 127 D7 ≈ S Tanzania
Great Saint Bernard Pass 61 A1 Pass, Italy/Switzerland
Great Salt Lake 103 C3 Salt lake, Utah, USA
Great Salt Lake Desert 103 C3 Plain, Utah, USA
Great Sand Sea 122 H3 Desert, Egypt/Libya
Great Sandy Desert 133 C3 Desert, Western Australia
Great Slave Lake 97 G5 ◎ NW Terr., NW Canada
Great Tobago 40 Island, W British Virgin Islands
Great Torrington 37 B4 SW England, UK
Great Victoria Desert 133 C4 Desert, S Australia/Western Australia
Great Wall of China 87 E3 Ancient monument, N China
Great Yarmouth 37 H2 E England, UK
Gredos, Sierra de 57 C3 ⛰ W Spain
Greece 65 D5 ◆ Republic, SE Europe
Greeley 103 E3 Colorado, USA
Green Bay 101 D2 Wisconsin, USA
Green Bay 101 D2 Lake bay, N USA
Greencastle 31 E3 S Northern Ireland, UK
Green Islands 137 D2 Island group, NE PNG
Greenland 92 Danish ◇ NE North America
Greenland Sea 139 C5 Sea, Arctic Ocean
Green Mountains 101 G2 ⛰ Vermont, USA
Greenock 33 D5 W Scotland, UK
Green River 137 A1 NW PNG
Green River 103 D2 Wyoming, USA
Green River 103 D3 ≈ W USA
Greensboro 101 F4 North Carolina, USA
Greenville 101 E5 South Carolina, USA
Greenwich 29 ◐ London borough, SE England, UK
Gregory Range 133 G3 ⛰ Queensland, E Australia
Greifswald 59 D2 NE Germany
Grenada 109 J6 ◆ Commonwealth republic, SE West Indies
Grenadines, The 109 K6 Island group, Grenada/St Vincent and the Grenadines
Grenoble 55 E5 E France
Gretna 33 E7 SW Scotland, UK
Grevenmacher 50 E9 E Luxembourg
Greymouth 135 B6 South Island, NZ
Grey Range 133 F4 ⛰ NSW/Queensland, E Australia
Greystones 31 E4 E Ireland
Grimari 124 H5 C CAR
Grimsby 35 F4 E England, UK
Groesbeek 50 E5 SE Netherlands
Grójec 63 F4 C Poland
Groningen 50 F2 NE Netherlands
Groote Eylandt 133 E2 Island, Northern Territory, N Australia
Grootfontein 128 C5 N Namibia
Groot Karasberge 128 C6 ⛰ S Namibia
Grosseto 61 C4 C Italy
Grossglockner 59 D8 ▲ W Austria
Groznyy 69 B9 SW Russ. Fed.
Grudziàdz 63 D2 N Poland
Grums 49 C5 C Sweden
Gryazi 69 B6 W Russ. Fed.
Gryfice 63 C2 NW Poland
Guabito 107 F6 NW Panama
Guadalajara 105 D5 C Mexico
Guadalajara 57 D3 C Spain
Guadalcanal 137 E3 Island, C Solomon Islands
Guadalquivir 57 C5 ≈ W Spain
Guadalupe 105 D4 C Mexico
Guadalupe Peak 103 E5 ▲ Texas, USA
Guadarrama, Sierra de 57 E3 ⛰ C Spain
Guadeloupe 109 K5 French ◇ E West Indies
Guadiana 57 B4 ≈ Portugal/Spain
Guadix 57 D5 S Spain
Guaimaca 107 D3 C Honduras
Gualaco 107 D3 C Honduras
Gualán 107 B3 C Guatemala
Gualeguaychú 117 C5 E Argentina
Guamúchil 105 C3 C Mexico
Guanabacoa 109 B2 W Cuba
Guana Island 40 Island, N British Virgin Islands
Guanajuato 105 E4 C Mexico
Guanare 115 C2 N Venezuela
Guangyuan 87 E4 C China
Guangzhou 87 F6 S China
Guantánamo 109 E4 SE Cuba
Guaporé, Rio 115 D5 ≈ Bolivia/Brazil
Guarda 57 B3 N Portugal
Guarumal 107 G7 S Panama
Guasave 105 C3 C Mexico
Guasopa 137 D3 SE PNG
Guatemala 107 A3 ◆ Republic, Central America
Guatemala Basin 14 Undersea feature, E Pacific Ocean
Guatemala City 107 B3 ● C Guatemala
Guaviare, Río 115 C2 ≈ E Colombia
Guayaquil 115 A4 SW Ecuador
Guayaquil, Golfo de 115 A4 Gulf, SW Ecuador
Guaymas 105 B3 NW Mexico
Gubadag 83 D2 N Turkmenistan
Guben 59 E4 E Germany
Gubkin 69 A6 W Russ. Fed.
Gudaut'a 79 F1 NW Georgia
Guéret 55 D4 C France
Guernsey 37 G6 UK ◇ NW Europe
Guerrero Negro 105 A3 NW Mexico
Guiana Basin 14 Undersea feature, W Atlantic Ocean
Guiana Highlands 115 E3 ⛰ N South America
Guider 124 G4 N Cameroon
Guidimouni 124 F3 S Niger
Guildford 37 F4 SE England, UK
Guilin 87 F5 S China
Guimarães 57 B2 N Portugal
Guinea 124 B4 ◆ Republic, W Africa
Guinea-Bissau 124 A4 ◆ Republic, W Africa
Guinea, Gulf of 124 E6 Gulf, E Atlantic Ocean
Guiyang 87 E5 S China
Gujarat 89 C4 Cultural region, W India
Gujranwala 89 D2 NE Pakistan
Gujrat 89 D2 E Pakistan
Gulbarga 89 D5 C India
Gulfport 101 C6 Mississippi, USA
Gulf, The 81 D3 Gulf, SW Asia
Guliston 83 F3 E Uzbekistan
Gulkana 97 D4 Alaska, USA
Gulu 127 C5 N Uganda
Gümüşhane 79 F2 NE Turkey
Güney Doğu Toroslar 79 F4 ⛰ SE Turkey
Gunnbjørn Fjeld 139 A6 ▲ C Greenland
Gunnedah 133 G5 NSW, SE Australia
Gurbantünggüt Shamo 87 C2 Desert, NW China
Gurktaler Alpen 59 E8 ⛰ S Austria
Gürün 79 E3 C Turkey
Gusau 124 E4 N Nigeria
Gusev 49 E7 W Russ. Fed.
Gustavus 97 E5 Alaska, USA
Güstrow 59 D2 NE Germany
Gütersloh 59 B4 W Germany
Guwahati 89 G3 NE India
Guyana 115 E2 ◆ Republic, N South America
Güzelyurt see Morfou
Gwadar 89 A3 SW Pakistan

CAR Central African Republic FYR Former Yugoslavian Rebublic NSW New South Wales NZ New Zealand PNG Papua New Guinea Russ. Fed. Russian Federation UAE United Arab Emirates UK United Kingdom USA United States of America

Gwalchmai 39 C1 NW Wales, UK
Gwalior 89 E3 C India
Gwanda 128 D5 SW Zimbabwe
Gweedore 31 C1 NW Ireland
Gwynedd 29 ◈ *Unitary auth.,* NW Wales, UK
Gwytherin 39 D2 N Wales, UK
Gyangzê 87 C5 W China
Gyaring Co 87 C4 ◎ W China
Gympie 133 H4 Queensland, E Australia
Gyomaendrőd 63 F8 SE Hungary
Gyöngyös 63 E7 NE Hungary
Győr 63 D7 NW Hungary
Gyumri 79 G2 W Armenia

H

Haacht 50 C6 C Belgium
Haaksbergen 50 F4 E Netherlands
Haarlem 50 C3 W Netherlands
Haast 135 B6 South Island, NZ
Hachijo-jima 85 G7 *Island,* Izu-shoto, SE Japan
Hachinohe 85 G3 C Japan
Hackney 29 ◈ *London borough,* SE England, UK
Haddington 33 E5 SE Scotland, UK
Hadejia 124 F4 N Nigeria
Hadejia 124 F4 ≈ N Nigeria
Hadleigh 37 G3 SE England, UK
Ha Dong 91 C2 N Vietnam
Hadramaut 81 D7 ⛰ S Yemen
Hadhdhunmathi Atoll 89 C9 Atoll, S Maldives
Haeju 85 A5 S North Korea
Hagåtña 130 ○ NW Guam
Hagondange 55 F2 NE France
Hag's Head 31 B5 *Headland,* W Ireland
Haguenau 55 F2 NE France
Haicheng 87 G3 NE China
Haifa 81 G5 N Israel
Haikou 87 F6 S China
Ha'il 81 B3 NW Saudi Arabia
Hailar 87 G1 N China
Hailsham 37 G4 SE England, UK
Hailuoto 49 E3 *Island,* W Finland
Hainan Dao 87 F6 *Island,* S China
Haines 97 E5 Alaska, USA
Hainichen 59 D5 E Germany
Hai Phong 91 C2 N Vietnam
Haiti 109 F4 ◆ *Republic,* C West Indies
Haiya 127 D2 NE Sudan
Hajdúhadház 63 F7 E Hungary
Hakodate 85 F2 NE Japan
Halberstadt 59 C4 C Germany
Halden 49 B5 S Norway
Halfmoon Bay 135 B8 Stewart Island, Southland, NZ
Halifax 99 G5 Nova Scotia, SE Canada
Halifax 35 D4 N England, UK
Halkirk 33 E2 N Scotland, UK
Halladale 33 D2 ≈ N Scotland, UK
Halle 50 C7 C Belgium
Halle 59 D4 C Germany
Halle-Neustadt 59 D4 C Germany
Halley 138 B3 *UK research station,* Antarctica
Halls Creek 133 D2 Western Australia
Halmahera, Pulau 91 G6 *Island,* E Indonesia
Halmahera Sea 91 G6 *Sea,* E Indonesia
Halmstad 49 C6 S Sweden
Halton 29 ◈ *Unitary auth.,* NW England, UK
Haltwhistle 35 C2 N England, UK
Hamada 85 D6 SW Japan
Hamadan 81 D2 W Iran
Hamah 81 B2 W Syria
Hamamatsu 85 F6 S Japan
Hamar 49 B5 S Norway
Hamburg 59 C3 N Germany
Hamd, Wadi al 81 A4 *Dry watercourse,* W Saudi Arabia
Hämeenlinna 49 E5 SW Finland
Hamersley Range 133 B3 ⛰ W Australia
Hamgyong-sanmaek 85 B4 ⛰ N North Korea
Hamhung 85 B4 C North Korea
Hami 87 D2 NW China
Hamilton 40 ○ C Bermuda
Hamilton 99 D6 Ontario, S Canada
Hamilton 135 D3 North Island, NZ
Hamilton 33 D6 S Scotland, UK
Hamim, Wadi al 122 G3 ≈ NE Libya
Hamm 59 B4 W Germany
Hammamet, Golfe de 70 E4 *Gulf,* NE Tunisia
Hammar, Hawr al 81 C3 ◎ SE Iraq
Hammersmith and Fulham 29 ◈ *London borough,* SE England, UK
Hampden 135 B7 South Island, NZ
Hampshire 29 ◈ *County,* S England, UK
Hamrun 70 B6 C Malta
Handan 87 F4 E China
Hangayn Nuruu 87 D2 ⛰ C Mongolia
Hangö *see* Hanko
Hangzhou 87 G4 SE China
Hanko 49 E5 SW Finland
Hanley 35 D5 C England, UK
Hanmer Springs 135 C6 South Island, NZ
Hannover *see* Hanover
Hanöbukten 49 C7 *Bay,* S Sweden
Hanoi 91 C2 ● N Vietnam
Hanover 59 C4 NW Germany
Han Shui 87 F4 ≈ C China
Hanzhong 87 E4 C China
Haora 89 G4 NE India
Haparanda 49 E3 N Sweden
Haradok 67 D1 N Belarus
Haramachi 85 G4 E Japan
Harare 128 E4 ● NE Zimbabwe
Harbel 124 B5 W Liberia
Harbin 87 H2 NE China
Hardangerfjorden 49 A5 *Fjord,* S Norway
Hardangervidda 49 B5 *Plateau,* S Norway
Hardenberg 50 F3 E Netherlands
Harelbeke 50 B6 W Belgium
Haren 50 F2 NE Netherlands
Harer 127 E3 E Ethiopia
Hargeysa 127 E3 NW Somalia
Harima-nada 85 E6 *Sea,* S Japan
Haringey 29 ◈ *London borough,* SE England, UK
Harirud 83 E5 ≈ Afghanistan/Iran
Harlech 39 C3 NW Wales, UK
Harlingen 50 D2 N Netherlands
Harlow 37 G3 E England, UK
Harney Basin 103 B2 *Basin,* Oregon, USA
Härnösand 49 D4 C Sweden
Har Nuur 87 D2 ◎ NW Mongolia
Harpenden 37 F3 E England, UK
Harper 124 C5 NE Liberia
Harricana 99 D4 ≈ Québec, SE Canada
Harris 33 B3 *Physical region,* NW Scotland, UK
Harrisburg 101 F3 Pennsylvania, USA
Harrison, Cape 99 G2 *Headland,* Newfoundland, E Canada
Harris, Sound of 33 B3 *Strait,* NW Scotland, UK
Harrogate 35 D4 N England, UK
Harrow 37 F3 SE England, UK
Harrow 29 ◈ *London borough,* SE England, UK
Harstad 49 C2 N Norway
Hartford 101 G3 Connecticut, USA
Hartland Point 37 B4 *Headland,* SW England, UK
Hartlepool 35 E3 N England, UK
Hartlepool 28 ◈ *Unitary auth.,* NE England, UK
Harwich 37 H3 E England, UK
Haryana 89 D2 *Cultural region,* N India
Harz 59 C4 ⛰ C Germany
Haslemere 37 F4 SE England, UK
Hasselt 50 D6 NE Belgium
Hastings 135 E4 North Island, NZ
Hastings 37 G4 SE England, UK
Hatfield 37 F3 E England, UK
Hattem 50 E3 E Netherlands
Hatteras, Cape 101 G5 *Headland,* North Carolina, USA
Hattiesburg 101 C6 Mississippi, USA
Hat Yai 91 B5 SW Thailand
Haugesund 49 A5 S Norway
Haukeligrend 49 B5 S Norway
Haukivesi 49 F4 ◎ SE Finland
Hauraki Gulf 135 D2 *Gulf,* North Island, N NZ
Hauroko, Lake 135 A8 ◎ South Island, NZ
Hautes Fagnes 50 E7 ⛰ E Belgium
Hauts Plateaux 122 D2 *Plateau,* Algeria/Morocco
Hauzenberg 59 E6 SE Germany
Havana 109 B2 ● W Cuba
Havant 37 F5 S England, UK
Havelock North 135 E4 North Island, NZ
Haverfordwest 39 B6 SW Wales, UK
Haverhill 37 G2 E England, UK
Havering 29 ◈ *London borough,* SE England, UK
Havířov 63 D5 E Czech Republic
Havre 103 D1 Montana, USA
Havre-St-Pierre 99 F4 Québec, E Canada
Hawaii 103 B6 ◈ *State,* USA, C Pacific Ocean
Hawea, Lake 135 B7 ◎ South Island, NZ
Hawera 135 D4 North Island, NZ
Hawes 35 D3 N England, UK
Hawick 33 E6 SE Scotland, UK
Hawke Bay 135 E4 *Bay,* North Island, NZ
Hawthorne 103 B3 Nevada, USA
Hay 133 F6 NSW, SE Australia
Hayes 99 A2 ≈ Manitoba, C Canada
Hay-on-Wye 39 E5 E Wales, UK
Hay River 97 G5 NW Terr., W Canada
Hays 103 F3 Kansas, USA
Haysyn 67 D5 C Ukraine
Haywards Heath 37 G4 SE England, UK
Hazar 83 B3 W Turkmenistan
Hearst 99 C4 Ontario, S Canada
Hebrides, Sea of the 33 B4 *Sea,* NW Scotland, UK
Hebron 81 H6 S West Bank
Heemskerk 50 C3 W Netherlands
Heerde 50 E3 E Netherlands
Heerenveen 50 E2 N Netherlands
Heerhugowaard 50 D3 NW Netherlands
Heerlen 50 E6 SE Netherlands
Hefei 87 G4 E China
Hegang 87 H1 NE China
Heide 59 B2 N Germany
Heidelberg 59 B6 SW Germany
Heidenheim an der Brenz 59 C6 S Germany
Heilbronn 59 B6 SW Germany
Heilong Jiang *see* Amur
Heiloo 50 C3 NW Netherlands
Heimdal 49 B4 S Norway
Hekimhan 79 E3 C Turkey
Helena 103 D1 Montana, USA
Helensburgh 33 D5 W Scotland, UK
Helensville 135 D2 North Island, NZ
Helgoländer Bucht 59 B2 *Bay,* NW Germany
Hellevoetsluis 50 C5 SW Netherlands
Hellín 57 E4 C Spain
Helmand, Darya-ye 83 D6 ≈ Afghanistan/Iran
Helmond 50 E5 S Netherlands
Helmsdale 33 E2 N Scotland, UK
Helmsley 35 E3 N England, UK
Helsingborg 49 C7 S Sweden
Helsinki 49 E5 ● S Finland
Helston 37 A6 SW England, UK
Helvellyn 35 C3 ▲ NW England, UK
Hengduan Shan 87 D5 ⛰ SW China
Hengelo 50 F4 E Netherlands
Hengyang 87 F5 S China
Heniches'k 67 F6 S Ukraine
Henley-on-Thames 37 F3 C England, UK
Hennebont 55 B3 NW France
Henzada 91 A3 SW Burma
Herat 83 D5 W Afghanistan
Heredia 107 E6 C Costa Rica
Hereford 35 C7 W England, UK
Herefordshire 29 ◈ *Unitary auth.,* W England, UK
Herford 59 B4 NW Germany
Herk-de-Stad 50 D6 NE Belgium
Herm 37 G6 *Island,* Channel Islands
Herma Ness 33 B5 *Headland,* NE Scotland, UK
Hermansverk 49 B5 S Norway
Hermit Islands 137 B1 *Island group,* N PNG
Hermon, Mount 81 H5 ▲ S Syria
Hermosillo 105 B2 NW Mexico
Herrera del Duque 57 C4 W Spain
Herselt 50 D6 C Belgium
Herstal 50 E7 E Belgium
Hertfordshire 29 ◈ *County,* E England, UK
Hessen 59 C5 *Cultural region,* C Germany
Hessle 35 F4 N England, UK
Hexham 35 D2 N England, UK
Hidalgo del Parral 105 D3 N Mexico
Hida-sanmyaku 85 E5 ⛰ Honshu, S Japan
Hienghène 137 G6 C New Caledonia
High Atlas 122 C2 ⛰ C Morocco
Highland 28 ◈ *Unitary auth.,* NW Scotland, UK
High Point 101 F4 North Carolina, USA
High Willhays 37 C5 ▲ SW England, UK
High Wycombe 37 F3 SE England, UK
Hiiumaa 49 D6 *Island,* W Estonia
Hikurangi 135 D2 North Island, NZ
Hildesheim 59 C4 N Germany
Hill Bank 107 B1 N Belize
Hill Cove Settlement 40 Falkland Islands
Hillegom 50 C4 W Netherlands
Hillingdon 29 ◈ *London borough,* SE England, UK
Hillsborough 31 E2 E Northern Ireland, UK
Hilo 103 B6 Hawaii, USA
Hilversum 50 D4 C Netherlands
Himalayas 89 E2 ⛰ S Asia
Himeji 85 E6 SW Japan
Hims 81 B2 C Syria
Hinchinbrook Island 133 G2 *Island,* Queensland, NE Australia
Hinds 135 C6 South Island, NZ
Hindu Kush 83 F4 ⛰ Afghanistan/Pakistan
Hinnøya 49 C2 *Island,* C Norway
Hirfanli Baraji 79 C3 ▣ C Turkey
Hirosaki 85 F3 C Japan
Hiroshima 85 D7 SW Japan
Hirson 55 E2 N France
Hisiu 137 B3 SW PNG
Hispaniola 109 F4 *Island,* Dominican Republic/Haiti
Hitachi 85 G5 S Japan
Hitra 49 B4 *Island,* S Norway
Hjälmaren 49 C6 ◎ C Sweden
Hjørring 49 B6 N Denmark
Hkakabo Razi 91 A1 ▲ Burma/China
Hlukhiv 67 E3 NE Ukraine
Hlybokaye 67 C2 N Belarus
Hoang Lien Son 91 C2 ⛰ N Vietnam
Hobart 133 G7 Tasmania, SE Australia
Hobro 49 B6 N Denmark
Ho Chi Minh 91 C4 S Vietnam
Hodeida 81 B6 W Yemen
Hódmezővásárhely 63 E8 SE Hungary
Hodna, Chott El 70 D4 *Salt lake,* N Algeria
Hodonín 63 D6 SE Czech Republic
Hoeryong 85 C3 NE North Korea
Hof 59 D5 SE Germany
Hofu 85 D7 SW Japan
Hohenems 59 C7 W Austria
Hohe Tauern 59 D8 ⛰ W Austria
Hohhot 87 F3 N China
Hokianga Harbour 135 C2 *Inlet,* SE Tasman Sea
Hokitika 135 B6 South Island, NZ
Hokkaido 85 F1 *Island,* NE Japan
Holguín 109 D3 SE Cuba
Hollabrunn 59 F6 NE Austria
Holland *see* Netherlands
Holman 97 G3 Victoria Island, NW Terr., N Canada
Holmsund 49 D4 N Sweden
Holon 81 G6 C Israel
Holstebro 49 B6 W Denmark
Holt 37 H1 E England, UK
Holt 39 E2 NE Wales, UK
Holycross 31 D5 S Ireland
Holyhead 39 B1 NW Wales, UK
Holyhead Bay 39 B1 *Bay,* NW Wales, UK
Holy Island 35 D1 *Island,* NE England, UK
Holy Island 39 B1 *Island,* NW Wales, UK
Holywell 39 E1 N Wales, UK
Hombori 124 D3 S Mali
Homyel' 67 D3 SE Belarus
Hondo 107 B1 ≈ Central America
Honduras 107 C3 ◆ *Republic,* Central America
Honduras, Gulf of 107 C2 *Gulf,* W Caribbean Sea
Hønefoss 49 B5 S Norway
Hong Gai 91 C2 N Vietnam
Hong Kong (Xianggang) 87 H6 *Special Administrative Region of China, Former UK dependency,* S China
Honiara 137 E3 ● C Solomon Islands
Honiton 37 C5 SW England, UK
Honjo 85 F4 C Japan
Honolulu 103 B6 Oahu, Hawaii, USA
Honshu 85 G5 *Island,* SW Japan
Hoogeveen 50 E3 NE Netherlands
Hoogezand-Sappemeer 50 F2 NE Netherlands
Hoorn 50 D3 NW Netherlands
Hopa 79 G2 NE Turkey
Hope 97 D4 British Columbia, SW Canada
Hope 39 E2 N Wales, UK
Hopedale 99 F2 Newfoundland, NE Canada
Horasan 79 G3 NE Turkey
Horki 67 D2 E Belarus
Horley 37 F4 SE England, UK
Horlivka 67 G5 E Ukraine
Hormuz, Strait of 81 E4 *Strait,* Iran/Oman
Hornby Mountains 40 *Hill range,* Falkland Islands
Horn, Cape 117 B9 *Headland,* S Chile
Horncastle 35 F5 E England, UK
Hornsea 35 F4 E England, UK
Horoshiri-dake 85 G2 ▲ N Japan
Horseleap 31 D4 C Ireland
Horsham 133 F6 Victoria, SE Australia
Horsham 37 F4 SE England, UK
Horst 50 E5 SE Netherlands
Horten 49 B5 S Norway
Horyn' 67 C4 ≈ NW Ukraine
Hosingen 50 E8 NE Luxembourg
Hotan 87 B3 NW China
Hotazel 128 C6 N South Africa
Hoting 49 C4 C Sweden
Houayxay 91 B2 N Laos
Houghton 101 D1 Michigan, USA
Houilles 55 C6 N France
Houlton 101 H2 Maine, USA
Hounslow 29 ◈ *London borough,* SE England, UK
Houston 103 G5 Texas, USA
Hovd 87 C2 W Mongolia
Hove 37 F5 SE England, UK
Hoverla, Hora 67 B5 ▲ W Ukraine
Hövsgöl Nuur 87 D1 ◎ N Mongolia
Howar, Wadi 127 B2 ≈ Chad/Sudan
Howth 31 E4 E Ireland
Hoy 33 E1 *Island,* N Scotland, UK
Hoyerswerda 59 E4 E Germany
Hradec Králové 63 C5 NE Czech Republic
Hranice 63 D6 E Czech Republic
Hrodna 67 B2 W Belarus
Huaihua 87 F5 S China
Huajuapan 105 F5 SE Mexico
Huambo 128 B4 C Angola
Huancayo 115 B5 C Peru
Huangshi 87 G4 C China
Huánuco 115 B5 C Peru
Huanuni 117 A4 W Bolivia
Huaraz 115 B5 W Peru
Huatabampo 105 C3 NW Mexico
Hubli 89 D6 SW India
Huch'ang 85 B4 N North Korea
Hucknall 35 E5 C England, UK
Huddersfield 35 D4 N England, UK
Hudiksvall 49 C5 C Sweden
Hudson Bay 99 B2 *Bay,* NE Canada
Hudson River 101 G2 ≈ NE USA
Hudson Strait 97 J4 *Strait,* Nunavut/Québec, NE Canada
Hue 91 C3 C Vietnam
Huehuetenango 107 A3 W Guatemala
Huelva 57 B5 SW Spain
Huesca 57 F2 NE Spain
Huéscar 57 E5 S Spain
Hughenden 133 G3 Queensland, NE Australia
Huich'on 85 B4 C North Korea
Huíla Plateau 128 B4 *Plateau,* S Angola
Huixtla 105 H6 SE Mexico
Hulingol 87 G2 N China
Hull 99 D5 Québec, SE Canada
Hull 35 F4 ≈ N England, UK
Hulst 50 C6 SW Netherlands
Hulun Nur 87 F2 ◎ NE China
Humaitá 115 D4 N Brazil
Humber 35 F4 *Estuary,* E England, UK
Humboldt River 103 B3 ≈ Nevada, USA
Humphreys Peak 103 D4 ▲ Arizona, USA
Humpolec 63 C6 C Czech Republic
Hunedoara 67 B6 SW Romania
Hünfeld 59 C5 C Germany
Hungary 63 D8 ◆ *Republic,* C Europe
Hunstanton 37 G1 E England, UK
Hunter Island 133 F7 *Island,* Tasmania, SE Australia
Huntingdon 37 F2 E England, UK
Huntington 101 E4 West Virginia, USA
Huntly 135 D3 North Island, NZ
Huntly 33 E3 NE Scotland, UK
Huntsville 101 D5 Alabama, USA
Huon Gulf 137 B2 *Gulf,* E PNG
Hurghada 122 J3 E Egypt
Huron, Lake 101 E2 ◎ Canada/USA
Hurunui 135 C6 ≈ South Island, NZ
Húsavík 49 A1 NE Iceland
Husum 59 B2 N Germany
Huy 50 D7 E Belgium
Hvannadalshnúkur 49 B1 ⚶ S Iceland
Hvar 65 B3 *Island,* S Croatia
Hwange 128 D5 W Zimbabwe
Hyargas Nuur 87 D2 ◎ NW Mongolia
Hyderabad 89 E5 C India
Hyderabad 89 B3 SE Pakistan
Hyères 55 E7 SE France
Hyères, Îles d' 55 E7 *Island group,* S France
Hyesan 85 B4 NE North Korea
Hythe 37 H4 SE England, UK
Hyvinkää 49 E5 S Finland

I

Ialomiţa 67 C7 ≈ SE Romania
Iaşi 67 C6 NE Romania
Ibadan 124 E5 SW Nigeria
Ibar 65 D2 ≈ C Serbia and Montenegro (Yugoslavia)
Ibarra 115 B3 N Ecuador
Iberian Peninsula 44 *Physical region,* Portugal/Spain
Ibérico, Sistema 57 E2 ⛰ NE Spain
Ibiza 57 G4 *Island,* Balearic Islands, Spain
Ica 115 B6 SW Peru
Iceland 49 A1 ◆ *Republic,* N Atlantic Ocean
Iceland Plateau 139 B6 *Undersea feature,* S Greenland Sea
Idaho 103 C2 ◈ *State,* NW USA
Idfu 122 J3 SE Egypt
Idîni 124 A2 W Mauritania
Idlib 81 B2 NW Syria
Idre 49 C4 C Sweden
Ieper 50 A6 W Belgium
Iferouâne 124 F2 N Niger
Ifôghas, Adrar des 124 E2 ⛰ NE Mali
Igarka 76 E3 N Russ. Fed.
Iglesias 61 A6 Sardinia, Italy
Igloolik 97 I3 Nunavut, N Canada
Igoumenítsa 65 D5 W Greece
Iguaçu, Rio 115 F8 ≈ Argentina/Brazil
Iguala 105 F5 S Mexico
Iguazu Falls 117 D4 *Waterfall,* Argentina/Brazil
Iguidi, 'Erg 122 C3 *Desert,* Algeria/Mauritania
Ihosy 128 G5 S Madagascar
Iisalmi 49 E4 C Finland
IJssel 50 E4 ≈ Netherlands
IJsselmeer 50 D3 ◎ N Netherlands
IJsselmuiden 50 E3 E Netherlands
Ijzer 50 A6 ≈ W Belgium
Ikaría 65 F6 *Island,* Dodecanese, Greece
Ikela 128 C2 C Dem. Rep. Congo
Iki 85 C7 *Island,* SW Japan
Ilagan 91 F3 Luzon, N Philippines
Iława 63 E2 N Poland
Ilebo 128 C2 W Dem. Rep. Congo
Île-de-France 55 D3 *Cultural region,* N France
Ilford 37 G3 SE England, UK
Ilfracombe 37 B4 SW England, UK
Ílhavo 57 B3 N Portugal
Ili 83 H1 ≈ China/Kazakhstan
Iligan 91 F5 Mindanao, S Philippines
Ilkeston 35 E5 C England, UK
Ilkley 35 D4 N England, UK
Illapel 117 A5 C Chile
Illichivs'k 67 E6 SW Ukraine
Illinois 101 C3 ◈ *State,* C USA
Iloilo 91 F4 Panay Island, C Philippines
Ilorin 124 E4 W Nigeria
Ilovlya 69 B7 SW Russ. Fed.
Imatra 49 F4 SE Finland
Imisli 79 I2 C Azerbaijan
Imola 61 C3 N Italy
Imperatriz 115 G4 NE Brazil
Imperia 61 A3 NW Italy
Imphal 89 H3 NE India
Inagh 31 B5 W Ireland
Inarijärvi 49 E1 ◎ N Finland
Inawashiro-ko 85 F5 ◎ Honshu, C Japan
İncesu 79 D4 C Turkey
Inch'on 85 B5 NW South Korea
India 89 D4 ◆ *Republic,* S Asia
Indiana 101 D3 ◈ *State,* N USA
Indianapolis 101 D3 Indiana, USA
Indian Church 107 B1 N Belize
Indian Ocean 15 *Ocean*
Indigirka 76 G2 ≈ NE Russ. Fed.
Indira Point 89 H6 *Headland,* Andaman and Nicobar Islands, India
Indonesia 91 C7 ◆ *Republic,* SE Asia
Indore 89 D4 C India
Indus 89 B3 ≈ S Asia
Indus, Mouths of the 89 B3 *Delta,* S Pakistan
İnebolu 79 D2 N Turkey
Infiernillo, Presa del 105 E5 ▣ S Mexico
Ingleborough 35 C4 ▲ N England, UK
Ingolstadt 59 C6 S Germany
Inhambane 128 E6 SE Mozambique
Inishannon 31 C7 S Ireland
Inishbofin 31 A4 *Island,* W Ireland
Inishkea North 31 A3 *Island,* NW Ireland
Inishkea South 31 A3 *Island,* NW Ireland
Inishmore 31 B4 *Island,* W Ireland
Inishshark 31 A4 *Island,* W Ireland
Inishtrahull 31 D1 *Island,* NW Ireland
Inishturk 31 A3 *Island,* W Ireland
Inn 59 D7 ≈ C Europe
Inner Hebrides 33 B5 *Island group,* W Scotland, UK
Inner Sound 33 C3 *Strait,* NW Scotland, UK
Innfield 31 E4 E Ireland
Inniscrone 31 C3 N Ireland
Innisfail 133 G2 Queensland, NE Australia
Innsbruck 59 C7 W Austria
Inowrocław 63 D3 C Poland
I-n-Salah 122 D3 C Algeria
Inta 69 E3 NW Russ. Fed.
Interlaken 59 B8 SW Switzerland
Inukjuak 99 D2 Québec, NE Canada
Inuvik 97 F4 NW Terr., NW Canada
Inver 31 C2 N Ireland
Inveraray 33 C5 W Scotland, UK
Inverbervie 33 F4 NE Scotland, UK
Invercargill 135 B8 South Island, NZ
Inverclyde 28 ◈ *Unitary auth.,* C Scotland, UK
Invergordon 33 D3 N Scotland, UK
Inverness 33 D3 N Scotland, UK
Inverurie 33 F3 NE Scotland, UK
Investigator Strait 133 E6 *Strait,* S Australia
Inyangani 128 E5 ▲ NE Zimbabwe
Ioánnina 65 D5 W Greece
Iona 33 B5 *Island,* W Scotland, UK
Iónia Nisiá *see* Ionian Islands
Ionian Islands 65 D5 *Island group,* W Greece
Ionian Sea 70 G3 *Sea,* C Mediterranean Sea
Íos 65 F6 *Island,* Cyclades, Greece
Iowa 103 G2 *State,* C USA
Iowa City 103 G2 Iowa, USA
Ipel' 63 E7 ≈ Hungary/Slovakia
Ipoh 91 B5 Peninsular Malaysia
Ippy 124 H5 C CAR
Ipswich 133 H5 Queensland, E Australia
Ipswich 37 H2 E England, UK
Iqaluit 97 J3 Baffin Island, Nunavut, NE Canada
Iquique 117 A3 N Chile
Iquitos 115 C4 N Peru
Irákleio 65 F7 Crete, Greece
Iran 81 E2 ◆ *Republic,* SW Asia
Iranian Plateau 81 E3 *Plateau,* N Iran
Irapuato 105 E4 C Mexico
Iraq 81 B2 ◆ *Republic,* SW Asia
Irbid 81 A2 N Jordan
Ireland, Republic of 31 C4 ◆ *Republic,* NW Europe
Irian Jaya *see* Papua
Iringa 127 D7 C Tanzania
Iriomote-jima 85 A8 *Island,* Sakishima-shoto, SW Japan
Iriona 107 D2 NE Honduras
Irish Sea 27 *Sea,* C British Isles
Irkutsk 76 F5 S Russ. Fed.
Iroise 55 A2 *Sea,* NW France
Irrawaddy 91 A2 ≈ W Burma
Irrawaddy, Mouths of the 91 A3 *Delta,* SW Burma
Irtysh 76 D4 ≈ C Asia
Irún 57 E1 N Spain
Iruña *see* Pamplona
Irvine 33 D6 W Scotland, UK
Irvinestown 31 D2 W Northern Ireland, UK
Isabela, Isla 115 A7 *Island,* Galapagos Islands, Ecuador
Isabella, Cordillera 107 D4 ⛰ NW Nicaragua
Isachsen 97 G2 Ellef Ringnes Island, Nunavut, N Canada
Ísafjördhur 49 A1 NW Iceland
Isbister 33 A6 NE Scotland, UK
Ise 85 F6 SW Japan
Isère 55 E5 ≈ E France
Isernia 61 D5 C Italy
Ise-wan 85 F6 *Bay,* S Japan
Isfahan 81 D2 C Iran
Ishigaki-jima 85 A8 *Island,* Sakishima-shoto, SW Japan
Ishikari-wan 85 F2 *Bay,* NE Japan
Ishim 76 C4 C Russ. Fed.
Ishim 76 D4 ≈ Kazakhstan/Russ. Fed.
Ishinomaki 85 G4 C Japan
Ishkoshim 83 G4 S Tajikistan
Isiro 128 D1 NE Dem. Rep. Congo
İskenderun 79 E5 S Turkey
Iskur 65 E3 ≈ NW Bulgaria
Iskur, Yazovir 65 E3 ▣ W Bulgaria
Isla Cristina 57 B5 S Spain
Islamabad 89 D1 ● NE Pakistan
I-n-Sakane, 'Erg 124 D2 *Desert,* N Mali
Islay 33 B6 *Island,* SW Scotland, UK
Isle 55 C5 ≈ W France
Isle of Anglesey 29 ◈ *Unitary auth.,* NW Wales, UK
Isle of Man 29 *UK* ◇ NW Europe
Isle of Wight 37 E5 ◈ *Unitary auth.,* S England, UK
Isles of Scilly 29 ◈ *Unitary auth.,* SW England, UK
Islington 29 ◈ *London borough,* SE England, UK
Ismâ'ilîya 122 I2 N Egypt
Isna 122 J3 SE Egypt

Isoka 128 E3 NE Zambia
İsparta 79 B4 Isparta, SW Turkey
İspir 79 F2 NE Turkey
Israel 81 G6 ◆ *Republic,* SW Asia
Issoire 55 D5 C France
Issyk-Kul', Ozero 83 H2 ◎ E Kyrgyzstan
Istanbul 79 B2 NW Turkey
Istra 65 A1 *Cultural region,* Croatia/Slovenia
Itabuna 115 H6 E Brazil
Itagüí 115 B2 W Colombia
Itaipú Dam 117 C4 *Dam,* Brazil/Paraguay
Itaipú, Represa de 115 F7 ⊠ Brazil/Paraguay
Itaituba 115 F4 NE Brazil
Italy 61 C4 ◆ *Republic,* S Europe
Itoigawa 85 F5 C Japan
Iturup, Ostrov 76 I5 *Island,* Kurile Islands, SE Russ. Fed.
Itzehoe 59 C2 N Germany
Ivalo 49 E2 N Finland
Ivanhoe 133 F5 NSW, SE Australia
Ivano-Frankivs'k 67 B5 W Ukraine
Ivanovo 69 B5 W Russ. Fed.
Ivoire, Côte d' *see* Ivory Coast
Ivory Coast 124 C5 ◆ *Republic,* W Africa
Ivujivik 99 D1 Québec, NE Canada
Iwaki 85 G5 N Japan
Iwakuni 85 D7 SW Japan
Iwanai 85 F2 NE Japan
Iwate 85 G3 N Japan
Ixtapa 105 E5 S Mexico
Ixtepec 105 G5 SE Mexico
Iyo-nada 85 D7 *Sea,* S Japan
Izabal, Lago de 107 B3 ◎ E Guatemala
Izad Khvast 81 D3 C Iran
Izegem 50 B6 W Belgium
Izhevsk 69 D6 NW Russ. Fed.
Izmayil 67 D7 SW Ukraine
İzmir 79 A4 W Turkey
İzmit 79 B2 NW Turkey
İznik Gölü 79 B2 ◎ NW Turkey
Izu-hanto 85 G6 *Peninsula,* Honshu, S Japan
Izu-shoto 85 G6 *Island group,* S Japan

J

Jabal ash Shifa 81 A3 *Desert,* NW Saudi Arabia
Jabalpur 89 E4 C India
Jaca 57 F2 NE Spain
Jacaltenango 107 A3 W Guatemala
Jackson 101 C5 Mississippi, USA
Jacksonville 101 E6 Florida, USA
Jacmel 109 F4 S Haiti
Jacobabad 89 C3 SE Pakistan
Jaén 57 D5 SW Spain
Jaffna 89 E7 N Sri Lanka
Jagdalpur 89 E5 C India
Jagdaqi 87 G1 N China
Jaipur 89 D3 N India
Jaisalmer 89 C3 NW India
Jakarta 91 C7 ● Java, C Indonesia
Jakobstad 49 D4 W Finland
Jalalabad 83 G5 E Afghanistan
Jalandhar 89 D2 N India
Jalapa 107 D3 NW Nicaragua
Jalpa 105 E4 C Mexico
Jalu 122 H3 NE Libya
Jamaame 127 E5 S Somalia
Jamaica 109 C5 ◆ *Commonwealth Republic,* W West Indies
Jamaica Channel 109 E4 *Channel,* Haiti/Jamaica
Jambi 91 C7 Sumatra, W Indonesia
James Bay 99 C3 *Bay,* Ontario/Québec, E Canada
James River 103 F2 ≈ N USA
Jamestown 40 ○ NW Saint Helena
Jammu 89 D2 NW India
Jammu and Kashmir 89 D2 *disputed region,* India/Pakistan
Jamnagar 89 C4 W India
Jamshedpur 89 F4 NE India
Jamuna 89 G4 ≈ Bangladesh
Janesville 101 D3 Wisconsin, USA
Jan Mayen 139 C6 *Norwegian* ◇ N Atlantic Ocean
Jánoshalma 63 E8 S Hungary
Japan 85 G4 ◆ *Monarchy,* E Asia
Japan, Sea of 85 D5 *Sea,* NW Pacific Ocean
Japiim 115 C5 W Brazil
Japurá, Rio 115 C3 ≈ Brazil/Colombia
Jaqué 107 I7 SE Panama
Jardines de la Reina, Archipiélago de los 109 C3 *Island group,* C Cuba
Jarocin 63 D4 C Poland
Jarosław 63 G5 SE Poland
Jarqo'rg'on 83 F4 S Uzbekistan
Jarvis Island 131 *US* ◇ C Pacific Ocean
Jasło 63 F5 SE Poland
Jason Islands 40 *Island group,* NW Falkland Islands
Jastrzębie-Zdrój 63 D5 S Poland
Jataí 115 F6 C Brazil
Jaunpur 89 F3 N India
Java 91 C8 *Island,* C Indonesia
Javalambre 57 E3 ▲ E Spain
Javari, Rio 115 C4 ≈ Brazil/ Peru
Java Sea 91 D7 *Sea,* W Indonesia
Jawhar 127 F5 S Somalia
Jaya, Puncak 91 H7 ▲ E Indonesia
Jayapura 91 I7 E Indonesia
Jaz Murian, Hamun-e 81 F3 ◎ SE Iran
Jebba 124 E4 W Nigeria
Jedburgh 33 F6 SE Scotland, UK
Jedda 81 B5 ● W Saudi Arabia
Jędrzejów 63 E5 S Poland
Jefferson City 103 G3 Missouri, USA
Jelenia Góra 63 C4 SW Poland
Jelgava 49 E6 C Latvia
Jemappes 50 B7 S Belgium
Jember 91 D8 Java, C Indonesia
Jena 59 C5 C Germany
Jenin 81 H6 N West Bank
Jérémie 109 E4 SW Haiti
Jeréz de la Frontera 57 C6 SW Spain
Jeréz de los Caballeros 57 C5 W Spain
Jericho 81 H6 E West Bank
Jerid, Chott el 122 E2 *Salt lake,* SW Tunisia
Jersey 37 G6 *UK* ◇ NW Europe
Jerusalem 81 H6 ● NE Israel
Jesenice 59 E8 NW Slovenia
Jessore 89 G4 W Bangladesh
Jesús María 117 B5 C Argentina
Jhansi 89 E3 N India
Jhelum 89 D2 NE Pakistan
Jiamusi 87 H2 NE China
Jiangmen 87 F6 S China
Jiaxing 87 G4 SE China
Jihlava 63 C6 S Czech Republic
Jilib 127 E5 S Somalia
Jilin 87 H2 NE China
Jima 127 D4 SW Ethiopia
Jiménez 105 D3 N Mexico
Jinan 87 G3 E China
Jingdezhen 87 G5 S China
Jinghong 87 D6 SW China
Jinhua 87 G4 SE China
Jining 87 G4 E China
Jinja 127 C5 S Uganda
Jinotega 107 D4 NW Nicaragua
Jinotepe 107 D5 SW Nicaragua
Jinsha Jiang 87 D4 ≈ SW China
Jinzhou 87 G3 NE China
Jiu 67 B7 ≈ S Romania
Jiujiang 87 G4 S China
Jixi 87 H2 NE China
Jizan 81 B6 SW Saudi Arabia
Jizzax 83 F3 C Uzbekistan
João Pessoa 115 I5 E Brazil
Jodhpur 89 C3 NW India
Joensuu 49 F4 SE Finland
Joetsu 85 F5 C Japan
Johannesburg 128 C6 NE South Africa
John o'Groats 33 E2 N Scotland, UK
Johnston 39 A6 SW Wales, UK
Johnston Atoll 42 *US* ◇ C Pacific Ocean
Johnstown 31 D5 SE Ireland
Johor Bahru 91 C6 Peninsular Malaysia
Joinville 115 G8 S Brazil
Jokkmokk 49 D3 N Sweden
Joliet 101 D3 Illinois, USA
Jonava 49 E7 C Lithuania
Jönköping 49 C6 S Sweden
Jonquière 99 E4 Québec, SE Canada
Jordan 83 G3 E Uzbekistan
Jordan 81 A3 ◆ *Monarchy,* SW Asia
Jorhat 89 H3 NE India
Jos 124 F4 C Nigeria
Jos Plateau 124 F4 *Plateau,* C Nigeria
Jost Van Dyke 40 *Island,* W British Virgin Islands
Jotunheimen 49 B5 ▲▲ S Norway
Joure 50 E2 N Netherlands
Joutseno 49 F5 SE Finland
Juan Aldama 105 D3 C Mexico
Juazeiro 115 H5 E Brazil
Juazeiro do Norte 115 H5 E Brazil
Juba 127 C4 S Sudan
Juba 127 E5 ≈ Ethiopia/Somalia
Júcar 57 E4 ≈ C Spain
Juchitán 105 G5 SE Mexico
Judenburg 59 E8 C Austria
Juigalpa 107 D5 S Nicaragua
Juiz de Fora 115 G7 SE Brazil
Juliaca 115 C6 SE Peru
Jumilla 57 E4 SE Spain
Juneau 97 E5 Alaska, USA
Junín 117 B5 E Argentina
Jur 127 B3 ≈ C Sudan
Jura 33 B5 *Island,* SW Scotland, UK
Jura 55 F4 ▲▲ France/Switzerland
Jura, Sound of 33 C5 *Strait,* W Scotland, UK
Jūrmala 49 E6 C Latvia
Juruá, Rio 115 C4 ≈ Brazil/Peru
Juruena, Rio 115 E5 ≈ W Brazil
Jutiapa 107 B3 S Guatemala
Juticalpa 107 D3 C Honduras
Jutland 49 B7 *Island,* W Denmark
Jyväskylä 49 E4 C Finland

K

K2 89 D1 ▲ China/Pakistan
Kaamanen 49 E1 N Finland
Kaaresuvanto 49 D2 N Finland
Kabale 127 C5 SW Uganda
Kabinda 128 D3 SE Dem. Rep. Congo
Kabompo 128 D4 ≈ W Zambia
Kabul 83 F5 ● E Afghanistan
Kabwe 128 D4 C Zambia
Kachchh, Gulf of 89 B4 *Gulf,* W India
Kachchh, Rann of 89 C4 *Salt marsh,* India/Pakistan
Kadavu 137 J5 *Island,* S Fiji
Kadavu Passage 137 J5 *Channel,* S Fiji
Kadugli 127 C3 S Sudan
Kaduna 124 F4 C Nigeria
Kadzhi-Say 83 H2 NE Kyrgyzstan
Kaédi 124 B3 S Mauritania
Kaesong 85 B5 S North Korea
Kafue 128 D4 SE Zambia
Kafue 128 D4 ≈ C Zambia
Kaga Bandoro 124 G5 C CAR
Kâghet 124 C1 *Physical region,* N Mauritania
Kagoshima 85 D8 SW Japan
Kahmard, Darya-ye 83 F4 ≈ NE Afghanistan
Kahramanmaraş 79 E4 S Turkey
Kaiapoi 135 C6 South Island, NZ
Kaifeng 87 F4 C China
Kai, Kepulauan 91 G7 *Island group,* Maluku, SE Indonesia
Kaikohe 135 C1 North Island, NZ
Kaikoura 135 C5 South Island, NZ
Kainji Reservoir 124 E4 ⊠ W Nigeria
Kaipara Harbour 135 C2 *Harbour,* North Island, NZ
Kairouan 122 F1 E Tunisia
Kaiserslautern 59 B6 SW Germany
Kaitaia 135 C1 North Island, NZ
Kajaani 49 F3 C Finland
Kaka 83 D4 S Turkmenistan
Kake 97 E5 Kupreanof Island, Alaska, USA
Kakhovs'ke Vodoskhovyshche 67 E5 ⊠ SE Ukraine
Kakinada 89 E5 E India
Kaktovik 97 E3 Alaska, USA
Kalahari Desert 128 C6 *Desert,* S Africa
Kalamariá 65 E4 N Greece
Kalamáta 65 E6 S Greece
Kalamazoo 101 D3 Michigan, USA
Kalat 83 F6 S Afghanistan
Kālat 89 B2 SW Pakistan
Kalbarri 133 A5 Western Australia
Kalecik 79 C3 N Turkey
Kalemie 128 D2 SE Dem. Rep. Congo
Kalgoorlie 133 C5 Western Australia
Kalima 128 D2 E Dem. Rep. Congo
Kalimantan 91 D6 *Geopolitical region,* C Indonesia
Kaliningrad 49 E7 W Russ. Fed.
Kaliningrad 49 F7 *Province,* W Russ. Fed.
Kalisz 63 D4 C Poland
Kalix 49 E3 N Sweden
Kalixälven 49 E3 ≈ N Sweden
Kalkarindji 133 D2 Northern Territory, N Australia
Kallavesi 49 F4 ◎ SE Finland
Kalloní 65 F5 Lesbos, E Greece
Kalmar 49 C6 S Sweden
Kalmthout 50 C5 N Belgium
Kaluga 69 A5 W Russ. Fed.
Kalyan 89 C5 W India
Kálymnos 65 F6 *Island,* Dodecanese, Greece
Kama 69 D5 ≈ NW Russ. Fed.
Kamchatka 76 I3 *Peninsula,* E Russ. Fed.
Kamensk-Shakhtinskiy 69 A7 SW Russ. Fed.
Kamina 128 D3 S Dem. Rep. Congo
Kamloops 97 F7 British Columbia, SW Canada
Kampala 127 C5 ● S Uganda
Kampong Cham 91 C4 C Cambodia
Kampong Saom 91 C4 SW Cambodia
Kampuchea *see* Cambodia
Kam"yanets'-Podil's'kyy 67 C5 W Ukraine
Kamyshin 69 B7 SW Russ. Fed.
Kananga 128 C2 S Dem. Rep. Congo
Kanash 69 C6 W Russ. Fed.
Kanazawa 85 F5 SW Japan
Kanchipuram 89 E6 SE India
Kandahar 83 E6 S Afghanistan
Kandalaksha 69 B2 NW Russ. Fed.
Kandangan 91 E7 C Indonesia
Kandi 124 E4 N Benin
Kandy 89 E8 C Sri Lanka
Kaneohe 103 B6 Oahu, Hawaii, USA
Kangan 81 D3 S Iran
Kangaroo Island 133 E6 *Island,* S Australia
Kanggye 85 B4 N North Korea
Kangnung 85 C5 NE South Korea
Kanivs'ke Vodoskhovyshche 67 D4 ⊠ C Ukraine
Kankaanpää 49 E4 SW Finland
Kankan 124 B4 E Guinea
Kano 124 F4 N Nigeria
Kanpur 89 E3 N India
Kansas 103 F3 ◐ *State,* C USA
Kansas City 103 G3 Kansas, USA
Kansas City 103 G3 Missouri, USA
Kansk 76 E5 S Russ. Fed.
Kantemirovka 69 A7 W Russ. Fed.
Kanto Plain 85 G5 *Plain,* Honshu, C Japan
Kanye 128 D6 SE Botswana
Kaohsiung 87 H6 S Taiwan
Kaolack 124 A3 W Senegal
Kapelle 50 C5 SW Netherlands
Kapellen 50 C6 N Belgium
Kaplangky, Plato 83 C2 *Ridge,* Turkmenistan/Uzbekistan
Kapoeta 127 C4 SE Sudan
Kaposvár 63 D8 SW Hungary
Kappeln 59 C2 N Germany
Kapuas, Sungai 91 D6 ≈ C Indonesia
Kapuskasing 99 C4 Ontario, S Canada
Kara-Balta 83 H2 N Kyrgyzstan
Karabük 79 C2 N Turkey
Karachi 89 B3 SE Pakistan
Karaganda 76 C5 C Kazakhstan
Karaginskiy, Ostrov 76 I3 *Island,* E Russ. Fed.
Karakol 83 H2 NE Kyrgyzstan
Karakol 83 I2 NE Kyrgyzstan
Karakoram Range 89 D1 ▲▲ C Asia
Karaman 79 C4 S Turkey
Karamay 87 C2 NW China
Karamea Bight 135 C5 *Gulf,* South Island, NZ
Kara-Say 83 I2 NE Kyrgyzstan
Karasburg 128 C6 S Namibia
Kara Sea 76 D2 *Sea,* Arctic Ocean
Kara Strait 69 E2 *Strait,* N Russ. Fed.
Karatau 76 C6 S Kazakhstan
Karatau, Khrebet 83 F2 ▲▲ S Kazakhstan
Karbala' 81 C2 S Iraq
Karditsa 65 D5 C Greece
Kargı 79 D2 N Turkey
Kariba 128 D4 N Zimbabwe
Kariba, Lake 128 D4 ⊠ Zambia/Zimbabwe
Karibib 128 B5 C Namibia
Karigasniemi 49 E1 N Finland
Karimata, Selat 91 C6 *Strait,* W Indonesia
Karimnagar 89 E5 C India
Karin 127 F3 N Somalia
Karkar Island 137 B2 *Island,* N PNG
Karkinits'ka Zatoka 67 E6 *Gulf,* S Ukraine
Karleby *see* Kokkola
Karlovac 65 B1 C Croatia
Karlovy Vary 63 A5 W Czech Republic
Karlskrona 49 C7 S Sweden
Karlsruhe 59 B6 SW Germany
Karlstad 49 C5 C Sweden
Karnal 89 D2 N India
Karnataka 89 D6 *Cultural region,* W India
Kárpathos 65 G7 Kárpathos, SE Greece
Kárpathos 65 G7 *Island,* SE Greece
Karpenísi 65 D5 C Greece
Kars 79 G2 NE Turkey
Karskoye More *see* Kara Sea
Karst 59 E8 *Physical region,* Croatia/Slovenia
Karyés 65 E4 N Greece
Kaş 79 B5 SW Turkey
Kasai 128 C3 ≈ Angola/Dem. Rep. Congo
Kasaji 128 C3 S Dem. Rep. Congo
Kasama 128 E3 N Zambia
Kasese 127 C5 SW Uganda
Kashan 81 D2 C Iran
Kashi 87 A3 NW China
Kasongo 128 D2 E Dem. Rep. Congo
Kasongo-Lunda 128 B3 SW Dem. Rep. Congo
Kásos 65 F7 *Island,* S Greece
Kaspiysk 69 B9 SW Russ. Fed.
Kassala 127 D2 E Sudan
Kassel 59 C4 C Germany
Kastamonu 79 D2 N Turkey
Kastsyukovichy 67 E2 E Belarus
Kasulu 127 C6 W Tanzania
Kasumiga-ura 85 G5 ◎ Honshu, S Japan
Katahdin, Mount 101 H1 ▲ Maine, USA
Katalla 97 D4 Alaska, USA
Katanning 133 B6 Western Australia
Katchall Island 89 H6 *Island,* Nicobar Islands, India
Kateríni 65 E4 N Greece
Katherine 133 D1 Northern Territory, N Australia
Kathmandu 89 F3 ● C Nepal
Katikati 135 D3 North Island, NZ
Katima Mulilo 128 D4 NE Namibia
Katiola 124 C5 C Ivory Coast
Katowice 63 E5 S Poland
Katsina 124 F4 N Nigeria
Kattaqo'rg'on 83 E3 C Uzbekistan
Kattegat 49 B7 *Strait,* N Europe
Kauai 103 A5 *Island,* Hawaii, USA
Kaufbeuren 59 C7 S Germany
Kaunas 49 E7 C Lithuania
Kauno Marios 63 G1 ⊠ S Lithuania
Kavála 65 E4 NE Greece
Kavali 89 E6 E India
Kavaratti 89 C7 Laccadive Islands, SW India
Kavarna 65 G2 NE Bulgaria
Kavieng 137 C1 NE PNG
Kavir, Dasht-e 81 E2 *Salt pan,* N Iran
Kawagoe 85 G5 S Japan
Kawasaki 85 G5 S Japan
Kawerau 135 E3 North Island, NZ
Kaya 124 D4 C Burkina
Kayan, Sungai 91 E6 ≈ C Indonesia
Kayes 124 B3 W Mali
Kayseri 79 D4 C Turkey
Kazach'ye 76 G3 NE Russ. Fed.
Kazakhstan 76 B5 ◆ *Republic,* C Asia
Kazakh Uplands 76 C5 *Plateau,* Kazakhstan
Kazan' 69 C6 W Russ. Fed.
Kazanlŭk 65 F3 C Bulgaria
Kazbek 79 G1 ▲ N Georgia
Kazerun 81 D3 S Iran
Kéa 65 F6 *Island,* Cyclades, Greece
Keady 31 E3 S Northern Ireland, UK
Kea, Mauna 103 B6 ▲ Hawaii, USA
Keban Barajı 79 F3 ◎ Turkey Asia
Kebkabiya 127 A2 W Sudan
Kebnekaise 49 C2 ▲ N Sweden
Kecskemét 63 E8 C Hungary
Kediri 91 D8 Java, C Indonesia
Keetmanshoop 128 C6 S Namibia
Kefalonía 65 D5 *Island,* Ionian Islands, Greece
Kehl 59 B6 SW Germany
Keïta 124 E3 C Niger
Keitele 49 E4 ◎ C Finland
Keith 133 F6 S Australia
Keith 33 E3 NE Scotland, UK
Këk-Art 83 H3 SW Kyrgyzstan
Kékes 63 E7 ▲ N Hungary
Kells 31 D5 S Ireland
Kells 31 E4 E Ireland
Kélo 124 G4 SW Chad
Kelowna 97 F7 British Columbia, SW Canada
Kelso 33 F6 SE Scotland, UK
Keluang 91 C6 Peninsular Malaysia
Kem' 69 B3 NW Russ. Fed.
Kemah 79 F3 E Turkey
Kemerovo 76 E5 C Russ. Fed.
Kemi 49 E3 NW Finland
Kemijärvi 49 E2 N Finland
Kemijoki 49 E3 ≈ NW Finland
Kemin 83 H2 N Kyrgyzstan
Kempele 49 E3 C Finland
Kemp Land 138 D4 *Physical region,* Antarctica
Kempten 59 C7 S Germany
Kendal 35 C3 NW England, UK
Kendari 91 F7 Celebes, C Indonesia
Kenema 124 B5 SE Sierra Leone
Keng Tung 91 B2 E Burma
Kenilworth 35 D6 C England, UK
Kénitra 122 C1 NW Morocco
Kenmare 31 B6 S Ireland
Kenora 99 A4 Ontario, S Canada
Kensington and Chelsea 29 ◐ *London borough,* SE England, UK
Kent 29 ◐ *County,* SE England, UK
Kentau 76 C6 S Kazakhstan
Kentucky 101 D4 ◐ *State,* C USA
Kentucky Lake 101 C4 ⊠ S USA
Kenya 127 D5 ◆ *Republic,* E Africa
Kępno 63 D4 C Poland
Kerala 89 D7 *Cultural region,* S India
Kerch 67 G6 SE Ukraine
Kerch Strait 67 G7 *Strait,* Black Sea/ Sea of Azov
Kerema 137 B2 S PNG
Kerguelen 15 *Island,* C French Southern and Antarctic Territories
Kerí 65 D6 Zákynthos, Greece
Kerikeri 135 D1 North Island, NZ
Kerkenah, Îles de 70 E4 *Island group,* E Tunisia
Kerkrade 50 E6 SE Netherlands
Kerkyra *see* Corfu
Kermadec Islands 131 *Island group,* NE New Zealand
Kerman 81 E3 C Iran
Kerry 29 ◐ *County,* SW Ireland
Kerry Head 31 A5 *Headland,* SW Ireland
Kerulen 87 F2 ≈ China/Mongolia
Kesennuma 85 G4 C Japan
Keswick 35 C3 NW England, UK
Keszthely 63 D8 SW Hungary
Ketchikan 97 E6 Revillagigedo Island, Alaska, USA
Kettering 37 F2 C England, UK
Keuruu 49 E4 C Finland
Kew 40 N Turks and Caicos Islands
Key Largo 101 F7 Key Largo, Florida, USA
Keynsham 37 D4 SW England, UK
Key West 101 E7 Florida Keys, Florida, USA
Khabarovsk 76 H5 SE Russ. Fed.
Khairpur 89 C3 SE Pakistan
Khambhat, Gulf of 89 C4 *Gulf,* W India
Khandwa 89 D4 C India
Khanka, Lake 76 H5 ◎ China/Russ. Fed.
Khanthabouli 91 C3 S Laos
Khanty-Mansiysk 76 D4 C Russ. Fed.
Khao Laem Reservoir 91 A3 ⊠ W Thailand
Kharagpur 89 G4 NE India
Kharkiv 67 F4 NE Ukraine
Khartoum 127 C2 ● C Sudan
Khartoum North 127 C2 C Sudan
Khasavyurt 69 B9 SW Russ. Fed.
Khash, Dasht-e 83 D6 *Desert,* SW Afghanistan
Khashm el Girba 127 D2 E Sudan
Khaskovo 65 F3 S Bulgaria
Khatanga 139 E3 N Russ. Fed.
Khaydarkan 83 G3 SW Kyrgyzstan
Kherson 67 E6 S Ukraine
Kheta 76 E3 ≈ N Russ. Fed.
Khiwa 83 D2 W Uzbekistan
Khmel'nyts'kyy 67 C5 W Ukraine
Kholm 83 F4 N Afghanistan
Khon Kaen 91 B3 E Thailand
Khor 76 H5 SE Russ. Fed.
Khorugh 83 G4 S Tajikistan
Khouribga 122 C2 C Morocco
Khowst 83 F5 E Afghanistan
Khujand 83 F3 N Tajikistan
Khulna 89 G4 SW Bangladesh
Khust 67 B5 W Ukraine
Khvoy 81 C1 NW Iran
Khyber Pass 89 C1 *Pass,* Afghanistan/Pakistan
Kia 137 E2 N Solomon Islands
Kibangou 128 B2 SW Congo
Kibombo 128 D2 E Dem. Rep. Congo
Kidderminster 35 D6 C England, UK
Kidlington 37 E3 C England, UK
Kidwelly 39 C6 S Wales, UK
Kiel 59 C2 N Germany
Kielce 63 E4 SE Poland
Kielder Water 35 C2 ◎ N England, UK
Kieler Bucht 59 C2 *Bay,* N Germany
Kiev 67 D4 ● N Ukraine
Kiev Reservoir 67 D4 ⊠ N Ukraine
Kiffa 124 B3 S Mauritania
Kigali 127 C6 ● C Rwanda
Kigoma 127 B6 W Tanzania
Kii-suido 85 E7 *Strait,* S Japan
Kikinda 65 D1 N Serbia and Montenegro (Yugoslavia)
Kikwit 128 C2 W Dem. Rep. Congo
Kilbaha 31 B5 W Ireland
Kilbeggan 31 D4 C Ireland
Kilchu 85 C4 NE North Korea
Kilcogy 31 D3 N Ireland
Kilcolgan 31 C4 W Ireland
Kilcormac 31 D4 C Ireland
Kildare 31 E4 E Ireland
Kildare 29 ◐ *County,* E Ireland
Kildorrery 31 C6 S Ireland
Kilgetty 39 B6 SW Wales, UK
Kilimanjaro 127 D6 ▲ NE Tanzania
Kilis 79 E5 S Turkey
Kilkee 31 B5 W Ireland
Kilkeel 31 F3 S Northern Ireland, UK
Kilkelly 31 C3 NW Ireland
Kilkenny 31 D5 S Ireland
Kilkenny 29 ◐ *County,* S Ireland
Kilkinlea 31 B6 SW Ireland
Kilkís 65 E4 N Greece
Killagan 31 E1 N Northern Ireland, UK
Killala 31 B3 NW Ireland
Killala Bay 31 B3 *Inlet,* NW Ireland
Killarney 31 B6 SW Ireland
Killeany 31 B4 W Ireland
Killeen 31 E3 S Northern Ireland, UK
Killeen 103 F5 Texas, USA
Killimer 31 B5 W Ireland
Killimor 31 C4 W Ireland
Killorglin 31 B6 SW Ireland
Killybegs 31 C2 NW Ireland
Killyleagh 31 F3 E Northern Ireland, UK
Kilmaine 31 B4 NW Ireland
Kilmarnock 33 D6 W Scotland, UK
Kilmurvy 31 B4 W Ireland
Kilrea 31 E2 N Northern Ireland, UK
Kilrush 31 B5 W Ireland
Kilwa Kivinje 127 D7 SE Tanzania
Kimbe 137 C2 E PNG
Kimberley 128 D6 C South Africa
Kimberley Plateau 133 C2 *Plateau,* Western Australia
Kimch'aek 85 C4 E North Korea
Kinabalu, Gunung 91 E5 ▲ East Malaysia
Kinbrace 33 D2 N Scotland, UK
Kincaslough 31 C1 N Ireland
Kinder Scout 35 D5 ▲ C England, UK
Kindersley 97 G7 Saskatchewan, S Canada
Kindia 124 B4 SW Guinea
Kindu 128 D2 C Dem. Rep. Congo
Kineshma 69 B5 W Russ. Fed.
King Island 133 F7 *Island,* Tasmania, SE Australia
Kingman Reef 131 *US* ◇ C Pacific Ocean
King's Lynn 37 G1 E England, UK
King Sound 133 C2 *Sound,* Western Australia
Kingston 99 D6 Ontario, SE Canada
Kingston 109 D5 ● E Jamaica
Kingston upon Hull 35 F4 E England, UK
Kingston upon Hull 29 ◐ *Unitary auth.,* N England, UK
Kingston upon Thames 29 ◐ *London borough,* SE England, UK
Kingstown 109 K6 ● Saint Vincent, Saint Vincent and the Grenadines
King William Island 97 H3 *Island,* Nunavut, N Canada
Kinnegad 31 D4 C Ireland
Kinrooi 50 E6 NE Belgium
Kinross 33 E5 C Scotland, UK
Kinsale 31 C7 SW Ireland
Kinsale 40 SW Montserrat
Kinsalebeg 31 D6 S Ireland
Kinshasa 128 B2 ● W Dem. Rep. Congo
Kintyre 33 C6 *Peninsula,* W Scotland, UK
Kintyre, Mull of 33 C6 *Headland,* W Scotland, UK
Kinvara 31 C4 W Ireland
Kinyeti 127 C4 ▲ S Sudan
Kipili 127 C7 W Tanzania
Kippure 31 E4 ▲ E Ireland
Kipushi 128 D3 SE Dem. Rep. Congo
Kirakira 137 F3 SE Solomon Islands
Kirghiz Range 83 G2 ▲▲ Kazakhstan/Kyrgyzstan
Kirghiz Steppe 76 C5 *Uplands,* C Kazakhstan
Kiribati 137 J1 ◆ *Republic,* C Pacific Ocean
Kırıkhan 79 E5 S Turkey
Kırıkkale 79 D3 C Turkey
Kirinyaga 127 D5 ▲ C Kenya
Kirishi 69 A4 NW Russ. Fed.
Kiritimati 131 *Island,* E Kiribati
Kiriwina Islands 137 C2 *Island group,* S PNG
Kirkby 35 C5 NW England, UK
Kirkby Stephen 35 D3 NW England, UK
Kirkcaldy 33 E5 E Scotland, UK
Kirkcudbright 33 D7 S Scotland, UK
Kirkenes 49 E1 N Norway
Kirkland Lake 99 C5 Ontario, S Canada
Kırklareli 79 A2 NW Turkey
Kirklees 29 ◐ *Unitary auth.,* N England, UK

CAR Central African Republic **FYR** Former Yugoslavian Rebublic **NSW** New South Wales **NZ** New Zealand **PNG** Papua New Guinea **Russ. Fed.** Russian Federation **UAE** United Arab Emirates **UK** United Kingdom **USA** United States of America

Kirkpatrick, Mount 138 C5 ▲ Antarctica
Kirksville 103 G3 Missouri, USA
Kirkuk 81 C2 N Iraq
Kirkwall 33 E1 NE Scotland, UK
Kirov 69 C5 W Russ. Fed.
Kirovo-Chepetsk 69 C5 NW Russ. Fed.
Kirovohrad 67 E5 C Ukraine
Kirriemuir 33 E4 E Scotland, UK
Kiruna 49 D2 N Sweden
Kisangani 128 D1 NE Dem. Rep. Congo
Kiskörei-víztároló 63 E7 ⊠ E Hungary
Kiskunfélegyháza 63 E8 C Hungary
Kislovodsk 69 A8 SW Russ. Fed.
Kismaayo 127 E5 S Somalia
Kissidougou 124 B4 S Guinea
Kissimmee, Lake 101 E7 ◎ SE USA
Kisumu 127 D5 W Kenya
Kisvárda 63 E9 E Hungary
Kita 124 B4 W Mali
Kitakyushu 85 C7 SW Japan
Kitami 85 G1 NE Japan
Kitchener 99 C6 Ontario, S Canada
Kitimat 97 E6 British Columbia, SW Canada
Kitinen 49 E2 ≈ N Finland
Kitob 83 F3 S Uzbekistan
Kitwe 128 D4 C Zambia
Kitzbühler Alpen 59 D7 ⛰ W Austria
Kiunga 137 A2 SW PNG
Kivalina 97 D3 Alaska, USA
Kivalo 49 E3 *Ridge*, C Finland
Kivu, Lake 128 D2 ◎ Dem. Rep. Congo/Rwanda
Kiwai Island 137 A3 *Island*, SW PNG
Kızıl Irmak 79 D2 ≈ C Turkey
Kladno 63 B5 NW Czech Republic
Klagenfurt 59 E8 S Austria
Klaipėda 49 E7 NW Lithuania
Klang 91 B6 Selangor, Peninsular Malaysia
Klarälven 49 C5 ≈ Norway/Sweden
Klatovy 63 A6 SW Czech Republic
Klazienaveen 50 F3 NE Netherlands
Klintsy 69 A5 W Russ. Fed.
Kłobuck 63 E4 S Poland
Klosters 59 C8 SE Switzerland
Kluczbork 63 D4 SW Poland
Klyuchevka 83 G2 NW Kyrgyzstan
Klyuchevskaya Sopka, Vulkan 76 H3 ⧍ E Russ. Fed.
Knaresborough 35 D4 N England, UK
Knighton 39 E4 E Wales, UK
Knock 31 C3 NW Ireland
Knocktopher 31 D6 SE Ireland
Knokke-Heist 50 B5 NW Belgium
Knowle 35 D6 C England, UK
Knowsley 29 ◐ *Unitary auth.*, NW England, UK
Knoxville 101 E4 Tennessee, USA
Knud Rasmussen Land 97 I1 *Physical region*, N Greenland
Kobe 85 E6 SW Japan
København *see* Copenhagen
Kobenni 124 B3 S Mauritania
Koblenz 59 B5 W Germany
Kobryn 67 B3 SW Belarus
K'obulet'i 79 G2 W Georgia
Kočevje 59 E9 S Slovenia
Koch Bihar 89 G3 NE India
Kochi 85 E7 Shikoku, SW Japan
Kodiak 97 D4 Kodiak Island, Alaska, USA
Kodiak Island 97 D5 *Island*, Alaska, USA
Kofu 85 F5 S Japan
Kogon 83 E3 C Uzbekistan
Kogum-do 85 B7 *Island*, S South Korea
Kohima 89 H3 E India
Kohtla-Järve 49 F5 NE Estonia
Koician 63 C3 W Poland
Koidu 124 B4 E Sierra Leone
Koje-do 85 C7 *Island*, S South Korea
Kokkola 49 E4 W Finland
Koko 124 E4 W Nigeria
Kokrines 97 D3 Alaska, USA
Kokshaal-Tau 83 H3 ⛰ China/Kyrgyzstan
Kokshetau 76 C5 N Kazakhstan
Koksijde 50 A6 W Belgium
Koksoak 99 D2 ≈ Québec, E Canada
Kokstad 128 D7 E South Africa
Kola Peninsula 69 C3 *Peninsula*, NW Russ. Fed.
Kolari 49 E2 NW Finland
Kolárovo 63 D7 SW Slovakia
Kolda 124 A3 S Senegal
Kolding 49 B7 C Denmark
Kolguyev, Ostrov 69 C2 *Island*, NW Russ. Fed.
Kolhapur 89 D5 SW India
Kolín 63 B5 C Czech Republic
Kolka 49 E6 NW Latvia
Kolkata 89 G4 NE India
Köln *see* Cologne
Koło 63 D3 C Poland
Kołobrzeg 63 C2 NW Poland
Kolokani 124 C3 W Mali
Kolomna 69 B5 W Russ. Fed.
Kolpa 65 B1 ≈ Croatia/Slovenia
Kolpino 69 A4 NW Russ. Fed.
Kol'skiy Poluostrov *see* Kola Peninsula
Kolwezi 128 D3 S Dem. Rep. Congo
Kolyma 76 H2 ≈ NE Russ. Fed.
Kolyma Range 76 H3 ⛰ E Russ. Fed.
Komatsu 85 F5 SW Japan
Komoé 124 C4 ≈ E Ivory Coast
Komotiní 65 F4 NE Greece
Komsomolets, Ostrov 76 E1 *Island*, N Russ. Fed.
Komsomol'sk-na-Amure 76 H5 SE Russ. Fed.
Kondopoga 69 B4 NW Russ. Fed.
Koné 137 G6 W New Caledonia
Köneürgenç 83 D2 N Turkmenistan
Kong Frederik VIII Land 139 B5 *Physical region*, NE Greenland
Kongolo 128 D2 E Dem. Rep. Congo
Kongor 127 C4 SE Sudan
Kongsberg 49 B5 S Norway
Konin 63 D3 C Poland
Kónitsa 65 D4 W Greece
Konosha 69 B4 NW Russ. Fed.
Konotop 67 E3 NE Ukraine
Konstanz 59 B7 S Germany
Konya 79 C4 C Turkey
Kopaonik 65 D3 ⛰ S Serbia and Montenegro (Yugoslavia)
Koper 59 E9 SW Slovenia
Köpetdag Gershi 83 C3 ⛰ Iran/Turkmenistan
Koppeh Dagh 81 E1 ⛰ Iran/Turkmenistan
Korat Plateau 91 B3 *Plateau*, E Thailand
Korçë 65 D4 SE Albania
Korčula 65 B3 *Island*, S Croatia
Korea Bay 87 G3 *Bay*, China/North Korea
Korea Strait 85 C7 *Channel*, Japan/South Korea
Korhogo 124 C4 N Ivory Coast
Korinthos *see* Corinth
Koriyama 85 G4 C Japan
Korla 87 C2 NW China
Körmend 63 C8 W Hungary
Koro 137 J5 *Island*, C Fiji
Koróni 65 E6 S Greece
Koror 130 ● N Palau
Koro Sea 137 J5 *Sea*, C Fiji
Korosten' 67 D4 NW Ukraine
Koro Toro 124 H3 N Chad
Kortrijk 50 B6 W Belgium
Koryak Range 76 I2 ⛰ NE Russ. Fed.
Koryazhma 69 C4 NW Russ. Fed.
Kos 65 G6 *Island*, Dodecanese, Greece
Ko-saki 85 C7 *Headland*, Tsushima, SW Japan
Kościerzyna 63 D2 NW Poland
Kosciuszko, Mount 133 G6 ▲ NSW, SE Australia
Koshikijima-retto 85 C8 *Island group*, SW Japan
Košice 63 F6 E Slovakia
Koson 83 E3 S Uzbekistan
Kosong 85 B5 SE North Korea
Kosovo 65 D3 *Cultural region*, S Serbia and Montenegro (Yugoslavia)
Kosovska Mitrovica 65 D3 S Serbia and Montenegro (Yugoslavia)
Kossou, Lac de 124 C5 ◎ C Ivory Coast
Kostanay 76 C4 N Kazakhstan
Kostroma 69 B5 NW Russ. Fed.
Kostyantynivka 67 G5 SE Ukraine
Koszalin 63 C2 NW Poland
Kota 89 D3 N India
Kota Bharu 91 B5 Peninsular Malaysia
Kota Kinabalu 91 D5 East Malaysia
Kotel'nyy, Ostrov 76 F2 *Island*, N Russ. Fed.
Kotka 49 F5 S Finland
Kotlas 69 C4 NW Russ. Fed.
Kotovs'k 67 D5 SW Ukraine
Kotto 125 I5 ≈ CAR/Dem. Rep. Congo
Kotuy 76 F3 ≈ N Russ. Fed.
Koudougou 124 D4 C Burkina
Koulamoutou 128 B2 C Gabon
Koulikoro 124 C4 SW Mali
Koumac 137 G6 W New Caledonia
Koumra 124 H4 S Chad
Kourou 115 F2 N French Guiana
Kousséri 124 G4 NE Cameroon
Koutiala 124 C4 S Mali
Kouvola 49 F5 S Finland
Kovel' 67 B4 NW Ukraine
Kozáni 65 D4 N Greece
Kozara 65 B2 ⛰ NW Bosnia and Herzegovina
Kozloduy 65 E2 NW Bulgaria
Kozu-shima 85 F6 *Island*, E Japan
Kpalimé 124 D5 SW Togo
Kragujevac 65 D2 C Serbia and Montenegro (Yugoslavia)
Kra, Isthmus of 91 B5 *Isthmus*, Malaysia/Thailand
Kraków 63 E5 S Poland
Kraljevo 65 D2 C Serbia and Montenegro (Yugoslavia)
Kramators'k 67 G5 SE Ukraine
Kramfors 49 D4 C Sweden
Kranj 59 E8 NW Slovenia
Krasnoarmeysk 69 B7 W Russ. Fed.
Krasnodar 69 A8 SW Russ. Fed.
Krasnokamensk 76 G5 S Russ. Fed.
Krasnokamsk 69 D5 W Russ. Fed.
Krasnoyarsk 76 E5 S Russ. Fed.
Krasnystaw 63 G4 SE Poland
Krasnyy Kut 69 C7 W Russ. Fed.
Krasnyy Luch 67 G5 E Ukraine
Krefeld 59 A4 W Germany
Kremenchuk 67 E5 NE Ukraine
Kremenchuk Reservoir 67 D5 ⊠ C Ukraine
Kreminna 67 G4 E Ukraine
Krishna 89 E5 ≈ C India
Krishnagiri 89 D6 SE India
Kristiansand 49 B6 S Norway
Kristianstad 49 C7 S Sweden
Kristiansund 49 B4 S Norway
Kriti *see* Crete
Kritikó Pélagos *see* Crete, Sea of
Krk 65 B1 *Island*, NW Croatia
Kronach 59 C5 E Germany
Kroonstad 128 D6 C South Africa
Kropotkin 69 A8 SW Russ. Fed.
Krosno 63 F5 SE Poland
Krosno Odrzańskie 63 B3 W Poland
Krško 59 F8 E Slovenia
Krung Thep, Ao 91 B4 *Bay*, S Thailand
Kruševac 65 D2 C Serbia and Montenegro (Yugoslavia)
Kryms'ki Hory 67 F7 ⛰ S Ukraine
Kryvyy Rih 67 E5 SE Ukraine
Ksar-el-Kebir 122 C1 NW Morocco
Kuala Lumpur 91 B6 ● Peninsular Malaysia
Kuala Terengganu 91 C5 Peninsular Malaysia
Kuantan 91 C6 Peninsular Malaysia
Kuban' 67 G6 ≈ SW Russ. Fed.
Kuching 91 D6 East Malaysia
Kuchnay Darweyshan 83 E6 S Afghanistan
Kudus 91 D8 Java, C Indonesia
Kugluktuk 97 G4 Nunavut, NW Canada
Kuhmo 49 F3 E Finland
Kuito 128 B4 C Angola
Kuji 85 G3 C Japan
Kula Kangri 89 G2 ▲ Bhutan/China
Kulob 83 F4 SW Tajikistan
Kulu 79 C3 W Turkey
Kulunda 76 D5 S Russ. Fed.
Kulunda Steppe 76 D5 *Grassland*, Kazakhstan/Russ. Fed.
Kuma 69 B8 ≈ SW Russ. Fed.
Kumamoto 85 D7 SW Japan
Kumanovo 65 D3 N FYR Macedonia
Kumasi 124 D5 C Ghana
Kumba 124 F5 W Cameroon
Kumertau 69 D7 W Russ. Fed.
Kumo 124 F4 E Nigeria
Kumon Range 91 B1 ⛰ N Burma
Kumul *see* Hami
Kunda 49 F5 NE Estonia
Kunduz 83 F4 NE Afghanistan
Kungsbacka 49 B6 S Sweden
Kungur 69 D5 NW Russ. Fed.
Kunlun Mountains 87 B3 ⛰ NW China
Kunming 87 E5 SW China
Kunsan 85 B6 W South Korea
Kununurra 133 D2 Western Australia
Kuopio 49 F4 C Finland
Kupang 91 F8 C Indonesia
Kupiano 137 C3 S PNG
Kup"yans'k 67 G4 E Ukraine
Kura 79 H2 ≈ SW Asia
Kurashiki 85 E6 SW Japan
Kurdistan 79 H4 *Cultural region*, SW Asia
Kurdzhali 65 F3 S Bulgaria
Kure 85 D7 SW Japan
Küre Dağları 79 D2 ⛰ N Turkey
Kurile Islands 76 I4 *Island group*, Russ. Fed.
Kurile Trench 15 *Undersea feature*, NW Pacific Ocean
Kuril'sk 76 I5 Kurile Islands, SE Russ. Fed.
Kuril'skiye Ostrova *see* Kurile Islands
Kurnool 89 D6 S India
Kursk 69 A6 W Russ. Fed.
Kuruktag 87 C3 ⛰ NW China
Kurume 85 D7 SW Japan
Kushiro 85 G2 NE Japan
Kütahya 79 B3 W Turkey
K'ut'aisi 79 G1 W Georgia
Kutno 63 E3 C Poland
Kuujjuaq 99 E2 Québec, E Canada
Kuusamo 49 F3 E Finland
Kuwait 81 D3 ● E Kuwait
Kuwait 81 C3 ◆ *Monarchy*, SW Asia
Kuybyshev Reservoir 69 B6 ⊠ W Russ. Fed.
Kuytun 87 C2 NW China
Kuznetsk 69 B6 W Russ. Fed.
Kvaløya 49 D1 *Island*, N Norway
Kvarnbergsvattnet 49 B3 ◎ N Sweden
Kvarner 65 B2 *Gulf*, W Croatia
Kwangju 85 B7 SW South Korea
Kwango 128 B3 ≈ Angola/Dem. Rep. Congo
Kwekwe 128 D5 C Zimbabwe
Kwidzyn 63 D2 N Poland
Kwigillingok 97 C3 Alaska, USA
Kwilu 128 C3 ≈ W Dem. Rep. Congo
Kyabé 124 H4 S Chad
Kyaikkami 91 B3 S Burma
Kyakhta 76 F5 S Russ. Fed.
Kyjov 63 D6 SE Czech Republic
Kyklades *see* Cyclades
Kyle of Lochalsh 33 C4 N Scotland, UK
Kymi 65 E5 C Greece
Kyoga, Lake 127 C5 ◎ C Uganda
Kyoto 85 E6 SW Japan
Kyrenia 70 C6 N Cyprus
Kyrgyzstan 83 G2 ◆ *Republic*, C Asia
Kythira 65 E6 *Island*, S Greece
Kythnos 65 E6 *Island*, Cyclades, Greece
Kythrea 70 D6 N Cyprus
Kyushu 85 A7 *Island*, SW Japan
Kyustendil 65 E3 W Bulgaria
Kyyiv *see* Kiev
Kyzyl 76 E5 C Russ. Fed.
Kyzyl Kum 83 E2 *Desert*, Kazakhstan/Uzbekistan
Kyzylorda 76 C5 S Kazakhstan
Kyzyl-Suu 83 I2 NE Kyrgyzstan

L

La Algaba 57 C5 S Spain
Laarne 50 B6 NW Belgium
Laâyoune 122 A3 ● NW Western Sahara
Labasa 137 J5 N Fiji
la Baule-Escoublac 55 B3 NW France
Labé 124 B4 NW Guinea
Laborec 63 F6 ≈ E Slovakia
Labrador 99 F2 *Cultural region*, Newfoundland, SW Canada
Labrador City 99 F3 Newfoundland, E Canada
Labrador Sea 99 F2 *Sea*, NW Atlantic Ocean
La Carolina 57 D5 S Spain
Laccadive Islands 89 C7 *Island group*, India, N Indian Ocean
La Ceiba 107 D2 N Honduras
La Chaux-de-Fonds 59 A8 W Switzerland
Lachlan River 133 G5 ≈ NSW, SE Australia
la Ciotat 55 E7 SE France
La Concepción 107 F7 W Panama
La Coruña *see* A Coruña
La Crosse 101 C2 Wisconsin, USA
La Cruz 107 D5 NW Costa Rica
Ladoga, Lake 69 A4 ◎ NW Russ. Fed.
Lae 137 B2 W PNG
La Esperanza 107 C3 SW Honduras
Lafayette 103 H5 Louisiana, USA
Lafia 124 F4 C Nigeria
la Flèche 55 C3 NW France
Lagdo, Lac de 124 F4 ◎ N Cameroon
Laghouat 122 D2 N Algeria
Lagos 124 E5 SW Nigeria
Lagos 57 A5 S Portugal
Lagos de Moreno 105 E4 SW Mexico
Lagouira 122 A4 SW Western Sahara
Lagunas 117 A3 N Chile
Lagunillas 117 B3 SE Bolivia
La Habana *see* Havana
Lahat 91 C7 Sumatra, W Indonesia
Laholm 49 C6 S Sweden
Lahore 89 D2 NE Pakistan
Lahr 59 B7 S Germany
Lahti 49 E5 S Finland
Laï 124 G4 S Chad
Lairg 33 D2 N Scotland, UK
Lake Charles 103 G5 Louisiana, USA
Lake District 35 C3 *Physical region*, NW England, UK
Lake King 133 B5 Western Australia
Lakeland 101 E6 Florida, USA
Lake of the Woods 99 A4 Minnesota, USA
Lakewood 103 E3 Colorado, USA
Lakonikós Kólpos 65 E6 *Gulf*, S Greece
Lakselv 49 E1 N Norway
Lakshadweep *see* Laccadive Islands
La Libertad 107 B2 N Guatemala
La Ligua 117 A5 C Chile
Lalín 57 B2 NW Spain
Lalitpur 89 F3 C Nepal
La Louvière 50 C7 S Belgium
la Maddalena 61 B5 Sardinia, Italy
La Marmora, Punta 61 A6 ▲ Sardinia, Italy
Lambaréné 128 A2 W Gabon
Lambert Glacier 138 D4 *Glacier*, Antarctica
Lambeth 29 ◐ *London borough*, SE England, UK
Lamego 57 B3 N Portugal
Lamezia 61 E7 SE Italy
Lamía 65 E5 C Greece
Lamiti 137 J5 C Fiji
Lammermuir Hills 33 E6 ⛰ SE Scotland, UK
Lampeter 39 C5 SW Wales, UK
Lanark 33 D6 S Scotland, UK
Lanbi Kyun 91 A4 *Island*, Mergui Archipelago, S Burma
Lancashire 29 ◐ *County*, N England, UK
Lancaster 35 C4 NW England, UK
Lancaster 101 F3 Pennsylvania, USA
Lancaster Sound 97 H2 *Sound*, Nunavut, N Canada
Landen 50 D7 C Belgium
Landerneau 55 A2 NW France
Landes 55 B5 *Cultural region*, SW France Europe
Land's End 37 A6 *Headland*, SW England, UK
Landshut 59 D7 SE Germany
Langar 83 E3 C Uzbekistan
Langholm 33 E7 S Scotland, UK
Langres 55 E3 N France
Langsa 91 B5 Sumatra, W Indonesia
Languedoc 55 D6 *Cultural region*, S France
Länkäran 79 J3 S Azerbaijan
Lansing 101 E3 Michigan, USA
Lanta, Ko 91 B5 *Island*, S Thailand
Lanzhou 87 E4 C China
Laois 29 ◐ *County*, C Ireland
Laon 55 E2 N France
La Orchila, Isla 109 I7 *Island*, N Venezuela
Laos 91 C3 ◆ *Republic*, SE Asia
La Palma 107 I6 SE Panama
La Paz 105 C4 NW Mexico
La Paz 117 A2 ● W Bolivia
La Paz, Bahía de 105 B3 *Bay*, W Mexico
La Perouse Strait 85 F1 *Strait*, Japan/Russ. Fed.
Lápithos 70 C6 NW Cyprus
Lapland 49 D2 *Cultural region*, N Europe
La Plata 117 C5 E Argentina
Lappeenranta 49 F5 SE Finland
Lapta *see* Lapithos
Laptev Sea 76 F2 *Sea*, Arctic Ocean
Lapua 49 E4 W Finland
Łapy 63 G3 E Poland
La Quiaca 117 B3 N Argentina
L'Aquila 61 D5 C Italy
Laredo 57 D1 N Spain
Laredo 103 F6 Texas, USA
Largo 101 E7 Florida, USA
Largo, Cayo 109 B3 *Island*, W Cuba
Largs 33 D6 W Scotland, UK
La Rioja 117 B4 NW Argentina
La Rioja 57 E2 *Cultural region*, N Spain
Lárisa 65 E5 C Greece
Lark 37 G2 ≈ E England, UK
Larkana 89 B3 SE Pakistan
Larnaca 70 D6 SE Cyprus
Lárnaka *see* Larnaca
Larne 31 F2 E Northern Ireland, UK
Larne 29 ◐ *District*, E Northern Ireland, UK
la Rochelle 55 B4 W France
la Roche-sur-Yon 55 B4 NW France
La Roda 57 E4 C Spain
La Romana 109 G4 E Dominican Republic
Las Cabezas de San Juan 57 C5 S Spain
La Seu d'Urgel 57 G2 NE Spain
La Serena 117 A5 C Chile
la Seyne-sur-Mer 55 E7 SE France
Lashio 91 B2 E Burma
Lashkar Gah 83 E6 S Afghanistan
La Sila 61 E7 ⛰ SW Italy
La Sirena 107 E4 E Nicaragua
Łask 63 E4 C Poland
Las Lomitas 117 C4 N Argentina
La Solana 57 D4 C Spain
La Spezia 61 B3 NW Italy
Las Tablas 107 G7 S Panama
Las Tunas 109 D3 Las Tunas, E Cuba
Las Vegas 103 C4 Nevada, USA
Lata 137 G3 Nendö, Solomon Islands
Latacunga 115 B3 C Ecuador
la Teste 55 B5 SW France
Latina 61 C5 C Italy
La Tortuga, Isla 109 I7 *Island*, N Venezuela
La Tuque 99 E5 Québec, SE Canada
Latvia 49 E6 ◆ *Republic*, NE Europe
Laugharne 39 C6 S Wales, UK
Lau Group 137 K5 *Island group*, E Fiji
Launceston 133 G7 Tasmania, SE Australia
Launceston 37 B5 SW England, UK
La Unión 107 D3 C Honduras
La Unión 57 F5 SE Spain
Laurentian Mountains 99 E4 *Plateau*, E Canada
Lauria 61 E6 S Italy
Lausanne 59 A8 SW Switzerland
Laut, Pulau 91 E7 *Island*, C Indonesia
Laval 99 E5 Québec, SE Canada
Laval 55 C3 NW France
Lavanggu 137 F3 Rennell, S Solomon Islands
La Vega 109 F4 C Dominican Republic
La Vila Joíosa *see* Villajoyosa
Lawton 103 F4 Oklahoma, USA
Layla 81 C5 C Saudi Arabia
Laytown 31 E4 E Ireland
Lazarev Sea 138 B2 *Sea*, Antarctica
Lázaro Cárdenas 105 E5 SW Mexico
Læsø 49 B6 *Island*, N Denmark
Leamington 99 C6 Ontario, S Canada
Leap 31 B7 S Ireland
Lebak 91 F5 Mindanao, S Philippines
Lebanon 81 A2 ◆ *Republic*, SW Asia
Lebap 83 D2 NE Turkmenistan
Lębork 63 D1 NW Poland
Lebrija 57 C6 S Spain
Lebu 117 A6 C Chile
le Cannet 55 F6 SE France
Lecce 61 F6 SE Italy
Lechainá 65 D5 S Greece
Leduc 97 G6 Alberta, SW Canada
Leeds 35 D4 N England, UK
Leeds 29 ◐ *Unitary auth.*, N England, UK
Leek 50 E2 NE Netherlands
Leek 35 D5 C England, UK
Leer 59 B3 NW Germany
Leeuwarden 50 E2 N Netherlands
Leeward Islands 109 K4 *Island group*, E West Indies
Lefkáda 65 D5 *Island*, Ionian Islands, Greece
Lefká Óri 65 E7 ⛰ Crete, Greece
Legaspi 91 F4 N Philippines
Legnica 63 C4 W Poland
le Havre 55 C2 N France
Leicester 35 E6 C England, UK
Leicester 29 ◐ *Unitary auth.*, C England, UK
Leicestershire 29 ◐ *County*, C England, UK
Leiden 50 C4 W Netherlands
Leie 50 B6 ≈ Belgium/France
Leighton Buzzard 37 F3 E England, UK
Leinster 31 D5 *Cultural region*, E Ireland
Leinster, Mount 31 E5 ▲ SE Ireland
Leipzig 59 D4 E Germany
Leiria 57 A4 C Portugal
Leirvik 49 A5 S Norway
Leitrim 29 ◐ *County*, NW Ireland
Leixlip 31 E4 E Ireland
Lek 50 D4 ≈ SW Netherlands
Leksand 49 C5 C Sweden
Lelystad 50 D3 C Netherlands
le Mans 55 C3 NW France
Lemesós *see* Limassol
Lena 76 G3 ≈ NE Russ. Fed.
Leningradskaya 138 D6 SW Russ. Fed.
Leninogorsk 76 D5 E Kazakhstan
Lenti 63 C8 SW Hungary
Leoben 59 E7 C Austria
Leominster 35 C7 W England, UK
León 105 E4 C Mexico
León 107 D4 NW Nicaragua
León 57 D1 NW Spain
Leonídio 65 E6 S Greece
Lepe 57 B5 S Spain
le Portel 55 D1 N France
le Puy 55 D5 C France
Léré 124 G4 SW Chad
Lérida *see* Lleida
Lerma 57 D2 N Spain
Léros 65 G6 *Island*, Dodecanese, Greece
Lerwick 33 B6 NE Scotland, UK
Lesbos 65 F5 *Island*, E Greece
Leshan 87 E5 C China
les Herbiers 55 B4 NW France
Leskovac 65 D3 SE Serbia and Montenegro (Yugoslavia)
Lesotho 128 D6 ◆ *Monarchy*, S Africa
les Sables-d'Olonne 55 B4 NW France
Lesser Antarctica 138 B5 *Physical region*, Antarctica
Lesser Antilles 109 I5 *Island group*, E West Indies
Lesser Caucasus 79 G2 ⛰ SW Asia
Lesser Sunda Islands 91 F8 *Island group*, C Indonesia
Leszno 63 C4 W Poland
Letchworth 37 F3 E England, UK
Lethbridge 97 G7 Alberta, SW Canada
Leti, Kepulauan 91 G8 *Island group*, E Indonesia
Letsôk-aw Kyun 91 A4 *Island*, Mergui Archipelago, S Burma
Letterkenny 31 D2 NW Ireland
Letterston 39 A5 SW Wales, UK
Leuven 50 C6 C Belgium
Leuze-en-Hainaut 50 B7 SW Belgium
Levanger 49 B4 C Norway
Leverkusen 59 A5 W Germany
Levice 63 D7 SW Slovakia
Levin 135 D4 North Island, NZ
Lewes 37 G4 SE England, UK
Lewis, Butt of 33 B2 *Headland*, NW Scotland, UK
Lewisham 29 ◐ *London borough*, SE England, UK
Lewis, Isle of 33 B2 *Island*, NW Scotland, UK
Lewiston 103 C1 Idaho, USA
Lexington 101 E4 Kentucky, USA
Leyland 35 C4 NW England, UK
Leyte 91 F4 *Island*, C Philippines
Leżajsk 63 F5 SE Poland
Lhasa 87 C4 W China
Lhazê 87 B4 W China
L'Hospitalet de Llobregat 57 G2 NE Spain
Liancourt Rocks 85 C5 *Island group*, Japan/South Korea
Lianyungang 87 G4 E China
Liaoyuan 87 G2 NE China
Libanus 39 E6 C Wales, UK
Liberec 63 B5 N Czech Republic
Liberia 107 D5 NW Costa Rica
Liberia 124 B5 ◆ *Republic*, W Africa
Libourne 55 C5 SW France
Libreville 128 A2 ● NW Gabon
Libya 122 F3 ◆ *Islamic state*, N Africa
Libyan Desert 122 H4 *Desert*, N Africa
Lichfield 35 D6 C England, UK
Lichtenfels 59 C5 SE Germany
Lichtenvoorde 50 F4 E Netherlands
Lichuan 87 F4 C China
Lida 67 C2 W Belarus
Lidköping 49 C6 S Sweden
Lidzbark Warmiński 63 E2 N Poland
Liechtenstein 59 C8 ◆ *Principality*, C Europe
Liège 50 D7 E Belgium
Lienz 59 D8 W Austria
Liepāja 49 E6 W Latvia
Liezen 59 E7 C Austria
Liffey 31 E5 ≈ E Ireland
Lifford 31 D2 NW Ireland
Lifou 137 G6 *Island*, Îles Loyauté, E New Caledonia
Ligger Bay 37 A5 *Bay*, SW England, UK
Lighthouse Reef 107 C1 *Reef*, E Belize
Ligure, Appennino 61 B2 ⛰ NW Italy
Ligurian Sea 61 A3 *Sea*, N Mediterranean Sea
Lihir Group 137 D1 *Island group*, NE PNG
Lihue 103 A5 Kauai, Hawaii, USA
Likasi 128 D3 SE Dem. Rep. Congo
Liknes 49 A6 S Norway
Lille 55 D1 N France
Lillehammer 49 B5 S Norway
Lillestrøm 49 B5 S Norway
Lilongwe 128 E4 ● W Malawi
Lima 115 B5 ● W Peru
Limanowa 63 E5 S Poland
Limassol 70 C6 SW Cyprus
Limavady 31 E1 NW Northern Ireland, UK
Limavady 29 ◐ *District*, N Northern Ireland, UK
Limerick 31 C5 SW Ireland
Limerick 29 ◐ *County*, SW Ireland
Límnos 65 F4 *Island*, E Greece
Limoges 55 C4 C France
Limón 107 F6 E Costa Rica
Limón 107 D2 NE Honduras
Limousin 55 C5 *Cultural region*, C France

◐ Administrative region ◆ Country ● Country capital ◇ Dependent territory ○ Dependent territory capital ⛰ Mountain range ▲ Mountain ⧍ Volcano ≈ River ◎ Lake ⊠ Reservoir

Limoux 55 D7 S France
Limpopo 128 E5 ≈ S Africa
Linares 117 A6 C Chile
Linares 105 E3 NE Mexico
Linares 57 D5 S Spain
Linchuan 87 G5 S China
Lincoln 35 F5 E England, UK
Lincoln 103 F3 Nebraska, USA
Lincoln Edge 35 F5 Ridge, E England, UK
Lincoln Sea 139 B4 Sea, Arctic Ocean
Lincolnshire 29 ◐ County, E England, UK
Linden 115 E2 E Guyana
Lindi 127 E7 SE Tanzania
Líndos 65 G6 Rhodes, Dodecanese, Greece
Line Islands 131 Island group, E Kiribati
Lingen 59 B3 NW Germany
Lingga, Kepulauan 91 C6 Island group, W Indonesia
Linköping 49 C6 S Sweden
Linnhe, Loch 33 C5 Inlet, W Scotland, UK
Linz 59 E7 N Austria
Lion, Golfe du 55 D7 Gulf, S France
Lipari 61 D7 Island, Aeolian Islands, S Italy
Lipetsk 69 B6 W Russ. Fed.
Lira 127 C5 N Uganda
Lisala 128 C1 N Dem. Rep. Congo
Lisboa see Lisbon
Lisbon 57 A4 ● W Portugal
Lisburn 31 E2 E Northern Ireland, UK
Lisburn 29 ◐ District, E Northern Ireland, UK
Lisdoonvarna 31 B5 W Ireland
Lisieux 55 C2 N France
Liski 69 A6 W Russ. Fed.
Lisnaskea 31 D3 W Northern Ireland, UK
Lisse 50 C4 W Netherlands
Listowel 31 B5 SW Ireland
Litang 87 D5 C China
Lithgow 133 G6 NSW, SE Australia
Lithuania 49 E7 ◆ Republic, NE Europe
Little Alföld 63 D7 Plain, Hungary/Slovakia
Little Andaman 89 H5 Island, Andaman Islands, India
Little Barrier Island 135 D2 Island, N NZ
Little Bay 40 Bay, S Gibraltar
Little Cayman 40 Island, E Cayman Islands
Littlehampton 37 F5 SE England, UK
Little Inagua 109 E3 Island, S Bahamas
Little Minch, The 33 B3 Strait, NW Scotland, UK
Little Nicobar 89 H6 Island, Nicobar Islands, India
Little Ouse 37 G2 ≈ E England, UK
Little Rock 103 G4 Arkansas, USA
Little Saint Bernard Pass 55 F5 Pass, France/Italy
Little Sandy Desert 133 B4 Desert, Western Australia
Liuzhou 87 F5 S China
Lively Island 40 Island, SE Falkland Islands
Liverpool 99 F5 Nova Scotia, SE Canada
Liverpool 35 C5 NW England, UK
Liverpool 28 ◐ Unitary auth., NW England, UK
Liverpool Bay 39 E1 Bay, England/Wales, UK
Livingston 33 E5 West Lothian, C Scotland, UK
Livingstone 128 D4 S Zambia
Livingstone Mountains 135 A7 ⛰ South Island, NZ
Livojoki 49 E3 ≈ C Finland
Livonia 101 E3 Michigan, USA
Livorno 61 B3 C Italy
Lizard Point 37 A6 Headland, SW England, UK
Ljubljana 59 E8 ● C Slovenia
Ljungby 49 C6 S Sweden
Ljusdal 49 C4 C Sweden
Ljusnan 49 C4 ≈ C Sweden
Llanaber 39 C3 NW Wales, UK
Llanaelhaearn 39 C2 NW Wales, UK
Llanarth 39 C5 W Wales, UK
Llanbedr 39 C3 NW Wales, UK
Llanbedrog 39 C3 NW Wales, UK
Llanberis 39 C2 NW Wales, UK
Llanbister 39 E4 C Wales, UK
Llanbrynmair 39 D3 C Wales, UK
Llandeilo 39 D6 S Wales, UK
Llandovery 39 D5 S Wales, UK
Llandrindod Wells 39 E5 E Wales, UK
Llandudno 39 D1 N Wales, UK
Llandybie 39 C6 S Wales, UK
Llandysul 39 C5 W Wales, UK
Llanelli 39 C6 SW Wales, UK
Llanerchymedd 39 C1 NW Wales, UK
Llanes 57 D1 N Spain
Llanfachraeth 39 B1 NW Wales, UK
Llanfaelog 39 C2 NW Wales, UK
Llanfair Caereinion 39 E3 C Wales, UK
Llanfair Talhaiarn 39 D2 N Wales, UK
Llanfihangel-nant-Melan 39 E5 C Wales, UK
Llanfyllin 39 E3 C Wales, UK
Llangadfan 39 E3 C Wales, UK
Llangadog 39 D5 S Wales, UK
Llangefni 39 C1 NW Wales, UK
Llangoed 39 C1 NW Wales, UK
Llangollen 39 E2 NE Wales, UK
Llangurig 39 D4 C Wales, UK
Llanharan 39 E7 S Wales, UK
Llanidloes 39 D4 C Wales, UK
Llanilar 39 D4 W Wales, UK
Llanllyfni 39 C2 NW Wales, UK
Llanon 39 C4 W Wales, UK
Llanos 115 C2 Physical region, Colombia/Venezuela
Llanrhaeadr-ym-Mochnant 39 E3 C Wales, UK
Llanrhidian 39 C6 S Wales, UK
Llanrhystud 39 C4 W Wales, UK
Llanrwst 39 D2 N Wales, UK
Llansteffan 39 C6 S Wales, UK
Llantrisant 39 E7 S Wales, UK
Llantwit Major 39 E7 S Wales, UK
Llanuwchllyn 39 D3 NW Wales, UK
Llanwrda 39 D5 S Wales, UK
Llanwrtyd Wells 39 D5 C Wales, UK
Llanybydder 39 C5 S Wales, UK
Lleida 57 F2 NE Spain
Lleyn Peninsula 39 C2 Peninsula, NW Wales, UK
Llucmajor 57 H4 Majorca, Spain
Llwyngwril 39 C3 NW Wales, UK
Llyn Brianne Reservoir 39 C5 ⊡ E Wales, UK
Llyswen 39 E5 C Wales, UK
Lobatse 128 D6 SE Botswana
Löbau 59 E4 E Germany
Lobito 128 B4 W Angola
Locarno 59 B8 S Switzerland
Lochboisdale 33 A4 NW Scotland, UK
Lochdon 33 C5 W Scotland, UK
Lochem 50 E4 E Netherlands
Lochgilphead 33 C5 W Scotland, UK
Lochinver 33 C2 N Scotland, UK
Lochmaddy 33 B3 NW Scotland, UK
Lochnagar 33 E4 ▲ C Scotland, UK
Lochy, Loch 33 C4 ◎ N Scotland, UK
Lockerbie 33 E7 S Scotland, UK
Lodja 128 C2 C Dem. Rep. Congo
Lodwar 127 D5 NW Kenya
Łódź 63 E4 C Poland
Lofoten 49 C2 Island group, C Norway
Logan, Mount 97 E5 ▲ Yukon Territory, W Canada
Logroño 57 E2 N Spain
Loibl Pass 59 E8 Pass, Austria/Slovenia
Loire 55 C3 ≈ C France
Loja 115 B4 S Ecuador
Lokitaung 127 D4 NW Kenya
Lokoja 124 E5 C Nigeria
Lolland 49 B7 Island, S Denmark
Lom 65 E2 NW Bulgaria
Lomami 128 D2 ≈ C Dem. Rep. Congo
Lomas de Zamora 117 C5 E Argentina
Lombardia see Lombardy
Lombardy 61 C2 Cultural region, N Italy
Lombok, Pulau 91 E8 Island, Nusa Tenggara, C Indonesia
Lomé 124 D5 ● S Togo
Lomela 128 C2 C Dem. Rep. Congo
Lommel 50 D6 N Belgium
Lomond, Loch 33 D5 ◎ C Scotland, UK
Lomonosov Ridge 139 C4 Undersea feature, Arctic Ocean
Łomża 63 F2 NE Poland
Loncoche 117 A6 C Chile
London 99 C6 Ontario, S Canada
London 37 G4 ● SE England, UK
London, City of 29 ◐ London borough, SE England, UK
Londonderry 31 D2 NW Northern Ireland, UK
Londonderry 29 ◐ District, NW Northern Ireland, UK
Londonderry, Cape 133 C1 Headland, Western Australia
Londrina 115 F7 S Brazil
Long Bay 101 F5 Bay, E USA
Long Beach 103 B4 California, USA
Longbluff 40 Headland, SW Tristan da Cunha
Long Eaton 35 E6 C England, UK
Longford 31 D4 C Ireland
Longford 29 ◐ County, C Ireland
Long Island 109 E2 Island, C Bahamas
Long Island 101 G3 Island, New York, USA
Long Island Sound 101 G3 Sound, NE USA
Longlac 99 B4 Ontario, S Canada
Longreach 133 G3 Queensland, E Australia
Long Strait 76 H1 Strait, NE Russ. Fed.
Long Swamp 40 C British Virgin Islands
Longview 103 B1 Washington, USA
Longwood 40 C Saint Helena
Longyan 87 G5 SE China
Longyearbyen 139 C5 ○ Spitsbergen, W Svalbard
Lons-le-Saunier 55 E4 E France
Loop Head 31 A5 Headland, W Ireland
Lop Nur 87 C3 Seasonal lake, NW China
Loppersum 50 F2 NE Netherlands
Lorca 57 E5 S Spain
Lorengau 137 B1 Manus Island, N PNG
Loreto 105 B3 W Mexico
Lorient 55 B3 NW France
Lorn, Firth of 33 B5 Inlet, W Scotland, UK
Lörrach 59 B7 S Germany
Lorraine 55 F2 Cultural region, NE France
Los Amates 107 B3 E Guatemala
Los Ángeles 117 A6 C Chile
Los Angeles 103 B4 California, USA
Lošinj 65 A2 Island, W Croatia
Los Mochis 105 C3 C Mexico
Los Roques, Islas 109 H7 Island group, N Venezuela
Lossiemouth 33 E3 NE Scotland, UK
Los Testigos 109 J7 Island, NE Venezuela
Lot 55 C5 Cultural region, C France
Lot 55 C6 ≈ S France
Lotagipi Swamp 127 D4 Wetland, Kenya/Sudan
Louangphabang 91 B3 N Laos
Loudéac 55 B2 NW France
Loudi 87 F5 S China
Louga 124 A3 NW Senegal
Loughborough 35 E6 C England, UK
Loughrea 31 C4 W Ireland
Louisburgh 31 B3 NW Ireland
Louisiade Archipelago 137 D3 Island group, SE PNG
Louisiana 103 G4 ◐ State, S USA
Louisville 101 D4 Kentucky, USA
Louisville Ridge 14 Undersea ridge, SW Pacific Ocean
Lourdes 55 C6 S France
Louth 31 E3 NE Ireland
Louth 35 F5 E England, UK
Louth 29 ◐ County, NE Ireland
Loutrá 65 E4 N Greece
Louvain-la Neuve 50 C7 C Belgium
Louviers 55 D2 N France
Lovosice 63 B5 NW Czech Republic
Lóvua 128 C3 NE Angola
Lower California 105 B3 Peninsula, NW Mexico
Lower Hutt 135 D5 North Island, NZ
Lower Lough Erne 31 D2 ◎ SW Northern Ireland, UK
Lower Red Lake 103 G1 ◎ Minnesota, USA
Lower Tunguska 76 E4 ≈ N Russ. Fed.
Lowestoft 37 H2 E England, UK
Loyauté, Îles 137 G6 Island group, S New Caledonia
Lualaba 128 D2 ≈ SE Dem. Rep. Congo
Luanda 128 B3 ● NW Angola
Luangwa 128 E4 ≈ Mozambique/Zambia
Luanshya 128 D4 C Zambia
Luarca 57 C1 N Spain
Lubaczów 63 G5 SE Poland
Lubań 63 B4 SW Poland
Lubango 128 B4 SW Angola
Lubao 128 D2 C Dem. Rep. Congo
Lübben 59 E4 E Germany
Lübbenau 59 E4 E Germany
Lubbock 103 F4 Texas, USA
Lübeck 59 C2 N Germany
Lubelska, Wyżyna 63 F4 Plateau, SE Poland
Lubin 63 C4 W Poland
Lublin 63 F4 E Poland
Lubliniec 63 D5 S Poland
Lubny 67 E4 NE Ukraine
Lubsko 63 B4 W Poland
Lubumbashi 128 D3 SE Dem. Rep. Congo
Lucan 31 E4 E Ireland
Lucano, Appennino 61 E6 ⛰ S Italy
Lucapa 128 C3 NE Angola
Lucca 61 C3 C Italy
Luce Bay 33 C7 Inlet, SW Scotland, UK
Lucena 91 F4 Luzon, N Philippines
Lucena 57 D5 S Spain
Lučenec 63 E7 S Slovakia
Lucknow 89 E3 N India
Luda Kamchiya 65 F3 ≈ E Bulgaria
Lüderitz 128 B6 SW Namibia
Ludhiana 89 D2 N India
Ludlow 35 C6 W England, UK
Ludvika 49 C5 C Sweden
Ludwigsburg 59 B6 SW Germany
Ludwigsfelde 59 D4 NE Germany
Ludwigshafen 59 B6 W Germany
Ludwigslust 59 C3 N Germany
Ludza 49 F6 E Latvia
Luena 128 C3 E Angola
Lufira 128 D3 ≈ SE Dem. Rep. Congo
Luga 69 A4 NW Russ. Fed.
Lugano 59 B8 S Switzerland
Luganville 137 G4 C Vanuatu
Lugenda, Rio 128 F4 ≈ N Mozambique
Lugnaquillia Mountain 31 E5 ▲ E Ireland
Lugo 57 B1 NW Spain
Lugoj 67 A6 W Romania
Luhans'k 67 G5 E Ukraine
Lukenie 128 C2 ≈ C Dem. Rep. Congo
Łuków 63 F4 E Poland
Lukuga 128 D3 ≈ SE Dem. Rep. Congo
Luleå 49 D3 N Sweden
Luleälven 49 D3 ≈ N Sweden
Lulimba 128 D2 E Dem. Rep. Congo
Lulonga 128 C1 ≈ NW Dem. Rep. Congo
Lumbo 128 F4 NE Mozambique
Lumi 137 A1 NW PNG
Lumsden 135 B7 South Island, NZ
Lund 49 C7 S Sweden
Lundy 37 B4 Island, SW England, UK
Lüneburg 59 C3 N Germany
Lungué-Bungo 128 C4 ≈ Angola/Zambia
Luninyets 67 C3 SW Belarus
Lunteren 50 D4 C Netherlands
Luoyang 87 F4 C China
Lurgan 31 E2 S Northern Ireland, UK
Lúrio 128 F4 NE Mozambique
Lúrio, Rio 128 F4 ≈ NE Mozambique
Lusaka 128 D4 ● SE Zambia
Lut, Dasht-e 81 F3 Desert, E Iran
Luti 137 E2 NW Solomon Islands
Luton 37 F3 E England, UK
Luton 29 ◐ Unitary auth., C England, UK
Łutselk'e 97 G5 NW Terr., W Canada
Luts'k 67 C4 NW Ukraine
Lützow-Holm Bay 138 D3 Bay, Antarctica
Luuq 127 E4 SW Somalia
Luwego 127 D7 ≈ S Tanzania
Luxembourg 50 E9 ● S Luxembourg
Luxembourg 50 E8 ◆ Monarchy, NW Europe
Luxor 122 J3 E Egypt
Luza 69 C4 NW Russ. Fed.
Luzern 59 B8 C Switzerland
Luzon 91 F3 Island, N Philippines
Luzon Strait 91 F3 Strait, Philippines/Taiwan
L'viv 67 B4 W Ukraine
Lycksele 49 D3 N Sweden
Lyepyel' 67 D2 N Belarus
Lyme Bay 37 C5 Bay, S England, UK
Lyme Regis 37 D5 S England, UK
Lymington 37 E5 S England, UK
Lynton 37 C4 SW England, UK
Lyon 55 E5 E France
Lysychans'k 67 G4 E Ukraine
Lytham St Anne's 35 C4 NW England, UK
Lyttelton 135 C6 South Island, NZ

M

Maamturk Mountains 31 B4 ⛰ W Ireland
Maaseik 50 E6 NE Belgium
Maastricht 50 E6 SE Netherlands
Mablethorpe 35 F5 E England, UK
Macao 87 G6 S China
Macapá 115 F3 N Brazil
Macbride Head 40 Headland, Falkland Islands
Macclesfield 35 D5 C England, UK
Macdonnell Ranges 133 D3 ⛰ Northern Territory, C Australia
Macduff 33 F3 NE Scotland, UK
Macedonia 65 D4 ◆ Republic, SE Europe
Maceió 115 I5 E Brazil
Macgillycuddy's Reeks 31 B6 ⛰ SW Ireland
Machala 115 A4 SW Ecuador
Machanga 128 E5 E Mozambique
Machilipatnam 89 E5 E India
Machynlleth 39 D3 C Wales, UK
Mackay 133 G3 Queensland, NE Australia
Mackay, Lake 133 D3 Salt lake, Northern Territory/Western Australia
Mackenzie 97 F4 ≈ NW Terr., NW Canada
Mackenzie Bay 138 E4 Bay, Antarctica
Mackenzie Mountains 97 E4 ⛰ NW Terr., NW Canada
Macleod, Lake 133 A4 ◎ Western Australia
Macomer 61 A6 Sardinia, Italy
Macon 101 E5 Georgia, USA
Mâcon 55 E4 C France
Macroom 31 B6 SW Ireland
Macuspana 105 H5 SE Mexico
Ma'daba 81 A2 NW Jordan
Madagascar 128 G5 ◆ Republic, W Indian Ocean
Madang 137 B2 N PNG
Made 50 C5 S Netherlands
Madeira, Rio 115 E4 ≈ Bolivia/Brazil
Madeleine, Îles de la 99 F4 Island group, Québec, E Canada
Madhya Pradesh 89 E4 Cultural region, C India
Madison 101 D2 Wisconsin, USA
Madiun 91 D8 Java, C Indonesia
Madras 89 E6 see Chennai
Madre de Dios, Río 117 A1 ≈ Bolivia/Peru
Madre del Sur, Sierra 105 F5 ⛰ S Mexico
Madre, Laguna 105 F3 Lagoon, NE Mexico
Madre Occidental, Sierra see Western Sierra Madre
Madre Oriental, Sierra see Eastern Sierra Madre
Madrid 57 D3 ● C Spain
Madrid 57 D3 Cultural region, C Spain
Madurai 89 D7 S India
Madura, Pulau 91 E8 Island, C Indonesia
Maebashi 85 G5 S Japan
Mae Nam Nan 91 B3 ≈ NW Thailand
Maentwrog 39 D2 NW Wales, UK
Maesteg 39 D6 S Wales, UK
Maéwo 137 G4 Island, C Vanuatu
Mafia 127 E7 Island, E Tanzania
Magadan 76 H3 E Russ. Fed.
Magarida 137 C3 SW PNG
Magdalena 105 B2 NW Mexico
Magdalena 117 B1 N Bolivia
Magdalena, Isla 105 B4 Island, W Mexico
Magdalena, Río 115 B3 ≈ C Colombia
Magdeburg 59 D4 C Germany
Magee, Island 31 F2 Island, E Northern Ireland, UK
Magelang 91 C8 Java, C Indonesia
Magellan, Strait of 117 B9 Strait, Argentina/Chile
Magerøya 49 D1 Island, N Norway
Maggiore, Lake 61 B1 ◎ Italy/Switzerland
Maghera 31 E2 C Northern Ireland, UK
Magherafelt 29 District, C Northern Ireland, UK
Maglie 61 F6 SE Italy
Magnitogorsk 76 C4 C Russ. Fed.
Magta' Lahjar 124 B3 SW Mauritania
Mahajanga 128 G4 NW Madagascar
Mahakam, Sungai 91 E6 ≈ C Indonesia
Mahalapye 128 D5 SE Botswana
Mahānadi 89 F4 ≈ E India
Maharashtra 89 D5 Cultural region, W India
Mahbubnagar 89 D5 C India
Mahia Peninsula 135 E4 Peninsula, North Island, NZ
Mahilyow 67 D2 E Belarus
Mahmud-e Raqi 83 F5 NE Afghanistan
Mahón 57 H3 Minorca, Spain
Maidenhead 37 F3 S England, UK
Maidens, The 31 F2 Island group, E Northern Ireland, UK
Maidstone 37 G4 SE England, UK
Maiduguri 124 G4 NE Nigeria
Main 59 C5 ≈ C Germany
Mai-Ndombe, Lac 128 C2 ◎ W Dem. Rep. Congo
Maine 101 H2 ◐ State, NE USA
Maine 55 C2 Cultural region, NW France
Maine, Gulf of 101 H2 Gulf, NE USA
Mainland 33 E1 Island, N Scotland, UK
Mainland 33 A6 Island, NE Scotland, UK
Mainz 59 B5 SW Germany
Maitri 138 C3 Indian research station, Antarctica
Maizhokunggar 87 C4 W China
Majorca 57 H4 Island, Balearic Islands, Spain
Makarov Basin 139 C4 Undersea feature, Arctic Ocean
Makassar Strait 91 E7 Strait, C Indonesia
Makay 128 G5 ⛰ SW Madagascar
Makeni 124 B4 C Sierra Leone
Makhachkala 69 B9 SW Russ. Fed.
Makiyivka 67 G5 E Ukraine
Makkovik 99 G2 Newfoundland, NE Canada
Makó 63 F8 SE Hungary
Makoua 128 B2 C Congo
Makran Coast 81 F4 Coastal region, SE Iran
Makrany 67 B3 SW Belarus
Makurdi 124 F5 C Nigeria
Malabo 124 F6 ● Isla de Bioco, NW Equatorial Guinea
Malacca, Strait of 91 B6 Strait, Indonesia/Malaysia
Malacky 63 C7 W Slovakia
Maladzyechna 67 C2 C Belarus
Málaga 57 D6 S Spain
Malahide 31 E4 E Ireland
Malaita 137 F3 Island, N Solomon Islands
Malakal 127 C3 S Sudan
Malang 91 D8 Java, C Indonesia
Malanje 128 B3 NW Angola
Mälaren 49 D5 ◎ C Sweden
Malatya 79 E4 SE Turkey
Malawi 128 E4 ◆ Republic, S Africa
Malay Peninsula 91 B5 Peninsula, Malaysia/Thailand
Malaysia 91 C5 ◆ Monarchy, SE Asia
Malbork 63 E2 N Poland
Malchin 59 D2 N Germany
Malden Island 131 Atoll, E Kiribati
Maldives 89 C9 ◆ Republic, N Indian Ocean
Male' 89 C8 ● N India
Malekula 137 G5 Island, W Vanuatu
Malheur Lake 103 C2 ◎ Oregon, USA
Mali 124 D3 ◆ Republic, W Africa
Mali Kyun 91 A4 Island, Mergui Archipelago, S Burma
Malin 31 D1 NW Ireland
Malindi 127 E6 SE Kenya
Malin Head 31 D1 Headland, NW Ireland
Mallaig 33 C4 N Scotland, UK
Mallawi 122 I3 C Egypt
Mallorca see Majorca
Mallow 31 C6 SW Ireland
Mallwyd 39 D3 NW Wales, UK
Malmberget 49 D2 N Sweden
Malmédy 50 F7 E Belgium
Malmö 49 C7 S Sweden
Małopolska 63 F5 Plateau, S Poland
Malozemel'skaya Tundra 69 D3 Physical region, NW Russ. Fed.
Malta 70 A6 ◆ Republic, C Mediterranean Sea
Malta Channel 61 D9 Strait, Italy/Malta
Malton 35 E4 N England, UK
Maluku see Moluccas
Malung 49 C5 C Sweden
Malvern Hills 35 C7 Hill range, W England, UK
Mamberamo, Sungai 91 I7 ≈ E Indonesia
Mamonovo 49 D7 W Russ. Fed.
Mamoré, Rio 117 B1 ≈ Bolivia/Brazil
Mamou 124 B4 W Guinea
Mamoudzou 128 G4 ○ C Mayotte
Mamuno 128 C5 W Botswana
Manacor 57 H4 Majorca, Spain
Manado 91 F6 Celebes, C Indonesia
Managua 107 D5 ● W Nicaragua
Managua, Lake 107 D4 ◎ W Nicaragua
Manakara 128 G5 SE Madagascar
Manama 81 D4 ● N Bahrain
Mananjary 128 G5 SE Madagascar
Manapouri, Lake 135 A7 ◎ South Island, NZ
Manas, Gora 83 F2 ▲ Kyrgyzstan/Uzbekistan
Manau 137 C2 S PNG
Manaus 115 E4 NW Brazil
Manavgat 79 C5 SW Turkey
Manbij 81 B1 N Syria
Manchester 101 G2 New Hampshire, USA
Manchester 35 D5 NW England, UK
Manchester 28 ◐ Unitary auth., NW England, UK
Mandalay 91 A2 C Burma
Mand, Rud-e 81 D3 ≈ S Iran
Mandurah 133 B5 Western Australia
Manduria 61 F6 SE Italy
Mandya 89 D6 C India
Manfredonia 61 E5 SE Italy
Mangai 128 C2 W Dem. Rep. Congo
Mangalmé 124 H4 SE Chad
Mangalore 89 D6 W India
Mangerton Mountain 31 B6 ▲ SW Ireland
Mangoky 128 F5 ≈ W Madagascar
Manicouagan, Réservoir 99 E4 ◎ Québec, E Canada
Manihiki 131 Atoll, N Cook Islands
Manila 91 F4 ● Luzon, N Philippines
Manisa 79 A3 W Turkey
Manitoba 97 H6 ◐ Province, S Canada
Manitoba, Lake 97 H6 ◎ Manitoba, S Canada
Manitoulin Island 99 C5 Island, Ontario, S Canada
Manizales 115 B2 W Colombia
Manjimup 133 B6 Western Australia
Manlleu 57 G2 NE Spain
Manmad 89 D4 W India
Mannar 89 E7 NW Sri Lanka
Mannar, Gulf of 89 D8 Gulf, India/Sri Lanka
Mannheim 59 B6 SW Germany
Manono 128 D3 SE Dem. Rep. Congo
Manorbier 39 B6 SW Wales, UK
Manorhamilton 31 C3 NW Ireland
Manosque 55 E6 SE France
Mansa 128 D3 N Zambia
Mansel Island 97 I4 Island, Québec, NE Canada
Mansfield 35 E5 C England, UK
Mansfield 101 E3 Ohio, USA
Mantova 61 C2 NW Italy
Manurewa 135 D2 North Island, NZ
Manus Island 137 B1 Island, N PNG
Manzanares 57 D4 C Spain
Manzanillo 109 D3 E Cuba
Manzanillo 105 D5 SW Mexico
Manzhouli 87 F1 N China
Mao 124 G3 W Chad
Maoke, Pegunungan 91 I7 ⛰ E Indonesia
Maoming 87 F6 S China
Maputo 128 E6 ● S Mozambique
Maraa 137 A6 W French Polynesia
Marabá 115 G4 NE Brazil
Maracaibo 115 C1 NW Venezuela
Maracaibo, Lake 115 B2 Inlet, NW Venezuela
Maradah 122 G3 N Libya
Maradi 124 F3 S Niger
Maragheh 81 C1 NW Iran
Marajó, Baía de 115 G3 Bay, N Brazil
Marajó, Ilha de 115 F3 Island, N Brazil
Maranhão 115 G4 ◐ State, E Brazil
Marañón, Río 115 B4 ≈ N Peru
Marathon 99 B4 Ontario, S Canada
Marbella 57 D6 S Spain
Marble Bar 133 B3 Western Australia
Marburg an der Lahn 59 B5 W Germany
March 37 G2 E England, UK
Marche 55 D4 Cultural region, C France
Marche-en-Famenne 50 D8 SE Belgium
Mar Chiquita, Laguna 117 B5 ◎ C Argentina
Mardan 89 C1 N Pakistan
Mar del Plata 117 C6 E Argentina
Mardin 79 F4 SE Turkey
Maré 137 G6 Island, Îles Loyauté, E New Caledonia
Mareeba 133 G2 Queensland, NE Australia
Maree, Loch 33 C3 ◎ N Scotland, UK
Margarita, Isla de 115 D1 Island, N Venezuela
Margate 37 H4 SE England, UK
Margherita, Lake 127 D4 ◎ SW Ethiopia
Margow, Dasht-e 83 D6 Desert, SW Afghanistan
Mari 137 A3 SW PNG
María Cleofas, Isla 105 C5 Island, C Mexico
Maria Island 133 G7 Island, Tasmania, SE Australia
María Madre, Isla 105 C4 Island, C Mexico
María Magdalena, Isla 105 C4 Island, C Mexico
Mariana Islands 15 Island group, Guam/Northern Mariana Islands
Mariana Trench 15 Undersea feature, W Pacific Ocean
Mariánské Lázně 63 A5 W Czech Republic
Maribor 59 F8 NE Slovenia
Maridi 127 B4 SW Sudan

Marie Byrd Land 138 B5 Physical region, Antarctica
Marie-Galante 109 K5 Island, SE Guadeloupe
Mariental 128 C6 SW Namibia
Mariestad 49 C6 S Sweden
Marília 115 F7 S Brazil
Marín 57 B2 NW Spain
Maringá 115 F7 S Brazil
Mariscal Estigarribia 117 C3 NW Paraguay
Maritsa 65 F3 ≈ SW Europe
Mariupol' 67 G5 SE Ukraine
Marka 127 F5 S Somalia
Market Harborough 35 E6 C England, UK
Markham, Mount 138 C5 ▲ Antarctica
Markounda 124 H5 NW CAR
Marktredwitz 59 D5 E Germany
Marmande 55 C5 SW France
Marmara, Sea of 79 A2 Sea, NW Turkey
Marmaris 79 A5 SW Turkey
Marne 55 E2 Cultural region, N France
Marne 55 E3 ≈ N France
Maro 124 H4 S Chad
Maroantsetra 128 G4 NE Madagascar
Maromokotro 128 G4 ▲ N Madagascar
Maroni River 115 F2 ≈ French Guiana/Surinam
Maroua 124 G4 N Cameroon
Marquises, Îles 131 Island group, N French Polynesia
Marrakech 122 C2 W Morocco
Marrawah 133 F7 Tasmania, SE Australia
Marree 133 E5 S Australia
Marsá al Burayqah 122 G3 N Libya
Marsabit 127 D5 N Kenya
Marsala 61 C8 Sicily, Italy
Mars Bay 40 Bay, Ascension Island, C Atlantic Ocean
Marsberg 59 B4 W Germany
Marseille 55 E7 SE France
Marshall Islands 131 ◆ Republic, W Pacific Ocean
Marsh Harbour 109 D1 Great Abaco, W Bahamas
Martigues 55 E6 SE France
Martin 63 E6 NW Slovakia
Martinique 109 K5 French ◇, E West Indies
Martinique Passage 109 K5 Channel, Dominica/Martinique
Marton 135 D4 North Island, NZ
Martos 57 D5 S Spain
Mary 83 D4 S Turkmenistan
Maryborough 133 H4 Queensland, E Australia
Maryland 101 F4 ⬖ State, NE USA
Masai Steppe 127 D6 Grassland, NW Tanzania
Masaka 127 C5 SW Uganda
Masan 85 C6 S South Korea
Masasi 127 D7 SE Tanzania
Masaya 107 D5 W Nicaragua
Maseru 128 D6 ● W Lesotho
Mashhad 81 F1 NE Iran
Masindi 127 C5 W Uganda
Masira, Gulf of 81 F5 Bay, E Oman
Mask, Lough 31 B4 ◎ W Ireland
Masqat see Muscat
Massa 61 B3 C Italy
Massachusetts 101 G3 ⬖ State, NE USA
Massawa 127 D2 E Eritrea
Massenya 124 G4 SW Chad
Massif Central 55 D5 Plateau, C France
Masterton 135 D5 North Island, NZ
Masuda 85 D7 SW Japan
Masvingo 128 E5 SE Zimbabwe
Matadi 128 B3 W Dem. Rep. Congo
Matagalpa 107 D4 C Nicaragua
Matale 89 E8 C Sri Lanka
Matamata 135 D3 North Island, NZ
Matamoros 105 F3 NE Mexico
Matane 99 F4 Québec, SE Canada
Matanzas 109 B2 NW Cuba
Matara 89 E8 S Sri Lanka
Mataram 91 E8 C Indonesia
Mataró 57 G2 E Spain
Mataura 135 B8 South Island, NZ
Mataura 135 B7 ≈ South Island, NZ
Matā'utu 137 K4 ○ Île Uvea, Wallis and Futuna
Matautu 137 B5 C Samoa
Mataveri 137 C6 Easter Island, Chile
Matera 61 E6 S Italy
Mathry 39 A5 SW Wales, UK
Matías Romero 105 G5 SE Mexico
Matlock 35 D5 C England, UK
Mato Grosso 115 E6 ⬖ State, W Brazil
Mato Grosso do Sul 115 E7 ⬖ State, S Brazil
Matosinhos 57 B3 NW Portugal
Matsue 85 D6 SW Japan
Matsumoto 85 F5 S Japan
Matsuyama 85 D7 Shikoku, SW Japan
Matterhorn 59 B9 ▲ Italy/Switzerland
Matthew Town 109 E3 S Bahamas
Maturín 115 D1 NE Venezuela
Mau 89 E3 N India
Maui 103 B6 Island, Hawaii, USA
Maun 128 C5 C Botswana
Mauritania 124 A2 ◆ Republic, W Africa
Mauritius 118 ◆ Republic, W Indian Ocean
Mawson 138 E4 Australian research station, Antarctica
Maya 107 B2 ≈ E Russ. Fed.
Mayaguana 109 F3 Island, SE Bahamas
Mayaguana Passage 109 E3 Passage, SE Bahamas
Mayagüez 109 H4 W Puerto Rico
Maybole 33 D6 W Scotland, UK
Maych'ew 127 D3 N Ethiopia
Maydan Shahr 83 F5 E Afghanistan
Mayfield 135 C6 South Island, NZ
May, Isle of 33 F5 Island, E Scotland, UK
Maykop 69 A8 SW Russ. Fed.
Maymyo 91 A2 C Burma
Mayo 29 ⬖ County, W Ireland
Mayor Island 135 D3 Island, NE NZ
Mayotte 128 G4 French ◇ E Africa
Mazabuka 128 D4 S Zambia
Mazar-e Sharif 83 F4 N Afghanistan
Mazatlán 105 D4 C Mexico
Mazury 63 F2 Physical region, NE Poland
Mazyr 67 D3 SE Belarus
Mbabane 128 E6 ● NW Swaziland
Mbala 128 E3 NE Zambia
Mbale 127 C5 E Uganda
Mbandaka 128 C2 NW Dem. Rep. Congo
M'Banza Congo 128 B3 NW Angola
Mbanza-Ngungu 128 B2 W Dem. Rep. Congo
Mbarara 127 C5 SW Uganda
Mbé 124 G5 N Cameroon
Mbeya 127 C7 Mbeya, SW Tanzania
Mbuji-Mayi 128 C3 S Dem. Rep. Congo
McAllen 103 F6 Texas, USA
McClintock Channel 97 G3 Channel, Nunavut, N Canada
McCook 103 F3 Nebraska, USA
McKinley, Mount 97 D4 ▲ Alaska, USA
McKinley Park 97 D4 Alaska, USA
McMurdo Base 138 C6 US research station, Antarctica
Mdantsane 128 D7 SE South Africa
Meath 29 ⬖ County, E Ireland
Mecca 81 B5 W Saudi Arabia
Mechelen 50 C6 C Belgium
Mecklenburger Bucht 59 C2 Bay, N Germany
Mecsek 63 D8 ⛰ SW Hungary
Medan 91 B6 Sumatra, E Indonesia
Medellín 115 B2 NW Colombia
Médenine 122 F2 SE Tunisia
Mediaş 67 B6 C Romania
Medicine Hat 97 G7 Alberta, SW Canada
Medina 81 B4 W Saudi Arabia
Medinaceli 57 E3 N Spain
Medina del Campo 57 D3 N Spain
Mediterranean Sea 70 D4 Sea, Africa/Asia/Europe
Médoc 55 B5 Cultural region, SW France
Medvezh'yegorsk 69 B3 NW Russ. Fed.
Medway 37 G4 ≈ SE England, UK
Medway 29 ⬖ Unitary auth., SE England, UK
Meekatharra 133 B4 Western Australia
Meerssen 50 E6 SE Netherlands
Meerut 89 D2 N India
Mehtarlam 83 G5 E Afghanistan
Mejillones 117 A3 N Chile
Mek'ele 127 D2 N Ethiopia
Meknès 122 C1 N Morocco
Mekong 91 C4 ≈ SE Asia
Mekong, Mouths of the 91 C5 Delta, S Vietnam
Melaka 91 B6 Peninsular Malaysia
Melanesia 137 G3 Island group, W Pacific Ocean
Melbourne 133 F6 Victoria, SE Australia
Melghir, Chott 122 E2 Salt lake, E Algeria
Melilla 122 D1 Spain, N Africa
Melita 97 H7 Manitoba, S Canada
Melitopol' 67 F6 SE Ukraine
Melle 50 B6 NW Belgium
Melleray, Mount 31 D6 ▲ S Ireland
Mellerud 49 C6 S Sweden
Mellieha 70 B6 E Malta
Mellizo Sur, Cerro 117 A8 ▲ S Chile
Melo 117 D5 NE Uruguay
Melsungen 59 C5 C Germany
Melton Mowbray 35 E6 C England, UK
Melun 55 D3 N France
Melville Island 133 D1 Island, Northern Territory, N Australia
Melville Island 97 G2 Island, Parry Islands, NW Terr./Nunavut, NW Canada
Melville, Lake 99 G3 ◎ Newfoundland, E Canada
Melville Peninsula 97 H3 Peninsula, Nunavut, NE Canada
Memmingen 59 C7 S Germany
Memphis 101 C4 Tennessee, USA
Menai Bridge 39 C2 NW Wales, UK
Menai Strait 39 C2 Strait, NW Wales, UK
Ménaka 124 E3 E Mali
Menaldum 50 D2 N Netherlands
Mende 55 D6 S France
Mendeleyev Ridge 139 C3 Undersea feature, Arctic Ocean
Mendi 137 B2 W PNG
Mendip Hills 37 D4 Hill range, S England, UK
Mendocino, Cape 103 A2 Headland, California, USA
Mendoza 117 A5 W Argentina
Menemen 79 A3 W Turkey
Menengiyn Tal 87 F2 Plain, E Mongolia
Menongue 128 B4 C Angola
Menorca see Minorca
Mentawai, Kepulauan 91 B7 Island group, W Indonesia
Meppel 50 E3 NE Netherlands
Merano 61 C1 N Italy
Mercedes 117 C4 NE Argentina
Meredith, Cape 40 Headland, Falkland Islands
Mergui 91 B4 S Burma
Mérida 105 H4 SW Mexico
Mérida 57 C4 W Spain
Mérida 115 C2 W Venezuela
Mérignac 55 B5 SW France
Merowe 127 C2 Desert, W Sudan
Merredin 133 B5 Western Australia
Merrick 33 D7 ▲ S Scotland, UK
Mersey 35 C5 ≈ NW England, UK
Mersin 79 D5 S Turkey
Merthyr Tydfil 39 E6 S Wales, UK
Merthyr Tydfil 29 ⬖ Unitary auth., S Wales, UK
Merton 37 F4 SE England, UK
Merton 29 ⬖ London borough, SE England, UK
Meru 127 D5 C Kenya
Merzifon 79 D2 N Turkey
Merzig 59 A6 SW Germany
Mesa 103 D4 Arizona, USA
Messalo, Rio 128 F4 ≈ NE Mozambique
Messina 61 D8 Sicily, Italy
Messina see Musina
Messina, Strait of 61 E8 Strait, C Mediterranean Sea
Mestia 79 G1 N Georgia
Mestre 61 D2 NE Italy
Metairie 103 H5 Louisiana, USA
Metán 117 B4 N Argentina
Metapán 107 B3 NW El Salvador
Meta, Río 115 C2 ≈ Colombia/Venezuela
Métsovo 65 D4 C Greece
Metz 55 F2 NE France
Meulaboh 91 A6 Sumatra, W Indonesia
Meuse 55 E2 ≈ W Europe
Mexborough 35 E5 N England, UK
Mexicali 105 A1 NW Mexico
Mexico 105 D3 ◆ Federal Republic, N Central America
Mexico City 105 E5 ● C Mexico
Mexico, Gulf of 92 G3 Gulf, W Atlantic Ocean
Meymaneh 83 E4 NW Afghanistan
Mezen' 69 C3 ≈ NW Russ. Fed.
Mezőtúr 63 F8 E Hungary
Mġarr 70 A6 N Malta
Miahuatlán 105 G6 SE Mexico
Miami 101 F7 Florida, USA
Miami Beach 101 F7 Florida, USA
Mianyang 87 E4 C China
Miastko 63 C2 NW Poland
Michalovce 63 F6 E Slovakia
Michigan 101 D2 ⬖ State, N USA
Michigan, Lake 101 D2 ◎ N USA
Michurinsk 69 B6 W Russ. Fed.
Micronesia 131 ◆ Federation, W Pacific Ocean
Mid-Indian Ridge 15 Undersea feature, C Indian Ocean
Mid-Atlantic Ridge 14 Undersea feature, Atlantic Ocean
Middelburg 50 B5 SW Netherlands
Middelharnis 50 C5 SW Netherlands
Middelkerke 50 A6 W Belgium
Middle Andaman 89 H5 Island, Andaman Islands, India
Middlesbrough 35 E3 N England, UK
Middlesbrough 28 ⬖ Unitary auth., N England, UK
Middletown 39 E3 C Wales, UK
Middlewich 35 C5 W England, UK
Midland 99 D5 Ontario, S Canada
Midland 103 F5 Texas, USA
Midleton 31 C6 SW Ireland
Midlothian 28 ⬖ Unitary auth., S Scotland, UK
Mid-Pacific Mountains 15 Undersea feature, NW Pacific Ocean
Midway Islands 42 US ◇ C Pacific Ocean
Miechów 63 E5 S Poland
Międzyrzecz 63 C3 W Poland
Międzyrzecz Podlaski 63 G3 E Poland
Mielec 63 F5 SE Poland
Miercurea-Ciuc 67 C6 C Romania
Mieres del Camino 57 C1 NW Spain
Mi'eso 127 E3 C Ethiopia
Miguel Asua 105 D3 C Mexico
Mijdrecht 50 D4 C Netherlands
Mikhaylovka 69 B7 SW Russ. Fed.
Mikun' 69 D4 NW Russ. Fed.
Mikura-jima 85 G6 Island, E Japan
Milan 61 B2 N Italy
Milano see Milan
Milas 79 A4 SW Turkey
Mildenhall 37 G2 E England, UK
Mildura 133 F5 Victoria, SE Australia
Miles 133 G4 Queensland, E Australia
Milford Haven 39 A6 SW Wales, UK
Milford Haven 39 A6 Inlet, SW Wales, UK
Milford Sound 135 A7 South Island, NZ
Mil'kovo 76 I3 E Russ. Fed.
Milk River 97 G7 Alberta, SW Canada
Milk River 103 D1 ≈ Montana, USA
Milk, Wadi el 127 B2 ≈ C Sudan
Mille Lacs Lake 103 F1 ◎ Minnesota, USA
Millennium Island 131 Atoll, Line Islands, E Kiribati
Millerovo 69 A7 SW Russ. Fed.
Millford 31 D1 NW Ireland
Mílos 65 F6 Island, Cyclades, Greece
Milton 135 B8 South Island, NZ
Milton Keynes 37 F3 SE England, UK
Milton Keynes 29 ⬖ Unitary auth., C England, UK
Milwaukee 101 D2 Wisconsin, USA
Minas Gerais 115 H7 ⬖ State, E Brazil
Minatitlán 105 G5 E Mexico
Minbu 91 A2 W Burma
Minch, The 33 C2 Strait, NW Scotland, UK
Mindanao 91 G5 Island, S Philippines
Mindelheim 59 C7 S Germany
Minden 59 B4 NW Germany
Mindoro 91 F4 Island, N Philippines
Mindoro Strait 91 E4 Strait, W Philippines
Minehead 37 C4 SW England, UK
Mingäçevir 79 I2 C Azerbaijan
Mingaora 89 C1 N Pakistan
Mingulay 33 A4 Island, NW Scotland, UK
Minho 57 B2 ≈ Portugal/Spain
Minicoy Island 89 C7 Island, SW India
Minna 124 E4 Niger, C Nigeria
Minneapolis 103 G2 Minnesota, USA
Minnesota 103 F1 ⬖ State, N USA
Miño 57 B2 ≈ Portugal/Spain
Minorca 57 H3 Island, Balearic Islands, Spain
Minsk 67 C2 ● C Belarus
Minskaya Wzvyshsha 67 C2 ⛰ C Belarus
Minto, Lac 99 D2 ◎ Québec, C Canada
Miraflores 105 C4 W Mexico
Miranda de Ebro 57 E2 N Spain
Miri 91 D5 East Malaysia
Mirim Lagoon 117 D5 Lagoon, Brazil/Uruguay
Mirjaveh 81 F3 SE Iran
Mirny 138 D5 Russian research station, Antarctica
Mirnyy 76 F4 NE Russ. Fed.
Mirpur Khas 89 C3 SE Pakistan
Mirtoan Sea 65 E6 Sea, S Greece
Miskitos, Cayos 107 F3 Island group, NE Nicaragua
Miskolc 63 F7 NE Hungary
Misool, Pulau 91 G7 Island, Maluku, E Indonesia
Misratah 122 F2 NW Libya
Mississippi 101 C5 ⬖ State, SE USA
Mississippi Delta 103 H5 Delta, Louisiana, USA
Mississippi River 101 C4 ≈ C USA
Missoula 103 D1 Montana, USA
Missouri 103 G3 ⬖ State, C USA
Missouri River 103 F2 ≈ C USA
Mistassini, Lac 99 D4 ◎ Québec, SE Canada
Mistelbach an der Zaya 59 F6 NE Austria
Misti, Volcán 115 C6 ※ S Peru
Mitchell 133 G4 Queensland, E Australia
Mitchell, Mount 101 E4 ▲ North Carolina, USA
Mitchell River 133 F2 ≈ Queensland, NE Australia
Mito 85 G5 S Japan
Mitú 115 C3 SE Colombia
Mitumba Range 128 D3 ⛰ E Dem. Rep. Congo
Miyako 85 G3 C Japan
Miyako-jima 85 G6 Island, SW Japan
Miyakonojō 85 D8 SW Japan
Miyazaki 85 D8 SW Japan
Mizen Head 31 A7 Headland, SW Ireland
Mizpe Ramon 81 G7 S Israel
Mjøsa 49 B5 ◎ S Norway
Mława 63 E3 C Poland
Mljet 65 C3 Island, S Croatia
Moa Island 133 F1 Island, Queensland, NE Australia
Moala 137 J5 Island, S Fiji
Moanda 128 B2 SE Gabon
Moate 31 D4 C Ireland
Moba 128 D3 E Dem. Rep. Congo
Mobaye 124 H5 S CAR
Mobile 101 D6 Alabama, USA
Mochudi 128 D6 SE Botswana
Mocímboa da Praia 128 F3 N Mozambique
Môco 128 B4 ▲ W Angola
Mocuba 128 F4 NE Mozambique
Modena 61 C3 N Italy
Modesto 103 B3 California, USA
Modica 61 D8 Sicily, Italy
Modimolle 128 D6 NE South Africa
Moe 133 F6 Victoria, SE Australia
Moelfre 39 C1 NW Wales, UK
Moelfre 39 D4 Hill, E Wales, UK
Moffat 33 E6 S Scotland, UK
Mogadishu 127 F5 ● S Somalia
Mogilno 63 D3 C Poland
Mohammedia 122 C1 NW Morocco
Mohéli 128 F4 Island, S Comoros
Mohoro 127 D7 E Tanzania
Moi 49 A6 S Norway
Mo i Rana 49 C3 C Norway
Mõisaküla 49 E6 S Estonia
Moissac 55 C6 S France
Mojácar 57 E5 S Spain
Mojave Desert 103 C4 Plain, California, USA
Mokp'o 85 B7 SW South Korea
Mol 50 D6 N Belgium
Mold 39 E2 NE Wales, UK
Moldavia see Moldova
Molde 49 B4 S Norway
Moldo-Too, Khrebet 83 H2 ⛰ C Kyrgyzstan
Moldova 67 C5 ◆ Republic, SE Europe
Molfetta 61 E6 SE Italy
Mölndal 49 B6 S Sweden
Molodezhnaya 138 E3 Russian research station, Antarctica
Molokai 103 B6 Island, Hawaii, USA
Molopo 128 C6 Seasonal river, Botswana/South Africa
Moluccas 91 G7 Island group, Indonesia
Molucca Sea 91 F6 Sea, E Indonesia
Mombacho, Volcán 107 D5 ※ SW Nicaragua
Mombasa 127 E6 SE Kenya
Møn 49 B7 Island, SE Denmark
Monach Islands 33 A3 Island group, NW Scotland, UK
Monaco 55 F6 ● S Monaco
Monaco 55 F6 ◆ Monarchy, W Europe
Monadhliath Mountains 33 D4 ⛰ N Scotland, UK
Monaghan 31 E3 N Ireland
Monaghan 29 ⬖ County, N Ireland
Mona, Isla 109 H4 Island, W Puerto Rico
Mona Passage 109 H4 Channel, Dominican Republic/Puerto Rico
Monbetsu 85 G1 NE Japan
Moncalieri 61 A2 NW Italy
Monchegorsk 69 B2 NW Russ. Fed.
Monclova 105 E3 NE Mexico
Moncton 99 F5 New Brunswick, SE Canada
Mondovì 61 A3 NW Italy
Moneygall 31 D5 C Ireland
Moneymore 31 E2 C Northern Ireland, UK
Monfalcone 61 D2 NE Italy
Monforte 57 B2 NW Spain
Mongo 124 H4 C Chad
Mongolia 87 D2 ◆ Republic, E Asia
Mongu 128 C4 W Zambia
Monkey Bay 128 E4 SE Malawi
Monkey River Town 107 C2 SE Belize
Monmouth 39 F6 SE Wales, UK
Monmouthshire 29 ⬖ Unitary auth., SE Wales, UK
Monovar 57 F5 E Spain
Monroe 103 H4 Louisiana, USA
Monrovia 124 B5 ● W Liberia
Mons 50 C7 S Belgium
Monselice 61 C2 NE Italy
Montana 65 E2 NW Bulgaria
Montana 103 D1 ⬖ State, NW USA
Montargis 55 D3 C France
Montauban 55 C6 S France
Montbéliard 55 F3 E France
Mont Cenis, Col du 55 F5 Pass, E France
Mont-de-Marsan 55 B6 SW France
Monteagudo 117 B3 S Bolivia
Monte Caseros 117 C5 NE Argentina
Monte Cristi 109 F4 NW Dominican Republic
Montego Bay 109 D4 W Jamaica
Montélimar 55 E6 E France
Montemorelos 105 E3 NE Mexico
Montenegro 65 C3 ⬖ Republic, SW Serbia and Montenegro (Yugoslavia)
Monte Patria 117 A5 N Chile
Monterey Bay 103 A3 Bay, California, USA
Montería 115 B2 NW Colombia
Montero 117 B2 C Bolivia
Monterrey 105 E3 NE Mexico
Montes Claros 115 G6 SE Brazil
Montevideo 117 C6 ● S Uruguay
Montgenèvre, Col de 55 F5 Pass, France/Italy
Montgomery 39 E4 E Wales, UK
Montgomery 101 D5 Alabama, USA
Monthey 59 A8 SW Switzerland
Montluçon 55 D4 C France
Montoro 57 D5 S Spain
Montpelier 101 G2 Vermont, USA
Montpellier 55 D6 S France
Montréal 99 E5 Québec, SE Canada
Montrose 33 F4 E Scotland, UK
Montserrat 40 UK ◇ E West Indies
Monywa 91 A2 C Burma
Monza 61 B2 N Italy
Monze 128 D4 S Zambia
Monzón 57 F2 NE Spain
Moonie 133 G4 Queensland, E Australia
Moora 133 B5 Western Australia
Moorea 137 A5 Island, Îles du Vent, W French Polynesia
Moore, Lake 133 B5 ◎ Western Australia
Moose 99 C4 ≈ Ontario, S Canada
Moosehead Lake 101 H2 ◎ Maine, USA
Moosonee 99 C4 Ontario, SE Canada
Mopti 124 C3 C Mali
Mora 49 C5 C Sweden
Morales 107 B3 E Guatemala
Morar, Loch 33 C4 ◎ N Scotland, UK
Moratalla 57 E5 SE Spain
Morava 63 D6 ≈ C Europe
Moravia 63 D6 Cultural region, E Czech Republic
Moray 28 ⬖ Unitary auth., N Scotland, UK
Moray Firth 33 D3 Inlet, N Scotland, UK
Morecambe 35 C4 NW England, UK
Morecambe Bay 35 B4 Inlet, NW England, UK
Moree 133 G5 NSW, SE Australia
Morelia 105 E5 S Mexico
Morena, Sierra 57 C5 ⛰ S Spain
Mórfou 70 C6 W Cyprus
Morghab, Darya-ye 83 E4 ≈ Afghanistan/Turkmenistan
Morioka 85 G3 C Japan
Morlaix 55 A2 NW France
Morocco 122 B2 ◆ Monarchy, N Africa
Morogoro 127 D6 E Tanzania
Moro Gulf 91 F5 Gulf, S Philippines
Morón 109 D3 C Cuba
Mörön 87 D1 N Mongolia
Morondava 128 G5 W Madagascar
Moroni 128 F4 ● Grande Comore, NW Comoros
Morotai, Pulau 91 G6 Island, Moluccas, E Indonesia
Morpeth 35 D2 N England, UK
Morrinsville 135 D3 North Island, NZ
Morris 40 S Montserrat
Morris Jesup, Kap 139 C4 Headland, N Greenland
Morvan 55 E4 Physical region, C France
Moscow 69 B5 ● Russ. Fed.
Mosel 59 A5 ≈ W Europe
Moselle 55 F3 ≈ W Europe
Mosgiel 135 B7 South Island, NZ
Moshi 127 D6 NE Tanzania
Mosjøen 49 C3 C Norway
Moskva 83 F4 SW Tajikistan
Moskva see Moscow
Mosonmagyaróvár 63 D7 NW Hungary
Mosquito Coast 107 E4 Physical region, Nicaragua
Mosquito Gulf 107 G6 Gulf, N Panama
Moss 49 B5 S Norway
Mosselbaai 128 C7 SW South Africa
Mossendjo 128 B2 SW Congo
Mossoró 115 I4 NE Brazil
Most 63 B5 NW Czech Republic
Mosta 70 B6 C Malta
Mostaganem 122 D1 NW Algeria
Mostar 65 C2 S Bosnia and Herzegovina
Mostyn 39 E1 N Wales, UK
Mosul 81 C2 N Iraq
Mota del Cuervo 57 E4 C Spain
Motagua, Río 107 B3 ≈ Guatemala/Honduras
Motherwell 33 D6 C Scotland, UK
Motril 57 D6 S Spain
Motueka 135 C5 South Island, NZ
Motul 105 H4 SE Mexico
Motu Nui 137 C6 Island, Easter Island, Chile
Mouchoir Passage 40 Passage, SE Turks and Caicos Islands
Mouila 128 A2 C Gabon
Mould Bay 97 G2 Prince Patrick Island, NW Terr., N Canada
Moulins 55 D4 C France
Moulmein 91 B3 S Burma
Moundou 124 G4 SW Chad
Mountain Ash 39 E6 S Wales, UK
Mountbellew Bridge 31 C4 C Ireland
Mount Cook see Aoraki
Mount Gambier 133 F6 S Australia
Mount Hagen 137 B2 C PNG
Mount Isa 133 F3 Queensland, C Australia
Mount Magnet 133 B4 Western Australia
Mount's Bay 37 A6 Inlet, SW England, UK
Mourne Mountains 31 E3 ⛰ SE Northern Ireland, UK
Mouscron 50 B7 W Belgium
Moussoro 124 G3 W Chad
Moycullen 31 B4 W Ireland
Moyen Atlas 122 C2 ⛰ N Morocco
Moyle 29 ⬖ District, N Northern Ireland, UK
Mo'ynoq 83 D1 NW Uzbekistan
Moyynkum, Peski 83 G1 Desert, S Kazakhstan
Mozambique 128 E5 ◆ Republic, S Africa
Mozambique Channel 128 F5 Strait, W Indian Ocean
Mpama 128 B2 ≈ C Congo
Mragowo 63 F2 NE Poland
Mtwara 127 E7 SE Tanzania
Muar 91 B6 Peninsular Malaysia
Muck 33 B4 Island, W Scotland, UK
Muckle Roe 33 A6 Island, NE Scotland, UK
Mucojo 128 F4 N Mozambique
Mudanjiang 87 H2 NE China
Mufulira 128 D4 C Zambia
Muğla 79 A4 SW Turkey
Muine Bheag 31 E5 SE Ireland
Mukacheve 67 B5 W Ukraine
Mula 57 E5 SE Spain
Mulhacén 57 D5 ▲ S Spain
Mulhouse 55 F3 E France
Mullaghmore 31 C2 N Ireland
Mullan 31 D3 W Northern Ireland, UK
Mullaranny 31 B3 NW Ireland
Muller, Pegunungan 91 D6 ⛰ C Indonesia
Müllheim 59 B7 SW Germany
Mullingar 31 D4 C Ireland
Mull, Isle of 33 B5 Island, W Scotland, UK
Mulongo 128 D3 SE Dem. Rep. Congo
Multan 89 C2 E Pakistan
Mumbai 89 C5 W India
Münchberg 59 D5 E Germany
München see Munich
Muncie 101 D3 Indiana, USA
Munda 137 E2 NW Solomon Islands
Mungbere 128 D1 NE Dem. Rep. Congo
Munich 59 D7 SE Germany
Munster 59 B4 NW Germany
Munster 31 B6 Cultural region, S Ireland
Muonio 49 E2 N Finland
Muonioälv 49 D2 Finland/Sweden
Muqdisho see Mogadishu
Mur 59 F8 ≈ C Europe
Muradiye 79 H3 E Turkey
Murchison River 133 B4 ≈ W Australia
Murcia 57 F5 SE Spain
Murcia 57 E5 Cultural region, SE Spain
Mureş 67 A6 ≈ Hungary/Romania

⬖ Administrative region ◆ Country ● Country capital ◇ Dependent territory ○ Dependent territory capital ⛰ Mountain range ▲ Mountain ※ Volcano ≈ River ◎ Lake ⊞ Reservoir

Murgap 83 D4 S Turkmenistan
Murgap 83 D4 ≈ SE Turkmenistan
Murghob 83 H3 SE Tajikistan
Murgon 133 H4 Queensland, E Australia
Müritz 59 D3 ◎ NE Germany
Murmansk 69 C2 NW Russ. Fed.
Murmashi 69 B2 NW Russ. Fed.
Murom 69 B5 W Russ. Fed.
Muroran 85 F2 NE Japan
Muros 57 A1 NW Spain
Murray, Lake 137 A2 ◎ SW PNG
Murray River 133 F5 ≈ SE Australia
Murrumbidgee River 133 F6 ≈ NSW, SE Australia
Murska Sobota 59 F8 NE Slovenia
Murupara 135 E3 North Island, NZ
Mururoa 131 *Atoll,* Îles Tuamotu, SE French Polynesia
Murwara 89 E4 N India
Murwillumbah 133 H5 NSW, SE Australia
Murzuq, Idhan 122 F4 *Desert,* SW Libya
Mürzzuschlag 59 F7 E Austria
Muş 79 G3 E Turkey
Musa, Gebel 122 I3 ▲ NE Egypt
Musala 65 E3 ▲ W Bulgaria
Muscat 81 F4 ● NE Oman
Musgrave Ranges 133 D4 ▲▲ S Australia
Musina 128 D5 NE South Africa
Musoma 127 C5 N Tanzania
Musters, Lago 117 A7 ◎ S Argentina
Muswellbrook 133 G5 NSW, SE Australia
Mut 79 C5 S Turkey
Mutare 128 E5 E Zimbabwe
Muy Muy 107 D4 C Nicaragua
Mwanza 127 C6 NW Tanzania
Mweelrea 31 A4 ▲ W Ireland
Mweka 128 C2 C Dem. Rep. Congo
Mwene-Ditu 128 C3 S Dem. Rep. Congo
Mweru, Lake 128 D3 ◎ Dem. Rep. Congo/Zambia
Myadzyel 67 C2 N Belarus
Myanmar *see* Burma
Myingyan 91 A2 C Burma
Myitkyina 91 B1 N Burma
Mykolayiv 67 E6 S Ukraine
Mykonos 65 F6 *Island,* Cyclades, Greece
Myrina 65 F4 Límnos, SE Greece
Myślibórz 63 B3 W Poland
Mysore 89 D6 W India
My Tho 91 C4 S Vietnam
Mytilíni 65 F5 Lesbos, E Greece
Mzuzu 128 E3 N Malawi

N

Naas 31 E4 C Ireland
Naberezhnyye Chelny 69 D6 W Russ. Fed.
Nacala 128 F4 NE Mozambique
Nadi 137 J5 Viti Levu, W Fiji
Nadur 70 A6 N Malta
Nadvoitsy 69 B3 NW Russ. Fed.
Nadym 76 D3 N Russ. Fed.
Náfpaktos 65 D5 C Greece
Náfplio 65 E6 S Greece
Naga 91 F4 N Philippines
Nagano 85 F5 S Japan
Nagaoka 85 F5 C Japan
Nagasaki 85 C8 SW Japan
Nagato 85 D7 Honshu, SW Japan
Nagercoil 89 D7 SE India
Nagles Mountains 31 C6 ▲ S Ireland
Nagornyy Karabakh 79 H2 *Former autonomous region,* SW Azerbaijan
Nagoya 85 F6 SW Japan
Nagpur 89 E4 C India
Nagqu 87 C4 W China
Nagykálló 63 F7 E Hungary
Nagykanizsa 63 C8 SW Hungary
Nagykörös 63 E8 C Hungary
Naha 85 A8 Okinawa, SW Japan
Nahariyya 81 H5 N Israel
Nahuel Huapi, Lago 117 A7 ◎ W Argentina
Nain 99 F2 Newfoundland, NE Canada
Nairn 33 D3 N Scotland, UK
Nairobi 127 D5 ● S Kenya
Najin 85 C3 NE North Korea
Najran 81 C6 S Saudi Arabia
Nakamura 85 E7 Shikoku, SW Japan
Nakatsugawa 85 F6 SW Japan
Nakhodka 76 H6 SE Russ. Fed.
Nakhon Ratchasima 91 B3 E Thailand
Nakhon Sawan 91 B3 W Thailand
Nakhon Si Thammarat 91 B5 SW Thailand
Nakuru 127 D5 SW Kenya
Nal'chik 69 A8 SW Russ. Fed.
Nalut 122 F2 NW Libya
Namangan 83 G3 E Uzbekistan
Nam Co 87 C4 ◎ W China
Nam Dinh 91 C2 N Vietnam
Namhae-do 85 B7 *Island,* S South Korea
Namib Desert 128 B5 *Desert,* W Namibia
Namibe 128 B4 SW Angola
Namibia 128 B5 ◆ *Republic,* S Africa
Nam Ou 91 B2 ≈ N Laos
Namp'o 85 A5 SW North Korea
Nampula 128 F4 NE Mozambique
Namsan-ni 85 A4 NW North Korea
Namsos 49 C3 C Norway
Namur 50 D7 SE Belgium
Namwon 85 B6 S South Korea
Nanaimo 97 E7 Vancouver Island, British Columbia, SW Canada
Nanchang 87 F5 S China
Nancy 55 F3 NE France
Nandaime 107 D5 SW Nicaragua
Nanded 89 D5 C India
Nandyal 89 E6 E India
Nangnim-sanmaek 85 B4 ▲▲ C North Korea
Nanjing 87 G4 E China
Nanning 87 F6 S China
Nanping 87 G5 SE China
Nansen Basin 139 D4 *Undersea feature,* Arctic Ocean
Nansen Cordillera 139 C4 *Undersea feature,* Arctic Ocean
Nanterre 55 D2 N France
Nantes 55 B3 NW France
Nantwich 35 C5 W England, UK
Nanumaga 137 I2 *Atoll,* NW Tuvalu
Nanumea Atoll 137 I2 *Atoll,* NW Tuvalu
Nanyang 87 F4 C China
Napier 135 E4 North Island, NZ
Naples 61 D6 S Italy
Napoli *see* Naples
Napo, Río 115 B3 ≈ Ecuador/Peru
Naracoorte 133 F6 S Australia
Narberth 39 B6 SW Wales, UK
Narbonne 55 D7 S France
Nares Strait 97 H1 *Strait,* Canada/Greenland
Narew 63 F3 ≈ E Poland
Narowlya 67 D3 SE Belarus
Närpes 49 D4 W Finland
Närpiö *see* Närpes
Narrabri 133 G5 NSW, SE Australia
Narrogin 133 B5 Western Australia
Narva 49 F5 NE Estonia
Narvik 49 D2 C Norway
Nar'yan-Mar 69 D3 NW Russ. Fed.
Naryn 83 H2 C Kyrgyzstan
Nashik 89 D5 W India
Nashville 101 D4 Tennessee, USA
Näsijärvi 49 E4 ◎ SW Finland
Nassau 109 D2 ● New Providence, N Bahamas
Nasser, Lake 122 J4 ◎ Egypt/Sudan
Nata 128 D5 NE Botswana
Natal 115 I4 E Brazil
Natchez 101 C5 Mississippi, USA
Natitingou 124 D4 NW Benin
Natuna, Kepulauan 91 C6 *Island group,* W Indonesia
Nauru 137 G1 ◆ *Republic,* W Pacific Ocean
Navan 31 E4 E Ireland
Navapolatsk 67 D1 N Belarus
Navarra 57 E2 *Cultural region,* N Spain
Navassa Island 109 D4 *US* ◇ C West Indies
Navoiy 83 E3 C Uzbekistan
Navojoa 105 C3 NW Mexico
Navolato 105 C3 C Mexico
Nawabshah 89 B3 S Pakistan
Naxcivan 79 H3 SW Azerbaijan
Náxos 65 F6 *Island,* Cyclades, Greece
Nayoro 85 G1 NE Japan
Nazareth 81 H5 N Israel
Nazca Ridge 14 *Undersea feature,* E Pacific Ocean
Naze 85 B7 SW Japan
Nazilli 79 A4 SW Turkey
Nazret 127 D3 C Ethiopia
N'Dalatando 128 B3 NW Angola
Ndélé 124 H4 N CAR
Ndendé 128 A2 S Gabon
Ndindi 128 A2 S Gabon
Ndjamena 124 G4 ● W Chad
Ndola 128 D4 C Zambia
Neagh, Lough 31 E2 ◎ E Northern Ireland, UK
Neápoli 65 E6 S Greece
Neápoli 65 D4 N Greece
Neath 39 D6 S Wales, UK
Neath Port Talbot 29 ⬖ *Unitary auth.,* S Wales, UK
Nebaj 107 A3 W Guatemala
Neblina, Pico da 115 C3 ▲ NW Brazil
Nebraska 103 F2 ⬖ *State,* C USA
Neckar 59 B6 ≈ SW Germany
Necochea 117 C6 E Argentina
Neder Rijn 50 D4 ≈ C Netherlands
Nederweert 50 E6 SE Netherlands
Neede 50 F4 E Netherlands
Neerpelt 50 D6 NE Belgium
Neftekamsk 69 D6 W Russ. Fed.
Nefyn 39 B2 NW Wales, UK
Negele 127 E4 S Ethiopia
Negev 81 G6 *Desert,* S Israel
Negombo 89 E8 SW Sri Lanka
Negotin 65 D2 E Serbia and Montenegro (Yugoslavia)
Negra, Punta 115 A4 *Headland,* NW Peru
Negro, Río 117 B6 ≈ E Argentina
Negro, Rio 115 D3 ≈ N South America
Negros 91 F5 *Island,* C Philippines
Neijiang 87 E5 C China
Nellore 89 E6 E India
Nelson 135 C5 South Island, NZ
Nelson 35 D4 NW England, UK
Nelson 97 H6 ≈ Manitoba, C Canada
Nelson Island 40 *Island,* N British Indian Ocean Territory
Néma 124 C3 SE Mauritania
Neman 49 E7 ≈ NE Europe
Nemours 55 D3 N France
Nemuro 85 H1 NE Japan
Nenagh 31 C5 C Ireland
Nendö 137 G3 *Island,* Santa Cruz Islands, E Solomon Islands
Nene 37 G2 ≈ E England, UK
Nepal 89 E3 ◆ *Monarchy,* S Asia
Nepean 99 D5 Ontario, SE Canada
Nephin 31 B3 ▲ W Ireland
Neretva 65 C2 ≈ Bosnia and Herzegovina/Croatia
Neringa 49 E7 SW Lithuania
Neris 67 C2 ≈ Belarus/Lithuania
Nerva 57 C5 S Spain
Neryungri 76 G4 NE Russ. Fed.
Neskaupstadhur 49 B1 E Iceland
Ness, Loch 33 D4 ◎ N Scotland, UK
Néstos 65 E4 ≈ Bulgaria/Greece
Netanya 81 G6 C Israel
Netherlands 50 D3 ◆ *Monarchy,* NW Europe
Netherlands Antilles 109 G7 *Dutch* ◇ S Caribbean Sea
Nettilling Lake 97 I3 ◎ Baffin Island, Nunavut, N Canada
Neubrandenburg 59 D3 NE Germany
Neuchâtel 59 A8 W Switzerland
Neuchâtel, Lac de 59 A8 ◎ W Switzerland
Neufchâteau 50 D8 SE Belgium
Neumünster 59 C2 N Germany
Neunkirchen 59 A6 SW Germany
Neuquén 117 A6 SE Argentina
Neuruppin 59 D3 NE Germany
Neusiedler See 59 F7 ◎ Austria/Hungary
Neustadt an der Weinstrasse 59 A6 SW Germany
Neustrelitz 59 D3 NE Germany
Neu-Ulm 59 C7 S Germany
Neuwied 59 B5 W Germany
Nevada 103 C3 ⬖ *State,* W USA
Nevers 55 D4 C France
Nevinnomyssk 69 A8 SW Russ. Fed.
Nevşehir 79 D4 C Turkey
Newala 127 D7 SE Tanzania
New Amsterdam 115 E2 E Guyana
Newark 101 G3 New Jersey, USA
Newark-on-Trent 35 E5 C England, UK
Newborough 39 C2 NW Wales, UK
Newbridge 31 C4 W Ireland
Newbridge 39 E6 S Wales, UK
Newbridge on Wye 39 E5 C Wales, UK
New Britain 137 C2 *Island,* E PNG
New Brunswick 99 F5 ⬖ *Province,* SE Canada
Newbury 37 E4 S England, UK
Newbury 29 ⬖ *Unitary auth.,* S England, UK
New Caledonia 137 D5 *French* ◇ SW Pacific Ocean
Newcastle 133 G5 NSW, SE Australia
Newcastle 31 F3 SE Northern Ireland, UK
Newcastle Emlyn 39 C5 S Wales, UK
Newcastle-under-Lyme 35 D5 C England, UK
Newcastle upon Tyne 35 D2 NE England, UK
Newcastle upon Tyne 28 ⬖ *Unitary auth.,* NE England, UK
Newcastle West 31 B5 SW Ireland
New Delhi 89 D3 ● N India
New England 101 G2 *Cultural region,* NE USA
New Forest 37 E5 *Physical region,* S England, UK
Newfoundland 99 G4 *Island,* Newfoundland, SE Canada
Newfoundland 99 G3 ⬖ *Province,* E Canada
New Georgia 137 E2 *Island,* New Georgia Islands, NW Solomon Islands
New Georgia Islands 137 D3 *Island group,* NW Solomon Islands
New Glasgow 99 G5 Nova Scotia, SE Canada
New Guinea 137 A2 *Island,* Indonesia/PNG
Newham 29 ⬖ *London borough,* SE England, UK
New Hampshire 101 G2 ⬖ *State,* NE USA
New Hanover 137 C1 *Island,* NE PNG
Newhaven 37 G5 SE England, UK
New Haven 101 G3 Connecticut, USA
New Ireland 137 C1 *Island,* NE PNG
New Island 40 *Island,* W Falkland Islands
New Jersey 101 G3 ⬖ *State,* NE USA
Newman 133 B3 Western Australia
Newmarket 37 G2 E England, UK
Newmarket on Fergus 31 C5 W Ireland
New Mexico 103 D4 ⬖ *State,* SW USA
New Orleans 103 H5 Louisiana, USA
New Plymouth 135 D4 North Island, NZ
Newport 37 E5 S England, UK
Newport 39 F7 SE Wales, UK
Newport 39 B5 SW Wales, UK
Newport 29 *Unitary auth.,* SE Wales, UK
Newport Bay 39 B5 *Bay,* SW Wales, UK
Newport News 101 F4 Virginia, USA
Newport Pagnell 37 F3 SE England, UK
New Providence 109 D1 *Island,* N Bahamas
Newquay 37 A5 SW England, UK
New Quay 39 C5 SW Wales, UK
New Ross 31 E6 SE Ireland
Newry 31 E3 SE Northern Ireland, UK
Newry and Mourne 29 ⬖ *District,* S Northern Ireland, UK
New Siberian Islands 76 F2 *Island group,* N Russ. Fed.
New South Wales 133 F5 ⬖ *State,* SE Australia
Newton Abbot 37 C5 SW England, UK
Newton Stewart 33 D7 S Scotland, UK
Newtown 31 C6 S Ireland
Newtown 39 E4 E Wales, UK
Newtownabbey 31 E2 E Northern Ireland, UK
Newtownabbey 29 ⬖ *District,* E Northern Ireland, UK
Newtown St Boswells 33 E6 S Scotland, UK
Newtownstewart 31 D2 W Northern Ireland, UK
New York 101 G3 New York, USA
New York 101 F3 ⬖ *State,* NE USA
New Zealand 135 A5 ◆ *Commonwealth Republic,* SW Pacific Ocean
Neyland 39 B6 SW Wales, UK
Neyveli 89 E7 SE India
Ngangze Co 87 B4 ◎ W China
Ngaoundéré 124 G5 N Cameroon
N'Giva 128 B4 S Angola
Ngo 128 B2 SE Congo
Ngoko 124 G6 ≈ Cameroon/Congo
Ngourti 124 G3 E Niger
Nguigmi 124 G3 SE Niger
Nguru 124 F4 NE Nigeria
Nha Trang 91 D4 S Vietnam
Nhulunbuy 133 E1 Northern Territory, N Australia
Niagara Falls 99 D6 Ontario, S Canada
Niagara Falls 101 F2 New York, USA
Niagara Falls 101 E3 *Waterfall,* Canada/USA
Niamey 124 E3 ● SW Niger
Niangay, Lac 124 D3 ◎ E Mali
Nia-Nia 128 D1 NE Dem. Rep. Congo
Nias, Pulau 91 A6 *Island,* W Indonesia
Nicaragua 107 D4 ◆ *republic,* C America
Nicaragua, Lake 107 E5 ◎ S Nicaragua
Nice 55 F6 SE France
Nicholls Town 109 D1 NW Bahamas
Nicobar Islands 89 H6 *Island group,* India, E Indian Ocean
Nicosia 70 C6 ● C Cyprus
Nicoya 107 D6 W Costa Rica
Nicoya, Golfo de 107 E6 *Gulf,* W Costa Rica
Nicoya, Península de 107 D6 *Peninsula,* NW Costa Rica
Nidzica 63 E2 N Poland
Nieuw-Bergen 50 E5 SE Netherlands
Nieuwegein 50 D4 C Netherlands
Nieuw Nickerie 115 E2 NW Surinam
Niğde 79 D4 C Turkey
Niger 124 E3 ◆ *Republic,* W Africa
Niger 124 E4 ≈ W Africa
Niger Delta 118 *Delta,* S Nigeria
Nigeria 124 E4 ◆ *Federal Republic,* W Africa
Niger, Mouths of the 124 E5 *Delta,* S Nigeria
Niigata 85 F4 C Japan
Niihama 85 E7 Shikoku, SW Japan
Niihau 103 A5 *Island,* Hawaii, USA
Nii-jima 85 G6 *Island,* E Japan
Nijkerk 50 D4 C Netherlands
Nijlen 50 C6 N Belgium
Nijmegen 50 E4 SE Netherlands
Nikel' 69 B2 NW Russ. Fed.
Nikiniki 91 F8 S Indonesia
Nikopol' 67 F5 SE Ukraine
Nikšić 65 C3 SW Serbia and Montenegro (Yugoslavia)
Nile 122 I3 ≈ N Africa
Nile Delta 122 I2 *Delta,* N Egypt
Nîmes 55 E6 S France
Nine Degree Channel 89 C7 *Channel,* India/Maldives
Ninetyeast Ridge 15 *Undersea feature,* E Indian Ocean
Ningbo 87 G4 SE China
Ninigo Group 137 A1 *Island group,* N PNG
Nioro 124 B3 W Mali
Niort 55 C4 W France
Nipigon 99 B4 Ontario, S Canada
Nipigon, Lake 99 B4 ◎ Ontario, S Canada
Niš 65 D2 SE Serbia and Montenegro (Yugoslavia)
Nisko 63 F5 SE Poland
Nísyros 65 G6 *Island,* Dodecanese, Greece
Nith 33 D6 ≈ S Scotland, UK
Nitra 63 D7 SW Slovakia
Nitra 63 D7 ≈ W Slovakia
Niue 131 *Self-governing* ◇ S Pacific Ocean
Niulakita 137 J3 *Atoll,* S Tuvalu
Niutao 137 J2 *Atoll,* NW Tuvalu
Nivernais 55 D4 *Cultural region,* C France
Nizamabad 89 D5 C India
Nizhnekamsk 69 C6 W Russ. Fed.
Nizhnevartovsk 76 D4 C Russ. Fed.
Nizhniy Novgorod 69 B5 W Russ. Fed.
Nizhniy Odes 69 D4 NW Russ. Fed.
Nizhyn 67 E4 NE Ukraine
Njombe 127 D7 S Tanzania
Nkayi 128 B2 S Congo
Nkongsamba 124 F5 W Cameroon
Nmai Hka 91 B1 ≈ N Burma
Nobeoka 85 D8 SW Japan
Noboribetsu 85 F2 NE Japan
Nogales 105 B2 NW Mexico
Nokia 49 E5 SW Finland
Nokou 124 G3 W Chad
Nola 124 G5 SW CAR
Nolinsk 69 C5 NW Russ. Fed.
Nome 139 B1 Alaska, USA
Noord-Beveland 50 B5 *Island,* SW Netherlands
Noordwijk aan Zee 50 C4 W Netherlands
Nora 49 C5 C Sweden
Norak 83 F3 W Tajikistan
Norddeutsches Tiefland 63 A2 *Plain,* N Germany
Norden 59 B3 NW Germany
Norderstedt 59 C3 N Germany
Nordfriesische Inseln *see* North Frisian Islands
Nordhausen 59 C4 C Germany
Nordhorn 59 A3 NW Germany
Nordkapp *see* North Cape
Nore 31 D5 ≈ S Ireland
Norfolk 101 G4 Virginia, USA
Norfolk 29 ⬖ *County,* E England, UK
Norfolk Island 131 *Australian* ◇ SW Pacific Ocean
Noril'sk 76 E3 N Russ. Fed.
Norman 103 F4 Oklahoma, USA
Normandie *see* Normandy
Normandy 55 C2 *Cultural region,* France
Norman Island 40 *Island,* S British Virgin Islands
Normanton 133 F2 Queensland, NE Australia
Norrköping 49 C6 S Sweden
Norrtälje 49 D5 C Sweden
Norseman 133 C5 Western Australia
Norsup 137 G5 Malekula, C Vanuatu
Northallerton 35 E3 N England, UK
Northam 133 B5 Western Australia
North America 92 *Continent*
North American Basin 14 *Undersea feature,* W Sargasso Sea
Northampton 37 F2 C England, UK
Northamptonshire 29 ⬖ *County,* C England, UK
North Andaman 89 H4 *Island,* Andaman Islands, India
North Arm 40 Falkland Islands
North Ayrshire 28 ⬖ *Unitary auth.,* W Scotland, UK
North Bay 99 D5 Ontario, S Canada
North Berwick 33 E5 SE Scotland, UK
North Caicos 40 *Island,* NW Turks and Caicos Islands
North Cape 135 C1 *Headland,* North Island, NZ
North Cape 49 E1 *Headland,* N Norway
North Carolina 101 E5 ⬖ *State,* SE USA
North Channel 33 B6 *Strait,* Northern Ireland/Scotland, UK
North Dakota 103 F1 ⬖ *State,* N USA
North Down 29 ⬖ *District,* E Northern Ireland, UK
North East Bay 40 *Bay,* Ascension Island, C Atlantic Ocean
North East Lincolnshire 29 ⬖ *Unitary auth.,* N England, UK
Northeim 59 C4 C Germany
Northern Cook Islands 131 *Island group,* N Cook Islands
Northern Dvina 69 C4 ≈ NW Russ. Fed.
Northern Ireland 29 *Political division,* Northern Ireland, UK
Northern Mariana Islands 131 *US* ◇ W Pacific Ocean
Northern Sporades 65 E5 *Island group,* E Greece
Northern Territory 133 D2 ⬖ *Territory,* N Australia
North Esk 33 E4 ≈ E Scotland, UK
North European Plain 44 *Plain,* N Europe
North Foreland 37 H3 *Headland,* SE England, UK
North Frisian Islands 59 B2 *Island group,* N Germany
North Geomagnetic Pole 139 A4 *Pole,* Arctic Ocean
North Island 135 B2 *Island,* N NZ
North Korea 85 C4 ◆ *Republic,* E Asia
North Lanarkshire 28 ⬖ *Unitary auth.,* C Scotland, UK
Northland 135 C1 *Cultural region,* North Island, NZ
North Lincolnshire 29 ⬖ *Unitary auth.,* N England, UK
North Little Rock 103 G4 Arkansas, USA
North Mole 40 *Harbour wall,* NW Gibraltar
North Platte River 103 E2 ≈ C USA
North Point 40 *Headland,* Ascension Island, C Atlantic Ocean
North Pole 139 C4 *Pole,* Arctic Ocean
North Ronaldsay 33 F1 *Island,* NE Scotland, UK
North Saskatchewan 97 G6 ≈ S Canada
North Sea 44 *Sea,* NW Europe
North Siberian Lowland 76 E3 *Lowlands,* N Russ. Fed.
North Somerset 29 ⬖ *Unitary auth.,* SW England, UK
North Sound 40 *Sound,* W Cayman Islands
North Sound 31 B4 *Sound,* W Ireland
North Sound, The 33 E1 *Sound,* N Scotland, UK
North Taranaki Bight 135 C3 *Gulf,* North Island, NZ
North Tyne 35 D2 ≈ N England, UK
North Tyneside 28 ⬖ *Unitary auth.,* NE England, UK
North Uist 33 A3 *Island,* NW Scotland, UK
Northumberland 29 ⬖ *County,* N England, UK
North West Bluff 40 *Headland,* N Montserrat
North West Highlands 33 C3 ▲▲ N Scotland, UK
Northwest Pacific Basin 15 *Undersea feature,* NW Pacific Ocean
Northwest Territories 97 F4 ⬖ *Territory,* NW Canada
Northwich 35 C5 C England, UK
Northwind Plain 139 B2 *Undersea feature,* Arctic Ocean
North York Moors 35 E3 *Moorland,* N England, UK
North Yorkshire 29 ⬖ *County,* N England, UK
Norton Sound 97 C3 *Inlet,* Alaska, USA
Norway 49 A4 ◆ *Monarchy,* N Europe
Norwegian Sea 49 A4 *Sea,* NE Atlantic Ocean
Norwich 37 H2 E England, UK
Noshiro 85 F3 C Japan
Nossob 128 C6 ≈ E Namibia
Noteć 63 D3 ≈ NW Poland
Nottingham 35 E5 C England, UK
Nottingham 29 ⬖ *Unitary auth.,* C England, UK
Nottinghamshire 29 ⬖ *County,* C England, UK
Nouâdhibou 124 A2 W Mauritania
Nouakchott 124 A2 ● SW Mauritania
Nouméa 137 G6 ○ S New Caledonia
Nova Gorica 59 E8 W Slovenia
Nova Iguaçu 115 G7 SE Brazil
Novara 61 B2 NW Italy
Nova Scotia 99 F5 ⬖ *Province,* SE Canada
Novaya Sibir', Ostrov 76 G2 *Island,* NE Russ. Fed.
Novaya Zemlya 69 E1 *Island group,* N Russ. Fed.
Novgorod 69 A4 W Russ. Fed.
Novi Sad 65 D1 N Serbia and Montenegro (Yugoslavia)
Novoazovs'k 67 G5 E Ukraine
Novocheboksarsk 69 C6 W Russ. Fed.
Novocherkassk 69 A7 SW Russ. Fed.
Novodvinsk 69 C3 NW Russ. Fed.
Novokazalinsk 76 B5 SW Kazakhstan
Novokuznetsk 76 E5 S Russ. Fed.
Novolazarevskaya 138 C3 *Russian research station,* Antarctica
Novo Mesto 59 E9 SE Slovenia
Novomoskovs'k 67 F5 E Ukraine
Novomoskovsk 69 B6 W Russ. Fed.
Novorossiysk 69 A8 SW Russ. Fed.
Novoshakhtinsk 69 A7 SW Russ. Fed.
Novosibirsk 76 D5 C Russ. Fed.
Novotroitsk 69 D7 W Russ. Fed.
Novyy Buh 67 E5 S Ukraine
Nowogard 63 C2 NW Poland
Nowy Dwór Mazowiecki 63 E3 C Poland
Nowy Sącz 63 F6 S Poland
Nowy Tomyśl 63 C3 W Poland
Noyon 55 D2 N France
Ntomba, Lac 128 B2 ◎ NW Dem. Rep. Congo
Nubian Desert 127 C1 *Desert,* NE Sudan
Nueva Gerona 109 B3 S Cuba
Nueva Guinea 107 E5 SE Nicaragua
Nueva Ocotepeque 107 B3 W Honduras
Nueva Rosita 105 E2 NE Mexico
Nuevitas 109 D3 E Cuba
Nuevo Casas Grandes 105 C2 N Mexico
Nuevo, Golfo 117 B7 *Gulf,* S Argentina
Nuevo Laredo 105 E2 NE Mexico
Nui Atoll 137 I2 *Atoll,* W Tuvalu
Nuku'alofa 131 ● Tongatapu, S Tonga
Nukufetau Atoll 137 I2 *Atoll,* C Tuvalu
Nukulaelae Atoll 137 J3 *Atoll,* E Tuvalu
Nukumanu Islands 137 E1 *Island group,* NE PNG
Nukus 83 D2 W Uzbekistan
Nullarbor Plain 133 D5 *Plateau,* S Australia/Western Australia
Nunavut 97 H4 ⬖ *Territory,* N Canada
Nuneaton 35 E6 C England, UK
Nunivak Island 97 B3 *Island,* Alaska, USA
Nunspeet 50 E4 E Netherlands
Nuoro 61 A6 Sardinia, Italy
Nuremberg 59 C6 S Germany
Nurmes 49 F4 E Finland
Nürnberg *see* Nuremberg
Nurota 83 E3 C Uzbekistan
Nusaybin 79 G4 SE Turkey
Nyagan' 76 D3 N Russ. Fed.
Nyainqêntanglha Shan 87 C4  W China
Nyala 127 B3 W Sudan
Nyamtumbo 127 D7 S Tanzania
Nyandoma 69 B4 NW Russ. Fed.
Nyantakara 127 C6 NW Tanzania
Nyasa, Lake 128 E4 ◎ E Africa
Nyeri 127 D5 C Kenya
Nyima 87 C4 W China
Nyíregyháza 63 F7 NE Hungary
Nykøbing 49 B7 SE Denmark
Nyköping 49 D6 S Sweden
Nylstroom *see* Modimolle
Nyngan 133 G5 NSW, SE Australia
Nyurba 76 F4 NE Russ. Fed.
Nzega 127 C6 C Tanzania
Nzérékoré 124 B5 SE Guinea
N'Zeto 128 B3 NW Angola

O

Oahu 103 B5 *Island,* Hawaii, USA
Oakham 35 E6 C England, UK

Oakland 103 B3 California, USA
Oamaru 135 B7 South Island, NZ
Oa, Mull of 33 B6 Headland, W Scotland, UK
Oaxaca 105 F5 SE Mexico
Ob' 76 D3 ≈ C Russ. Fed.
Oban 33 C5 W Scotland, UK
Ob, Gulf of 76 D3 Gulf, N Russ. Fed.
Obihiro 85 G2 NE Japan
Obo 124 I5 E CAR
Obock 127 E3 E Djibouti
Oborniki 63 C3 W Poland
Ocaña 57 D3 C Spain
O Carballiño 57 B2 NW Spain
Occidental, Cordillera 117 A2 ⛰ Bolivia/Chile
Ocean Falls 97 E6 British Columbia, SW Canada
Oceanside 103 C4 California, USA
Och'amch'ire 79 G1 W Georgia
Ochil Hills 33 E5 ⛰ C Scotland, UK
Ocotal 107 D4 NW Nicaragua
Ocozocuautla 105 G5 SE Mexico
October Revolution Island 76 F2 Island, N Russ. Fed.
Ocú 107 G7 S Panama
Odate 85 G3 C Japan
Ödemiş 79 A4 SW Turkey
Odense 49 B7 C Denmark
Oder 59 E3 ≈ C Europe
Oderhaff 63 B2 Bay, Germany/Poland
Odesa 67 E6 SW Ukraine
Odessa 103 F5 Texas, USA
Odienné 124 C4 NW Ivory Coast
Odoorn 50 F2 NE Netherlands
Of 79 F2 NE Turkey
Ofanto 61 E6 ≈ S Italy
Offaly 29 ◈ County, C Ireland
Offenbach 59 B5 W Germany
Offenburg 59 B7 SW Germany
Ogaden 127 F4 Plateau, Ethiopia/Somalia
Ogaki 85 F6 SW Japan
Ogbomosho 124 E5 W Nigeria
Ogden 103 D3 Utah, USA
Ohio 101 E3 ◈ State, N USA
Ohio River 101 D4 ≈ N USA
Ohrid, Lake 65 D4 ◎ Albania/FYR Macedonia
Ohura 135 D3 North Island, NZ
Oirschot 50 D5 S Netherlands
Oise 55 D2 ≈ N France
Oita 85 D7 Kyushu, SW Japan
Ojinaga 105 D2 N Mexico
Ojos del Salado, Cerro 117 A4 ▲ W Argentina
Okaihau 135 C1 North Island, NZ
Okara 89 D2 E Pakistan
Okavango 128 C5 ≈ S Africa
Okavango Delta 128 C5 Wetland, N Botswana
Okayama 85 E6 SW Japan
Okazaki 85 F6 C Japan
Okeechobee, Lake 101 E7 ◎ SE USA
Okehampton 37 C5 SW England, UK
Okhotsk 76 H3 E Russ. Fed.
Okhotsk, Sea of 76 H4 Sea, NW Pacific Ocean
Okhtyrka 67 F4 NE Ukraine
Okinawa 85 A8 SW Japan
Okinawa-shoto 85 A8 Island group, SW Japan
Oki-shoto 85 D6 Island group, SW Japan
Oklahoma 103 F4 ◈ State, C USA
Oklahoma City 103 F4 Oklahoma, USA
Oko, Wadi 127 D1 ≈ NE Sudan
Oktyabr'skiy 69 D6 SW Russ. Fed.
Okushiri-to 85 F2 Island, NE Japan
Öland 49 D7 Island, S Sweden
Olavarría 117 C6 E Argentina
Oława 63 D4 SW Poland
Olbia 61 B5 Sardinia, Italy
Oldebroek 50 E3 E Netherlands
Oldenburg 59 B3 NW Germany
Oldenburg 59 C2 N Germany
Oldenzaal 50 F4 E Netherlands
Oldham 35 D5 NW England, UK
Oldham 28 ◈ Unitary auth., NW England, UK
Old Head of Kinsale 31 C7 Headland, SW Ireland
Olëkma 76 G4 ≈ C Russ. Fed.
Olëkminsk 76 G4 NE Russ. Fed.
Oleksandriya 67 E5 C Ukraine
Olenegorsk 69 B2 NW Russ. Fed.
Olenëk 76 F3 ≈ NE Russ. Fed.
Oléron, Île d' 55 B4 Island, W France
Olevs'k 67 C4 N Ukraine
Ölgiy 87 C1 W Mongolia
Olhão 57 B5 S Portugal
Olifa 128 B4 NW Namibia
Oliva 57 F4 E Spain
Olivet 55 D3 C France
Olmaliq 83 F3 E Uzbekistan
Olomouc 63 D6 E Czech Republic
Olonets 69 B4 NW Russ. Fed.
Olovyannaya 76 G5 S Russ. Fed.
Olpe 59 B5 W Germany
Olsztyn 63 E2 N Poland
Olt 67 B7 ≈ S Romania
Olvera 57 C6 S Spain
Olverston 40 ○ W Montserrat
Olympia 103 B1 Washington, USA
Olympus, Mount 65 D4 ▲ N Greece
Omagh 31 D2 W Northern Ireland, UK
Omagh 29 ◈ District, W Northern Ireland, UK
Omaha 103 G3 Nebraska, USA
Oman 81 E6 ◆ Monarchy, SW Asia
Oman, Gulf of 81 F4 Gulf, N Arabian Sea
Omboué 128 A2 W Gabon
Omdurman 127 C2 C Sudan
Ometepe, Isla de 107 D5 Island, S Nicaragua
Ommen 50 E3 E Netherlands
Omsk 76 D5 C Russ. Fed.
Omuta 85 D7 SW Japan
Onda 57 F3 E Spain
Öndörhaan 87 F2 E Mongolia
Onega 69 B3 NW Russ. Fed.
Onega 69 B4 ≈ NW Russ. Fed.
Onega, Lake 69 B4 ◎ NW Russ. Fed.
Onex 59 A8 SW Switzerland
Ongjin 85 A5 SW North Korea
Ongole 89 E6 E India
Onitsha 124 F5 S Nigeria
Onon Gol 87 F2 ≈ N Mongolia
Onslow 133 A3 Western Australia
Onslow Bay 101 F5 Bay, North Carolina, USA
Ontario 99 B4 ◈ Province, S Canada
Ontario, Lake 101 F2 ◎ Canada/USA
Ontinyent 57 F4 E Spain
Ontong Java Atoll 137 E2 Atoll, N Solomon Islands
Oostakker 50 B6 NW Belgium
Oostburg 50 B5 SW Netherlands
Oostende see Ostend
Oosterbeek 50 E4 SE Netherlands
Oosterhout 50 D5 S Netherlands
Opava 63 D5 E Czech Republic
Opmeer 50 D3 NW Netherlands
Opochka 69 A4 W Russ. Fed.
Opole 63 D5 SW Poland
Oporto 57 B3 NW Portugal
Opotiki 135 E3 North Island, NZ
Oqtosh 83 E3 C Uzbekistan
Oradea 67 B6 NW Romania
Oran 122 D1 NW Algeria
Orange 133 G5 NSW, SE Australia
Orange 55 E6 SE France
Orange River 128 C6 ≈ S Africa
Orange Walk 107 C1 N Belize
Oranienburg 59 D3 NE Germany
Oranjemund 128 B6 SW Namibia
Oranjestad 109 G7 ○ W Aruba
Oranmore 31 C4 W Ireland
Orbetello 61 C4 C Italy
Orcadas 138 A2 Argentinian research station, South Orkney Islands, Antarctica
Ord River 133 D2 ≈ N Australia
Ordu 79 E2 N Turkey
Örebro 49 C5 C Sweden
Oregon 103 B2 State, NW USA
Orël 69 A6 W Russ. Fed.
Orem 103 D3 Utah, USA
Ore Mountains 59 D5 ⛰ Czech Republic/Germany
Orenburg 69 D7 W Russ. Fed.
Orense see Ourense
Orford Ness 37 H2 Headland, E England, UK
Oriental, Cordillera 117 B3 ⛰ Bolivia/Peru
Orihuela 57 F5 E Spain
Orikhiv 67 F5 SE Ukraine
Orinoco, Río 115 D2 ≈ Colombia/Venezuela
Oriomo 137 A3 SW PNG
Orissa 89 F5 Cultural region, NE India
Oristano 61 A6 Sardinia, Italy
Orkney Islands 28 ◈ Unitary auth., N Scotland, UK
Orkney Islands 33 D1 Island group, N Scotland, UK
Orlando 101 E6 Florida, USA
Orléanais 55 D3 Cultural region, C France
Orléans 55 D3 C France
Ormskirk 35 C5 NW England, UK
Örnsköldsvik 49 D4 C Sweden
Orohena, Mont 137 B6 🌋 W French Polynesia
Oromocto 99 F5 New Brunswick, SE Canada
Orsha 67 D2 NE Belarus
Orsk 69 D7 W Russ. Fed.
Orthez 55 B6 SW France
Ortona 61 D5 C Italy
Oruro 117 A2 W Bolivia
Orwell 37 H2 ≈ E England, UK
Osaka 85 E6 SW Japan
Osa, Península de 107 E7 Peninsula, S Costa Rica
Osh 83 G3 SW Kyrgyzstan
Oshakati 128 B5 N Namibia
Oshawa 99 D6 Ontario, SE Canada
Oshikango 128 B4 N Namibia
O-shima 85 G6 Island, S Japan
Oshkosh 101 D2 Wisconsin, USA
Osijek 65 C1 E Croatia
Oskarshamn 49 C6 S Sweden
Oslo 49 B5 ● S Norway
Osmaniye 79 E5 S Turkey
Osnabrück 59 B4 NW Germany
Osorno 117 A7 C Chile
Oss 50 D5 S Netherlands
Ossa, Serra d' 57 B4 ⛰ SE Portugal
Ossora 76 I3 E Russ. Fed.
Ostend 50 A6 NW Belgium
Östersund 49 C4 C Sweden
Ostfriesische Inseln see East Frisian Islands
Ostiglia 61 C2 N Italy
Ostrava 63 D5 E Czech Republic
Ostróda 63 E2 N Poland
Ostrołęka 63 F3 NE Poland
Ostrov 69 A4 W Russ. Fed.
Ostrowiec Świętokrzyski 63 F4 SE Poland
Ostrów Mazowiecka 63 F3 NE Poland
Ostrów Wielkopolski 63 D4 C Poland
Osumi-shoto 85 A7 Island group, SW Japan
Osumit, Lumi i 65 D4 ≈ SE Albania
Osuna 57 C5 S Spain
Oswestry 35 C6 W England, UK
Otago Peninsula 135 B7 Peninsula, South Island, NZ
Otaki 135 D5 North Island, NZ
Otaru 85 F2 NE Japan
Otavi 128 B5 N Namibia
Otira 135 C6 South Island, NZ
Otjiwarongo 128 B5 N Namibia
Otley 35 D4 N England, UK
Otorohanga 135 D3 North Island, NZ
Otranto 70 G3 SE Italy
Otranto, Strait of 61 F7 Strait, Albania/Italy
Otrokovice 63 D6 SE Czech Republic
Otsu 85 E6 Honshu, SW Japan
Ottawa 99 D5 ● Ontario, SE Canada
Ottawa Islands 99 C2 Island group, Québec, C Canada
Otterburn 35 D2 N England, UK
Ottignies 50 C7 C Belgium
Ouachita Mountains 103 G4 ⛰ C USA
Ouachita River 103 H4 ≈ C USA
Ouagadougou 124 D4 ● C Burkina
Ouahigouya 124 D3 NW Burkina
Oualâta 124 C3 SE Mauritania
Ouanda Djallé 124 I4 NE CAR
Ouarâne 124 B2 Desert, C Mauritania
Ouargla 122 E2 NE Algeria
Ouarzazate 122 C2 S Morocco
Oubangui 124 H5 ≈ C Africa
Ouessant, Île d' 55 A2 Island, NW France
Ouésso 128 B1 NW Congo
Oughterard 31 B4 W Ireland
Oujda 122 D1 NE Morocco
Oujeft 124 B2 C Mauritania
Oulu 49 E3 C Finland
Oulujärvi 49 E3 ◎ C Finland
Oulujoki 49 E3 ≈ C Finland
Ounasjoki 49 E2 ≈ N Finland
Ounianga Kébir 124 H2 N Chad
Oupeye 50 D7 E Belgium
Our 50 E8 ≈ NW Europe
Ourense 57 B2 NW Spain
Ourique 57 B5 S Portugal
Ourthe 50 D8 ≈ E Belgium
Ou-sanmyaku 85 G3 ⛰ Honshu, C Japan
Ouse 35 E4 ≈ N England, UK
Outer Hebrides 33 A3 Island group, NW Scotland, UK
Out Skerries 33 B6 Island group, NE Scotland, UK
Ouvéa 137 G6 Island, Îles Loyauté, NE New Caledonia
Ouyen 133 F6 Victoria, SE Australia
Ovalle 117 A5 N Chile
Ovar 57 B3 N Portugal
Overflakkee 50 B5 Island, SW Netherlands
Overijse 50 C7 C Belgium
Overton 39 F2 NE Wales, UK
Oviedo 57 C1 NW Spain
Owando 128 B2 C Congo
Owase 85 F6 SW Japan
Owen, Mount 135 C5 ▲ South Island, NZ
Owensboro 101 D4 Kentucky, USA
Owen Stanley Range 137 B3 ⛰ S PNG
Owerri 124 F5 S Nigeria
Oxford 135 C6 South Island, NZ
Oxford 37 E3 S England, UK
Oxford Canal 37 E2 Canal, S England, UK
Oxfordshire 29 ◈ County, S England, UK
Oxkutzcab 105 H4 SE Mexico
Oyama 85 G5 Honshu, S Japan
Oyem 128 A1 N Gabon
Oykel 33 D3 ≈ N Scotland, UK
Oyo 128 B2 C Congo
Oyo 124 E5 W Nigeria
Ozark Plateau 103 G4 Plain, C USA
Ozarks, Lake of the 103 G3 ▣ Missouri, USA
Ózd 63 E7 NE Hungary
Ozieri 61 A5 Sardinia, Italy

P

Pabbay 33 A3 Island, NW Scotland, UK
Pabna 89 G3 W Bangladesh
Pachuca 105 F5 C Mexico
Pacific Ocean 14 Ocean
Padang 91 B6 Sumatra, W Indonesia
Paderborn 59 B4 NW Germany
Padova see Padua
Padre Island 103 G6 Island, Texas, USA
Padua 61 C2 NE Italy
Paektu-san 85 B3 ▲ China/North Korea
Paengnyong-do 85 A5 Island, NW South Korea
Paeroa 135 D3 North Island, NZ
Páfos 70 C6 W Cyprus
Pag 65 B2 Island, C Croatia
Pago Pago 131 ○ W American Samoa
Pahiatua 135 D4 North Island, NZ
Paignton 37 C5 SW England, UK
Paihia 135 D1 North Island, NZ
Päijänne 49 E4 ◎ S Finland
Paine, Cerro 117 A9 ▲ S Chile
Painted Desert 103 D4 Desert, Arizona, USA
Paisley 33 D6 W Scotland, UK
País Valenciano 57 F3 Cultural region, NE Spain
País Vasco see Basque Country, The
Pakistan 89 B2 ◆ Republic, S Asia
Pakokku 91 A2 C Burma
Pakruojis 49 E7 N Lithuania
Paks 63 E8 S Hungary
Pakwach 127 C5 NW Uganda
Pakxé 91 C3 S Laos
Palafrugell 57 H2 NE Spain
Palagruža 65 B3 Island, SW Croatia
Palamós 57 H2 NE Spain
Palanpur 89 C4 W India
Palapye 128 D5 SE Botswana
Palau 91 H6 ◆ Republic, W Pacific Ocean
Palawan 91 E5 Island, W Philippines
Palawan Passage 91 E4 Passage, W Philippines
Palembang 91 C7 Sumatra, W Indonesia
Palencia 57 D2 NW Spain
Palermo 61 C7 Sicily, Italy
Pali 89 C3 N India
Palikir 131 ● Pohnpei, E Micronesia
Palk Strait 89 E7 Strait, India/Sri Lanka
Palliser, Cape 135 D5 Headland, North Island, NZ
Palma de Mallorca 57 H4 Majorca, Spain
Palma del Río 57 C5 S Spain
Palmar Sur 107 F6 SE Costa Rica
Palma Soriano 109 E4 E Cuba
Palmer 138 A4 US research station, Antarctica
Palmer Land 138 B4 Physical region, Antarctica
Palmerston North 135 D4 North Island, NZ
Palmi 61 E8 SW Italy
Palmyra Atoll 131 US ◇ C Pacific Ocean
Palu 91 E6 Celebes, C Indonesia
Pamiers 55 C7 S France
Pamir 83 G4 ≈ Afghanistan/Tajikistan
Pamirs 83 G4 ⛰ C Asia
Pamlico Sound 101 G5 Sound, North Carolina, USA
Pampas 117 B6 Plain, C Argentina
Pamplona 57 E2 N Spain
Panaji 89 C6 W India
Panama 107 G7 ◆ Republic, Central America
Panama Canal 107 G6 Canal, E Panama
Panama City 107 H6 ● C Panama
Panama, Gulf of 107 H7 Gulf, S Panama
Panama, Isthmus of 107 H6 Isthmus, E Panama
Panay Island 91 E4 Island, C Philippines
Pančevo 65 D2 N Serbia and Montenegro (Yugoslavia)
Panevėžys 49 E7 C Lithuania
Pangkalpinang 91 C7 W Indonesia
Pantanal 115 E6 Swamp, SW Brazil
Pantelleria 61 B8 Sicily, Italy
Pantelleria, Isola di 70 F4 Island, SW Italy
Pánuco 105 F4 E Mexico
Paola 70 B6 E Malta
Papagayo, Golfo de 107 D5 Gulf, NW Costa Rica
Papakura 135 D2 North Island, NZ
Papantla 105 F4 E Mexico
Papa Stour 33 A6 Island, NE Scotland, UK
Papa Westray 33 E1 Island, NE Scotland, UK
Papeete 137 A5 ○ W French Polynesia
Papua 91 I7 Province, E Indonesia
Papua, Gulf of 137 B3 Gulf, S PNG
Papua New Guinea 137 B2 ◆ Commonwealth Republic, NW Melanesia
Papuk 65 C1 ⛰ NE Croatia
Pará 115 F4 ◈ State, NE Brazil
Paracel Islands 91 C3 Disputed ◇ SE Asia
Paraguay 117 B3 ◆ Republic, C South America
Paraguay 117 C3 ≈ C South America
Paraíba 115 I5 ◈ State, E Brazil
Parakou 124 E4 C Benin
Paramaribo 115 F2 ● N Surinam
Paramushir, Ostrov 76 I4 Island, SE Russ. Fed.
Paraná 117 C5 E Argentina
Paraná 115 F8 ◈ State, S Brazil
Paraná 117 C5 ≈ C South America
Paraparaumu 135 D5 North Island, NZ
Parchim 59 D3 N Germany
Parczew 63 G4 E Poland
Pardubice 63 C5 C Czech Republic
Parecis, Chapada dos 117 B1 ⛰ W Brazil
Parepare 91 E7 Celebes, C Indonesia
Paria, Gulf of 109 J7 Gulf, Trinidad and Tobago/Venezuela
Paris 55 D2 ● Paris, N France
Parkes 133 G5 NSW, SE Australia
Parma 61 C3 N Italy
Parnaíba 115 H4 E Brazil
Pärnu 49 E6 SW Estonia
Páros 65 F6 Island, Cyclades, Greece
Parral 117 A6 C Chile
Parramatta 133 G6 NSW, SE Australia
Parras 105 E3 NE Mexico
Parrett 37 D4 ≈ SW England, UK
Partney 35 F5 E England, UK
Partry 31 B3 NW Ireland
Partry Mountains 31 B4 ⛰ W Ireland
Pasadena 103 B4 California, USA
Pasadena 103 G5 Texas, USA
Pasewalk 59 E3 NE Germany
Pasinler 79 G3 NE Turkey
Pasłęk 63 E2 N Poland
Pasni 89 A3 SW Pakistan
Paso de Indios 117 A7 S Argentina
Passau 59 D6 SE Germany
Passo Fundo 115 F8 S Brazil
Pasto 115 B3 SW Colombia
Patagonia 117 B7 Physical region, Argentina/Chile
Patea 135 D4 North Island, NZ
Paterson 101 G3 New Jersey, USA
Pátmos 65 F6 Island, Dodecanese, Greece
Patna 89 F3 N India
Patnos 79 G3 E Turkey
Patos, Lagoa dos 115 F9 Lagoon, S Brazil
Pátra 65 D5 S Greece
Patrickswell 31 C5 SW Ireland
Patuca, Río 107 E3 ≈ E Honduras
Pau 55 B6 SW France
Paulatuk 97 F3 NW Terr., NW Canada
Pavia 61 B2 N Italy
Pavlodar 76 D5 NE Kazakhstan
Pavlohrad 67 F5 E Ukraine
Pawn 91 B3 ≈ C Burma
Paxoí 65 D5 Island, Ionian Islands, Greece
Paysandú 117 C5 W Uruguay
Pazar 79 F2 NE Turkey
Pazardzhik 65 E3 SW Bulgaria
Peak District 35 D5 Physical region, C England, UK
Peak, The 40 ▲ C Ascension Island
Pearl Islands 107 H6 Island group, SE Panama
Pearl Lagoon 107 F4 Lagoon, E Nicaragua
Pearl River 101 C5 ≈ S USA
Pebble Island Settlement 40 N Falkland Islands
Peć 65 D3 S Serbia and Montenegro (Yugoslavia)
Pechora 69 D4 NW Russ. Fed.
Pechora 69 D3 ≈ NW Russ. Fed.
Pechora Sea 69 D2 Sea, NW Russ. Fed.
Pecos River 103 F5 ≈ SW USA
Pécs 63 D9 SW Hungary
Pedro Juan Caballero 117 C3 E Paraguay
Peebles 33 E6 SE Scotland, UK
Peel 35 A3 W Isle of Man
Peer 50 D6 NE Belgium
Pegasus Bay 135 C6 Bay, South Island, NZ
Pegu 91 B3 SW Burma
Pehuajó 117 B6 E Argentina
Peine 59 C4 C Germany
Peipus, Lake 49 E5 ◎ Estonia/Russ. Fed.
Peiraiás see Piraeus
Pekalongan 91 D7 Java, C Indonesia
Pekanbaru 91 B6 Sumatra, W Indonesia
Peking see Beijing
Pelagie 61 C9 Island group, SW Italy
Pelly Bay 97 H3 Nunavut, N Canada
Peloponnese 65 D6 Peninsula, S Greece
Pematangsiantar 91 A6 Sumatra, W Indonesia
Pemba 128 F4 NE Mozambique
Pemba 127 E6 Island, E Tanzania
Pembrey 39 C6 S Wales, UK
Pembroke 99 D5 Ontario, SE Canada
Pembroke 39 B6 SW Wales, UK
Pembroke Dock 39 B6 SW Wales, UK
Pembrokeshire 29 ◈ Unitary auth., SW Wales, UK
Penarth 39 E7 S Wales, UK
Penas, Golfo de 117 A8 Gulf, S Chile
Pencoed 39 E7 S Wales, UK
Pendine 39 B6 S Wales, UK
Pendleton 103 C1 Oregon, USA
Peniche 57 A4 W Portugal
Penmaenmawr 39 D1 N Wales, UK
Pennine Alps 59 A8 ⛰ Italy/Switzerland
Pennines 35 D3 ⛰ N England, UK
Pennsylvania 101 G3 ◈ State, NE USA
Penong 133 E5 S Australia
Penonomé 107 G6 C Panama
Penrhyn 131 N Cook Islands
Penrith 35 C3 NW England, UK
Pensacola 101 D6 Florida, USA
Pentecost 137 H4 Island, C Vanuatu
Pentland Firth 33 E1 Strait, N Scotland, UK
Pentland Hills 33 E6 Hill range, S Scotland, UK
Pentraeth 39 C1 NW Wales, UK
Pentrefoelas 39 D2 N Wales, UK
Penybont 39 E4 C Wales, UK
Pen y Fan 39 E6 ▲ SE Wales, UK
Pen y Garn 39 D4 ▲ W Wales, UK
Pen-y-ghent 35 D3 ▲ N England, UK
Penygroes 39 C2 NW Wales, UK
Penza 69 B6 W Russ. Fed.
Penzance 37 A6 SW England, UK
Peoria 101 D3 Illinois, USA
Perchtoldsdorf 59 F7 NE Austria
Percival Lakes 133 C3 Lakes, Western Australia
Perdido, Monte 57 F2 ▲ NE Spain
Pergamino 117 C5 E Argentina
Périgueux 55 C5 SW France
Perito Moreno 117 A8 S Argentina
Perleberg 59 D3 N Germany
Perm' 69 D5 NW Russ. Fed.
Pernambuco 115 H5 State, E Brazil
Pernik 65 E3 W Bulgaria
Peros Banhos 40 Island, N British Indian Ocean Territory
Perote 105 F5 E Mexico
Perpignan 55 D7 S France
Perth 133 B5 Western Australia
Perth 33 E5 C Scotland, UK
Perth and Kinross 28 ◈ Unitary auth., C Scotland, UK
Peru 117 A2 ◆ Republic, W South America
Peru-Chile Trench 14 Undersea feature, E Pacific Ocean
Peru Basin 14 Undersea feature, E Pacific Ocean
Perugia 61 C4 C Italy
Péruwelz 50 B7 SW Belgium
Pervomays'k 67 E5 S Ukraine
Pervyy Kuril'skiy Proliv 76 I4 Strait, E Russ. Fed.
Pesaro 61 D3 C Italy
Pescara 61 D5 C Italy
Peshawar 89 C1 N Pakistan
Pessac 55 B5 SW France
Petah Tiqwa 81 H6 C Israel
Pétange 50 E9 SW Luxembourg
Petén Itzá, Lago 107 B2 ◎ N Guatemala
Peterborough 133 E5 S Australia
Peterborough 99 D6 Ontario, SE Canada
Peterborough 37 F2 E England, UK
Peterborough 29 ◈ Unitary auth., E England, UK
Peterhead 33 F3 NE Scotland, UK
Peter Island 40 Island, S British Virgin Islands
Peter I Island 138 A4 Norwegian ◇ Antarctica
Peterlee 35 E3 N England, UK
Petersfield 37 F4 S England, UK
Peto 105 H4 SE Mexico
Petrich 65 E4 SW Bulgaria
Petrodvorets 69 A4 NW Russ. Fed.
Petropavlovsk 76 C4 N Kazakhstan
Petropavlovsk-Kamchatskiy 76 I3 E Russ. Fed.
Petrozavodsk 69 B4 NW Russ. Fed.
Pevek 76 H2 NE Russ. Fed.
Pezinok 63 D7 SW Slovakia
Pforzheim 59 B6 SW Germany
Pfungstadt 59 B6 W Germany
Phangan, Ko 91 B4 Island, SW Thailand
Phetchaburi 91 B4 SW Thailand
Philadelphia 101 G3 Pennsylvania, USA
Philippines 91 D4 ◆ Republic, SE Asia
Philippine Sea 91 F3 Sea, W Pacific Ocean
Philippine Trench 15 Undersea feature, W Philippine Sea
Phitsanulok 91 B3 C Thailand
Phnom Penh 91 C4 ● S Cambodia
Phnum Dangrek 91 C4 ⛰ Cambodia/Thailand
Phoenix 103 D4 Arizona, USA
Phoenix Islands 131 Island group, C Kiribati
Phra Thong, Ko 91 A5 Island, SW Thailand
Phuket 91 B5 SW Thailand
Phuket, Ko 91 A5 Island, SW Thailand
Piacenza 61 B2 N Italy
Piatra-Neamț 67 C6 NE Romania
Piauí 115 G5 ◈ State, E Brazil
Picardie see Picardy
Picardy 55 D2 Cultural region, N France
Pichilemu 117 A5 C Chile
Pickering 35 E3 N England, UK
Picos 115 H4 E Brazil
Picton 135 D5 South Island, NZ
Piedmont 61 A2 Cultural region, NW Italy
Piedras Negras 105 E2 NE Mexico
Pielinen 49 F4 ◎ E Finland
Piemonte see Piedmont
Pierre 103 F2 South Dakota, USA
Piešťany 63 D6 W Slovakia
Pietarsaari see Jakobstad
Pietermaritzburg 128 D6 E South Africa
Pietersburg see Polokwane
Pigs, Bay of 109 C3 Bay, SE Cuba
Pijijiapán 105 H6 SE Mexico
Piła 63 C3 NW Poland
Pilar 117 C4 S Paraguay
Pilcomayo 117 C3 ≈ C South America
Pillar Bay 40 Bay, Ascension Island, C Atlantic Ocean
Pinar del Río 109 B2 W Cuba
Pindus Mountains 65 D5 ⛰ C Greece
Pine Bluff 103 H4 Arkansas, USA
Pine Creek 133 D1 Northern Territory, N Australia
Pinega 69 C4 ≈ NW Russ. Fed.
Pineiós 65 E4 ≈ C Greece
Pingdingshan 87 F4 C China
Ping, Mae Nam 91 B3 ≈ W Thailand
Pins, Île des 137 G6 Island, E New Caledonia
Pinotepa Nacional 105 F6 SE Mexico
Pinsk 67 C3 SW Belarus
Piombino 61 B4 C Italy
Piotrków Trybunalski 63 E4 C Poland
Piraeus 65 E5 C Greece
Piripiri 115 H4 E Brazil
Pirna 59 E5 E Germany
Pisa 61 B3 C Italy
Pisco 115 B6 SW Peru
Písek 63 B6 SW Czech Republic
Pishan 87 B3 NW China
Pistoia 61 C3 C Italy
Pisz 63 F2 NE Poland
Pita 124 B4 NW Guinea
Pitcairn Islands 131 UK ◇ S Pacific Ocean
Piteå 49 D3 N Sweden
Pitești 67 B7 S Romania
Pitlochry 33 D4 C Scotland, UK

◈ Administrative region ◆ Country ● Country capital ◇ Dependent territory ○ Dependent territory capital ⛰ Mountain range ▲ Mountain 🌋 Volcano ≈ River ◎ Lake ▣ Reservoir

Pittsburgh 101 F3 Pennsylvania, USA
Piura 115 A4 NW Peru
Pivdennyy Buh 67 E5 ≈ S Ukraine
Placetas 109 C3 C Cuba
Plano 103 G4 Texas, USA
Plasencia 57 C3 W Spain
Plate, River 117 C5 *Estuary,* Argentina/Uruguay
Platinum 97 C4 Alaska, USA
Plauen 59 D5 E Germany
Play Cu 91 C4 C Vietnam
Plenty, Bay of 135 E3 *Bay,* North Island, NZ
Plérin 55 B2 NW France
Plesetsk 69 C4 NW Russ. Fed.
Pleszew 63 D4 C Poland
Pleven 65 E2 N Bulgaria
Płock 63 E3 C Poland
Plöcken Pass 59 D8 *Pass,* SW Austria
Ploieşti 67 C7 SE Romania
Płońsk 63 E3 C Poland
Plovdiv 65 F3 C Bulgaria
Plymouth 40 SW Montserrat
Plymouth 109 J5 Trinidad and Tobago
Plymouth 37 B5 SW England, UK
Plymouth 29 ◐ *Unitary auth.,* SW England, UK
Plynlimon 39 D4 ▲ C Wales, UK
Plzeň 63 A5 W Czech Republic
Po 61 C3 ≈ N Italy
Pobedy, Pik 87 B2 ▲ China/Kyrgyzstan
Pochinok 69 A5 W Russ. Fed.
Pocking 59 D7 SE Germany
Pocklington Reef 137 E3 *Reef,* SE PNG
Poděbrady 63 B5 C Czech Republic
Podgorica 65 C3 SW Serbia and Montenegro (Yugoslavia)
Podil's'ka Vysochyna 67 C5 ⛰ SW Ukraine
Podol'sk 69 A5 W Russ. Fed.
P'ohang 85 C6 E South Korea
Poinsett, Cape 138 E5 *Headland,* Antarctica
Pointe-à-Pitre 109 J5 C Guadeloupe
Pointe-Noire 128 A2 S Congo
Point Lay 97 D2 Alaska, USA
Poitiers 55 C4 W France
Poitou 55 B4 *Cultural region,* W France
Pokhara 89 F3 C Nepal
Pola de Lena 57 C1 N Spain
Poland 63 D4 ◆ *Republic,* C Europe
Polatlı 79 C3 C Turkey
Polatsk 67 D1 N Belarus
Pol-e Khomri 83 F4 NE Afghanistan
Pólis 70 C6 W Cyprus
Pollença 57 H3 Majorca, Spain
Polokwane 128 D6 NE South Africa
Poltava 67 F4 NE Ukraine
Polyarnyy 69 C2 NW Russ. Fed.
Polynesia 131 *Island group,* C Pacific Ocean
Pomerania 63 C2 *Cultural Region,* Poland
Pomeranian Bay 59 E2 *Bay,* Germany/Poland
Pomio 137 C2 E PNG
Pomorskiy Proliv 69 D3 *Strait,* NW Russ. Fed.
Ponce 109 H4 C Puerto Rico
Pondicherry 89 E6 SE India
Pond Inlet 139 A4 Baffin Island, NW Terr., NE Canada
Ponferrada 57 C2 NW Spain
Poniatowa 63 F4 E Poland
Ponta Grossa 115 F8 S Brazil
Pontardawe 39 D6 S Wales, UK
Pontardulais 39 C6 S Wales, UK
Pontarlier 55 F4 E France
Ponteareas 57 B2 NW Spain
Ponte da Barca 57 B2 N Portugal
Ponterwyd 39 D4 W Wales, UK
Pontevedra 57 B2 NW Spain
Pontiac 101 E3 Michigan, USA
Pontianak 91 D6 C Indonesia
Pontivy 55 B3 NW France
Pontoise 55 D2 N France
Pontrhydfendigaid 39 D4 W Wales, UK
Pontycymer 39 D6 S Wales, UK
Pontypool 39 E6 S Wales, UK
Pontypridd 39 E6 S Wales, UK
Ponziane Island 61 C6 *Island,* C Italy
Poole 37 E5 S England, UK
Poole 29 ◐ *Unitary auth.,* S England, UK
Poole Bay 37 E5 *Bay,* S England, UK
Popayán 115 B3 SW Colombia
Poperinge 50 A6 W Belgium
Popocatépetl 105 F5 ▲ S Mexico
Popondetta 137 C3 S PNG
Poprad 63 E6 NE Slovakia
Poprád 63 E6 ≈ Poland/Slovakia
Porbandar 89 C4 W India
Pordenone 61 D2 NE Italy
Pori 49 E5 SW Finland
Porirua 135 D5 North Island, NZ
Porkhov 69 A4 W Russ. Fed.
Póros 65 D5 Kefallinía, Greece
Porpoise Point 40 *Headland,* Falkland Islands
Porsangerfjorden 49 E1 *Fjord,* N Norway
Porsgrunn 49 B5 S Norway
Portadown 31 E2 S Northern Ireland, UK
Portaferry 31 F3 E Northern Ireland, UK
Portalegre 57 B4 E Portugal
Port Alfred 128 D7 S South Africa
Port Askaig 33 B6 W Scotland, UK
Port Augusta 133 E5 S Australia
Port-au-Prince 109 ● C Haiti
Port Blair 89 H5 Andaman Islands, SE India
Port Dinorwic 39 C2 NW Wales, UK
Port Douglas 133 G2 Queensland, NE Australia
Port Elizabeth 128 D7 S South Africa
Port Ellen 33 B6 W Scotland, UK
Port Erin 35 A4 SW Isle of Man
Port-Eynon 39 C7 S Wales, UK
Port-Gentil 128 A2 W Gabon
Port Harcourt 124 E5 S Nigeria
Port Hardy 97 E7 Vancouver Island, British Columbia, SW Canada
Porthcawl 39 D7 S Wales, UK
Port Hedland 133 B3 Western Australia
Porthmadog 39 C2 NW Wales, UK
Port Howard Settlement 40 Falkland Islands
Portimão 57 B5 S Portugal
Port Isaac Bay 37 A5 *Bay,* SW England, UK
Portishead 37 D4 SW England, UK
Portland 133 F6 Victoria, SE Australia
Portland 101 H2 Maine, USA
Portland 103 B1 Oregon, USA
Portland Bill 37 D5 *Headland,* S England, UK
Portland, Isle of 37 D5 *Island,* SW England, UK
Portlaoise 31 D5 C Ireland
Port Lincoln 133 E6 S Australia
Port Louis 40 Falkland Islands
Port Louis 119 ● NW Mauritius
Port Macquarie 133 H5 NSW, SE Australia
Port Moresby 137 B3 ● New Guinea, SW Papua New Guinea
Porto *see* Oporto
Porto Alegre 115 F8 S Brazil
Portobelo 107 H6 N Panama
Portoferraio 61 B4 C Italy
Port of Ness 33 B2 NW Scotland, UK
Port-of-Spain 109 K7 ● Trinidad, Trinidad and Tobago
Portogruaro 61 D2 NE Italy
Porto-Novo 124 E5 ● S Benin
Porto Torres 61 A5 Sardinia, Italy
Porto Velho 115 D5 W Brazil
Portoviejo 115 A4 W Ecuador
Port Pirie 133 E5 S Australia
Portree 33 B3 N Scotland, UK
Portrush 31 E1 N Northern Ireland, UK
Port Said 122 I2 N Egypt
Port San Carlos 40 East Falkland, Falkland Islands
Portskerra 33 D2 N Scotland, UK
Portsmouth 37 F5 S England, UK
Portsmouth 101 F4 Virginia, USA
Portsmouth 29 ◐ *Unitary auth.,* S England, UK
Port Stephens Settlement 40 Falkland Islands
Port Sudan 127 D1 NE Sudan
Port Talbot 39 D7 S Wales, UK
Portugal 57 A3 ◆ *Republic,* SW Europe
Port Vila 137 H5 ● Éfaté, C Vanuatu
Porvenir 117 A1 NW Bolivia
Porvenir 117 B9 S Chile
Porvoo 49 E5 S Finland
Posadas 117 C4 NE Argentina
Posterholt 50 E6 SE Netherlands
Postojna 59 E9 SW Slovenia
Potenza 61 E6 S Italy
P'ot'i 79 G1 W Georgia
Potiskum 124 F4 NE Nigeria
Potosí 117 B3 S Bolivia
Potsdam 59 D3 NE Germany
Pouébo 137 G6 C New Caledonia
Poulton-le-Fylde 35 C4 NW England, UK
Po Valley 61 C3 *Valley,* N Italy
Považská Bystrica 63 D6 NW Slovakia
Poverty Bay 135 E4 *Inlet,* North Island, NZ
Póvoa de Varzim 57 B2 NW Portugal
Powell, Lake 103 D3 ◎ Utah, USA
Powys 29 ◐ *Unitary auth.,* E Wales, UK
Poza Rica 105 F4 E Mexico
Poznań 63 C3 W Poland
Pozoblanco 57 D5 S Spain
Pozzallo 61 D9 Sicily, Italy
Prachatice 63 B6 SW Czech Republic
Prague 63 ● NW Czech Republic
Praha *see* Prague
Praia 119 ● Santiago, S Cape Verde
Prato 61 C3 C Italy
Pravia 57 C1 N Spain
Prenzlau 59 D3 NE Germany
Přerov 63 D6 E Czech Republic
Preseli, Mynydd 39 B5 ⛰ SW Wales, UK
Prešov 63 F6 NE Slovakia
Prespa, Lake 65 D4 ◎ SE Europe
Prestatyn 39 E1 N Wales, UK
Presteigne 39 F4 C Wales, UK
Preston 35 C4 NW England, UK
Prestwick 33 D6 W Scotland, UK
Pretoria 128 D6 ● NE South Africa
Préveza 65 D5 W Greece
Prilep 65 D4 S FYR Macedonia
Prince Albert 97 G6 Saskatchewan, S Canada
Prince Edward Island 99 G5 ◐ *Province,* SE Canada
Prince George 97 F6 British Columbia, SW Canada
Prince of Wales Island 133 F1 *Island,* Queensland, E Australia
Prince of Wales Island 97 H3 *Island,* Queen Elizabeth Islands, Nunavut, NW Canada
Prince Patrick Island 97 F2 *Island,* Parry Islands, NW Terr., NW Canada
Prince Rupert 97 E6 British Columbia, SW Canada
Princess Charlotte Bay 133 G1 *Bay,* Queensland, NE Australia
Princess Elizabeth Land 138 D4 *Physical region,* Antarctica
Príncipe 124 E6 *Island,* N Sao Tome and Principe
Prinzapolka 107 E4 NE Nicaragua
Pripet 67 C3 ≈ Belarus/Ukraine
Pripet Marshes 67 C3 *Wetland,* Belarus/Ukraine
Priština 65 D3 S Serbia and Montenegro (Yugoslavia)
Privas 55 E5 E France
Prizren 65 D3 S Serbia and Montenegro (Yugoslavia)
Probolinggo 91 D8 Java, C Indonesia
Progreso 105 H4 SE Mexico
Prokhladnyy 69 B8 SW Russ. Fed.
Prome 91 A3 C Burma
Promyshlennyy 69 E3 NW Russ. Fed.
Prostějov 63 D6 SE Czech Republic
Provence 55 E6 *Cultural region,* SE France
Providence 101 G3 Rhode Island, USA
Providenciales 40 *Island,* W Turks and Caicos Islands
Provideniya 139 C1 NE Russ. Fed.
Provo 103 D3 Utah, USA
Prudhoe Bay 97 E3 Alaska, USA
Pruszków 63 E3 C Poland
Prut 67 D6 ≈ E Europe
Prydz Bay 138 E4 *Bay,* Antarctica
Pryluky 67 E4 NE Ukraine
Przemyśl 63 G5 SE Poland
Psará 65 F5 *Island,* E Greece
Psël 67 F4 ≈ Russ. Fed./Ukraine
Pskov 69 A4 W Russ. Fed.
Ptsich 67 D3 ≈ SE Belarus
Ptuj 59 F8 NE Slovenia
Pucallpa 115 B5 C Peru
Puck 63 D1 N Poland
Pudasjärvi 49 E3 C Finland
Puebla 105 F5 S Mexico
Pueblo 103 E3 Colorado, USA
Puerto Acosta 117 A2 W Bolivia
Puerto Aisén 117 A7 S Chile
Puerto Ángel 105 G6 SE Mexico
Puerto Ayacucho 115 D2 SW Venezuela
Puerto Baquerizo Moreno 115 B7 Galapagos Islands, Ecuador
Puerto Barrios 107 C2 E Guatemala
Puerto Cabezas 107 E3 NE Nicaragua
Puerto Cortés 107 C2 NW Honduras
Puerto Deseado 117 B8 SE Argentina
Puerto Escondido 105 F6 SE Mexico
Puerto Lempira 107 E3 E Honduras
Puertollano 57 D4 C Spain
Puerto Maldonado 115 C5 E Peru
Puerto Montt 117 A7 C Chile
Puerto Natales 117 A9 S Chile
Puerto Obaldía 107 I6 NE Panama
Puerto Plata 109 G4 N Dominican Republic
Puerto Princesa 91 E4 Palawan, W Philippines
Puerto Rico 109 H4 *US* ◇ C West Indies
Puerto San Julián 117 B8 SE Argentina
Puerto Suárez 117 C2 E Bolivia
Puerto Vallarta 105 D5 SW Mexico
Puerto Varas 117 A7 C Chile
Puerto Viejo 107 E5 NE Costa Rica
Puglia *see* Apulia
Pukaki, Lake 135 B6 ◎ South Island, NZ
Pukatikei, Maunga 137 D6 ▲ Easter Island, Chile
Pukch'ong 85 B4 E North Korea
Pukekohe 135 D3 North Island, NZ
Pula 65 A2 NW Croatia
Puławy 63 F4 E Poland
Pułtusk 63 F3 C Poland
Pumsaint 39 D5 S Wales, UK
Pune 89 C5 W India
Punjab 89 D2 *Cultural region,* India/Pakistan
Puno 115 C6 SE Peru
Punta Alta 117 B6 E Argentina
Punta Arenas 117 A9 S Chile
Punta Gorda 107 E5 SE Nicaragua
Punta Gorda 107 B2 SE Belize
Puntarenas 107 E6 W Costa Rica
Pupuya, Nevado 117 A2 ▲ W Bolivia
Puri 89 F5 E India
Purmerend 50 D3 C Netherlands
Purus, Rio 115 D4 ≈ Brazil/Peru
Pusan 85 C6 SE South Korea
Püspökladány 63 F7 E Hungary
Putorana Mountains 76 E3 ⛰ N Russ. Fed.
Puttalam 89 E7 W Sri Lanka
Puttgarden 59 C2 N Germany
Putumayo, Río 115 C4 ≈ NW South America
Pwllheli 39 C3 NW Wales, UK
Pyatigorsk 69 A8 SW Russ. Fed.
Pyle 39 D7 S Wales, UK
Pyongyang 85 A5 ● SW North Korea
Pyramid Lake 103 B3 ◎ Nevada, USA
Pyrenees 57 F2 ⛰ SW Europe
Pyrgos 65 D6 S Greece
Pyrzyce 63 B3 NW Poland

Q

Qaidam Pendi 87 D3 *Basin,* C China
Qal'aikhum 83 G3 S Tajikistan
Qal'eh-ye Now 83 E4 NW Afghanistan
Qamdo 87 D4 W China
Qarokul 83 G3 E Tajikistan
Qarshi 83 E3 S Uzbekistan
Qasr Farafra 122 I3 W Egypt
Qatar 81 D4 ◆ *Monarchy,* SW Asia
Qattara Depression 122 I3 *Desert,* NW Egypt
Qazimämmäd 79 J2 SE Azerbaijan
Qazvin 81 D2 NW Iran
Qena 122 J3 E Egypt
Qilian Shan 87 D3 ⛰ N China
Qingdao 87 G3 E China
Qinghai Hu 87 D3 ◎ C China
Qinhuangdao 87 G3 E China
Qinzhou 87 F6 S China
Qiqihar 87 G2 NE China
Qira 87 B3 NW China
Qitai 87 C2 NW China
Qizilrabot 83 H4 SE Tajikistan
Qom 81 D2 N Iran
Qo'ng'irot 83 D2 NW Uzbekistan
Qo'qon 83 G3 E Uzbekistan
Quang Ngai 91 D3 C Vietnam
Quanzhou 87 F5 S China
Quanzhou 87 G5 SE China
Qu'Appelle 97 H7 ≈ Saskatchewan, S Canada
Quarles, Pegunungan 91 E7 ⛰ Celebes, C Indonesia
Quartu Sant' Elena 61 A6 Sardinia, Italy
Quba 79 I2 N Azerbaijan
Québec 99 D3 Québec, SE Canada
Québec 99 E5 ◐ *Province,* SE Canada
Queen Charlotte Islands 97 D6 *Island group,* British Columbia, SW Canada
Queen Charlotte Sound 97 D6 *Sea area,* British Columbia, W Canada
Queen Elizabeth Islands 97 G2 *Island group,* NW Terr./Nunavut, N Canada
Queen Mary's Peak 40 ▲ C Tristan da Cunha
Queensferry 39 E2 N Wales, UK
Queensland 133 F3 ◐ *State,* N Australia
Queenstown 135 B7 South Island, NZ
Queenstown 128 D7 S South Africa
Quelimane 128 E5 NE Mozambique
Quepos 107 E6 S Costa Rica
Querétaro 105 E4 C Mexico
Quesada 107 E6 N Costa Rica
Quetta 89 B2 SW Pakistan
Quezaltenango 107 A3 W Guatemala
Quilon 89 D7 SW India
Quilty 31 B5 W Ireland
Quimper 55 A2 NW France
Quimperlé 55 A3 NW France
Quito 115 B3 ● N Ecuador
Qurghonteppa 83 F4 SW Tajikistan
Quy Nhon 91 D4 C Vietnam

R

Raahe 49 E3 W Finland
Raalte 50 E3 E Netherlands
Raamsdonksveer 50 D5 S Netherlands
Raasay 33 B3 *Island,* NW Scotland, UK
Rába 63 C8 ≈ Austria/Hungary
Rabat 70 A5 W Malta
Rabat 122 C1 ● NW Morocco
Rabaul 137 D1 E PNG
Rabinal 107 B3 C Guatemala
Rabka 63 E6 S Poland
Rabyanah, Ramlat 122 G4 *Desert,* SE Libya
Race, Cape 99 H4 *Headland,* Newfoundland, E Canada
Rach Gia 91 C4 S Vietnam
Racine 101 D3 Wisconsin, USA
Radom 63 F4 C Poland
Radomsko 63 E4 C Poland
Radzyń Podlaski 63 F4 E Poland
Raetihi 135 D4 North Island, NZ
Rafaela 117 B5 E Argentina
Raga 127 B4 SW Sudan
Ragged Island Range 109 D3 *Island group,* S Bahamas
Raglan 39 F6 SE Wales, UK
Ragusa 61 D8 Sicily, Italy
Rahimyar Khan 89 C3 SE Pakistan
Raichur 89 D5 C India
Rainier, Mount 103 B1 ▲ Washington, USA
Rainy Lake 99 A4 ◎ Canada/USA
Raipur 89 E4 C India
Rajahmundry 89 E5 E India
Rajang, Batang 91 D6 ≈ East Malaysia
Rajapalaiyam 89 D7 SE India
Rajasthan 89 C3 *Cultural region,* NW India
Rajkot 89 C4 W India
Rajshahi 89 G3 W Bangladesh
Rakaia 135 C6 ≈ South Island, NZ
Raleigh 101 F4 North Carolina, USA
Râmnicu Vâlcea 67 B7 C Romania
Ramree Island 91 A3 *Island,* W Burma
Ramsey 35 A3 NE Isle of Man
Ramsey Island 39 A6 *Island,* SW Wales, UK
Ramsgate 37 H4 SE England, UK
Rancagua 117 A5 C Chile
Ranchi 89 F4 N India
Randers 49 B6 C Denmark
Rangiora 135 C6 South Island, NZ
Rangitikei 135 D4 ≈ North Island, NZ
Rangoon 91 A3 ● S Burma
Rangpur 89 G3 N Bangladesh
Rankin Inlet 97 H4 Nunavut, C Canada
Rannoch Moor 33 D4 *Heathland,* C Scotland, UK
Rapid City 103 E2 South Dakota, USA
Räpina 49 F6 SE Estonia
Rarotonga 131 *Island,* S Cook Islands
Rasht 81 D1 NW Iran
Ratan 49 C4 C Sweden
Rathfriland 31 E3 SE Northern Ireland, UK
Rathkeale 31 C5 SW Ireland
Rathlin Island 31 E1 *Island,* N Northern Ireland, UK
Ráth Luirc 31 C6 S Ireland
Rathmelton 31 D1 N Ireland
Rathmore 31 B6 SW Ireland
Rathmullan 31 D1 N Ireland
Rathnew 31 E5 E Ireland
Rat Islands 97 A3 *Island group,* Aleutian Islands, Alaska, USA
Ratlam 89 D4 C India
Ratnapura 89 E8 S Sri Lanka
Rättvik 49 C5 C Sweden
Raufarhöfn 49 B1 NE Iceland
Raukumara Range 135 E3 ⛰ North Island, NZ
Răulakela 89 F4 E India
Rauma 49 D5 SW Finland
Ravenglass 35 B3 NW England, UK
Ravenna 61 C3 N Italy
Ravi 89 C2 ≈ India/Pakistan
Rawalpindi 89 D1 NE Pakistan
Rawa Mazowiecka 63 E4 C Poland
Rawicz 63 C4 W Poland
Rawlinna 133 C5 Western Australia
Rawson 117 B7 SE Argentina
Rayong 91 B4 S Thailand
Razazah, Buhayrat ar 81 B2 ◎ C Iraq
Razgrad 65 F2 NE Bulgaria
Razim, Lacul 67 D7 *Lagoon,* NW Black Sea
Reading 37 F4 S England, UK
Reading 101 G3 Pennsylvania, USA
Reading 29 ◐ *Unitary auth.,* S England, UK
Real, Cordillera 110 ⛰ C Ecuador
Realicó 117 B5 C Argentina
Rebecca, Lake 133 C5 ◎ Western Australia
Rebun-to 85 F1 *Island,* NE Japan
Recife 115 I5 E Brazil
Recklinghausen 59 A4 W Germany
Recogne 50 D8 SE Belgium
Reconquista 117 C4 C Argentina
Redbridge 29 ◐ *London borough,* SE England, UK
Redcar 35 E3 N England, UK
Redcar and Cleveland 28 ◐ *Unitary auth.,* N England, UK
Red Deer 97 G7 Alberta, SW Canada
Redditch 35 D7 W England, UK
Redhill 37 F4 SE England, UK
Redon 55 B3 NW France
Red River 91 B2 ≈ China/Vietnam
Red River 103 G4 ≈ S USA
Redruth 37 A6 SW England, UK
Red Sea 81 A4 *Sea,* Africa/Asia
Red Wharf Bay 39 C1 *Bay,* N Wales, UK
Reefton 135 C5 South Island, NZ
Ree, Lough 31 D4 ◎ C Ireland
Refahiye 79 F3 C Turkey
Regensburg 59 D6 SE Germany
Regenstauf 59 D6 SE Germany
Reggane 122 D3 C Algeria
Reggio di Calabria 61 E8 SW Italy
Reggio nell' Emilia 61 C3 N Italy
Regina 97 H7 Saskatchewan, S Canada
Rehoboth 128 B5 C Namibia
Rehovot 81 G6 C Israel
Reid 133 D5 Western Australia
Ré, Île de 55 B4 *Island,* W France
Reims 55 E2 N France
Reindeer Lake 97 H5 ◎ Manitoba/Saskatchewan, C Canada
Reinga, Cape 135 C1 *Headland,* North Island, NZ
Reinosa 57 D1 N Spain
Reliance 97 G5 NW Terr., C Canada
Rendsburg 59 C2 N Germany
Renfrewshire 28 ◐ *Unitary auth.,* W Scotland, UK
Rengat 91 B6 Sumatra, W Indonesia
Rennell 137 E3 *Island,* S Solomon Islands
Rennes 55 B3 NW France
Reno 103 B3 Nevada, USA
Repulse Bay 97 I3 Nunavut, N Canada
Resistencia 117 C4 NE Argentina
Reşiţa 67 A7 W Romania
Resolute 97 H2 Cornwallis Island, Nunavut, N Canada
Resolution Island 99 E1 *Island,* NW Terr., NE Canada
Resolven 39 D6 S Wales, UK
Réthymno 65 F7 Crete, Greece
Réunion 128 H6 *French* ◇ W Indian Ocean
Reus 57 G3 E Spain
Reutlingen 59 B7 S Germany
Reuver 50 E6 SE Netherlands
Revillagigedo, Islas 105 B5 *Island group,* W Mexico
Reyes 117 A2 NW Bolivia
Rey, Isla del 107 H6 *Island,* Archipiélago de las Perlas, SE Panama
Reykjavík 49 A1 ● W Iceland
Reynosa 105 F3 C Mexico
Rezé 55 B3 NW France
Rhayader 39 D4 C Wales, UK
Rheidol 39 C4 ≈ W Wales, UK
Rhein *see* Rhine
Rheine 59 B4 NW Germany
Rheinisches Schiefergebirge 59 A5 ⛰ W Germany
Rhine 50 E4 ≈ W Europe
Rhinelander 101 D2 Wisconsin, USA
Rhinog Fawr 39 C3 ▲ NW Wales, UK
Rho 61 B2 N Italy
Rhode Island 101 H3 ◐ *State,* NE USA
Rhodes 65 G6 *Island,* Dodecanese, Greece
Rhodope Mountains 65 E3 ⛰ Bulgaria/Greece
Rhondda Cynon Taff 29 ◐ *Unitary auth.,* S Wales, UK
Rhône 55 E6 ≈ France/Switzerland
Rhoose 39 E7 S Wales, UK
Rhos 39 C5 S Wales, UK
Rhosllanerchrugog 39 E2 NE Wales, UK
Rhosneigr 39 B2 NW Wales, UK
Rhossili 39 C7 S Wales, UK
Rhum 33 B4 *Island,* W Scotland, UK
Rhyl 39 D1 NE Wales, UK
Rhymney 39 E6 S Wales, UK
Ribble 35 C4 ≈ NW England, UK
Ribeirão Preto 115 G7 S Brazil
Riberalta 117 B1 N Bolivia
Richard Toll 124 A3 N Senegal
Richmond 135 C5 South Island, NZ
Richmond 35 D3 N England, UK
Richmond 101 F4 Virginia, USA
Richmond Range 135 C5 ⛰ South Island, NZ
Richmond upon Thames 29 ◐ *London borough,* SE England, UK
Ricobayo, Embalse de 57 B2 *Reservoir,* NW Spain
Ridsdale 35 D2 N England, UK
Ried im Innkreis 59 D7 NW Austria
Riemst 50 D7 NE Belgium
Riesa 59 D4 E Germany
Riga 49 E6 ● C Latvia
Riga, Gulf of 49 E6 *Gulf,* Estonia/Latvia
Rigestan 83 E6 *Desert region,* S Afghanistan
Riihimäki 49 E5 S Finland
Rijeka 65 B1 NW Croatia
Rijn *see* Rhine
Rijssen 50 E4 E Netherlands
Rimah, Wadi ar 81 C4 *Dry watercourse,* C Saudi Arabia
Rimini 61 D3 N Italy
Rimouski 99 E4 Québec, SE Canada
Ringebu 49 B4 S Norway
Ringkøbing Fjord 49 A7 *Fjord,* W Denmark
Ringvassøya 49 C1 *Island,* N Norway
Ringwood 37 E5 S England, UK
Rio Branco 115 D5 W Brazil
Río Bravo 105 F3 C Mexico
Río Cuarto 117 B5 C Argentina
Rio de Janeiro 115 H7 SE Brazil
Río Gallegos 117 B9 S Argentina
Río Grande 117 B9 S Argentina
Rio Grande 115 F9 S Brazil
Río Grande 105 D4 C Mexico
Rio Grande do Norte 115 I4 ◐ *State,* E Brazil
Rio Grande do Sul 115 F8 ◐ *State,* S Brazil
Ríohacha 115 C1 N Colombia
Río Lagartos 105 I4 SE Mexico
Riom 55 D5 C France
Río Verde 105 E4 C Mexico
Ripoll 57 G2 NE Spain
Ripon 35 D4 N England, UK
Risca 39 E6 S Wales, UK
Rishiri-to 85 F1 *Island,* NE Japan
Rivas 107 D5 SW Nicaragua
Rivera 117 C5 NE Uruguay
Riverside 103 C4 California, USA
Riverstown 31 C6 S Ireland
Riverton 135 A8 South Island, NZ
Rivière-du-Loup 99 E5 Québec, SE Canada
Rivne 67 C4 NW Ukraine
Rivoli 61 A2 NW Italy
Riyadh 81 C4 ● C Saudi Arabia
Rize 79 F2 NE Turkey
Rkîz 124 A3 W Mauritania
Road Town 40 ○ C British Virgin Islands
Roag, Loch 33 A2 *Inlet,* NW Scotland, UK
Roanne 55 E4 E France
Roanoke 101 F4 Virginia, USA
Roanoke River 101 F4 ≈ SE USA
Roatán 107 D2 N Honduras
Robin Hood's Bay 35 E3 N England, UK
Robson, Mount 97 F6 ▲ British Columbia, SW Canada
Roca Partida, Isla 105 B5 *Island,* W Mexico
Rocas, Atol das 115 I4 *Island,* E Brazil
Rochdale 35 D4 NW England, UK
Rochdale 28 ◐ *Unitary auth.,* NW England, UK
Rochefort 50 D8 SE Belgium
Rochefort 55 B4 W France
Rochester 103 G2 Minnesota, USA
Rochester 101 F3 New York, USA
Rockford 101 D3 Illinois, USA
Rockhampton 133 H4 Queensland, E Australia
Rock Sound 109 E2 Eleuthera Island, C Bahamas
Rocky Mountains 92 ⛰ Canada/USA
Roden 50 E2 NE Netherlands
Rodez 55 D6 S France
Rodos *see* Rhodes
Roermond 50 E6 SE Netherlands
Roeselare 50 B6 W Belgium
Roi Et 91 C3 E Thailand
Rokiškis 49 F7 NE Lithuania
Rokycany 63 B5 W Czech Republic
Roma 133 G4 Queensland, E Australia
Roma *see* Rome
Roman 67 C6 NE Romania

Romania 67 B6 ◆ *Republic,* SE Europe
Rome 61 C5 ● C Italy
Romford 37 G3 SE England, UK
Romney Marsh 37 G4 *Physical region,* SE England, UK
Romny 67 E4 NE Ukraine
Rømø 49 A7 *Island,* SW Denmark
Romsey 37 E4 S England, UK
Ronda 57 C6 S Spain
Rondônia 115 D5 ◐ *State,* W Brazil
Rondonópolis 115 F6 W Brazil
Rønne 49 C7 E Denmark
Ronne Ice Shelf 138 B4 *Ice shelf,* Antarctica
Roosendaal 50 C5 S Netherlands
Roosevelt Island 138 C6 *Island,* Antarctica
Roraima 115 D3 ◐ *State,* N Brazil
Roraima, Mount 115 D2 ▲ N South America
Røros 49 B4 S Norway
Rosa, Lake 109 E3 ◎ S Bahamas
Rosalia, Punta 137 C5 *Headland,* Easter Island, Chile
Rosario 117 C5 C Argentina
Rosario 117 C3 C Paraguay
Rosarito 105 A1 NW Mexico
Roscommon 31 C4 C Ireland
Roscommon 101 E2 Michigan, USA
Roscommon 29 *County,* C Ireland
Roscrea 31 D5 C Ireland
Roseau 109 K5 ● SW Dominica
Rosengarten 59 C3 N Germany
Rosenheim 59 D7 S Germany
Rosia 40 W Gibraltar
Rosia Bay 40 *Bay,* SW Gibraltar
Roslavl' 69 A5 W Russ. Fed.
Rosmalen 50 D5 S Netherlands
Ross 135 B6 South Island, NZ
Rossano 61 E7 SW Italy
Ross Carbery 31 B7 S Ireland
Ross Ice Shelf 138 C5 *Ice shelf,* Antarctica
Rosslare 31 E6 SE Ireland
Rosslare Harbour 31 E6 SE Ireland
Rosso 124 A3 SW Mauritania
Ross-on-Wye 35 C7 W England, UK
Rossosh' 69 A7 W Russ. Fed.
Ross Sea 138 C6 *Sea,* Antarctica
Rostock 59 D2 NE Germany
Rostov-na-Donu 69 A7 SW Russ. Fed.
Rother 37 F4 ≈ S England, UK
Rothera 138 A4 *UK research station,* Antarctica
Rotherham 35 E5 N England, UK
Rotherham 29 ◐ *Unitary auth.,* N England, UK
Rothesay 33 C6 W Scotland, UK
Rotorua 135 D3 North Island, NZ
Rotorua, Lake 135 D3 ◎ North Island, NZ
Rotterdam 50 C4 SW Netherlands
Rottweil 59 B7 S Germany
Rotuma 137 I4 *Island,* NW Fiji
Roubaix 55 D1 N France
Rouen 55 D2 N France
Roundstone 31 B4 W Ireland
Roundwood 31 E5 E Ireland
Rousay 33 E1 *Island,* N Scotland, UK
Roussillon 55 D7 *Cultural region,* S France
Rouyn-Noranda 99 D5 Québec, SE Canada
Rovaniemi 49 E3 N Finland
Rovigo 61 C3 NE Italy
Rovuma, Rio 128 F4 ≈ Mozambique/Tanzania
Roxas City 91 F4 Panay Island, N Philippines
Royale, Isle 101 D1 *Island,* Michigan, USA
Royal Leamington Spa 35 E7 C England, UK
Royal Tunbridge Wells 37 G4 SE England, UK
Royan 55 B4 W France
Roy Cove Settlement 40 Falkland Islands
Royston 37 G3 E England, UK
Rožňava 63 E6 E Slovakia
Ruabon 39 E2 NE Wales, UK
Ruapehu, Mount 135 D4 ⛛ North Island, NZ
Ruapuke Island 135 B8 *Island,* SW NZ
Ruatoria 135 E3 North Island, NZ
Ruawai 135 D2 North Island, NZ
Rubizhne 67 G4 E Ukraine
Rudnyy 76 C4 N Kazakhstan
Rufiji 127 D7 ≈ E Tanzania
Rufino 117 B5 C Argentina
Rugby 35 E6 C England, UK
Rugeley 35 D6 C England, UK
Rügen 59 D2 *Headland,* NE Germany
Ruhr Valley 59 A4 *Industrial region,* W Germany
Rukwa, Lake 127 C7 ◎ SE Tanzania
Rumbek 127 B4 S Sudan
Rum Cay 109 E2 *Island,* C Bahamas
Rumia 63 D1 N Poland
Rumney 39 E7 S Wales, UK
Runanga 135 C5 South Island, NZ
Runcorn 35 C5 C England, UK
Rundu 128 C5 NE Namibia
Ruoqiang 87 C3 NW China
Rupel 50 C6 ≈ N Belgium
Rupert, Rivière de 99 D4 ≈ Québec, C Canada
Ruse 65 F2 N Bulgaria
Rushden 37 F2 C England, UK
Russian Federation 76 D4 ◆ *Republic,* Asia/Europe
Rust'avi 79 H2 SE Georgia
Ruthin 39 E2 NE Wales, UK
Rutland 29 ◐ *Unitary auth.,* C England, UK
Rutland Water 35 E6 ◎ C England, UK
Rutog 87 A4 W China
Ruvuma 127 D7 ≈ Mozambique/Tanzania
Ruwenzori 127 B5 ⛰ Dem. Rep. Congo/Uganda
Ružomberok 63 E6 N Slovakia
Rwanda 127 B6 ◆ *Republic,* C Africa
Ryazan' 69 B6 W Russ. Fed.
Rybinsk 69 B5 W Russ. Fed.
Rybnik 63 D5 S Poland
Rye 37 G4 SE England, UK
Rye 35 E3 ≈ N England, UK
Ryki 63 F4 E Poland
Rypin 63 E3 C Poland
Rysy 63 E6 ▲ S Poland
Ryukyu Islands 85 A7 *Island group,* SW Japan
Rzeszów 63 F5 SE Poland
Rzhev 69 A5 W Russ. Fed.

S

Saale 59 D4 ≈ C Germany
Saalfeld 59 C5 C Germany
Saarbrücken 59 A6 SW Germany
Saaremaa 49 D6 *Island,* W Estonia
Saariselkä 49 E2 N Finland
Šabac 65 D2 W Serbia and Montenegro (Yugoslavia)
Sabadell 57 G2 E Spain
Sabah 91 E5 *Cultural region,* Borneo, E Malaysia
Sab'atayn, Ramlat as 81 C7 *Desert,* C Yemen
Sabaya 117 A3 S Bolivia
Saberi, Hamun-e 81 F3 ◎ Afghanistan/Iran
Sabha 122 F3 C Libya
Sabinas 105 E2 NE Mexico
Sabinas Hidalgo 105 E3 NE Mexico
Sable, Île de 137 E5 *Island,* NW New Caledonia
Sable Island 99 G5 *Island,* Nova Scotia, SE Canada
Sabzevar 81 E1 NE Iran
Sachsen *see* Saxony
Sachs Harbour 97 F3 Banks Island, NW Terr., N Canada
Sacramento 103 B3 California, USA
Sacramento Mountains 103 E4 ⛰ New Mexico, USA
Sacramento River 103 B3 ≈ California, USA
Sacramento Valley 103 B3 *Valley,* California, USA
Sa'dah 81 C6 NW Yemen
Sado 85 F4 *Island,* C Japan
Säffle 49 C5 C Sweden
Saffron Walden 37 G3 SE England, UK
Safi 122 B2 W Morocco
Safid Kuh, Selseleh-ye 83 D5 ⛰ W Afghanistan
Saga 85 D7 Kyūshū, SW Japan
Sagaing 91 A2 C Burma
Sagami-nada 85 G6 *Inlet,* SW Japan
Sagar 89 E4 C India
Saginaw 101 E2 Michigan, USA
Saginaw Bay 101 E2 *Lake bay,* Michigan, USA
Sagua la Grande 109 C2 C Cuba
Sagunt *see* Sagunto
Sagunto 57 F4 E Spain
Sahara 124 D2 *Desert,* N Africa
Saharan Atlas 122 D2 ⛰ Algeria/Morocco
Sahel 124 E3 *Physical region,* C Africa
Sahiwal 89 D2 E Pakistan
Saidpur 89 F3 NW Bangladesh
Saimaa 49 F4 ◎ SE Finland
St Albans 37 F3 E England, UK
St Aldhelm's Head 37 E5 *Headland,* S England, UK
St Andrews 33 E5 E Scotland, UK
St. Anne 37 H5 Alderney, Channel Islands
St.Anthony 99 G3 Newfoundland, SE Canada
St Arvans 39 F6 SE Wales, UK
St Asaph 39 E1 N Wales, UK
St Austell 37 B5 SW England, UK
St Austell Bay 37 B6 *Bay,* SW England, UK
St-Barthélemy 109 J4 *Island,* N Guadeloupe
St Bees Head 35 B3 *Headland,* NW England, UK
St Brides Bay 39 A6 *Inlet,* SW Wales, UK
St-Brieuc 55 B2 NW France
St. Catherines 99 D6 Ontario, S Canada
St Catherine's Point 37 E5 *Headland,* S England, UK
St-Chamond 55 E5 E France
St-Claude 55 E4 E France
St Clears 39 B6 S Wales, UK
St Croix 109 I4 *Island,* S Virgin Islands (US)
St David's 39 A6 SW Wales, UK
St David's Head 39 A5 *Headland,* SW Wales, UK
St David's Island 40 *Island,* E Bermuda
St-Dié 55 F3 NE France
St-Egrève 55 E5 E France
Saintes 55 B4 W France
St-Étienne 55 E5 E France
St-Flour 55 D5 C France
St-Gaudens 55 C6 S France
Saint George 133 G4 Queensland, E Australia
St George 40 N Bermuda
St-Georges 99 E5 Québec, SE Canada
St George's 109 K7 ● SW Grenada
St George's Channel 31 F6 *Channel,* Ireland/Wales, UK
St George's Island 40 *Island,* E Bermuda
St Govan's Head 39 A7 *Headland,* SW Wales, UK
Saint Helena 40 *UK* ◇ C Atlantic Ocean
St.Helena Bay 128 B7 *Bay,* SW South Africa
St Helens 35 C5 NW England, UK
St Helens 28 ◐ *Unitary auth.,* NW England, UK
Saint Helens, Mount 103 B1 ⛛ Washington, USA
St Helier 37 H6 ○ S Jersey, Channel Islands
St Ives 37 A6 E England, UK
St Ives 37 B3 SW England, UK
St-Jean, Lac 99 E4 ◎ Québec, SE Canada
St John 37 H6 Jersey, Channel Islands
Saint John 99 F5 New Brunswick, SE Canada
Saint John 101 H1 ≈ Canada/USA
St John's 109 J4 ● Antigua, Antigua and Barbuda
St.John's 99 H4 Newfoundland, E Canada
St John's 40 N Montserrat
St John's Point 31 C2 *Headland,* N Ireland
Saint Joseph 103 G3 Missouri, USA
St Julian's 70 B6 N Malta
St Kilda 53 B3 *Island,* NW Scotland, UK
St.Lawrence 101 G2 ≈ Canada/USA
St. Lawrence, Gulf of 99 F4 *Gulf,* NW Atlantic Ocean
St-Lô 55 C2 N France
St-Louis 55 F3 NE France
Saint Louis 124 A3 NW Senegal
Saint Louis 103 H3 Missouri, USA
St Lucia 109 J6 ◆ *Commonwealth Republic,* SE West Indies
St Lucia Channel 109 K6 *Channel,* Martinique/Saint Lucia
St Magnus Bay 33 A6 *Bay,* N Scotland, UK
St-Malo 55 B2 NW France
St-Malo, Golfe de 55 B2 *Gulf,* NW France
St Margaret's Hope 33 E1 NE Scotland, UK
St-Martin 109 J4 *Island,* N Guadeloupe
St Mary 37 H6 Jersey, Channel Islands
St.Matthias Group 137 C1 *Island group,* NE PNG
St Mellons 39 E7 S Wales, UK
St.Moritz 59 C8 SE Switzerland
St-Nazaire 55 B3 NW France
St Neots 37 F2 E England, UK
St-Omer 55 D1 N France
Saint Paul 103 G2 Minnesota, USA
St. Peter Port 37 G6 ○ C Guernsey, Channel Islands
Saint Petersburg 69 A4 NW Russ. Fed.
Saint Petersburg 101 E7 Florida, USA
St Pierre and Miquelon 99 G4 *French* ◇ NE North America
St-Quentin 55 D2 N France
Saint Vincent 109 J6 *Island,* N Saint Vincent and the Grenadines
Saint Vincent and the Grenadines 109 I6 ◆ *Commonwealth Republic,* SE West Indies
Saint Vincent Passage 109 K6 *Passage,* Saint Lucia/Saint Vincent and the Grenadines
Sajama, Nevado 117 A2 ▲ W Bolivia
Sajószentpéter 63 F7 NE Hungary
Sakakawea, Lake 103 E1 ⊡ North Dakota, USA
Sakata 85 F4 Honshu, C Japan
Sakhalin 76 I4 *Island,* SE Russ. Fed.
Saki 79 I2 NW Azerbaijan
Sakishima-shoto 85 A8 *Island group,* SW Japan
Sala 49 C5 C Sweden
Sala Consilina 61 E6 S Italy
Salado, Río 117 B4 ≈ E Argentina
Salado, Río 117 B5 ≈ C Argentina
Salalah 81 E6 SW Oman
Salamá 107 B3 C Guatemala
Salamanca 117 A5 C Chile
Salamanca 57 C3 NW Spain
Salang Tunnel 83 F4 *Tunnel,* C Afghanistan
Salantai 49 E7 NW Lithuania
Salavat 69 D6 W Russ. Fed.
Šalčininkai 49 F7 SE Lithuania
Salcombe 37 C6 SW England, UK
Sale 133 G6 Victoria, SE Australia
Salé 122 C1 NW Morocco
Salekhard 76 D3 N Russ. Fed.
Salelologa 137 A5 C Samoa
Salem 89 D7 SE India
Salem 40 W Montserrat
Salem 103 B1 Oregon, USA
Salerno 61 D6 S Italy
Salerno, Gulf of 61 D6 *Gulf,* S Italy
Salford 35 C5 NW England, UK
Salford 28 ◐ *Unitary auth.,* NW England, UK
Salihorsk 67 C3 S Belarus
Salina Cruz 105 G6 SE Mexico
Salinas 103 B3 California, USA
Salisbury 37 E4 S England, UK
Salisbury Plain 37 E4 *Plain,* S England, UK
Salo 49 E5 SW Finland
Salomon Atoll 40 *Atoll,* N British Indian Ocean Territory
Salon-de-Provence 55 E6 SE France
Salonica 65 E4 N Greece
Sal'sk 69 A8 SW Russ. Fed.
Salta 117 B4 NW Argentina
Saltash 37 B5 SW England, UK
Saltillo 105 E3 NE Mexico
Salt Island 40 *Island,* SE British Virgin Islands
Salt Lake City 103 D3 Utah, USA
Salto 117 C5 N Uruguay
Salton Sea 103 C4 ◎ California, USA
Salvador 115 H6 E Brazil
Salween 91 B2 ≈ SE Asia
Salyan 89 E3 W Nepal
Salzburg 59 D7 N Austria
Salzgitter 59 C4 C Germany
Salzwedel 59 C3 N Germany
Samalayuca 105 C2 N Mexico
Samar 91 F4 *Island,* C Philippines
Samara 69 C6 W Russ. Fed.
Samarinda 91 E6 C Indonesia
Samarqand 83 F3 C Uzbekistan
Samaxi 79 I2 C Azerbaijan
Sambalpur 89 F4 E India
Sambava 128 H4 NE Madagascar
Sambir 67 B4 NW Ukraine
Sambre 55 E1 ≈ Belgium/France
Samfya 128 D3 N Zambia
Samoa 137 B4 ◆ *Monarchy,* W Polynesia
Sámos 65 F5 *Island,* Dodecanese, Greece
Samothráki 65 F4 *Island,* NE Greece
Sampit 91 D7 C Indonesia
Samsun 79 E2 N Turkey
Samtredia 79 G1 W Georgia
Samui, Ko 91 B5 *Island,* SW Thailand
San 124 C3 C Mali
San 63 G5 ≈ SE Poland
Sana 81 C6 ● W Yemen
Sana 65 B2 ≈ NW Bosnia and Herzegovina
San'a' *see* Sana
Sanae 138 B3 *South African research station,* Antarctica
Sanaga 124 G5 ≈ C Cameroon
Sanandaj 81 C2 W Iran
San Andrés, Isla de 107 F4 *Island,* NW Colombia
San Andrés Tuxtla 105 G5 E Mexico
San Angelo 103 F5 Texas, USA
San Antonio 107 B2 S Belize
San Antonio 117 A5 C Chile
San Antonio 103 F5 Texas, USA
San Antonio Oeste 117 B7 E Argentina
Sanaw 81 D6 NE Yemen
San Benedicto, Isla 105 B5 *Island,* W Mexico
San Benito 107 B2 N Guatemala
San Bernardino 103 C4 California, USA
San Blas 105 C3 C Mexico
San Blas, Cordillera de 107 H6 ⛰ NE Panama
San Carlos 107 E5 S Nicaragua
San Carlos de Bariloche 117 A7 SW Argentina
San Cristobal 137 F3 *Island,* SE Solomon Islands
San Cristóbal 115 C2 W Venezuela
San Cristóbal de Las Casas 105 H5 SE Mexico
San Cristóbal, Isla 115 B7 *Island,* Galapagos Islands, Ecuador
Sancti Spíritus 109 C3 C Cuba
Sancy, Puy de 55 D5 ▲ C France
Sandakan 91 E5 East Malaysia
Sandanski 65 E3 SW Bulgaria
Sanday 33 E1 *Island,* NE Scotland, UK
Sandbach 35 D5 W England, UK
San Diego 103 C4 California, USA
Sandnes 49 A5 S Norway
Sandomierz 63 F5 SE Poland
Sandoway 91 A3 W Burma
Sandown 37 E5 S England, UK
Sandray 33 A4 *Island,* NW Scotland, UK
Sandvika 49 B5 S Norway
Sandviken 49 D5 C Sweden
Sandwell 29 ◐ *Unitary auth.,* C England, UK
Sandy Bay 40 *Bay,* S Saint Helena
Sandy Lake 99 A3 ◎ Ontario, C Canada
San Esteban 107 D3 C Honduras
San Fernando 57 C6 S Spain
San Fernando 109 K7 Trinidad, Trinidad and Tobago
San Fernando del Valle de Catamarca 117 B4 NW Argentina
San Francisco 103 B3 California, USA
San Francisco del Oro 105 D3 N Mexico
San Francisco de Macorís 109 G4 C Dominican Republic
Sangan, Kuh-e 83 E5 ⛰ C Afghanistan
Sangir, Kepulauan 91 F6 *Island group,* N Indonesia
Sangli 89 D5 W India
Sangmélima 124 G6 S Cameroon
San Ignacio 107 B2 W Belize
San Ignacio 117 B2 N Bolivia
San Ignacio 105 B3 W Mexico
San Joaquin Valley 103 B3 *Valley,* California, USA
San Jorge, Golfo 117 B8 *Gulf,* S Argentina
San José 117 C2 E Bolivia
San José 107 E6 ● C Costa Rica
San José 107 A4 S Guatemala
San Jose 103 B3 California, USA
San José del Guaviare 115 C3 S Colombia
San Juan 117 A5 W Argentina
San Juan 109 H4 ○ NE Puerto Rico
San Juan Bautista 117 C4 S Paraguay
San Juan de Alicante 57 F5 E Spain
San Juan del Norte 107 E5 SE Nicaragua
San Juanito, Isla 105 C4 *Island,* C Mexico
San Juan Mountains 103 E3 ⛰ Colorado, USA
San Juan, Río 107 E5 ≈, S Nicaragua
Sankt-Peterburg *see* Saint Petersburg
Sankt Gallen 59 B7 NE Switzerland
Sankt Pölten 59 E7 N Austria
Sankuru 128 C2 ≈ C Dem. Rep. Congo
Şanlıurfa 79 F4 S Turkey
San Lorenzo 117 B3 S Bolivia
Sanlúcar de Barrameda 57 C6 S Spain
San Lucas Cape 105 C4 *Headland,* W Mexico
San Luis 117 B5 C Argentina
San Luis 107 B2 NE Guatemala
San Luis 105 A1 NW Mexico
San Luis Obispo 103 B4 California, USA
San Luis Potosí 105 E4 C Mexico
San Marcos 107 A3 W Guatemala
San Marino 61 D3 ● C San Marino
San Marino 61 D3 ◆ *Republic,* S Europe
San Martín 138 A4 C Argentina
San Matías 117 C2 E Bolivia
San Matías, Gulf of 117 B7 *Gulf,* E Argentina
Sanmenxia 87 F4 C China
San Miguel 107 B4 SE El Salvador
San Miguel 105 D2 N Mexico
San Miguel de Tucumán 117 B4 N Argentina
San Miguelito 107 E5 S Nicaragua
San Miguelito 107 G5 C Panama
San Miguel, Río 117 B2 ≈ E Bolivia
Sanok 63 F6 SE Poland
San Pablo 117 B3 S Bolivia
San Pedro 107 C1 NE Belize
San-Pédro 124 C5 S Ivory Coast
San Pedro 105 D3 NE Mexico
San Pedro de la Cueva 105 C2 NW Mexico
San Pedro Mártir, Sierra 105 A2 ⛰ NW Mexico
San Pedro Sula 107 C3 NW Honduras
San Rafael 117 A5 W Argentina
San Ramón de la Nueva Orán 117 B3 N Argentina
San Remo 61 A3 NW Italy
San Salvador 107 B4 ● SW El Salvador
San Salvador 109 E2 *Island,* E Bahamas
San Salvador de Jujuy 117 B3 N Argentina
Sansanné-Mango 124 D4 N Togo
Sansepolcro 61 C4 C Italy
San Severo 61 E5 SE Italy
Santa Ana 117 B2 N Bolivia
Santa Ana 107 B4 NW El Salvador
Santa Ana 103 B4 California, USA
Santa Barbara 105 D3 N Mexico
Santa Barbara 103 B4 California, USA
Santa Catalina 107 G6 W Panama
Santa Catarina 115 F8 ◐ *State,* S Brazil
Santa Clara 109 C3 C Cuba
Santa Comba 57 B1 NW Spain
Santa Cruz 117 B2 C Bolivia
Santa Cruz del Quiché 107 A3 W Guatemala
Santa Cruz, Isla 115 B7 *Island,* Galapagos Islands, Ecuador
Santa Cruz Islands 137 G3 *Island group,* E Solomon Islands
Santa Cruz, Río 117 A8 ≈ S Argentina
Santa Elena 107 B2 W Belize
Santa Fe 117 C5 C Argentina
Santa Fe 103 E4 New Mexico, USA
Santa Genoveva 105 B4 ▲ W Mexico
Santa Isabel 137 E2 *Island,* N Solomon Islands
Santa Margarita, Isla 105 B4 *Island,* W Mexico
Santa Maria 115 F8 S Brazil
Santa Maria 137 G4 *Island,* Banks Islands, N Vanuatu
Santa María, Isla 115 A7 *Island,* Galapagos Islands, Ecuador
Santa Marta 115 B1 N Colombia
Santander 57 D1 N Spain
Santarém 115 F4 N Brazil
Santarém 57 A4 W Portugal
Santa Rosa 117 B6 C Argentina
Santa Rosa 103 B3 California, USA
Santa Rosa de Copán 107 B3 W Honduras
Santa Uxía de Ribeira 57 A2 NW Spain
Sant Carles de la Ràpita 57 F3 NE Spain
Santiago 117 A5 ● C Chile
Santiago 109 G4 N Dominican Republic
Santiago 107 G7 S Panama
Santiago de Compostela 57 B1 NW Spain
Santiago de Cuba 109 E4 E Cuba
Santiago del Estero 117 B4 C Argentina
Santo Domingo 109 G4 ● SE Dominican Republic
Santos 115 G7 S Brazil
Santo Tomé 117 C4 NE Argentina
San Valentín, Cerro 117 A8 ▲ S Chile
San Vicente 107 C4 C El Salvador
São Francisco, Rio 115 G6 ≈ E Brazil
Sao Hill 127 D7 S Tanzania
São João da Madeira 57 B3 N Portugal
São Luís 115 G4 NE Brazil
São Manuel, Rio 115 E5 ≈ C Brazil
Saona, Isla 109 G4 *Island,* SE Dominican Republic
Saône 55 E5 ≈ E France
São Paulo 115 G7 S Brazil
São Paulo 115 F7 ◐ *State,* S Brazil
São Roque, Cabo de 115 I4 *Headland,* E Brazil
São Tomé 124 E6 ● S Sao Tome and Principe
São Tomé 124 F6 *Island,* S Sao Tome and Principe
Sao Tome and Principe 124 E6 ◆ *Republic,* E Atlantic Ocean
São Vicente, Cabo de 57 A5 *Headland,* S Portugal
Sapele 124 E5 S Nigeria
Sa Pobla 57 H4 Majorca, Spain
Sappir 81 H7 S Israel
Sapporo 85 F2 NE Japan
Sapri 61 E6 S Italy
Saqqez 81 C2 NW Iran
Sarahs 83 D4 S Turkmenistan
Sarajevo 65 C2 ● SE Bosnia and Herzegovina
Saraktash 69 D7 W Russ. Fed.
Saran' 76 C5 C Kazakhstan
Sarandë 65 D4 S Albania
Saransk 69 B6 W Russ. Fed.
Saratov 69 B7 W Russ. Fed.
Sarawak 91 D6 *Cultural region,* S Malaysia
Sardegna *see* Sardinia
Sardinia 61 B6 *Island,* Italy
Sargodha 89 C2 NE Pakistan
Sarh 124 H4 S Chad
Sari 81 D1 N Iran
Sária 65 G7 *Island,* SE Greece
Sarıkamış 79 G2 NE Turkey
Sarikol Range 83 H3 ⛰ China/Tajikistan
Sariwon 85 A5 SW North Korea
Sark 37 H6 *Island,* Channel Islands
Şarkışla 79 E3 C Turkey
Sarmiento 117 B7 S Argentina
Sarnia 99 C6 Ontario, S Canada
Sarny 67 C4 NW Ukraine
Sarpsborg 49 B5 S Norway
Sartène 55 G6 Corsica, France
Sarthe 55 C3 *Cultural region,* N France
Sárti 65 E4 N Greece
Sary-Tash 83 G3 SW Kyrgyzstan
Sasebo 85 C7 SW Japan
Saskatchewan 97 G5 ◐ *Province,* SW Canada
Saskatchewan 97 H6 ≈ Manitoba/Saskatchewan, C Canada
Saskatoon 97 G7 Saskatchewan, S Canada
Sasovo 69 B6 W Russ. Fed.
Sassandra 124 C5 S Ivory Coast
Sassandra 124 C5 ≈ S Ivory Coast
Sassari 61 A5 Sardinia, Italy
Sassenheim 50 C4 W Netherlands
Sassnitz 59 D2 NE Germany
Sátoraljaújhely 63 F7 NE Hungary
Satpura Range 89 D4 ⛰ C India
Satsunan-shoto 85 A7 *Island group,* SW Japan
Sattanen 49 E2 NE Finland
Satu Mare 67 B5 NW Romania
Saudi Arabia 81 C5 ◆ *Monarchy,* SW Asia
Saulkrasti 49 E6 C Latvia
Sault Ste.Marie 99 C5 Ontario, S Canada
Sault Sainte Marie 101 E2 Michigan, USA
Saumur 55 C3 NW France
Saundersfoot 39 B6 SW Wales, UK
Saunders Island Settlement 40 NW Falkland Islands
Saurimo 128 C3 NE Angola
Savá 107 D2 N Honduras
Sava 65 D2 ≈ SE Europe
Savai'i 137 A4 *Island,* NW Samoa
Savannah 101 E5 Georgia, USA
Savannah River 101 E5 ≈ SE USA
Save, Rio 128 E5 ≈ Mozambique/Zimbabwe
Saverne 55 F3 NE France
Savigliano 61 A2 NW Italy
Savinskiy 69 C4 NW Russ. Fed.
Savissivik 139 A4 N Greenland
Savoie 55 E5 *Cultural region,* E France
Savona 61 B3 NW Italy
Savu Sea 91 F8 *Sea,* S Indonesia
Sawel 31 E2 ▲ C Northern Ireland, UK
Sawqirah 81 E6 S Oman
Saxony 59 D4 *Cultural region,* E Germany
Sayaxché 107 B2 N Guatemala
Saýat 83 E3 E Turkmenistan
Sayhut 81 D6 E Yemen
Saynshand 87 F2 SE Mongolia
Say'un 81 D6 C Yemen
Scafell Pike 35 B3 ▲ NW England, UK
Scandinivia 44 *Geophysical region,* NW Europe
Scapa Flow 33 E1 *Sea basin,* N Scotland, UK
Scarborough 109 K7 Trinidad and Tobago
Scarborough 35 F3 N England, UK
Scarp 33 A2 *Island,* NW Scotland, UK
Schaerbeek 50 C6 C Belgium
Schaffhausen 59 B7 N Switzerland
Schagen 50 C3 NW Netherlands
Scheessel 59 C3 NW Germany
Schefferville 99 E3 Québec, E Canada
Scheldt 50 C6 ≈ W Europe
Schiermonnikoog 50 E1 *Island,* Waddeneilanden, N Netherlands
Schijndel 50 D5 S Netherlands
Schiltigheim 55 F3 NE France

◐ Administrative region ◆ Country ● Country capital ◇ Dependent territory ○ Dependent territory capital ⛰ Mountain range ▲ Mountain ⛛ Volcano ≈ River ◎ Lake ⊡ Reservoir

Schleswig 59 C2 N Germany
Schleswig-Holstein 59 C2 *Cultural region*, N Germany
Schönebeck 59 D4 C Germany
Schoten 50 C6 N Belgium
Schouwen 50 B5 *Island*, SW Netherlands
Schwäbische Alb 59 B7 ⛰ S Germany
Schwandorf 59 D6 SE Germany
Schwarzwald *see* Black Forest
Schwaz 59 D7 W Austria
Schweinfurt 59 C5 SE Germany
Schwerin 59 C3 N Germany
Schwyz 59 B8 C Switzerland
Scilly, Isles of 37 A3 *Island group*, SW England, UK
Scotch Corner 35 D3 N England, UK
Scotia Sea 138 A2 *Sea*, SW Atlantic Ocean
Scotland 33 C4 *National region*, UK
Scott Base 138 C6 *NZ research station*, Antarctica
Scottish Borders 28 ◐ *Unitary auth.*, S Scotland, UK
Scottsdale 103 D4 Arizona, USA
Scousburgh 33 A7 NE Scotland, UK
Scranton 101 F3 Pennsylvania, USA
Scunthorpe 35 E4 E England, UK
Scutari, Lake 65 C3 ◎ Albania/Serbia and Montenegro (Yugoslavia)
Seaford 37 G5 SE England, UK
Sea Lion Islands 40 *Island group*, SE Falkland Islands
Seascale 35 B3 NW England, UK
Seattle 103 B1 Washington, USA
Sébaco 107 D4 W Nicaragua
Sebastián Vizcaín, Bahía 105 A2 *Bay*, NW Mexico
Secunderabad 89 E5 C India
Sedan 55 E2 N France
Seddon 135 D5 South Island, NZ
Seddonville 135 C5 South Island, NZ
Sédhiou 124 A4 SW Senegal
Seesen 59 C4 C Germany
Sefton 28 ◐ *Unitary auth.*, NW England, UK
Segezha 69 B3 NW Russ. Fed.
Ségou 124 C3 C Mali
Segovia 57 D3 C Spain
Séguédine 124 G2 NE Niger
Segura 57 E5 ≈ S Spain
Seinäjoki 49 E4 W Finland
Seine 55 D2 ≈ N France
Seine, Baie de la 55 C2 *Bay*, N France
Sekondi-Takoradi 124 D5 S Ghana
Selby 35 E4 N England, UK
Selenga 87 E2 ≈ Mongolia/Russ. Fed.
Sélestat 55 F3 NE France
Selfoss 49 A1 SW Iceland
Sélibabi 124 B3 S Mauritania
Selkirk 33 E6 SE Scotland, UK
Semarang 91 D8 Java, C Indonesia
Sembé 128 B1 NW Congo
Seminole, Lake 101 E6 ⊡ SE USA
Semipalatinsk 76 D5 E Kazakhstan
Semnān 81 E2 N Iran
Semois 50 D8 ≈ SE Belgium
Sendai 85 G4 C Japan
Sendai 85 D8 SW Japan
Sendai-wan 85 G4 *Bay*, E Japan
Senec 63 D7 W Slovakia
Senegal 124 A3 ◆ *Republic*, W Africa
Senegal 124 A3 ≈ W Africa
Senftenberg 59 E4 E Germany
Sênggê Zangbo 87 B4 ≈ W China
Senica 63 D6 W Slovakia
Senja 49 C1 *Island*, N Norway
Senkaku-shoto 85 A8 *Island group*, SW Japan
Senlis 55 D2 N France
Sennar 127 C3 C Sudan
Sennybridge 39 D5 C Wales, UK
Sens 55 D3 C France
Seoul 85 B6 ● NW South Korea
Sepik 137 A2 ≈ Indonesia/PNG
Sept-Îles 99 F4 Québec, SE Canada
Seraing 50 D7 E Belgium
Seram, Pulau 91 G7 *Island*, Maluku, E Indonesia
Serang 91 C7 Java, C Indonesia
Serasan, Selat 91 D6 *Strait*, Indonesia/Malaysia
Serbia 65 D2 ◐ *Republic*, Serbia and Montenegro (Yugoslavia)
Serbia and Montenegro 65 C3 ◆ *Federal Republic*, SE Europe
Serdar 83 C3 W Turkmenistan
Seremban 91 B6 Peninsular Malaysia
Serengeti Plain 127 C6 *Plain*, N Tanzania
Serenje 128 D4 E Zambia
Serhetabat 83 D4 S Turkmenistan
Sérifos 65 E6 *Island*, Cyclades, Greece
Serov 76 C4 C Russ. Fed.
Serowe 128 D5 SE Botswana
Serpukhov 69 A5 W Russ. Fed.
Sesto San Giovanni 61 B2 N Italy
Sète 55 D6 S France
Setesdal 49 B5 *Valley*, S Norway
Sétif 122 E1 N Algeria
Setté Cama 128 A2 SW Gabon
Settle 35 D4 N England, UK
Setúbal 57 A4 W Portugal
Setúbal, Baía de 57 A5 *Bay*, W Portugal
Seul, Lac 99 A4 ◎ Ontario, S Canada
Sevan 79 H2 C Armenia
Sevan, Lake 79 H2 ◎ E Armenia
Sevastopol' 67 F7 S Ukraine
Sevenoaks 37 G4 SE England, UK
Severn 99 B3 ≈ Ontario, S Canada
Severn 37 D3 ≈ England/Wales, UK
Severnaya Zemlya 76 E2 *Island group*, N Russ. Fed.
Severn, Mouth of the 39 F7 *Estuary*, England/Wales, UK
Severnyy 69 E3 NW Russ. Fed.
Severodvinsk 69 C3 NW Russ. Fed.
Severomorsk 69 C2 NW Russ. Fed.
Sevilla *see* Seville
Seville 57 B5 S Spain
Seychelles 118 ◆ *Republic*, W Indian Ocean
Seydhisfjördhur 49 B1 E Iceland
Seýdi 83 E3 E Turkmenistan
Sfântu Gheorghe 67 C6 C Romania
Sfax 122 F2 E Tunisia
's-Gravenhage *see* The Hague
's-Gravenzande 50 C4 W Netherlands
Sgurr Na Lapaich 33 C3 ▲ NW Scotland, UK
Shache 87 A3 NW China
Shackleton Ice Shelf 138 E5 *Ice shelf*, Antarctica
Shaftesbury 37 D4 S England, UK
Shahany, Ozero 67 D6 ◎ SW Ukraine
Shahrak 83 E5 C Afghanistan
Shahr-e Kord 81 D2 C Iran
Shahrud 81 E1 N Iran
Shanghai 87 G4 E China
Shangrao 87 G5 S China
Shannon 31 C5 W Ireland
Shannon 31 B5 ≈ W Ireland
Shannon Erne Waterway 31 D3 *Canal*, N Ireland
Shannon, Mouth of the 31 A5 *Estuary*, W Ireland
Shan Plateau 91 B2 *Plateau*, E Burma
Shantou 87 G5 S China
Shaoguan 87 F5 S China
Shapinsay 33 E1 *Island*, NE Scotland, UK
Shar 76 D5 E Kazakhstan
Sharjah 81 E4 NE UAE
Shark Bay 133 A4 *Bay*, E Indian Ocean
Shashe 128 D5 ≈ Botswana/Zimbabwe
Shchëkino 69 A6 W Russ. Fed.
Shchors 67 E3 N Ukraine
Shchuchinsk 76 C5 N Kazakhstan
Shchuchyn 67 B2 W Belarus
Shebekino 69 A6 W Russ. Fed.
Shebeli 127 E4 ≈ Ethiopia/Somalia
Sheberghan 83 E4 N Afghanistan
Shebshi Mountains 124 F4 ⛰ E Nigeria
Sheelin, Lough 31 D3 ◎ C Ireland
Sheerness 37 G4 SE England, UK
Sheffield 35 E5 N England, UK
Sheffield 29 ◐ *Unitary auth.*, N England, UK
Shelekhov Gulf 76 H3 *Gulf*, E Russ. Fed.
Shendi 127 C2 NE Sudan
Shenyang 87 G2 NE China
Shepherd Islands 137 H5 *Island group*, C Vanuatu
Shepparton 133 F6 Victoria, SE Australia
Shepton Mallet 37 D4 SW England, UK
Sherbrooke 99 E5 Québec, SE Canada
Shereik 127 C1 N Sudan
's-Hertogenbosch 50 D5 S Netherlands
Shetland Islands 33 A7 *Island group*, NE Scotland, UK
Shetland Islands 28 ◐ *Unitary auth.*, NE Scotland, UK
Shevchenko *see* Aktau
Shiant Islands 33 B3 *Island group*, NW Scotland, UK
Shibetsu 85 G1 NE Japan
Shibushi-wan 85 D8 *Bay*, SW Japan
Shihezi 87 C2 NW China
Shijiazhuang 87 F3 E China
Shikarpur 89 C3 S Pakistan
Shikoku 85 E7 *Island*, SW Japan
Shilabo 127 F4 SE Ethiopia
Shildon 35 D3 N England, UK
Shiliguri 89 G3 NE India
Shilka 76 G5 ≈ S Russ. Fed.
Shillelagh 31 E5 E Ireland
Shillong 89 G3 NE India
Shimbiris 127 F3 ▲ N Somalia
Shimoga 89 D6 W India
Shimonoseki 85 D7 Honshu, SW Japan
Shinano-gawa 85 F5 ≈ Honshu, C Japan
Shindand 83 D5 W Afghanistan
Shingu 85 F7 Honshu, SW Japan
Shinjo 85 G4 Honshu, C Japan
Shin, Loch 33 D2 ◎ N Scotland, UK
Shinyanga 127 C6 NW Tanzania
Shiraz 81 D3 S Iran
Shivpuri 89 D3 C India
Shizugawa 85 G4 NE Japan
Shizuoka 85 F6 Honshu, S Japan
Shkodër 65 D3 NW Albania
Shoreham-by-Sea 37 F5 SE England, UK
Shostka 67 E3 NE Ukraine
Shreveport 103 G4 Louisiana, USA
Shrewsbury 35 C6 W England, UK
Shropshire 29 ◐ *County*, W England, UK
Shu 76 C6 SE Kazakhstan
Shumen 65 F2 NE Bulgaria
Shuqrah 81 C7 SW Yemen
Shymkent 76 B6 S Kazakhstan
Sialum 137 B2 C PNG
Šiauliai 49 E7 N Lithuania
Sibay 69 D7 W Russ. Fed.
Siberia 76 E4 *Physical region*, Russ. Fed.
Siberut, Pulau 91 A6 *Island*, Kepulauan Mentawai, W Indonesia
Sibi 89 B2 SW Pakistan
Sibiti 128 B2 S Congo
Sibiu 67 B6 C Romania
Sibolga 91 B6 Sumatra, W Indonesia
Sibu 91 D6 East Malaysia
Sibut 124 H5 S CAR
Sibuyan Sea 91 F4 *Sea*, W Pacific Ocean
Sichon 91 B5 SW Thailand
Sichuan Pendi 87 E4 *Basin*, C China
Sicilia *see* Sicily
Sicily 61 C8 *Island*, Italy
Sicily, Strait of 61 B8 *Strait*, C Mediterranean Sea
Siderno 61 E8 SW Italy
Sîdi Barrâni 122 H2 NW Egypt
Sidi Bel Abbès 122 D1 NW Algeria
Sidlaw Hills 33 E5 ⛰ E Scotland, UK
Sidley, Mount 138 B5 ▲ Antarctica
Sidmouth 37 C5 SW England, UK
Siedlce 63 F3 E Poland
Siegen 59 B5 W Germany
Siemiatycze 63 G3 E Poland
Siena 61 C4 C Italy
Sieradz 63 D4 C Poland
Sierpc 63 E3 C Poland
Sierra Leone 124 A5 ◆ *Republic*, W Africa
Sierra Madre 107 A3 ⛰ Guatemala/Mexico
Sierra Madre Occidental 105 C3 ⛰ C Mexico
Sierra Madre Oriental 105 E4 ⛰ C Mexico
Sierra Morena 70 B4 ⛰ SW Spain Europe
Sierra Nevada 57 D6 ⛰ S Spain
Sierra Nevada 103 B3 ⛰ W USA
Sífnos 65 E6 *Island*, Cyclades, Greece
Sigli 91 A5 Sumatra, W Indonesia Asia
Siglufjördhur 49 A1 N Iceland
Signy 138 A3 *UK research station*, South Orkney Islands, Antarctica
Siguatepeque 107 C3 W Honduras
Siguiri 124 B4 NE Guinea
Siilinjärvi 49 F4 C Finland
Siirt 79 G4 SE Turkey
Sikasso 124 C4 S Mali
Siklós 63 D9 SW Hungary
Silchar 89 H3 NE India
Silesia 63 D4 *Physical region*, SW Poland
Silifke 79 D5 S Turkey
Siling Co 87 C4 ◎ W China
Silisili 137 A4 ▲ C Samoa
Silistra 65 F2 NE Bulgaria
Šilutė 49 E7 W Lithuania
Silvan 79 F4 SE Turkey
Silverek 79 F4 SE Turkey
Simav 79 B3 W Turkey
Simav Çayı 79 A3 ≈ NW Turkey
Simeto 61 D8 ≈ Sicily, Italy
Simeulue, Pulau 91 A6 *Island*, NW Indonesia
Simferopol' 67 F7 S Ukraine
Simpelveld 50 E6 SE Netherlands
Simplon Pass 59 B8 *Pass*, S Switzerland
Simpson Desert 133 E4 *Desert*, Northern Territory/S Australia
Sinai 122 J2 *Physical region*, NE Egypt
Sincelejo 115 B2 NW Colombia
Sind 89 B3 *Cultural region*, SE Pakistan
Sindelfingen 59 B6 SW Germany
Sines 57 A5 S Portugal
Singapore 91 C6 ● SE Asia
Singapore 91 C6 ◆ *Republic*, SE Asia
Singen 59 B7 S Germany
Singida 127 D6 C Tanzania
Singkawang 91 D6 C Indonesia
Siniscola 61 B5 Sardinia, Italy
Sinmi-do 85 A5 *Island*, NW North Korea
Sinoie, Lacul 67 D7 *Lagoon*, SE Romania
Sinop 79 D2 N Turkey
Sinp'o 85 B4 E North Korea
Sinsheim 59 B6 SW Germany
Sint-Michielsgestel 50 D5 S Netherlands
Sint-Niklaas 50 C6 N Belgium
Sint-Pieters-Leeuw 50 B7 C Belgium
Sintra 57 A4 W Portugal
Sinuiju 85 A4 W North Korea
Sinujiif 127 F3 NE Somalia
Sion 59 A8 SW Switzerland
Sion Mills 31 D2 W Northern Ireland, UK
Sioux City 103 F2 Iowa, USA
Sioux Falls 103 F2 South Dakota, USA
Siping 87 G2 NE China
Siple, Mount 138 A5 ▲ Siple Island, Antarctica
Siquirres 107 F6 E Costa Rica
Siracusa 61 D8 Sicily, Italy
Sir Edward Pellew Group 133 E2 *Island group*, Northern Territory, NE Australia
Siret 67 C6 ≈ Romania/Ukraine
Sir Francis Drake Channel 40 *Channel*, E Caribbean Sea
Sirikit Reservoir 91 B3 ◎ N Thailand
Sirjan 81 E3 S Iran
Şırnak 79 G4 SE Turkey
Sirte, Gulf of 122 G2 *Gulf*, N Libya
Sisimiut 139 A5 S Greenland
Sitges 57 G3 NE Spain
Sittang 91 A3 ≈ S Burma
Sittard 50 E6 SE Netherlands
Sittwe 91 A2 W Burma
Siuna 107 E3 NE Nicaragua
Sivas 79 E3 C Turkey
Sivers'kyy Donets' 67 F4 ≈ Russian Federation/Ukraine
Siwa 122 H3 NW Egypt
Six-Fours-les-Plages 55 E7 SE France
Siyäzän 79 J2 NE Azerbaijan
Sjælland 49 B7 *Island*, E Denmark
Skagerrak 49 B6 *Channel*, N Europe
Skalka 49 D2 ◎ N Sweden
Skegness 35 F5 E England, UK
Skellefteå 49 D3 N Sweden
Skellefteälven 49 D3 ≈ N Sweden
Skerries 31 E4 E Ireland
Ski 49 B5 S Norway
Skiddaw 35 C3 ▲ NW England, UK
Skikda 122 E1 NE Algeria
Skipton 35 D4 N England, UK
Skokholm Island 39 A6 *Island*, SW Wales, UK
Skomer Island 39 A6 *Island*, SW Wales, UK
Skopje 65 D3 ● N FYR Macedonia
Skovorodino 76 G5 SE Russ. Fed.
Skrīveri 49 E6 S Latvia
Skull 31 B7 SW Ireland
Skye, Isle of 33 B3 *Island*, NW Scotland, UK
Skýros 65 F5 *Island*, Vóreioi Sporádes, Greece
Slagelse 49 B7 E Denmark
Slane 31 E4 E Ireland
Slaney 31 E5 ≈ SE Ireland
Slatina 67 B7 S Romania
Slavonski Brod 65 C1 NE Croatia
Sławno 63 C2 NW Poland
Sleaford 35 F5 E England, UK
Sleat, Sound of 33 C4 *Strait*, NW Scotland, UK
Sliema 70 B6 N Malta
Slieve Gamph 31 C3 ⛰ N Ireland
Slieve League 31 C2 ⛰ N Ireland Europe
Slieve Mish Mountains 31 B6 ⛰ SW Ireland
Slievenamon 31 D6 ▲ S Ireland
Sligo 31 C3 NW Ireland
Sligo 29 ◐ *County*, NW Ireland
Sligo Bay 31 C2 *Inlet*, NW Ireland
Sliven 65 F3 E Bulgaria
Slough 37 F3 S England, UK
Slough 29 ◐ *Unitary auth.*, S England, UK
Slovakia 63 E6 ◆ *Republic*, C Europe
Slovenia 59 E8 ◆ *Republic*, SE Europe
Slovenské rudohorie 63 E6 ⛰ C Slovakia
Slov"yans'k 67 G4 E Ukraine
Słubice 63 B3 W Poland
Sluch 67 C4 ≈ NW Ukraine
Słupsk 63 D1 NW Poland
Slutsk 67 C3 S Belarus
Slyne Head 31 A4 *Headland*, W Ireland
Smallwood Reservoir 99 F3 ◎ Newfoundland, S Canada
Smara 122 B3 N Western Sahara
Smederevo 65 D2 N Serbia and Montenegro (Yugoslavia)
Smederevska Palanka 65 E2 C Serbia and Montenegro (Yugoslavia)
Smøla 49 B4 *Island*, W Norway
Smolensk 69 A5 W Russ. Fed.
Snaefell 35 A3 ▲ C Isle of Man
Snake River 103 C2 ≈ NW USA
Snake River Plain 103 D2 *Plain*, Idaho, USA
Sneek 50 E2 N Netherlands
Sneem 31 B6 SW Ireland
Sněžka 63 C5 ▲ N Czech Republic
Snina 63 F6 E Slovakia
Snowdon 39 C2 ▲ NW Wales, UK
Snowdonia 39 C2 ⛰ NW Wales, UK
Sobradinho, Represa de 115 G5 ⊡ E Brazil
Sochi 69 A8 SW Russ. Fed.
Society Islands 131 *Island group*, W French Polynesia
Socorro, Isla 105 B5 *Island*, W Mexico
Socotra 81 D7 *Island*, SE Yemen
Socuéllamos 57 E4 C Spain
Sodankylä 49 E2 N Finland
Söderhamn 49 D5 C Sweden
Södertälje 49 D5 C Sweden
Sodiri 127 B2 C Sudan
Sofia 65 E3 ● W Bulgaria
Sofiya *see* Sofia
Sogamoso 115 C2 C Colombia
Sognefjorden 49 A5 *Fjord*, NE North Sea
Sohag 122 I3 C Egypt
Sokch'o 85 B5 N South Korea
Söke 79 A4 SW Turkey
Sokhumi 79 F1 NW Georgia
Sokodé 124 D4 C Togo
Sokol 69 B4 NW Russ. Fed.
Sokolov 63 A5 W Czech Republic
Sokone 124 A3 W Senegal
Sokoto 124 E4 NW Nigeria
Sokoto 124 E4 ≈ NW Nigeria
Solapur 89 D5 W India
Sol, Costa del 57 D6 *Coastal region*, S Spain
Solec Kujawski 63 D3 W Poland
Solihull 35 D6 C England, UK
Solihull 29 ◐ *Unitary auth.*, C England, UK
Solikamsk 69 D5 NW Russ. Fed.
Sol'-Iletsk 69 D7 W Russ. Fed.
Solingen 59 A4 W Germany
Sollentuna 49 D5 C Sweden
Solomon Islands 137 F2 ◆ *Commonwealth Republic*, W Pacific Ocean
Solomon Sea 137 C2 *Sea*, W Pacific Ocean
Soltau 59 C3 NW Germany
Sol'tsy 69 A4 W Russ. Fed.
Solva 39 A6 SW Wales, UK
Solway Firth 35 B3 *Inlet*, England/Scotland, UK
Solwezi 128 D4 NW Zambia
Soma 85 G4 C Japan
Somalia 127 F4 ◆ *Republic*, E Africa
Somali Plain 15 *Undersea feature*, W Indian Ocean
Sombrero 109 J4 *Island*, N Anguilla
Someren 50 E5 SE Netherlands
Somerset 40 W Bermuda
Somerset 29 ◐ *County*, SW England, UK
Somerset Island 40 *Island*, W Bermuda
Somerset Island 97 H2 *Island*, Queen Elizabeth Islands, Nunavut, NW Canada
Somme 55 D1 ≈ N France
Somotillo 107 D4 NW Nicaragua
Somoto 107 D4 NW Nicaragua
Songea 127 D7 S Tanzania
Songkhla 91 B5 SW Thailand
Sonoran Desert 103 C4 *Desert*, Mexico/USA
Sonsonate 107 B4 W El Salvador
Sopot 63 D2 N Poland
Sopron 63 C7 NW Hungary
Sorgues 55 E6 SE France
Sorgun 79 D3 C Turkey
Soria 57 E2 N Spain
Sorong 91 G6 E Indonesia
Sørøya 49 D1 *Island*, N Norway
Sortavala 69 A3 NW Russ. Fed.
Sotkamo 49 F3 C Finland
Soufriére Hills 40 ⛰ E Montserrat
Sŏul *see* Seoul
Soúrpi 65 E5 C Greece
Sousse 122 F1 NE Tunisia
South Africa 128 C7 ◆ *Republic*, S Africa
South America 117 *Continent*
Southampton 37 E4 S England, UK
Southampton 29 ◐ *Unitary auth.*, S England, UK
Southampton Island 97 I4 *Island*, Nunavut, NE Canada
South Andaman 89 H5 *Island*, Andaman Islands, India
South Australia 133 D4 ◐ *State*, S Australia
South Ayrshire 29 ◐ *Unitary auth.*, W Scotland, UK
South Bend 101 D3 Indiana, USA
South Bruny Island 133 G7 *Island*, Tasmania, SE Australia
South Caicos 40 *Island*, S Turks and Caicos Islands
South Carolina 101 E5 ◐ *State*, SE USA
South China Sea 91 E3 *Sea*, SE Asia
South Dakota 103 E2 ◐ *State*, N USA
South Downs 37 F4 *Hill range*, SE England, UK
Southeast Indian Ridge 15 *Undersea feature*, Indian Ocean/Pacific Ocean
South East Point 40 *Headland*, SE Ascension Island
South East Point 133 F7 *Headland*, Victoria, S Australia
Southend-on-Sea 37 G3 E England, UK
Southend-on-Sea 29 ◐ *Unitary auth.*, SE England, UK
Southern Alps 135 B6 ⛰ South Island, NZ
Southern Cook Islands 131 *Island group*, S Cook Islands
Southern Cross 133 B5 Western Australia
Southern Indian Lake 97 H5 ◎ Manitoba, C Canada
Southern Ocean 14 *Ocean*, Atlantic Ocean/Indian Ocean/Pacific Ocean
Southern Uplands 33 D6 ⛰ S Scotland, UK
South Esk 33 E4 ≈ E Scotland, UK
South Foreland 37 H4 *Headland*, SE England, UK
South Geomagnetic Pole 138 C5 *Pole*, Antarctica
South Georgia 138 A2 *Island*, South Georgia and the South Sandwich Islands, SW Atlantic Ocean
South Gloucestershire 29 ◐ *Unitary auth.*, W England, UK
South Goulburn Island 133 E1 *Island*, Northern Territory, N Australia
South Indian Basin 15 *Undersea basin*, S Indian Ocean
South Island 135 C6 *Island*, S NZ
South Korea 85 A6 ◆ *Republic*, E Asia
South Lanarkshire 28 ◐ *Unitary auth.*, C Scotland, UK
South Molton 37 C4 SW England, UK
South Orkney Islands 138 A3 *Island group*, Antarctica
South Point 40 *Headland*, S Ascension Island
South Pole 138 C5 *Pole*, Antarctica
Southport 35 C4 NW England, UK
South Ronaldsay 33 E1 *Island*, NE Scotland, UK
South Sandwich Islands 138 A2 *Island group*, SE South Georgia and South Sandwich Islands
South Sandwich Trench 138 B2 *Undersea feature*, SW Atlantic Ocean
South Shetland Islands 138 A3 *Island group*, Antarctica
South Shields 35 E2 NE England, UK
South Sound 40 E British Virgin Islands
South Sound 31 B5 *Sound*, W Ireland
South Taranaki Bight 135 C4 *Bight*, SE Tasman Sea
South Town 40 Little Cayman, C Cayman Islands
South Tyne 35 C2 ≈ N England, UK
South Tyneside 28 ◐ *Unitary auth.*, NE England, UK
South Uist 33 A3 *Island*, NW Scotland, UK
Southwark 29 ◐ *London borough*, SE England, UK
South West Cape 135 A8 *Headland*, Stewart Island, NZ
Southwest Indian Ridge 15 *Undersea feature*, SW Indian Ocean
Southwest Pacific Basin 14 *Undersea feature*, SE Pacific Ocean
South West Point 40 *Headland*, SW Saint Helena
Southwold 37 H2 E England, UK
Soweto 128 D6 NE South Africa
Spain 57 C3 ◆ *Monarchy*, SW Europe
Spalding 35 F6 E England, UK
Spanish Town 40 E British Virgin Islands
Spanish Town 109 D4 C Jamaica
Spárti 65 E6 S Greece
Speedwell Island Settlement 40 S Falkland Islands
Spencer Gulf 133 E6 *Gulf*, S Australia
Spennymoor 35 D3 N England, UK
Spey 33 E3 ≈ NE Scotland, UK
Spijkenisse 50 C4 SW Netherlands
Spin Buldak 83 E6 S Afghanistan
Spitsbergen 139 C5 *Island*, NW Svalbard
Split 65 B2 S Croatia
Spokane 103 C1 Washington, USA
Spot Bay 40 NE Cayman Islands
Spratly Islands 91 D4 *Disputed* ◇ SE Asia
Spree 59 E4 ≈ E Germany
Springfield 101 D3 Illinois, USA
Springfield 103 G3 Missouri, USA
Springfield 101 D3 Ohio, USA
Spring Point 40 Falkland Islands
Springs Junction 135 C5 South Island, NZ
Springsure 133 G4 Queensland, E Australia
Spruce Knob 101 E4 ▲ West Virginia, USA
Spurn Head 35 F4 *Headland*, E England, UK
Sri Aman 91 D6 East Malaysia
Sri Jayawardanapura 89 E8 W Sri Lanka
Srikakulam 89 F5 E India
Sri Lanka 89 D8 ◆ *Republic*, S Asia
Srinagar 89 D1 N India
Srpska, Republika 65 ◐ *Republic*, Bosnia & Herzegovina
Stabroek 50 C5 N Belgium
Stack Skerry 33 D1 *Island*, N Scotland, UK
Stade 59 C3 NW Germany
Stadskanaal 50 F2 NE Netherlands
Stafford 35 D6 C England, UK
Staffordshire 29 ◐ *County*, C England, UK
Staines 37 F4 SE England, UK
Staithes 35 E3 N England, UK
Stakhanov 67 G4 E Ukraine
Stalowa Wola 63 F5 SE Poland
Stamford 35 F6 E England, UK
Stamford 101 G3 Connecticut, USA
Stanhope 35 D3 N England, UK
Stanley 40 ○ Falkland Islands
Stanley 35 D2 N England, UK
Stanthorpe 133 H5 Queensland, E Australia
Staphorst 50 E3 E Netherlands
Starachowice 63 F4 SE Poland
Stara Zagora 65 F3 C Bulgaria
Starbuck Island 131 *Island*, E Kiribati
Stargard Szczeciński 63 B2 NW Poland
Starobil's'k 67 G4 E Ukraine
Starogard Gdański 63 D2 N Poland
Starominskaya 69 A7 SW Russ. Fed.
Start Bay 37 C6 *Bay*, SW England, UK
Start Point 37 C6 *Headland*, SW England, UK
Staryy Oskol 69 A6 W Russ. Fed.
Stavanger 49 A5 S Norway
Stavropol' 69 A8 SW Russ. Fed.
Steenwijk 50 E3 N Netherlands
Steinkjer 49 C4 C Norway
Stendal 59 D3 C Germany
Sterlitamak 69 D6 W Russ. Fed.
Stevenage 37 F3 E England, UK
Stewart Island 135 A8 *Island*, S NZ
Steyr 59 E7 N Austria
Stickford 35 F5 E England, UK
Stirling 33 D5 C Scotland, UK
Stirling 28 ◐ *Unitary auth.*, C Scotland, UK
Stjørdalshalsen 49 B4 C Norway
Stockach 59 B7 S Germany
Stockholm 49 D5 ● C Sweden
Stockport 35 D5 NW England, UK
Stockport 28 ◐ *Unitary auth.*, NW England, UK
Stockton 103 B3 California, USA
Stockton-on-Tees 35 E3 N England, UK
Stockton-on-Tees 28 ◐ *Unitary auth.*, NE England, UK
Stoke-on-Trent 35 D5 C England, UK
Stoke-on-Trent 29 ◐ *Unitary auth.*, C England, UK
Stone 35 D6 C England, UK
Stonehaven 33 F4 NE Scotland, UK
Stonyhill Point 40 *Headland*, S Tristan da Cunha
Støren 49 B4 S Norway
Stornoway 33 B2 NW Scotland, UK
Storsjön 49 C4 ◎ C Sweden

CAR Central African Republic **FYR** Former Yugoslavian Rebublic **NSW** New South Wales **NZ** New Zealand **PNG** Papua New Guinea **Russ. Fed.** Russian Federation **UAE** United Arab Emirates **UK** United Kingdom **USA** United States of America

Storuman 49 D3 N Sweden
Storuman 49 C3 ◎ N Sweden
Stour 37 D4 ≈ E England, UK
Stour 37 H3 ≈ S England, UK
Stourport-on-Severn 35 D7 W England, UK
Stowmarket 37 G2 E England, UK
Strabane 31 D2 W Northern Ireland, UK
Strabane 29 ◐ *District*, W Northern Ireland, UK
Stradbally 31 D5 C Ireland
Strakonice 63 B6 SW Czech Republic
Stralsund 59 D2 NE Germany
Strangford Lough 31 F3 *Inlet*, E Northern Ireland, UK
Stranraer 33 C7 S Scotland, UK
Strasbourg 55 F3 NE France
Stratford 135 D4 North Island, NZ
Stratford-upon-Avon 35 D7 C England, UK
Strathy Point 33 D2 *Headland*, N Scotland, UK
Straubing 59 D6 SE Germany
Strehaia 67 B7 SW Romania
Strelka 76 E4 C Russ. Fed.
Strickland 137 A2 ≈ SW PNG
Stromboli 61 D7 ✱ Isola Stromboli, SW Italy
Stromeferry 33 C3 N Scotland, UK
Stromness 33 E1 N Scotland, UK
Strömstad 49 B6 S Sweden
Strömsund 49 C4 C Sweden
Stronsay 33 E1 *Island*, NE Scotland, UK
Stroud 37 D3 C England, UK
Strumble Head 39 A5 *Headland*, SW Wales, UK
Strymónas 65 E4 ≈ Bulgaria/Greece
Stryy 67 B5 NW Ukraine
Studholme 135 B7 South Island, NZ
Stuttgart 59 B6 SW Germany
Stykkishólmur 49 A1 W Iceland
Styr 67 C4 ≈ Belarus/Ukraine
Suakin 127 D1 NE Sudan
Subotica 65 D1 N Serbia and Montenegro (Yugoslavia)
Suceava 67 C5 NE Romania
Suck 31 C4 ≈ C Ireland
Suckling, Mount 137 C3 ▲ S PNG
Sucre 117 B3 ● S Bolivia
Sudan 127 B3 ◆ *Republic*, N Africa
Sudbury 99 C5 Ontario, S Canada
Sudbury 37 G2 E England, UK
Sudd 127 B4 *Swamp region*, S Sudan
Sudeten 63 C5 ⛰ Czech Republic/Poland
Sue 127 B4 ≈ S Sudan
Sueca 57 F4 E Spain
Suez 122 I2 NE Egypt
Suez Canal 122 I2 *Canal*, NE Egypt
Suez, Gulf of 70 J6 *Gulf*, NE Egypt
Suffolk 29 ◐ *County*, E England, UK
Sugar Loaf Point 40 *Headland*, N Saint Helena
Suğla Gölü 79 B4 ◎ SW Turkey
Suhar 81 E4 N Oman
Sühbaatar 87 E1 N Mongolia
Suhl 59 C5 C Germany
Suir 31 D6 ≈ S Ireland
Sujawal 89 B3 SE Pakistan
Sukabumi 91 C8 Java, C Indonesia
Sukagawa 85 G5 C Japan
Sukhona 69 C4 ≈ NW Russ. Fed.
Sukkur 89 C3 SE Pakistan
Sukumo 85 E7 Shikoku, SW Japan
Sulaiman Range 89 C2 ⛰ C Pakistan
Sula, Kepulauan 91 F7 *Island group*, C Indonesia
Sulawesi *see* Celebes
Sule Skerry 33 D1 *Island*, N Scotland, UK
Sullana 115 A4 NW Peru
Sulu Archipelago 91 F5 *Island group*, SW Philippines
Sulu Sea 91 E5 *Sea*, SW Pacific Ocean
Sulyukta 83 F3 SW Kyrgyzstan
Sumatra 91 B6 *Island*, W Indonesia
Sumba, Pulau 91 E8 *Island*, Nusa Tenggara, C Indonesia
Sumba, Selat 91 E8 *Strait*, Nusa Tenggara, S Indonesia
Sumbawanga 127 C7 W Tanzania
Sumbe 128 B3 W Angola
Sumburgh 33 A7 NE Scotland, UK
Sumburgh Head 33 A7 *Headland*, NE Scotland, UK
Sumeih 127 B3 S Sudan
Summer Isles 33 C3 *Island group*, NW Scotland, UK
Summit 40 ▲ C Gibraltar
Sumqayit 79 J2 E Azerbaijan
Sumy 67 F4 NE Ukraine
Sunch'on 85 B7 S South Korea
Sunda, Selat 91 C7 *Strait*, Java/Sumatra, SW Indonesia
Sunderland 35 E2 NE England, UK
Sunderland 28 ◐ *Unitary auth.*, NE England, UK
Sundsvall 49 D4 C Sweden
Sungaipenuh 91 B7 Sumatra, W Indonesia
Suntar 76 F4 NE Russ. Fed.
Sunyani 124 D5 W Ghana
Suomussalmi 49 F3 E Finland
Suoyarvi 69 B3 NW Russ. Fed.
Superior 101 C1 Wisconsin, USA
Superior, Lake 101 D1 ◎ Canada/USA
Sur 81 F5 NE Oman
Surabaya 91 D8 Java, C Indonesia
Surakarta 91 D8 Java, S Indonesia
Šurany 63 D7 SW Slovakia
Surat 89 C4 W India
Sur, Cabo 137 C6 *Headland*, Easter Island, Chile
Sûre 50 E8 ≈ W Europe
Surendranagar 89 C4 W India
Surfers Paradise 133 H5 Queensland, E Australia
Surgut 76 D4 C Russ. Fed.
Surinam 115 E2 ◆ *Republic*, N South America
Surkhob 83 G3 ≈ C Tajikistan
Surrey 29 ◐ *County*, SE England, UK
Surt 122 G2 N Libya
Surtsey 49 A2 *Island*, S Iceland
Suruga-wan 85 G6 *Bay*, SE Japan
Susa 61 A2 NE Italy
Susteren 50 E6 SE Netherlands
Susuman 76 H3 E Russ. Fed.
Sutlej 89 C2 ≈ India/Pakistan
Sutton 37 F4 SE England, UK
Sutton 29 ◐ *London borough*, SE England, UK
Sutton Coldfield 35 D6 C England, UK
Suva 137 J5 ● Viti Levu, W Fiji
Suwałki 63 G2 NE Poland
Suwon 85 B6 NW South Korea
Svalbard 139 C5 *Norwegian* ◇ Arctic Ocean
Svartisen 49 C3 *Glacier*, C Norway
Sveg 49 C4 C Sweden
Svenstavik 49 C4 C Sweden
Svetlograd 69 A8 SW Russ. Fed.
Svobodnyy 76 H5 SE Russ. Fed.
Svyataya Anna Trough 139 D4 *Undersea feature*, N Kara Sea
Svyetlahorsk 67 D3 SE Belarus
Swakopmund 128 B5 W Namibia
Swale 35 E4 ≈ N England, UK
Swanage 37 E5 S England, UK
Swan Islands 107 E1 *Island group*, NE Honduras
Swanlinbar 31 D3 N Ireland
Swansea 39 D6 S Wales, UK
Swansea 29 ◐ *Unitary auth.*, S Wales, UK
Swansea Bay 39 C7 *Bay*, S Wales, UK
Swarzędz 63 D3 W Poland
Swaziland 128 E6 ◆ *Monarchy*, S Africa
Sweden 49 C4 ◆ *Monarchy*, N Europe
Świdnica 63 C5 SW Poland
Świdwin 63 C2 NW Poland
Świebodzice 63 C4 SW Poland
Świebodzin 63 C3 W Poland
Świecie 63 D2 N Poland
Swilly, Lough 31 D1 *Inlet*, N Ireland
Swindon 37 E3 S England, UK
Swindon 29 ◐ *Unitary auth.*, C England, UK
Swinford 31 C3 NW Ireland
Świnoujście 63 B2 NW Poland
Switzerland 59 A8 ◆ *Federal Republic*, C Europe
Swords 31 E4 E Ireland
Sydney 133 G6 NSW, SE Australia
Sydney 99 G5 Cape Breton Island, Nova Scotia, SE Canada
Syeverodonets'k 67 G4 E Ukraine
Syktyvkar 69 D4 NW Russ. Fed.
Sylhet 89 G3 NE Bangladesh
Syowa 138 D3 *Japanese research station*, Antarctica
Syracuse 101 F2 New York, USA
Syr Darya 76 B5 ≈ C Asia
Syria 81 B2 ◆ *Republic*, SW Asia
Syrian Desert 81 B2 *Desert*, SW Asia
Sýros 65 F6 *Island*, Cyclades, Greece
Syvash, Zatoka 67 F6 *Inlet*, S Ukraine
Syzran' 69 C6 W Russ. Fed.
Szamotuły 63 C3 W Poland
Szczecin 63 B2 NW Poland
Szczecinek 63 C2 NW Poland
Szczytno 63 F2 NE Poland
Szeged 63 E8 SE Hungary
Székesfehérvár 63 D8 W Hungary
Szekszárd 63 D8 S Hungary
Szolnok 63 E8 C Hungary
Szombathely 63 C8 W Hungary
Szprotawa 63 C4 W Poland

T

Tábor 63 B6 SW Czech Republic
Tabora 127 C6 W Tanzania
Tabriz 81 C1 NW Iran
Tabuaeran 131 *Island*, E Kiribati
Tabubil 137 A2 SW PNG
Tabūk 81 A3 NW Saudi Arabia
Tabwemasana, Mount 137 F4 ▲ W Vanuatu
Täby 49 D5 C Sweden
Tacaná, Volcán 107 A3 ✱ Guatemala/Mexico
Tachov 63 A5 W Czech Republic
Tacloban 91 F4 Leyte, C Philippines
Tacna 115 C6 SE Peru
Tacoma 103 B1 Washington, USA
Tacuarembó 117 C5 C Uruguay
Tademait, Plateau du 122 D3 *Plateau*, C Algeria
Tadine 137 G6 E New Caledonia
T'aebaek-sanmaek 85 B5 ⛰ E South Korea
Taedong-gang 85 B4 ≈ C North Korea
Taegu 85 C6 SE South Korea
Taejon 85 B6 C South Korea
Taff 39 E7 ≈ SE Wales, UK
Taganrog 69 A7 SW Russ. Fed.
Taganrog, Gulf of 67 G5 *Gulf*, Russian Federation/Ukraine
Taghmon 31 E6 SE Ireland
Taguatinga 115 G5 C Brazil
Tagula Island 137 D3 *Island*, SE PNG
Tagus 57 B4 ≈ Portugal/Spain
Tahat 122 E4 ▲ SE Algeria
Tahiti 137 B6 *Island*, Îles du Vent, W French Polynesia
Tahoe, Lake 103 B3 ◎ W USA
Tahoua 124 E3 W Niger
Taiarapu, Presqu'île de 137 B6 *Peninsula*, W French Polynesia
T'aichung 87 H5 C Taiwan
Taieri 135 B7 ≈ South Island, NZ
Taihape 135 D4 North Island, NZ
Tailem Bend 133 F6 S Australia
Tain 33 D3 N Scotland, UK
T'ainan 87 H5 S Taiwan
Taipei 87 H5 ● N Taiwan
Taiping 91 B5 Peninsular Malaysia
Taiwan 91 F2 ◆ *Republic*, E Asia
Taiwan 87 H6 *Island*, E Asia
Taiwan Strait 87 G5 *Strait*, China/Taiwan
Taiyuan 87 F3 C China
Ta'izz 81 C7 SW Yemen
Tajikistan 83 F3 ◆ *Republic*, C Asia
Takamatsu 85 E7 Shikoku, SW Japan
Takaoka 85 F5 Honshu, SW Japan
Takapuna 135 D2 North Island, NZ
Takikawa 85 G2 NE Japan
Takla Makan Desert 87 B3 *Desert*, NW China
Takuu Islands 137 E2 *Island group*, NE PNG
Talamanca, Cordillera de 107 F6 ⛰ S Costa Rica
Talara 115 A4 NW Peru
Talas 83 G2 NW Kyrgyzstan
Talaud, Kepulauan 91 G6 *Island group*, E Indonesia
Talavera de la Reina 57 D3 C Spain
Talca 117 A6 C Chile
Talcahuano 117 A6 C Chile
Taldykorgan 76 D6 SE Kazakhstan
Talgarth 39 E5 C Wales, UK
Tallahassee 101 E6 Florida, USA
Tallinn 49 E5 ● NW Estonia
Tallow 31 C6 S Ireland
Talnakh 76 E3 N Russ. Fed.
Taloqan 83 F4 NE Afghanistan
Taltal 117 A4 N Chile
Talvik 49 D1 N Norway
Talybont 39 D4 W Wales, UK
Tamabo, Banjaran 91 E6 ⛰ E Malaysia
Tamale 124 D4 C Ghana
Tamanrasset 122 E4 S Algeria
Tamar 37 B5 ≈ SW England, UK
Tamazunchale 105 F4 C Mexico
Tambacounda 124 B3 SE Senegal
Tambea 137 E3 C Solomon Islands
Tambov 69 B6 W Russ. Fed.
Tambura 127 B4 SW Sudan
Tâmchekket 124 B3 S Mauritania
Tameside 28 ◐ *Unitary auth.*, NW England, UK
Tamiahua, Laguna de 105 F4 *Lagoon*, E Mexico
Tamil Nadu 89 E7 *Cultural region*, SE India
Tampa 101 E7 Florida, USA
Tampere 49 E5 SW Finland
Tampico 105 F4 C Mexico
Tamworth 133 G5 NSW, SE Australia
Tamworth 35 D6 C England, UK
Tana 49 E1 ≈ Finland/Norway
Tana 127 E5 ≈ SE Kenya
Tanabe 85 E7 Honshu, SW Japan
Tana Bru 49 E1 N Norway
Tana, Lake 127 D3 ◎ NW Ethiopia
Tanami Desert 133 D2 *Desert*, Northern Territory, N Australia
Tanat 39 E3 ≈ E Wales, UK
Tandil 117 C6 E Argentina
Tane Range 91 B3 ⛰ W Thailand
Tanga 127 D6 E Tanzania
Tanganyika, Lake 127 B6 ◎ E Africa
Tangaroa, Maunga 137 C6 ✱ Easter Island, Chile
Tangier 122 C1 NW Morocco
Tanggula Shan 87 C4 ⛰ W China
Tangra Yumco 87 B4 ◎ W China
Tangshan 87 G3 E China
Tanimbar, Kepulauan 91 G8 *Island group*, Maluku, E Indonesia
Tanna 137 H5 *Island*, S Vanuatu
Tan-Tan 122 B2 SW Morocco
Tanzania 127 C6 ◆ *Republic*, E Africa
Taoudenni 124 C1 N Mali
Tapachula 105 H6 SE Mexico
Tapajós, Rio 115 E4 ≈ NW Brazil
Tarabulus *see* Tripoli
Taranaki, Mount 135 C4 ✱ North Island, NZ
Tarancón 57 E3 C Spain
Taransay 33 A3 *Island*, NW Scotland, UK
Taranto 61 F6 SE Italy
Taranto, Gulf of 61 E7 *Gulf*, S Italy
Tarare 55 E5 E France
Tarascon 55 E6 SE France
Taravao 137 B6 W French Polynesia
Taraz 76 C6 S Kazakhstan
Tarazona 57 E2 NE Spain
Tarbat Ness 33 D3 *Headland*, N Scotland, UK
Tarbert 33 C6 W Scotland, UK
Tarbert 33 B3 NW Scotland, UK
Tarbes 55 C6 S France
Tarcoola 133 E5 S Australia
Taree 133 H5 NSW, SE Australia
Târgoviște 67 C7 S Romania
Târgu Jiu 67 B7 W Romania
Târgu Mureș 67 B6 C Romania
Tarija 117 B3 S Bolivia
Tarim 81 D6 C Yemen
Tarim Basin 87 B3 *Basin*, NW China
Tarim He 87 B3 ≈ NW China
Tarn 55 D6 *Cultural region*, France
Tarn 55 D6 ≈ S France
Tarnobrzeg 63 F5 SE Poland
Tarnów 63 F5 SE Poland
Taron 137 D2 NE PNG
Tarragona 57 G3 E Spain
Tàrrega 57 G2 NE Spain
Tarsus 79 D5 S Turkey
Tartu 49 E6 SE Estonia
Tartus 81 A2 W Syria
Tarvisio 61 D2 NE Italy
Tashkent 83 F2 ● E Uzbekistan
Tash-Kumyr 83 G2 W Kyrgyzstan
Tasikmalaya 91 C8 Java, C Indonesia
Tasman Bay 135 C5 *Inlet*, South Island, NZ
Tasmania 133 F7 ◐ *State*, SE Australia
Tasman Sea 130 *Sea*, SW Pacific Ocean
Tassili-n-Ajjer 122 E4 *Plateau*, E Algeria
Tatabánya 63 D7 NW Hungary
Tathlith 81 C5 S Saudi Arabia
Tatra Mountains 63 E6 ⛰ Poland/Slovakia
Tatvan 79 G4 SE Turkey
Taumarunui 135 D3 North Island, NZ
Taunggyi 91 A2 C Burma
Taunton 37 C4 SW England, UK
Taupo 135 D3 North Island, NZ
Taupo, Lake 135 D3 ◎ North Island, NZ
Tauranga 135 D3 North Island, NZ
Taurus Mountains 79 C5 ⛰ S Turkey
Tautira 137 B6 W French Polynesia
Tavas 79 B4 SW Turkey
Taveuni 137 J5 *Island*, N Fiji
Tavira 57 B5 S Portugal
Tavoy 91 B4 S Burma
Tavy 37 B5 ≈ SW England, UK
Taw 37 C5 ≈ SW England, UK
Tawau 91 E5 East Malaysia
Taxco 105 F5 S Mexico
Taxiatosh 83 D2 W Uzbekistan
Taxtako'pir 83 D2 NW Uzbekistan
Tay 33 D4 ≈ C Scotland, UK
Tay, Firth of 33 E5 *Inlet*, E Scotland, UK
Tay, Loch 33 D5 ◎ C Scotland, UK
Tayma' 81 B3 NW Saudi Arabia
Taymyr, Ozero 76 F3 ◎ N Russ. Fed.
Taymyr, Poluostrov 76 E2 *Peninsula*, N Russ. Fed.
Taz 76 E3 ≈ N Russ. Fed.
Tbilisi 79 H2 ● SE Georgia
Tczew 63 D2 N Poland
Teahupoo 137 B6 W French Polynesia
Te Anau 135 A7 South Island, NZ
Te Anau, Lake 135 A7 ◎ South Island, NZ
Teapa 105 G5 SE Mexico
Tecomán 105 D5 SW Mexico
Tecpan 105 E5 S Mexico
Tees 35 D3 ≈ N England, UK
Tefé 115 D4 N Brazil
Tegal 91 D7 Java, C Indonesia
Tegelen 50 E5 SE Netherlands
Tegucigalpa 107 C3 ● SW Honduras
Tehran 81 D2 ● N Iran
Tehuacán 105 F5 S Mexico
Tehuantepec 105 G5 SE Mexico
Tehuantepec, Gulf of 105 G6 *Gulf*, S Mexico
Tehuantepec, Isthmus of 105 F5 *Isthmus*, SE Mexico
Teifi 39 B5 ≈ SW Wales, UK
Teignmouth 37 C5 SW England, UK
Tejen 83 D4 S Turkmenistan
Te Kao 135 C1 North Island, NZ
Tekax 105 H4 SE Mexico
Tekeli 76 D6 SE Kazakhstan
Tekirdağ 79 A2 NW Turkey
Tekong, Pulau 91 C6 *Island*, E Singapore
Te Kuiti 135 D3 North Island, NZ
Tela 107 C2 NW Honduras
Tel Aviv-Yafo 81 G6 C Israel
Telford 35 C6 W England, UK
Telford and Wrekin 29 ◐ *Unitary auth.*, C England, UK
Tell Atlas 122 D2 ⛰ N Algeria
Tembagapura 91 H7 E Indonesia
Teme 39 E4 ≈ England/Wales, UK
Temirtau 76 C5 C Kazakhstan
Tempio Pausania 61 A5 Sardinia, Italy
Templemore 31 D5 C Ireland
Templeton 39 B6 SW Wales, UK
Temuco 117 A6 C Chile
Temuka 135 C7 South Island, NZ
Tenby 39 B6 SW Wales, UK
Ten Degree Channel 89 H5 *Strait*, India, E Indian Ocean
Ténenkou 124 C3 C Mali
Ténéré 124 F2 *Physical region*, C Niger
Tengger Shamo 87 E3 *Desert*, N China
Tengréla 124 C4 N Ivory Coast
Tenkodogo 124 D4 S Burkina
Tennant Creek 133 E3 Northern Territory, C Australia
Tennessee 101 D4 ◐ *State*, SE USA
Tennessee River 101 D5 ≈ S USA
Tepic 105 D4 C Mexico
Teplice 63 B5 NW Czech Republic
Tequila 105 D4 SW Mexico
Teraina 131 *Atoll*, Line Islands, E Kiribati
Teramo 61 D4 C Italy
Tercan 79 F3 NE Turkey
Teresina 115 H4 NE Brazil
Terevaka, Maunga 137 C5 ✱ Easter Island, Chile
Términos, Laguna de 105 G5 *Lagoon*, SE Mexico
Termiz 83 F4 S Uzbekistan
Termoli 61 E5 C Italy
Terneuzen 50 B5 SW Netherlands
Terni 61 C4 C Italy
Ternopil' 67 C4 W Ukraine
Terracina 61 D5 C Italy
Terrassa 57 G2 E Spain
Terre Adélie 138 D6 *Physical region*, Antarctica
Terre Haute 101 D3 Indiana, USA
Terschelling 50 D1 *Island*, Waddeneilanden, N Netherlands
Teruel 57 F3 E Spain
Tervuren 50 C6 C Belgium
Teseney 127 D2 W Eritrea
Tessalit 124 D2 NE Mali
Tessaoua 124 F3 S Niger
Tessenderlo 50 D6 NE Belgium
Test 37 E4 ≈ S England, UK
Tete 128 E4 NW Mozambique
Teterow 59 D2 NE Germany
Tétouan 122 C1 N Morocco
Tevere *see* Tiber
Teviot 33 E6 ≈ SE Scotland, UK
Te Waewae Bay 135 A8 *Bay*, South Island, NZ
Texas 103 F5 ◐ *State*, S USA
Texel 50 C2 *Island*, Waddeneilanden, NW Netherlands
Teziutlán 105 F5 S Mexico
Thailand 91 B3 ◆ *Monarchy*, SE Asia
Thailand, Gulf of 91 B4 *Gulf*, SE Asia
Thai Nguyên 91 C2 N Vietnam
Thakhèk 91 C3 C Laos
Thamarit 81 E6 SW Oman
Thame 37 F3 C England, UK
Thames 135 D3 North Island, NZ
Thames 37 F3 ≈ S England, UK
Thar Desert 89 C3 *Desert*, India/Pakistan
Tharthar, Buhayrat ath 81 B2 ◎ C Iraq
Thásos 65 F4 Thásos, E Greece
Thásos 65 F4 *Island*, E Greece
Thatcham 37 E4 S England, UK
Thaton 91 B3 S Burma
Thayetmyo 91 A3 C Burma
The Hague 50 C4 ● W Netherlands
The Mumbles 39 D7 S Wales, UK
The Pas 97 H6 Manitoba, C Canada
Thermaic Gulf 65 E4 *Gulf*, N Greece
The Rock 40 E Gibraltar
The Settlement 40 Anegada, N British Virgin Islands
Thessaloniki *see* Salonica
Thetford 37 G2 E England, UK
The Vale of Glamorgan 29 ◐ *Unitary auth.*, S Wales, UK
The Vale of Glamorgan 39 E7 *Cultural region*, S Wales, UK
The Valley 109 J4 ○ E Anguilla
Thiers 55 D5 C France
Thiès 124 A3 W Senegal
Thimphu 89 G3 ● W Bhutan
Thio 137 G6 C New Caledonia
Thionville 55 F2 NE France
Thíra 65 F6 *Island*, Cyclades, Greece
Thirsk 35 E3 N England, UK
Tholen 50 C5 *Island*, SW Netherlands
Thompson 97 H6 Manitoba, C Canada
Thonon-les-Bains 55 F4 E France
Thorlákshöfn 49 A1 SW Iceland
Thornbury 37 D3 SW England, UK
Thornhill 33 D6 S Scotland, UK
Thouars 55 C4 W France
Thracian Sea 65 F4 *Sea*, Greece/Turkey
Three Brothers 40 *Island group*, C British Indian Ocean Territory
Three Kings Islands 135 B1 *Island group*, N NZ
Thuin 50 C7 S Belgium
Thun 59 B8 W Switzerland
Thunder Bay 99 B4 Ontario, S Canada
Thuner See 59 A8 ◎ C Switzerland
Thung Song 91 B5 SW Thailand
Thurles 31 D5 S Ireland
Thurrock 29 ◐ *Unitary auth.*, SE England, UK
Thurso 33 E2 N Scotland, UK
Thyamis 65 D5 ≈ W Greece
Tianjin 87 G3 E China
Tianshui 87 E4 C China
Tiarei 137 B6 W French Polynesia
Ti'avea 137 B5 SE Samoa
Tiber 61 C4 ≈ C Italy
Tiberias, Lake 81 H5 ◎ N Israel
Tibesti 124 G2 ⛰ N Africa
Tibet 87 B4 *Cultural region*, W China
Tibet, Plateau of 87 B4 *Plateau*, S Asia
Tiburón, Isla 105 B2 *Island*, NW Mexico
Tîchît 124 B2 C Mauritania
Ticul 105 H4 SE Mexico
Tidjikja 124 B2 C Mauritania
Tienen 50 D7 C Belgium
Tien Shan 83 H2 ⛰ C Asia
Tierp 49 D5 C Sweden
Tierra del Fuego 117 B9 *Island*, Argentina/Chile
Tighina 67 D6 E Moldova
Tigris 81 C3 ≈ Iraq/Turkey
Tiguentourine 122 E3 E Algeria
Tijuana 105 A1 NW Mexico
Tikhoretsk 69 A8 SW Russ. Fed.
Tikhvin 69 B4 NW Russ. Fed.
Tiksi 76 G3 NE Russ. Fed.
Tilburg 50 D5 S Netherlands
Tillabéri 124 D3 W Niger
Tílos 65 G6 *Island*, Dodecanese, Greece
Timan Ridge 69 D3 *Ridge*, NW Russ. Fed.
Timanskiy Kryazh *see* Timan Ridge
Timaru 135 C7 South Island, NZ
Timbedgha 124 C3 SE Mauritania
Timbuktu 124 D3 N Mali
Timișoara 67 A6 W Romania
Timmins 99 C4 Ontario, S Canada
Timor 91 F8 *Island*, Nusa Tenggara, C Indonesia
Timor Sea 91 G8 *Sea*, E Indian Ocean
Timrå 49 D4 C Sweden
Tindouf 122 B3 W Algeria
Tineo 57 C1 N Spain
Tínos 65 F6 *Island*, Cyclades, Greece
Tipitapa 107 D4 W Nicaragua
Tipperary 31 C5 S Ireland
Tipperary 29 ◐ *County*, S Ireland
Tip Top Mountain 99 B4 ▲ Ontario, S Canada
Tirana 65 D4 ● C Albania
Tiranë *see* Tirana
Tiraspol 67 D6 E Moldova
Tiree 33 B5 *Island*, W Scotland, UK
Tirol 59 C8 *Cultural region*, W Austria
Tiruchchiappalli 89 E7 SE India
Tisza 65 D1 ≈ SE Europe
Tiszakécske 63 E8 C Hungary
Titicaca, Lake 115 C6 ◎ Bolivia/Peru
Titule 128 D1 N Dem. Rep. Congo
Tiverton 37 C5 SW England, UK
Tivoli 61 C5 C Italy
Tizimín 105 I4 SE Mexico
Tizi Ouzou 122 E1 N Algeria
Tiznit 122 B2 SW Morocco
Tlaquepaque 105 E5 C Mexico
Tlaxcala 105 F5 C Mexico
Tlemcen 122 D1 NW Algeria
Toamasina 128 G5 E Madagascar
Toba, Danau 91 A6 ◎ Sumatra, W Indonesia
Tobago 109 K7 *Island*, NE Trinidad and Tobago
Toba Kakar Range 89 B2 ⛰ NW Pakistan
Tobermory 33 B4 W Scotland, UK
Tobol 76 C4 ≈ Kazakhstan/Russ. Fed.
Tobol'sk 76 D4 C Russ. Fed.
Tobruk 122 H2 NE Libya
Tocantins 115 G5 ◐ *State*, C Brazil
Tocantins, Rio 115 G4 ≈ N Brazil
Tocoa 107 D2 N Honduras
Tocopilla 117 A3 N Chile
Todi 61 C4 C Italy
Todos os Santos, Baía de 115 I6 *Bay*, E Brazil
Togo 124 D4 ◆ *Republic*, W Africa
Tokanui 135 B8 South Island, NZ
Tokar 127 D2 NE Sudan
Tokat 79 E3 N Turkey
Tokelau 131 *NZ* ◇ S Pacific Ocean
Tokmak 83 H2 N Kyrgyzstan
Tokoroa 135 D3 North Island, NZ
Tokounou 124 B4 C Guinea
Tokushima 85 E7 Shikoku, SW Japan
Tokyo 85 F5 ● Honshu, S Japan
Toledo 57 D4 C Spain
Toledo 101 E3 Ohio, USA
Toledo Bend Reservoir 103 G5 ▣ SW USA
Toliara 128 F6 SW Madagascar
Tolmin 59 E8 W Slovenia
Tolna 63 D8 S Hungary
Tolosa 57 E1 N Spain
Toluca 105 F5 S Mexico
Tol'yatti 69 C6 W Russ. Fed.
Tomakomai 85 G2 NE Japan
Tomar 57 B4 W Portugal
Tomaszów Lubelski 63 G5 SE Poland
Tomaszów Mazowiecki 63 E4 C Poland
Tombigbee River 101 D5 ≈ S USA
Tombua 128 B4 SW Angola
Tomelloso 57 E4 C Spain
Tomini, Gulf of 91 F6 *Bay*, Celebes, C Indonesia
Tomintoul 33 E4 N Scotland, UK
Tommot 76 G4 NE Russ. Fed.
Tomsk 76 D5 C Russ. Fed.
Tonga 137 K6 ◆ *Monarchy*, SW Pacific Ocean
Tongatapu 137 K6 *Island*, Tongatapu Group, S Tonga
Tonga Trench 14 *Undersea feature*, S Pacific Ocean
Tongchuan 87 F4 C China
Tongeren 50 D7 NE Belgium
Tonghae 85 C5 NE South Korea
Tongking, Gulf of 91 C3 *Gulf*, China/Vietnam
Tongliao 87 G2 N China
Tongtian He 87 C4 ≈ C China
Tongue 33 D2 N Scotland, UK
Tonj 127 B4 SW Sudan
Tônlé Sap 91 C4 ◎ W Cambodia
Tonopah 103 C3 Nevada, USA
Tonosí 107 G7 S Panama
Toormore 31 B7 S Ireland
Toowoomba 133 H4 Queensland, E Australia
Topeka 103 G3 Kansas, USA
Topoľčany 63 D6 W Slovakia
Tor Bay 37 C5 *Bay*, SW England, UK
Torbay 29 ◐ *Unitary auth.*, SW England, UK
Torez 67 G5 SE Ukraine
Torfaen 29 ◐ *Unitary auth.*, SE Wales, UK
Torgau 59 D4 E Germany
Torhout 50 B6 W Belgium
Torino *see* Turin
Toriu 137 C2 E PNG
Torneträsk 49 D2 ◎ N Sweden
Tornio 49 E3 NW Finland
Tornionjoki 49 E2 ≈ Finland/Sweden
Toro 57 C2 N Spain

◐ Administrative region ◆ Country ● Country capital ◇ Dependent territory ○ Dependent territory capital ⛰ Mountain range ▲ Mountain ✱ Volcano ≈ River ◎ Lake ▣ Reservoir

Toronto 99 D6 Ontario, S Canada
Toros Dağları see Taurus Mountains
Torquay 37 C5 SW England, UK
Torre, Alto da 57 A3 ▲ C Portugal
Torre del Greco 61 D6 S Italy
Torrejón de Ardoz 57 D3 C Spain
Torrelavega 57 D1 N Spain
Torrens, Lake 133 E5 Salt lake, S Australia
Torrente 57 F4 E Spain
Torreón 105 D3 NE Mexico
Torres Islands 137 G4 Island group, N Vanuatu
Torres Strait 137 A3 Strait, Australia/PNG
Torres Vedras 57 A4 C Portugal
Torridge 37 B5 ≈ SW England, UK
Torridon, Loch 33 C3 Inlet, NW Scotland, UK
To'rtko'l 83 D2 W Uzbekistan
Tortola 40 Island, C British Virgin Islands
Tortosa 57 F3 E Spain
Toruń 63 D3 C Poland
Tory Island 31 C1 Island, NW Ireland
Tory Sound 31 C1 Sound, N Ireland
Torzhok 69 A5 W Russ. Fed.
Tosa-wan 85 F7 Bay, SW Japan
Toscana see Tuscany
Toscano, Archipelago 61 B4 Island group, C Italy
Toshkent see Tashkent
Totana 57 E5 SE Spain
Tottori 85 E6 SW Japan
Touâjîl 124 B2 N Mauritania
Toubkal, Jbel 122 B2 ▲ W Morocco
Touggourt 122 E2 NE Algeria
Toukoto 124 B3 W Mali
Toul 55 E3 NE France
Toulon 55 E7 SE France
Toulouse 55 C6 S France
Touraine 55 C3 Cultural region, C France
Tourcoing 55 D1 N France
Tournai 50 B7 SW Belgium
Tours 55 C3 C France
Tovarkovskiy 69 B6 W Russ. Fed.
Towcester 37 E2 C England, UK
Tower Hamlets 29 ◐ London borough, SE England, UK
Townsville 133 G3 Queensland, NE Australia
Towraghoudi 83 D4 NW Afghanistan
Towuti, Danau 91 F7 ◎ Celebes, C Indonesia
Toyama 85 F5 SW Japan
Toyama-wan 85 F5 Bay, W Japan
Toyota 85 F6 SW Japan
Tozeur 122 E2 W Tunisia
Trabzon 79 F2 NE Turkey
Trafford 28 ◐ Unitary auth., NW England, UK
Traiskirchen 59 F7 NE Austria
Tralee 31 B6 SW Ireland
Tralee Bay 31 A6 Bay, SW Ireland
Transantarctic Mountains 138 C5 ▲▲ Antarctica
Transylvania 67 B6 Cultural region, NW Romania
Transylvanian Alps 67 B7 ▲▲ C Romania
Trapani 61 C7 Sicily, Italy
Traralgon 133 G6 Victoria, SE Australia
Trasimeno, Lago 61 C4 ◎ C Italy
Trawsfynydd 39 D3 NW Wales, UK
Trbovlje 59 E8 C Slovenia
Třebíč 63 C6 S Czech Republic
Trebišov 63 F6 E Slovakia
Tredegar 39 E6 SE Wales, UK
Treffgarne 39 B6 SW Wales, UK
Tregaron 39 D5 W Wales, UK
Trélazé 55 C3 NW France
Trelew 117 B7 SE Argentina
Tremadog Bay 39 C3 Bay, NW Wales, UK
Tremelo 50 C6 C Belgium
Trenčín 63 D6 W Slovakia
Trenque Lauquen 117 B6 E Argentina
Trent 35 E4 ≈ C England, UK
Trento 61 C2 N Italy
Trenton 101 G3 New Jersey, USA
Treorchy 39 D6 S Wales, UK
Tres Arroyos 117 C6 E Argentina
Tres Marías, Islas 105 C5 Island group, C Mexico
Tretower 39 E6 C Wales, UK
Treviso 61 D2 NE Italy
Trevose Head 37 A5 Headland, SW England, UK
Trichur 89 D7 SW India
Trier 59 A6 SW Germany
Trieste 61 D2 NE Italy
Tríkala 65 D5 C Greece
Trim 31 E4 E Ireland
Trincomalee 89 E7 NE Sri Lanka
Trinidad 117 B2 N Bolivia
Trinidad 117 C5 S Uruguay
Trinidad 103 E3 Colorado, USA
Trinidad 109 K7 Island, C Trinidad and Tobago
Trinidad and Tobago 109 K7 ◆ Republic, SE West Indies
Trípoli 65 E6 S Greece
Tripoli 81 A2 N Lebanon
Tripoli 122 F2 ● NW Libya
Tristan da Cunha 40 St.Helena ◇ SE Atlantic Ocean
Trivandrum 89 D7 SW India
Trnava 63 D7 W Slovakia
Troglav 65 B2 ▲ Bosnia and Herzegovina/Croatia
Trois-Rivières 99 E5 Québec, SE Canada
Trollhättan 49 C6 S Sweden
Tromsø 49 D1 N Norway
Trondheim 49 B4 S Norway
Trondheimsfjorden 49 B4 Fjord, S Norway
Troódos 70 C6 ▲▲ C Cyprus
Troon 33 D6 W Scotland, UK
Trowbridge 37 D4 S England, UK
Troy 101 G3 New York, USA
Troyes 55 E3 N France
Trujillo 107 D2 NE Honduras
Trujillo 115 B5 NW Peru
Trujillo 57 C4 W Spain
Truro 99 G5 Nova Scotia, SE Canada
Truro 37 A6 SW England, UK
Trwyn Cilan 39 B3 Headland, NW Wales, UK
Trzcianka 63 C3 NW Poland
Trzebnica 63 C4 SW Poland
Tsalka 79 H2 S Georgia
Tsarevo 65 G3 SE Bulgaria
Tsetserleg 87 E2 C Mongolia
Tshela 128 B2 W Dem. Rep. Congo
Tshikapa 128 C3 SW Dem. Rep. Congo
Tshuapa 128 C2 ≈ C Dem. Rep. Congo
Tsu 85 F6 SW Japan
Tsugaru-kaikyo 85 F3 Strait, N Japan
Tsumeb 128 C5 N Namibia
Tsuruga 85 E6 SW Japan
Tsuruoka 85 F4 C Japan
Tsushima 85 C7 Island group, SW Japan
Tuam 31 C4 W Ireland
Tuamotu Islands 131 Island group, N French Polynesia
Tuapi 107 E3 NE Nicaragua
Tuapse 69 A8 SW Russ. Fed.
Tubbergen 50 F3 E Netherlands
Tubize 50 C7 C Belgium
Tubmanburg 124 B5 NW Liberia
Tucker's Town 40 E Bermuda
Tucson 103 D5 Arizona, USA
Tucuruí, Represa de 115 G4 ⊡ NE Brazil
Tudela 57 E2 N Spain
Tudweiliog 39 B3 NW Wales, UK
Tufi 137 C3 S PNG
Tuguegarao 91 F3 N Philippines
Tuktoyaktuk 97 F3 NW Terr., NW Canada
Tula 69 A6 W Russ. Fed.
Tulancingo 105 F5 C Mexico
Tulcán 115 B3 N Ecuador
Tulcea 67 D7 E Romania
Tullamore 31 D4 C Ireland
Tulle 55 D5 C France
Tulln 59 F7 NE Austria
Tullow 31 E5 SE Ireland
Tully 133 G2 Queensland, NE Australia
Tulsa 103 G4 Oklahoma, USA
Tulsk 31 C3 C Ireland
Tuluá 115 B3 W Colombia
Tulun 76 E5 S Russ. Fed.
Tulun Islands 137 D2 Island group, NE PNG
Tumbes 115 A4 NW Peru
Tumen 85 B3 ≈ E Asia
Tumkur 89 D6 W India
Tummel 33 D4 ≈ C Scotland, UK
Tunduru 127 D7 S Tanzania
Tungsten 97 F5 NW Terr., W Canada
Tunis 122 F1 ● NE Tunisia
Tunis, Golfe de 70 E4 Gulf, NE Tunisia
Tunisia 122 E2 ◆ Republic, N Africa
Tunja 115 C2 C Colombia
Tupiza 117 B3 S Bolivia
Turangi 135 D4 North Island, NZ
Turan Lowland 83 D2 Plain, C Asia
Turayf 81 B2 NW Saudi Arabia
Turbat 89 A3 SW Pakistan
Turda 67 B6 NW Romania
Turín 61 A2 El Salvador
Turin 61 A2 NW Italy
Turkana, Lake 127 D5 ◎ N Kenya
Turkestan 76 C6 S Kazakhstan
Turkey 79 C3 ◆ Republic, SW Asia
Turkish Republic of Northern Cyprus 70 D6 ◇ Disputed Territory Cyprus
Türkmenabat 83 E3 E Turkmenistan
Türkmen Aylagy 83 B3 Lake gulf, W Turkmenistan
Türkmenbashy 83 B2 W Turkmenistan
Turkmenistan 83 B3 ◆ Republic, C Asia
Turks and Caicos Islands 40 UK ◇ N West Indies
Turks Islands 40 Island group, SE Turks and Caicos Islands
Turku 49 E5 SW Finland
Turnagain, Cape 135 D5 Headland, North Island, NZ
Turnhout 50 D6 N Belgium
Turnov 63 B5 N Czech Republic
Turpan 87 C2 NW China
Turriff 33 F3 NE Scotland, UK
Tuscaloosa 101 D5 Alabama, USA
Tuscany 61 C4 Cultural region, C Italy
Tuticorin 89 D7 SE India
Tuvalu 137 H2 ◆ Commonwealth Republic, SW Pacific Ocean
Tuwayq, Jabal 81 C5 ▲▲ C Saudi Arabia
Tuxpan 105 E5 C Mexico
Tuxpan 105 D4 C Mexico
Tuxpán 105 F4 E Mexico
Tuxtepec 105 G5 S Mexico
Tuxtla 105 H5 SE Mexico
Tuy Hoa 91 D4 S Vietnam
Tuzla 65 C2 NE Bosnia and Herzegovina
Tuz, Lake 79 D3 ◎ C Turkey
Tver' 69 A5 W Russ. Fed.
Tweed 33 E6 ≈ England/Scotland, UK
Tweedmouth 35 D1 N England, UK
Twin Falls 103 C2 Idaho, USA
Tychy 63 E5 S Poland
Tyler 103 G4 Texas, USA
Tympáki 65 F7 Crete, Greece
Tynda 76 G5 SE Russ. Fed.
Tyne 33 F7 ≈ N England, UK
Tynemouth 35 D2 NE England, UK
Tyrrhenian Sea 61 B6 Sea, N Mediterranean Sea
Tyumen' 76 C4 C Russ. Fed.
Tyup 83 I2 NE Kyrgyzstan
Tywi 39 C6 ≈ S Wales, UK
Tywyn 39 C4 W Wales, UK
Tuong Duong 91 C3 N Vietnam

U

Ubangi 124 H5 ≈ C Africa
Ube 85 D7 SW Japan
Ubeda 57 D5 S Spain
Uberaba 115 G7 SE Brazil
Uberlândia 115 F7 SE Brazil
Ubon Ratchathani 91 C3 E Thailand
Ubrique 57 C6 S Spain
Ucayali, Río 115 B4 ≈ C Peru
Uchiura-wan 85 F2 Bay, NW Pacific Ocean
Uchquduq 83 E2 N Uzbekistan
Uchtagan, Peski 83 C2 Desert, NW Turkmenistan
Uckfield 37 G5 SE England, UK
Udaipur 89 D3 N India
Uddevalla 49 B6 S Sweden
Udine 61 D2 NE Italy
Udon Thani 91 B3 N Thailand
Udupi 89 D6 SW India
Uele 128 C1 ≈ NE Dem. Rep. Congo
Uelzen 59 C3 N Germany
Ufa 69 D6 W Russ. Fed.
Uganda 127 C5 ◆ Republic, E Africa
Uglovka 69 A4 W Russ. Fed.
Uig 33 B3 N Scotland, UK
Uíge 128 B3 NW Angola
Uitenhage 128 D7 S South Africa
Uithoorn 50 D4 C Netherlands
Ujungpandang 91 E7 Celebes, C Indonesia
Ukhta 69 D4 NW Russ. Fed.
Ukmergė 49 E7 C Lithuania
Ukraine 67 C4 ◆ Republic, SE Europe
Ulaanbaatar see Ulan Bator
Ulaangom 87 D1 NW Mongolia
Ulan Bator 87 E2 ● C Mongolia
Ulanhot 87 G2 N China
Ulan-Ude 76 F5 S Russ. Fed.
Ulft 50 E4 E Netherlands
Ullapool 33 C3 N Scotland, UK
Ullswater 35 C3 ◎ NW England, UK
Ulm 59 C7 S Germany
Ulsan 85 C6 SE South Korea
Ulsta 33 B6 NE Scotland, UK
Ulster 31 D2 Cultural region, Ireland/Northern Ireland, UK
Ulungur Hu 87 C2 ◎ NW China
Uluru 133 D4 Rocky outcrop, Northern Territory, C Australia
Ulverston 35 C4 NW England, UK
Ul'yanovsk 69 C6 W Russ. Fed.
Umán 105 H4 SE Mexico
Uman' 67 D5 C Ukraine
Umbro-Marchigiano, Appennino 61 D4 ▲▲ C Italy
Umeå 49 D4 N Sweden
Umeälven 49 D3 ≈ N Sweden
Umm Buru 127 A2 W Sudan
Umm Ruwaba 127 C3 C Sudan
Umtata 128 D7 SE South Africa
Una 65 B1 ≈ Bosnia and Herzegovina/Croatia
Unac 65 B2 ≈ W Bosnia and Herzegovina
Uncía 117 B2 C Bolivia
Uncompahgre Peak 103 E3 ▲ Colorado, USA
Ungava Bay 99 E2 Bay, Québec, E Canada
Ungava Peninsula 99 D1 Peninsula, Québec, SE Canada
United Arab Emirates 81 E4 ◆ Federation, SW Asia
United Kingdom 29 ◆ Monarchy, NW Europe
United States of America 93 ◆ Federal Republic, North America
Unst 33 B5 Island, NE Scotland, UK
Ünye 79 E2 W Turkey
Upala 107 E5 NW Costa Rica
Upemba, Lac 128 D3 ◎ SE Dem. Rep. Congo
Upolu 137 B5 Island, SE Samoa
Upper Chapel 39 E5 C Wales, UK
Upper Klamath Lake 103 B2 ◎ Oregon, USA
Upper Lough Erne 31 D3 ◎ SW Northern Ireland, UK
Upper Red Lake 103 F1 ◎ Minnesota, USA
Uppsala 49 D5 C Sweden
Ural 76 B4 ≈ Kazakhstan/Russ. Fed.
Ural Mountains 76 C3 ▲▲ Kazakhstan/Russ. Fed.
Ural'sk 76 B4 NW Kazakhstan
Ural'skiye Gory see Ural Mountains
Ure 35 D3 ≈ N England, UK
Uren' 69 C5 W Russ. Fed.
Urganch 83 D2 W Uzbekistan
Urgut 83 F3 C Uzbekistan
Urlingford 31 D5 SE Ireland
Urmia, Lake 81 C1 ◎ NW Iran
Uroteppa 83 F3 NW Tajikistan
Uruapan 105 E5 SW Mexico
Uruguay 117 C5 ◆ Republic, E South America
Uruguay 117 C5 ≈ E South America
Ürümqi 87 C2 NW China
Urup, Ostrov 76 I4 Island, Kurile Islands, SE Russ. Fed.
Uruzgan 83 F5 C Afghanistan
Usa 69 E3 ≈ NW Russ. Fed.
Uşak 79 B3 W Turkey
Usborne, Mount 40 ▲ Falkland Islands
Ushuaia 117 B9 S Argentina
Usinsk 69 D3 NW Russ. Fed.
Usk 39 F6 SE Wales, UK
Usk 39 F6 ≈ SE Wales, UK
Usk Reservoir 39 D5 ⊡ S Wales, UK
Usol'ye-Sibirskoye 76 F5 C Russ. Fed.
Ussel 55 D5 C France
Ussuriysk 76 H6 SE Russ. Fed.
Ustica 61 C7 Sicily, SW Italy
Ust'-Ilimsk 76 F4 C Russ. Fed.
Ústí nad Labem 63 B5 N Czech Republic
Ustka 63 C1 NW Poland
Ust'-Kamchatsk 76 I3 E Russ. Fed.
Ust'-Kamenogorsk 76 D5 E Kazakhstan
Ust'-Kut 76 F5 C Russ. Fed.
Ust'-Olenëk 76 F3 NE Russ. Fed.
Ustyurt Plateau 83 C1 Plateau, Kazakhstan/Uzbekistan
Usulután 107 C4 SE El Salvador
Usumacinta, Río 107 A2 ≈ Guatemala/Mexico
Utah 103 D3 ◐ State, W USA
Utrecht 50 D4 C Netherlands
Utsunomiya 85 G5 S Japan
Uttar Pradesh 89 E3 Cultural region, N India
Uttoxeter 35 D6 C England, UK
Utupua 137 G3 Island, Santa Cruz Islands, E Soloman Islands
Uulu 49 E6 SW Estonia
Uvs Nuur 87 D1 ◎ Mongolia/Russ. Fed.
'Uwaynāt, Jabal al 127 B1 ▲ Libya/Sudan
Uyo 124 F5 S Nigeria
Uyuni 117 B3 W Bolivia
Uzbekistan 83 D2 ◆ Republic, C Asia
Uzhhorod 67 B5 W Ukraine

V

Vaal 128 D6 ≈ C South Africa
Vaals 50 E7 SE Netherlands
Vaasa 49 D4 W Finland
Vaassen 50 E4 E Netherlands
Vác 63 E7 N Hungary
Vadodara 89 C4 W India
Vaduz 59 C8 ● W Liechtenstein
Váh 63 D6 ≈ W Slovakia
Vaitupu 137 J2 Atoll, C Tuvalu
Valdai Hills 69 A5 Hill range, Russ. Fed.
Valday 69 A4 W Russ. Fed.
Valdecañas, Embalse de 57 C4 ⊡ W Spain
Valdepeñas 57 D4 C Spain
Valdés, Península 117 B7 Peninsula, SE Argentina
Valdivia 117 A6 C Chile
Val-d'Or 99 D5 Québec, SE Canada
Valence 55 E5 E France
Valencia 57 F4 E Spain
Valencia 115 D1 N Venezuela
Valencia, Gulf of 57 F4 Gulf, Spain
Valencia Island 31 A6 Island, SW Ireland
Valenciennes 55 E1 N France
Valjevo 65 D2 W Serbia and Montenegro (Yugoslavia)
Valkenswaard 50 D5 S Netherlands
Valladolid 105 I4 SE Mexico
Valladolid 57 D2 NW Spain
Vall D'Uxó 57 F4 E Spain
Vallejo 103 B3 California, USA
Vallenar 117 A4 N Chile
Valletta 70 B6 ● E Malta
Válljohka 49 E1 N Norway
Valls 57 G3 NE Spain
Valparaíso 117 A5 C Chile
Valverde del Camino 57 C5 S Spain
Van 79 G3 E Turkey
Vanadzor 79 H2 N Armenia
Vancouver 97 F7 British Columbia, SW Canada
Vancouver Island 97 E7 Island, British Columbia, SW Canada
Van Diemen Gulf 133 D1 Gulf, Northern Territory, N Australia
Vänern 49 C6 ◎ S Sweden
Vangaindrano 128 G6 SE Madagascar
Van Gölü see Van, Lake
Vanikolo 137 G3 Island, Santa Cruz Islands, E Solomon Islands
Vanimo 137 A1 NW PNG
Van, Lake 79 G4 Salt lake, E Turkey
Vannes 55 B3 NW France
Vantaa 49 E5 S Finland
Vanua Lava 137 G4 Island, Banks Islands, N Vanuatu
Vanua Levu 137 J5 Island, N Fiji
Vanuatu 137 E4 ◆ Republic, SW Pacific Ocean
Vao 137 G6 S New Caledonia
Varanasi 89 F3 N India
Varangerfjorden 49 F1 Fjord, N Norway
Varangerhalvøya 49 E1 Peninsula, N Norway
Varaždin 65 B1 N Croatia
Varberg 49 B6 S Sweden
Vardar 65 E4 ≈ FYR Macedonia/Greece
Varde 49 B7 W Denmark
Varese 61 B2 N Italy
Vârful Moldoveanu 67 B6 ▲ C Romania
Varkaus 49 F4 C Finland
Varna 65 G2 NE Bulgaria
Varnenski Zaliv 79 A1 Bay, E Bulgaria
Vasa see Vaasa
Vasilikí 65 D5 Lefkáda, Ionian Islands, Greece
Vaslui 67 D6 C Romania
Västerås 49 C5 C Sweden
Vatican City 61 C5 ◆ Papal state, S Europe
Vatnajökull 49 A1 Glacier, SE Iceland
Vättern 49 C6 ◎ S Sweden
Vaupés, Río 115 C3 ≈ Brazil/Colombia
Vavuniya 89 E7 N Sri Lanka
Vawkavysk 67 B3 W Belarus
Växjö 49 C6 S Sweden
Vaygach, Ostrov 69 E2 Island, NW Russ. Fed.
Veendam 50 F2 NE Netherlands
Veenendaal 50 D4 C Netherlands
Vega 49 C3 Island, C Norway
Veisiejai 49 E7 S Lithuania
Vejer de la Frontera 57 C6 S Spain
Veldhoven 50 D5 S Netherlands
Velebit 65 B2 ▲▲ C Croatia
Velenje 59 E8 N Slovenia
Velika Morava 65 D2 ≈ C Serbia and Montenegro (Yugoslavia)
Velikiye Luki 69 A5 W Russ. Fed.
Veliko Turnovo 65 F3 N Bulgaria
Vel'ký Krtíš 63 E7 S Slovakia
Vella Lavella 137 D2 Island, New Georgia Islands, NW Solomon Islands
Vellore 89 E6 SE India
Velsen-Noord 50 C3 W Netherlands
Vel'sk 69 C4 NW Russ. Fed.
Vendôme 55 C3 C France
Venezia see Venice
Venezuela 115 C2 ◆ Republic, N South America
Venezuela, Gulf of 115 C1 Gulf, NW Venezuela
Venice 61 D2 NE Italy
Venice, Gulf of 61 D3 Gulf, N Adriatic Sea
Venlo 50 E5 SE Netherlands
Venta 49 E6 ≈ Latvia/Lithuania
Vent, Îles du 137 A6 Island group, Archipel de la Société, W French Polynesia
Ventimiglia 61 A3 NW Italy
Ventspils 49 E6 NW Latvia
Vera 117 C4 C Argentina
Veracruz 105 F5 E Mexico
Vercelli 61 B2 NW Italy
Verdal 49 C4 C Norway
Verde, Costa 57 D1 Coastal region, N Spain
Verden 59 B3 NW Germany
Verkhoyanskiy Khrebet 76 G3 ▲▲ NE Russ. Fed.
Vermont 101 G2 ◐ State, NE USA
Verona 61 C2 NE Italy
Versailles 55 D2 N France
Verviers 50 E7 E Belgium
Vesdre 50 E7 ≈ E Belgium
Vesoul 55 F3 E France
Vesterålen 49 C2 Island, NW Norway
Vestfjorden 49 C2 Fjord, C Norway
Vestmannaeyjar 49 A2 S Iceland
Vesuvio 61 D6 ▲ S Italy
Veszprém 63 D8 W Hungary
Veurne 50 A6 W Belgium
Viacha 117 A2 W Bolivia
Viana do Castelo 57 B2 NW Portugal
Vianen 50 D4 C Netherlands
Viareggio 61 B3 C Italy
Viborg 49 B6 NW Denmark
Vic 57 G2 NE Spain
Vicenza 61 C2 NE Italy
Vichy 55 D4 C France
Victoria 97 E7 Vancouver Island, British Columbia, SW Canada
Victoria 70 A6 NW Malta
Victoria 119 ● SW Seychelles
Victoria 103 G5 Texas, USA
Victoria 133 F6 ◐ State, SE Australia
Victoria Falls 128 C5 Waterfall, Zambia/Zimbabwe
Victoria Island 97 G3 Island, NW Terr./Nunavut, NW Canada
Victoria, Lake 127 C5 ◎ E Africa
Victoria Land 138 D6 Physical region, Antarctica
Victoria, Mount 137 I5 ▲ Viti Levu, W Fiji
Victoria River 133 D2 ≈ Western Australia
Vidin 65 E2 NW Bulgaria
Viedma 117 B7 E Argentina
Vienna 59 F7 ● NE Austria
Vienne 55 E5 E France
Vienne 55 C4 ≈ W France
Vientiane 91 B3 ● C Laos
Vierzon 55 D3 C France
Vietnam 91 C4 ◆ Republic, SE Asia
Vieux Fort 109 K6 S Saint Lucia
Vigo 57 B2 NW Spain
Vijayawada 89 E5 SE India
Vila do Conde 57 B2 NW Portugal
Vilafranca del Penedès 57 G2 NE Spain
Viļaka 49 F6 NE Latvia
Vilalba 57 B1 NW Spain
Vila Nova de Gaia 57 B3 NW Portugal
Vila Real 57 B3 N Portugal
Vilhelmina 49 C3 N Sweden
Viliya 67 C2 ≈ W Belarus
Villa Acuña 105 E2 NE Mexico
Villa Bella 117 B1 N Bolivia
Villacarrillo 57 E5 S Spain
Villach 59 E8 S Austria
Villacidro 61 A6 Sardinia, Italy
Villafranca de los Barros 57 C4 W Spain
Villahermosa 105 H5 SE Mexico
Villajoyosa 57 F4 E Spain
Villa María 117 B5 C Argentina
Villa Martín 117 A3 SW Bolivia
Villanueva 105 E4 C Mexico
Villanueva de la Serena 57 C4 W Spain
Villanueva de los Infantes 57 E4 C Spain
Villarrica 117 C4 SE Paraguay
Villavicencio 115 C2 C Colombia
Villaviciosa 57 C1 N Spain
Villazón 117 B3 S Bolivia
Villena 57 F4 E Spain
Villeurbanne 55 E5 E France
Villingen-Schwenningen 59 B7 S Germany
Vilnius 49 F7 ● SE Lithuania
Vilvoorde 50 C6 C Belgium
Vilyuy 76 G4 ≈ NE Russ. Fed.
Viña del Mar 117 A5 C Chile
Vinaròs 57 F3 E Spain
Vindhya Range 89 D4 ▲▲ N India
Vineland 101 G3 New Jersey, USA
Vinh 91 C3 N Vietnam
Vinnytsya 67 D5 C Ukraine
Vinson Massif 138 A4 ▲ Antarctica
Viranşehir 79 F4 SE Turkey
Virgin Gorda 40 Island, C British Virgin Islands
Virginia 31 D3 N Ireland
Virginia 103 G1 Minnesota, USA
Virginia 101 F4 ◐ State, NE USA
Virginia Beach 101 G4 Virginia, USA
Virgin Islands (US) 109 H4 US ◇ E West Indies
Virovitica 65 C1 NE Croatia
Virton 50 D9 SE Belgium
Vis 65 B3 Island, S Croatia
Visakhapatnam 89 F5 SE India
Visby 49 D6 Gotland, SE Sweden
Viscount Melville Sound 97 G2 Sound, Arctic Ocean, N Canada
Visé 50 E7 E Belgium
Viseu 57 B3 N Portugal
Vistula 63 E2 ≈ C Poland
Vistula Lagoon 63 E1 Lagoon, Poland/Russ. Fed.
Viterbo 61 C4 C Italy
Vitiaz Strait 137 B2 Strait, NE PNG
Viti Levu 137 I5 Island, W Fiji
Vitim 76 G5 ≈ C Russ. Fed.
Vitória 115 H7 SE Brazil
Vitória da Conquista 115 H6 E Brazil
Vitoria-Gasteiz 57 E2 N Spain
Vitré 55 B3 NW France
Vitsyebsk 67 D2 NE Belarus
Vittoria 61 D8 Sicily, Italy
Vizianagaram 89 F5 E India
Vlaardingen 50 C4 SW Netherlands
Vladikavkaz 69 B9 SW Russ. Fed.
Vladimir 69 B5 W Russ. Fed.
Vladivostok 76 H6 SE Russ. Fed.
Vlagtwedde 50 F2 NE Netherlands
Vlieland 50 C2 Island, Waddeneilanden, N Netherlands
Vlijmen 50 D5 S Netherlands
Vlissingen 50 B5 SW Netherlands
Vlorë 65 C4 SW Albania
Vöcklabruck 59 E7 NW Austria
Vohimena, Tanjona 128 F6 Headland, S Madagascar
Voiron 55 E5 E France
Vojvodina 65 D1 Cultural region, N Serbia and Montenegro (Yugoslavia)
Volga 69 B7 ≈ NW Russ. Fed.
Volga Uplands 69 B6 ▲▲ W Russ. Fed.
Volgodonsk 69 A7 SW Russ. Fed.
Volgograd 69 B7 SW Russ. Fed.
Volkhov 69 A4 NW Russ. Fed.
Volnovakha 67 G5 SE Ukraine
Volodymyr-Volyns'kyy 67 B4 NW Ukraine
Vologda 69 B4 W Russ. Fed.
Vólos 65 E5 C Greece
Vol'sk 69 C6 W Russ. Fed.
Volta 124 D5 ≈ SE Ghana
Volta, Lake 124 D5 ⊡ SE Ghana
Volturno 61 D5 ≈ S Italy
Volzhskiy 69 B7 SW Russ. Fed.
Voorst 50 E4 E Netherlands
Vorderrhein 59 B8 ≈ SE Switzerland
Vorkuta 69 E3 NW Russ. Fed.
Voronezh 69 A6 W Russ. Fed.
Võrtsjärv 49 E6 ◎ SE Estonia
Võru 49 F6 SE Estonia
Vosges 55 F3 ▲▲ NE France
Vostok 138 D5 Russian research station, Antarctica
Vranov nad Topľou 63 F6 E Slovakia
Vratsa 65 E3 NW Bulgaria
Vrbas 65 C1 NW Serbia and Montenegro (Yugoslavia)
Vrbas 65 C2 ≈ N Bosnia and Herzegovina
Vršac 65 D1 NE Serbia and Montenegro (Yugoslavia)
Vsetín 63 D6 E Czech Republic
Vukovar 65 C1 E Croatia
Vulcano 61 D7 Island, Aeolian Islands, S Italy
Vung Tau 91 C4 S Vietnam

Vunisea 137 J5 SE Fiji
Vyatka 69 C5 〰 NW Russ. Fed.
Vyborg 69 A4 NW Russ. Fed.
Vyrnwy 39 E3 〰 E Wales, UK

W

Wa 124 D4 NW Ghana
Waal 50 D4 〰 S Netherlands
Waala 137 F6 W New Caledonia
Waddan 122 G3 NW Libya
Waddeneilanden see West Frisian Islands
Waddenzee 50 D2 Sea, SE North Sea
Waddington, Mount 97 E7 ▲ British Columbia, SW Canada
Wadebridge 37 B5 SW England, UK
Wadi Halfa 127 C1 N Sudan
Wad Medani 127 C2 C Sudan
Waflia 91 G7 E Indonesia
Wagga Wagga 133 G6 NSW, SE Australia
Wagin 133 B5 Western Australia
Wah 89 C1 NE Pakistan
Wahai 91 G7 E Indonesia
Wahiawa 103 A5 Oahu, Hawaii, USA
Wahibah Sands 81 E5 Desert, N Oman
Waiau 135 A8 〰 South Island, NZ
Waigeo, Pulau 91 G6 Island, Maluku, E Indonesia
Waikaremoana, Lake 135 E3 ◎ North Island, NZ
Wailuku 103 B6 Maui, Hawaii, USA
Waimate 135 B7 South Island, NZ
Waiouru 135 D4 North Island, NZ
Waipara 135 C6 South Island, NZ
Waipawa 135 D4 North Island, NZ
Waipukurau 135 D4 North Island, NZ
Wairau 135 C5 〰 South Island, NZ
Wairoa 135 E4 North Island, NZ
Wairoa 135 D2 〰 North Island, NZ
Waitaki 135 B7 〰 South Island, NZ
Waitara 135 C4 North Island, NZ
Waiuku 135 D3 North Island, NZ
Wakasa-wan 85 E6 Bay, C Japan
Wakatipu, Lake 135 B7 ◎ South Island, NZ
Wakayama 85 E6 SW Japan
Wakefield 35 E4 N England, UK
Wakefield 29 ⬖ Unitary auth., N England, UK
Wakkanai 85 F1 NE Japan
Wałbrzych 63 C5 SW Poland
Walcourt 50 C8 S Belgium
Wałcz 63 C2 NW Poland
Wales 97 C2 Alaska, USA
Wales 39 D4 National region, United Kingdom
Walgett 133 G5 NSW, SE Australia
Wallachia 67 B7 Cultural region, S Romania
Wallasey 35 C5 NW England, UK
Wallis and Futuna 137 I4 French ◇ C Pacific Ocean
Wallis, Îles 137 K4 Island group, N Wallis and Futuna
Walney, Isle of 35 B4 Island, NW England, UK
Walsall 35 D6 C England, UK
Walsall 29 ⬖ Unitary auth., C England, UK
Waltham Forest 29 ⬖ London borough, SE England, UK
Walvis Bay 128 B5 NW Namibia
Wanaka 135 B7 South Island, NZ
Wanaka, Lake 135 A7 ◎ South Island, NZ
Wandel Sea 139 C5 Sea, Arctic Ocean
Wandsworth 29 ⬖ London borough, SE England, UK
Wanganui 135 D4 North Island, NZ
Wangaratta 133 G6 Victoria, SE Australia
Wanlaweyn 127 F5 SW Somalia
Wanxian 87 F4 C China
Warangal 89 E5 C India
Warburg 59 B4 W Germany
Ware 97 E6 British Columbia, W Canada
Waremme 50 D7 E Belgium
Waren 59 D3 NE Germany
Warkworth 135 D2 North Island, NZ
Warminster 37 D4 S England, UK
Warnemünde 59 D2 NE Germany
Warnes 117 B2 C Bolivia
Warrego River 133 G5 Seasonal river, NSW/Queensland, E Australia
Warren 101 E3 Michigan, USA
Warren 101 E3 Ohio, USA
Warri 124 E5 S Nigeria
Warrington 35 C5 C England, UK
Warrington 29 ⬖ Unitary auth., NW England, UK
Warrnambool 133 F6 Victoria, SE Australia
Warsaw 63 F3 ● C Poland
Warszawa see Warsaw
Warta 63 D4 〰 W Poland
Warwick 133 H5 Queensland, E Australia
Warwick 35 D7 C England, UK
Warwickshire 29 ⬖ County, C England, UK
Washington 35 D2 NE England, UK
Washington 103 B1 ⬖ State, NW USA
Washington DC 101 F4 ● District of Columbia, NE USA
Washington, Mount 101 G2 ▲ New Hampshire, USA
Wash, The 37 G1 Inlet, E England, UK
Waspam 107 E3 NE Nicaragua
Waterford 31 D6 S Ireland
Waterford 29 ⬖ County, S Ireland
Waterloo 103 G2 Iowa, USA
Watertown 103 F2 South Dakota, USA
Waterville 31 A6 SW Ireland
Watford 37 F3 E England, UK
Watsa 128 D1 NE Dem. Rep. Congo
Watts Bar Lake 101 D5 ▣ Tennessee, USA
Wau 127 B4 S Sudan
Waukesha 101 D2 Wisconsin, USA
Waveney 37 H2 〰 E England, UK
Wavre 50 C7 C Belgium
Wawa 99 C5 Ontario, S Canada
Wawa, Río 107 E3 〰 NE Nicaragua
Waycross 101 E6 Georgia, USA
Wé 137 G6 E New Caledonia
Weald, The 37 G4 Lowlands, SE England, UK
Weam 137 A3 SW PNG
Wear 35 D3 〰 N England, UK
Weddell Plain 138 B3 Undersea feature, SW Atlantic Ocean
Weddell Sea 138 B3 Sea, SW Atlantic Ocean
Weddell Settlement 40 W Falkland Islands
Weener 59 B3 NW Germany
Weert 50 E6 SE Netherlands
Weesp 50 D4 C Netherlands
Węgorzewo 63 F2 NE Poland
Weimar 59 C5 C Germany
Weissenburg 59 C6 SE Germany
Weiswampach 50 E8 N Luxembourg
Wejherowo 63 D1 NW Poland
Weldiya 127 E3 N Ethiopia
Welkom 128 D6 C South Africa
Welland 35 F6 〰 C England, UK
Wellesley Islands 133 F2 Island group, Queensland, N Australia
Wellingborough 37 F2 C England, UK
Wellington 135 D5 ● North Island, NZ
Wellington 37 C4 SW England, UK
Wellington, Isla 117 A8 Island, S Chile
Wells 103 C3 Nevada, USA
Wellsford 135 D2 North Island, NZ
Wells, Lake 133 C4 ◎ Western Australia
Wells-next-the-Sea 37 G1 E England, UK
Wels 59 E7 N Austria
Welshpool 39 E3 E Wales, UK
Wemmel 50 C6 C Belgium
Wenchi 124 D5 W Ghana
Wenquan 87 C4 C China
Wenvoe 39 E7 S Wales, UK
Wenzhou 87 G5 SE China
Werkendam 50 D5 S Netherlands
Weser 59 B3 〰 NW Germany
Wessel Islands 133 E1 Island group, Northern Territory, N Australia
West Bank 81 H6 Disputed region, SW Asia
West Bay 40 W Cayman Islands
West Bengal 89 F4 Cultural region, NE India
West Bromwich 35 D6 C England, UK
West Burra 33 A6 Island, NE Scotland, UK
West Caicos 40 Island, W Turks and Caicos Islands
West Dunbartonshire 28 ⬖ Unitary auth., W Scotland, UK
West End 40 W British Virgin Islands
West End 40 NE Cayman Islands
Westerland 59 B2 N Germany
Western Australia 133 B3 ⬖ State, W Australia
Western Dvina 49 F6 〰 W Europe
Western Ghats 89 C5 ⛰ SW India
Western Sahara 122 A3 Disputed ◇ N Africa
Western Sayans 76 E5 ⛰ S Russ. Fed.
Westerschelde 50 B5 Inlet, S North Sea
West Falkland 40 Island, W Falkland Islands
West Frisian Islands 50 D1 Island group, Netherlands
West Lothian 28 ⬖ Unitary auth., S Scotland, UK
Westmeath 29 ⬖ County, C Ireland
Westminster 29 ⬖ London borough, SE England, UK
Weston-super-Mare 37 D4 SW England, UK
West Palm Beach 101 F7 Florida, USA
Westpoint Island Settlement 40 NW Falkland Islands
Westport 31 B3 W Ireland
Westport 135 C5 South Island, NZ
Westray 33 E1 Island, NE Scotland, UK
West Siberian Plain 76 D4 Plain, C Russ. Fed.
West Sussex 29 ⬖ County, S England, UK
West Virginia 101 E3 ⬖ State, NE USA
Wetar, Pulau 91 E8 Island, Kepulauan Damar, E Indonesia
Wetherby 35 E4 N England, UK
Wetzlar 59 B5 W Germany
Wewak 137 A1 NW PNG
Wexford 31 E6 SE Ireland
Wexford 29 ⬖ County, SE Ireland
Weyburn 97 H7 Saskatchewan, S Canada
Weymouth 37 D5 S England, UK
Wezep 50 E3 E Netherlands
Whakatane 135 E3 North Island, NZ
Whale Cove 97 H4 Nunavut, C Canada
Whalsay 33 B6 Island, NE Scotland, UK
Whangarei 135 D2 North Island, NZ
Wharfe 35 D4 〰 N England, UK
Whataroa 135 B6 South Island, NZ
Wheeler Peak 103 E4 ▲ New Mexico, USA
Whernside 35 C3 ▲ N England, UK
Whitby 35 E3 N England, UK
Whitchurch 35 C6 W England, UK
Whitehaven 35 B3 NW England, UK
Whitehead 31 F2 E Northern Ireland, UK
Whitehorse 97 E5 Yukon Territory, W Canada
White Nile 127 C3 〰 SE Sudan
White Sea 69 B3 Sea, Arctic Ocean
Whites Town 31 E3 NE Ireland
White Volta 124 D4 〰 Burkina/Ghana
Whithorn 33 D7 S Scotland, UK
Whitianga 135 D2 North Island, NZ
Whitland 39 B6 S Wales, UK
Whitley Bay 35 D2 NE England, UK
Whitstable 37 H4 SE England, UK
Whitsunday Group 133 H3 Island group, Queensland, E Australia
Whyalla 133 E5 S Australia
Wichita 103 F3 Kansas, USA
Wichita Falls 103 F4 Texas, USA
Wick 33 E2 N Scotland, UK
Wicklow 31 E5 E Ireland
Wicklow 29 ⬖ County, E Ireland
Wicklow Mountains 31 E5 ⛰ E Ireland
Widnes 35 C5 NW England, UK
Wieliczka 63 E5 S Poland
Wieluń 63 D4 C Poland
Wien see Vienna
Wiener Neustadt 59 F7 E Austria
Wierden 50 F3 E Netherlands
Wiesbaden 59 B5 W Germany
Wigan 35 C5 NW England, UK
Wigan 28 ⬖ Unitary auth., NW England, UK
Wigston 35 E6 C England, UK
Wigton 35 C2 NW England, UK
Wigtown 33 D7 S Scotland, UK
Wigtown Bay 33 D7 Bay, SW Scotland, UK
Wijchen 50 E5 SE Netherlands
Wijk bij Duurstede 50 D4 C Netherlands
Wilcannia 133 F5 NSW, SE Australia
Wilhelm, Mount 137 A2 ▲ C PNG
Wilhelmshaven 59 B3 NW Germany
Wilkes Land 138 E5 Physical region, Antarctica
Willebroek 50 C6 C Belgium
Willemstad 109 H7 ○ Curacao, Netherlands Antilles
Wilmington 101 G3 Delaware, USA
Wilmslow 35 D5 W England, UK
Wilrijk 50 C6 N Belgium
Wiltshire 29 ⬖ County, S England, UK
Winchester 37 E4 S England, UK
Windermere 35 C3 ◎ NW England, UK
Windhoek 128 B5 ● C Namibia
Windorah 133 F4 Queensland, C Australia
Windsor 99 C6 Ontario, S Canada
Windsor 37 F3 S England, UK
Windsor and Maidenhead 29 ⬖ Unitary auth., S England, UK
Windward Islands 109 K6 Island group, E West Indies
Windward Passage 109 E4 Channel, Cuba/Haiti
Winisk 99 C3 Ontario, C Canada
Winisk 99 C3 〰 Ontario, S Canada
Winnebago, Lake 101 C2 ◎ Wisconsin, USA
Winnemucca 103 C2 Nevada, USA
Winnipeg 97 H7 Manitoba, S Canada
Winnipeg, Lake 97 H6 ◎ Manitoba, C Canada
Winschoten 50 F2 NE Netherlands
Winsen 59 C3 N Germany
Winston Salem 101 F4 North Carolina, USA
Winsum 50 D2 NE Netherlands
Winterswijk 50 F4 E Netherlands
Winterthur 59 B7 NE Switzerland
Winton 133 F3 Queensland, E Australia
Winton 135 B8 South Island, NZ
Wirral 28 ⬖ Unitary auth., NW England, UK
Wisbech 37 G2 E England, UK
Wisconsin 101 C2 ⬖ State, N USA
Wismar 59 C2 N Germany
Wisła see Vistula
Witham 37 G3 SE England, UK
Witham 35 F5 〰 E England, UK
Withernsea 35 F4 E England, UK
Witney 37 E3 S England, UK
Wittenberge 59 D3 N Germany
Wittlich 59 A5 SW Germany
Wittstock 59 D3 NE Germany
Witu Islands 137 C2 Island group, E PNG
Władysławowo 63 D1 N Poland
Włocławek 63 E3 C Poland
Włodawa 63 G4 SE Poland
Wlotzkasbaken 128 B5 W Namibia
Wodonga 133 G6 Victoria, SE Australia
Wodzisław Śląski 63 D5 S Poland
Woking 37 F4 SE England, UK
Wokingham 37 F4 S England, UK
Wokingham 29 ⬖ Unitary auth., S England, UK
Wolds, The 35 F5 Hill range, E England, UK
Wolds, The 35 E4 Hill range, N England, UK
Wolfsberg 59 E8 SE Austria
Wolfsburg 59 C4 N Germany
Wolgast 59 D2 NE Germany
Wollaston Lake 97 H5 Saskatchewan, C Canada
Wollongong 133 G6 NSW, SE Australia
Wolvega 50 E2 N Netherlands
Wolverhampton 35 D6 C England, UK
Wolverhampton 29 ⬖ Unitary auth., C England, UK
Wonju 85 B5 N South Korea
Wonsan 85 B5 SE North Korea
Woodlark Island 137 C3 Island, SE PNG
Woods, Lake of the 103 G1 ◎ Canada/USA
Woodville 135 D4 North Island, NZ
Wooler 35 D1 N England, UK
Wootton Bassett 37 E3 S England, UK
Worcester 128 C7 SW South Africa
Worcester 35 D7 W England, UK
Worcestershire 29 ⬖ County, C England, UK
Workington 35 B3 NW England, UK
Worksop 35 E5 C England, UK
Worms 59 B6 SW Germany
Worthing 37 F5 SE England, UK
Worthington 103 G2 Minnesota, USA
Woudrichem 50 D5 S Netherlands
Wragby 35 F5 E England, UK
Wrangel Island 76 H1 Island, NE Russ. Fed.
Wrangel Plain 139 C3 Undersea feature, Arctic Ocean
Wrath, Cape 33 C2 Headland, N Scotland, UK
Wrexham 39 F2 NE Wales, UK
Wrexham 29 ⬖ Unitary auth., NE Wales, UK
Wrocław 63 C4 SW Poland
Września 63 D3 C Poland
Wuday 'ah 81 C6 S Saudi Arabia
Wuhai 87 E3 N China
Wuhan 87 F4 C China
Wuhu 87 G4 E China
Wukari 124 F5 E Nigeria
Wuliang Shan 87 D5 ⛰ SW China
Wuppertal 59 A4 W Germany
Würzburg 59 C5 SW Germany
Wuxi 87 G4 E China
Wye 39 F6 〰 England/Wales, UK
Wyndham 133 D2 Western Australia
Wyoming 103 D2 ⬖ State, C USA
Wyre 35 C4 〰 NW England, UK
Wyszków 63 F3 NE Poland
Wyżyna Lubelska 63 F4 Physical region, SW Poland

X

Xaafuun, Raas 127 G3 Headland, NE Somalia
Xaçmaz 79 I1 N Azerbaijan
Xai-Xai 128 E6 S Mozambique
Xalapa 105 F5 SE Mexico
Xankändi 79 I3 SW Azerbaijan
Xánthi 65 F4 NE Greece
Xátiva 57 F4 E Spain
Xiamen 87 G5 SE China
Xi'an 87 F4 C China
Xianggang see Hong Kong
Xiangkhoang, Plateau de 91 B2 Plateau, N Laos
Xiangtan 87 F5 S China
Xiao Hinggan Ling 87 G1 ⛰ NE China
Xichang 87 E5 C China
Xigazê 87 C4 W China
Xi Jiang 91 D2 〰 S China
Xilinhot 87 F2 N China
Xingu, Rio 115 F5 〰 C Brazil
Xingxingxia 87 D3 C China
Xining 87 E4 C China
Xinxiang 87 F4 C China
Xinyang 87 F4 C China
Xinzo de Limia 57 B2 NW Spain
Xixón see Gijón
Xuddur 127 E4 SW Somalia
Xuwen 87 F6 S China
Xuzhou 87 G4 E China

Y

Ya'an 87 E5 C China
Yabelo 127 D4 S Ethiopia
Yablis 107 E3 NE Nicaragua
Yablonovyy Khrebet 76 G5 ⛰ S Russ. Fed.
Yabrai Shan 87 E3 ⛰ NE China
Yafran 122 F2 NW Libya
Yahualica 105 E4 SW Mexico
Yakima 103 B1 Washington, USA
Yakutsk 76 G4 NE Russ. Fed.
Yalong Jiang 87 D4 〰 C China
Yalova 79 B2 NW Turkey
Yalta 67 F7 S Ukraine
Yalu 85 A4 〰 China/North Korea
Yamagata 85 G4 C Japan
Yamaguchi 85 D7 SW Japan
Yamal, Poluostrov 76 D3 Peninsula, N Russ. Fed.
Yambio 127 B4 S Sudan
Yambol 65 F3 E Bulgaria
Yamdena, Pulau 91 G8 Island, Kepulauan Tanimbar, E Indonesia
Yamoussoukro 124 C5 ● C Ivory Coast
Yamuna 89 E3 〰 N India
Yana 76 G3 〰 NE Russ. Fed.
Yanbu 'al Bahr 81 A4 W Saudi Arabia
Yandina 137 E3 Russell Islands, C Solomon Islands
Yangambi 128 D1 N Dem. Rep. Congo
Yangiyo'l 83 F2 E Uzbekistan
Yangtze 87 F4 〰 C China
Yangzhou 87 G4 E China
Yantai 87 G3 E China
Yaoundé 124 F5 ● S Cameroon
Yapen, Pulau 91 H7 Island, E Indonesia
Yaqui, Río 105 C2 〰 NW Mexico
Yaransk 69 C5 NW Russ. Fed.
Yare 37 H2 〰 E England, UK
Yarega 69 D4 NW Russ. Fed.
Yarmouth 99 F5 Nova Scotia, SE Canada
Yaroslavl' 69 B5 W Russ. Fed.
Yasawa Group 137 I5 Island group, NW Fiji
Yasyel'da 67 C3 〰 SW Belarus
Yatsushiro 85 D8 SW Japan
Yaviza 107 I6 SE Panama
Yazd 81 E3 C Iran
Yecheng 87 A3 NW China
Yefremov 69 A6 W Russ. Fed.
Yekaterinburg 76 C4 C Russ. Fed.
Yelets 69 A6 W Russ. Fed.
Yell 33 B6 Island, NE Scotland, UK
Yellowknife 97 G5 NW Terr., W Canada
Yellow River 87 G3 〰 C China
Yellow Sea 87 G4 Sea, E Asia
Yellowstone Lake 103 D2 ◎ Wyoming, USA
Yellowstone River 103 E1 〰 NW USA
Yell Sound 33 A6 Strait, N Scotland, UK
Yelwa 124 E4 W Nigeria
Yemen 81 C6 ◆ Republic, SW Asia
Yemva 69 D4 NW Russ. Fed.
Yenakiyeve 67 G5 E Ukraine
Yendi 124 D4 NE Ghana
Yengisar 87 A3 NW China
Yenierenköy see Agialousa
Yenisey 76 E4 〰 Mongolia/Russ. Fed.
Yeovil 37 D4 SW England, UK
Yeppoon 133 H4 Queensland, E Australia
Yerevan 79 H3 ● C Armenia
Yeu, Île d' 55 B4 Island, NW France
Yevlax 79 I2 C Azerbaijan
Yevpatoriya 67 F7 S Ukraine
Yeya 67 G5 〰 SW Russ. Fed.
Yichang 87 F4 C China
Yıldızeli 79 E3 N Turkey
Yinchuan 87 E3 N China
Yining 87 B2 NW China
Y Llethr 39 D3 ▲ NW Wales, UK
Yogyakarta 91 C8 Java, C Indonesia
Yokohama 85 G6 S Japan
Yokote 85 G4 C Japan
Yola 124 G4 E Nigeria
Yonago 85 E6 SW Japan
Yong'an 87 G5 SE China
Yonghung 85 B5 E North Korea
Yonne 55 D3 〰 C France
York 35 E4 N England, UK
York 29 ⬖ Unitary auth., N England, UK
York, Cape 133 G1 Headland, Queensland, NE Australia
Yorkshire Dales 35 D3 Physical region, N England, UK
Yorkton 97 H7 Saskatchewan, S Canada
Yoro 107 C3 C Honduras
Yoshkar-Ola 69 C5 W Russ. Fed.
Youghal 31 D6 S Ireland
Youngstown 101 E3 Ohio, USA
Yreka 103 B2 California, USA
Ystalyfera 39 D6 S Wales, UK
Ystrad Aeron 39 C5 W Wales, UK
Ystradgynlais 39 D6 C Wales, UK
Ystrad Mynach 39 E6 SE Wales, UK
Ythan 33 F3 〰 NE Scotland, UK
Yucatan Channel 105 I3 Channel, Cuba/Mexico
Yucatan Peninsula 105 H4 Coastal feature, Guatemala/Mexico
Yuci 87 F3 C China
Yueyang 87 G5 S China
Yugoslavia see Serbia and Montenegro
Yukon River 97 E3 〰 Canada/USA
Yukon Territory 97 E4 Territory, NW Canada
Yulin 87 F6 S China
Yumen 87 D3 N China
Yushu 87 D4 C China
Yuty 117 C4 S Paraguay
Yuzhno-Sakhalinsk 76 I5 SE Russ. Fed.
Ýylanly 83 D2 N Turkmenistan

Z

Zaanstad 50 D3 C Netherlands
Zabaykal'sk 76 G5 S Russ. Fed.
Zabid 81 B7 W Yemen
Ząbkowice Śląskie 63 C5 SW Poland
Zábřeh 63 C5 E Czech Republic
Zacapa 107 B3 E Guatemala
Zacatecas 105 E4 C Mexico
Zacatepec 105 F5 S Mexico
Zadar 65 B2 W Croatia
Zadetkyi Kyun 91 A4 Island, Mergui Archipelago, S Burma
Zafra 57 C4 W Spain
Żagań 63 C4 W Poland
Zagazig 122 I2 N Egypt
Zagreb 65 B1 ● N Croatia
Zagros Mountains 81 D3 ⛰ W Iran
Zahedan 81 F3 SE Iran
Záhony 63 F6 NE Hungary
Zaire see Dem. Rep. Congo
Zákynthos 65 D6 Island, Ionian Islands, Greece
Zalaegerszeg 63 G2 W Hungary
Zalău 67 B6 NW Romania
Zalim 81 B5 W Saudi Arabia
Zambezi 128 C4 W Zambia
Zambezi 128 E4 〰 S Africa
Zambia 128 D4 ◆ Republic, S Africa
Zamboanga 91 F5 S Philippines
Zambrów 63 F3 E Poland
Zamora 57 C2 NW Spain
Zamora de Hidalgo 105 E5 SW Mexico
Zamość 63 G5 SE Poland
Zanda 87 A4 W China
Zanjan 81 D1 NW Iran
Zanzibar 127 D6 E Tanzania
Zanzibar 127 E6 Island, E Tanzania
Zaozhuang 87 G4 E China
Zapadna Morava 65 D2 〰 C Serbia and Montenegro (Yugoslavia)
Zapadnaya Dvina 69 A5 W Russ. Fed.
Zapala 117 A6 W Argentina
Zapolyarnyy 69 B2 NW Russ. Fed.
Zaporizhzhya 67 F5 SE Ukraine
Zaqatala 79 I1 NW Azerbaijan
Zara 79 E3 C Turkey
Zarafshon 83 E2 N Uzbekistan
Zaragoza 57 F2 NE Spain
Zaranj 83 D6 SW Afghanistan
Zarasai 49 F7 E Lithuania
Zárate 117 C5 E Argentina
Zarautz 57 E1 N Spain
Zarghun Shahr 83 F5 SE Afghanistan
Zaria 124 F4 C Nigeria
Żary 63 B4 W Poland
Zaunguzskiye Garagumy 83 C3 Desert, N Turkmenistan
Zawiercie 63 E5 S Poland
Zawilah 122 F3 C Libya
Zaysan, Ozero 76 D6 ◎ E Kazakhstan
Zduńska Wola 63 E4 C Poland
Zealand 49 B7 Island, Denmark
Zeebrugge 50 B5 NW Belgium
Zeewolde 50 D3 C Netherlands
Zeidskoye Vodokhranilishche 83 D4 ▣ E Turkmenistan
Zeist 50 D4 C Netherlands
Zele 50 C6 NW Belgium
Zelenoborskiy 69 B2 NW Russ. Fed.
Zelenograd 69 B5 W Russ. Fed.
Zelenogradsk 49 D7 W Russ. Fed.
Zelzate 50 B6 NW Belgium
Zemst 50 C6 C Belgium
Zemun 65 D2 N Serbia and Montenegro (Yugoslavia)
Zenica 65 C2 C Bosnia and Herzegovina
Zeravshan 83 F3 〰 Tajikistan/Uzbekistan
Zermatt 59 B8 SW Switzerland
Zevenaar 50 E4 SE Netherlands
Zevenbergen 50 C5 S Netherlands
Zeya Reservoir 76 G4 ▣ SE Russ. Fed.
Zgierz 63 E4 C Poland
Zgorzelec 63 B4 SW Poland
Zhanaozen 76 B5 W Kazakhstan
Zhangjiakou 87 F3 E China
Zhangzhou 87 G5 SE China
Zhanjiang 87 F6 S China
Zhaoqing 87 F6 S China
Zheleznogorsk 69 A6 W Russ. Fed.
Zhengzhou 87 F4 C China
Zhezkazgan 76 C5 C Kazakhstan
Zhlobin 67 D3 SE Belarus
Zhodzina 67 D2 C Belarus
Zhongshan 138 D4 Chinese research station, Antarctica
Zhovkva 67 B4 NW Ukraine
Zhovti Vody 67 E5 E Ukraine
Zhytomyr 67 D4 NW Ukraine
Zibo 87 G3 E China
Zielona Góra 63 C4 W Poland
Zierikzee 50 C5 SW Netherlands
Zigong 87 E5 C China
Ziguinchor 124 A4 SW Senegal
Žilina 63 D6 NW Slovakia
Zimbabwe 128 E5 ◆ Republic, S Africa
Zimovniki 69 B7 SW Russ. Fed.
Zinder 124 F3 S Niger
Zittau 59 E5 E Germany
Zlín 63 D6 SE Czech Republic
Złotów 63 D2 NW Poland
Żnin 63 D3 W Poland
Znojmo 63 C6 S Czech Republic
Zoetermeer 50 C4 W Netherlands
Zomba 128 E4 S Malawi
Zongo 128 C1 N Dem. Rep. Congo
Zonguldak 79 C2 NW Turkey
Zonhoven 50 D6 NE Belgium
Żory 63 D5 S Poland
Zouar 124 G2 N Chad
Zouérat 124 B1 N Mauritania
Zrenjanin 65 D1 N Serbia and Montenegro (Yugoslavia)
Zug 59 B8 C Switzerland
Zugspitze 59 C7 ▲ S Germany
Zuid-Beveland 50 B5 Island, SW Netherlands
Zuider Zee see IJsselmeer
Zuidhorn 50 E2 NE Netherlands
Zuidlaren 50 F2 NE Netherlands
Zula 127 D2 E Eritrea
Zundert 50 C5 S Netherlands
Zunyi 87 E5 S China
Zürich 59 B7 N Switzerland
Zurich, Lake 59 B8 ◎ NE Switzerland
Zürichsee see Lake Zurich
Zutphen 50 E4 E Netherlands
Zuwarah 122 F2 NW Libya
Zuyevka 69 D5 NW Russ. Fed.
Zvenyhorodka 67 E5 C Ukraine
Zvishavane 128 D5 S Zimbabwe
Zvolen 63 E6 C Slovakia
Zwedru 124 C5 E Liberia
Zwettl 59 E6 NE Austria
Zwevegem 50 B7 W Belgium
Zwickau 59 D5 E Germany
Zwolle 50 E3 E Netherlands
Zyryanovsk 76 D5 E Kazakhstan

NORTH AMERICA

CANADA

UNITED STATES OF AMERICA

MEXICO

BELIZE

COSTA RICA

EL SALVADOR

GUATEMALA

HONDURAS

GRENADA

HAITI

JAMAICA

ST KITTS & NEVIS

ST LUCIA

ST VINCENT & THE GRENADINES

TRINIDAD & TOBAGO

SOUTH AMERICA

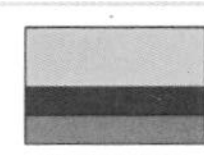
COLOMBIA

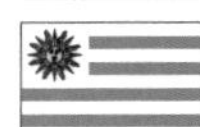
URUGUAY

CHILE

PARAGUAY

AFRICA

ALGERIA

EGYPT

LIBYA

MOROCCO

TUNISIA

LIBERIA

MALI

MAURITANIA

NIGER

NIGERIA

SENEGAL

SIERRA LEONE

TOGO

BURUNDI

DJIBOUTI

ERITREA

ETHIOPIA

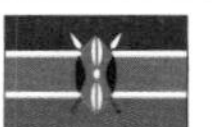
KENYA

RWANDA

SOMALIA

SUDAN

SOUTH AFRICA

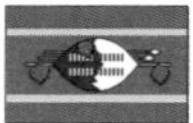
SWAZILAND

ZAMBIA

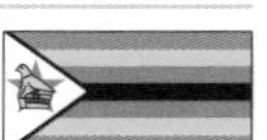
ZIMBABWE

EUROPE

DENMARK

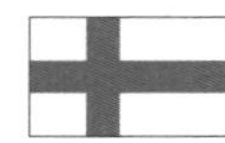
FINLAND

ICELAND

NORWAY

MONACO

ANDORRA

PORTUGAL

SPAIN

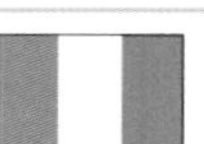
ITALY

SAN MARINO

VATICAN CITY

AUSTRIA

BOSNIA & HERZEGOVINA

CROATIA

MACEDONIA

SERBIA & MONTENEGRO (YUGOSLAVIA)

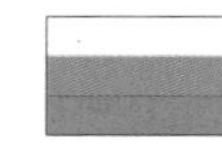
BULGARIA

GREECE

MOLDOVA

ROMANIA

ASIA

ARMENIA

AZERBAIJAN

GEORGIA

TURKEY

IRAQ

ISRAEL

JORDAN

LEBANON

IRAN

KAZAKHSTAN

KYRGYZSTAN

TAJIKISTAN

TURKMENISTAN

UZBEKISTAN

AFGHANISTAN

PAKISTAN

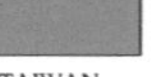
TAIWAN

JAPAN

BRUNEI

INDONESIA

EAST TIMOR

MALAYSIA

SINGAPORE

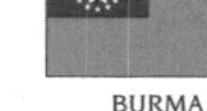
BURMA

MAURITIUS

SEYCHELLES

AUSTRALASIA & OCEANIA

AUSTRALIA

NEW ZEALAND

PAPUA NEW GUINEA

SOLOMON ISLANDS

MARSHALL ISLANDS

MICRONESIA